# Usborne
# Illustrated
# English
# Thesaurus

Jane Bingham and Fiona Chandler

Designed by Susie McCaffrey
and Matthew Hart

Cover designed by Karen Tomlins

Illustrated by
David Cuzik, Gerald Wood, Nicholas Hewetson,
Ian Jackson, Ann Johns and Gary Bines

Additional contributions by John McIlwain,
Jessica Feinstein, Rachel Wardley and Shelley Harris

# What is a thesaurus?

A thesaurus is a book which gives lists of words with similar meanings. This thesaurus will help you choose the best words for your writing.

*Is there a more exciting word for "new"?*

If you know the word that you need, but want to say it in a more interesting way, your thesaurus will provide you with a list of alternative words, or "synonyms", for that word.

Your thesaurus can help you avoid using the same word over and over again. Really overused words, such as "nice" and "good", have panels with synonyms arranged in lists to help you make the right choices.

This thesaurus contains illustrated panels on lots of different subjects to give you ideas for writing and to help get your imagination working. You can see a list of panels on the page opposite.

*A night in the forest*

Slowly darkness enveloped the
The sky was star-studded and v
I stood still and listened carefull
hedgehog snuffled about in the
an owl hooted and in the di nce
siren began to wail.
Shadowy shapes of ba ter
silvery in the moonlig

You can also use your thesaurus to find a word that you know, but just can't remember.

*What's that word that means "noise" and begins with "d"?*

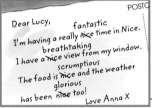

Dear Lucy,
I'm having a really nice time in Nice. fantastic
breathtaking
I have a nice view from my window.
scrumptious
The food is nice and the weather
glorious
has been nice too!
Love Anna X

---

## Looking at an entry

**headword** All headwords are arranged in alphabetical order.

**part of speech** shows the part that the word plays in a sentence. Look at the **Guide to parts of speech** on the page facing this one.

**opposite** gives an opposite word or words.

**number** introduces each new meaning of the word.

**list of synonyms** gives you a choice of alternative words, with the most suitable ones first. Most of the synonyms fit exactly into the example sentence, so you can try out each one until you find the word you like.

You may not recognize all the synonyms in a list. Always use a dictionary to check unfamiliar words.

### frantic
*(adj) You'll be frantic when you hear the news.* beside yourself, at your wits' end, desperate, panic-stricken, distraught, hysterical, overwrought, worked up, frenzied.
OPPOSITE: calm.

### fraud
**1** *(n) Dodgy Dave is guilty of fraud.* swindling, cheating, deception, sharp practice, double-dealing, embezzlement, trickery.
**2** *(n) (informal) That man is a fraud.* impostor, phoney *(informal)*, fake, cheat, con man *(informal)*, swindler, double-dealer, charlatan, quack *(doctor)*.

**example sentence** or **phrase** demonstrates how the word is used and helps you to find the meaning that you want.

**word-use label** shows that a word is informal, slang or old-fashioned. Informal words are not normally used in formal or official writing.

Word-use labels also show when a word is plural or if it should only be used in a certain situation.

# What's in your thesaurus?

*chameleon*

*leaping goalkeeper*

## List of panels

*staring eyes*

*treasure island*

*spicy stir-fry*

*jester*

*perplexed*

*sorcerer's castle*

---

## Other helpful features

**word lists** give groups of related words for you to choose from. Some of these lists are illustrated.

**song**
*(n)* TYPES OF SONG: anthem, aria, ballad, calypso, canon, carol, chant, folk song, hymn, jingle, love song, lullaby, madrigal, nursery rhyme, pop song, psalm, round, sea shanty, serenade, spiritual.

**cross-references** point you to the headword where you will find the list of words you want. The number shows you which meaning you need to look for.

**prod** *see* **poke** 2.

**cross-references to panels** direct you to a range of related words in an illustrated panel.

**castle**
*(n)* fortress, fort, stronghold, citadel, palace, chateau.
❖ *Also see* **medieval life**.

If you can't find the word you want, look for a similar word. For example, for "slowly", look up "slow".

## Guide to parts of speech

**noun** *(n)* Nouns give the name of a person, animal or thing. They tell you who or what a sentence is about. "Sofa" and "happiness" are nouns.
Some nouns, such as "ruins", which are normally used in the plural form, have a label *(plural n)*.

**pronoun** *(pronoun)* Pronouns refer to a person or thing without naming it. They act like nouns. "We" and "it" are pronouns.

**adjective** *(adj)* Adjectives are descriptive words which tell you more about a person or thing. They are used with nouns and pronouns. "Huge" and "busy" are adjectives.

**verb** *(v)* Verbs are action words. They tell you what someone or something does, thinks or feels. "Destroy" and "imagine" are verbs.

**adverb** *(adv)* Adverbs tell you how, when, where or why something happens. They are used with verbs. "Suddenly" and "sadly" are adverbs.

**preposition** *(prep)* Prepositions show where people or things are, or what relation they have to each other. "Under" and "near" are prepositions.

**phrase** *(phrase)* This thesaurus also contains phrases which are made up of several parts of speech. "Fall in love with" and "take advantage of" are phrases.

noun  Chloë

and

pronoun I

verb clambered

adverb cautiously

preposition up

the

adjective craggy

noun cliff.

# Choosing and using words

You can transform your writing by choosing interesting words. Try to avoid repeating the same words and use your thesaurus to find exciting alternatives.

Before you start to write, think carefully about the effect you want to create. The examples on this page will give you ideas for using words in different ways.

## Creating atmosphere

To make a scene really come to life, try to use all your senses to describe what you see, hear, smell and feel.

*Fire swept through the forest, devouring everything in its path. Flames licked around the blackened trees and lit up the night sky with a weird orange glow. Branches snapped and crackled in the blaze and the air was thick with the acrid smell of smoke.*

## Conveying action and excitement

Lots of verbs (action words) and short sentences will give your writing a sense of speed and drama.

*Buzz dived for the ball, grabbed it and raced off. Bouncing the ball in front of him, he dodged and swerved up the court. Suddenly he stopped, took aim and shot. It was a goal! The crowd roared with delight. Buzz had saved the match.*

## Describing people

Make your characters interesting and convincing by describing their features, their expressions, their build and the way they move. Details of hair and clothing will help to create a realistic picture.

*A burly figure strode along the quay, his crimson frockcoat flapping in the breeze. Where his left hand should have been, a silver hook gleamed from under a lacy cuff. One eye was hidden by a black patch, but the other glittered greedily. Beneath his tangled beard, his mouth looked thin and cruel and a deep scar ran across his weather-beaten cheek.*

WANTED
Dead or Alive

## Writing conversation

To make a conversation sound natural, think about the way people talk in real life. Try to find different ways of saying "said" (see panel on page 127) and begin a new line whenever a different person starts to speak.

Poppy inquired

Is that a love letter?

It's none of your business!

Ben snapped

*"Is that a love letter?" inquired Poppy, nosily, leaning over Ben's shoulder.*
*"It's none of your business!" snapped Ben, blushing furiously. "Now clear off and leave me alone!"*
*"Is it to Sophie?" she continued. Ben was silent. "Because, if so, I'm sure she'll be very happy..." Poppy tailed off, miserably.*
*"Sophie? No way!" Ben retorted. He took a deep breath. "It's actually to you."*

## Starting a story

There are lots of different ways to begin a story. You can introduce a character, or set a scene, or even jump straight in with an exciting piece of action or an intriguing conversation. A really dramatic opening will grab your readers' attention and make them want to read on.

*Thump!*
*A large, scaly, orange dragon landed at Todd's feet.*
*"Excuse me," said Todd, stepping carefully over its tail. "You're blocking the pavement."*
*"Not for long!" cried the dragon. "Come on, there isn't a moment to lose. We might already be too late!"*

## Ending a story

You can finish a story by tidying everything up, but sometimes it's fun to leave a mystery unsolved.

*It was time to leave Netherfield Manor. Of course it wasn't haunted, it was just a creaky, draughty old house. As I fumbled for my key, I glanced in the hall mirror. Was it just the reflection of the candle flame or was there someone there, calling to me? I locked the door behind me and walked away for ever.*

# Aa

**abandon**
1 *(v) When the river flooded, we had to abandon our homes.* leave, desert, leave behind, vacate, quit, evacuate.
2 *(v) Rain forced us to abandon the match.* discontinue, stop, scrap, give up.

**ability**
1 *(n) I know I have the ability to do better.* potential, capacity, power, capability.
2 *(n) Pablo has great ability in art.* skill, talent, expertise, flair, aptitude.

**able**
*(adj) Vikram is an able tennis player.* capable, competent, proficient, accomplished, practised, skilled, skilful, expert, gifted, talented, clever.

**abnormal** *see* **strange 1.**

**abolish**
*(v) The government wants to abolish smoking in public places.* stamp out, put an end to, do away with, eradicate, wipe out, get rid of, eliminate, stop.

**about**
*(adv) Jo has about 20 hats!* approximately, roughly, around, more or less, close to, nearly, approaching, nearing.
OPPOSITE: exactly.

**abroad**
*(adv) Mum is abroad this week.* overseas, out of the country, in a foreign country.

**abrupt**
1 *(adj) My ride came to an abrupt end.* sudden, rapid, swift, hasty, unexpected, surprising, unanticipated, unforeseen.
OPPOSITES: gradual, slow.
2 *(adj) Alice gave an abrupt reply.* curt, blunt, brusque, brisk, terse, snappy, direct.

**absent** *see* **away 1.**

**absent-minded**
*(adj) Professor Peabody is so absent-minded.* forgetful, scatterbrained, vague, dreamy, distracted, preoccupied, inattentive, lost in thought.

**absolute**
*(adj) That goal was absolute magic!* pure, sheer, complete, total, utter, perfect.

**absolutely**
*(adv) This is absolutely ridiculous!* completely, totally, altogether, utterly, perfectly, positively, thoroughly, entirely.

**absorb**
1 *(v) Use a cloth to absorb the water.* soak up, mop up, suck up, drink up.
2 *(v) I can't absorb all this information at once. See* **take in.**
3 *(v) This book will absorb you for hours.* enthral, captivate, engross, fascinate, rivet.

**absorbing** *see* **fascinating.**
**absurd** *see* **ridiculous.**

**abuse**
1 *(v) Don't abuse your computer.* misuse, ill-treat, damage, harm, manhandle.
2 *(v) It's wrong to abuse animals.* ill-treat, maltreat, be cruel to, harm, hurt, injure, beat, batter, molest.
3 *(n) I've had enough of this abuse.* rudeness, insults *(plural)*, attacks *(plural)*, character assassination, invective, ridicule, derision, slander *(spoken)*, libel *(written)*, cursing, swearing.

**accelerate** *see* **speed up 1.**

**accept**
1 *(v) I hope you will accept this gift.* take, receive, welcome.
OPPOSITES: reject, refuse.
2 *(v) I can't accept this behaviour!* allow, tolerate, put up with *(informal)*, take, stand, bear.
3 *(v) I hope you can accept our plan.* agree to, approve, consent to, go along with, resign yourself to, submit to.
OPPOSITE: reject.

**accident**
1 *(n) Our holiday consisted of one accident after another.* mishap, disaster, misfortune, calamity, catastrophe, blow.
2 *(n) There's been an accident on the motorway. See* **crash 2.**
3 *(n) I broke the plate by accident.* mistake, bad luck.
4 *(n) We met by accident.* chance, coincidence, luck, fluke, serendipity.

**accidental**
*(adj) An accidental meeting.* chance, unexpected, unintentional, unplanned, unforeseen, casual, fluky *(informal)*.

**accompany** *see* **go with 1.**
**accomplish** *see* **achieve.**

**account**
*(n) A written account.* report, record, description, narrative, explanation, statement, diary, journal, log, history.

**accurate**
1 *(adj) Accurate measurements.* exact, precise, correct, spot-on *(informal)*, strict, unerring, faultless, careful, meticulous.
OPPOSITES: approximate, rough.
2 *(adj) An accurate newspaper report.* correct, factual, true, truthful, faithful.
OPPOSITES: inaccurate, false.

**accuse**
*(v) I don't want to accuse you of stealing.* blame you for, charge you with, denounce you for, take you to task for.

**ache**
*(v) My knee is starting to ache.* hurt, throb, pound, be painful, be sore, smart.

**achieve**
*(v) See what you can achieve in an hour.* accomplish, manage, bring about, do, complete, finish, carry out.

**achievement**
*(n) Climbing the mountain was a great achievement.* accomplishment, attainment, feat, triumph, exploit, success.

**act**
1 *(v) Hugh loves to act in his own plays.* perform, appear, take part, star, play.
2 *(v) Act your age!* behave.
3 *(v) This medicine should act quickly.* work, take effect, react, function.
4 *(n) Saving Fido was a courageous act.* deed, feat, action, undertaking, enterprise, exploit, effort, move, step, operation, accomplishment, achievement.
5 *(n) Rosie's shyness is just an act.* pose, pretence, show, sham, front, façade, mask, cover-up, fake, counterfeit.

**action**
1 *(n) That was a brave action. See* **act 4.**
2 *(n) The film was packed with action.* activity, drama, excitement, adventure, movement, energy, incident.

**active**
1 *(adj) Gran is very active.* lively, sprightly, energetic, sporty, vigorous, nimble, spry.
OPPOSITES: sluggish, slow.
2 *(adj) Sally has an active life.* busy, full, energetic, bustling, action-packed.
OPPOSITES: sedentary, idle.
3 *(adj) Marco is an active member of the group.* enthusiastic, hard-working, energetic, involved, committed, dedicated.

**activity**
1 *(n) The classroom was full of activity.* action, movement, bustle, hustle and bustle, life, commotion.
2 *(n) Football is my favourite leisure activity.* pursuit, occupation, pastime, interest, hobby, project, undertaking.

**actor, actress**
*(n)* performer, player, film star, star, lead, supporting actor, character actor, bit player, extra, starlet, dramatic artist.

**adapt**
1 *(v) I want to adapt my bike so it can go faster.* modify, alter, adjust, convert, remodel, reconstruct, rebuild, change.
2 *(v) Dan plans to adapt his book for TV.* alter, change, modify, tailor, edit, rewrite.
3 *(v) It's hard to adapt to life in a new country.* acclimatize, adjust, get used, accustom yourself, fit in.

**adaptable** *see* **flexible 3.**

**add**
1 *(v) Add one more name to the list.* append, attach, tack on *(informal)*, include, insert, affix.
2 *(v) Add these figures together. See* **add up 1.**

**addict**
1 *(n) A drug addict.* user *(informal)*, junkie *(informal)*, crack-head *(slang)*.
2 *(n) A computer addict.* enthusiast, fanatic, devotee, freak *(informal)*, buff *(informal)*, nut *(slang)*, fiend *(informal)*.

# **a**ddicted

**addicted**
1 *(adj) Alice is addicted to computer games.* hooked on, obsessed by, crazy about, devoted to.
2 *(adj) Ziggy is addicted to drugs.* hooked on, dependent on.

**additional** *see* **extra**.

**add up**
1 *(v) Add up these figures.* add, count up, tot up, total, reckon up, find the sum of.
2 *(v) How much does my bill add up to?* amount to, come to, total.
3 *(v) I'm not sure that our story will add up.* make sense, sound convincing, ring true, hold water, be plausible.

**adequate**
1 *(adj) Do you have adequate supplies for your voyage?* sufficient, enough, ample.
OPPOSITES: inadequate, insufficient.
2 *(adj) Your work is adequate, but nothing more.* satisfactory, fair, passable, acceptable, tolerable, good enough, O.K. *(informal)*, all right, so-so *(informal)*.
OPPOSITE: unsatisfactory.

**adjust**
1 *(v) Are you starting to adjust to your new life?* adapt, acclimatize, get used, accustom yourself, reconcile yourself.
2 *(v) We need to adjust our TV.* tune, retune, regulate, fix, fiddle with *(informal)*.
3 *(v) Adjust the straps until they fit tightly.* alter, change, move, fiddle with *(informal)*.

**admire**
1 *(v) I do admire Uncle Jim.* respect, look up to, think highly of, rate *(slang)*, approve of, idolize, revere, appreciate, value.
OPPOSITE: despise.
2 *(v) Let's all admire Gary's new car.* praise, marvel at, wonder at, delight in.

**admirer**
*(n) Do you have an admirer?* fan, follower, devotee, supporter, disciple, suitor, lover, wooer, worshipper.

**admiring**
*(adj) An admiring glance.* appreciative, adoring, approving, delighted, devoted.
OPPOSITES: scornful, disdainful.

**admission**
1 *(n) Admission to the concert is free.* entrance, entry, admittance, access.
2 *(n) Burglar Beryl made an admission of guilt. See* **confession**.

**admit**
1 *(v) How many pupils will the school admit?* accept, take in, give a place to, allow in, receive, welcome.
OPPOSITE: exclude.
2 *(v) You must admit that you're lying.* confess, own up, acknowledge, concede, accept, recognize, grant.
OPPOSITE: deny.

**adolescence**
*(n) Dad remembers his adolescence with affection.* teenage years *(plural)*, teens *(plural)*, youth, puberty.

**adolescent**
*(n)* teenager, youngster, youth, juvenile.

**adopt**
1 *(v) Let's adopt Fran's idea.* take up, follow, accept, go in for, support, endorse.
OPPOSITE: reject.
2 *(v) Will you adopt this injured duck?* take in, befriend, foster, parent, take under your wing.

**adorable**
*(adj) An adorable little kitten.* lovable, appealing, endearing, charming, delightful, sweet, cute, cuddly, winsome.
OPPOSITES: revolting, repellent.

**adore**
1 *(v) Juliet, I adore you. See* **love** 1.
2 *(v) (informal) I adore fudge. See* **like** 1.

**adult**
1 *(n) Wait until you're an adult.* grown-up.
OPPOSITE: child.
2 *(adj) Rosie seems very adult.* mature, grown-up, experienced, sensible.
OPPOSITES: immature, childish.

**advance**
1 *(v) The army began to advance.* move forward, move onward, press on, proceed, progress, approach, come near, bear down.
OPPOSITES: retreat, withdraw.
2 *(v) I hope to advance rapidly this term. See* **improve** 1.
3 *(v) The money will help to advance research.* promote, further, develop, boost, accelerate.
OPPOSITES: hinder, obstruct.
4 *(v) Please advance me some money.* lend, loan.
5 *(n) This is a major advance in space technology.* development, step, improvement, breakthrough.
OPPOSITE: setback.

**advanced**
1 *(adj) An advanced new computer system.* modern, up-to-date, state-of-the-art, progressive, sophisticated.
OPPOSITES: out of date, obsolete.
2 *(adj) Advanced maths.* complicated, complex, higher, difficult, hard.
OPPOSITES: elementary, basic.

**advantage**
1 *(n) A good memory is an advantage if you want to learn a language.* asset, help, benefit, bonus, boon, blessing.
OPPOSITES: disadvantage, handicap.
2 **take advantage of** *see* **take advantage of**.

**adventure**
1 *(n) Crossing the rapids was a great adventure.* feat, escapade, experience, exploit, enterprise, undertaking, venture.
2 *(n) Amanda longed for adventure.* excitement, drama, thrills *(plural)*, thrills and spills *(plural)*, danger.

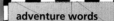

## adventure words

### adventures can be...

| | |
|---|---|
| action-packed | incredible |
| amazing | intriguing |
| astonishing | nail-biting |
| baffling | nerve-racking |
| dangerous | perilous |
| exciting | perplexing |
| exhilarating | puzzling |
| extraordinary | remarkable |
| fascinating | scary *(informal)* |
| frightening | strange |
| hair-raising | terrifying |
| hazardous | thrilling |

### adventure clues

| | |
|---|---|
| ancient manuscript | last will and testament |
| chart | map |
| cryptic message (message in code) | newspaper cutting |
| cypher (code) | parchment scroll |
| diary | photograph |
| footprints | riddle |
| inscription | sealed letter |
| | secret symbols |
| | tape recording |

*cryptic message*

*penknife*

### equipment for adventures

| | |
|---|---|
| binoculars | rope ladder |
| camera | rucksack |
| codebook | survival kit |
| compass | torch |
| magnifying glass | vine cutters |
| map | water bottle |
| notebook | |
| penknife | |

*compass*

*binoculars*

## LOST CITY

**in the city you see...**
bridge
canal
city walls
courtyard
lake
market place
mosaic pavement
palace
pyramid
river
temple
tombs
winding streets

**the city is...**
ancient
beautiful
deserted
fabled
forbidding
forgotten
hidden
legendary
magnificent
mysterious
remote
ruined
sinister
undiscovered
unexplored

*courtyard*

*temple*

*plan of labyrinth*

**under the lost city**
cavern
dead end
labyrinth
(network of tunnels)
maze
pillar
sealed passage
secret entrance
stone steps
tunnel
underground chamber
underground passage
underground waterway

**the tunnels under the city are...**
airless
bewildering
claustrophobic
confusing
creepy (informal)
crooked
dark
disorientating
endless
meandering
musty
narrow
shadowy
silent
stuffy
tortuous
twisting
winding

*underground passage*

## TEMPLES AND TOMBS

**in the temples and tombs you see...**
burial chamber
carved symbols
coffin
corridor
engravings
flaming torch
gilded shrine
gilded throne
hidden entrance
hieroglyphics
(picture writing)
mummy
(embalmed body)

pillar
sacrificial altar
sarcophagus
(stone coffin)
shrine
skull rack
staircase
statue
stone slab
stone tablet
treasure chamber
tunnel
wall painting

*hieroglyphics*

*sarcophagus*

*statue*

**the temple is...**
awe-inspiring
colossal
crumbling
immense
imposing
magnificent
majestic
massive
monumental
towering
vast

**inside the temple it is...**
cool
dim
dingy
eerie
gloomy
menacing
murky
mysterious
sinister
smoky

**treasures of the tombs**
amulet (lucky charm)
armlet
bowl
bracelet
chalice
(drinking cup)
coin
dagger
diadem
(light crown)
flagon (jug)
goblet
golden casket
golden mask
helmet
idol
jewelled collar
medallion
necklace
pendant
shield
sword

*golden mask*

*goblet*

*dagger*

*necklace*

*coins*

*shield*

*Also see* **fantasy words, ghosts & hauntings, jungle, pirates & shipwrecks, space adventure, treasure words.**

# adventurous

**adventurous**
1 *(adj) Gerry is an adventurous climber.*
See **daring**.
2 *(adj) Kit loves adventurous holidays.*
exciting, challenging, dangerous, risky.

**advertise**
*(v) Let's advertise our play in the paper.*
publicize, announce, draw attention to,
plug *(informal)*, promote, push.

**advertisement**
*(n)* advert *(informal)*, ad *(informal)*, plug
*(informal)*, announcement.
TYPES OF ADVERTISEMENT: blurb *(book
jacket)*, brochure, classified advertisement
*(newspaper)*, commercial *(TV and radio)*,
display, flier, hand-out, leaflet, notice,
placard, poster, promotion, publicity stunt,
sandwich board, small ad *(newspaper)*
*(informal)*.

**advice**
*(n) I need some advice on how to mend
my bicycle.* suggestions *(plural)*, hints
*(plural)*, tips *(plural)*, guidance, help.

**advise**
*(v) I advise that you try again.* suggest,
recommend, urge, counsel, encourage.

**affair**
1 *(n) I'll handle this; it's my affair.*
business, concern, problem, responsibility.
2 *(n) Kurt's disappearance was a strange
affair.* business, occurrence, event,
incident, episode, matter, case.
3 *(n) Romeo and Juliet had a passionate
affair.* love affair, romance, relationship,
attachment, involvement, liaison.
4 *(n) The party was a grand affair.*
occasion, event, do *(informal)*, function.

**affect**
*(v) The weather can affect my mood.*
influence, have an effect on, have an
impact on, sway, alter, change, transform.

**affection**
*(n) Kate looked at her mum with affection.*
fondness, tenderness, warmth, devotion,
love, liking, friendship.

**affectionate** see **loving**.

**afford**
*(v) I can't afford a new pair of jeans.* pay
for, spare the money for, meet the cost of,
find the cash for, bear the expense of.

**afraid** see **scared** 1, 2.

**age**
1 *(n) We're studying the Elizabethan age.*
period, era, days *(plural)*, time, epoch.
2 *(v) We all age as time passes.* grow old,
decline, deteriorate, fade, grow older,
grow up, mature, come of age.
3 **ages** *(plural n) I haven't seen Hugo for
ages.* a long time, a long while, weeks
*(plural)*, months *(plural)*, years *(plural)*,
aeons *(plural)*, yonks *(plural)* *(informal)*.

**aggravate**
1 *(v) Complaining will only aggravate the
problem.* make worse, worsen, magnify,
intensify, heighten, exacerbate.

2 *(v) (informal) Practical jokes aggravate
Mrs Badger.* See **annoy** 1.

**aggressive**
*(adj) Roger is so aggressive; he's always
starting fights.* quarrelsome, belligerent,
pugnacious, argumentative, antagonistic,
provocative, hostile, violent.
OPPOSITES: submissive, friendly.

**agile**
*(adj) Monkeys are agile in their
movements.* nimble, lithe, sprightly,
acrobatic, lively, supple, limber, flexible.
OPPOSITES: awkward, stiff.

**agitated**
*(adj) The long wait made me feel agitated.*
uneasy, edgy, restless, fidgety, nervous,
worked up, anxious, perturbed, unnerved,
disconcerted, troubled, worried.
OPPOSITES: calm, serene.

**agonizing**
*(adj) An agonizing pain.* excruciating,
racking, stabbing, shooting, piercing,
searing, acute, intense, unbearable.

**agony**
1 *(n) When he broke his ankle, Marvin
was in agony.* pain, torment, distress,
paroxysms *(plural)*.
2 *(n) Parting from Peter was agony.*
misery, torture, torment, anguish.

**agree**
1 *(v) Do you agree that this is a good film?*
acknowledge, admit, accept, recognize.
OPPOSITE: deny.
2 *(v) Let's agree a date to play tennis.* fix,
decide on, arrange, settle on, arrive at.
3 *(v) I wish you two would agree!*
get on, see eye to eye, be united, concur.
OPPOSITES: disagree, quarrel.
4 **agree with** *(v) I agree with animal
rights.* See **support** 3.
5 **agree with** *(v) Does your version of
events agree with mine?* correspond to,
coincide with, match, fit, conform to, tally
with, square with.
OPPOSITE: differ from.
6 **agree to** *(v) I hope that Nat will agree
to our plan.* consent to, accept, go along
with, comply with, assent to, approve.

**agreement**
*(n) The two sides reached an agreement.*
understanding, consensus, settlement,
arrangement, deal *(informal)*, bargain,
contract, pact, truce, treaty.

**aid**
1 *(n) Many countries offered aid to victims
of the earthquake.* help, assistance, relief,
support, backing, a helping hand.
2 *(v) The money we raise will aid starving
children.* See **help** 3.

**aim**
1 *(n) My aim is to become a pilot.*
ambition, goal, target, intention, plan,
objective, wish, dream, hope, aspiration.
2 *(v) I aim to be famous one day.* intend,
plan, mean, want, wish, aspire, propose.

3 *(v) Aim the arrow at the bull's-eye.*
point, direct, line up with, zero in on.

**aimless**
*(adj) Amy wandered around in an aimless
way.* pointless, purposeless, futile,
haphazard, random, rambling, desultory.
OPPOSITE: purposeful.

**air**
1 *(n) The kite soared high into the air.* sky,
atmosphere, heavens *(plural)*, ether.
2 *(n) The air felt cool on my face.* fresh air,
breeze, wind, draught, breath of air.
3 *(n) The house had an air of mystery.*
appearance, look, atmosphere, feeling,
sense, aura, mood, impression.

**aircraft**
*(n)* plane, aeroplane,
flying machine
*(old-fashioned)*.
TYPES OF AIRCRAFT:
airliner, airship,
biplane, bomber, cargo
plane, executive jet,
fighter, glider, hang-
glider, helicopter, hot-air
balloon, jet, jumbo jet, jump
jet, microlight, reconnaissance
plane, rescue helicopter,
seaplane, stealth bomber,
supersonic jet, tanker, triplane.
❖ Also see **journey words**.

*hot-air
balloon*

**airport**
*(n)* aerodrome, airfield, heliport.

**airy**
*(adj) The room was light and airy.* fresh,
well-ventilated, draughty, spacious, open.
OPPOSITE: stuffy.

**alarm**
1 *(n) If you hear the alarm, run for cover!*
siren, bell, buzzer, signal, warning, alert.
2 *(n) Seb shrank back in alarm.* dismay,
panic, consternation, fear, fright, terror.
3 *(v) This news may alarm you.* startle,
frighten, scare, worry, panic, unnerve, put
the wind up *(informal)*, upset, disturb,
distress, shock, dismay.
OPPOSITE: reassure.

**alert**
1 *(adj) You seem very alert this morning.*
wide-awake, sharp, quick, perceptive,
attentive, on the ball *(informal)*, on your
toes, lively, quick off the mark *(informal)*.
OPPOSITES: lethargic, slow.
2 *(adj) The guards stayed alert all night.*
See **awake**.
3 *(v) Alert the police!* See **warn** 1.

**alien**
1 *(n) An alien stepped from the
spacecraft.* extraterrestial, space creature.
2 *(adj) The new school seemed alien to
me.* See **strange** 3.

**alike**
*(adj) The twins look alike.* identical, the
same, similar, like peas in a pod *(informal)*.
OPPOSITE: different.

**alive**
1 *(adj) Our rabbits are still alive.* living,
breathing, alive and kicking, in the land of
the living *(informal),* surviving, flourishing.
OPPOSITE: dead.
2 *(adj) There are no dinosaurs alive today.*
living, existing, in existence.
OPPOSITE: extinct.

**alley**
*(n)* alleyway, backstreet, passage, lane.

**almost** *see* **nearly.**

**alone**
1 *(adj) Are you alone in the house?* on
your own, by yourself, unaccompanied,
unattended, solitary, solo.
2 *(adj) After my friends left, I felt alone.*
lonely, solitary, isolated, friendless, forlorn,
abandoned, forsaken, deserted, desolate.

**aloof** *see* **cold 4.**

**a lot** *see* **many.**

**amazing**
*(adj) Arthur made an amazing discovery.*
astonishing, incredible, remarkable,
extraordinary, unusual, startling,
astounding, staggering, stunning,
breathtaking, miraculous, phenomenal,
electrifying, sensational *(informal).*

**ambition**
1 *(n) My ambition is to become a pilot.*
See **aim 1.**
2 *(n) Joel has plenty of ambition.* drive,
enthusiasm, eagerness, enterprise, get-up-
and-go *(informal),* oomph *(informal).*

**ambitious**
*(adj) An ambitious businessman.* go-
getting *(informal),* pushy *(informal),* go-
ahead, forceful, purposeful, enterprising.
OPPOSITE: unambitious.

**ammunition**
*(n)* TYPES OF AMMUNITION: blank
cartridge, bullet, cannonball, cartridge,
grenade, missile, rocket, rubber bullet,
shell, shot, shrapnel.

**amount**
1 *(n) We bought a large amount of jelly
babies.* quantity, number, supply.
2 *(n) The reservoir holds a large amount of
water.* quantity, volume, mass, expanse.
3 *(n) What was the final amount that you
raised?* sum, total, grand total, sum total.
4 **amount to** *(v) Lord Lucre's savings
amount to millions.* See **add up 2.**

**amuse**
1 *(v) I think this joke will amuse you.* make
you laugh, tickle you *(informal),* cheer you
up, raise a smile.
2 *(v) This game will amuse you for hours.*
entertain, keep you amused, occupy,
absorb, engross, interest, fascinate.
OPPOSITE: bore.

**amusement**
1 *(n) The joke caused much amusement.*
laughter, hilarity, mirth, merriment.
OPPOSITES: boredom, sadness.
2 *(n) What do you do for amusement?*
fun, pleasure, entertainment, enjoyment,
interest, recreation, leisure, pastime, sport.

**amusing**
1 *(adj) An amusing joke.* See **funny 1.**
2 *(adj) An amusing game of cards.* See
**entertaining**.

**analyse**
*(v) Let's analyse the situation.* examine,
think through, investigate, study, consider,
review, inquire into, scrutinize, evaluate.

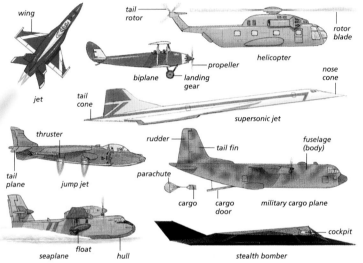

wing

tail
rotor

rotor
blade

helicopter

propeller

nose
cone

biplane

landing
gear

jet

tail
cone

supersonic jet

thruster

rudder

tail fin

fuselage
(body)

tail
plane

jump jet

parachute

cargo

cargo
door

military cargo plane

cockpit

seaplane

float

hull

stealth bomber

**allow**
1 *(v) Will your dad allow you to go?* give
you permission, permit, let, authorize, give
you leave, give you the green light, give
you the go-ahead *(informal).*
OPPOSITE: forbid.
2 *(v) Mrs Badger will not allow talking in
class.* permit, tolerate, stand for *(informal),*
put up with *(informal),* endure, sanction.
OPPOSITES: forbid, prohibit.

**allowance**
1 *(n) Each refugee had an allowance of
food.* share, portion, ration, measure,
amount, quota, allocation.
2 *(n) A clothes allowance.* grant, subsidy.

**all right**
1 *(adj) Is it all right to come in?* O.K.
*(informal),* permitted, in order, acceptable.
2 *(adj) I had an accident but I'm all right.*
O.K. *(informal),* unharmed, uninjured, safe,
safe and sound, healthy, well.
3 *(adj) The food was all right.* adequate,
acceptable, satisfactory, average, fair, O.K.
*(informal),* reasonable, tolerable, passable.

**ally**
*(n) America was an ally of Britain in World
War II.* partner, associate, colleague,
friend, helper.
OPPOSITE: enemy.

**also**
*(adv)* too, as well, besides, in addition,
additionally, furthermore, on top of that.

**alter**
1 *(v) Let's alter our plans.* See **change 1.**
2 *(v) I need to alter my trousers.* adjust,
take in, take up, let out, let down, shorten,
lengthen, remodel, revamp, transform.

**alternative**
1 *(adj) Let's try an alternative plan.*
different, other, substitute, back-up.
2 *(n) Do I have an alternative?* choice,
option, fall-back.

**always**
1 *(adv) Fifi is always late.* consistently,
invariably, without exception, regularly,
repeatedly, unfailingly, constantly,
continually, perpetually, forever.
OPPOSITES: never, rarely.
2 *(adv) I will love you always.* forever,
forever and ever, evermore, eternally,
unceasingly, until the end of time.

**amaze** *see* **astonish.**

**amazed** *see* **astonished.**

**amazement**
*(adj) Tiggy looked at me in amazement.*
astonishment, surprise, shock, confusion,
bewilderment, wonder, admiration.

**ancient**
1 *(adj) How did people live in ancient
times?* early, past, bygone, olden *(old-
fashioned),* primeval, prehistoric, primitive.
OPPOSITES: modern, recent.
2 *(adj) Our school buildings are ancient.*
old, aged, archaic, antiquated, timeworn,
out of date, old-fashioned, outmoded,
antediluvian, out of the ark *(informal).*
OPPOSITES: modern, state-of-the-art.

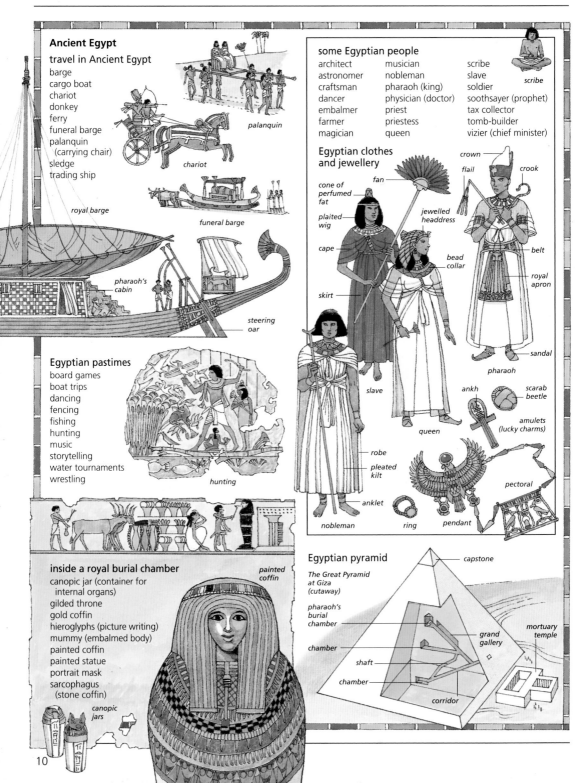

## Ancient Egypt

### travel in Ancient Egypt
barge
cargo boat
chariot
donkey
ferry
funeral barge
palanquin
  (carrying chair)
sledge
trading ship

*palanquin*

*chariot*

*royal barge*

*funeral barge*

*pharaoh's cabin*

*steering oar*

### Egyptian pastimes
board games
boat trips
dancing
fencing
fishing
hunting
music
storytelling
water tournaments
wrestling

*hunting*

### some Egyptian people
| | | |
|---|---|---|
| architect | musician | scribe |
| astronomer | nobleman | slave |
| craftsman | pharaoh (king) | soldier |
| dancer | physician (doctor) | soothsayer (prophet) |
| embalmer | priest | tax collector |
| farmer | priestess | tomb-builder |
| magician | queen | vizier (chief minister) |

*scribe*

### Egyptian clothes and jewellery

*cone of perfumed fat*
*plaited wig*
*cape*
*skirt*
*fan*
*jewelled headdress*
*bead collar*
*crown*
*flail*
*crook*
*belt*
*royal apron*
*sandal*

*pharaoh*

*slave*
*queen*
*ankh*
*scarab beetle*
*amulets (lucky charms)*

*robe*
*pleated kilt*
*anklet*
*nobleman*
*ring*
*pendant*
*pectoral*

### inside a royal burial chamber
canopic jar (container for
  internal organs)
gilded throne
gold coffin
hieroglyphs (picture writing)
mummy (embalmed body)
painted coffin
painted statue
portrait mask
sarcophagus
  (stone coffin)

*painted coffin*

*canopic jars*

### Egyptian pyramid

*The Great Pyramid at Giza (cutaway)*

*capstone*
*pharaoh's burial chamber*
*chamber*
*shaft*
*chamber*
*grand gallery*
*mortuary temple*
*corridor*

---

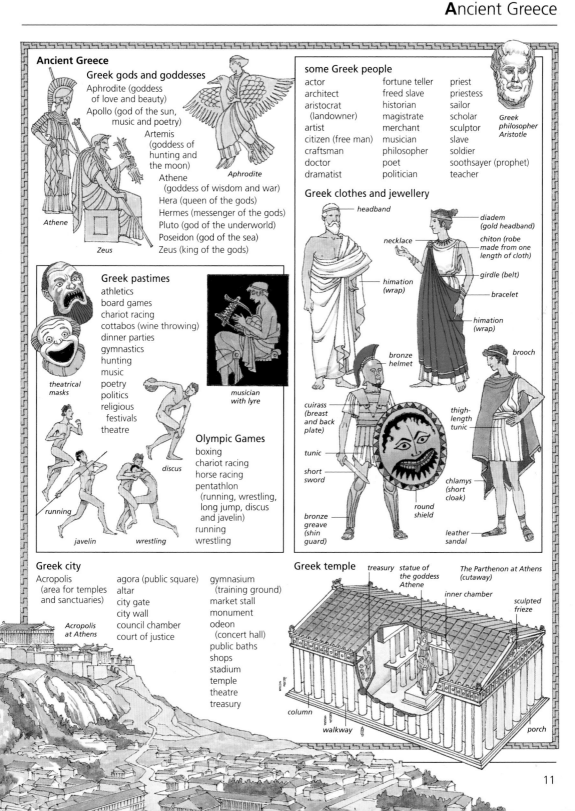

## Ancient Greece

### Greek gods and goddesses

Aphrodite (goddess of love and beauty)
Apollo (god of the sun, music and poetry)
Artemis (goddess of hunting and the moon)
Athene (goddess of wisdom and war)
Hera (queen of the gods)
Hermes (messenger of the gods)
Pluto (god of the underworld)
Poseidon (god of the sea)
Zeus (king of the gods)

*Athene*

*Aphrodite*

*Zeus*

### Greek pastimes

athletics
board games
chariot racing
cottabos (wine throwing)
dinner parties
gymnastics
hunting
music
poetry
politics
religious festivals
theatre

*theatrical masks*

*musician with lyre*

### Olympic Games

boxing
chariot racing
horse racing
pentathlon (running, wrestling, long jump, discus and javelin)
running
wrestling

*running*

*javelin*

*wrestling*

*discus*

### some Greek people

actor
architect
aristocrat (landowner)
artist
citizen (free man)
craftsman
doctor
dramatist
fortune teller
freed slave
historian
magistrate
merchant
musician
philosopher
poet
politician
priest
priestess
sailor
scholar
sculptor
slave
soldier
soothsayer (prophet)
teacher

*Greek philosopher Aristotle*

### Greek clothes and jewellery

headband
himation (wrap)
diadem (gold headband)
necklace
chiton (robe made from one length of cloth)
girdle (belt)
bracelet
himation (wrap)
bronze helmet
brooch
cuirass (breast and back plate)
thigh-length tunic
tunic
short sword
round shield
bronze greave (shin guard)
chlamys (short cloak)
leather sandal

### Greek city

Acropolis (area for temples and sanctuaries)

*Acropolis at Athens*

agora (public square)
altar
city gate
city wall
council chamber
court of justice

gymnasium (training ground)
market stall
monument
odeon (concert hall)
public baths
shops
stadium
temple
theatre
treasury

### Greek temple

treasury
statue of the goddess Athene
inner chamber
sculpted frieze

*The Parthenon at Athens (cutaway)*

column
walkway
porch

# anger

**anger**
1 *(n) Mum turned purple with anger.*
rage, fury, wrath, indignation, annoyance, exasperation, irritation, outrage.
2 *(v) Your giggles will anger Mrs Badger.*
infuriate, enrage, madden, incense, rile, annoy, exasperate, irritate, provoke.
OPPOSITES: pacify, placate.

**angry**
*(adj) Dad was angry that I hadn't told the truth.* furious, livid, irate, incensed, fuming, seething, raging, enraged, mad *(informal)*, apoplectic, cross, annoyed, indignant.

**animal**
*(n) A wild animal.* creature, beast.

**announce**
1 *(v) I heard the head announce that the trip was cancelled.* state, declare, give out, reveal, disclose, make known, make public.
2 *(v) Will you announce the next act in the talent show?* introduce, present, lead into.

**announcement**
*(n) Did you hear the announcement?*
notice, statement, message, bulletin, communication, advertisement, report, declaration, disclosure.

**announcer**
*(n)* presenter, broadcaster, anchorman, newsreader, newscaster, commentator, master of ceremonies, town crier.

**annoy**
1 *(v) Doesn't your brother annoy you?*
irritate, exasperate, infuriate, get on your nerves *(informal)*, madden, provoke, rile, bug *(informal)*, rub you up the wrong way, aggravate *(informal)*, needle *(informal)*, get to *(informal)*, get up your nose *(slang)*, nark *(slang)*, get on your wick *(slang)*.
2 *(v) Don't annoy Dad when he's busy.*
disturb, bother, trouble, pester, hassle *(informal)*, badger, harass, worry.

**annoyed**
*(adj) Kim was annoyed that she hadn't got her own way.* irritated, exasperated, cross, indignant, displeased, vexed, riled, miffed *(informal)*, peeved *(informal)*, piqued.
OPPOSITE: pleased.

**annoying**
*(adj) Are you being deliberately annoying?*
irritating, infuriating, maddening, exasperating, aggravating *(informal)*, tiresome, trying, irksome, troublesome.

**anonymous**
1 *(adj) The writer wishes to remain anonymous.* nameless, unnamed, unidentified, unknown, unacknowledged, uncredited, incognito.
2 *(adj) An anonymous letter.* unsigned.

**answer**
1 *(v) You didn't answer my question.* reply to, respond to, react to, acknowledge.
OPPOSITE: ask.
2 *(v) "Never!" I heard Luke answer.* reply, respond, retort, return, rejoin, retaliate.
OPPOSITES: ask, inquire.

3 *(n) Kay gave no answer to my question.*
reply, response, reaction, comeback *(informal)*, acknowledgment, rejoinder.
OPPOSITE: question.
4 *(n) What is the answer to this problem?*
solution, explanation, key.

**answer back**
*(v) Don't answer back!* talk back, argue, contradict, be cheeky, be impertinent.

**anticlimax** *see* **letdown**.

**antisocial**
*(adj) Antisocial behaviour.* disruptive, anarchic, rebellious, uncooperative, offensive, disagreeable, hostile, disorderly, unruly, antagonistic.

**anxiety** *see* **worry** 3.

**anxious**
1 *(adj) Sally is anxious about her exams.*
worried, apprehensive, concerned, nervous, tense, uneasy, edgy, on edge, uptight *(informal)*, jittery *(informal)*, troubled, agitated, perturbed, fretful, fearful, distressed, overwrought.
OPPOSITES: calm, confident.
2 *(adj) We are anxious to get started.*
*See* **eager** 2.

**apathetic** *see* **indifferent**.

**apologetic** *see* **sorry** 1.

**apologize**
*(v) You ought to apologize for breaking the window.* say sorry, say you are sorry, make an apology, express regret, be penitent about, ask forgiveness, beg pardon, eat humble pie.

**apology**
*(n) Mum accepted my apology.* expression of regret, confession, explanation, excuse, plea, defence, justification.

**appalling** *see* **dreadful** 1, 2, 3.

**apparent** *see* **obvious**.

**appeal**
1 *(n) A charity appeal.* campaign.
2 *(n) Burglar Beryl made an appeal for mercy.* plea, request, cry, call, petition.
3 *(v) We will appeal for more volunteers.* ask, put in a plea, beg, plead, call, request, petition, canvass.
4 **appeal to** *(v) This film will appeal to young children.* interest, delight, attract, fascinate, captivate, enthral, enchant, charm, please.
OPPOSITES: bore, repulse, alienate.

**appealing** *see* **charming**.

**appear**
1 *(v) We watched the ship appear over the horizon.* come into view, come into sight, emerge, loom, materialize, surface.
OPPOSITES: disappear, vanish.
2 *(v) What time did you appear at the party?* arrive, turn up, show up *(informal)*, roll up *(informal)*, come.
OPPOSITES: leave, depart.
3 *(v) Do you appear in the play?* feature, figure, perform, act, take part, play a part.

4 *(v) You appear fit and well.* look, seem, give the impression of being.
5 *(v) The next issue of "Rap Weekly" will appear on Monday.* come out, be published, become available, come on the market, hit the shops *(informal)*.

**appearance**
1 *(n) Can you describe Samantha's appearance?* looks *(plural)*, bearing, demeanour, figure, image, expression, air.
2 *(n) Ed gives the appearance of being confident.* impression, illusion, outward appearance, show, semblance, pretence.
OPPOSITE: reality.
3 *(n) The sudden appearance of rain spoiled the barbecue.* arrival, advent, coming, presence.
OPPOSITE: disappearance.

## appearance words

| tall | thin | strong |
|------|------|--------|
| lanky | bony | athletic |
| leggy | emaciated | beefy |
| towering | gaunt | *(informal)* |
| | lanky | brawny |
| **short** | lean | broad- |
| diminutive | scraggy | shouldered |
| dumpy | scrawny | burly |
| little | skeletal | hulking |
| petite | skinny | muscular |
| pint-sized | spare | powerful |
| *(informal)* | spindly | sinewy |
| small | waiflike | stocky |
| squat | | strapping |
| tiny | **slim** | sturdy |
| | dainty | thickset |
| **fat** | elfin | well-built |
| chubby | lithe | wiry |
| corpulent | slender | |
| flabby | slight | **weak** |
| heavy | svelte | anaemic |
| hefty | sylphlike | delicate |
| obese | trim | feeble |
| overweight | willowy | fragile |
| paunchy | | frail |
| plump | **curvy** | puny |
| podgy | bosomy | sickly |
| portly | busty | weedy |
| potbellied | buxom | *(informal)* |
| stout | curvaceous | wimpish |
| tubby | shapely | *(informal)* |
| weighty | voluptuous | |
| | | **upright** |
| | | erect |
| | | straight |
| | | straight- |
| | | backed |
| | | unbending |

*hulking sumo wrestler*

## appetite
(n) Indiana has an appetite for adventure. taste, thirst, hunger, need, desire, passion, liking, longing, craving, yearning, hankering, eagerness, zest.
OPPOSITES: dislike, aversion.

## appetizing see delicious.

## applaud
(v) The audience are sure to applaud. clap, cheer, whistle, give you a standing ovation, give you a big hand (informal), put their hands together, ask for an encore.
OPPOSITES: boo, heckle.

## apply
1 (v) Apply the lotion twice a day. use, smear on, put on, rub in, spread on, administer, cover with.

| hunched | smart |
| --- | --- |
| bent | dapper |
| bowed | neat |
| crooked | spruce |
| drooping | tidy |
| slouching | well-dressed |
| stooping | well-groomed |
| | |
| young | messy |
| boyish | bedraggled |
| girlish | dishevelled |
| youthful | scruffy |
| | shabby |
| old | tatty |
| aged | unkempt |
| elderly | untidy |
| | |
| graceful | fashionable |
| agile | chic |
| dignified | trendy (informal) |
| elegant | smart |
| lithe | stylish |
| poised | up-to-date |
| | |
| clumsy | unfashionable |
| awkward | dowdy |
| blundering | old-fashioned |
| bumbling | |
| gangling | sophisticated |
| gauche | classy (slang) |
| gawky | debonair |
| lumbering | elegant |
| shambling | glamorous |
| uncoordinated | refined |
| ungainly | suave |

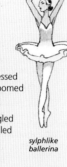

*sylphlike ballerina*

*wiry gymnast*

Also see **faces & features, hair & hairstyles**.

2 (v) This comment could apply to you. refer, relate, be relevant, be applicable, be pertinent, have a bearing on, pertain.
3 **apply for** (v) Did you apply for the job? make an application for, put in for, try for, inquire after, request.
4 **apply yourself** (v) You need to apply yourself to your work. See **concentrate** 2.

## appointment
(n) I have an appointment at four o'clock. engagement, meeting, date, rendezvous, interview, consultation (medical).

## appreciate
1 (v) I will always appreciate your help. value, be grateful for, be thankful for, be appreciative of, be indebted to you for, welcome.
OPPOSITE: be ungrateful for.
2 (v) Aunt Bertha will never appreciate pop music. enjoy, approve of, admire, think much of, think highly of, rate (slang), understand.
OPPOSITE: despise.
3 (v) Do you appreciate how long it took to make this meal? See **realize**.

## apprehensive see anxious 1.

## approach
1 (v) The army began to approach. draw near, come closer, move nearer, edge nearer, bear down, near, advance, push forward, catch up.
OPPOSITES: move away, back off.
2 (v) I intend to approach Dad about my pocket money. speak to, talk to, tackle, sound out, appeal to, make a proposal to.
3 (v) I'm not sure how to approach this essay. tackle, set about, go about, start, begin, embark on, make a start on.

## approachable see friendly.

## appropriate see suitable 1, 2.

## approve
1 (v) The chairman must approve the plan first. accept, agree to, authorize, pass, endorse, consent to, give the go-ahead to (informal), rubber-stamp (informal).
2 **approve of** (v) I hope you'll approve of what I've done. be pleased with, like, applaud, admire, think highly of, have a good opinion of, appreciate, respect.
OPPOSITE: disapprove of.

## approximately see about.

## area
1 (n) I have a lot of friends in this area. district, neighbourhood, locality, part of the world, region, vicinity.
2 (n) The fire destroyed a large area of forest. expanse, stretch, patch, tract.

## arena
(n) A sports arena. stadium, ground, field, ring, pitch, bowl, oval, rink.

## argue
1 (v) My brothers argue all the time. quarrel, squabble, bicker, row, fight, fall out (informal), disagree, wrangle.
OPPOSITES: agree, get on.

2 (v) My cousins argue that eating animals is wrong. claim, assert, declare, maintain, insist, reason, hold, contend.

## argument
1 (n) We had an argument over who should pay. row, quarrel, squabble, disagreement, dispute, difference of opinion, clash, fight, tiff (informal), bust-up (informal), set-to (informal).
OPPOSITE: agreement.
2 (n) The argument about violence on TV continues. debate, discussion, controversy.
3 (n) Your argument is very convincing. reasoning, logic, evidence, defence, justification, case, reasons (plural), grounds (plural).

## armed
1 (adj) The robber is armed. carrying weapons, armed to the teeth.
OPPOSITES: unarmed, defenceless.
2 (adj) The soldiers were armed with swords. equipped, fitted out, supplied, provided, issued.

## armour
(n) protection.
TYPES OF ARMOUR: body armour, bulletproof vest, chain mail, flak jacket, plate armour, riot shield, suit of armour.

helmet
visor
cuirass (breast and back plate)
gauntlet
cuisse (thigh guard)
greave (shin guard)
*suit of armour*

## aroma see smell 1.

## arrange
1 (v) Would you arrange these ornaments for me? display, set out, put out, tidy, position, line up, align, put in order.
2 (v) Can you arrange these words in alphabetical order? sort, group, organize, set out, rank, classify, categorize, collate.
3 (v) Let's arrange a party. organize, plan, fix up, set up, prepare, schedule.

## arrangement
1 (n) The arrangement is that we use the gym on Tuesdays. agreement, understanding, deal (informal), set-up (informal), system, plan, scheme.
2 (n) What a beautiful arrangement of flowers! display, array, show.

## arrest
(v) The police decided to arrest Burglar Beryl. take into custody, detain, apprehend, catch, capture, seize, haul in, collar (informal), run in (informal), pick up (informal), nab (informal), nick (slang).

**arrive**
1 *(v) When do you think Tracy will arrive?* appear, turn up, show up *(informal),* come, roll up *(informal),* get here, put in an appearance, show *(informal).*
OPPOSITES: leave, depart.
2 *(v) When will we arrive in New York?* land, touch down, dock, berth, disembark.
OPPOSITES: leave, take off, set sail.

**arrogant** *see* **proud** 2.

**art**
1 *(n) Lysander is studying art.* the visual arts *(plural),* design, fine art, art history.
TYPES OF ART: architecture, carving, computer art, drawing, engraving, etching, graphics, illustration, installation art, mosaic making, painting, photography, printing, sculpture, stained glass, tapestry.
*Also see* **drawing**, **painting**.
2 *(n) We admired the potter's art.*
*See* **skill**.

**article**
1 *(n) There's an interesting article in the newspaper.* item, feature, story, report, write-up, piece, column, exclusive, scoop *(informal),* editorial, leader.
2 *(n) What's that odd-looking article on the table?* object, thing, item.

**artificial**
1 *(adj) Lycra is an artificial fibre.* synthetic, man-made, manufactured.
OPPOSITE: natural.
2 *(adj) Artificial pearls are cheaper than real ones.* imitation, fake, simulated, synthetic, sham, mock, pseudo *(informal).*
OPPOSITES: genuine, natural.
3 *(adj) Araminta gave me an artificial smile.* insincere, forced, false, feigned, affected, phoney *(informal),* put-on.
OPPOSITES: genuine, sincere.

**ascend** *see* **rise** 1.

**ash**
*(n) The ash from the volcano glowed red-hot.* cinders *(plural),* embers *(plural).*

**ashamed**
*(adj) Ben looked ashamed that he'd lost his temper.* guilty, conscience-stricken, sorry, mortified, embarrassed, shamefaced, sheepish, red-faced, repentant, remorseful, rueful, abashed, chastened, humiliated.
OPPOSITE: unrepentant.

**ask**
1 *(v) Jon wants to ask if his answer is right.* inquire, enquire, query, question.
OPPOSITES: reply, answer.
2 *(v) The police want to ask Burglar Beryl about the robbery.* question, interrogate, cross-examine, quiz, grill *(informal),* pump, give the third degree to.
3 *(v) Wait for the doctor to ask you into the surgery.* invite, summon, order, bid.
4 **ask for** *(v) Jo decided to ask for more pocket money.* request, appeal for, beg for, plead for, demand, call for, claim, press for, petition for, apply for.

5 **ask for** *(v) You did rather ask for that punch on the nose!* deserve, bring on yourself, provoke, cause, encourage.

**asleep**
*(adj) Dad's asleep on the sofa.* sleeping, fast asleep, sound asleep, dozing, snoozing *(informal),* napping, having a kip *(slang),* slumbering *(old-fashioned),* crashed out *(slang),* dead to the world *(informal).*
OPPOSITE: awake.

**assault** *see* **attack** 2, 4, 5.

**assemble**
1 *(v) Mrs Badger told us to assemble in the hall.* See **meet** 3.
2 *(v) The workers began to assemble the car.* construct, build, put together, manufacture, piece together.
OPPOSITES: dismantle, take apart.

**assembly** *see* **meeting** 2.

**assertive**
1 *(adj) You should try to be more assertive.* confident, self-assured, firm, decisive, positive, emphatic, forceful.
OPPOSITE: passive.
2 *(adj) Pat is becoming too assertive.* domineering, overbearing, aggressive, opinionated, dogmatic, forceful, strong-willed, pushy *(informal).*
OPPOSITE: submissive.

**assistance** *see* **help** 5.

**assistant**
*(n)* helper, deputy, second-in-command, right-hand man or woman, henchman *(informal),* subordinate.

**associate**
1 *(v) Don't associate with those boys!* See **mix** 3.
2 *(v) I always associate that smell with school dinners.* connect, identify, link, lump together, relate to.

**assorted** *see* **mixed** 1.

**assortment** *see* **mixture** 1.

**assume**
*(v) I assume you like chocolate.* presume, take it for granted, expect, suppose, imagine, suspect, believe, guess *(informal).*

**assure**
*(v) Can you assure me that I won't be in danger?* promise, give your word, swear, guarantee, reassure, convince, persuade.

**astonish**
*(v) Marvello the Magician will astonish you with his tricks.* amaze, astound, stun, stagger, leave you speechless, startle, surprise, dazzle, take your breath away, leave you open-mouthed, wow *(slang).*

**astonished**
*(adj) I was astonished to hear the news.* amazed, astounded, stunned, staggered, surprised, startled, taken aback, shocked, flabbergasted *(informal),* dumbfounded, gobsmacked *(slang),* thunderstruck.

**astonishing** *see* **amazing**.

**astound** *see* **astonish**.

**astronaut**
*(n)* spaceman, spacewoman, cosmonaut *(Russian),* space traveller, shuttle crew member. ❖ *Also see* **space adventure**.

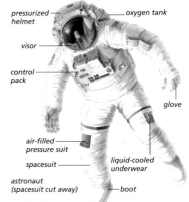

pressurized helmet — oxygen tank
visor
control pack
glove
air-filled pressure suit
spacesuit — liquid-cooled underwear
astronaut (spacesuit cut away) — boot

**athletics**
*(n)* track and field events *(plural),* games *(plural).*
TYPES OF ATHLETICS EVENT: cross-country, decathlon, discus, hammer throw, heptathlon, high jump, hurdles, javelin, long jump, marathon, pentathlon, pole vault, relay, running, shot put, sprint, steeplechase, triple jump, walking.
❖ *Also see* **sport words**.

**atmosphere**
1 *(n) The spaceship blasted into the atmosphere.* air, sky, heavens *(plural),* space, ether.
2 *(n) There was a strange atmosphere at the party.* feeling, mood, ambience, air, aura, vibrations *(plural) (informal),* vibes *(plural) (slang).*

**atrocious** *see* **dreadful** 1, 2, 3.

**attach**
*(v) Attach the pieces together.* fasten, join, fix, link, connect, stick, pin, tie, secure.
OPPOSITES: detach, separate.

**attack**
1 *(v) The soldiers will attack the city by night.* invade, storm, charge, strike, fall upon, descend on, bombard, raid, rush.
OPPOSITES: defend, protect.
2 *(v) The robbers threatened to attack the guard.* assault, beat up *(informal),* mug *(informal),* jump on, set on, set about, lay into *(informal),* put the boot in *(slang).*
3 *(v) The newspapers often attack the government.* criticize, find fault with, blame, slate *(informal),* have a go at *(informal),* lay into *(informal),* snipe at, get at, harangue, censure, berate.
OPPOSITE: defend.
4 *(n) The commanders planned their attack.* assault, charge, invasion, offensive, strike, raid, sortie, foray, onslaught, bombardment, blitz (air raid).
OPPOSITE: defence.

**5** (n) We were shocked by the attack on the old lady. assault, mugging (informal).
**6** (n) Lord Lucre was upset by the newspaper's attack. criticism, slating (informal), censure, tirade, onslaught, character assassination, denigration.
**7** (n) Joseph had an attack of coughing. fit, bout, spell, outbreak.

**attempt** see **try** 1, 2.

**attend**
**1** (v) Are you planning to attend the club meeting? go to, be present at, be at, turn up for, put in an appearance at, show up at (informal).
**2** attend to (v) Please attend to your work. See **concentrate** 2.
**3** attend to (v) The doctor will attend to you now. See **see to**.

**attic**
(n) loft, roof space, garret (old-fashioned).

**attitude**
**1** (n) What's your attitude towards fox-hunting? opinion of, view on, reaction to, position on, point of view on, perspective on, stance on, thoughts on (plural).
**2** (n) I don't like your attitude. approach, outlook, manner, behaviour, disposition, frame of mind, mood, air, demeanour.

**attract**
(v) This window display is bound to attract customers. draw, pull (informal), bring in, entice, lure, seduce, tempt, appeal to, interest, fascinate, captivate, enchant.
OPPOSITES: repel, drive away, put off.

**attractive**
(adj) Sam is really attractive. good-looking, handsome, pretty, striking, stunning (informal), beautiful, gorgeous, fetching (informal), charming, enchanting, alluring.
OPPOSITES: unattractive, ugly.

**audible**
(adj) Jon's yells were audible all over the school. easy to hear, clear, loud, distinct, detectable, perceptible.
OPPOSITE: inaudible.

**audience**
(n) crowd, spectators (plural) (sport), viewers (plural) (TV), listeners (plural) (radio), congregation (religious meeting).

**author** see **writer**.

**authority**
**1** (n) Do you have authority to use this computer? See **permission**.
**2** (n) The headteacher has authority over us. power, control, command, influence.

**authorize** see **approve** 1.

**automatic**
**1** (adj) An automatic machine. automated, mechanized, mechanical, computerized, programmable, push-button, robotic.
OPPOSITES: manual, hand-operated.
**2** (adj) An automatic gesture. instinctive, involuntary, unconscious, spontaneous, unthinking, mechanical, reflex.
OPPOSITES: conscious, deliberate.

**available**
**1** (adj) There are still some seats available. See **free** 3.
**2** (adj) There is lots more food available. to hand, on tap, at your disposal, obtainable, ready, handy, convenient, accessible.
OPPOSITE: unavailable.

**avenue** see **road**.

**average**
**1** (adj) Brownchester is an average small town. ordinary, typical, everyday, normal, standard, run-of-the-mill, commonplace, unremarkable, unexceptional.
OPPOSITES: unusual, extraordinary.
**2** (adj) The meal was average. mediocre, middling, so-so (informal), not bad, tolerable, passable, fair, indifferent.
OPPOSITES: outstanding, exceptional.

**avoid**
**1** (v) I think that Sasha is trying to avoid me. keep away from, steer clear of, hide from, evade, elude, shun, ignore.
**2** (v) Josh managed to avoid doing the washing-up. get out of, escape, evade, dodge, wriggle out of, duck out of (informal), shirk, sidestep.

**awake**
(adj) The guards stayed awake all night. wide-awake, alert, aware, conscious, wakeful, watchful, vigilant, attentive, on the lookout, on guard, on the alert.
OPPOSITE: asleep.

**award**
**1** (v) Who will award the prizes on Sports Day? See **present** 5.
**2** (n) Finn won an award for his poem. See **prize** 1.

**aware of**
**1** (adj) Patsy was aware of the danger. conscious of, mindful of, sensitive to, heedful of, alive to, wise to (slang).
OPPOSITES: unaware of, oblivious to.
**2** (adj) Are you aware of the rules about school uniform? familiar with, acquainted with, conversant with, knowledgeable about, clued-up on (informal).
OPPOSITES: unaware of, ignorant of.

**away**
**1** (adj) Nathan is away today. absent, not here, not present, off.
**2** (adj) Our neighbours are away. not here, not at home, on holiday, abroad.

**awe**
**1** (n) I looked at the painting with awe. wonder, amazement, astonishment, admiration, reverence, respect.
**2** (n) We gazed at the monster with awe. dread, fear, horror, terror, alarm.

**awful** see **dreadful** 1, 2, 3.

**awkward**
**1** (adj) Penny is so awkward; she's always dropping things. clumsy, uncoordinated, butter-fingered (informal), ham-fisted (informal), inept, bungling, all thumbs.
OPPOSITE: dexterous.

**2** (adj) The robot moved with awkward steps. clumsy, uncoordinated, ungainly, stiff, jerky, gawky, lumbering, blundering, ungraceful, inelegant, gauche.
OPPOSITE: graceful.
**3** (adj) This parcel is a really awkward shape. inconvenient, difficult, unwieldy, unmanageable, cumbersome, bulky, troublesome.
OPPOSITES: convenient, handy.
**4** (adj) Nina is being deliberately awkward. difficult, uncooperative, unhelpful, perverse, obstinate, stubborn, stroppy (informal), bolshie (informal), bloody-minded (informal), impossible (informal).
OPPOSITES: cooperative, obliging.
**5** (adj) This is a really awkward problem to solve. difficult, tricky, perplexing, baffling, thorny, troublesome, problematic.
OPPOSITE: straightforward.
**6** (adj) Gus found himself in an awkward situation. difficult, tricky, delicate, embarrassing, uncomfortable, unpleasant, ticklish, problematic, sticky (informal), cringe-making (informal), compromising.

**babble** see **prattle**.

**baby**
(n) infant, child, newborn child, babe (old-fashioned), sprog (slang), rug rat (slang).

**babyish** see **childish**.

**back**
**1** (n) Jed has hurt his back. spine, spinal column, backbone, vertebrae (plural).
**2** (n) I sat at the back of the bus. rear, rear end, far end, tail end, end, stern (ship).
OPPOSITE: front.
**3** (adj) The horse kicked its back legs in the air. hind, rear.
OPPOSITES: fore, front.
**4** (v) Jack began to back along the ledge. retreat, move back, reverse, backtrack.
OPPOSITE: advance.
**5** (v) Jo will back my idea. See **support** 3.

**background**
**1** (n) Tell me a bit about your background. upbringing, education, family history, family circumstances (plural), experience, qualifications (plural), credentials (plural).
**2** (n) Choose a dramatic background for your picture. backdrop, setting, backcloth, scene, surroundings (plural), context.

**back out**
(v) You can't back out now - I need you! drop out, pull out, resign, withdraw, get cold feet, chicken out (informal).

**back up**
(v) Will you back me up if I tell the truth? support, side with, stand by, stand up for, stick up for (informal), vouch for.

# **b**ad

## bad

| a bad person | a bad accident | a bad smell | bad work | bad weather | Smoking is bad for you. | I feel bad about what I have done. |
|---|---|---|---|---|---|---|
| corrupt | appalling | disgusting | abysmal | awful | damaging | ashamed |
| criminal | catastrophic | foul | awful | dismal | dangerous | awful |
| crooked (informal) | disastrous | horrible | diabolical (informal) | dreadful | detrimental | conscience-stricken |
| depraved | dreadful | loathsome | dreadful | dreary | harmful | contrite |
| dishonest | horrendous | nasty | inadequate | filthy | risky | dreadful |
| evil | horrific | nauseating | inferior | foul | unhealthy | embarrassed |
| immoral | nasty | offensive | poor | murky | | guilty |
| sinful | serious | repulsive | substandard | nasty | **After you left I felt bad.** | mortified |
| villainous | terrible | revolting | unacceptable | | awful | red-faced |
| wicked | tragic | sickening | unsatisfactory | **Overeating makes you feel bad.** | blue | regretful |
| | | unpleasant | | dreadful | depressed | remorseful |
| **a bad child** | **a bad film** | vile | **a bad mood** | ill | down | rueful |
| badly behaved | abysmal | | angry | nauseous | dreadful | sad |
| cheeky | appalling | **bad food** | bad-tempered | off colour | glum | shamefaced |
| difficult | atrocious | decayed | cross | poorly (informal) | low | sheepish |
| disobedient | diabolical (informal) | mildewed | grouchy (informal) | queasy | melancholy | sorry |
| mischievous | dire (informal) | mouldy | grumpy | rotten (informal) | miserable | terrible |
| naughty | lousy (slang) | off | irritable | sick | sad | uncomfortable |
| rebellious | pathetic (informal) | putrid | peevish | terrible | unhappy | uneasy |
| rude | | rancid | ratty (informal) | unwell | wretched | upset |
| uncooperative | rotten (informal) | rotten | sulky | | | |
| unruly | terrible | sour | | | | |
| | | spoiled | | | | |

---

**badge**
(n) I sewed the badge on to my sweater. emblem, crest, logo, symbol, insignia.

**badger** see **pester**.

**bad-tempered**
(adj) Dad gets bad-tempered when we're late. irritable, cross, short-tempered, grumpy, grouchy (informal), ratty (informal), crabby, crotchety (informal), cantankerous, snappy, touchy, fractious, peevish, testy, morose, surly.
OPPOSITE: good-humoured.

**baffle** see **puzzle** 2.

**bag**
(n) TYPES OF BAG: backpack, basket, briefcase, carrier bag, handbag, holdall, knapsack, rucksack, sack, satchel, shopping bag, shoulder bag, sports bag, suitcase.

**baggy** see **loose** 1.

**baking** see **hot** 1.

**balance**
1 (v) Can you balance a ball on your nose? support, keep steady, steady, poise.
2 (v) Try to make the scales balance. even up, be equal, be level, counterbalance, reach equilibrium, be steady, stabilize.

**ball**
1 (n) A ball of fire. sphere, globe, orb.
2 (n) A masked ball. dance, party.

**ban**
(v) The judge decided to ban Dave from driving. prohibit, bar, prevent, stop, disqualify.
OPPOSITES: permit, authorize.

**band**
1 (n) My skirt has a blue band round the bottom. stripe, strip, line, ribbon.
2 (n) Fasten the bundle with a leather band. strap, strip, thong, belt, hoop.
3 (n) William has a large band of friends. See **group** 3.
4 (n) Let's listen to the band. group, ensemble, orchestra.

jazz band, sousaphone, piano, trumpet, drums, trombone, banjo, clarinet

**bang**
1 (n) I heard a loud bang from the science lab. explosion, blast, crash, thud, thump, boom, pop, report.
2 (v) Don't bang your head on that shelf! See **hit** 2.

**banish**
(v) The king decided to banish the magician. exile, send away, expel, cast out, outlaw, throw out, deport.
OPPOSITES: admit, welcome.

**bank**
1 (n) We walked along the river bank. side, shore, edge, embankment, brink.
2 (n) We climbed a grassy bank. mound, slope, embankment, knoll, ridge, rise, hill.

**bankrupt**
(adj) Flash Frank is bankrupt. ruined, insolvent, broke (informal).
OPPOSITE: solvent.

**banquet**
(n) The king laid on a magnificent banquet. feast, dinner, spread (informal), meal.

**bar**
1 (n) A metal bar. rod, pole, post, stake, railing, girder, crowbar, jemmy.
2 (n) A bar of chocolate. slab, block, piece, hunk, chunk.
3 (n) We had drinks in a local bar. pub, inn, wine bar, public house, tavern (old-fashioned), boozer (informal).
4 (v) Don't bar my way! block, obstruct.

**bare**
1 (adj) The boys were bare to the waist. naked, stripped, undressed, unclothed, uncovered, nude, exposed.
OPPOSITES: dressed, clothed.
2 (adj) The room was completely bare. unfurnished, empty, vacant, stripped.
OPPOSITES: full, cluttered.
3 (adj) We climbed the bare hillside. bleak, barren, desolate, windswept, exposed.
4 (adj) Give me a bare outline of what happened. basic, simple, straightforward, plain, stark, bald, unembellished, unvarnished, unadorned.
OPPOSITE: elaborate.

**barely** see **hardly**.

**bargain**
1 (n) Ann has found a bargain. good deal, good buy, special offer, reduction, discount, steal (informal), snip (informal).

**2** (n) *The two sides made a bargain.* deal (informal), agreement, arrangement, pact, contract, settlement, treaty.
**3** (v) *You have to bargain for food in the market.* haggle, barter, negotiate.

**bark**
(v) *The dog began to bark.* yap, woof, growl, snarl, howl, yelp, bay, bow-wow.

**barrel**
(n) cask, keg, tub, vat, drum.

**base**
**1** (n) *The base of the statue is cracked.* bottom, foot, foundation, plinth, stand, pedestal, support.
OPPOSITE: top.
**2** (n) *All troops must return to their base.* headquarters (plural), camp, station, quarters (plural), billet, garrison, base camp, starting point.
**3** (v) *Base your essay on your own experience.* model, ground, construct, build, develop from, derive from.

**bash** (informal) see **hit** 1, 2, 4.

**basic**
**1** (adj) *What are the basic points in your essay?* fundamental, key, central, underlying, main, chief, essential.
**2** (adj) *I'm learning basic Italian.* elementary, simple, easy, rudimentary.
OPPOSITE: advanced.

**bath**
**1** (n) *Fill the bath with water.* tub.
**2** (n) *Matt had a bath after the match.* soak, wash, scrub, sponge down, shower.

**bathe**
**1** (v) *Is it safe to bathe here? See* **swim** 2.
**2** (v) *Bathe your feet in warm water.* soak, immerse, douse, dip, wash, cleanse.

**batter**
(v) *Don't batter the door like that!* pound, hammer, thump, bash (informal), beat, pummel, thrash, smash, buffet.

**battered**
**1** (adj) *A battered old suitcase.* worn-out, beaten-up, scruffy, damaged, squashed, scarred, dilapidated, weather-beaten.
**2** (adj) *Claude emerged battered from the fight.* bruised, beaten, hurt, injured, bleeding, wounded, scarred.

**battle**
**1** (n) *The battle was long and bloody.* fight, conflict, struggle, skirmish, confrontation, clash, combat, campaign, siege, dogfight, shoot-out, rebellion.
**2** (v) *Carl had to battle to win the game.* struggle, fight, strive.

**bay**
(n) *The yacht sheltered in the bay.* cove, estuary, inlet, natural harbour.

**beach**
**1** (n) *Let's go to the beach today.* seaside, coast, seashore, shore. ❖ *Also see* **sea & seashore, seaside words**.
**2** (n) *We played tennis on the beach.* sand, sands (plural), shingle.

**beam**
**1** (v) *The sight of his new bike made Ben beam.* grin, smile, grin from ear to ear.
**2** (n) *A beam of sunlight shone through the curtains.* ray, shaft, streak, stream, gleam, glimmer, glow.
**3** (n) *Don't remove that beam or the ceiling will collapse.* plank, support, joist, girder, rafter, timber, prop, brace, spar.

**bear**
**1** (v) *Can you bear my weight?* take, support, carry, shoulder.
**2** (v) *I can't bear the noise! See* **stand** 4.

**beast**
**1** (n) *A wild beast.* animal, creature.
**2** (n) *A beast with two heads. See* **monster** 1.

**beastly** (informal) see **mean** 6.

**beat**
**1** (v) *Teachers used to beat their pupils.* hit, strike, thrash, cane, whip, flog, belt (slang), clout (informal), wallop (informal), thump, batter, birch.
**2** (v) *I'm bound to beat you at chess.* defeat, thrash, get the better of, hammer (informal), slaughter (informal), clobber (informal), wipe the floor with (informal), lick (informal), blow you out of the water (informal), run rings round (informal), triumph over.
**3** (v) *The suspense made my heart beat fast.* pound, thump, hammer, bang, palpitate, pulsate, pulse.
**4** (v) *Beat the egg whites until they are stiff.* whisk, whip, stir, mix, blend.
**5** (n) *This song has a very strong beat.* rhythm, pulse, stress, accent.

**beat up**
(v) (informal) *Don't let Bozo beat you up.* assault, attack, batter, lay into (informal), knock you about, rough you up (informal), beat the living daylights out of (informal), work you over (slang), duff you up (slang), put the boot in (slang).

**beckon** see **signal** 2.

**become**
(v) *This caterpillar will become a butterfly.* turn into, change into, develop into, grow into, be transformed into.

**bed**
(n) TYPES OF BED: air bed, berth, bunk bed, camp bed, cot, cradle, divan, double bed, four-poster bed, futon, hammock, single bed, sofa bed, water bed.

**beg**
**1** (v) *The poor woman had to beg for food.* scrounge (informal), ask, cadge.
**2** (v) *I'll beg Dad to let us go.* plead with, implore, entreat, beseech (old-fashioned).

**begin**
**1** (v) *Let's begin!* start, get started, get going, get moving, get the show on the road (informal), take the plunge (informal), start the ball rolling, kick off (informal).
OPPOSITE: stop.
**2** (v) *It's time to begin our work.* start, set about, commence, embark on.
OPPOSITE: finish.
**3** (v) *Don't begin an argument.* start, provoke, initiate, trigger off, spark off, cause, instigate, incite.
OPPOSITE: end.
**4** (v) *When did life on earth begin?* start, appear, originate, come into being, come into existence, emerge, arise, burst forth.
OPPOSITES: cease, end.

**beginner**
(n) *I'm just a beginner.* novice, learner, fledgling, greenhorn, new recruit.

**beginning**
**1** (n) *I was there at the beginning of the project.* start, birth, outset, onset, starting point, commencement, inception, origin.
OPPOSITES: end, conclusion.
**2** (n) *We've missed the beginning of the film.* start, opening, introduction, kickoff (informal), prologue (play), preface (book).
OPPOSITES: end, conclusion.

| beautiful a beautiful woman | beautiful weather | beautiful music | beautiful scenery |
|---|---|---|---|
| alluring | brilliant | bewitching | awe-inspiring |
| attractive | delightful | captivating | breathtaking |
| dazzling | fabulous | enchanting | glorious |
| fetching | (informal) | entrancing | impressive |
| (informal) | fair | exquisite | incredible |
| good-looking | fine | glorious | magnificent |
| gorgeous | glorious | haunting | marvellous |
| lovely | gorgeous | heavenly | picturesque |
| pretty | lovely | (informal) | spectacular |
| radiant | magnificent | inspiring | striking |
| ravishing | marvellous | lovely | stunning |
| striking | perfect | magnificent | (informal) |
| stunning | superb | poignant | superb |
| (informal) | wonderful | sublime | wonderful |

# behave

**behave**
1 *(v) I'm sure you'll behave sensibly.* act, conduct yourself, acquit yourself.
2 *(v) When will you learn to behave?* be polite, remember your manners, mind your manners, control yourself.
OPPOSITES: misbehave, be rude.

**behind**
*(adv) Nat is behind with his project.* late, behind schedule, overdue.
OPPOSITE: ahead.

**believable**
*(adj) Your story is not believable.* credible, plausible, convincing, possible, probable, likely, conceivable, trustworthy.
OPPOSITES: unbelievable, implausible.

**believe**
1 *(v) It's hard to believe your story.* trust, accept, credit, feel convinced by, have faith in, be certain of, be sure of, swallow *(informal)*, buy *(informal)*, count on, fall for.
2 *(v) I used to believe that girls were stupid.* think, be convinced, feel, consider, be of the opinion, be certain.
3 *(v) I believe this is for me.* think, assume, guess *(informal)*, presume, suppose, imagine, reckon, gather, suspect.

**bellow** see **shout**.

**belongings** see **things**.

**bend**
1 *(v) The road should bend just here.* turn, curve, twist, wind, swerve, veer.
2 *(v) Can you bend this metal rod?* twist, flex, curve, shape, wind, loop, contort, buckle, warp.
3 *(v) Bend down to get through the tunnel.* stoop, crouch, bow, lean, squat.
4 *(n) Watch out for the bend!* curve, turn, corner, twist, hairpin bend, loop, zigzag.

**bendy** see **flexible** 1.

**bent**
1 *(adj) A bent bicycle wheel.* twisted, buckled, crooked, warped, contorted.
OPPOSITE: straight.
2 *(adj) (slang) A bent cop. See* **corrupt** 1.

**best**
1 *(adj) Jon is the best runner in the team.* finest, top, foremost, leading, outstanding, unrivalled, unsurpassed, supreme.
OPPOSITE: worst.
2 *(adj) What's the best thing to do?* right, correct, most appropriate, most suitable, most fitting.
OPPOSITE: worst.

**bet** see **gamble** 1, 2.

**betray**
1 *(v) I hope your friend won't betray you.* deceive, be disloyal to, stab you in the back *(informal)*, inform on, give you away, double-cross, sell you out *(informal)*, sell you down the river *(informal)*.
2 *(v) Don't betray the one you love.* deceive, be unfaithful to, cheat on *(informal)*, two-time *(informal)*.
3 *(v) Try not to betray your true feelings.* reveal, show, give away, expose, lay bare, let slip, blurt out, indicate.

**better**
1 *(adj) There's a better way of doing that.* preferable, easier, more effective, more appropriate, more acceptable.
OPPOSITE: worse.
2 *(adj) Are you better now?* fully recovered, well, fit, cured, on the mend, fitter, stronger, back on your feet.
OPPOSITE: worse.

**beware of**
*(v) Beware of falling rocks.* watch out for, look out for, be careful of, keep clear of, steer clear of, be on your guard against.

**bewildered** see **confused**.

**biased**
*(adj) A biased magazine article.* one-sided, unfair, prejudiced, distorted, slanted.
OPPOSITES: impartial, unbiased.

**bicycle**
*(n)* bike, cycle, pushbike, two-wheeler, mountain bike, racing bike, touring bike, BMX (motocross bicycle), tandem.

**bill**
*(n) Send me the bill.* account, invoice, statement, reckoning, charge.

**billow**
1 *(v) We watched the sails billow in the wind.* swell, bulge, fill out, balloon, puff out.
2 *(v) As the storm approached, the waves began to billow.* swell, rise, surge, roll, heave.

**bind** see **tie** 1.

**bird**
*(n)* fowl, feathered friend *(informal)*, cock *(male)*, hen *(female)*, chick, nestling, fledgling.
TYPES OF BIRD: bird of paradise, blackbird, budgerigar, canary, chaffinch, chicken, cockatoo, crane, crow, cuckoo, dove, duck, eagle, emu, falcon, finch, flamingo, goose, grouse, gull, hawk, heron, hummingbird, jackdaw, jay, kingfisher, kiwi, kookaburra, lark, macaw, magpie, mina bird, moorhen, nightingale, ostrich, owl, parakeet, parrot, partridge, peacock, pelican, penguin, pheasant, pigeon, puffin, quail, raven, robin, rook, seagull, sparrow, starling, stork, swallow, swift, thrush, tit, toucan, turkey, turtledove, vulture, woodpecker, wren.

## big

| a big person | a big building | a big mountain | a big bag | a big bang |
|---|---|---|---|---|
| beefy *(informal)* | enormous | enormous | bulky | almighty *(informal)* |
| burly | huge | high | capacious | colossal |
| fat | immense | huge | enormous | deafening |
| heavy | large | lofty | heavy | ear-splitting |
| hefty | massive | massive | huge | enormous |
| obese | roomy | towering | large | loud |
| overweight | spacious | | mammoth | mighty |
| stout | tall | **a big helping of pudding** | voluminous | resounding |
| strapping | towering | ample | | terrific |
| tall | vast | enormous | **a big wardrobe** | tremendous |
| towering | | generous | capacious | |
| | **a big monster** | huge | enormous | **a big decision** |
| **a big desert** | colossal | jumbo *(informal)* | huge | critical |
| enormous | elephantine | large | immense | crucial |
| extensive | enormous | liberal | large | grave |
| huge | gigantic | mammoth | massive | important |
| immense | ginormous *(informal)* | mega *(informal)* | sizable | major |
| vast | hulking | mountainous | **a big sister** | momentous |
| | humongous *(informal)* | substantial | elder | serious |
| *gigantic blue whale* | | | grown-up | significant |
| | | | older | weighty |

## bird words

### bird moves

| | |
|---|---|
| circle | plummet |
| dart | plunge |
| dive | pounce |
| drop | preen |
| flit | rise |
| float | roost |
| flutter | sail |
| fly | skim |
| glide | soar |
| hop | splash |
| hover | strut |
| land | swim |
| paddle | swoop |
| peck | take off |
| perch | waddle |

*claw*
*dazzling bird of paradise*

*hovering tern*
*tail feathers*
*crown*
*beak*
*diving kingfisher*

### bird sounds

| | |
|---|---|
| cackle | honk |
| call | hoot |
| caw | peep |
| chatter | pipe |
| cheep | quack |
| chirp | screech |
| chirrup | shriek |
| coo | sing |
| crow | squawk |
| cry | trill |
| gabble | tweet |
| gaggle | twitter |
| gobble | warble |
| hiss | whistle |

### a bird's feathers can be...

| | |
|---|---|
| bedraggled | gleaming |
| colourful | iridescent |
| dazzling | ruffled |
| downy | smooth |
| dull | speckled |

*wing*
*throat*
*breast*
*warbling blackbird*

---

**bit**
1 *(n) I'd love a bit of cheese.* piece, lump, chunk, hunk, block, slab, wedge, slice, morsel, scrap, fragment, crumb.
2 *(n) Would you like a bit of my orange?* piece, share, segment, section, part, portion, slice.
3 *(n) I'll be there in a bit. See* **moment** 1.

**bitchy** *(informal) see* **spiteful**.

**bite**
1 *(v) Bite on this apple.* chew, nibble, gnaw, chomp, crunch.
2 *(v) That insect might bite.* sting, nip.
3 *(n) Can I have a bite of your biscuit?* nibble, taste, bit, piece, mouthful, morsel.

**biting** *see* **cold** 2.

**bitter**
1 *(adj) This drink has a bitter taste.* sour, sharp, tart, acid, vinegary, pungent, acrid.
OPPOSITE: sweet.
2 *(adj) Does Jo's success make you feel bitter?* resentful, sore, embittered, begrudging, aggrieved, sour, jealous, envious, put out, wounded, hurt.
OPPOSITES: glad, grateful.
3 *(adj) The girls had a bitter row.* fierce, angry, violent, heated, acrimonious, vicious, savage.
4 *(adj) I have bitter memories of that time.* painful, agonizing, unhappy, distressing, heartbreaking, poignant, bittersweet.
OPPOSITES: happy, pleasant.
5 *(adj) The wind was bitter. See* **cold** 2.

**bizarre** *see* **strange** 1.

**black**
*(adj) Count Dracula wore a black cloak.* coal-black, jet-black, pitch-black, inky, sable, ebony, raven *(hair).*

**blame**
1 *(v) I blame you for starting this row.* hold you responsible, accuse you of, charge you with, condemn, reproach, criticize, find fault with, censure.

2 *(n) Max accepted the blame for the incident.* responsibility, liability, censure, criticism, rap *(slang),* stick *(informal).*

**bland**
1 *(adj) A bland sauce.* mild, tasteless, flavourless, insipid, weak, nondescript.
OPPOSITES: tasty, spicy.
2 *(adj) A bland speech.* dull, boring, uninspiring, uninteresting, unexciting, humdrum, flat, monotonous, tedious.
OPPOSITES: exciting, stimulating.

**blank**
1 *(adj) Take a blank sheet of paper.* clean, empty, new, unused, unmarked, bare.
2 *(adj) Marcus looked blank when I questioned him.* vacant, glazed, at a loss, uncomprehending, flummoxed, puzzled, bewildered, confused, at sea.

**blaze** *see* **burn** 1, 2.

**bleak**
1 *(adj) We surveyed the bleak landscape.* bare, barren, exposed, windswept, desolate, deserted.
2 *(adj) The future looks bleak.* grim, depressing, gloomy, dismal, hopeless, dreary, forbidding, sombre.
OPPOSITES: hopeful, bright.

**blend** *see* **mix** 1.

**blind**
1 *(adj) Great Grandma is blind.* unable to see, sightless, visually impaired.
2 *(adj) How could I be so blind?* unaware, blinkered, unobservant, unsuspecting, insensitive, inattentive, heedless, dim, stupid, inconsiderate, thoughtless.
OPPOSITES: aware, sensitive.

**blissful** *see* **heavenly** 2.

**blizzard**
*(n) snowstorm.* ❖ *Also see* **ice, frost & snow**.

**blob**
*(n) A blob of cream.* drop, spot, dollop *(informal),* splodge.

**block**
1 *(n) Please will you move this block of stone?* slab, lump, piece, chunk, hunk, mass, brick, cube, wedge.
2 *(v) Leaves sometimes block our drainpipe.* clog, stop up, obstruct, choke, fill, bung up.
3 *(v) Don't try to block my progress.* bar, obstruct, impede, interfere with, check, hinder, thwart, prevent, halt, stop.

**bloke** *(informal) see* **man** 1, 2.

**blond, blonde**
1 *(adj) James is blond; Jenny is blonde too.* fair-haired, golden-haired, fair, tow-headed, flaxen-haired *(old-fashioned).*
2 *(adj) Millie has blonde hair.* fair, golden, ash-blonde, platinum-blonde, strawberry-blonde, honey-coloured, straw-coloured, sandy, yellow, peroxide-blonde, bleached, flaxen *(old-fashioned).*

**bloodthirsty** *see* **savage** 2.

**bloody**
1 *(adj) A bloody wound.* bleeding, gory.
2 *(adj) A bloody shirt.* bloodstained, blood-soaked, blood-spattered.
3 *(adj) A bloody fight.* gory, fierce, ferocious, savage, violent, vicious.

**bloom** *see* **flower** 1, 2.

**blot**
1 *(n) My work was spoilt by a large blot of ink.* spot, blotch, smear, smudge, blob, splodge, splotch, patch.
2 *(n) That shed is a blot on the landscape.* blemish, eyesore, flaw, scar.

**blotchy**
*(adj) Nancy's face looks blotchy.* mottled, spotty, patchy, blemished.

**blow**
1 *(v) Blow on the paint to make it dry.* breathe, puff, huff, breathe out, exhale.
2 *(v) The leaves began to blow around.* whirl, flutter, waft, swirl, flap, whisk.
3 *(n) Bozo is recovering from a blow on the head.* bang, knock, bump, hit, smack, whack, bash *(informal),* thump, punch, wallop *(informal),* belt *(informal).*
4 *(n) Losing the match was a real blow.* disappointment, disaster, catastrophe, calamity, setback, upset, misfortune, bombshell, shock, tragedy.

**blow up**
1 *(v) This bomb may blow up without any warning.* explode, detonate, go off.
2 *(v) The soldiers were ordered to blow up the bridge.* bomb, dynamite, destroy, blast.
3 *(v) You need to blow up your bicycle tyres.* inflate, pump up.
4 *(v) (informal) Please don't blow up when you see the mess. See* **lose your temper**.

**blue**
1 *(n) SHADES OF BLUE:* aquamarine, azure, cobalt, cornflower, cyan, forget-me-not, indigo, navy, powder blue, royal blue, sapphire, sky blue, turquoise, ultramarine.
2 *(adj) Kim is feeling blue. See* **depressed**.

## blunt

**blunt**
1 *(adj)* This blade is blunt. not sharp, unsharpened, dull, rounded.
OPPOSITE: sharp.
2 *(adj)* Carl's blunt comment upset me. frank, candid, forthright, direct, tactless, insensitive, outspoken, curt, brusque, rude.
OPPOSITES: tactful, polite.

**blurred**
*(adj)* Without my glasses, everything is blurred. out of focus, fuzzy, hazy, misty, foggy, unclear, indistinct, faint.
OPPOSITES: clear, sharp, in focus.

**blush**
*(v)* I wish I wouldn't blush whenever I'm embarrassed. go red, go pink, redden, colour, turn scarlet, turn crimson, flush.

**boast**
*(v)* Don't boast about your success. brag, show off *(informal)*, crow, swank *(informal)*, swagger, exaggerate, blow your own trumpet, sing your own praises.

**boastful**
*(adj)* Leah is so boastful; she's always showing off. conceited, bigheaded *(informal)*, swollen-headed *(informal)*, cocky, vain, puffed up, arrogant.
OPPOSITES: modest, self-effacing.

**boat**
*(n)* ship, vessel, craft.
TYPES OF BOAT: aircraft carrier, barge, battleship, cabin cruiser, canoe, catamaran, clipper, coracle, cruise liner, cruiser, destroyer, dhow, dugout, ferry, fishing boat, freighter, frigate, galleon, galley, gondola, houseboat, hovercraft, hydrofoil, hydroplane, inflatable dinghy, junk, kayak, launch, lifeboat, liner, man o' war, minesweeper, motorboat, narrow boat, paddle steamer, powerboat, punt, raft, rowing boat, sailing boat, sailing dinghy, schooner, skiff, speedboat, steamship, supertanker, tanker, trawler, trireme, tug, warship, yacht.
❖ Also see **journey words**.

*Ancient Greek galley*

**body**
1 *(n)* Jason has a muscular body. build, physique, figure, frame, form, torso, trunk.
PARTS OF THE BODY: OUTSIDE: Adam's apple, ankle, arm, armpit, back, breast, buttock, calf, cheek, chest, chin, ear, elbow, eye, face, finger, foot, forehead, genitals *(plural)*, groin, hand, head, heel, hip, jaw, knee, knuckle, leg, limb, lip, midriff, mouth, navel, neck, nipple, nose, nostril, scalp, shin, shoulder, stomach, thigh, thumb, toe, waist, wrist. INSIDE: abdomen, adenoid, anus, aorta, appendix, artery, bladder, bone, bowel, brain, cartilage, colon, diaphragm, duodenum, eardrum, epiglottis, gall bladder, gland, gum, heart, intestine, kidney, larynx (voice box), ligament, liver, lung, muscle, nerve, oesophagus (gullet), ovary, pancreas, rectum, rib, sinew, spine, spleen, stomach, tendon, throat, tongue, tonsil, trachea (windpipe), uterus (womb), vein, vocal cords *(plural)*. Also see **bone**.
2 *(n)* The police found a body in the woods. dead body, corpse, remains *(plural)*, stiff *(slang)*.

**bog**
*(n)* marsh, marshland, peat bog, fen, swamp, quagmire, wetlands *(plural)*.

**boil**
*(v)* Wait for the water to boil. come to the boil, bubble, simmer, seethe, steam.
OPPOSITE: freeze.

**boiling** see **hot** 1, 2, 3.

**boisterous** see **rowdy**.

pennant · yard · 15th-century galleon
topsail
mast
mizzen sail
mainsail
foresail
bowsprit
poop deck
stern
prow
rudder

deck · hull

19th-century paddle steamer

paddle wheel

bridge
lifeboat

funnel

tanker

radio aerial
radar antenna
bridge
hull
passenger area
strut
helipad

foil · hydrofoil

**bold**
1 *(adj)* A bold knight. intrepid, daring, audacious, brave, courageous, fearless, adventurous, heroic, valiant *(old-fashioned)*, gallant *(old-fashioned)*.
OPPOSITES: cowardly, fearful.
2 *(adj)* A bold reply. See **cheeky**.
3 *(adj)* Bold colours. bright, strong, vivid, striking, loud, eye-catching, conspicuous.
OPPOSITES: pale, unobtrusive.

**bolshie** *(informal)* see **awkward** 4.

**bolt**
1 *(v)* Please bolt the door. See **lock** 1.
2 *(v)* Burglar Beryl tried to bolt when she saw the police. See **run away**.

**bomb**
1 *(n)* The soldiers made the bomb safe. explosive, device.
TYPES OF BOMB: atom bomb, car bomb, depth charge, grenade, H-bomb (hydrogen bomb), incendiary device (firebomb), land mine, letter bomb, mine, napalm bomb, nuclear bomb, petrol bomb, time bomb.
2 *(v)* Terrorists tried to bomb the building. See **blow up** 2.

**bone**
*(n)* TYPES OF BONE: backbone, clavicle (collarbone), cranium (skull), femur (thighbone), mandible (jawbone), patella (kneecap), pelvis (hipbone), rib, scapula (shoulder blade), sternum (breastbone), tibia (shinbone), vertebra.

**bony** see **thin** 1.

**boo**
*(v)* When the villain appeared, we all began to boo. jeer, heckle, catcall, hiss.
OPPOSITES: cheer, applaud.

**book**
1 *(n)* A best-selling book. title, publication, work, paperback, hardback, volume.
2 *(n)* Write your ideas in your book. jotter, notebook, notepad, pad, exercise book.
3 *(v)* We need to book a room in advance. reserve, organize, arrange, order, secure.

**booty** see **loot** 1.

**border**
1 *(n)* We crossed the border into Germany. frontier, boundary, borderline.
2 *(n)* My writing paper has a blue border. edge, margin, surround, frame.
3 *(n)* Susie's skirt has a red border. edging, hem, trimming, frill, fringe.

**bore**
1 *(v)* This film will bore you. send you to sleep, bore you to death, bore you to tears, bore you out of your mind, leave you cold *(informal)*, turn you off *(informal)*, pall on, tire, weary.
OPPOSITES: interest, fascinate.
2 *(v)* The miners had to bore deep into the rock. drill, penetrate, tunnel, mine.
3 *(n)* Shopping can be a bore. drag *(informal)*, yawn *(informal)*, turn-off *(informal)*, nuisance, bother, pain *(informal)*, pain in the neck *(informal)*.

**bored**
*(adj) Learning endless facts can make you feel bored.* bored to death, bored to tears, bored out of your mind, fed up *(informal),* switched off *(informal),* indifferent, apathetic, weary, listless, jaded, restless. OPPOSITES: interested, fascinated.

**boring**
*(adj) A boring job.* dull, tedious, uninteresting, monotonous, repetitive, routine, humdrum, unvaried, mind-numbing, unexciting, uninspiring, dreary. OPPOSITES: interesting, fascinating.

**borrow**
*(v) Can I borrow some paper?* have, use, scrounge *(informal),* cadge, have the loan of, touch you for *(slang).* OPPOSITE: lend.

**boss**
*(n) (informal)* employer, manager, supervisor, director, gaffer *(informal).*

**bossy**
*(adj) My sister is so bossy; she's always ordering me around.* domineering, overbearing, dictatorial, high-handed, imperious, autocratic, tyrannical, bullying. OPPOSITES: meek, submissive.

**bother**
1 *(v) I don't want to bother you, but I need a lift.* trouble, disturb, put you out, impose on, inconvenience, pester, hassle *(informal),* harass, nag.
2 *(v) Doesn't it bother you that someone's been in your room?* worry, concern, upset, annoy, irritate, trouble, disturb, perturb, distress, alarm, dismay.
3 *(v) Dad didn't seem to bother about the mess.* mind, care, be bothered, be concerned, be worried, object to.
4 *(n) Our new car has given us a lot of bother. See* **trouble** 1.

**bottom**
1 *(n) The bottom of the statue was set in concrete.* foot, base, foundation, pedestal, plinth, support. OPPOSITE: top.
2 *(n) What's that muck on the bottom of your shoe?* sole, underside, underneath.
3 *(n) Joe slipped and fell on his bottom.* behind *(informal),* backside *(informal),* bum *(slang),* rear, rear end, posterior, rump.
4 *(n) The submarine sank to the bottom of the sea.* depths *(plural),* bed, floor.

**boulder** *see* **rock** 1.

**bounce**
1 *(v) We watched the kangaroos bounce across the plain.* bound, spring, leap, jump.
2 *(v) Can you make this ball bounce off the wall?* rebound, ricochet.

**bouncy**
1 *(adj) A bouncy diving board.* springy, flexible, bendy, elastic, resilient, rubbery. OPPOSITES: rigid, stiff.
2 *(adj) A bouncy girl. See* **lively** 1.

**bound** *see* **leap** 1, 3.

**box**
*(n)* TYPES OF BOX: carton, case, casket, chest, coffer, coffin, crate, jewellery box, lunch box, matchbox, shoe box, trunk.

**boy**
*(n)* lad, youth, schoolboy, young man.

**brain**
*(n) Crosswords exercise your brain.* mind, intellect, brains *(plural) (informal),* powers of reasoning *(plural),* brainpower, grey matter *(informal),* intelligence.

**brainy** *(informal) see* **clever** 1.

**branch**
1 *(n) A branch of a tree.* bough, limb, twig, stem, sprig.
2 *(n) A branch of a bank.* division, local office, department, section, subdivision.

**brash**
*(adj) A brash salesman.* over-confident, cocky, assertive, aggressive, pushy *(informal),* bumptious, swaggering, self-important, boastful, bigheaded *(informal).* OPPOSITES: timid, retiring.

**brave**
*(adj) A brave knight.* courageous, fearless, intrepid, plucky, gutsy *(informal),* heroic, valiant *(old-fashioned),* gallant *(old-fashioned),* daring, bold, lion-hearted. OPPOSITES: cowardly, fearful.

**bravery** *see* **courage**.

**break**
1 *(v) Don't break that plate!* smash, shatter, smash to smithereens, crack, splinter, chip, fracture *(bone).*
2 *(v) That branch could break at any moment.* crack, snap, split, splinter, give way, come away, disintegrate, fragment.
3 *(v) Don't break my radio!* damage, ruin, wreck, destroy, bust *(informal).*
4 *(v) If you break the rules, you'll be in trouble.* disobey, disregard, defy, flout, infringe, violate. OPPOSITES: obey, abide by.
5 *(n) The break from revision will do you good.* rest, breather *(informal),* time off, time out, breathing space, respite.
6 *(n) Cross when there's a break in the traffic.* lull, gap, let-up *(informal),* interval, pause, interruption.

**breakable** *see* **fragile**.

**break down**
1 *(v) I hope the car doesn't break down.* stop, stop working, conk out *(informal),* die, seize up, go kaput *(informal).*
2 *(v) Anji will break down when she hears the news.* go to pieces, collapse, lose control, be overcome, crack up *(informal),* fall apart *(informal).*

**break-in**
*(n) Police are investigating the break-in.* burglary, forced entry, robbery, theft, raid.

**break up**
1 *(v) The yacht hit the rocks and began to break up.* disintegrate, break into pieces, break apart, smash up, splinter, shatter.

2 *(v) When will school break up? See* **end** 6.
3 *(v) Justin thinks his parents may break up. See* **separate** 3.

**breasts**
*(plural n) Pam has large breasts.* bust, bosom, chest, boobs *(plural) (slang).*

**breathe**
*(v) Don't forget to breathe!* take a breath, inhale, exhale, take a gulp of air.

**breathless**
*(adj) Giles was breathless after his run.* out of breath, out of puff, panting, gasping, wheezing, winded.

**breed**
1 *(v) Jamie's rabbits have started to breed.* reproduce, multiply, produce young.
2 *(n) What breed of cat do you like best? See* **kind** 3.

**breezy** *see* **windy** 1.

**bribe**
1 *(v) Burglar Beryl tried to bribe the police.* buy off, influence, corrupt, pay off *(informal),* grease the palm of *(slang).*
2 *(n) Beryl offered the judge a bribe.* incentive, tip, pay-off *(informal),* backhander *(slang),* sweetener *(slang).*

**bridge**
*(n)* footbridge, flyover, overpass, viaduct, aqueduct, ropebridge, drawbridge.

**brief**
1 *(adj) Dad gave a brief account of the accident. See* **short** 2.
2 *(adj) We paid a brief visit to Aunt Bertha. See* **short** 3.
3 *(v) The coach will brief you before the match.* instruct, give you the facts, inform, fill you in *(informal),* put you in the picture *(informal),* give you the lowdown *(informal),* prepare, prime, advise.

**bright**
1 *(adj) A bright light.* dazzling, blinding, glaring, shining, blazing, beaming, intense, brilliant, radiant, incandescent. OPPOSITES: dull, dim.
2 *(adj) Bright colours.* vivid, bold, vibrant, intense, rich, brilliant, glowing, luminous, fluorescent, loud, glaring, gaudy, garish. OPPOSITES: dull, pale.
3 *(adj) Bright weather.* sunny, clear, fair, cloudless, pleasant. OPPOSITES: dull, cloudy.
4 *(adj) A bright student. See* **clever** 1.
5 *(adj) A bright future. See* **hopeful** 2.

**brilliant**
1 *(adj) A brilliant diamond.* dazzling, sparkling, glittering, scintillating, flashing, shining, glistening, shimmering, gleaming, lustrous, bright, flashy, showy. OPPOSITE: dull.
2 *(adj) A brilliant child.* gifted, talented, accomplished, bright, clever, intelligent, brainy *(informal),* precocious, exceptional. OPPOSITES: stupid, slow.
3 *(adj) A brilliant party. See* **fantastic** 3.

# bring

**bring**
1 *(v) A boat will bring supplies from the mainland.* fetch, carry, take, deliver, transport, ferry, convey, transfer.
2 *(v) Did someone bring you home?* See **take** 3.
3 *(v) Hooligans bring trouble.* cause, create, produce, provoke, give rise to, lead to, result in, generate, attract.

**bring up**
1 *(v) It's hard to bring up children on your own.* raise, rear, look after, support, care for, nurture, educate, train.
2 *(v) Stop leaping about or you'll bring up your lunch.* See **vomit**.
3 *(v) Don't bring up the subject of homework.* See **mention** 2.

**brisk**
1 *(adj) Will walked at a brisk pace.* quick, fast, swift, rapid, spanking *(informal),* speedy, energetic, vigorous, sprightly. OPPOSITES: leisurely, sluggish.
2 *(adj) Mrs Badger has a brisk manner.* businesslike, no-nonsense, crisp, decisive, bustling, lively, bright. OPPOSITE: lethargic.

**bristly** see **hairy** 2.

**brittle** see **fragile**.

**broad**
1 *(adj) Lawrence surveyed the broad stretch of desert.* wide, vast, large, extensive, expansive, sweeping, boundless. OPPOSITE: narrow.
2 *(adj) This shop sells a broad range of magazines.* wide, extensive, large, varied, comprehensive, wide-ranging, all-embracing, unlimited, encyclopedic. OPPOSITES: narrow, limited.
3 *(adj) Chloë gave a broad description of the thief.* see **general** 2.

**broad-minded** see **tolerant** 1.

**broke**
*(adj) (informal) Flash Frank will be broke if his business fails.* penniless, bankrupt, ruined, insolvent, poverty-stricken, impoverished, destitute, stony-broke *(slang),* skint *(slang),* strapped for cash *(slang),* cleaned out *(slang).* OPPOSITES: solvent, flush *(informal).*

**broken**
1 *(adj) This bone is broken.* fractured, cracked, chipped, shattered, smashed, crushed, splintered, snapped, severed.
2 *(adj) Our washing machine is broken.* out of order, faulty, defective, broken-down, inoperative, damaged, on the blink *(slang),* clapped out *(informal),* bust *(informal),* kaput *(informal).*
3 *(adj) Since his business failed, Frank is a broken man.* demoralized, dispirited, discouraged, humbled, humiliated, crushed, ruined, beaten, defeated.
4 *(adj) The tourist spoke in broken English.* halting, faltering, disjointed, hesitating, stammering, imperfect.

**broken-down** see **broken** 2.

**brown**
1 *(n)* SHADES OF BROWN: beige, bronze, buff, chocolate, cinnamon, cocoa, coffee, copper, donkey brown, dun, fawn, ginger, hazel, khaki, russet, rust, sepia, tan, terracotta, umber.
2 *(adj) Brown hair.* dark, brunette, mousy, sandy, tawny, chestnut, auburn, coppery.
3 *(adj) Brown skin.* See **tanned**.

**bruise**
1 *(n) Darren has a bruise on his forehead.* black mark, shiner *(informal),* bump, swelling, lump, contusion.
2 *(v) Be careful not to bruise your shins.* bump, bang, bash *(informal),* knock, hit, injure, hurt, mark, make black and blue.

**brush**
1 *(n) Where's the brush?* broom, floor brush, scrubbing brush, clothes brush.
2 *(v) I must brush my hair.* comb, tidy, straighten, neaten, untangle, smooth.
3 *(v) Please brush the floor.* sweep, clean.

**brutal** see **savage** 2.

**bubble**
1 *(v) The sauce began to bubble.* See **boil**.
2 *(v) Look at the lemonade bubble.* fizz, sparkle, effervesce, foam, froth.
3 *(n) A bubble of paint ran down the tin.* bead, globule, drop, droplet, blob, blister.
4 **bubbles** *(plural n) Soap bubbles.* suds *(plural),* lather, foam, froth.

**bubbly**
1 *(adj) Bubbly lemonade.* See **fizzy**.
2 *(adj) A bubbly personality.* See **lively** 1.

**buckle**
1 *(v) Buckle the straps on your rucksack.* fasten, do up, secure, close, clip, clasp.
2 *(v) The collision made my bicycle wheel buckle.* crumple, warp, twist, fold, bend, bulge, become contorted, collapse.

**budge**
*(v) Rick found a good seat and wouldn't budge.* move, shift, stir, give way.

**bug**
1 *(n) There's a bug hiding under that stone.* insect, creepy-crawly *(informal).*
2 *(n) (informal) This bug is making me feel sick.* virus, infection, germ.
3 *(n) (informal) There's a bug in my computer program.* error, fault, defect, failing, flaw, virus, gremlin, malfunction, snarl-up *(informal).*
4 *(v) (informal) The detectives decided to bug Beryl's phone calls.* tap, listen in on, monitor, eavesdrop on.
5 *(v) (informal) Rodney's jokes really bug me.* See **annoy** 1.

**build**
1 *(v) It took Dad ages to build the shed.* construct, put up, erect, assemble, put together, make, knock together *(informal).* OPPOSITES: demolish, dismantle.
2 *(n) Ed has a muscular build.* frame, body, physique, figure, form, shape.

**building**
*(n)* structure, edifice, construction, premises *(plural),* pile *(informal).*

## buildings can be...

| | | |
|---|---|---|
| austere | graceful | outlandish |
| awe-inspiring | hideous | plain |
| | historic | rambling |
| beautiful | imposing | ruined |
| crumbling | impressive | simple |
| dazzling | lofty | solemn |
| elaborate | magical | stark |
| exotic | magnificent | striking |
| flamboyant | majestic | sumptuous |
| futuristic | massive | towering |
| gleaming | monstrous | ugly |
| glittering | ornate | vast |

## MOSQUE

**outside a mosque**
cupola (small dome)
dome
onion dome
minaret
outer wall

*mosaic design*

**inside a mosque**

| | |
|---|---|
| ablution fountain (washing fountain) | kiblah (wall facing Mecca) |
| arcade (row of arches) | mihrab (niche showing direction of Mecca) |
| calligraphy (decorative writing) | minbar (pulpit) |
| carpets | mosaics |
| courtyard | pointed arch |
| enamel tiles | prayer hall |
| jali (latticed screen) | women's section |

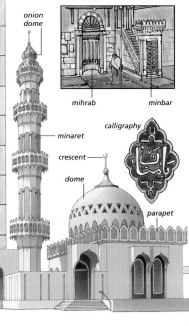

onion dome

mihrab

minbar

calligraphy

minaret

crescent

dome

parapet

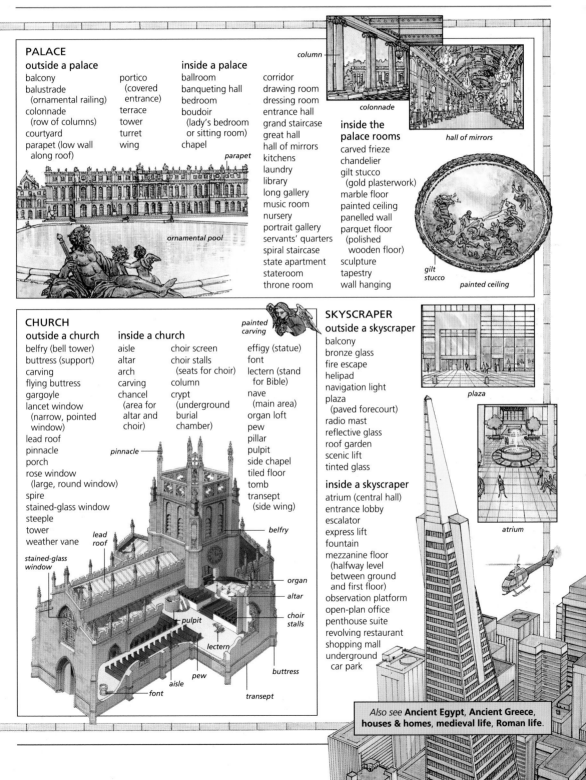

## PALACE

### outside a palace

balcony
balustrade
  (ornamental railing)
colonnade
  (row of columns)
courtyard
parapet (low wall
  along roof)

portico
  (covered
  entrance)
terrace
tower
turret
wing

### inside a palace

ballroom
banqueting hall
bedroom
boudoir
  (lady's bedroom
  or sitting room)
chapel

corridor
drawing room
dressing room
entrance hall
grand staircase
great hall
hall of mirrors
kitchens
laundry
library
long gallery
music room
nursery
portrait gallery
servants' quarters
spiral staircase
state apartment
stateroom
throne room

### inside the palace rooms

carved frieze
chandelier
gilt stucco
  (gold plasterwork)
marble floor
painted ceiling
panelled wall
parquet floor
  (polished
  wooden floor)
sculpture
tapestry
wall hanging

*column*

*colonnade*

*hall of mirrors*

*parapet*

*ornamental pool*

*gilt stucco*

*painted ceiling*

## CHURCH

### outside a church

belfry (bell tower)
buttress (support)
carving
flying buttress
gargoyle
lancet window
  (narrow, pointed
  window)
lead roof
pinnacle
porch
rose window
  (large, round window)
spire
stained-glass window
steeple
tower
weather vane

### inside a church

aisle
altar
arch
carving
chancel
  (area for
  altar and
  choir)

choir screen
choir stalls
  (seats for choir)
column
crypt
  (underground
  burial
  chamber)

effigy (statue)
font
lectern (stand
  for Bible)
nave
  (main area)
organ loft
pew
pillar
pulpit
side chapel
tiled floor
tomb
transept
  (side wing)

*painted carving*

*pinnacle*

*lead roof*

*stained-glass window*

*belfry*

*organ*

*altar*

*choir stalls*

*pulpit*

*lectern*

*pew*

*aisle*

*font*

*buttress*

*transept*

## SKYSCRAPER

### outside a skyscraper

balcony
bronze glass
fire escape
helipad
navigation light
plaza
  (paved forecourt)
radio mast
reflective glass
roof garden
scenic lift
tinted glass

### inside a skyscraper

atrium (central hall)
entrance lobby
escalator
express lift
fountain
mezzanine floor
  (halfway level
  between ground
  and first floor)
observation platform
open-plan office
penthouse suite
revolving restaurant
shopping mall
underground
  car park

*plaza*

*atrium*

*Also see* **Ancient Egypt, Ancient Greece, houses & homes, medieval life, Roman life**.

# **b**uild-up

**build-up**
(n) After all the build-up, the concert was disappointing. hype, publicity, promotion, advertising, ballyhoo (informal), fuss.

**build up**
1 (v) Jet has managed to build up a huge collection of CDs. amass, assemble, accumulate, collect, put together, construct, create, establish.
2 (v) Jet aims to build up her collection even further. See **increase** 3.
3 (v) Don't let the noise build up any more. See **increase** 2.

**bulging**
1 (adj) The monster had bulging eyes. protruding, sticking out, popping out, bug.
2 (adj) My bag is bulging. bursting at the seams, straining at the seams, overstuffed, swollen, distended.

**bulky**
(adj) A bulky parcel. large, enormous, massive, unwieldy, unmanageable, cumbersome, hulking, heavy, weighty.

**bullet**
(n) shot, slug, pellet, rubber bullet.

**bully**
1 (v) I didn't mean to bully you. intimidate, frighten, terrorize, push you around (slang), browbeat, torment, persecute, tyrannize, bulldoze (informal), bludgeon.
2 (n) I tried to escape from the bully. bully boy, tormentor, persecutor, tyrant, tough, thug, heavy (slang).

**bump**
1 (n) Guy has a bump on his knee. lump, swelling, bulge.
2 (n) Ed fell out of bed with a bump. thud, thump, crash, bang, jolt, smack, clunk.
3 (v) Don't bump your head! See **hit** 2.
4 (v) We watched the jeep bump across the field. bounce, jolt, rattle, jerk.

**bump into** see **crash into**.

**bumpy**
1 (adj) A bumpy track. rough, uneven, potholed, rutted, pitted, lumpy.
OPPOSITES: smooth, even.
2 (adj) A bumpy ride. rough, bouncy, bone-breaking, jolting, jerky, jarring.
OPPOSITE: smooth.
3 (adj) A bumpy sea crossing. rough, choppy, stormy, turbulent.
OPPOSITE: smooth.

**bunch**
1 (n) Romeo clutched a bunch of flowers. bouquet, posy, spray, arrangement.
2 (n) I've lost a bunch of papers. set, bundle, collection, sheaf, batch, stack, heap, pile, group, number, quantity, mass, clump, cluster, assortment.
3 (n) (informal) A bunch of people watched the juggler. See **crowd** 1.

**bundle**
1 (n) A bundle of papers. sheaf, bunch, batch, pile, bale, heap, stack, group, collection, mass, package, packet.

2 (v) Please bundle these newspapers together. tie, bind, fasten, pack, roll, heap.
3 (v) Did you see the kidnappers bundle a man into their car? shove, push, hustle, hurry, rush, thrust, throw.

**bung**
(v) (slang) Bung your trainers in the wardrobe. throw, shove (informal), sling (informal), dump, stick (informal), put, plonk, drop, stuff.

**bungle** see **make a mess of**.

**burglar**
(n) housebreaker, robber, thief, cat burglar, intruder, ram raider (informal).

**burglary**
1 (n) Beryl was arrested for burglary. housebreaking, robbery, stealing, theft, breaking and entering, ram raiding (informal).
2 (n) Police are investigating the burglary. See **break-in**.

**burn**
1 (v) The forest could burn for days. blaze, be on fire, be in flames, be alight, be ablaze, smoulder, glow, smoke.
2 (v) Matilda watched the candle burn. flicker, glow, blaze, flare, flash.
3 (v) We need to burn this garden rubbish. set fire to, incinerate, set alight, set on fire, reduce to ashes, ignite, kindle.
4 (v) If the iron is too hot it will burn your top. singe, scorch, char, sear, scald (liquid).
5 (v) My skin is starting to burn. go red, go pink, redden, blister, peel, sting, smart, tingle, prickle.

**burning**
1 (adj) We watched the burning coals. blazing, flaming, glowing, fiery, red-hot, smouldering, sizzling, smoking.
2 (adj) A burning smell came from the science lab. smoky, pungent, acrid.
3 (adj) Jan has a burning desire to change the world. passionate, intense, ardent, fervent, all-consuming, deep, sincere, earnest, raging, frenzied, frantic.

**burp**
(v) (informal) belch, bring up wind.

**burst**
1 (v) Our pipes might burst. crack, split, break, break open, rupture, fracture, explode, shatter, disintegrate, tear apart.
2 (v) Shall I burst this balloon? pop, puncture, prick, pierce, stab.
3 (v) Don't burst into the room like that! rush, charge, barge (informal), crash, dash.
4 (n) Dan had a sudden burst of energy. spurt, surge, rush.

**bury**
(v) Pirate Peg plans to bury the treasure in her garden. conceal, hide, stow away, stash (informal), secrete, cover up.

**bus**
(n) We travelled by bus. coach, double-decker, minibus, charabanc (old-fashioned), omnibus (old-fashioned).

**bush**
(n) Hide behind this bush! shrub, hedge, shrubbery, plant.

**bushy**
(adj) Bushy hair. thick, shaggy, wiry, bristly, fuzzy, frizzy, tangled, unruly, luxuriant.

**business**
1 (n) A computer business. See **firm** 6.
2 (n) This company has a lot of business with Japan. trade, commerce, trading, buying and selling, dealings (plural), transactions (plural).
3 (n) It's my business how I spend my money. See **affair** 1.

**businessman**, **businesswoman**
(n) executive, tycoon, financier, industrialist, trader, entrepreneur, manager, director.

**bust**
1 (n) This T-shirt is too tight round the bust. chest, bosom, breasts (plural).
2 (adj) (informal) My radio is bust. See **broken** 2.

**busy**
1 (adj) You always seem to be busy. occupied, fully occupied, active, bustling about, on the go (informal), up to your eyes (informal), working, hard at work, slaving away, on duty.
OPPOSITES: idle, at a loose end.
2 (adj) Jem is busy doing her homework. hard at work, involved in, engaged in, occupied with, absorbed in, engrossed in, preoccupied with.
3 (adj) We stayed in a busy seaside resort. bustling, lively, buzzing, humming (informal), crowded, swarming, teeming, hectic, frenetic.
OPPOSITES: quiet, sleepy.

**butt in** see **interrupt** 1.

**buy**
(v) Let's buy a TV. purchase, get, acquire, invest in (informal), obtain, pay for.
OPPOSITE: sell.

**by accident**
(phrase) Timmy hit me by accident. accidentally, by mistake, by chance, unintentionally, inadvertently, unwittingly.

**cadge** see **scrounge**.

**café**
(n) snack bar, coffee shop, tea shop, restaurant, buffet, cafeteria.

**cake**
(n) gateau, sponge cake, layer cake, fruitcake, swiss roll, gingerbread, cupcake, bun, pastry, éclair, doughnut.

**calamity** see **disaster**.

**calculate** see **figure out** 1.

**call**
1 *(v) Did you call for help?* shout, yell, cry, cry out, scream, holler *(informal)*, bellow.
2 *(v) Call the boys to come in for tea.* summon, order, instruct, invite, assemble, rally, gather, collect, muster.
3 *(v) What shall we call our gang? See* **name** 1.
4 *(v) I'll call you later. See* **phone** 1.
5 *(v) Can I call this morning?* drop in *(informal)*, come round, visit, pop in *(informal)*, look in *(informal)*, stop by, pay you a visit, look you up.
6 **call for** *(v) Did Ali call for the parcel?* come for, collect, fetch, pick up.

**callous**
*(adj) Bozo is so callous about other people's feelings.* uncaring, unfeeling, heartless, hardhearted, cold, cruel, unsympathetic, insensitive, thick-skinned.
OPPOSITES: caring, sympathetic.

**calm**
1 *(adj) The sea was calm.* still, smooth, motionless, tranquil, unruffled, glassy.
OPPOSITES: rough, choppy.
2 *(adj) Claire always seems so calm.* serene, peaceful, untroubled, placid, tranquil, unflustered, relaxed, laid-back *(informal)*, self-possessed, cool, composed, level-headed, unflappable *(informal)*.
OPPOSITES: agitated, frantic.
3 *(v) Heather tried to calm the crying baby.* soothe, settle, quieten, pacify, hush.

**camouflage** see **disguise** 1, 3.

**cancel**
*(v) Let's cancel the match.* call off, scrap, drop, ditch *(slang)*, abandon, write off.

**capable** see **able**.

**capture** see **catch** 2.

**car**
*(n)* motorcar, motor, vehicle, automobile *(old-fashioned)*, wheels *(plural) (informal)*, banger *(informal)*.
TYPES OF CAR: classic car, convertible, estate, family car, hatchback, limousine, off-road vehicle, people carrier, racing car, rally car, saloon, sports car, stretch limo *(informal)*, veteran car, vintage car.

**care**
1 *(v) You should care about the future.* mind, be concerned, concern yourself, be bothered, be interested in, worry.
2 *(n) Act with care. See* **caution**.
3 **care for** *(v) Can you care for my rat while I'm away? See* **look after**.

**career** see **job** 2.

**careful**
1 *(adj) Neesha always does careful work.* painstaking, meticulous, methodical, well-organized, neat, accurate, thoughtful.
OPPOSITES: careless, slapdash.
2 *(adj) Be careful crossing the road.* wary, attentive, alert, cautious, on your guard, observant, watchful.

**careless**
1 *(adj) Careless work.* slapdash, sloppy *(informal)*, scrappy, untidy, shoddy, slipshod, rushed, disorganized, inaccurate.
OPPOSITES: careful, meticulous.
2 *(adj) Careless actions.* thoughtless, inconsiderate, negligent, irresponsible.
OPPOSITES: careful, considerate.

**carry**
1 *(v) Carry your luggage to the car.* take, bring, transfer, move, shift, cart, lug, haul, hump *(informal)*, ferry, transport, deliver.
2 *(v) Can you carry my weight?* support, bear, take, hold, shoulder, sustain.

**carry on** see **continue** 1, 2, 3.

**carry out**
*(v) We must carry out our plan.* execute, accomplish, complete, carry through, fulfil.

**carve**
*(v) Try to carve a figure.* sculpt, hew, chisel, whittle, form, shape, engrave, etch.

**case**
1 *(n) I'll carry your case.* suitcase, bag, holdall, trunk, luggage, baggage.
2 *(n) Put that away in its case.* container, holder, wrapper, cover, box, cabinet.

**castle**
*(n)* fortress, fort, stronghold, citadel, palace, chateau. ❖ *Also see* **medieval life**.

**casual**
1 *(adj) A casual manner.* nonchalant, blasé, informal, free and easy, offhand, careless, relaxed, laid-back *(informal)*.
2 *(adj) Casual clothes.* informal, leisure, comfortable, ordinary, everyday, sporty.

**cat**
*(n)* pussy *(informal)*, pussycat *(informal)*, puss *(informal)*, moggy *(informal)*, kitten, tomcat *(male)*, tom *(male)*, mouser.
TYPES OF CAT: Burmese, chinchilla, long-haired cat, Manx, Persian, short-haired cat, Siamese, tabby, tortoiseshell.

**catastrophe** see **disaster**.

**catch**
1 *(v) Catch the ball.* grab, seize, grasp, clutch, snatch, get, intercept.
2 *(v) The police are trying to catch a thief.* capture, seize, trap, snare, arrest, nick *(slang)*, nab *(informal)*, collar *(informal)*.
3 *(v) I don't want to catch another cold.* get, contract, pick up, develop, go down with, succumb to, get infected with.
4 *(n) What's the catch?* snag, drawback, disadvantage, hitch, trap, trick.

**catching**
*(adj) Is this disease catching?* infectious, contagious.

**catty** *(informal)* see **spiteful**.

**cause**
1 *(v) This decision may cause problems.* create, produce, lead to, bring about, give rise to, generate, start, trigger off, spark off, stir up, provoke, make.
2 *(n) What was the cause of the problem?* root, source, reason for, origin.
3 *(n) Please support this cause.* campaign, movement, project, enterprise, charity.

**caution**
*(n) Act with caution.* care, attention, watchfulness, vigilance, forethought.

**cautious**
1 *(adj) A cautious swimmer.* careful, wary, unadventurous.
OPPOSITES: careless, reckless.
2 *(adj) A cautious reply.* guarded, careful, cagey *(informal)*, noncommittal, discreet, circumspect.
OPPOSITES: careless, unguarded.

---

**cat words**

**cat moves**

| | |
|---|---|
| claw | paw |
| creep | pounce |
| crouch | prowl |
| curl up | scratch |
| dash | slink |
| dive | sprawl |
| drop | spring |
| leap | stalk |
| nuzzle | stretch |
| pad | |

*pouncing Siamese*

*playful kittens*

**cat sounds**
caterwaul
cough
hiss
mew
miaow
purr
screech
spit
squeak
yelp
yowl

**a cat's coat can be...**
bedraggled
flea-bitten
fluffy
mangy
matted
shaggy
shiny
silky
sleek
smooth
soft

**a cat can seem...**

| | |
|---|---|
| adventurous | independent |
| affectionate | inquisitive |
| alert | lazy |
| aloof | mischievous |
| contented | playful |
| crazy | quizzical |
| curious | supercilious |
| dignified | timid |
| friendly | wild |

— *muzzle*

— *chest*

*sleek tabby*

*ruff*

*frill*

*fluffy long-haired cat*

# cave

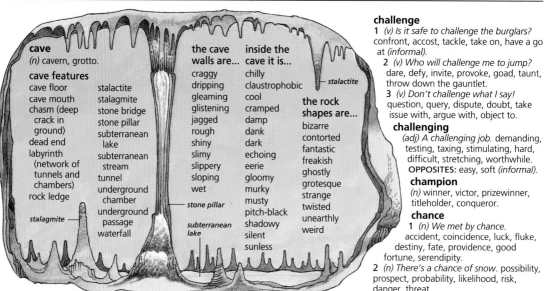

**cave**
(n) cavern, grotto.

**cave features**
cave floor
cave mouth
chasm (deep crack in ground)
dead end
labyrinth (network of tunnels and chambers)
rock ledge

stalactite
stalagmite
stone bridge
stone pillar
subterranean lake
subterranean stream
tunnel
underground chamber
underground passage
waterfall

*stalagmite*

**the cave walls are...**
craggy
dripping
gleaming
glistening
jagged
rough
shiny
slimy
slippery
sloping
wet

*stone pillar*

*subterranean lake*

**inside the cave it is...**
chilly
claustrophobic
cool
cramped
damp
dank
dark
echoing
eerie
gloomy
murky
musty
pitch-black
shadowy
silent
sunless

*stalactite*

**the rock shapes are...**
bizarre
contorted
fantastic
freakish
ghostly
grotesque
strange
twisted
unearthly
weird

---

**cease** see **stop** 3.

**ceaseless**
(adj) I can't stand this ceaseless noise. constant, continual, incessant, never-ending, nonstop, continuous, everlasting, endless, unending, unceasing, perpetual, relentless, persistent, interminable.
OPPOSITES: occasional, intermittent.

**celebrate**
1 (v) Do you celebrate St Patrick's Day? observe, commemorate, keep, mark.
2 (v) You should celebrate on your birthday. enjoy yourself, party (informal), whoop it up (informal), live it up (informal), make merry, paint the town red (informal).

**celebration**
(n) The celebration lasted all weekend. festivity, merrymaking, revelry, jollification, festivities (plural), party, shindig (informal), bash (informal), rave (slang), feast, carnival, gala, jubilee, festival.

**celebrity**
(n) Jason has become a TV celebrity. star, personality, idol, superstar, VIP (very important person), big name, big shot (informal), megastar.

**cellar**
(n) basement, vault, crypt (church).

**cemetery**
(n) graveyard, burial ground, churchyard.

**central**
1 (adj) The central part of the city. inner, middle, innermost, interior, core, focal.
OPPOSITE: outer.
2 (adj) The central point of an argument. main, key, focal, pivotal, principal, major, dominant, leading, most important, chief, basic, fundamental, essential.

**centre**
1 (n) Drive to the centre of the city. middle, heart, midpoint.
OPPOSITES: edge, outskirts (plural).
2 (n) This office is the centre of our operation. hub, heart, focal point, nerve centre, core, focus, nucleus, crux.

**ceremony**
(n) Is there a ceremony to mark the end of term? event, function, gathering, celebration, do (informal), service, ritual.

**certain**
1 (adj) Chas was certain he had seen a ghost. sure, positive, in no doubt, confident, convinced, satisfied, assured, persuaded, definite.
2 (adj) The detectives need certain proof. definite, absolute, conclusive, undeniable, unquestionable, indisputable, irrefutable, clear, unmistakable, reliable.
3 (adj) Is it certain that Dad will lose his job? definite, settled, guaranteed, inevitable, unavoidable, inescapable, inexorable, sure, fixed, destined, fated.
4 (adj) The shop is closed on certain days. specific, particular, special, individual, established, fixed, set.

**chain**
1 (n) A chain of disasters. See **series**.
2 **chains** (plural n) The prisoners were kept in chains. irons (plural), shackles (plural), fetters (plural), handcuffs (plural), manacles (plural), leg irons (plural).

**chair**
(n) seat.
TYPES OF CHAIR: armchair, deck chair, dining chair, easy chair, office chair, reclining chair, rocking chair, sun lounger, swivel chair, throne.

**challenge**
1 (v) Is it safe to challenge the burglars? confront, accost, tackle, take on, have a go at (informal).
2 (v) Who will challenge me to jump? dare, defy, invite, provoke, goad, taunt, throw down the gauntlet.
3 (v) Don't challenge what I say! question, query, dispute, doubt, take issue with, argue with, object to.

**challenging**
(adj) A challenging job. demanding, testing, taxing, stimulating, hard, difficult, stretching, worthwhile.
OPPOSITES: easy, soft (informal).

**champion**
(n) winner, victor, prizewinner, titleholder, conqueror.

**chance**
1 (n) We met by chance. accident, coincidence, luck, fluke, destiny, fate, providence, good fortune, serendipity.
2 (n) There's a chance of snow. possibility, prospect, probability, likelihood, risk, danger, threat.
3 (n) Will you take a chance? risk, gamble, leap in the dark.
4 (n) You will have another chance to win soon. opportunity, occasion, time, turn.
5 (adj) It was a chance meeting. accidental, coincidental, unexpected, unintentional, unplanned, unforeseen, random, casual, fluke, fortuitous.

**change**
1 (v) We must change our plans. alter, revise, amend, modify, adapt, vary, reform.
2 (v) I want to change my room. alter, rearrange, transform, make over, redo, reorganize, remodel, revamp.
3 (v) The frog began to change into a prince. turn, be transformed, morph (informal), mutate, metamorphose, transmute, become.
4 (v) Can I change this jumper for a smaller one? exchange, swap, switch, trade, substitute, replace with.
5 (v) Let's change our direction. switch, alter, shift, reverse.
6 (n) There's been a change in Guy's attitude. shift, switch, alteration, transformation, turnaround, sea change, reversal, metamorphosis.
7 (n) This is a pleasant change. variation, departure, diversion, break, novelty.
8 (n) I need some change for the bus. coins (plural), small change, loose change, cash, coppers (plural), silver.

**change your mind**
(phrase) Why don't you change your mind and stay? revise your opinion, think better of it, think twice, reconsider, rethink.

**chaos**
(n) There was chaos in the classroom. confusion, disorder, pandemonium, bedlam, turmoil, uproar, tumult, anarchy.

**chaotic**
*(adj) The office was chaotic.* disorganized, jumbled, muddled, topsy-turvy, shambolic *(informal)*, out of control, riotous, anarchic.

**character**
1 *(n) Marie has a very gentle character.* personality, nature, temperament, disposition, make-up.
2 *(n) Yves is a strange character.* person, individual, type *(informal)*, sort *(informal)*.
3 *(n) (informal) Eddie's a real character!* individual, eccentric, clown, comic, case *(informal)*, oddball *(informal)*.
4 *(n) This village has a special character.* quality, atmosphere, feel, personality.

**characteristic**
*(n) Untidiness is a characteristic of many teenagers.* quality, attribute, trait, feature, peculiarity, idiosyncrasy, mark, property.

**charge**
1 *(n) What is the charge for entering the museum?* cost, fee, price, rate, payment.
2 *(v) The troops began to charge the enemy.* attack, storm, assault, rush at.
3 *(v) The police will charge Beryl with burglary.* accuse of, indict, prosecute for.

**charm**
1 *(n) Oz has a mysterious charm.* appeal, charisma, allure, magnetism, fascination.
2 *(n) A wizard's charm. See* **spell**.
3 *(n) A lucky charm.* amulet, talisman.
4 *(v) Kamala will charm you with her singing.* delight, captivate, enchant, bewitch, beguile, fascinate, mesmerize.

**charming**
*(adj) A charming smile.* appealing, attractive, enchanting, captivating, winning, bewitching, engaging, irresistible, disarming, fetching *(informal)*.

**chart**
*(n) Study this chart.* plan, map, table, diagram, graph, blueprint.

**chase**
*(v) Fido loves to chase Pickles.* run after, pursue, follow, tail, hunt, stalk, trail.

**chat** see **talk 1, 5, 6.**

**chatter** see **prattle.**

**chatterbox**
*(n) (informal) Sophie is a real chatterbox!* gossip, chatterer, prattler, motormouth *(slang)*, windbag *(slang)*.

**chatty**
*(adj) (informal) Zoë sent me a chatty letter.* gossipy, newsy, friendly, informal.

**cheap**
1 *(adj) This CD is cheap.* inexpensive, reasonable, moderately priced, good value, economical, cut-price, reduced.
OPPOSITE: expensive.
2 *(adj) This cheap furniture won't last.* poor-quality, inferior, shoddy, trashy, tacky *(informal)*, tawdry, rubbishy, crappy *(slang)*, crummy *(slang)*, worthless.
OPPOSITES: high-quality, superior.
3 *(adj) What a cheap trick! See* **mean 6.**

**cheat**
1 *(v) Watch out for Dodgy Dave or he'll cheat you.* trick, swindle, con *(informal)*, screw *(informal)*, sting *(informal)*, bamboozle *(informal)*, dupe, do *(informal)*, fleece, rip you off *(slang)*, take you for a ride *(informal)*, pull a fast one on *(slang)*, hoodwink, defraud.
2 *(v) Don't cheat in this test.* break the rules, bend the rules, copy, crib *(informal)*.
3 *(n) That man's a cheat.* swindler, con man *(informal)*, rogue, shark *(informal)*, double-dealer, double-crosser, fraud *(informal)*, crook *(informal)*, impostor.

**check**
*(v) Check your bike carefully before you set off.* examine, inspect, check out, test, try out, give it the once-over *(informal)*, look over, scrutinize.

**checkup**
*(n) A medical checkup.* examination, medical *(informal)*, physical *(informal)*.

**cheeky**
*(adj) I've had enough of your cheeky comments!* impertinent, impudent, rude, saucy, bold, insolent, disrespectful, insulting, pert, fresh *(informal)*, forward.
OPPOSITES: polite, respectful.

**cheer**
*(v) When we heard the score, we all began to cheer.* applaud, clap, whoop, whistle, yell, stamp, give a standing ovation.

**cheerful**
*(adj) Sally is always cheerful.* happy, good-humoured, cheery, light-hearted, jolly, sunny, chirpy *(informal)*, perky, merry, bright, breezy, buoyant, optimistic.
OPPOSITES: miserable, depressed.

**cheer up**
1 *(v) Try to cheer up.* perk up *(informal)*, buck up *(informal)*, take heart, rally, brighten, snap out of it *(informal)*.
2 *(v) How can I cheer you up?* encourage, comfort, buck you up *(informal)*, give you new heart, buoy you up, jolly you along *(informal)*, gladden, hearten.

**chest**
1 *(n) A person's chest.* ribcage, breast *(old-fashioned)*.
2 *(n) A storage chest.* trunk, box, crate, container, case, strongbox, coffer, casket.

**chew**
*(v) Chew your food thoroughly.* munch, crunch, chomp, gnaw, grind up, nibble.

**chief**
1 *(adj) Amy was the chief bridesmaid.* principal, senior, head, leading, main.
2 *(adj) What is your chief reason for leaving? See* **main.**

**child**
*(n) kid (informal)*, youngster, young person, boy, girl, little one, nipper *(informal)*, brat, kiddywink *(informal)*, sprog *(slang)*, infant, toddler, tot, tiny tot, adolescent, teenager, juvenile, minor.

**childish**
*(adj) Childish behaviour.* infantile, juvenile, immature, babyish, puerile, foolish, silly.

**chilly**
1 *(adj) A chilly morning.* cold, icy, frosty, crisp, cool, nippy, fresh, raw, wintry.
OPPOSITE: warm.
2 *(adj) A chilly response.* cool, frosty, unfriendly, aloof, standoffish, cold, hostile.
OPPOSITES: friendly, warm.

**chip**
1 *(n) My mug has a chip in it.* nick, crack, split, flaw, notch, scratch, dent, gash.
2 *(n) I knocked a chip off the table.* splinter, sliver, shaving, flake, piece, fragment, chunk, wedge.

**choice**
1 *(n) Do I have a choice?* option, alternative, vote, say, voice.
2 *(n) There was a wide choice of desserts.* selection, range, variety, array, assortment.
3 *(n) Have you made your choice?* selection, pick, decision, preference.

**choke**
1 *(v) The thick smoke made us choke.* gasp, gag, retch, cough, suffocate.
2 *(v) The villain tried to choke his victim.* strangle, throttle, garrotte, suffocate, smother, stifle, overwhelm, overpower.
3 *(v) Leaves often choke the stream.* block, clog, stop up, obstruct, dam, bung up, constrict, congest.

**choose**
1 *(v) I think we should choose Bill as our captain.* select, pick, elect, appoint, decide on, opt for, settle on, fix upon.
2 *(v) You may choose to walk alone.* decide, prefer, opt, elect, see fit, wish, resolve, make up your mind, determine.

**choosy** *(informal) see* **fussy.**

**chop**
1 *(v) Can you chop this log in two?* split, cut, cleave, hew, hack, slice, divide, sever.
2 *(v) Chop the carrots finely.* chop up, cut up, slice, dice, cube, mince.

**choppy**
*(adj) A choppy sea.* rough, ruffled, stormy, squally, turbulent, heaving.
OPPOSITES: smooth, calm.

**chore** see **task.**

**chubby** see **plump.**

**chuck** *(informal) see* **throw 1.**

**chuckle** see **giggle.**

**chuffed** *(slang) see* **pleased.**

**chunk**
*(n) A chunk of cheese.* block, hunk, slab, lump, wedge, slice, wodge *(informal)*.

**circle**
1 *(n) Draw a circle.* ring, loop, disc, hoop, band, round shape, circular shape.
2 *(v) The road will circle the city.* surround, enclose, encircle, ring, skirt, hem in, orbit.
3 *(v) Watch the dancers circle round the room. See* **whirl.**

# city

| city | | on the pavement you can see... | people may... | the traffic may be... | you can shop at... | the city may be... |
|---|---|---|---|---|---|---|
| (n) metropolis, town. | | beggar | brush past | at a standstill | boutique | bewildering |
| | | busker | crowd | bumper-to- | chain store | bustling |
| **city sights** | **city streets** | bus stop | dawdle | bumper | covered market | busy |
| art gallery | alley | entertainer | hurry | chock-a-block | department | buzzing |
| bridge | avenue | flower seller | jostle | crawling | store | congested |
| cathedral | backstreet | fruit stall | loiter | slow-moving | kiosk | crowded |
| cinema | boulevard | lamppost | mill about | snarled up | open-air | dirty |
| city hall | crescent | litter | rush | solid | market | dynamic |
| concert hall | cul-de-sac | newspaper | wander | tailed back | shopping mall | exciting |
| fountain | flyover | vendor | window-shop | | supermarket | grimy |
| hotel | lane | pedestrian | | **traffic sounds** | | high-tech |
| ice rink | one-way street | police officer | **city transport** | beep | **you can eat and drink at...** | historic |
| leisure complex | passage | road sweeper | bicycle | chug | | lively |
| library | plaza | shopper | bus | growl | bistro | noisy |
| mosque | ring road | street artist | car | honk | burger bar | overwhelming |
| museum | square | tourist | open-topped | hum | café | packed |
| nightclub | subway | | bus | purr | coffee shop | polluted |
| opera house | (underground | | taxi | roar | pavement café | pulsing |
| park | passage) | | tram | screech | pub | run-down |
| skyscraper | | *city skyline* | tube | squeal | restaurant | shabby |
| sports stadium | | | underground | toot | snack bar | smart |
| temple | | | | wail | tea shop | smoggy |
| theatre | | | | | wine bar | smoky |
| tower | | | | | | spectacular |
| block | | | | | | throbbing |

*Also see* **building.**

## claim
1 (v) I've come to claim my money. demand, ask for, collect, pick up, request.
2 (v) I still claim that I was right. insist, maintain, argue, assert, affirm, declare.

## clammy see damp 3.

## clap see applaud.

## class
(n) Which class are you in at school? form, group, set, stream, year, level.

## clean
1 (v) I must clean everything in my room. wash, wipe, mop, scrub, scour, sponge, dust, soap, sweep, vacuum, cleanse, launder, rinse, disinfect.
2 (adj) Everything in my room is clean. spotless, immaculate, squeaky-clean, fresh, sanitary, hygienic, unsoiled, unstained, washed, laundered, swept, scrubbed, scoured, dusted, disinfected.
OPPOSITES: dirty, soiled.
3 (adj) You must only drink clean water. pure, uncontaminated, unpolluted, purified, sterile, clear, unadulterated.
OPPOSITES: polluted, contaminated.
4 (adj) Use a clean sheet of paper. blank, new, empty, unused, unmarked, fresh.

## clear
1 (adj) A clear stream. transparent, limpid, pure, crystal clear, crystalline.
OPPOSITES: muddy, cloudy.

2 (adj) A clear signal. definite, plain, distinct, recognizable, unmistakable.
OPPOSITES: unclear, confusing.
3 (adj) Clear writing. legible, bold, neat.
OPPOSITE: illegible.
4 (adj) A clear day. See **fine 3.**
5 (adj) A clear outline. clean, clear-cut, definite, distinct, sharp, well-defined.
OPPOSITE: fuzzy.
6 (adj) A clear voice. audible, distinct, penetrating, piercing.
OPPOSITES: indistinct, muffled.
7 (adj) A clear argument. clear-cut, coherent, simple, straightforward, easy to follow, unambiguous, lucid.
OPPOSITES: confusing, complicated.
8 (adj) A clear space. See **empty 1.**
9 (v) I must clear this rubbish from my room. get rid of, remove, empty, strip, unload, unpack, disentangle.
10 (v) I wish the mist would clear. disappear, evaporate, melt away, lift.

## clear up
1 (v) Clear up the kitchen. See **tidy 3.**
2 (v) Let's clear up this problem. sort out, settle, resolve, clarify, unravel, put right.
3 (v) I hope your cold will clear up soon. go away, disappear, get better.

## clever
1 (adj) A clever student. intelligent, bright, able, quick, brainy (informal), smart, gifted, talented, capable, knowledgeable.

2 (adj) A clever trick. cunning, crafty, ingenious, shrewd, smart, slick, inventive.

## cliff
(n) precipice, rockface, crag, escarpment.
❖ Also see **sea & seashore.**

## climax
(n) The climax of Jackson's career was winning the gold medal. high point, high spot, highlight, culmination, crowning point, pinnacle, peak.

## climb
1 (v) We tried to climb the mountain. scale, clamber up, go up, ascend, shin up.
OPPOSITES: descend, go down.
2 (v) I think prices will climb. See **rise 2.**
3 (v) The road began to climb. See **rise 4.**

## cling on to see hold on to.

## clip see fasten 2.

## clog see block 2.

## close
1 (v) Close the gate. See **shut 1.**
2 (adj) Bill and Ben are close friends. See **intimate 1.**
3 (adj) The match was close. evenly matched, well-matched, hard-fought, neck and neck.
4 close to (adj) I live close to the park. See **near 1.**

## cloth see material.

**clothes** (*plural n*) clothing, garments (*plural*), gear (*informal*), togs (*plural*) (*informal*), get-up (*informal*), dress, costume, attire (*old-fashioned*).

## trousers and shorts

bermuda shorts
chinos
corduroys
culottes
cut-offs
cycling shorts
drainpipes
dungarees
flannels

flares
jeans
jodhpurs
knickerbockers
leggings
palazzo pants
pedal pushers
plus fours
ski pants

## suits

boiler suit
dress suit
lounge suit
morning suit
overalls
pinstripe suit
safari suit
sailor suit
shell suit
three-piece suit
tracksuit
trouser suit

## skirts

flared skirt
gathered skirt
kilt
miniskirt
pleated skirt
puffball skirt
sarong
split skirt
straight skirt
tiered skirt
wrapover skirt

## dresses

ball gown
cocktail dress
gym slip
kimono
maternity dress
minidress
pinafore
sari
shift dress
sundress

*three-piece suit*

*safari suit*

*waistband*

*chinos*

*culottes*

*palazzo pants*

*puffball skirt*

*wrapover skirt*

*pinafore dress*

*shift dress*

## tops

blouse
body
camisole top
cardigan
crew-neck jumper
cropped top
lumberjack shirt
polo-neck jumper
polo shirt
pullover

rugby shirt
smock
sweater
sweatshirt
tanktop
T-shirt
turtleneck jumper
vest top
V-neck jumper
waistcoat

*blouse*

*camisole top*

*cropped top*

## fabrics

acrylic
cashmere
chiffon
corduroy
cotton
crushed velvet
denim
fur
jersey
lamé
leather
lycra
satin
silk
suede
taffeta
tweed
velvet
wool

## patterns

checked
floral
gingham
paisley
polka dot
striped
tartan

*gingham*

*floral*

*tartan*

## some clothes have...

beads
embroidery
flounces
frills
fringes
ruffles
sequins
tassels
tiers

*sequin*

*bead*

## coats and jackets

anorak
blazer
bomber jacket
cagoule
cape
cloak
combat jacket
dinner jacket
double-breasted jacket
duffle coat
fleece
fur coat
greatcoat
mackintosh
overcoat
raincoat
shawl
sports jacket
tail coat
trench coat
waxed jacket

*double-breasted jacket*

*collar*

*lapel*

*trench coat*

## accessories

bag
belt
bow tie
braces
cravat
cummerbund

gloves
jewellery
sash
scarf
shoes
tie

## clothes can look...

baggy
casual
chic
clingy
comfortable
daring
dashing
drab
elegant
fashionable
feminine
figure-hugging
flamboyant

flattering
floating
flowing
formal
frilly
frumpy
fun
fussy
glamorous
glittering
neat
old-fashioned
outrageous

practical
revealing
roomy
scruffy
see-through
severe
skintight
slinky
smart
sophisticated
sporty
tight-fitting

## clothes can be...

backless
cropped
fitted
flared
gathered
padded
pleated
ribbed
sleeveless
strapless
tailored
tapered

*Also see* **hat**, **jewellery**, **shoe**.

**cloudy**
1 *(adj) A cloudy sky.* overcast, hazy, grey, dull, gloomy, dismal, dark, leaden, heavy, thundery, threatening, sunless, starless.
OPPOSITES: clear, cloudless.
2 *(adj) Cloudy water.* murky, muddy, milky, opaque.
OPPOSITES: clear, transparent.

**club**
*(n) Please join our club!* group, society, organization, association, circle, clique, company, league, union, federation.

**clue**
*(n) This clue may help solve the crime.* lead, pointer, information, evidence, tip-off, suggestion, hint, sign, key, idea.

**clumsy** *see* **awkward** 1, 2.

**clutch** *see* **grip**.

**clutter**
1 *(n) Tidy up this clutter! See* **mess** 1.
2 *(v) Don't clutter the lounge with your comics.* litter, mess up, strew, make untidy.

**coach**
1 *(n) We travelled by coach. See* **bus**.
2 *(n) We've got a new tennis coach.* instructor, trainer, teacher, tutor, mentor.
3 *(v) Who'll coach the team? See* **train** 4.

**coarse**
1 *(adj) Coarse material.* rough, scratchy, bristly, prickly, hairy, thick, homespun.
OPPOSITES: fine, soft.
2 *(adj) Coarse jokes. See* **crude**.

**coast** *see* **shore**.

**coat**
1 *(n) Put on your coat.* ❖ *See* **clothes**.
2 *(n) An animal's coat keeps it warm in winter.* fur, hair, fleece, wool, pelt, hide.
3 *(n) Apply a coat of varnish. See* **layer** 1.

**coax** *see* **persuade**.

**cocky** *see* **conceited**.

**coil** *see* **loop** 1, 2.

**cold**
1 *(adj) It was a cold winter's day.* chilly, freezing, frosty, icy, crisp, nippy, raw, bitter, bleak, perishing *(informal)*, wintry.
OPPOSITES: warm, hot.
2 *(adj) A cold wind blew in off the sea.* chill, icy, freezing, bitter, keen, biting, cutting, piercing, penetrating, arctic.
OPPOSITES: warm, balmy.
3 *(adj) I'm cold!* chilly, freezing, frozen, frozen stiff, perishing *(informal)*, chilled to the bone, shivering, numbed.
OPPOSITES: warm, hot.
4 *(adj) Mr Steel is a rather cold person.* distant, remote, aloof, reserved, unfriendly, standoffish, impersonal, unemotional, unfeeling, unsympathetic, uncaring.
OPPOSITES: warm, friendly.

**collapse**
1 *(v) Let's hope the roof doesn't collapse.* fall in, cave in, give way, subside, tumble down, crumble, disintegrate, fall to pieces, fall apart, crumple, buckle.

2 *(v) Jenny may collapse when she hears the bad news.* faint, pass out, lose consciousness, keel over, swoon *(old-fashioned)*, break down, go to pieces.
3 *(n) The collapse of Communism.* fall, ruin, downfall, destruction, break-up.

**collect**
1 *(v) Fran has started to collect old comics.* save, keep, accumulate, amass, pile up, gather together, stockpile, hoard.
2 *(v) We'll collect you from the station.* fetch, come and get, pick you up, call for.
3 *(v) A crowd began to collect around the juggler.* gather, assemble, congregate, converge, cluster, flock, concentrate, mass.
OPPOSITES: disperse, scatter.

**collection**
*(n) Melissa has a collection of stamps.* set, assortment, array, hoard, mass, pile, stack.

**collision** *see* **crash** 2.

**colossal** *see* **huge**.

**colour**
1 *(n) That colour of blue suits you.* shade, tone, tint, tinge, hue.
2 *(v) Colour the background green.* paint, shade, tint, dye, stain, tinge, colourwash.

**colourful**
*(adj) A colourful shirt.* brightly coloured, bright, vivid, vibrant, multicoloured, gaudy, jazzy *(informal)*, psychedelic.
OPPOSITES: dull, colourless.

**column**
1 *(n) A stone column. See* **pillar**.
2 *(n) A column of people. See* **line** 3.
3 *(n) A newspaper column. See* **article** 1.

**combine**
*(v) Let's combine the teams to create a winning side.* merge, put together, pool, mix, unite, join, integrate, amalgamate.
OPPOSITES: separate, divide.

**come**
1 *(v) The enemy will come under cover of darkness.* approach, advance, move closer, draw near, close in, bear down.
OPPOSITE: go.
2 *(v) Please come on time. See* **arrive** 1.
3 **come to** *(v) Stop when you come to the lights.* reach, get to, arrive at, get as far as.

**comedy**
*(n)* light entertainment, humour, fun.
TYPES OF COMEDY: black comedy, clowning, farce, improvisation, pantomime, parody, revue, satire, sitcom (situation comedy), sketch, skit, slapstick, spoof *(informal)*, stand-up comedy.

**come in** *see* **enter** 1.

**come round**
1 *(v) Please come round soon. See* **call** 5.
2 *(v) We waited anxiously for Jo to come round after her fall.* come to, regain consciousness, revive, recover, wake up.

**come up**
*(v) Did any problems come up?* crop up *(informal)*, arise, occur, emerge, happen.

**comfort**
1 *(v) Gina tried to comfort her sobbing sister.* console, soothe, calm, reassure, encourage, cheer up, sympathize with.
2 *(n) Lord Lucre enjoys a life of comfort.* ease, contentment, wellbeing, cosiness, luxury, affluence, opulence.
OPPOSITE: hardship.

**comfortable**
1 *(adj) A comfortable sofa.* comfy *(informal)*, soft, squashy, well-padded, well-cushioned, cosy, snug, roomy.
OPPOSITE: uncomfortable.
2 *(adj) Comfortable clothes.* comfy *(informal)*, loose-fitting, roomy, baggy, sloppy, stretchy, snug, casual, sporty.
OPPOSITES: uncomfortable, tight-fitting.

**command** *see* **order** 1, 3.

**comment**
1 *(v) Beth was quick to comment that I looked better.* remark, point out, mention, observe, note, say.
2 *(n) Ben made a nasty comment about my hair.* remark, observation, statement.

**commit**
*(v) Beryl may commit another crime.* carry out, perpetrate, execute, be guilty of.

**common**
1 *(adj) Red buses are a common sight in London.* normal, familiar, usual, everyday, frequent, regular, daily, ordinary, routine, commonplace, run-of-the-mill, standard.
OPPOSITES: rare, uncommon.
2 *(adj) There's a common theory that chocolate gives you spots. See* **popular** 3.
3 *(adj) Araminta says I'm common.* coarse, uncouth, vulgar, crude, rough, yobbish *(informal)*, loutish, ill-bred, inferior.
OPPOSITES: refined, well-bred.

**communicate**
1 *(v) Please communicate this message.* convey, pass on, relay, spread, transmit.
2 *(v) We try to communicate regularly.* be in touch, make contact, talk, converse, speak, correspond, write, e-mail.

**company**
1 *(n) I enjoy Orlando's company.* friendship, companionship.
2 *(n) We have company for dinner.* guests *(plural)*, visitors *(plural)*, callers *(plural)*.
3 *(n) An electronics company. See* **firm** 6.

**compare**
1 *(v) Compare your results with mine.* check against, contrast, set against.
2 **compare with** *(v) This restaurant can compare with any in the area.* equal, rival, match, measure up to, bear comparison with, hold a candle to *(informal)*.

**compete**
1 *(v) Are you going to compete on Sports Day?* take part, participate, join in, enter, be a contestant, be in the running.
2 *(v) Six teams will compete for the cup.* contend, vie, battle, fight, rival each other.

**competent** *see* **able**.

## competition

1 *(n) Who won the competition?* contest, championship, tournament, match, game, race, event, challenge, rally, quiz.
2 *(n) There's a lot of competition for places at the school.* rivalry, one-upmanship *(informal)*, opposition.

## competitive

1 *(adj) Tony is so competitive.* ambitious, pushy *(informal)*, aggressive, combative.
2 *(adj) We live in a competitive society.* dog-eat-dog, cutthroat, aggressive.

## competitor

*(n) Are you a competitor in this race?* contestant, contender, challenger, participant, entrant, runner, candidate.

## complain

*(v) I'm tired of hearing you complain.* criticize, find fault, make a fuss, protest, grumble, moan, grouse, whine, whinge *(informal)*, gripe *(informal)*, carp, groan *(informal)*, beef *(slang)*, bellyache *(slang)*.

## complaint

*(n) Please see the manager with your complaint.* grievance, criticism, objection, protest, grouse, gripe *(informal)*.

## complete

1 *(adj) Do you have the complete set?* See **whole**.
2 *(adj) The match was a complete disaster.* absolute, total, utter, unqualified, out-and-out, outright, thoroughgoing, perfect.
3 *(v) We must complete our project today.* See **finish** 1.

## completely see **absolutely**.

## complex

*(n) Nathan has a complex about being short.* obsession, fixation, phobia, preoccupation, hang-up *(informal)*.

## complicated

*(adj) Complicated directions.* complex, involved, elaborate, convoluted, intricate, difficult, perplexing, puzzling.
OPPOSITES: simple, straightforward.

## compliment

*(n) Freddie's compliment made me blush.* flattering remark, praise, admiration, tribute, flattery, congratulations *(plural)*.

## compose see **write** 2.

## compromise

*(v) We couldn't agree, so we had to compromise.* make concessions, meet halfway, make a deal *(informal)*, strike a balance, find the middle ground, give and take, find a solution.

## compulsory

*(adj) At my school, wearing uniform is compulsory.* obligatory, required, mandatory, necessary, stipulated.
OPPOSITE: optional.

## computer

*(n)* TYPES OF COMPUTER: hand-held, laptop, mainframe, notebook, palmtop, PC (personal computer), server, word processor, work station.

*(n)* PARTS OF A COMPUTER: CD-ROM (compact disc with read-only memory), CD-ROM drive, CD-writer, CPU (central processing unit), disk drive, floppy disk, hard disk, keyboard, memory expansion card, modem, monitor, mouse, printer, scanner, screen, sound card, speaker, VDU (visual display unit).

## con

1 *(n) (informal) This offer is a real con!* swindle, cheat, con trick *(informal)*, rip-off *(slang)*, swiz *(informal)*, scam *(slang)*.
2 *(v) (informal) Dodgy Dave will con you out of your money.* See **cheat** 1.

## conceal see **hide** 1, 2, 3.

## conceited

*(adj) Jack is so conceited; he's always boasting.* vain, bigheaded *(informal)*, swollen-headed *(informal)*, puffed up, proud, arrogant, self-important, self-satisfied, boastful, cocky, bumptious.
OPPOSITES: modest, self-effacing.

## concentrate

1 *(v) Do you find it hard to concentrate?* focus your thoughts, focus your attention, pay attention, stop your mind wandering.
2 **concentrate on** *(v) Concentrate on your work.* keep your mind on, focus on, give your full attention to, apply yourself to, attend to.

## concern

1 *(v) This decision will concern you all.* affect, involve, apply to, relate to, be relevant to, be of interest to, matter to.
2 *(v) Don't let this problem concern you.* See **worry** 2.
3 *(n) Granny's illness has caused us a lot of concern.* See **worry** 3.
4 *(n) Show some concern for your sister!* consideration, care, sympathy, regard.
5 *(n) This mess is not my concern.* affair, business, responsibility, problem.

## conclusion

1 *(n) We had to leave before the conclusion.* See **end** 1.
2 *(n) After all that thinking, what's your conclusion?* decision, judgment, verdict, opinion, deduction, answer, solution.

## condemn

1 *(v) Don't condemn Ziggy for being different.* criticize, blame, denounce, censure, reproach, damn, slam *(slang)*.
2 *(v) The judge decided to condemn Burglar Beryl.* See **convict** 1.

## condescending

*(adj) Araminta is so condescending; she looks down on everyone.* patronizing, superior, supercilious, disdainful, snobbish, snooty *(informal)*, toffee-nosed *(slang)*.

## condition

1 *(n) Are you in good condition?* health, shape, trim, nick *(informal)*, form.
2 *(n) Our school is in a dreadful condition.* state, state of repair, order, situation, position, predicament, plight.

3 **conditions** *(plural n) The conditions in the prison were terrible.* circumstances *(plural)*, surroundings *(plural)*, environment, situation, way of life.

## confess

1 *(v) Did Beryl confess that she was guilty?* admit, own up, acknowledge, concede, declare, reveal, disclose, blurt out, confide.
2 *(v) If you broke the window you should confess.* own up, accept responsibility, plead guilty, come clean *(informal)*, make a clean breast of it, spill the beans *(informal)*.

## confession

*(n) A confession of guilt.* admission, acknowledgment, declaration, profession.

## confide in

*(v) You can confide in me; I won't tell a soul.* open your heart to, unburden yourself to, tell your secrets to, tell all to *(informal)*, trust, have confidence in.

## confident

1 *(adj) Izzy is confident in new situations.* self-confident, self-assured, poised, self-possessed, composed, assertive, fearless.
OPPOSITES: diffident, insecure.
2 *(adj) I'm confident that it will be sunny.* certain, sure, convinced, positive, optimistic, hopeful.
OPPOSITE: doubtful.

## confidential see **private** 2.

## confirm

*(v) Sid's actions confirm my suspicions about him.* bear out, verify, prove, substantiate, corroborate, validate, back up, support, strengthen, reinforce.

## confiscate

*(v) Mrs Badger will confiscate that comic.* seize, remove, take away, impound.

## confront

*(v) Are you brave enough to confront Bozo?* face, face up to, stand up to, resist, oppose, defy, challenge, tackle, accost.

## confuse

1 *(v) Complicated instructions confuse me.* bewilder, perplex, baffle, puzzle, muddle, flummox, faze, mystify, bemuse.
2 **confuse with** *(v) I often confuse you with your twin brother.* mistake you for, mix you up with, take you for.

## confused

*(adj) Don't speak so fast; it makes me feel confused.* bewildered, dazed, muddled, disorientated, befuddled, at sixes and sevens, at sea, perplexed, baffled, flummoxed, nonplussed, puzzled.

## confusing

*(adj) These instructions are confusing.* baffling, bewildering, perplexing, mystifying, puzzling, misleading, ambiguous, unclear, complicated.
OPPOSITES: clear, straightforward.

## confusion

*(n) A scene of total confusion met my eyes.* chaos, turmoil, muddle, disorder, disarray, disorganization, jumble, clutter, shambles.

# congratulate

**congratulate**
(v) *I'll be the first to congratulate you if you win.* shake your hand, pat you on the back *(informal)*, compliment, praise, offer you good wishes, wish you joy.
OPPOSITE: commiserate with.

**conjurer** *see* **magician 2.**

**connect**
1 (v) *Connect the cable to the television.* join, attach, link up, fix, fasten, secure.
OPPOSITE: disconnect.
2 (v) *I always connect that smell with school dinners. See* **associate 2.**

**connection**
(n) *Is there a connection between air pollution and asthma?* link, correlation, relationship, association, tie-in, parallel.

**conquer**
1 (v) *The army managed to conquer their enemy.* defeat, beat, overcome, subdue, overthrow, overpower, triumph over, crush, thrash, rout, vanquish, subjugate.
2 (v) *I'm trying to conquer my fear of flying.* overcome, get the better of, quell, subdue, master, rise above.

**conscience**
(n) *Dodgy Dave has no conscience when it comes to lying.* scruples *(plural)*, misgivings *(plural)*, qualms *(plural)*, principles *(plural)*, standards *(plural)*, morals *(plural)*, ethics *(plural)*, sense of right and wrong.

**conscientious**
(adj) *Oliver is conscientious about his work.* diligent, careful, meticulous, thorough, painstaking, dedicated, hard-working.
OPPOSITES: careless, slack.

**conscious**
1 (adj) *Fergus bumped his head, but remained conscious.* aware, awake, alert, compos mentis, with it *(informal)*.
OPPOSITES: unconscious, out cold.
2 (adj) *Annie made a conscious decision to stay out late. See* **deliberate.**

**consequence** *see* **result 1.**

**consider**
1 (v) *Consider the consequences before you take action.* think about, weigh up, give thought to, reflect on, examine, contemplate, ponder, mull over, chew over, turn over in your mind.
2 (v) *I consider fox-hunting to be wrong.* believe, regard, judge, deem, hold, think.

**considerate** *see* **thoughtful 1.**

**consistent**
1 (adj) *Toby is a consistent worker.* steady, dependable, reliable, predictable, stable, unchanging, unvarying, unfailing.
2 (adj) *The reports are consistent on this point.* compatible, in agreement, the same, matching, all of a piece.

**consist of**
(v) *The new maths course will consist of ten different modules.* be made up of, be composed of, comprise, include, contain, involve, incorporate.

**console** *see* **comfort 1.**

**conspicuous** *see* **noticeable.**

**conspiracy** *see* **plot 1.**

**constant**
1 (adj) *I can't stand this constant noise.* continuous, continual, incessant, never-ending, nonstop, ceaseless, perpetual, relentless, unremitting, interminable, unending, unceasing, persistent.
OPPOSITES: intermittent, occasional.
2 (adj) *Mum drove at a constant speed.* steady, even, consistent, uniform, fixed, unchanging, unvarying, invariable.
OPPOSITES: erratic, varying.

**constantly**
(adv) *Fifi talks constantly.* all the time, nonstop, continuously, continually, incessantly, without stopping, night and day, endlessly, unceasingly, relentlessly, perpetually, interminably, always.
OPPOSITES: occasionally, now and then.

**construct** *see* **build 1.**

**consult**
(v) *I'd like to consult you before I make up my mind.* ask, ask your advice, speak to, confer with, discuss something with, compare notes with, refer to, turn to.

**contact**
(v) *I must contact Mandy.* get in touch with, get hold of, communicate with, reach, ring, call, phone, speak to, write to, e-mail, text, fax.

**contain**
1 (v) *What does this file contain?* hold, include, consist of, comprise, incorporate.
2 (v) *I couldn't contain my laughter.* control, restrain, hold in, keep in, keep back, suppress, stifle, curb, check.

**contaminate**
(v) *Industrial waste can contaminate the water supply.* pollute, make impure, poison, infect, taint, dirty, foul, blight.
OPPOSITES: purify, decontaminate.

**contemplate**
1 (v) *This is a good spot to contemplate the view. See* **look at 3.**
2 (v) *I need to contemplate what I should do next. See* **consider 1.**
3 (v) *Ziggy loves to sit cross-legged and contemplate. See* **think 4.**

**contemporary** *see* **modern.**

**contempt** *see* **scorn 2.**

**contented**
(adj) *I feel quite contented about how things have turned out.* content, pleased, satisfied, gratified, glad, happy, cheerful, relaxed, at ease, comfortable, serene.
OPPOSITES: discontented, dissatisfied.

**contents**
(plural n) *The contents of a book.* content, subject matter, subject, theme, topic, sections *(plural)*, chapters *(plural)*.

**contest** *see* **competition 1.**

**contestant** *see* **competitor.**

**continual** *see* **constant 1.**

**continually** *see* **constantly.**

**continue**
1 (v) *We must continue walking.* keep, keep on, carry on, go on, persevere with, stick at, persist in.
2 (v) *This storm could continue for hours.* last, carry on, drag on, go on, persist.
3 (v) *You can continue your painting next week.* carry on with, return to, resume, proceed with, take up, pick up where you left off, start again, recommence.

**continuous** *see* **constant 1.**

**continuously** *see* **constantly.**

**contract**
1 (v) *This metal pipe will contract if you cool it.* get smaller, get shorter, get narrower, shrink, reduce, narrow, tighten, compress, draw in, close up.
OPPOSITE: expand.
2 (n) *Be sure you understand the contract before you sign.* agreement, settlement, arrangement, deal *(informal)*, bargain, transaction, commitment, pact, lease.

**contradict**
(v) *Don't contradict what I say!* argue with, dispute, disagree with, deny, challenge, oppose, object to.
OPPOSITES: agree with, support.

**contrast**
1 (v) *Contrast these two photos to see how Jack has changed.* compare, set side by side, set one against the other.
2 (v) *Your explanations contrast radically. See* **differ 1.**
3 (n) *Notice the contrast between the two pictures. See* **difference.**

**contribute**
1 (v) *Please contribute generously to the school fund. See* **give 2.**
2 **contribute to** (v) *Fine weather will contribute to a successful barbecue.* lead to, play a part in, add to, be conducive to, be partly responsible for, help.
OPPOSITE: detract from.

**control**
1 (v) *It's the headteacher's job to control the school's affairs.* manage, be in charge of, be in control of, direct, govern, run, administer, supervise, oversee, preside over, look after, deal with, handle, be in the driver's seat, hold the purse strings.
2 (v) *Try to control your giggles.* keep under control, keep in check, hold back, contain, restrain, curb, suppress, subdue.
3 (v) *Who has control over these men?* command, charge, authority, power, management, supervision, supremacy.

**controversial**
(adj) *The referee's decision was controversial.* contentious, open to question, questionable, debatable, arguable, disputed, widely discussed.
OPPOSITE: noncontroversial.

**convalesce** *see* **recover 1.**

**convenient**
1 *(adj) A convenient shop. See* **handy** 2.
2 *(adj) A convenient date. See* **suitable** 2.

**conventional**
1 *(adj) Black is the conventional colour to wear to a funeral.* standard, customary, usual, normal, correct, proper, orthodox.
OPPOSITES: unconventional, unorthodox.
2 *(adj) Jet thinks her parents are too conventional.* conservative, traditional, conformist, unadventurous, stuffy, strait-laced, rigid, bourgeois.
OPPOSITE: unconventional.

**conversation** *see* **talk** 5, 6.

**convert**
1 *(v) I want to convert my bike so it can take a passenger. See* **adapt** 1.
2 *(v) Don't worry; I'm not trying to convert you.* change your mind, persuade, convince, reform, re-educate.

**convict**
1 *(v) The judge decided to convict Burglar Beryl.* find guilty, declare guilty, condemn, sentence.
OPPOSITE: acquit.
2 *(n) A convict has escaped from prison.* prisoner, jailbird, con *(slang)*, criminal, offender, felon.

**convince**
*(v) How can I convince you that I'm right?* prove to, satisfy, assure, persuade, talk you round, bring you round, win you over.

**convincing**
1 *(adj) That's quite a convincing argument.* powerful, persuasive, plausible, credible, telling, cogent, conclusive.
OPPOSITES: unconvincing, weak.
2 *(adj) Our team had a convincing win.* decisive, conclusive, impressive, definite.
OPPOSITES: unconvincing, inconclusive.
3 *(adj) Ella gave a convincing impression of Mrs Badger. See* **realistic** 2.

**cook**
*(v) Dad offered to cook lunch.* make, prepare, rustle up *(informal)*, concoct, put together, heat up, warm up.
WAYS TO COOK: bake, barbecue, boil, braise, broil, casserole, deep-fry, fry, grill, microwave, poach, roast, sauté, scramble, simmer, steam, stew, stir-fry, toast.

**cool**
1 *(adj) A cool breeze blew in off the sea.* fresh, refreshing, chilly, cold, nippy.
OPPOSITE: warm.
2 *(adj) Stay cool in a crisis. See* **calm** 2.
3 *(adj) Araminta gave us a cool welcome.* lukewarm, unenthusiastic, offhand, half-hearted, unemotional, apathetic, indifferent, reserved, chilly, aloof, distant, standoffish, unfriendly, unwelcoming.
OPPOSITES: warm, friendly.
4 *(adj) (informal) Jet looks cool in those clothes. See* **fashionable**.
5 *(adj) (informal) What a cool idea! See* **great** 9.

6 *(v) Cool the mixture.* chill, refrigerate.
OPPOSITES: warm up, heat.

**cooperate**
*(v) Let's all cooperate to get the job done fast.* work together, pull together, join forces, help each other, collaborate, work as a team, pitch in, pool resources, unite.
OPPOSITE: compete.

**cooperative**
*(adj) Oscar was very cooperative about the move.* obliging, accommodating, helpful, supportive, willing.

**cope**
1 *(v) Life is hard but I'm sure you'll cope.* manage, survive, get by *(informal)*, muddle through, struggle through, win through, hold your own, rise to the occasion.
2 **cope with** *(v) Alex has a lot to cope with.* deal with, handle, contend with, bear, endure, grapple with, wrestle with.

**copy**
1 *(n) Pirate Peg made a copy of the map.* duplicate, replica, photocopy, carbon copy, facsimile, transcript, tracing.
2 *(n) This painting is a copy; the original is in Paris.* reproduction, replica, print, imitation, fake, forgery, counterfeit, sham.
3 *(v) Selena decided to copy her friend's work.* duplicate, reproduce, photocopy, print, crib *(informal)*, forge, counterfeit.
4 *(v) Donna can copy Aunt Bertha's voice.* imitate, mimic, impersonate, ape, echo.

**cord**
*(n)* string, rope, twine, cable, line.

**core** *see* **centre** 2.

**corner**
1 *(n) The car took the corner too fast.* bend, turn, curve, hairpin bend, turning, junction, intersection.
2 *(n) Find a dark corner to hide.* nook, niche, recess, cranny, crevice, hole, hideaway, hide-out, hidey-hole *(informal)*.
3 *(v) The police managed to corner the thieves. See* **trap** 2.

**corny**
1 *(adj) (slang) A corny joke.* unfunny, old, familiar, tired, stale, clichéd, hackneyed.
2 *(adj) (slang) A corny love song. See* **sentimental** 2.

**corpse** *see* **body** 2.

**correct**
1 *(adj) Is this the correct answer? See* **right** 1.
2 *(adj) What's the correct way to address a king?* right, proper, conventional, standard, acceptable, appropriate, fitting.
OPPOSITES: wrong, inappropriate.
3 *(v) Please correct your spelling mistakes.* put right, rectify, amend, remedy, improve.
4 *(v) Mrs Badger will correct your work. See* **mark** 7.

**correspond**
1 *(v) Our stories must correspond or no one will believe us.* match, agree, tally, be consistent, coincide, square.

2 *(v) My cousin and I try to correspond regularly.* write, exchange letters, communicate, be in touch, be in contact.

**corridor**
*(n)* passage, passageway, hallway, aisle.

**corrode** *see* **wear away**.

**corrupt**
1 *(adj) A corrupt official.* dishonest, crooked *(informal)*, bent *(slang)*, bribable, fraudulent, unscrupulous, untrustworthy.
2 *(v) Can violence on television corrupt children?* lead astray, be a bad influence on, warp, brutalize, deprave, pervert.

**cost**
1 *(v) How much will a new TV cost?* come to, set you back *(informal)*, sell for, fetch, go for, be worth.
2 *(n) Can we afford the cost of a room in this hotel? See* **price** 1.

**costume**
*(n) Your costume is perfect for the fancy-dress party.* outfit, get-up *(informal)*, garb, gear *(informal)*, clothes *(plural)*, dress, attire *(old-fashioned)*, period costume, national costume, uniform, livery.

**cosy**
*(adj) A cosy cottage.* snug, comfortable, comfy *(informal)*, homely, warm, secure.

**cough**
*(n) Have you taken anything for that cough?* tickle in your throat, hacking cough, bark, frog in your throat.

**count**
1 *(v) Let's count how much money we've made.* count up, add up, tot up, calculate, reckon up, total, tally.
2 *(v) Your result won't count if you're disqualified.* matter, mean anything, count for anything, amount to anything, signify, be taken into consideration, carry weight.

**count on** *see* **depend on** 1, 2.

**country**
1 *(n) A European country.* nation, state, land, kingdom, realm *(old-fashioned)*, republic, principality, people *(plural)*.
2 *(n) A house in the country.* countryside, rural area, green belt, farmland, outback *(Australia)*, bush *(Australia)*, backwoods *(plural)*, wilds *(plural)*, sticks *(plural)* *(informal)*, back of beyond.

**couple**
1 *(n) We're a couple now.* twosome, pair, item *(informal)*, duo, married couple, husband and wife, girlfriend and boyfriend, partners *(plural)*.
2 **a couple of** *(phrase) I need a couple of nails.* two, two or three, a few, several.

**courage**
*(n) The rescuers showed great courage.* bravery, fearlessness, guts *(plural)* *(informal)*, heroism, valour *(old-fashioned)*, gallantry, nerve, pluck, spirit, grit, bottle *(slang)*, boldness, daring, audacity.
OPPOSITE: cowardice.

**courageous** *see* **brave**.

## course

**course**
1 (n) I'm having a course of tennis lessons. series, sequence, programme.
2 (n) Are you taking the new maths course? syllabus, programme, module, curriculum, classes (plural), lessons (plural), lectures (plural).
3 (n) We worked out the ship's course. route, path, bearings (plural), direction.

**court**
(n) Beryl's case will be tried in a court. law court, high court, crown court, magistrates' court, county court.

**cover**
1 (v) Cover the statue with a cloth. drape, wrap, cloak, veil, swathe, shroud, envelop, curtain, clothe, spread over, lay over.
OPPOSITE: uncover.
2 (v) Use this scarf to cover your face. shield, protect, hide, conceal, veil, shade, screen, obscure, mask, disguise.
OPPOSITE: expose.
3 (v) A sprinkling of snow began to cover the ground. carpet, blanket, cloak, coat.
4 (v) This book should cover all you need to know. contain, include, incorporate, encompass, embrace, deal with, examine, consider, describe, survey.
5 (v) This should cover your train fare. pay for, be enough for, be sufficient for, meet.
6 (n) Is there a cover for this? See **top** 2.
7 (n) Do you need a cover for your bed? duvet, bedspread, quilt, blanket, rug, sheet, eiderdown, coverlet (old-fashioned).
8 (n) We ran for cover. shelter, protection, refuge, safety, sanctuary.
9 (n) The troops need some cover. protection, support, covering fire.
10 (n) Beryl dropped her cover to reveal her true identity. disguise, front, mask, pretence, façade, cover-up, smoke screen.

**cover up**
(v) It's no use trying to cover up your mistake. conceal, hide, hush up, keep secret, suppress, cover your tracks, keep it under your hat.

**cowardly**
(adj) Sir Lancelittle was too cowardly to attack the dragon. timid, fearful, scared, afraid, spineless, faint-hearted, chicken (informal), yellow (informal), weak-kneed (informal), nervous, anxious.
OPPOSITES: brave, courageous.

**cower**
(v) Don't cower in the corner! cringe, grovel, skulk, crouch, shrink, quail, tremble, shiver, flinch.

**crack**
1 (n) This plate has a crack in it. split, chip, break, fracture, flaw.
2 (n) The explorers squeezed through a crack in the rock. chink, cleft, slit, crevice, cranny, fissure, rift, split, rent, gash.
3 (n) I heard a loud crack. snap, bang, crackle, smack, pop.
4 (v) Don't crack the plate. See **break** 1.

5 (v) Let's crack this problem. See **solve**.
6 (v) Mel may crack under pressure. crack up (informal), break down, go to pieces, fall apart (informal), collapse, lose control.

**cracked**
(adj) A cracked mug. chipped, split, broken, crazed, flawed, damaged.

**crackle** see **crack** 3.

**crack up** (informal) see **crack** 6.

**craft**
(n) A craft exhibition. handicraft, art.

**crafty** see **cunning**.

**cram**
1 (v) Don't cram so many chocolates into your mouth! stuff, jam, ram, shove, force, pack, squash, squeeze, press, crowd.
2 (v) (informal) Celia is trying to cram for her exams. See **study** 1.

**cramped**
(adj) This room is so cramped! tiny, small, narrow, confined, constricting, oppressive, claustrophobic, crowded, overcrowded.
OPPOSITES: spacious, roomy.

**crash**
1 (n) The tray landed with a tremendous crash. bang, clatter, thump, thud, clang, clash, clunk, boom, din, racket.
2 (n) There's been a crash in the high street. collision, accident, smash, smash-up (informal), pile-up (informal), multiple pile-up (informal), prang (informal).
3 (v) We watched the tower crash to the ground. fall, topple, plunge, collapse, hurtle, clatter, overbalance.
4 (v) Dad is scared that Leo will crash his car. smash, smash up (informal), bump, prang (informal), write off (informal), total (slang), wreck, trash (slang).
5 (v) Frank's firm may crash. See **fail** 4.

**crash into**
(v) Don't crash into me. bump into, collide with, career into, barge into (informal).

**crave** see **long** 3.

**crawl**
1 (v) You'll have to crawl along this ledge. go on all fours, go on your hands and knees, worm your way, edge, inch, creep, slither, wriggle, drag yourself, squirm.
2 (v) The car began to crawl forwards. creep, edge, inch, move at a snail's pace.
3 (v) Trust Calvin to crawl to the teacher. grovel, toady, suck up (informal), butter up, flatter, fawn, pander.

**craze**
(n) What's the latest craze? trend, fashion, fad, thing (informal), novelty, mania, passion, enthusiasm, excitement.

**crazy** see **mad** 2, 3, 5.

**creak**
(v) Listen to the gate creak! squeak, grind, grate, scrape, screech, squeal, rasp.

**cream**
(n) SHADES OF CREAM: buttermilk, ivory, off-white, oyster, pearl.

**creamy**
(adj) A creamy sauce. smooth, rich, thick, velvety, buttery.

**crease**
1 (v) Don't crease your dress! crumple, crush, rumple, wrinkle, pucker, ruck up, scrunch up, screw up.
2 (n) There's a crease in this material. fold, tuck, pleat, wrinkle, pucker, crumple.

**create**
1 (v) Callum plans to create a model village. make, build, construct, produce, devise, design, develop, dream up, invent, concoct, fabricate, form, bring into being.
2 (v) This decision may create problems. See **cause** 1.

**creation**
(n) We're learning about the creation of the universe. origin, birth, dawning, beginning, formation, shaping, genesis.

**creative**
(adj) Ben's written work is very creative. imaginative, inventive, inspired, original.

**creature**
(n) An odd creature. animal, beast, being.

**credible** see **believable**.

**creep**
1 (v) The snail began to creep along the path. crawl, slither, inch, wriggle, worm, squirm, glide, dawdle, go at a snail's pace.
2 (v) Emma tried to creep past her sleeping sister. slip, sneak, steal, tiptoe, sidle, edge, inch, slink.
3 (n) (slang) Calvin is such a creep! toady, groveller, bootlicker (informal), sneak, telltale.

**creepy** (informal) see **spooky**.

**crest**
1 (n) Our pet cockatoo has a scarlet crest. plume, tuft, comb, topknot.
2 (n) We climbed to the crest of the hill. summit, top, peak, brow, ridge, crown.

**crime**
1 (n) Crime is increasing. lawbreaking, misconduct, delinquency, corruption, villainy, wrongdoing, foul play, vice.
2 (n) What crime did Beryl commit? offence, misdeed, misdemeanour, violation, wrong, atrocity, outrage, trespass, felony (old-fashioned).
TYPES OF CRIME: abduction, armed robbery, arson, assassination, assault, attempted murder, blackmail, breaking and entering, bribery and corruption, burglary, conspiracy to murder, criminal damage, drink-driving, drug pushing, drug trafficking, extortion, forgery, fraud, GBH (grievous bodily harm), hijacking, hit and run, hold-up, indecent assault, joyriding, kidnapping, looting, manslaughter, money laundering, mugging (informal), murder, poaching, racial attack, ram raiding (informal), shoplifting, smuggling, speeding, trespassing, rape, robbery, terrorism, theft, vandalism.

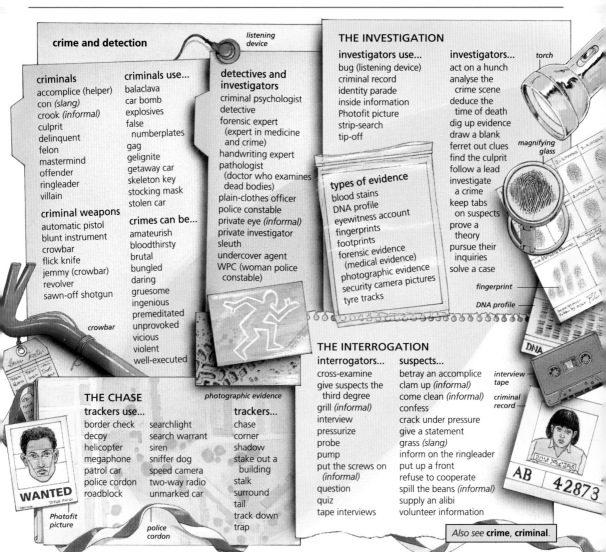

## crime and detection

### criminals
accomplice (helper)
con (slang)
crook (informal)
culprit
delinquent
felon
mastermind
offender
ringleader
villain

### criminal weapons
automatic pistol
blunt instrument
crowbar
flick knife
jemmy (crowbar)
revolver
sawn-off shotgun

### criminals use...
balaclava
car bomb
explosives
false
 numberplates
gag
gelignite
getaway car
skeleton key
stocking mask
stolen car

### crimes can be...
amateurish
bloodthirsty
brutal
bungled
daring
gruesome
ingenious
premeditated
unprovoked
vicious
violent
well-executed

*crowbar*

*listening device*

### detectives and investigators
criminal psychologist
detective
forensic expert
 (expert in medicine
 and crime)
handwriting expert
pathologist
 (doctor who examines
 dead bodies)
plain-clothes officer
police constable
private eye (informal)
private investigator
sleuth
undercover agent
WPC (woman police
 constable)

## THE INVESTIGATION

### investigators use...
bug (listening device)
criminal record
identity parade
inside information
Photofit picture
strip-search
tip-off

### investigators...
act on a hunch
analyse the
 crime scene
deduce the
 time of death
dig up evidence
draw a blank
ferret out clues
find the culprit
follow a lead
investigate
 a crime
keep tabs
 on suspects
prove a
 theory
pursue their
 inquiries
solve a case

*torch*

*magnifying glass*

### types of evidence
blood stains
DNA profile
eyewitness account
fingerprints
footprints
forensic evidence
 (medical evidence)
photographic evidence
security camera pictures
tyre tracks

*fingerprint*

*DNA profile*

## THE INTERROGATION

### interrogators...
cross-examine
give suspects the
 third degree
grill (informal)
interview
pressurize
probe
pump
put the screws on
 (informal)
question
quiz
tape interviews

### suspects...
betray an accomplice
clam up (informal)
come clean (informal)
confess
crack under pressure
give a statement
grass (slang)
inform on the ringleader
put up a front
refuse to cooperate
spill the beans (informal)
supply an alibi
volunteer information

*interview tape*

*criminal record*

*DNA*

## THE CHASE

*photographic evidence*

### trackers use...
border check
decoy
helicopter
megaphone
patrol car
police cordon
roadblock

searchlight
search warrant
siren
sniffer dog
speed camera
two-way radio
unmarked car

### trackers...
chase
corner
shadow
stake out a
 building
stalk
surround
tail
track down
trap

*WANTED*
*Photofit picture*

*police cordon*

*AB 42873*

*Also see crime, criminal.*

---

### criminal
(n) TYPES OF CRIMINAL: assassin, bandit, blackmailer, bomber, burglar, computer hacker, drug dealer, forger, gangster, gunman, hijacker, hit man (slang), joyrider, kidnapper, mugger (informal), murderer, pickpocket, poacher, rapist, robber, shoplifter, swindler, terrorist, thief, vandal.

### cringe
(v) Dad's jokes make me cringe. wince, flinch, shudder, quail, blush, blench, recoil.

### crisis
1 (n) If this pipe bursts, we'll have a crisis. problem, emergency, disaster, catastrophe, panic, alarm, predicament, mess.

2 (n) The meeting reached a crisis. turning point, climax, critical stage, moment of truth, crunch (informal), culmination, crux.

### crisp
1 (adj) A crisp cracker. crispy, crunchy, brittle, hard, dry, crumbly.
OPPOSITES: soft, soggy.
2 (adj) A crisp winter's day. See cold 1.

### critical
1 (adj) Critical remarks. scathing, derogatory, disapproving, disparaging, censorious, nit-picking (informal), nagging, niggling, uncomplimentary, hypercritical.
OPPOSITES: complimentary, flattering.
2 (adj) A critical decision. See vital.

### criticize
1 (v) I'll try not to criticize you. find fault with, knock (informal), snipe at, pick on, censure, denigrate, disparage, pick holes in, nitpick (informal), cast aspersions on, slate (informal), pan (informal), bad-mouth (slang), slag you off (slang).
OPPOSITES: praise, compliment.
2 (v) Please criticize this poem. analyse, review, evaluate, discuss, assess, comment on, give your opinion of.

### croak
(v) Your cold is making you croak. speak huskily, speak hoarsely, have a frog in your throat, rasp, wheeze, squawk, caw (bird).

# crooked

**crooked**
1 *(adj) A crooked path.* winding, twisting, curving, zigzag, meandering, tortuous.
OPPOSITE: straight.
2 *(adj) A crooked branch. See* **twisted** 1.
3 *(adj) That poster is crooked.* tilted, at an angle, slanting, sloping, askew, skewwhiff *(informal)*, lopsided, off-centre.
OPPOSITES: straight, level.
4 *(adj) (informal) Don't get involved in Dave's crooked deals.* dishonest, criminal, illegal, corrupt, fraudulent, unscrupulous, dodgy *(informal)*, dubious, questionable, shady *(informal)*, underhand, deceitful.
OPPOSITES: honest, legal.

**cross**
1 *(adj) Liz is cross that she wasn't invited.* annoyed, indignant, put out, disgruntled, upset, offended, peeved *(informal),* miffed *(informal),* irritated, piqued, vexed, cheesed off *(slang),* hacked off *(slang),* in a bad mood, sulky, in a huff.
OPPOSITES: pleased, contented.
2 *(adj) Dad was really cross when I broke the CD player. See* **angry**.
3 *(adj) Aunt Bertha always seems so cross. See* **bad-tempered**.
4 *(v) How will we cross the desert?* get across, travel across, journey across, traverse, cut across, ford *(river).*
5 *(v) The new bridge will cross the railway line.* span, pass over, stretch across, bridge.
6 *(v) Where do the two streets cross?* intersect, meet, join, converge, crisscross.

**cross out**
*(v) Cross out my name from the list.* strike out, delete, rub out, scratch out, erase.

**crouch**
*(v) Let's crouch behind this bush.* squat, bend down, hunker down, duck, kneel, stoop, hunch over, cower.

**crowd**
1 *(n) A crowd of people gathered in the square.* group, bunch *(informal),* gang, cluster, knot, throng, horde, mass, flock, swarm, mob, pack, army, crush, rabble, multitude, collection, company, assembly.
2 *(v) We watched the fans crowd into the stadium.* swarm, flock, throng, stream, surge, pile, push, shove, jostle, elbow, pack, squeeze, squash, press, cram, jam.

**crowded**
*(adj) The stadium was crowded.* packed, jam-packed, full, overcrowded, congested, overflowing, swarming, thronging, cramped, full to bursting.

**crown**
*(n) The queen wore a glittering golden crown.* coronet, diadem, tiara, circlet.

**crucial** *see* **vital**.

**crude**
*(adj) Crude jokes.* coarse, vulgar, rude, uncouth, crass, tasteless, indecent, dirty, smutty, bawdy, lewd, obscene, offensive.
OPPOSITES: polite, sophisticated.

**cruel**
1 *(adj) A cruel murder.* brutal, vicious, savage, barbaric, bloodthirsty, sadistic, cold-blooded, callous, heartless, ruthless, pitiless, inhuman, diabolical, fiendish.
OPPOSITES: kind, gentle.
2 *(adj) A cruel remark.* hurtful, unkind, spiteful, malicious, vicious, cutting, heartless, callous, hardhearted, unfeeling.
OPPOSITE: kind.

**crumb**
*(n) A crumb of food.* morsel, bit, fragment, scrap, shred, speck, grain, particle, atom.

**crumble**
*(v) The old castle will crumble if it isn't repaired.* disintegrate, collapse, fall apart, fall to pieces, break up, fall into decay, go to rack and ruin.

**crumple** *see* **crease** 1, 2.

**crunch**
*(v) Don't crunch your carrot so noisily!* munch, chomp, chew, gnaw, champ.

**crush**
1 *(v) Try not to crush the strawberries.* squash, squeeze, bruise, flatten, pulp, mash, mangle, pulverize.
2 *(v) Crush the biscuits into little pieces.* grind, pound, smash, crumble, pulverize, shatter, crunch, break.
3 *(v) Don't crush your skirt. See* **crease** 1.

**cry**
1 *(v) Todd began to cry when he heard the news.* weep, sob, shed tears, blubber, snivel, whimper, wail, howl, bawl.
2 *(v) Gina tried to cry for help. See* **call** 1.
3 *(n) I heard a cry.* call, shout, scream, shriek, yell, screech, squeal, yelp, howl.

**cuddle**
*(v) Henry loves to cuddle his bunny.* hug, snuggle up to, fondle, caress, embrace, nestle against, hold, clasp.

**cunning**
*(adj) A cunning plan.* crafty, wily, devious, sneaky, artful, tricky, deceitful, sly, shrewd, clever, ingenious, subtle.

**cup**
*(n)* TYPES OF CUP: beaker, chalice, coffee cup, goblet, mug, tankard, teacup, trophy.

**cure**
*(v) Will this ointment cure my rash?* heal, make better, clear up, put right, help, treat, ease, relieve, alleviate, remedy.
OPPOSITES: aggravate, make worse.

**curious**
1 *(adj) I'm curious to know what really happened.* interested, intrigued, puzzled, burning with curiosity, inquisitive.
OPPOSITES: incurious, indifferent.
2 *(adj) Curious neighbours. See* **nosy**.
3 *(adj) A curious hat. See* **strange** 1.

**curl**
1 *(n) A curl of hair.* wave, coil, kink, ringlet, corkscrew, twist, spiral, lock.
2 *(v) Did you curl your hair yourself?* crimp, kink, coil, wave, perm, frizz.

3 *(v) The snake began to curl round my leg.* coil, wind, loop, spiral, twist, twine, twirl, writhe, snake, curve, bend.

**curly**
*(adj) Curly hair.* curling, wavy, frizzy, fuzzy, curled, crimped, permed, corkscrew.
OPPOSITE: straight.

**current**
*(adj) Marcie likes to keep up with current fashions.* present-day, contemporary, modern, up-to-date, up-to-the-minute, popular, fashionable, happening *(informal)*, existing, prevailing.
OPPOSITES: past, out of date.

**curse**
1 *(v) Please don't curse! See* **swear** 1.
2 *(n) Duncan let out a curse.* oath, swearword, obscenity, expletive, profanity.
3 *(n) The wizard put a curse on the village.* jinx, spell, malediction, the evil eye.

**curt** *see* **abrupt** 2.

**curve** *see* **bend** 1, 2, 4.

**curved**
*(adj) A curved surface.* bent, rounded, arched, bowed, bulging, convex, concave.
OPPOSITES: flat, level.

**custom**
*(n) Kissing under the mistletoe is a popular custom.* tradition, practice, convention, institution, procedure, ritual, ceremony.

**cut**
1 *(v) How did you cut your finger?* gash, slash, slit, nick, graze, lacerate, wound.
2 *(v) We need to cut some wood for the fire. See* **chop** 1.
3 *(v) Will you cut my hair?* trim, clip, crop, snip, shape, layer, shave.
4 *(v) We must cut that low branch.* trim, prune, clip, lop off, hack off, mow *(grass).*
5 *(v) Don't cut your name in the desk!* carve, gouge, score, scratch, chisel, engrave, inscribe, chip, notch, whittle.
6 *(v) You need to cut this essay.* shorten, trim, prune, abridge, condense, abbreviate, summarize, précis.
7 *(v) Is it a good idea to cut violent films for TV?* edit, censor, clean up, sanitize.
8 *(v) Supermarkets may cut their prices. See* **reduce** 1.
9 *(n) Zina has a cut on her leg.* gash, nick, slash, scratch, graze, laceration, wound.
10 *(n) We expect a cut in prices. See* **decrease** 1.

**cute** *see* **sweet** 3.

**cutting**
1 *(adj) A cutting remark.* hurtful, scathing, barbed, sarcastic, caustic, acerbic, vicious, malicious, spiteful, vitriolic, wounding.
2 *(adj) A cutting wind. See* **cold** 2.

**cut up** *see* **chop** 2.

**cynical**
*(adj) Cyril has a cynical approach to life.* sceptical, negative, pessimistic, mocking, ironic, sneering, suspicious, distrustful.
OPPOSITES: positive, optimistic, trusting.

# Dd

**dab**
1 *(v) Dab some lotion on that itchy bite.* pat, daub, dot, smear, stroke, wipe, tap.
2 *(n) You've got a dab of paint on your nose.* drop, spot, speck, blob, smudge.

**dabble**
1 *(v) If you dabble about in the stream you'll get wet.* paddle, splash, slosh *(informal)*, wade, wallow.
2 **dabble in** *(v) Sylvie likes to dabble in astrology.* dip into, play at, toy with, trifle with, tinker with, potter about with.

**daft** *(informal) see* **silly** 1, 2.

**dainty**
1 *(adj) A dainty ballerina.* graceful, petite, small-boned, trim, elegant, pretty.
OPPOSITES: clumsy, ungainly.
2 *(adj) Dainty stitching.* neat, delicate, fine, exquisite.
OPPOSITES: clumsy, coarse.

**dam**
*(n) If the dam bursts the valley will be flooded.* barrier, barrage, dyke, wall, barricade, embankment.

**damage**
1 *(n) The hurricane caused widespread damage.* destruction, devastation, havoc, ruin, harm, injury, suffering, loss.
2 *(v) Vandals damage other people's property.* spoil, deface, wreck, destroy, ruin, vandalize, abuse, harm, mar, tamper with, play havoc with, devastate.
3 *(v) Reading in poor light can damage your eyesight.* harm, impair, weaken, strain, injure, hurt.

**damaging** *see* **harmful** 1.

**damp**
1 *(adj) Damp ground.* moist, dewy, wet, soggy, sodden, sopping, waterlogged.
OPPOSITE: dry.
2 *(adj) A damp day on the moor.* wet, drizzly, rainy, misty, foggy, dank.
OPPOSITE: dry.
3 *(adj) A damp day in the jungle.* humid, muggy, clammy, steamy, sticky, sweaty.
OPPOSITE: dry.
4 *(adj) A damp cave. See* **dank**.

**dance**
1 *(n) Alexander is interested in dance.* dancing, choreography.
2 *(n) I went to the dance with Carl.* disco, discotheque, rave *(slang)*, hop *(informal)*, ball, barn dance, dinner-dance.
3 *(v) Let's dance!* bop *(informal)*, boogie *(slang)*, jive, rock, move to the music, take the floor, trip the light fantastic.
4 *(v) Mo began to dance about when she heard the news.* leap, jump, skip, prance, bounce, hop, caper, romp, frolic, cavort.

---

## dance words

### types of dance
ballet
ballroom dancing
belly dancing
break dancing
contemporary dance
country dancing
disco dancing
flamenco dancing
folk dancing
formation dancing
hip-hop
jazz dance
Latin American dancing
limbo dancing
line dancing
morris dancing
old-time dancing
rock 'n' roll
square dancing
tap

### ballroom dances
cha-cha-cha
foxtrot
jive
quickstep
rumba
samba
tango
waltz

*break dancing*

### folk dances
highland fling
hornpipe
jig
reel

### other dances
cancan
conga
jitterbug
minuet
polka
salsa
twist

### ballet words
arabesque
ballerina
choreographer (dance creator)
corps de ballet (group of dancers)
*arabesque* grand jeté (leap)

pas-de-deux (dance for two)
pirouette
prima ballerina (leading ballerina)
principal dancer
tutu (ballet dress)

### dancers can be...
acrobatic
agile
athletic
balletic
clumsy
dainty
elegant
energetic
expressive
exuberant
graceful
lithe
lively
lumbering
nimble
poised
rhythmic
skilful
sprightly
stately
supple

### dancers may...
boogie *(slang)*
bop *(informal)*
dart
glide
gyrate
hop
jiggle
jive
jump
kick
leap
pogo
prance
rock
shuffle
skip
slide
spin
spring
stomp *(informal)*
stretch
strut
sway
swing
swirl
swivel
teeter
totter
twirl
twist
whirl
wiggle

*contemporary dance*

*ballroom dancing*

*jazz dance*

*grand jeté*

*tap dancing*

---

**danger**
1 *(n) There's a danger of snow.* risk, threat, chance, possibility.
2 *(n) Indiana encountered one danger after another.* hazard, threat, peril, risk, menace, pitfall, crisis.

**dangerous**
1 *(adj) Indiana set out on a dangerous expedition.* hazardous, perilous, risky, treacherous, hairy *(slang)*, dicey *(informal)*.
OPPOSITE: safe.
2 *(adj) That bridge looks dangerous.* precarious, unsafe, insecure, unstable, unreliable, dodgy *(informal)*, shaky, rickety.
OPPOSITES: safe, secure.

3 *(adj) The robber is armed and dangerous.* violent, unpredictable, ruthless, desperate, threatening, menacing.
OPPOSITE: harmless.
4 *(adj) Acid is a dangerous substance.* hazardous, harmful, poisonous, toxic, noxious, deadly, destructive.
OPPOSITES: harmless, safe.

**dangle**
*(v) Relax and let your arms dangle by your side.* hang, hang down, swing, droop, trail, fall, flop, sway, flap.

**dank**
*(adj) A dank cave.* damp, wet, chilly, clammy, dripping, slimy.

# dare

**dare**
1 (v) *Would you dare to sleep in a haunted house?* have the nerve, have the courage, be brave enough, risk, venture.
2 (v) *If you dare me to jump into the river I will!* challenge, defy, goad, taunt, provoke, throw down the gauntlet.
3 (n) *I did it for a dare.* challenge, bet.

**daring**
(adj) *A daring climber.* fearless, intrepid, adventurous, bold, audacious, plucky, brave, undaunted, daredevil, reckless, rash.
OPPOSITES: timid, cowardly.

**dark**
1 (adj) *A dark dungeon.* dim, dingy, pitch-dark, unlit, shadowy, murky, gloomy, dismal, drab, cheerless, grim, sombre.
OPPOSITES: bright, cheerful.
2 (adj) *A dark sky.* black, pitch-black, inky, jet-black, moonless, starless, sunless, cloudy, overcast, leaden, ominous.
OPPOSITES: bright, light.
3 (adj) *Dark hair.* brown, brunette, black, jet-black, raven, ebony, sable.
OPPOSITES: fair, blonde.
4 (adj) *Dark skin.* brown, black, swarthy, tanned, dusky, olive, sallow.
OPPOSITE: fair.

**darkness**
(n) *A figure vanished into the darkness.* dark, blackness, night, gloom, shadows (plural), shade, gathering gloom, dusk.

**dart** see **dash** 2.

**dash**
1 (v) *I must dash! See* **hurry** 1.
2 (v) *I saw a rabbit dash across the field.* run, race, tear, hurtle, sprint, dart, shoot, scoot, bolt, speed, flash, whiz (informal).

**data**
(n) information, facts (plural), figures (plural), details (plural), statistics (plural), info (informal), lowdown (informal).

**date**
1 (n) *I have a date with Paula on Saturday.* meeting, rendezvous, appointment, engagement, assignation.
2 (n) *Luke and Lucy have set a date for their wedding.* day, time, specific day.

**daunting**
(adj) *Facing the dragon was a daunting prospect for Sir Lancelittle.* alarming, unnerving, frightening, terrifying, intimidating, disconcerting, off-putting (informal), discouraging, disheartening.

**dawdle**
(v) *If you dawdle we'll be late.* delay, waste time, lag behind, go at a snail's pace, straggle, loiter, linger, dally, hang about.

**dawn**
1 (n) *We got up at dawn.* daybreak, sunrise, break of day, crack of dawn, first light, sunup, cockcrow.
OPPOSITES: dusk, sunset.
2 **dawn on** (v) *It didn't dawn on me until it was too late. See* **occur** 2.

**day**
1 (n) *Vampires sleep during the day.* daytime, daylight hours (plural), daylight.
OPPOSITE: night.
2 (n) *Luke and Lucy have decided on a day for their wedding.* date, time, specific day.
3 (n) *In my granddad's day there were no computers.* time, era, age, period, generation, heyday.

**daydream**
1 (v) *Sebastian likes to sit and daydream.* dream, stargaze, fantasize, imagine, muse.
2 (n) *I was in a daydream. See* **dream** 2.

**dazed**
1 (adj) *The blow from the ball left Leah dazed. See* **stunned** 1.
2 (adj) *Naresh felt dazed when he heard the news. See* **stunned** 2.
3 (adj) *I felt dazed with everyone shouting at once. See* **confused**.

**dazzle**
1 (v) *Bright lights dazzle me.* blind, confuse, daze, disorientate.
2 (v) *Marvello will dazzle you with his magic tricks. See* **astonish**.

**dazzling**
1 (adj) *A dazzling jewel. See* **brilliant** 1.
2 (adj) *A dazzling display of acrobatics. See* **spectacular**.

**dead**
1 (adj) *Queen Victoria is dead.* deceased, dead and buried, passed away, departed, gone, no more, perished.
OPPOSITES: alive, living.
2 (adj) *The man lay dead on the ground.* lifeless, inert, cold, rigid, stiff.
3 (adj) *The dodo is a dead species.* extinct, defunct, died out.
OPPOSITES: existing, living.
4 (adj) *My fingers feel dead. See* **numb**.
5 (adj) *At night the town is dead.* lifeless, deserted, quiet, boring, dull, uninteresting.
OPPOSITES: lively, buzzing.
6 (adj) *The radio is dead.* not working, useless, out of order, inoperative.
OPPOSITES: working, operational.

**deadly**
1 (adj) *Deadly fumes.* lethal, poisonous, toxic, noxious, dangerous, hazardous, venomous (snake), virulent (disease).
2 (adj) *A deadly wound.* lethal, fatal, mortal, death-dealing, terminal (illness).
3 (adj) *Deadly enemies.* mortal, bitter, hated, sworn, out-and-out, irreconcilable, remorseless, implacable, murderous.
4 (adj) *A deadly aim.* accurate, sure, true, unerring, unfailing, exact, precise.

**deafening** see **loud** 1.

**deal**
1 (n) (informal) *The businessmen made a deal.* arrangement, agreement, bargain, pact, contract, transaction.
2 (v) *Does Dodgy Dave still deal in second-hand cars?* trade, do business, buy and sell, stock, traffic (drugs).

3 (v) *It's your turn to deal the cards.* give out, dole out, distribute, hand out, divide.
4 **deal with** (v) *Can you deal with this problem?* handle, see to, take care of, tackle, cope with, manage, sort out.
5 **deal with** (v) *What issues will your essay deal with?* be about, be concerned with, have to do with, cover, consider, discuss, examine, explore, treat.

**dear**
1 (adj) *Lopa is a dear friend.* close, much-loved, intimate, valued, cherished, treasured, beloved, adored, bosom.
2 (adj) *That watch is much too dear. See* **expensive**.
3 (n) *What's the matter, dear?* darling, love, honey, pet, sweetheart, dearest, beloved (old-fashioned).

**death**
1 (n) *The death of the king saddened the nation.* passing, demise, loss, dying.
OPPOSITE: birth.
2 (n) *There's been a death in the family.* bereavement, loss.
3 (n) *The crash resulted in only one death.* fatality, casualty.

**debate**
1 (n) *We had a debate about the death penalty.* discussion, argument, dispute.
2 (v) *Nina was keen to debate the issue of animal rights. See* **discuss**.

**debris**
(n) *Rescuers sifted through the debris.* rubble, wreckage, remains (plural), ruins (plural), wreck, fragments (plural), pieces (plural), bits (plural), rubbish, litter, waste.

**decay** see **rot** 1, 2, 3.

**deceitful**
(adj) *A deceitful politician.* untruthful, untrustworthy, dishonest, insincere, hypocritical, two-faced, double-dealing, duplicitous, devious, underhand, tricky, sneaky, slippery, shifty, crafty, cunning, sly.
OPPOSITES: honest, truthful.

**deceive**
1 (v) *Keep your wits about you or Dodgy Dave will deceive you.* trick, fool, mislead, delude, pull the wool over your eyes, take you in (informal), dupe, hoodwink, double-cross, bamboozle (informal), kid (informal), cheat, swindle, con (informal), diddle (informal), take you for a ride (informal), pull a fast one on you (slang).
2 (v) *Don't deceive the one you love.* be unfaithful to, betray, cheat on (informal), two-time (informal).

**decent**
1 (adj) *Mum thinks this top is not decent.* respectable, presentable, seemly, proper, dignified, modest, fitting, appropriate, suitable, tasteful, fit to be seen.
OPPOSITES: indecent, improper.
2 (adj) *My bedroom is a decent size.* reasonable, adequate, acceptable, satisfactory, ample, sufficient, average.
OPPOSITES: inadequate, unsatisfactory.

**3** *(adj) Mr Badger is a decent man.* good, kind, honest, honourable, trustworthy, thoughtful, helpful, obliging, generous, polite, courteous, respectable, upright.
**4** *(adj) (informal) This band's really decent!* See **great** 9.

**decide**
**1** *(v) Decide which book you want.* make up your mind, choose, select, pick, come to a decision about.
**2** *(v) Once you decide to do something you should see it through.* make up your mind, make a decision, resolve, determine, commit yourself.
**3** *(v) Let's decide the argument by tossing a coin.* settle, resolve, clinch, put an end to, clear up, sort out, end, conclude.

**decipher**
*(v) Can you decipher this secret message?* decode, work out, figure out *(informal)*, understand, read, interpret, translate, unravel, solve, crack, suss out *(slang)*.

**decision**
**1** *(n) It's a hard decision to make.* choice.
**2** *(n) The judge gave her decision.* verdict, judgment, ruling, conclusion, finding.

**decisive**
**1** *(adj) Our team won a decisive victory.* See **convincing** 2.
**2** *(adj) Jon is a decisive person.* firm, strong-minded, forceful, purposeful, resolute, determined, definite, incisive.
OPPOSITES: indecisive, hesitant.

**declare**
*(v) Declare your loyalty to the king - or die!* announce, proclaim, profess, swear, state, make known, assert, affirm, confirm.

**decline**
**1** *(v) I'm afraid I'll have to decline your offer.* See **refuse** 1.
**2** *(v) Pupil numbers are expected to decline.* See **decrease** 2.

**decorate**
**1** *(v) It's my turn to decorate the tree.* trim, adorn, embellish, festoon, trick out.
**2** *(v) I helped Dad to decorate the front room.* paint, paper, do up *(informal)*, spruce up, refurbish, renovate, revamp.

**decoration**
**1** *(n) Hang this decoration on the Christmas tree.* ornament, bauble, trinket, streamer, tinsel, spangle, trimming.
**2** *(n) Granny wore a plain dress with no decoration.* trimming, embroidery, frill, flounce, ruffle, fringe, tassel, frippery.

**decorative**
*(adj) A decorative bow.* ornamental, fancy, pretty, elaborate, ornate, nonfunctional.
OPPOSITES: functional, plain.

**decrease**
**1** *(n) There has been a decrease in the number of crimes.* drop, fall, decline, reduction, cut, downturn, falling off, dwindling, lessening, slump, ebb.
OPPOSITE: increase.

**2** *(v) Pupil numbers are expected to decrease.* fall, drop, decline, fall off, drop off, dwindle, lower, go down, tumble, slump, slide, plummet, plunge, nose-dive.
OPPOSITE: increase.
**3** *(v) The wind began to decrease.* drop, subside, lessen, abate, let up, die down.
OPPOSITE: increase.
**4** *(v) Decrease your speed. See **reduce** 3.

**decrepit** *see* **dilapidated**.

**dedicated**
*(adj) A dedicated nurse.* committed, single-minded, enthusiastic, keen, devoted.

**deed** *see* **act** 4.

**deep**
**1** *(adj) A deep crack opened up in the earth.* bottomless, yawning, gaping, fathomless, unfathomable, cavernous.
OPPOSITE: shallow.
**2** *(adj) Our new carpet is a deep shade of blue.* dark, rich, strong, vivid, intense.
OPPOSITES: pale, light.
**3** *(adj) The giant spoke in a deep voice.* low, low-pitched, bass, rich, booming, rumbling, resounding, resonant, sonorous.
OPPOSITES: high, high-pitched.
**4** *(adj) Ned has a deep dislike of spiders.* profound, deep-seated, deep-rooted, intense, strong, extreme, heartfelt, fervent.

**defeat**
**1** *(v) The soldiers were determined to defeat the enemy. See **conquer** 1.
**2** *(v) I hope we defeat the other team.* See **beat** 2.
**3** *(n) The match ended in a defeat for our team.* beating, thrashing, pasting *(slang)*, drubbing, failure, setback, humiliation, disappointment, frustration.
OPPOSITES: victory, triumph.

**defect** *see* **fault** 1.

**defence**
*(n) The police used shields as a defence against the rioters.* protection, safeguard, guard, screen, shield, shelter, deterrent.

**defenceless**
*(adj) Without weapons the soldiers were defenceless.* vulnerable, open to attack, helpless, powerless, unprotected, unarmed, exposed, in danger.

**defend**
**1** *(v) The soldiers did their best to defend the castle.* protect, guard, fortify, secure, safeguard, keep safe, shield, preserve, keep from harm, watch over, fight for.
**2** *(v) Nathan tried to defend his point of view.* justify, explain, give reasons for, make a case for, argue for, vindicate.
**3** *(v) Burglar Beryl has a lawyer to defend her.* speak for, plead for, support, back, stand up for, stick up for *(informal)*.

**defiant**
*(adj) The defiant child refused to go to bed.* disobedient, rebellious, insolent, truculent, recalcitrant, mutinous.
OPPOSITES: obedient, meek.

**definite**
**1** *(adj) Is it definite that you can't come?* certain, sure, decided, settled, final, cut and dried *(informal)*, guaranteed, positive.
OPPOSITE: uncertain.
**2** *(adj) Do you have any definite plans for the future?* specific, particular, explicit, precise, clear, clear-cut, clearly defined, set, fixed, confirmed, categorical.
OPPOSITES: vague, obscure.
**3** *(adj) Your work shows a definite improvement.* marked, noticeable, obvious, distinct, unmistakable, pronounced, decided, perceptible, positive.
OPPOSITES: imperceptible, slight.

**definitely**
*(adv) Carl is definitely the best-looking boy in the school.* certainly, without doubt, undoubtedly, undeniably, unquestionably, beyond a shadow of a doubt, for certain, clearly, obviously, easily, far and away.

**deformed**
*(adj) The monster was horribly deformed.* misshapen, disfigured, contorted, bent, twisted, crooked, gnarled, maimed, mutilated, unsightly, grotesque, ugly.

**defy**
**1** *(v) Rick doesn't dare to defy his parents.* disobey, disregard, fly in the face of, flout, challenge, confront, resist, stand up to.
OPPOSITES: obey, submit to.
**2** *(v) I defy you to jump into the river. See **dare** 2.

**degrading**
*(adj) Living conditions in the prison were degrading.* demeaning, humiliating, shameful, disgraceful, contemptible, debasing, dehumanizing, brutalizing.

**dejected** *see* **depressed**.

**delay**
**1** *(v) If you delay any longer, you won't get a ticket.* wait, hesitate, hang around, stall, dither, pause, procrastinate, dawdle.
OPPOSITE: hurry.
**2** *(v) I hope the traffic doesn't delay you.* hold you up, slow you down, keep you back, make you late, detain, keep you waiting, hamper, bog you down.
**3** *(v) Mrs Badger agreed to delay the test for a week. See **postpone**.
**4** *(n) There was no delay on the journey.* hold-up, interruption, setback, stoppage.

**delete**
*(v) Delete that word from your essay.* remove, cut out, take out, omit, edit out, eradicate, scrub *(informal)*, erase, rub out, cross out, strike out, wipe.

**deliberate**
*(adj) Anji took a deliberate risk.* intentional, conscious, calculated, considered, studied, intended, planned, premeditated *(crime)*.
OPPOSITES: accidental, unintentional.

**delicacy**
*(n) Caviar is a great delicacy.* luxury, speciality, treat, gourmet food.

# **d**elicate

## delicate
1 *(adj) Delicate lace curtains.* fine, dainty, exquisite, intricate, flimsy, fragile, gauzy, wispy, silky, gossamer, cobwebby.
OPPOSITES: coarse, tough.
2 *(adj) A delicate child.* frail, weak, sickly, ailing, unhealthy, feeble, peaky, unwell.
OPPOSITES: robust, healthy.
3 *(adj) A delicate shade of blue.* soft, subtle, subdued, gentle, muted, pastel.
OPPOSITES: strong, bright.
4 *(adj) A delicate flavour.* See **mild** 3.
5 *(adj) A delicate situation.* difficult, sensitive, tricky, sticky *(informal)*, ticklish, dicey *(informal)*, critical, precarious.
6 *(adj) This situation needs delicate handling.* careful, sensitive, tactful, discreet, diplomatic, kidglove.
OPPOSITES: tactless, indiscreet.

## delicious
*(adj) A delicious meal.* tasty, appetizing, mouthwatering, scrumptious *(informal)*, yummy *(slang)*, delectable, luscious, flavoursome, moreish *(informal)*.
OPPOSITES: unappetizing, revolting.

## delight
1 *(n) The birth of the baby caused great delight.* See **happiness**.
2 *(v) Gemma's singing will delight you.* captivate, charm, thrill, enchant, enthral, entrance, entertain, amuse, please, cheer.

## delighted *see* **pleased**.

## delightful
1 *(adj) We spent a delightful day by the river.* See **lovely** 2.
2 *(adj) Carrie is a delightful girl.* charming, lovely, pleasant, agreeable, attractive, enchanting, engaging, bewitching.
OPPOSITES: unpleasant, disagreeable.

## delirious
1 *(adj) Without water, the travellers were soon delirious.* light-headed, feverish, incoherent, raving, babbling, hallucinating, demented, deranged, crazy, irrational.
OPPOSITES: rational, clear-headed.
2 *(adj) Maria was delirious about meeting Famous Fred.* See **ecstatic**.

## deliver
1 *(v) A boat will deliver supplies to the island.* bring, carry, take, transport, convey.
2 *(v) Ahmed is in a hurry to deliver his invitations.* distribute, give out, hand out, dish out *(informal)*, send, post, dispatch.

## demand
1 *(v) I know Dad will demand an apology.* insist on, expect, require, ask for, call for, request, press for.
2 *(v) These problems demand urgent action.* call for, require, need, necessitate, cry out for, want.

## demanding
1 *(adj) A demanding job.* See **difficult** 2.
2 *(adj) A demanding child.* nagging, insistent, hard to please, fussy, impatient, fractious, clamorous.

## demolish
*(v) It didn't take long to demolish the building.* knock down, pull down, tear down, destroy, dismantle, break down, wreck, flatten, level, raze to the ground, bulldoze, blow up, dynamite.

## demonstrate
1 *(v) Can you demonstrate how to make an omelette?* show, illustrate, give an idea of, make clear, explain, describe, teach.
2 *(v) Demonstrate your loyalty by voting for me.* show, indicate, display, prove, confirm, express, testify to.
3 *(v) We decided to demonstrate against the new road.* protest, lobby, march, picket, hold a rally, hold a sit-in.

## demonstration
1 *(n) A demonstration of country dancing.* display, exhibition, show, presentation, illustration, explanation, exposition.
2 *(n) A demonstration against nuclear weapons.* protest, demo *(informal)*, march, rally, mass rally, sit-in, picket, parade.

## demoralized *see* **discouraged**.

## den
1 *(n) The animal hid in its den.* See **hole** 4.
2 *(n) Bozo's gang has a den in the woods.* hide-out, base, hiding place, hideaway, secret place, retreat, hang-out, haunt.

## dense
1 *(adj) Dense undergrowth.* See **thick** 4.
2 *(adj) Dense fog.* See **thick** 5.
3 *(adj) The crowd was so dense we couldn't move.* solid, tightly packed, jam-packed, jammed together, crammed together, compacted, close-knit.
OPPOSITES: sparse, scattered.
4 *(adj) Don't be so dense!* See **stupid** 1.

## dent
*(v) I didn't mean to dent the car door.* knock in, make a dent in, bash in *(informal)*, push in, dint, buckle, crumple.

## deny
1 *(v) Burglar Beryl was quick to deny the charges.* reject, declare untrue, dispute, contradict, disagree with, repudiate, refute, rebuff, disclaim.
2 *(v) Your parents seem to deny you nothing.* refuse, deprive you of, begrudge, forbid, withhold from you.

## depart *see* **leave** 1.

## department
*(n) Which department does your dad work in?* section, branch, division, segment.

## dependable *see* **reliable** 1, 2.

## depend on
1 *(v) All Bethan's friends depend on her.* rely on, count on, lean on, trust, have confidence in, turn to, confide in.
2 *(v) You can depend on Tim being early.* rely on, count on, bank on, be sure of, reckon on, calculate on, bet on.
3 *(v) Our plans must depend on the weather.* hang on, hinge on, turn on, be determined by, be subject to, rest on.

## depressed
*(adj) Jessica is feeling depressed.* unhappy, sad, miserable, down, blue, low, glum, gloomy, down in the dumps *(informal)*, dejected, downhearted, despondent, melancholy, discouraged, disheartened, dispirited, moody, morose, suicidal.
OPPOSITES: cheerful, happy.

## depressing
1 *(adj) This is such a depressing film.* sad, gloomy, dreary, dismal, bleak, black, dark, morbid, sombre, melancholy, cheerless, heartbreaking, distressing, harrowing.
OPPOSITES: cheerful, happy.
2 *(adj) It's depressing when you always lose.* See **discouraging**.

## derelict
*(adj) A derelict cottage.* dilapidated, tumbledown, ramshackle, run-down, crumbling, ruined, rickety, broken-down, neglected, abandoned, deserted.

## descend
1 *(v) The plane began to descend.* go down, come down, drop, fall, sink, plummet, plunge, nose-dive, tumble.
OPPOSITES: ascend, climb.
2 *(v) The road starts to descend here.* go down, slope, drop, dip, fall, slant, incline.
OPPOSITES: ascend, rise, climb.

## describe
1 *(v) Ned was eager to describe how he caught the thief.* relate, explain, report, outline, tell, give an account of, give details of, put into words, recount, narrate.
2 *(v) How would you describe your sister?* define, characterize, portray, label, depict.

## description
1 *(n) Write a description of your first day at this school.* account, report, chronicle, narration, narrative, commentary.
2 *(n) Write a detailed description of your brother.* characterization, portrayal, depiction, pen portrait, sketch.

## descriptive
*(adj) A descriptive piece of writing.* expressive, vivid, graphic, detailed, colourful, striking, imaginative.

## desert
1 *(v) Don't desert your friends.* abandon, leave, forsake, turn your back on, walk out on *(informal)*, leave in the lurch, leave high and dry, run out on *(informal)*, cast off.
2 *(v) The demoralized troops decided to desert.* run away, abscond, make off, escape, bolt, turn tail, go AWOL (absent without leave), flee, fly, decamp, defect.
3 *(n) The travellers were lost in the desert.* wilderness, wasteland, wilds *(plural)*.
4 *(adj) Few plants can survive in desert conditions.* dry, arid, moistureless, parched, hot, burning, barren, infertile.

## deserted
*(adj) A deserted farmhouse.* abandoned, neglected, empty, vacant, uninhabited, unoccupied, isolated, desolate, lonely.

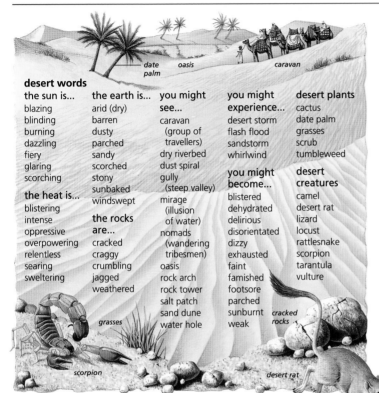

**desert words**

**the sun is...**
blazing
blinding
burning
dazzling
fiery
glaring
scorching

**the heat is...**
blistering
intense
oppressive
overpowering
relentless
searing
sweltering

**the earth is...**
arid (dry)
barren
dusty
parched
sandy
scorched
stony
sunbaked
windswept

**the rocks are...**
cracked
craggy
crumbling
jagged
weathered

**you might see...**
caravan
 (group of travellers)
dry riverbed
dust spiral
gully
 (steep valley)
mirage
 (illusion of water)
nomads
 (wandering tribesmen)
oasis
rock arch
rock tower
salt patch
sand dune
water hole

**you might experience...**
desert storm
flash flood
sandstorm
whirlwind

**you might become...**
blistered
dehydrated
delirious
disorientated
dizzy
exhausted
faint
famished
footsore
parched
sunburnt
weak

**desert plants**
cactus
date palm
grasses
scrub
tumbleweed

**desert creatures**
camel
desert rat
lizard
locust
rattlesnake
scorpion
tarantula
vulture

*date palm*   *oasis*   *caravan*

*grasses*   *cracked rocks*

*scorpion*   *desert rat*

**deserve**
1 *(v) Your painting must surely deserve a prize.* warrant, merit, be worthy of, justify, be qualified for, be entitled to, win.
2 *(v) You've worked hard enough to deserve a holiday.* be entitled to, have a right to, earn.

**design**
1 *(n) Rajesh is working on a design for a toy plane.* drawing, sketch, plan, blueprint, draft, outline, diagram, model, prototype.
2 *(n) I don't like the design on that wallpaper.* pattern, motif, decoration.
3 *(n) The design of this book cover is striking.* layout, composition, format, style, arrangement, organization.
4 *(n) Our car is the latest design. See* **model** 2.
5 *(v) Mel was asked to design a cover for the school magazine.* draw up, devise, create, think up, dream up, conceive, originate, plan, draft, map out, sketch, outline, draw.

**desirable**
1 *(adj) This house is in a desirable neighbourhood.* attractive, popular, sought-after, fashionable, enviable, pleasant, appealing, agreeable, excellent, good, advantageous, in demand.
2 *(adj) A desirable person. See* **sexy** 1.

**desire**
1 *(v) The genie will bring you anything you desire.* wish for, want, fancy, set your heart on, long for, yearn for, hunger for, thirst for, hanker after, crave, covet, need.
2 *(n) Sir Lancelittle had no desire for adventure.* wish, appetite, thirst, hunger, craving, longing, hankering, yearning, urge, need.
3 *(n) Cinderella's beauty filled the prince with desire.* passion, ardour, love, lust, the hots *(plural) (slang)*.
4 *(n) The sight of the gold filled Pirate Peg with desire. See* **greed** 2.

**desolate**
*(adj) The wind howled across the desolate moor.* bleak, barren, bare, windswept, wild, inhospitable, lonely, remote, isolated, empty, deserted, uninhabited.

**despair**
1 *(v) The marooned sailors began to despair.* lose hope, give up hope, lose heart, be discouraged, be despondent.
2 *(n) Mirza tried to conquer her feelings of despair.* desperation, hopelessness, dejection, despondency, depression, gloom, pessimism, misery, wretchedness, distress, anguish.
OPPOSITES: hope, optimism.

**despairing** *see* **desperate** 4.

**desperate**
1 *(adj) The travellers were desperate for water.* in urgent need of, in want of.
2 *(adj) Indiana made a desperate bid to escape.* frantic, daring, death-defying, bold, audacious, determined, risky, dangerous, hazardous, reckless, rash, hasty, foolhardy, harebrained, madcap.
3 *(adj) The climbers found themselves in a desperate situation.* hopeless, impossible, perilous, precarious, dangerous, life-threatening, serious, critical, dire, drastic, appalling, dreadful, terrible, awful.
4 *(adj) Juliet felt desperate when she saw that Romeo was dead.* despairing, hopeless, distraught, grief-stricken, brokenhearted, heartbroken, inconsolable, distressed, wretched, anguished, suicidal.
OPPOSITES: hopeful, optimistic.

**despise** *see* **scorn** 1.

**dessert**
*(n) What's for dessert?* sweet, pudding, afters *(plural) (informal)*.

**destined**
1 *(adj) The expedition was destined to fail.* doomed, bound, certain, meant, fated.
2 *(adj) It was destined that we should fall in love.* inevitable, unavoidable, inescapable, ordained, written in the stars, predestined, meant.

**destiny** *see* **fate** 1, 2.

**destroy**
1 *(v) Earthquakes can destroy whole cities.* wreck, devastate, demolish, ruin, flatten, level, wipe out, lay waste to, raze to the ground, wreak havoc on, ravage, smash, shatter.
2 *(v) The soldiers were ordered to destroy the enemy.* annihilate, wipe out, obliterate, exterminate, liquidate, kill, slay, slaughter, massacre, decimate, waste *(informal)*.

**destruction**
*(n) The earthquake caused widespread destruction.* devastation, desolation, havoc, ruin, wreckage, damage.

**detached**
*(adj) Try to remain detached; don't take sides.* objective, disinterested, impartial, unbiased, unprejudiced, dispassionate, aloof, unemotional, unconcerned.

**detail**
1 *(n) Check every detail of the plan.* aspect, element, part, item, point, feature, particular, component.
2 *details (plural n) Samir asked Mrs Badger for details about the French trip.* information, particulars *(plural)*, facts *(plural)*, specifics *(plural)*.

**detailed**
*(adj) Bart gave a detailed account of the match.* full, thorough, comprehensive, in-depth, exhaustive, complete, meticulous, precise, blow-by-blow, elaborate.
OPPOSITES: brief, general.

# **d**etective

**detective**
(n) investigator, sleuth (informal), private detective, private investigator, private eye (informal). ❖ Also see **crime & detection**.

**deteriorate** see **get worse**.

**determination**
(n) Chris showed great determination in finishing the race. perseverance, tenacity, persistence, willpower, drive, resolve, single-mindedness, dedication, guts (plural) (informal), grit, spirit.

**determined**
1 (adj) Patsy is a very determined person. persistent, tenacious, single-minded, strong-willed, assertive, firm, gutsy (informal), obstinate, stubborn, dogged. OPPOSITES: indecisive, weak-willed.
2 (adj) I don't want to go, but Nat is determined. resolved, immovable, insistent, set on it, bent on it, intent on it. OPPOSITES: unsure, wavering.

**detest** see **hate** 1.

**detour**
(n) We took a detour to get home. diversion, indirect route, roundabout route, long way round, scenic route.

**develop**
1 (v) Nadia should develop once she starts her new school. mature, blossom, flourish, grow up, make progress, progress, grow, fill out, shoot up.
2 (v) Dad wants to develop his grocery business. See **expand** 2.
3 (v) Tom may develop a taste for modern art. acquire, pick up, cultivate, form.
4 (v) I might develop mumps. See **catch** 3.
5 (v) It's a good idea, but you need to develop it. enlarge on, elaborate on, expand, flesh out, pad out, fill out.

**development**
(n) We're studying the development of modern medicine. progress, advance, evolution, growth, improvement, spread, expansion, history, course.

**devious** see **cunning**.

**devoted**
1 (adj) Mo is a devoted friend. See **loyal**.
2 (adj) Sally is devoted to caring for sick animals. dedicated, committed.

**devour** see **eat** 2.

**diagram**
(n) Study this diagram. representation, figure, sketch, drawing, line drawing, outline, chart, plan, map, graph, table.

**diarrhoea**
(n) the runs (plural) (informal), the trots (plural) (informal), holiday tummy (informal), Delhi belly (informal), dysentery.

**diary**
1 (n) Jo keeps a diary to record her secret thoughts. journal, record, chronicle, log.
2 (n) Priscilla entered the meeting in her diary. personal organizer, appointments book, engagement book, calendar.

**dictate**
1 (v) You dictate and I'll take notes. read aloud, speak slowly, recite.
2 (v) I can't dictate what you should think. tell you, lay down the law about, decree, impose, direct, order, determine, ordain.

**die**
1 (v) Everyone must die eventually. expire, pass away, pass on, decease, snuff it (informal), kick the bucket (informal), bite the dust (informal), give up the ghost (informal), croak (slang).
2 (v) Soldiers sometimes die in battle. perish, fall, lose their lives, give their lives.
3 (v) Those flowers will die without water. wither, wilt, shrivel up, droop, fade.

**diet**
1 (v) I must diet to fit into this skirt. lose weight, slim, eat sparingly, fast.
2 (n) You need to go on a special diet. programme, regimen, regime, fast.
3 (n) Is this your usual diet? food, nutrition, nourishment, fare.

**differ**
1 (v) Our tastes in music tend to differ. be different, contrast, vary, conflict, diverge.
2 (v) Matt and I differ about which team is best. See **disagree** 1.

**difference**
(n) Note the difference in price between the two items. contrast, disparity, divergence, discrepancy, inconsistency. OPPOSITE: similarity.

**different**
1 (adj) Mum and I have different opinions on clothes. differing, dissimilar, contrasting, conflicting, opposing, contradictory, clashing, incompatible. OPPOSITES: similar, identical.
2 (adj) We stock a range of different chocolates. various, assorted, mixed, varied, miscellaneous, multifarious.
3 (adj) Try a different approach. new, fresh, other, original, changed, altered.
4 (adj) Every fingerprint is different. individual, distinct, unique, special, distinctive, separate, unrelated, personal.
5 (adj) With his purple hair, Ziggy is certainly different. See **unusual** 2.

**difficult**
1 (adj) A difficult maths problem. hard, tough, knotty (informal), advanced, complicated, complex, challenging, testing, baffling, thorny, puzzling. OPPOSITES: easy, straightforward.
2 (adj) A difficult assault course. hard, challenging, demanding, testing, taxing, strenuous, tough, gruelling, exhausting, killing (informal), backbreaking, arduous. OPPOSITES: easy, undemanding.
3 (adj) A difficult child. demanding, hard to please, fussy, fractious, unmanageable, uncooperative, unruly, obstreperous, bolshie (informal), stroppy (informal), wilful, awkward, obstinate, stubborn. OPPOSITES: cooperative, undemanding.

4 (adj) A difficult situation. See **awkward** 6.

**difficulty**
1 (n) Gran has had a life full of difficulty. See **trouble** 2.
2 (n) Don't let this little difficulty put you off. problem, complication, obstacle, snag, stumbling block, hurdle, pitfall, hiccup (informal), hassle (informal), hindrance.

**dig**
1 (v) The climbers tried to dig a hole in the snow. scoop out, gouge out, hollow out, excavate, shovel, burrow, tunnel.
2 (v) Mum asked me to dig the flowerbed. turn over, fork over.
3 **dig up** (v) Pirate Peg began to dig up the treasure. unearth, excavate, uncover.

**dignified**
1 (adj) The duchess has a dignified manner. stately, solemn, formal, proud, lofty, majestic, upright, elegant, refined. OPPOSITES: undignified, coarse.
2 (adj) Hetty gave a dignified reply. calm, composed, restrained, solemn, grave. OPPOSITES: rude, unrestrained.

**dilapidated**
(adj) A dilapidated farmhouse. run-down, decaying, decrepit, ramshackle, tumbledown, neglected, crumbling, broken-down, rickety, shabby, uncared-for. OPPOSITE: well-maintained.

**dilute**
(v) You need to dilute this sauce. water down, weaken, thin, add water to. OPPOSITES: condense, thicken.

**dim**
1 (adj) A dim cave. dark, gloomy, murky, dingy, dull, poorly lit, ill-lit, shadowy. OPPOSITES: bright, well-lit, sunny.
2 (adj) A dim figure in the mist. faint, indistinct, shadowy, pale, vague, hazy, fuzzy, bleary, blurred, ill-defined, misty. OPPOSITES: clear, distinct.
3 (adj) Don't be so dim! See **stupid** 1.

**din** see **noise** 2.

**dingy**
(adj) A dingy attic. drab, dreary, dark, gloomy, ill-lit, shabby, grimy, cheerless. OPPOSITES: bright, clean, cheerful.

**dip**
1 (n) Do you want a dip in the river? swim, bathe, dunk, splash, plunge, soaking, ducking.
2 (n) Watch out for that dip in the ground. hollow, depression, dent, hole, pit, incline, slope.
3 (v) Dip your mug in the stream. plunge, dunk, submerge, immerse, lower, rinse.
4 (v) The plane began to dip. See **drop** 2.

**direct**
1 (adj) Take the direct road. straight, shortest, undeviating, unswerving. OPPOSITES: indirect, winding.
2 (adj) Take the direct train. nonstop, express, through.

**3** (adj) You can rely on Nat to give a direct answer. See **frank**.
**4** (adj) We need a direct response. See **immediate**.
**5** (v) Greg will direct operations. supervise, oversee, take charge of, control, run, manage, handle, lead, mastermind.
**6** (v) Let me direct you to the school. show you the way, guide, point, lead, steer.

**direction**
(n) Which direction should we take? way, route, path, track, course, bearing.

**directions**
(plural n) Follow the directions carefully. instructions (plural), guidelines (plural), rules (plural), recommendations (plural), suggestions (plural).

**dirt**
(n) We must get rid of all this dirt. grime, filth, muck, sludge, slime, mud, dust, crud (informal), gunge (informal), gunk (informal), grot (slang), mess, pollution.

**dirty**
**1** (adj) This room is really dirty. filthy, grimy, mucky, grubby, squalid, sordid, foul, grotty (slang), grungy (slang), dusty, muddy, sooty, smoky, black, stained, soiled, spattered, streaked, insanitary. OPPOSITES: clean, spotless.
**2** (adj) Don't tell dirty jokes. blue, risqué, smutty, rude, filthy, indecent, crude, vulgar, obscene, pornographic. OPPOSITES: clean, decent.
**3** (adj) George was sent off the pitch for dirty play. See **foul 5**.
**4** (v) Try not to dirty your clothes. soil, stain, muddy, mess up, make a mess of, muck up (slang), smear, spatter, spot.

**disabled**
(adj) handicapped, incapacitated, infirm, paralysed, paraplegic, quadriplegic. OPPOSITE: able-bodied.

**disadvantage**
(n) It's a disadvantage to live a long way from school. handicap, drawback, inconvenience, hindrance, nuisance, pain (informal), hardship, fly in the ointment. OPPOSITES: advantage, benefit.

**disagree**
**1** (v) We often disagree about which team is best. argue, quarrel, row, squabble, bicker, fall out (informal), clash, differ. OPPOSITE: agree.
**2 disagree with** (v) Why do you disagree with everything I say? object to, take issue with, quarrel with, argue with, dispute, oppose, contradict. OPPOSITE: agree with.
**3 disagree with** (v) Do spicy meals disagree with you? upset, make you ill, give you indigestion, cause you problems, bother, nauseate.

**disagreement**
**1** (n) We had a disagreement over who should pay. See **argument 1**.

**2** (n) There's been a lot of disagreement about this matter. conflict, dissent, division, difference of opinion, debate. OPPOSITES: harmony, agreement.

**disappear**
(v) Slowly, the figure began to disappear. vanish, fade away, melt away, become invisible, vanish into thin air, leave no trace, dissolve, evaporate, dematerialize. OPPOSITES: appear, materialize.

**disappoint**
(v) I'm sorry to disappoint you. let you down, dash your hopes, disillusion, disenchant, fail, fail to live up to your expectations, dishearten, sadden, dismay, displease, upset, frustrate, thwart.

**disappointed**
(adj) I felt disappointed when I learnt the truth. let down, dejected, despondent, crestfallen, downcast, disenchanted, disillusioned, saddened, discouraged, downhearted, miffed (informal), fed up (informal), disgruntled, dissatisfied. OPPOSITES: satisfied, gratified.

**disapprove**
**1** (v) My parents disapprove when I play loud music. object, protest, take exception. OPPOSITE: approve.
**2 disapprove of** (v) I disapprove of fox-hunting. take exception to, have a low opinion of, take a dim view of (informal), frown on, condemn, deplore. OPPOSITE: approve of.

**disapproving** see **critical 1**.

**disaster**
(n) We must try to avoid another disaster. catastrophe, calamity, tragedy, misfortune, mishap, accident, fiasco, cataclysm.

**disastrous**
(adj) The pilot made a disastrous mistake. catastrophic, fatal, tragic, terrible, devastating, horrendous, calamitous, grievous, ill-fated, unlucky, cataclysmic. OPPOSITES: fortunate, lucky.

**discipline**
**1** (v) The coach will discipline the players. train, instruct, school, drill, control.
**2** (v) If you break the rules, I will have to discipline you. punish, penalize, reprimand, teach you a lesson, bring you into line, rebuke, chastise, chasten, correct, scold.
**3** (n) Good athletes need discipline. self-discipline, self-control, strictness, firmness, routine, order, training.

**discourage**
(v) What can I do to discourage you from going? dissuade, deter, prevent, stop, talk you out of, put you off, advise you against. OPPOSITE: encourage.

**discouraged**
(adj) We were discouraged by the bad news. disheartened, demoralized, dismayed, daunted, depressed, crushed, deterred, cowed, put off, unnerved. OPPOSITES: encouraged, reassured.

**discouraging**
(adj) It's discouraging when you always lose. demoralizing, disheartening, depressing, disappointing, demotivating, dispiriting, daunting, off-putting (informal). OPPOSITES: encouraging, heartening.

**discover**
**1** (v) It didn't take me long to discover that Oz was lying. find out, learn, become aware, realize, detect, spot, discern, work out, deduce, suss out (slang), ascertain.
**2** (v) The explorers were lucky to discover the treasure. See **find 1**.
**3** (v) The journalist was determined to discover the truth. find out, uncover, bring to light, ferret out, dig up, expose, reveal.

**discovery**
(n) This is an amazing discovery. invention, find, revelation, innovation, breakthrough.

**discreet**
(adj) You can trust Tony; he's always discreet. careful, guarded, reserved, cautious, tactful, diplomatic, prudent. OPPOSITES: indiscreet, rash.

**discrimination**
(n) I hate discrimination of all kinds. prejudice, bigotry, unfairness, favouritism, bias, racism, sexism, chauvinism, ageism. OPPOSITE: tolerance.

**discuss**
(v) Can we discuss this later? talk about, consider, debate, examine, exchange views on, argue about, confer about, go into, thrash out, argue the toss on (informal).

**discussion**
(n) We had a discussion about where to go on holiday. conversation, debate, exchange of views, argument, talk, powwow, dialogue, conference.

**disease** see **illness 1, 2**.

**disgrace**
(n) Burglar Beryl has brought disgrace to her family. shame, embarrassment, humiliation, dishonour, scandal, ignominy. OPPOSITES: honour, credit.

**disgraceful**
**1** (adj) Disgraceful behaviour. appalling, shameful, scandalous, shocking, outrageous, disgusting, deplorable, despicable, contemptible, disreputable.
**2** (adj) A disgraceful defeat. See **humiliating**.

**disguise**
**1** (n) I'll need a good disguise to get into the house. cover, front, screen, façade, camouflage, alias.
**2** (n) Sally looks wonderful in her disguise. fancy dress, costume, outfit, get-up (informal), mask, veil, make-up, face paint.
**3** (v) The soldiers used bushes to disguise the tank. camouflage, hide, cover up, conceal, screen, mask, shroud, veil.
**4** (v) Burglar Beryl decided to disguise herself as the milkman. dress up as, pretend to be, impersonate, imitate.

# **d**isgust

**disgust**
1 (n) The details of the crime filled me with disgust. loathing, distaste, revulsion, repugnance, contempt, hatred, antipathy.
OPPOSITES: delight, approval.
2 (v) Doesn't bad language disgust you? sicken, revolt, appal, nauseate, turn your stomach, repel, offend, put you off.
OPPOSITES: delight, attract.

**disgusted**
(adj) Gran was disgusted by Mark's jokes. appalled, sickened, outraged, offended, scandalized, shocked, nauseated, repelled.
OPPOSITE: delighted.

**disgusting**
1 (adj) A disgusting smell. revolting, repulsive, nauseating, sickening, loathsome, offensive, obnoxious, foul, vile.
OPPOSITES: delightful, lovely.
2 (adj) Disgusting behaviour. appalling, obnoxious, offensive, odious, detestable, abominable, shocking, scandalous.
OPPOSITES: delightful, pleasing.

**dishonest**
(adj) A dishonest businessman. deceitful, fraudulent, lying, crooked (informal), bent (slang), immoral, untrustworthy, unscrupulous, corrupt, double-dealing, treacherous, slippery, shady (informal), tricky, wily, two-faced, hypocritical.
OPPOSITES: honest, truthful.

**dishonesty**
(n) Dad cannot stand dishonesty. deceit, deceitfulness, untruthfulness, insincerity, deviousness, lies (plural), cheating, double-dealing, sharp practice, fraud, hypocrisy.
OPPOSITES: honesty, truthfulness.

**dish up**
(v) Dad will dish up the vegetables. serve, serve up, dole out, give out, hand out.

**disillusioned** see **disappointed**.

**disintegrate**
1 (v) The yacht hit the rocks and began to disintegrate. See **break up** 1.
2 (v) The wallpaper is starting to disintegrate. crumble, rot, moulder away, decay, decompose, fall apart, fall to pieces.

**dislike**
1 (v) I dislike bullies. See **hate** 1.
2 (n) George surveyed his broccoli with dislike. distaste, displeasure, disgust, loathing, revulsion, repugnance, hatred, hostility, detestation, animosity.
OPPOSITES: liking, delight.

**disloyal**
(adj) A disloyal friend. false, unfaithful, two-faced, untrustworthy, treacherous.
OPPOSITES: loyal, faithful.

**dismal**
1 (adj) Dismal weather. See **dull** 1.
2 (adj) A dismal story. See **depressing** 1.

**dismay**
(n) I gazed at the mountain with dismay. alarm, apprehension, anxiety, trepidation, consternation, dread, distress, fear, horror.

**dismiss**
1 (v) The boss may have to dismiss you. give you notice, sack (informal), fire (informal), let you go, release, make you redundant, lay you off, give you your cards (informal), show you the door (informal).
2 (v) Don't dismiss my idea without thinking about it first. reject, discount, spurn, pooh-pooh (informal), disregard.

**disobedient**
(adj) A disobedient child. rebellious, uncooperative, defiant, badly behaved, disruptive, naughty, wilful, wayward, unruly, uncontrollable, unmanageable.
OPPOSITE: obedient.

**disobey**
1 (v) Mum will be angry if you disobey her. defy, refuse to obey, resist, rebel against, revolt against, go your own way.
OPPOSITE: obey.
2 (v) Don't disobey the school rules. break, flout, disregard, ignore, infringe, overstep.
OPPOSITE: obey.

**disorganized**
1 (adj) Daisy is such a disorganized person. scatterbrained, undisciplined, scatty (informal), muddleheaded, untogether (slang), shambolic (informal), chaotic.
OPPOSITE: well-organized.
2 (adj) This essay is very disorganized. jumbled, muddled, confused, chaotic, unstructured, unplanned, illogical, haphazard, unsystematic, unmethodical.
OPPOSITES: well-organized, clear.

**display**
1 (n) We went to see the display. demonstration, exhibition, presentation, show, array, pageant, spectacle, parade.
2 (v) The makers were keen to display their products. show, demonstrate, exhibit, present, unveil, reveal, show off, flaunt.

**disprove**
(v) Burglar Beryl's lawyer set out to disprove the charges. refute, prove false, discredit, invalidate, contradict.
OPPOSITE: prove.

**disqualified**
(adj) Our team is disqualified from the competition. banned, eliminated, debarred, out of the running, knocked out.

**disrespectful**
(adj) Don't be so disrespectful to your father! rude, impertinent, insolent, cheeky, impolite, impudent, irreverent, insulting.
OPPOSITE: respectful.

**dissatisfied**
(adj) I feel dissatisfied with the way I've been treated. displeased, unhappy, disgruntled, disappointed, discontented, fed up (informal), cheesed off (slang).
OPPOSITES: satisfied, contented.

**dissolve**
(v) Wait for the stock cube to dissolve. melt, break up, disintegrate, disperse, liquefy, soften, thaw, disappear.

**distance**
1 (n) A short distance. space, span, gap, interval, length, breadth, width.
2 (n) A long distance. stretch, extent, range, length, breadth, width.

**distant**
(adj) Distant lands. faraway, far-flung, far-off, remote, out-of-the-way, outlying.
OPPOSITES: nearby, neighbouring.

**distinct**
1 (adj) A distinct signal. See **clear** 2.
2 (adj) A distinct outline. See **clear** 5.
3 (adj) A distinct voice. See **clear** 6.
4 (adj) The two companies are quite distinct. different, separate, unconnected, dissimilar, distinguishable, detached.

**distinguish**
(v) Can you distinguish between frogs and toads? tell the difference, differentiate, discriminate, tell apart.

**distort** see **twist** 5.

**distract**
(v) Will it distract you if I watch television? put you off, disturb, bother, ruin your concentration, faze, disconcert, sidetrack, unsettle, worry, confuse, annoy.

**distress**
1 (n) Your news caused me much distress. pain, heartache, misery, anguish, torment, worry, anxiety, grief, agony, upset.
OPPOSITE: comfort.
2 (v) This film might distress you. See **disturb** 2.

**distressing** see **disturbing**.

**distribute** see **give out**.

**distrust** see **suspect** 1.

**disturb**
1 (v) I don't want to disturb you while you're working. bother, interrupt, distract, put you off, pester, hassle (informal), butt in on, annoy, trouble, disrupt.
2 (v) It might disturb you to know the truth. upset, alarm, distress, unsettle, worry, trouble, perturb, fluster, disconcert.

**disturbed**
1 (adj) When I read your letter, I felt disturbed. uneasy, worried, troubled, concerned, upset, distressed, alarmed, anxious, apprehensive, agitated, nervous.
2 (adj) A disturbed teenager. troubled, confused, unbalanced, neurotic, maladjusted, screwed up (informal).
OPPOSITE: well-adjusted.

**disturbing**
(adj) I found the film really disturbing. upsetting, distressing, worrying, unsettling, disquieting, troubling, perturbing, harrowing, alarming, frightening.

**ditch**
1 (n) Henry fell into a ditch. gully, trench, dyke, channel, hollow, pit, moat, drain.
2 (v) (slang) Jason wants to ditch his girlfriend. See **drop** 6.

**dither** see **hesitate**.

**dive**
1 *(v) We watched Alexis dive into the river.* plunge, jump, leap, fall, belly-flop, plummet, go under.
2 *(v) Suddenly, the plane began to dive.* drop, sink, plunge, plummet, fall, descend, swoop, dip, nose-dive, tumble, submerge *(submarine).*
OPPOSITE: rise.
3 *(v) The goalkeeper prepared to dive for the ball.* lunge, pounce on, swoop on, fall upon, leap, jump.

**diver**
*(n)* frogman, scuba diver.

**divide**
1 *(v) Where does the path divide?* branch, fork, split, separate, diverge, subdivide.
2 *(v) Can you divide this apple for me?* cut up, halve, split, bisect.
3 *(v) Let's divide the money between us.* share, share out, split, distribute, dole out, deal out, allocate, allot, apportion, go halves, go fifty-fifty *(informal).*
4 *(v) Please divide these papers into groups. See* **sort** 3.

**divine**
*(adj) A divine being.* heavenly, celestial, holy, sacred, godlike, angelic, spiritual, supernatural, immortal, superhuman.

**divorce**
*(v) Joe's parents have decided to divorce.* split up, separate, part, break up.

**dizzy**
*(adj) After her fall, Fran felt dizzy.* giddy, faint, light-headed, woozy *(informal),* groggy *(informal),* reeling, weak at the knees, shaky, dazed, wobbly, unsteady.

**do**
1 *(v) I have lots of things to do.* undertake, carry out, get on with, achieve, accomplish, perform, complete, finish.
2 *(v) Let's ask Mrs Bunn to do the teas.* make, prepare, organize, handle, deal with, take care of, see to, manage, look after, arrange, be responsible for.
3 *(v) This will do for our needs.* be good enough, be adequate, be sufficient, suffice, be useful, be acceptable.
4 *(v) Can you do this puzzle?* solve, answer, complete, work out, figure out *(informal),* crack, find the solution to.
5 *(v) You may do as you please.* behave, act, live, lead your life, carry on.
6 *(v) This may do some good.* result in, cause, bring about, give rise to, lead to.
7 *(v) William should do better at his new school.* manage, get on, get along, cope, progress, advance, make out, fare.
8 *(v) I must do my room.* tidy, straighten up, sort out, organize, arrange, neaten.
9 *(v) Sunita hopes to do drama at college.* study, learn, take up, go in for.
10 *(v) This car will do 130 miles per hour.* travel at, go at, reach.
11 *(v) (informal) Watch out for Dodgy Dave or he'll do you! See* **cheat** 1.

**dock**
1 *(n) We moored our boat at the dock.* quay, wharf, jetty, harbour, landing stage.
2 *(v) When will the boat dock?* berth, moor, tie up, anchor, drop anchor.

**doctor**
*(n)* medical practitioner, medic *(informal),* doc *(informal),* quack *(informal).*
TYPES OF DOCTOR: anaesthetist, brain surgeon, consultant, GP (general practitioner), gynaecologist, homeopath, neurologist, obstetrician, orthopaedic surgeon, osteopath, paediatrician, plastic surgeon, psychiatrist, specialist, surgeon.

**dodge**
1 *(v) I threw a pillow at Kevin, but he managed to dodge it.* avoid, evade, escape, sidestep, swerve, duck, turn aside.
2 *(v) Oz tries to dodge work. See* **avoid** 2.

**dodgy**
1 *(adj) (informal) Dave made a dodgy deal. See* **crooked** 4.
2 *(adj) (informal) That bridge looks dodgy. See* **dangerous** 2.

**dog**
*(n)* hound, bitch *(female),* pup, puppy, mutt *(informal),* pooch *(slang),* mongrel, cur, canine, man's best friend.
TYPES OF DOG: Afghan hound, Alsatian, beagle, bloodhound, boxer, bulldog, Chihuahua, collie, corgi, dachshund, Dalmatian, Doberman, foxhound, Great Dane, greyhound, gundog, husky, Labrador, Pekingese, pointer, poodle, pug, retriever, Rottweiler, St Bernard, setter, sheepdog, spaniel, terrier, whippet, wolfhound.

**dominate**
1 *(v) Do your big brothers dominate you?* tyrannize, keep you under their thumb, rule, domineer over, boss you around *(informal),* take you over, have the whip hand over, take control of, monopolize.
2 *(v) The skyscrapers dominate the city.* tower over, overshadow, dwarf, look down on, loom over, soar above.

**domineering** see **bossy.**

**donate** see **give** 2.

**done for**
*(adj) (informal) After the fight, Lee felt he was done for.* finished, ruined, defeated, destroyed, dead, doomed, lost.

**done in** *(informal)* see **exhausted.**

**doodle** see **scribble** 2.

**doomed**
*(adj) I'm afraid our love is doomed.* cursed, ill-fated, fated, luckless, condemned, star-crossed, ill-omened, hopeless.

**door**
*(n)* doorway, entrance, entry, exit, gate, gateway, opening.

**dope** see **drug** 2, 3.

**dopey**
1 *(adj) (informal) I felt dopey after my operation.* groggy *(informal),* drowsy, woozy *(informal),* dazed, sleepy, muzzy, sluggish, lethargic, drugged.
2 *(adj) (slang) Don't be so dopey! See* **stupid** 1.

**dot**
*(n) Remove that dot.* spot, speck, fleck, mark, dab, blob, full stop, decimal point.

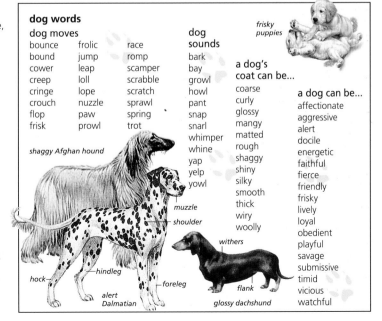

**dog words**

**dog moves**
| | | |
|---|---|---|
| bounce | frolic | race |
| bound | jump | romp |
| cower | leap | scamper |
| creep | loll | scrabble |
| cringe | lope | scratch |
| crouch | nuzzle | sprawl |
| flop | paw | spring |
| frisk | prowl | trot |

*shaggy Afghan hound*

**dog sounds**
bark
bay
growl
howl
pant
snap
snarl
whimper
whine
yap
yelp
yowl

*frisky puppies*

**a dog's coat can be...**
coarse
curly
glossy
mangy
matted
rough
shaggy
shiny
silky
smooth
thick
wiry
woolly

**a dog can be...**
affectionate
aggressive
alert
docile
energetic
faithful
fierce
friendly
frisky
lively
loyal
obedient
playful
savage
submissive
timid
vicious
watchful

*muzzle*
*shoulder*
*withers*
*alert Dalmatian*
*hindleg*
*hock*
*foreleg*
*flank*
*glossy dachshund*

# **d**ouble

**double**
1 *(adj) Double railway tracks.* dual, twin, paired.
2 *(n) I've just seen your double.* twin, spitting image *(informal)*, lookalike, clone, counterpart.
3 *(v) We aim to double our numbers.* increase, multiply, expand, duplicate.

**doubt**
1 *(v) I'm starting to doubt if Oz will come.* be uncertain, be unsure, have doubts about, be dubious, wonder, question.
OPPOSITES: be sure, be certain.
2 *(v) I have reason to doubt your motives.* See **suspect** 1.
3 *(n) There's no doubt about Beryl's guilt.* uncertainty, question, debate, ambiguity.
OPPOSITE: certainty.
4 *(n) I have some doubt about your story.* suspicions *(plural)*, misgivings *(plural)*, reservations *(plural)*, qualms *(plural)*, scepticism, distrust, disbelief, incredulity.

**doubtful**
1 *(adj) It's doubtful whether the story is true.* uncertain, unclear, arguable, debatable, questionable, iffy *(informal)*.
OPPOSITES: certain, definite.
2 *(adj) Ellen was doubtful about her chances.* uncertain, dubious, unsure, unconvinced, hesitant, tentative.
OPPOSITES: confident, certain.

**do up** *(informal)* see **decorate** 2.

**dowdy**
*(adj) Aunt Bertha wears such dowdy clothes.* frumpy, drab, dreary, unattractive, unfashionable, old-fashioned, dull, dingy.
OPPOSITES: smart, fashionable.

**down** see **depressed**.

**down-and-out** see **homeless**.

**down-to-earth**
*(adj) Roger has a down-to-earth approach.* realistic, practical, hard-headed, no-nonsense, matter-of-fact, common-sense, sensible, sane, pragmatic.
OPPOSITES: unrealistic, impractical.

**doze**
*(v) Granny likes to doze after lunch.* snooze *(informal)*, catnap, sleep, take a nap, have forty winks *(informal)*, nod off *(informal)*, drop off *(informal)*, get some shuteye *(informal)*, have a kip *(slang)*.

**drab**
*(adj) A drab bedsit.* dreary, dingy, dismal, cheerless, gloomy, shabby, dull.
OPPOSITES: bright, cheerful.

**drag**
1 *(v) Drag that carpet over here.* pull, haul, tow, lug, tug, yank, trail, draw.
2 *(n) (informal) Shopping can be such a drag.* See **bore** 3.
3 **drag behind** *(v) Don't drag behind the others.* See **drop behind**.

**drain**
1 *(n) A drain for waste water.* ditch, pipe, sewer, trench, channel, gutter, drainpipe.

2 *(v) We watched the water drain away.* seep, ooze, trickle, ebb, leak, flow, escape.
3 *(v) Drain the water from the pond.* empty, draw off, siphon off, bleed, tap.

**drama**
1 *(n) We are staging a new drama.* See **play** 5.
2 *(n) Melissa wants to study drama.* acting, stagecraft, the theatre, the dramatic arts *(plural)*.
3 *(n) There was some drama in town.* crisis, incident, excitement, commotion, fuss, scene, turmoil, histrionics *(plural)*.

**dramatic** see **exciting**.

**drastic**
*(adj) Drastic action is needed.* radical, extreme, forceful, strong, serious, severe, desperate, rigorous, harsh, far-reaching.

**draw**
1 *(v) I want to draw a cat.* sketch, depict, portray, trace, outline, design, pen, pencil.
2 *(v) Draw a number from the bag.* pick, select, take out, pull out, choose, extract.
3 *(v) Horses draw carts.* See **pull**.
4 *(v) I think the teams will draw.* tie, finish equal, be neck and neck, be even, be level.
5 *(v) This game should draw a big crowd.* See **attract**.
6 *(n) The match ended in a draw.* tie, dead heat, stalemate, deadlock, impasse.
7 *(n) Are you entering the draw?* lottery, raffle, sweepstake, competition.

**drawback** see **disadvantage**.

**drawing**
*(n)* picture, study, design.
TYPES OF DRAWING: caricature, cartoon, charcoal drawing, comic strip, doodle, illustration, line drawing, pen-and-ink drawing, portrait, sketch, still life.

**drawn** see **haggard**.

**draw on**
*(v) You can draw on your own experience for this story.* make use of, use, employ, rely on, utilize, exploit, fall back on.

**dread**
1 *(v) There's no need to dread visiting the dentist.* fear, be afraid of, be apprehensive about, be scared of, shrink from, cringe at, shudder at, tremble at, flinch from, have cold feet, have butterflies in your stomach.
2 *(n) The sight of the monster filled Cedric with dread.* See **fear** 1.

**dreadful**
1 *(adj) A dreadful crime.* appalling, terrible, horrible, horrific, horrifying, horrendous, shocking, frightful, atrocious, awful, ghastly, vile, foul, hideous, gruesome, grisly, monstrous, sickening, harrowing, distressing, despicable, deplorable, unspeakable, tragic.
2 *(adj) A dreadful essay.* awful, terrible, atrocious, appalling, abysmal, abominable, diabolical *(informal)*, disgraceful, dire *(informal)*, deplorable, bad, lousy *(slang)*.
OPPOSITES: wonderful, excellent.

3 *(adj) Dreadful weather.* awful, terrible, horrible, atrocious, appalling, bad, foul, filthy, dirty, rough, miserable, dismal, murky, bleak, wet, rainy, stormy, wild.
OPPOSITES: wonderful, brilliant.

**dream**
1 *(n) I thought I could fly, but it was only a dream.* nightmare, daydream, fantasy, illusion, delusion, hallucination, speculation, vision.
2 *(n) You're in a dream again.* daydream, trance, daze, world of your own, reverie.
3 *(n) Eddie's dream is to be a star.* fantasy, hope, wish, desire, ideal, aspiration, ambition, goal, vision.
4 *(adj) This is my dream house.* ideal, perfect, fantasy.
5 *(v) Do you ever dream that you can fly?* imagine, fancy, fantasize, envisage, visualize, daydream, muse.
6 **dream up** *(v) Gita loves to dream up new recipes.* See **think up**.

**dreamy**
*(adj) Daisy is so dreamy, she never knows where she is.* absent-minded, airy-fairy, vague, faraway, abstracted, distracted.

**dreary**
1 *(adj) Dreary weather.* dull, depressing, dismal, gloomy, murky, bleak, grey, wet.
OPPOSITES: cheerful, bright.
2 *(adj) A dreary lesson.* See **boring**.

**drenched** see **soaking**.

**dress**
1 *(v) It's time to dress for the party.* get dressed, get changed, change, put your clothes on, dress up.
2 *(n) Poppy wore a red dress.* frock, gown, robe. ❖ *Also see* **clothes**.
3 *(n) Formal dress is required.* clothes *(plural)*, clothing, wear, gear *(informal)*, attire *(old-fashioned)*, costume, get-up *(informal)*, garments *(plural)*, togs *(plural)* *(informal)*, kit.

**dress up**
*(v) It's time to dress up and go out.* dress up to the nines *(informal)*, dress for dinner, put on your glad rags *(informal)*, tart yourself up *(slang)*, doll yourself up *(slang)*.

**dribble**
1 *(v) Look at Fido dribble!* drool, slobber, slaver, salivate, water at the mouth.
2 *(v) Don't let the syrup dribble out of the bottle.* trickle, drip, leak, ooze, seep, run.

**drift**
1 *(v) The boat began to drift downstream.* float, glide, sail, be carried, coast.
2 *(v) I love to drift around town.* See **wander** 1.
3 *(n) Zak fell into a drift of snow.* bank, mound, ridge, heap, pile, mass.

**drill**
1 *(v) Can you drill through this wood?* bore, pierce, penetrate, punch, puncture.
2 *(v) Our coach will drill us every day.* See **train** 4.

**drink**
1 *(v) Drink your milk.* sip, swallow, down, swig *(informal)*, gulp, guzzle, drain, knock back *(informal)*, quaff *(old-fashioned)*.
2 *(n) Bring some drink for the journey.* liquid, refreshment, beverage.
3 *(n) Supermarkets sell alcoholic drink.* liquor, spirits *(plural)*, booze *(informal)*, plonk *(informal)*, grog *(informal)*.
4 *(n) Take a drink from the bottle.* sip, swig *(informal)*, slug, swallow, gulp, suck.
5 *(n) Dodgy Dave went out for a drink.* tipple, tot, dram, booze-up *(slang)*.

**drip**
1 *(v) Look at the water drip from the ceiling!* trickle, splash, dribble, fall in drops, plop, leak, drop, seep, sprinkle, drizzle.
2 *(n) Clem could hear the steady drip of water.* dripping, trickle, dribble, splash.
3 *(n) (informal) Cyril is a real drip!* wimp *(informal)*, weed *(informal)*, wet *(informal)*, softy *(informal)*, mummy's boy *(informal)*, nerd *(slang)*, weakling.

**drive**
1 *(v) Let's drive home.* motor, travel, journey, go by car, ride.
2 *(v) Do you know how to drive this car?* handle, steer, control, operate.
3 *(v) How can I drive you to work harder?* force, spur you on, goad, push, compel, motivate, prompt, prod, incite, coerce, dragoon, oblige, urge, press.
4 *(n) We went for a drive in the car.* run, ride, spin *(informal)*, whirl *(informal)*, trip, journey, jaunt, outing, excursion.
5 *(n) Jacob has lots of drive.* ambition, determination, energy, push *(informal)*, motivation, enthusiasm, oomph *(informal)*.

**drive out**
*(v) The king tried to drive out the sorcerer.* banish, send away, send packing, cast out, throw out, expel, exile, evict, turf out *(informal)*, drum out, kick out *(informal)*.

**droop**
1 *(v) Don't let the scarf droop over your face.* hang down, sag, dangle, flop, trail.
2 *(v) The tulips are starting to droop.* wilt, go limp, sag, go floppy, hang down, flag, slump, wither, shrivel.

**droopy** *see* **floppy**.

**drop**
1 *(v) Don't drop that vase!* let go of, lose your grip on, let fall, let slip.
2 *(v) Suddenly the plane began to drop.* fall, sink, descend, dip, dive, plunge, plummet, tumble, nose-dive.
OPPOSITE: rise.
3 *(v) Prices may drop. See* **decrease** 2.
4 *(v) Can I drop my flute lessons?* give up, stop, discontinue, abandon, finish with.
5 *(v) We'll have to drop you from the team.* exclude, eliminate, leave you out of, kick you off *(informal)*, axe *(informal)*.
6 *(v) Holly decided to drop her boyfriend.* finish with, leave, dump *(informal)*, chuck *(informal)*, ditch *(slang)*, jilt.

7 *(n) A drop of paint ran down the tin.* droplet, bubble, globule, drip, bead, blob.
8 *(n) Add just a drop of sauce.* dash, spot, trace, dribble, bit, little, sprinkle, trickle, taste, pinch, soupçon, smidgen *(informal)*.
9 *(n) There's been a drop in crime. See* **decrease** 1.
10 *(n) The path led to a steep drop.* chasm, precipice, abyss, cliff, slope.

**drop behind**
*(v) Try not to drop behind!* fall behind, lag behind, straggle behind, trail behind, drag behind, dawdle, linger, loiter, dally, bring up the rear *(informal)*.

**drop in** *(informal) see* **call** 5.

**drop off**
1 *(v) Dad will drop you off at school.* set you down, let you off, leave, deposit.
2 *(v) (informal) Gran tends to drop off in front of the TV.* fall asleep, doze off, nod off *(informal)*, snooze *(informal)*, catnap, drowse, have forty winks *(informal)*.

**drown**
1 *(v) The pirates may drown if their ship sinks.* go under, go down, go to a watery grave, go to Davy Jones's locker.
2 *(v) The new reservoir will drown the village. See* **flood** 2.

**drowsy** *see* **sleepy** 1.

**drug**
1 *(n) Dr Dose wasn't sure which drug to prescribe.* medication, medicine, remedy, treatment, tonic, painkiller, antibiotic, tranquillizer, sedative, stimulant, antidepressant.
2 *(n) Cannabis is a type of drug.* narcotic, dope *(informal)*.
3 *(v) The vet had to drug the wild tiger.* dope, tranquillize, sedate, knock out, anaesthetize, put to sleep, inject.

**drum**
*(v) Listen to the rain drum on the roof.* beat, rap, tap, pound, thrum, reverberate.

**drunk**
1 *(adj) Dad said Dodgy Dave was drunk.* intoxicated, inebriated, tipsy, under the influence *(informal)*, tiddly *(informal)*, merry *(informal)*, legless *(informal)*, sozzled *(informal)*, paralytic *(informal)*, plastered *(slang)*, smashed *(slang)*, sloshed *(slang)*.
OPPOSITE: sober.
2 *(n) Dodgy Dave is a real drunk.* drunkard, alcoholic, hard drinker, heavy drinker, boozer *(informal)*, wino *(informal)*.
OPPOSITE: teetotaller.

**dry**
1 *(adj) The travellers crossed the dry desert.* arid, parched, dried up, barren, torrid, waterless, moistureless, scorched.
OPPOSITES: wet, humid.
2 *(adj) Lauren's dad has a dry sense of humour.* keen, sharp, shrewd, wry, ironic, laconic, sarcastic, deadpan, droll.
3 **dry up** *(v) Don't let the plants dry up.* wither, shrivel up, wilt, dehydrate, dry out.

**duck**
1 *(n) A duck paddled across the pond.* drake *(male)*, duckling.
2 *(v) You'll have to duck to avoid that beam.* stoop, bend down, lower your head, bob down, crouch down, dodge.
3 *(v) I'll duck you in the deep end!* dunk, push you under, submerge, plunge, dip, douse, immerse.

**dull**
1 *(adj) The sky has been dull all day.* cloudy, overcast, grey, gloomy, murky, leaden, dark, dismal, dreary, sunless.
OPPOSITES: bright, clear.
2 *(adj) Mrs Badger's lessons are never dull. See* **boring**.
3 *(adj) Aunt Bertha wears such dull colours.* drab, dreary, sombre, muted, subdued, dark, faded, colourless.
OPPOSITE: bright.
4 *(adj) Are you being deliberately dull? See* **stupid** 1.
5 *(adj) The prisoner stared with dull eyes.* lifeless, listless, expressionless, indifferent, apathetic, dead, blank, lacklustre.
OPPOSITES: bright, lively.

**dumb**
1 *(adj) I was dumb with fear.* speechless, unable to speak, tongue-tied, at a loss for words, silent, mute, mum.
2 *(adj) (informal) Don't be dumb! See* **stupid** 1.

**dump**
1 *(n) Take your rubbish to the dump.* tip, rubbish dump, rubbish tip, scrapheap, refuse centre, waste disposal site, junkyard, scrap yard, recycling centre.
2 *(n) (informal) This place is a dump.* hole *(informal)*, dive *(informal)*, tip *(informal)*, slum, pigsty, hovel, the pits *(informal)*.
3 *(v) Don't dump your bag on the floor.* drop, throw, plonk, sling *(informal)*, fling, toss, deposit, park *(informal)*.
4 *(v) (informal) You should dump that rubbish. See* **throw away** 1.
5 *(v) (informal) Holly decided to dump her boyfriend. See* **drop** 6.

**dumpy**
*(adj) Mrs Bunn is a dumpy woman.* squat, short, tubby, stubby, chubby, plump, stout, chunky, roly-poly, podgy, pudgy.
OPPOSITE: lanky.

**dungeon**
*(n) The traitors were thrown into a dark dungeon.* prison, cell, underground chamber, vault, lockup, pit.

**dusk**
*(n) I must be home before dusk.* nightfall, twilight, evening, sunset, sundown.
OPPOSITES: dawn, sunrise.

**dust**
1 *(n) The floor is covered in dust.* grime, dirt, grit, powder.
2 *(v) Dust the table.* wipe, clean, polish.
3 *(v) Dust the cake with icing sugar.* sprinkle, powder, cover, scatter.

**dusty**
1 (adj) The attic was dusty. dirty, grimy, grubby, filthy, mucky, sooty, unswept.
2 (adj) The earth was dry and dusty. crumbly, powdery, sandy, chalky, fine.

**duty**
1 (n) It's my duty to tidy up. responsibility, obligation, job, task, business, role, function, mission, vocation, calling.
2 (n) Nigel worked late out of a sense of duty. responsibility, loyalty, obligation, allegiance, obedience, respect, service.

**dwindle**
(v) Seth's strength began to dwindle. diminish, decline, weaken, decrease, lessen, shrink, wane, fade, peter out, ebb, sink, subside, abate, wither, disappear.
OPPOSITES: increase, strengthen.

**dye**
(v) Let's dye this shirt. colour, tint, stain.

**dying**
1 (adj) The old man was dying. declining, sinking, failing, fading fast, at death's door, breathing his last, expiring.
2 (adj) I'm dying to know who won. See **eager** 2.

**dynamic**
(adj) A dynamic salesperson. energetic, lively, vigorous, active, forceful, driving, go-getting (informal), high-powered, go-ahead, zappy (slang), aggressive.

# Ee

**eager**
1 (adj) An eager student. enthusiastic, keen, interested, motivated, committed, zealous, diligent, hard-working.
OPPOSITES: apathetic, indifferent.
2 (adj) Jade was eager to open her presents. keen, impatient, bursting, dying (informal), itching (informal), anxious, longing, yearning, hungry, raring.
OPPOSITE: reluctant.

**early**
1 (adv) I bet Kit will arrive early. in good time, ahead of time, in advance, too soon.

OPPOSITE: late.
2 (adj) An early manuscript. old, ancient, primitive.
3 (adj) Early humans hunted for food. primitive, prehistoric, primeval, primordial.

**earn**
1 (v) Nic is hoping to earn a lot of money. make, bring in, obtain, gain, take home, rake in (informal), collect, clear, gross, net.
2 (v) You've worked hard enough to earn a holiday. See **deserve** 2.
3 (v) I want to earn a medal. See **win** 2.

**earnest** see **serious** 1, 2.

**earth**
1 (n) The earth is round. world, globe, planet.
2 (n) Dan dug up the earth. ground, soil, land, clay, loam, topsoil, dirt, dust, turf.

---

**earthquake**
(n) earth tremor, quake (informal).

**earthquakes...**
destroy
devastate
flatten
ravage
shatter
smash
wreck

**the earth may...**
cave in
crack
gape
jolt
judder (informal)
open up
quake
quiver
shake
shift
subside
tremble
vibrate
yawn

**buildings may...**
buckle
collapse
crack
crumble
crumple
disintegrate
lurch
rock
shake
shudder
sway
tilt
topple
totter
tumble
wobble

**you might see...**
chasms
cracks
crushed cars
debris
dust
fallen trees
flames
rubble
ruins
smoke
trapped victims
wreckage

**earthquake dangers**
broken cables
burst dam
burst water main
collapsed bridge
cracked pipes
falling masonry
fire
flying glass
gas explosion
landslide
tidal wave

**earthquake words**
aftershock
epicentre (earthquake centre)
seismic wave (shock wave)

rubble

chasm     crack

water gushing from burst water main

---

**easy**
1 (adj) The test was easy! simple, straightforward, uncomplicated, a doddle (informal), a piece of cake (informal), child's play (informal), a pushover (slang).
OPPOSITES: hard, difficult.
2 (adj) Declan thinks his new job is really easy. undemanding, cushy (informal), effortless, painless, light, soft (informal).
OPPOSITES: hard, demanding.
3 (adj) Lord Lucre has an easy life. comfortable, carefree, untroubled, pleasant, relaxed, leisurely, contented, calm, tranquil, secure, affluent.
OPPOSITES: harsh, difficult, stressful.
4 (adj) Dom's parents are too easy on him. lenient with, lax with, indulgent towards, liberal with, tolerant towards.
OPPOSITES: hard, strict.

**easy-going**
(adj) Omar is so easy-going; nothing ever bothers him. even-tempered, placid, calm, relaxed, laid-back (informal), carefree, happy-go-lucky, nonchalant, flexible, amenable, undemanding, tolerant.
OPPOSITES: uptight (informal), intolerant.

**eat**
1 (v) I need to eat. have a meal, feed, dine, take food, take nourishment.
2 (v) I can eat a huge amount. consume, devour, swallow, put away, demolish.
WAYS TO EAT: bite, bolt, champ, chew, chomp, crunch, gnaw, gobble, gorge, grind, gulp, guzzle, lick, make a pig of yourself (informal), munch, nibble, overeat, peck at, pick at, pig out (slang), scoff (informal), slurp (informal), stuff yourself, suck, tuck into (informal), wolf down.
3 eat away (v) Eventually the sea will eat away the rocks. See **wear away**.

**eavesdrop**
(v) I didn't mean to eavesdrop on your conversation. listen in, snoop, overhear, bug (informal), tap.

**eccentric**
1 (adj) Ziggy's behaviour is quite eccentric. bizarre, peculiar, weird, strange, odd, unconventional, outlandish, quirky, idiosyncratic, cranky (informal), wacky (slang), off-the-wall (slang), abnormal.
2 (n) Professor Peabody is a real eccentric. oddity, character (informal), oddball (informal), crank (informal), crackpot (informal), weirdo (informal), nut (slang).

**echo**
1 (v) We heard the screams echo round the cave. reverberate, ring, resound, sound, repeat.
2 (v) Don't echo what I say. See **repeat** 2.

**ecstatic**
(adj) I was ecstatic when I won. delighted, overjoyed, thrilled, elated, thrilled to bits (informal), over the moon (informal), on cloud nine (informal), delirious, euphoric, in raptures, frenzied, hysterical.
OPPOSITES: wretched, dejected.

## edge
1 (n) Go to the edge of the field. end, side, boundary, limit, perimeter, border, margin, kerb (street), verge (road), outskirts (town) (plural).
OPPOSITES: centre, middle.
2 (n) Theo filled the jug up to the edge. rim, brim, lip.
3 (n) Lucy caught the edge of her skirt on a nail. hem, border, fringe, edging, trimming, bottom.
4 (n) The expedition is on the edge of disaster. brink, threshold, verge, point.
5 (v) Try to edge forwards. inch, creep, ease, crawl, sidle, worm your way, work your way, steal, sneak, slink.

## edgy see nervous.

## education
(n) Your education must come first. schooling, teaching, tuition, training, instruction, coaching, drilling.

## educational
(adj) An educational film. informative, instructive, edifying, enlightening, improving, cultural.

## eerie see spooky.

## effect
1 (n) One effect of the fire was to make us more careful. result, consequence, outcome, upshot, aftereffect, side effect, knock-on effect, aftermath.
2 (n) Going to France had a great effect on me. influence, impact, impression.

## efficient
1 (adj) An efficient worker. capable, competent, well-organized, businesslike, proficient, productive, effective, skilful.
OPPOSITES: inefficient, incompetent.
2 (adj) An efficient business. productive, cost-effective, streamlined, well-run, well-organized, economical, cost-cutting, energy-saving, timesaving.
OPPOSITES: inefficient, wasteful.

## effort
1 (n) Let's make an effort to break the record. attempt, bid, try, endeavour, stab (informal), shot (informal), crack (informal).
2 (n) You must have put lots of effort into making this. exertion, work, energy, power, force, muscle, labour, toil, trouble.

## elaborate
1 (adj) An elaborate ballgown. extravagant, ornate, fancy, decorative, fussy, showy, ostentatious.
OPPOSITES: plain, simple.
2 (adj) Elaborate plans. See complicated.

## elect see choose 1, 2.

## elegant
1 (adj) Mel looks elegant in that suit. smart, sophisticated, stylish, chic (female), debonair (male), suave (male), dashing, fashionable, handsome (male), poised.
2 (adj) What an elegant room! tasteful, stylish, exquisite, classical, beautiful, splendid, luxurious, sumptuous, stately.

## embarrass
(v) Would it embarrass you if Dad wore his tank top? humiliate, make you uncomfortable, make you self-conscious, make you blush, mortify, shame, upset, distress, show you up (informal).

## embarrassed
(adj) Mr Plod felt embarrassed when his wig fell off. self-conscious, uncomfortable, humiliated, mortified, ashamed, red in the face (informal), flustered, disconcerted.

## embarrassing
(adj) This is such an embarrassing situation. awkward, humiliating, uncomfortable, mortifying, cringe-making (informal), upsetting, distressing, compromising.

## embrace see hug.

## embroidery
(n) needlework, sewing, tapestry.

## emerge
(v) Wait for the train to emerge from the tunnel. come out, appear, come into view, become visible, surface.

## emergency
(n) If there's an emergency, ring for help. crisis, danger, difficulty, predicament, panic stations (plural) (informal).

## emotion see feeling 3.

## emotional
1 (adj) Letty is such an emotional person. excitable, highly strung, temperamental, sensitive, sentimental, passionate, hot-blooded, intense, melodramatic.
OPPOSITE: unemotional.
2 (adj) An emotional film. See moving 2.

## emphasize
(v) I must emphasize the importance of safety. stress, underline, highlight, play up, point out, lay emphasis on, lay stress on, insist on, press home, accentuate.
OPPOSITE: play down.

## empty
1 (adj) This cupboard is completely empty. bare, clear, free.
OPPOSITES: full, stuffed.
2 (adj) Dustin handed in an empty page. See blank 1.
3 (adj) The house next door is empty. vacant, unoccupied, uninhabited, deserted, unfurnished, bare, free.
OPPOSITES: occupied, furnished.
4 (adj) I wasted the day in empty pursuits. meaningless, pointless, futile, purposeless, aimless, hollow, frivolous, worthless, trivial.
OPPOSITES: worthwhile, valuable.
5 (v) Empty the rubbish into the bin. tip, dump, unload, pour, clear, drain.

## enchant
1 (v) Erica will enchant you with her singing. See delight 2.
2 (v) The magician planned to enchant the princess. bewitch, cast a spell on, charm, hypnotize, mesmerize.

## enchanting see delightful 2.

## encourage
1 (v) I think this result will encourage you. reassure, cheer you up, inspire, give you confidence, give you hope, spur you on, comfort, console, hearten, buoy you up.
OPPOSITES: discourage, demoralize.
2 (v) We all turned out to encourage the team. support, spur on, urge on, cheer, applaud, rally, rouse, egg on.
3 (v) Parents should encourage their children to read. urge, persuade, prompt, help, assist, aid.
OPPOSITES: discourage, dissuade.

## encouraging
(adj) This is an encouraging result. reassuring, heartening, comforting, promising, favourable, satisfactory.
OPPOSITES: discouraging, demoralizing.

## end
1 (n) Let's wait until the end of the show. finish, conclusion, completion, ending, close, finale, climax, final curtain (theatre).
OPPOSITES: start, beginning, opening.
2 (n) This is the end of the school grounds. limit, boundary, edge, border, perimeter, margin.
3 (n) Our expedition reached its end. destination, goal, target, journey's end.
OPPOSITE: starting point.
4 (n) Get to the end of the queue. back, rear, tail, tail end.
OPPOSITES: front, head.
5 (n) What caused the end of the Roman Empire? fall, ruin, demise, destruction, collapse, death, dissolution, extinction.
OPPOSITES: birth, beginning.
6 (v) When does school end for the summer? stop, finish, close, break up, come to an end, cease, wind up.
OPPOSITES: start, open.
7 (v) Mrs Badger decided to end the lesson early. finish, stop, bring to an end, conclude, wind up, break off, discontinue.
OPPOSITES: start, begin.

## ending
(n) What a sad ending! end, conclusion, finish, resolution, finale, climax, outcome, upshot, result.
OPPOSITES: beginning, opening.

## endless
1 (adj) The desert seemed endless. unending, never-ending, limitless, infinite, boundless, measureless.
2 (adj) The city was invaded by an endless stream of tourists. constant, continuous, never-ending, perpetual, nonstop, uninterrupted, incessant, interminable.

## endure
1 (v) I can't endure any more suffering. bear, stand, put up with (informal), tolerate, take, cope with, handle, suffer, go through, undergo, experience, stomach, swallow, brave, withstand, stick (slang).
2 (v) The poet's fame will endure for ever. See live 4.

**enemy**
1 (n) Japan was Britain's enemy in World War II. opponent, foe, adversary, rival.
OPPOSITES: ally, friend.
2 **the enemy** (n) Sir Blackheart has joined the enemy. the other side, the opposition.

**energetic**
1 (adj) Emma always seems so energetic. lively, dynamic, active, full of life, full of beans (informal), spirited, animated, vibrant, zippy (informal), tireless.
OPPOSITES: lethargic, listless.
2 (adj) Squash is an energetic sport. strenuous, vigorous, fast-moving, active.

**energy**
1 (n) I admire Marco's energy. vitality, stamina, strength, vigour, drive, get-up-and-go (informal), enthusiasm, liveliness, spirit, verve, zest, sparkle, exuberance, oomph (informal).
2 (n) Are you in favour of nuclear energy? power, fuel.

**enjoy**
1 (v) I enjoy cycling. See **like** 2.
2 (v) My parents enjoy good food. love, appreciate, relish, take pleasure in, have a taste for, delight in, revel in, savour.
OPPOSITES: dislike, hate.
3 **enjoy yourself** (v) Enjoy yourself at the party! have a good time, have fun, have a laugh (informal), have a ball (informal), let your hair down, have the time of your life.

**enjoyable**
(adj) An enjoyable holiday. pleasant, delightful, fun, amusing, entertaining, pleasurable, lovely, great (informal).

**enlarge**
(v) The council plans to enlarge the local sports field. extend, expand, make bigger, make larger, widen, lengthen, add to, develop, supplement, augment, blow up (photograph) (informal), magnify (image).
OPPOSITE: reduce.

**enormous**
(adj) Marcie eats an enormous amount of chocolate. huge, vast, massive, immense, colossal, gigantic, tremendous, prodigious, monstrous, mountainous, astronomic, stupendous, humongous (informal), mammoth, monster.
OPPOSITES: tiny, minute.

**enough**
(adj) I think we have enough supplies for the journey. sufficient, adequate, ample, abundant, plenty of.
OPPOSITES: insufficient, inadequate.

**enquire** see **ask** 1.

**enter**
1 (v) I let Mrs Badger enter in front of me. go in, come in, move in, pass in.
OPPOSITE: leave.
2 (v) Will you enter the competition? take part in, participate in, sign up for, put your name down for, go in for, volunteer for, enrol in, be a competitor in.

3 (v) Enter the results of the experiment in your notebook. record, note down, write, take down, jot down, log, list, insert.

**entertain**
1 (v) This game will entertain you while you're ill. amuse, keep you amused, occupy, keep you occupied, cheer you up, divert, distract, delight, please, interest.
2 (v) My parents like to entertain guests. receive, invite, welcome, show hospitality to, play host to, wine and dine, put up.

**entertaining**
(adj) An entertaining novel. amusing, interesting, enjoyable, light-hearted, witty, funny, humorous, comical, hilarious, delightful, charming, enchanting.

**entertainment** see **amusement** 2.

**enthralling** see **fascinating**.

**enthusiasm**
(n) Tristan approaches his work with enthusiasm. eagerness, interest, relish, zest, excitement, keenness, passion, fervour, zeal, devotion, delight.
OPPOSITES: apathy, indifference.

**enthusiastic**
1 (adj) Alice is an enthusiastic football fan. keen, avid, eager, ardent, fervent, passionate, fanatical, zealous, mad keen (informal), devoted, committed, earnest.
OPPOSITES: apathetic, half-hearted.
2 (adj) Halim is always so enthusiastic. positive, optimistic, exuberant, spirited, ebullient, lively, willing.
OPPOSITES: apathetic, indifferent.

**entire** see **whole**.

**entrance**
1 (n) Don't block the entrance. way in, entry, gateway, gate, doorway, door, drive, opening, access, approach.
OPPOSITE: exit.
2 (n) Entrance to the museum is free. admission, admittance, entry, access.
3 (n) Famous Fred made a dramatic entrance. entry, appearance, arrival.
OPPOSITE: exit.

**envious**
(adj) Toby looked envious when he saw my new bike. jealous, green with envy, green-eyed, resentful, grudging, covetous.

**environment**
1 (n) I like to see animals in their natural environment. surroundings (plural), setting, habitat, location, territory, domain.
2 (n) I can't work in this environment. surroundings (plural), situation, conditions (plural), atmosphere.

**envy**
1 (n) Toby was filled with envy when he saw my new bike. jealousy, covetousness, desire, resentment, bitterness, discontent, the green-eyed monster (informal).
2 (v) It's pointless to envy other people's success. be envious of, be jealous of, resent, begrudge, covet.

**episode**
1 (n) Did you see the last episode of "WestEnders"? instalment, part, section, scene, chapter.
2 (n) I'd rather forget that embarrassing episode. See **event** 1.

**equal**
1 (adj) The boys are equal in their ability. identical, alike, the same, comparable, evenly matched, evenly balanced, level, neck and neck, at level pegging (informal).
2 (adj) Two dozen is equal to 24. equivalent, identical, the same as.
3 (v) Two plus two will always equal four. be equal to, make, add up to, total, amount to, correspond to, equate to.
4 (v) We managed to equal the scores by half-time. level, even up, balance, equalize.
5 (v) Nothing can equal a steaming hot bath. compare with, match, be as good as, match up to, touch, rival, measure up to, come near, hold a candle to (informal).

**equipment**
(n) Do you have all your equipment for the expedition? gear, tackle, stuff, apparatus, tools (plural), baggage, supplies (plural).

**erase**
(v) Erase that word from your essay. remove, delete, rub out, wipe out, scratch out, cross out, strike out, cancel, expunge.

**erode** see **wear away**.

**errand**
(n) Mum gave me an errand to do in town. job, task, message, assignment, mission.

**error** see **mistake** 1.

**escape**
1 (v) Burglar Beryl longs to escape from prison. get away, run away, break loose, break free, break out of, bolt, abscond, scarper (slang), do a bunk (slang), do a runner (slang), flit (informal), flee, fly.
2 (v) Don't let the oil escape from the barrel. See **leak** 2.
3 (v) Sid always tries to escape the washing-up. avoid, evade, shirk, dodge, get out of, wriggle out of, duck (informal).
4 (n) Burglar Beryl plans to make her escape tonight. getaway, break-out, flight.

**essay**
(n) I have to write an essay for homework. composition, piece, story, report, paper, extended essay, dissertation, review.

**essential**
(adj) Essential instructions. necessary, vital, crucial, indispensable, important, basic, fundamental, key.
OPPOSITES: inessential, unnecessary.

**establish**
1 (v) Mum aims to establish a successful business. set up, start, begin, found, get going, get off the ground (informal), create, form, build, construct, originate.
2 (v) I need to establish exactly what happened. find out, ascertain, determine, confirm, prove, verify, authenticate.

**estimate**
1 *(v) Try to estimate the cost of this dress.* assess, evaluate, guess, judge, work out, calculate, reckon, weigh up, gauge.
2 *(n) Annie supplied an estimate for her work.* quotation, price, costing, valuation.

**eternal**
*(adj) Eternal life.* everlasting, endless, never-ending, without end, immortal, infinite, limitless, undying, timeless.
OPPOSITES: ephemeral, transitory.

**even**
1 *(adj) An even surface.* level, flat, smooth, horizontal, straight, flush.
OPPOSITES: uneven, rough, sloping.
2 *(adj) An even flow of water.* steady, regular, consistent, constant, unvarying, smooth, continuous, uninterrupted.
OPPOSITES: erratic, irregular.
3 *(adj) The scores are even.* level, equal, identical, all square, at level pegging *(informal)*, tied, drawn, neck and neck.
OPPOSITE: unequal.

**evening**
*(n)* dusk, nightfall, twilight, sunset, sundown, gloaming *(old-fashioned)*.

**event**
1 *(n) I'd rather forget that unfortunate event.* incident, episode, affair, business, matter, occasion, occurrence, experience.
2 *(n) We've been planning this event for months.* activity, do *(informal)*, function, occasion, ceremony, entertainment.
3 *(n) A sports event. See* **competition** 1.

**eventually** *see* **finally** 1.

**evidence**
1 *(n) The detectives need evidence.* proof, confirmation, documentation, data.
2 *(n) Is there any evidence of damage?* indication, sign, trace, symptoms *(plural)*.

**evident** *see* **obvious**.

**evil**
1 *(adj) This evil deed must be punished.* wicked, sinful, bad, diabolical, fiendish, villainous, vile, depraved, immoral, corrupt, atrocious, vicious, malicious, wrong.
OPPOSITES: good, virtuous.
2 *(n) We must overcome evil.* wickedness, sin, sinfulness, depravity, corruption, vice, immorality, villainy, wrongdoing, malice.
OPPOSITE: good.

**exact**
1 *(adj) Are these measurements exact? See* **accurate** 1.
2 *(adj) At that exact moment, I sneezed.* very, precise, specific, particular, actual.
3 *(adj) An exact copy.* faithful, identical, perfect, precise, strict, true, flawless.
OPPOSITE: rough.

**exaggerate**
*(v) Jo tends to exaggerate her problems.* overstate, overemphasize, magnify, overplay, dramatize, embellish, embroider, make too much of, play up, inflate.
OPPOSITES: play down, understate.

**examination**
1 *(n) A school examination.* exam, test, assessment, oral, practical.
2 *(n) A medical examination.* checkup, investigation, observation, inspection, test, scan, probe, once-over *(informal)*.

**examine**
*(v) Detectives will examine the evidence.* look at, inspect, study, look into, go over, go through, sift through, scrutinize, survey, check, consider, weigh up, analyse, check out, investigate, explore, probe, test.

**example**
1 *(n) This is an example of Finn's bad behaviour.* instance, illustration, case, case in point, sample, specimen.
2 *(n) Rosa has set an example for you to follow.* model, pattern, standard, ideal.

**exasperate** *see* **annoy** 1.

**excellent**
*(adj) An excellent film.* superb, brilliant, fantastic *(informal)*, wonderful, terrific *(informal)*, marvellous, outstanding, great, first-class, first-rate, impressive, magnificent, splendid, fine, exceptional, superlative, remarkable, extraordinary, tremendous *(informal)*, sensational *(informal)*, stunning *(informal)*.
OPPOSITES: terrible, inferior.

**exception**
*(n) It's usually warm in July; this snow is an exception.* rarity, freak, oddity, peculiarity, special case, quirk, anomaly, irregularity.

**exceptional**
1 *(adj) This hot weather is exceptional for March. See* **unusual** 1.
2 *(adj) Your work is exceptional. See* **excellent**.

**exchange**
*(v) May I exchange this shirt for a bigger one?* swap, change, switch, replace with, trade.

**excited**
*(adj) Everyone was excited before the party.* animated, worked up, wound up *(informal)*, agitated, overwrought, high *(informal)*, hyper *(informal)*, restless, wild, feverish, frantic, frenzied, hysterical.

**excitement**
1 *(n) Gemma was beside herself with excitement.* eagerness, anticipation, exhilaration, enthusiasm, elation, agitation.
2 *(n) I like films that are full of excitement.* tension, suspense, thrills *(plural)*, action, adventure, drama, kicks *(plural)* *(informal)*.
3 *(n) What's all the excitement about?* commotion, fuss, activity, confusion, furore, hubbub, kerfuffle *(informal)*.

**exciting**
*(adj) An exciting film.* thrilling, dramatic, exhilarating, electrifying, fast-moving, action-packed, cliffhanging, nail-biting, heart-stopping, spine-tingling, stirring, gripping, compelling, riveting.
OPPOSITES: boring, dull.

**exclude**
*(v) If you try to spoil the game we'll exclude you.* leave you out, ostracize, ignore, pass you over, leave you out in the cold *(informal)*, shut you out, bar, ban, throw you out, kick you out *(informal)*.

**excruciating** *see* **agonizing**.

**excuse**
1 *(v) I can't excuse your behaviour.* forgive, pardon, condone, make allowances for, overlook, ignore, tolerate.
2 *(v) Dodgy Dave tried to excuse his actions.* defend, justify, explain, vindicate, give reasons for.
3 *(n) What's your excuse for arriving so late?* reason, justification, grounds *(plural)*, defence, alibi *(legal)*, pretext.

**exercise**
1 *(v) You'll get fat if you don't exercise.* keep fit, work out, train, play sport, exert yourself, pump iron *(slang)*.
2 *(n) Exercise is good for you.* activity, training, exertion, sport, games *(plural)*, working out, pumping iron *(slang)*, physical jerks *(plural)* *(informal)*.

**exhausted**
*(adj) After the race I was exhausted.* tired out, worn out, ready to drop, shattered *(informal)*, dead tired, weary, drained, dead beat *(informal)*, done in *(informal)*, whacked *(informal)*, zonked *(slang)*.

**exhausting**
*(adj) An exhausting job.* tiring, gruelling, arduous, strenuous, draining, punishing, backbreaking, killing *(informal)*, difficult, hard, laborious, taxing, testing.

**exhibition** *see* **display** 1.

**exhilarating** *see* **exciting**.

**expand**
1 *(v) Pipes expand when water freezes in them.* swell, enlarge, increase in size, widen, thicken, lengthen, dilate, fill out.
OPPOSITES: contract, shrink.
2 *(v) Dad wants to expand his business.* develop, build up, extend, enlarge.
3 *(v) It's a good idea, but you need to expand it. See* **develop** 5.

**expect**
1 *(v) I expect that Danni will arrive late.* assume, presume, suppose, imagine, reckon, guess *(informal)*, think, believe, envisage, anticipate, predict, foretell.
2 *(v) Can we expect some improvement?* look forward to, anticipate, look for, hope for, reckon on, bank on.
3 *(v) Dad will expect an apology.* insist on, demand, require, look for, call for, want.

**expedition**
*(n) The explorers set out on an expedition.* journey, voyage, trip, mission, quest, exploration, trek, safari, hike, tramp, tour.

**expel**
*(v) The head may expel you from school.* exclude, dismiss, ban, send you away, throw you out, turf you out *(informal)*.

## expensive

*(adj) An expensive holiday.* dear, pricey *(informal)*, costly, overpriced, exorbitant, extortionate, extravagant, steep *(informal)*.
OPPOSITES: cheap, inexpensive.

## experience

1 *(n) What an amazing experience!* incident, occurrence, adventure, episode, affair, happening, event, ordeal.
2 *(n) For this job, you need the right experience.* skill, know-how *(informal)*, practical knowledge, training, background.
3 *(n) You will learn by experience.* doing, taking part, practice, participation, involvement, familiarity.
4 *(v) You may have to experience hardship.* undergo, suffer, endure, face, go through, live through, encounter, meet.

## experienced

*(adj) Bo is an experienced cook.* practised, seasoned, skilled, accomplished, expert, proficient, competent, trained, qualified.
OPPOSITE: inexperienced.

## experiment

1 *(n) Write up the results of your experiment.* investigation, practical, inquiry, test, trial, demonstration, research.
2 *(v) I love to experiment when I cook.* try things out, improvise, explore.

## expert

1 *(n) We need an expert to mend our computer.* specialist, professional, consultant, authority, pro *(informal)*, pundit, boffin *(informal)*, anorak *(slang)*.
OPPOSITE: novice.
2 *(n) Dean is an expert at juggling.* master, genius, wizard, ace *(informal)*, virtuoso, past master, maestro, whiz *(informal)*, whiz kid *(informal)*, dab hand *(informal)*.
3 *(adj) An expert footballer. See **skilful**.

## explain

1 *(v) Can you explain what this means?* make clear, clarify, spell out, throw light on, elucidate, interpret, define, describe.
2 *(v) Please explain why you are late.* give an explanation for, give a reason for, account for, justify.

## explode

*(v) This bomb may explode without any warning.* blow up, go off, detonate, erupt.

## exploit *see* **take advantage of**.

## explore

*(v) Let's explore the castle.* investigate, scout around, take a look around, check out *(informal)*, survey, reconnoitre, tour.

## explorer

*(n)* discoverer, traveller, voyager.

## explosion

*(n) The explosion made the windows shake.* blast, bang, boom, rumble, crash, detonation, report.

## expose

1 *(v) Dad rolled up his trousers to expose his hairy legs. See **reveal** 1.

2 *(v) The journalist was determined to expose the truth.* uncover, bring to light, make known, lay bare, unmask, reveal, disclose, divulge, leak, blow wide open *(slang)*, blow the whistle on *(informal)*.

## express

1 *(v) Nasim was keen to express his views.* state, put into words, voice, make known, air, put across, communicate, point out, give vent to, articulate, verbalize.
2 *(adj) Take the express train.* high-speed, fast, nonstop, direct, through.

## expression

1 *(n) Sim's face wore a strange expression.* look, appearance, aspect, air.
2 *(n) Where did you hear that expression?* word, phrase, saying, turn of phrase, idiom, term, choice of words, remark.

## extend

1 *(v) Extend the elastic. See **stretch** 1.
2 *(v) The desert seemed to extend for miles. See **stretch** 4.
3 *(v) We plan to extend our house.* enlarge, build on to, add on to, make bigger, make larger, expand.

## extinct

*(adj) That species is extinct.* dead, defunct, vanished, lost, died out, wiped out, gone.
OPPOSITES: surviving, extant.

## extra

*(adj) This extension will give us extra space.* more, additional, further, added, spare, surplus, excess, leftover, superfluous.

## extraordinary

1 *(adj) Carl's artistic talent is extraordinary.* exceptional, outstanding, unique, out of the ordinary, unprecedented, remarkable, amazing, phenomenal, unusual, rare.
OPPOSITES: unexceptional, ordinary.
2 *(adj) Ziggy wears some extraordinary clothes. See **strange** 1.

## extravagant

1 *(adj) Letty is so extravagant; she's always wasting money.* wasteful, careless with money, self-indulgent, lavish, imprudent.
OPPOSITES: thrifty, economical.
2 *(adj) What an extravagant gift!* lavish, costly, expensive, flashy, showy, over the top, overgenerous, excessive, immoderate, outrageous, OTT *(slang)*.

## extreme

1 *(adj) Extreme pain.* severe, intense, acute, great.
2 *(adj) Extreme measures. See **drastic**.
3 *(adj) Extreme political views.* fanatical, radical, uncompromising, unreasonable, hardline, way-out *(informal)*, outrageous, exaggerated, excessive, immoderate.
OPPOSITE: moderate.

## extrovert

*(adj) Kylie is so extrovert; she's the life and soul of the party.* outgoing, lively, vivacious, bubbly, sociable, gregarious, friendly, confident, exuberant, animated.
OPPOSITES: introverted, withdrawn.

**fabric** *see* **material**.
**fabulous** *(informal) see* **fantastic** 3.

## face

1 *(n) Burglar Beryl has a distinctive face.* features *(plural)*, appearance, countenance *(old-fashioned)*, mug *(slang)*, kisser *(slang)*.
2 *(n) Lisa made a horrible face.* scowl, grimace, frown, smirk, pout.
3 *(v) Our new house will face the sea.* overlook, look onto, look towards, front onto, be opposite.
4 *(v) The explorers will face many dangers.* encounter, experience, come up against, come across, meet, be confronted by.
5 *(v) I can't face this problem on my own.* deal with, cope with, face up to, tackle, confront, meet head-on, brave, get to grips with, come to terms with.

### faces and features

| faces | complexions | |
|---|---|---|
| angular | ashen | pasty |
| babyish | black | peaches- |
| chubby | blotchy | and-cream |
| craggy | bronzed | pimply |
| flabby | brown | pitted |
| fleshy | clear | radiant |
| gaunt | coarse | rosy |
| haggard | dark | rough |
| heart-shaped | delicate | ruddy |
| long | dusky | sallow |
| oval | fair | scarred |
| pinched | florid | shiny |
| plump | flushed | sickly |
| podgy | freckled | smooth |
| round | fresh | spotty |
| square | glowing | stubbly |
| strong-jawed | greasy | swarthy |
| triangular | healthy | tanned |
| | ivory | unshaven |
| *heart-shaped* | oily | wan |
| *face* | olive | white |
| | pale | wrinkled |
| | pallid | |

*stubbly complexion*

*haggard face*

## fact
**1** *(n) The fact is that pigs can't fly.* truth, reality, naked truth, actuality, certainty.
OPPOSITE: fiction.
**2** *facts (plural n) Give me the facts.* details *(plural)*, particulars *(plural)*, information, data, whole story, lowdown *(informal)*, info *(informal)*, gen *(informal)*.

## factual
*(adj) Write a factual account of your holiday.* true, accurate, true-to-life, truthful, honest, faithful, authentic, realistic, matter-of-fact, exact, precise, objective, unbiased, unvarnished.
OPPOSITES: fictional, imaginary.

## fade
**1** *(v) I hope my shirt doesn't fade in the wash.* lose colour, become pale, become bleached, become washed out, whiten.
**2** *(v) Bright sunlight will fade the carpet.* bleach, discolour, dull, whiten.
**3** *(v) The light began to fade.* die away, wane, dwindle, fail, diminish, weaken, grow faint, dim, disappear, vanish.

## fail
**1** *(v) I bet I'll fail in the exam.* be unsuccessful, not pass, not make the grade *(informal)*, not come up to scratch *(informal)*, come to grief, come a cropper *(informal)*, flunk *(informal)*.
OPPOSITES: succeed, pass.
**2** *(v) Henry's plan is bound to fail.* fall through, be unsuccessful, fall flat, misfire, miscarry, come to nothing, be frustrated, founder, flop *(informal)*, fizzle out.
OPPOSITES: succeed, pass.
**3** *(v) I hope the engine doesn't fail.* cut out, give out, stop working, break down, die, conk out *(informal)*, cease to function.
**4** *(v) Flash Frank is afraid his business will fail.* collapse, crash, go bankrupt, go under, go to the wall, close down, go out of business, fold *(informal)*, flop *(informal)*, go bust *(informal)*, go broke *(informal)*.
OPPOSITES: succeed, prosper, thrive.
**5** *(v) Aunt Bertha's eyesight is starting to fail.* deteriorate, weaken, decline, get worse, degenerate, go.
OPPOSITES: improve, strengthen.

**6** *(v) I won't fail you.* let you down, disappoint, abandon, desert, forsake.

## failing see **weakness** 1.

## failure
**1** *(n) The match ended in failure.* defeat, disaster, disappointment, frustration.
OPPOSITE: success.
**2** *(n) The play was a failure.* disaster, fiasco, flop *(informal)*, catastrophe, nonstarter, washout *(informal)*.
OPPOSITE: success.
**3** *(n) Cyril thinks he's a failure.* loser, no-hoper *(informal)*, ne'er-do-well, non-achiever, disappointment, incompetent.
OPPOSITE: success.
**4** *(n) The storm caused a power failure.* cut, loss, breakdown, stoppage, outage.

## faint
**1** *(v) Simone will faint when she sees all this blood.* pass out, black out, lose consciousness, keel over *(informal)*, collapse, swoon *(old-fashioned)*.
**2** *(adj) Anjali felt faint after her run.* dizzy, giddy, light-headed, muzzy, woozy *(informal)*, unsteady, weak, exhausted.
**3** *(adj) There's a faint pink glow in the sky.* pale, soft, delicate, hazy, misty, vague.
OPPOSITES: bright, distinct.
**4** *(adj) Sarah spoke in a faint voice.* weak, feeble, low, soft, scarcely audible, hushed, whispered, subdued, muffled, muted.
OPPOSITES: loud, clear.

## fair
**1** *(adj) Jenny has fair hair.* See **blonde** 2.
**2** *(adj) Mrs Badger may be strict, but she is always fair.* just, impartial, even-handed, fair-minded, unbiased, unprejudiced, objective, open-minded.
OPPOSITES: unfair, unjust.
**3** *(adj) I hope the weather will be fair tomorrow.* fine, dry, clear, bright, sunny, cloudless, favourable, clement.
OPPOSITE: foul.
**4** *(adj) Your work is fair.* adequate, satisfactory, acceptable, passable, reasonable, respectable, decent, not bad, all right, pretty good, average, middling, mediocre, tolerable, so-so *(informal)*.
**5** *(n) We went on lots of rides at the fair.* See **funfair**.
**6** *(n) The school fair was a success.* fête, bazaar, sale, gala, carnival, festival.
**7** *(n) Our village is putting on a craft fair.* exhibition, show, display, exhibit.

## fairly see **quite** 1.

## fairy
*(n)* pixie, elf, sprite, imp, brownie, leprechaun. ❖ *Also see* **fantasy words**.

## faithful
**1** *(adj) A faithful friend.* loyal, devoted, true, reliable, dependable, trustworthy, trusty, constant, staunch, unwavering.
OPPOSITES: disloyal, faithless.
**2** *(adj) Is this a faithful account of the accident?* See **true** 2.

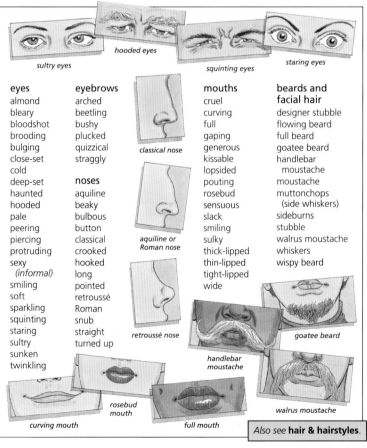

sultry eyes

hooded eyes

squinting eyes

staring eyes

classical nose

aquiline or Roman nose

retroussé nose

goatee beard

handlebar moustache

rosebud mouth

curving mouth

full mouth

walrus moustache

| eyes | eyebrows | mouths | beards and facial hair |
|---|---|---|---|
| almond | arched | cruel | designer stubble |
| bleary | beetling | curving | flowing beard |
| bloodshot | bushy | full | full beard |
| brooding | plucked | gaping | goatee beard |
| bulging | quizzical | generous | handlebar |
| close-set | straggly | kissable |   moustache |
| cold | | lopsided | moustache |
| deep-set | **noses** | pouting | muttonchops |
| haunted | aquiline | rosebud |   (side whiskers) |
| hooded | beaky | sensuous | sideburns |
| pale | bulbous | slack | stubble |
| peering | button | smiling | walrus moustache |
| piercing | classical | sulky | whiskers |
| protruding | crooked | thick-lipped | wispy beard |
| sexy | hooked | thin-lipped | |
|   (informal) | long | tight-lipped | |
| smiling | pointed | wide | |
| soft | retroussé | | |
| sparkling | Roman | | |
| squinting | snub | | |
| staring | straight | | |
| sultry | turned up | | |
| sunken | | | |
| twinkling | | | |

*Also see* **hair & hairstyles**.

# fake

**fake**
1 (n) *This painting is a fake.* copy, forgery, imitation, reproduction, sham, counterfeit. OPPOSITE: original.
2 (n) *That man is a fake.* impostor, fraud (informal), phoney (informal), charlatan.
3 (adj) *Dodgy Dave deals in fake money.* counterfeit, forged, false, bogus, sham, phoney (informal), imitation.
OPPOSITES: genuine, authentic.
4 (v) *Carol tried to fake an attack of flu.* feign, put on, sham, simulate, counterfeit.

**fall**
1 (v) *Be careful you don't fall.* trip, slip, fall over, trip over, overbalance, stumble, go head over heels, come a cropper (informal), tumble, collapse, fall in a heap.
2 (v) *The plane began to fall.* See **drop** 2.
3 (v) *Watch the leaves fall to the ground.* drift, float, waft, flutter, swirl, tumble.
4 (v) *The flood water started to fall.* sink, subside, recede, ebb, abate, lower.
OPPOSITE: rise.
5 (v) *Pupil numbers are expected to fall.* See **decrease** 2.
6 (n) *Nat had a bad fall.* tumble, spill.
7 (n) *There has been a fall in the number of crimes* See **decrease** 1.
8 (n) *We're studying the fall of the Roman Empire.* See **collapse** 3.

**fall apart** see **disintegrate** 2.

**fall asleep**
(v) *Gran tends to fall asleep in front of the TV.* go to sleep, doze off, nod off (informal), drop off (informal).
OPPOSITE: wake up.

**fall in love with**
(phrase) *Could you ever fall in love with me?* fall for, become fond of, lose your heart to, take a fancy to, become infatuated with, be smitten by, be bowled over by (informal), become attached to.

**fall out** (informal) see **argue** 1.

**fall over** see **fall** 1.

**fall through** see **fail** 2.

**false**
1 (adj) *It's false to say that pigs can fly.* incorrect, untrue, wrong, inaccurate, mistaken, erroneous, misleading.
OPPOSITES: true, correct.
2 (adj) *Dodgy Dave has a false passport.* See **fake** 3.
3 (adj) *Burglar Beryl uses a false name.* made-up, assumed, fictitious, invented, phoney (informal), spurious, unreal.
OPPOSITES: real, genuine.

**familiar**
1 (adj) *That's a familiar sight.* well-known, common, recognizable, everyday, normal, commonplace, routine, frequent, ordinary.
OPPOSITES: unfamiliar, strange.
2 **familiar with** (adj) *Are you familiar with the rules of football?* acquainted with, knowledgeable about, conversant with, well up on, versed in, informed about.

**family**
1 (n) *Dad stayed at home to look after the family.* children (plural), offspring, brood.
2 (n) *When did you last see your family?* relatives (plural), relations (plural), nearest and dearest, people (plural), flesh and blood, kin, kith and kin.
3 (n) *Hugh comes from a noble family.* dynasty, clan, line, tribe, ancestors (plural).

**famous**
(adj) *A famous musician.* well-known, world-famous, prominent, renowned, celebrated, legendary, notable, eminent, distinguished, leading, illustrious.
OPPOSITES: unknown, obscure.

**fan**
1 (n) *Hanif is a computer fan.* fanatic, addict, enthusiast, buff (informal), freak (informal), fiend (informal), nut (slang).
2 (n) *Maisie is a fan of Famous Fred.* supporter, admirer, follower, groupie (slang), devotee.

**fanatical**
1 (adj) *Sonia is a fanatical football supporter.* See **enthusiastic** 1.
2 (adj) *Dan holds fanatical views.* extreme, irrational, extremist, dogmatic, obsessive, radical, militant, bigoted, narrow-minded.

**fancy**
1 (adj) *A fancy vase.* See **decorative**.
2 (v) *I fancy a night out.* feel like, would like, could do with, feel the need for, want, long for, hanker after, yearn for.
3 (v) (informal) *Mel will really fancy you in that shirt.* go for, fall for, like the look of, be attracted by, take to, take a liking to, be captivated by, be crazy about (informal), desire, lust after.

**fantastic**
1 (adj) *I saw a fantastic creature with two heads.* strange, peculiar, weird, odd, grotesque, outlandish, freakish, exotic, fabulous, fantastical, fairy-tale.
2 (adj) (informal) *I've put a fantastic amount of work into this project.* huge, enormous, massive, great, tremendous, terrific, overwhelming.
3 (adj) (informal) *I had a fantastic time.* great, wonderful, brilliant, excellent, terrific (informal), marvellous, amazing (informal), incredible (informal), fabulous (informal), superb, tremendous (informal), smashing (informal), sensational (informal), mega (slang), wicked (slang).
OPPOSITES: awful, terrible.

**fantasy**
1 (n) *I love reading tales of fantasy.* make-believe, imagination, invention, fiction.
2 (n) *It's just a fantasy; it isn't real.* dream, daydream, flight of fancy, figment of the imagination, illusion, hallucination, vision, delusion, apparition, invention, fabrication.
3 (adj) *Miranda lives in a fantasy world.* dream, imaginary, make-believe, pretend, unreal, fairy-tale.

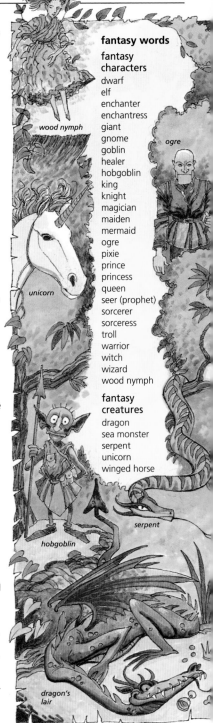

wood nymph

ogre

unicorn

hobgoblin

serpent

dragon's lair

**fantasy words**

fantasy characters
dwarf
elf
enchanter
enchantress
giant
gnome
goblin
healer
hobgoblin
king
knight
magician
maiden
mermaid
ogre
pixie
prince
princess
queen
seer (prophet)
sorcerer
sorceress
troll
warrior
witch
wizard
wood nymph

fantasy creatures
dragon
sea monster
serpent
unicorn
winged horse

## ENCHANTED FOREST

winged horse

sorcerer's castle

**fantasy characters can be...**
beautiful
bewitching
cruel
cunning
dazzling
enchanting
evil
fantastical
frightening
incredible
invisible
magical
malevolent
menacing
mesmerizing
monstrous
terrifying
unearthly
wonderful

**sorcerers can...**
bewitch
cast spells
change shape
enchant
enslave
entice
imprison
vanish

**sorcerers use...**
charms
curses
elixir
 (magic potion)
enchantment
incantations
 (magic spells)
magic ring
magic staff
sleeping potion
sorcery
spells
sword
talisman
 (lucky charm)
thunderbolt
wand

**in the forest**
creeper
dragon's lair
enchanted river
forest floor
glade (clearing)
magic stream
moss
path
poisoned pool
swamp
trailing ivy
undergrowth
vanishing lake
waterfall

**the forest is...**
ancient
bewitched
dank
dark
dense
gloomy
hushed
impenetrable
magical
misty
mysterious
shadowy
silent
strange
uninhabited

**the trees are...**
alive
decaying
gnarled
hostile
knotted
menacing
tangled
threatening
towering
twisted
watchful
wizened

waterfall

elf

sorcerer

poisoned pool

troll

magic staff

**heroes and heroines must...**
accomplish a task
do battle
encounter danger
escape
go on a quest
outwit sorcerers
overcome evil
pursue
rescue
search
solve riddles
vanquish the enemy
withstand ordeals

**fantasy clues**
dream
inscription
legend
prophecy
revelation
riddle
runes
 (ancient
 writing)
sign
symbol
vision

## SORCERER'S CASTLE

**in the castle**
battlements
dungeon
gatehouse
labyrinth
 (network of
 tunnels)
library
maze
moat
parapet
secret passage
spiral staircase
subterranean
 chamber
throne room
tower
treasure chamber
tunnel
turret
winding corridors

**the castle is...**
cloaked in mist
eerie
enchanted
forbidding
hidden
inaccessible
lonely
magnificent
menacing
mysterious
ominous

talisman

sword

runes

pixie

Lizard Blood

Elixir of eternal life

magic potions

**far**
(adv) Have you travelled far? a long way, a great distance, a good way, miles.

**faraway** see **distant**.

**far-fetched** see **incredible 1**.

**farm**
(n) TYPES OF FARM: arable farm, croft (Scotland), dairy farm, fish farm, fruit farm, hill farm, hop garden, livestock farm, market garden, organic farm, pig farm, plantation (tropical countries), poultry farm, ranch (North America), sheep station (Australia, New Zealand), smallholding, stud farm (horse-breeding farm), vineyard.

**farming**
(n) agriculture.

**fascinate**
(v) This film will fascinate you. intrigue, enthral, engross, hold you spellbound, mesmerize, transfix, rivet, entrance, captivate, bewitch, tantalize.

**fascinating**
(adj) A fascinating story. intriguing, enthralling, compelling, gripping, riveting, engrossing, absorbing, spellbinding, mesmerizing, captivating, tantalizing.

**fashion**
1 (n) These new jeans are the latest fashion. style, trend, thing, look, cut, craze, fad, vogue, rage.
2 (n) Jake is interested in fashion. clothes (plural), clothes design, the rag trade (informal), the clothing industry, couture.

**fashionable**
(adj) Minty always wears fashionable clothes. the latest, up-to-date, trendy (informal), stylish, chic, smart, up-to-the-minute, modern, in, happening (informal), cool (informal), hip (slang).
OPPOSITES: unfashionable, frumpy.

**fast**
1 (adj) We had a fast tour of the castle. quick, rapid, swift, brisk, speedy, hasty, hurried, flying, breakneck.
OPPOSITES: slow, leisurely.
2 (adj) Flash Frank drives a fast car. speedy, nippy (informal), express (train), high-speed (train), supersonic (plane).
OPPOSITE: slow.
3 (adv) Rory finished his homework fast. quickly, rapidly, in no time, swiftly, speedily, hurriedly, hastily, in a flash, like a shot (informal), posthaste, pdq (slang).

**fasten**
1 (v) Fasten your bike to the railings. secure, attach, chain, lock, padlock, bolt, tie, lash, fix, clamp, screw.
OPPOSITES: unfasten, detach.
2 (v) Fasten these papers together. attach, secure, clip, clasp, staple, pin, tack, tie, bind, tape, fix, stick, paste.
OPPOSITES: unfasten, detach.
3 (v) Phil bent down to fasten his shoe. do up, tie, lace, knot, buckle, strap.
OPPOSITE: undo.

4 (v) My jeans won't fasten. close, button, zip up, meet.

**fat**
1 (adj) A fat man. overweight, obese, flabby, stout, large, corpulent, paunchy, portly, plump, podgy, pudgy, chubby, tubby, potbellied, beefy (informal).
OPPOSITE: thin.
2 (adj) A fat book. thick, weighty, bulky.
OPPOSITE: slim.

**fatal**
1 (adj) A fatal disease. deadly, lethal, terminal, killer, incurable, inoperable, malignant, mortal (wound).
OPPOSITES: harmless, minor.
2 (adj) The pilot made a fatal mistake. See **disastrous**.

**fate**
1 (n) Fate brought us together. destiny, providence, the stars (plural), fortune.
2 (n) Sir Lancelittle accepted his fate. destiny, doom, lot, future, end.

**father**
(n) dad (informal), daddy (informal), pop (informal), pa (informal), papa (informal), old man (informal), old boy (informal).

**fatty**
(adj) Chips are a fatty food. greasy, oily.

**fault**
1 (n) There's a fault in this computer program. flaw, defect, bug (informal), malfunction, mistake, error, inaccuracy, weakness, failing, shortcoming, snag.
2 (n) It's all my fault. responsibility.

**faulty**
(adj) Our new toaster is faulty. broken, not working, defective, out of order, inoperative, on the blink (informal), damaged, unusable, useless.

**favourite**
1 (adj) Who is your favourite singer? preferred, best-loved, most-liked, ideal.
2 (n) Benji is Mrs Badger's favourite. pet, darling, blue-eyed boy (informal).

**fear**
1 (n) Sir Lancelittle shrank back in fear. terror, dread, horror, fright, panic, trepidation, alarm, dismay, consternation, fear and trembling, awe.
2 (n) Paul has a fear of heights. horror, dread, terror, phobia about, thing about (informal), hang-up about (informal).
3 (n) My greatest fear is that I might fail. worry, concern, anxiety, doubt, suspicion.
4 (v) There's no need to fear going to the dentist. See **dread 1**.

**fearless** see **brave**.

**feast**
(n) banquet, dinner, slap-up meal (informal), spread (informal), nosh-up (slang), blowout (slang).

**feat**
(n) Crossing the rapids was an amazing feat. achievement, exploit, deed, act, stunt, accomplishment, performance.

**feathers**
(plural n) Birds' feathers. plumage, down.

**feathery**
(adj) The clouds looked feathery. wispy, fluffy, fleecy, downy.

**feature**
1 (n) Which feature of this book do you like best? aspect, detail, facet, side, characteristic, quality, attribute, point.
2 (n) Amit wrote a feature for the school magazine. See **article 1**.
3 (v) The film will feature an unknown actress. star, present, highlight, turn the spotlight on, give prominence to, promote.
4 features (plural n) Can you describe Beryl's features? See **face 1**.

**fed up with**
(adj) (informal) I'm fed up with your constant complaining. tired of, sick of (informal), sick and tired of (informal), weary of, bored with, browned off with (informal), cheesed off with (slang), hacked off with (slang), irritated by, irked by.

**feeble**
1 (adj) Hattie felt feeble after her illness. See **weak 1**.
2 (adj) Don't be so feeble! See **weak 3**.
3 (adj) That's a feeble excuse. weak, poor, lame, flimsy, unconvincing, implausible, pathetic, inadequate.
OPPOSITE: convincing.

**feed**
(v) It costs a lot to feed a family of four. provide for, cater for, give food to, nourish, sustain.

**feel**
1 (v) Feel the kitten's fur! touch, stroke, run your hands over, fondle, caress, handle, finger, paw (informal).
2 (v) You won't feel any pain. sense, be aware of, be conscious of, notice, perceive, experience, suffer, go through, undergo.
3 (v) Do my hands feel cold? seem, appear, strike you as.
4 (v) Dom tried to feel for the light switch. fumble, grope, feel around, explore.
5 (v) What do you feel about fox-hunting? See **think 1**.
6 feel like (v) I feel like a night out. See **fancy 2**.

**feeling**
1 (n) Veronica lost all feeling in her fingers. sensation, sense of touch, sensitivity, awareness.
2 (n) I have a feeling I've been here before. idea, funny feeling, hunch, notion, gut feeling (informal), suspicion, sneaking suspicion, inkling, sense, impression.
3 (n) Celia spoke with great feeling. emotion, passion, fervour, warmth, enthusiasm, sentiment, affection.
4 (n) There's a strange feeling in this room. See **atmosphere 2**.
5 feelings (plural n) It hurts my feelings when people laugh at me. self-esteem, ego, sensibilities (plural).

## feelings

| happy | sad | excited | annoyed | upset | surprised | worried |
|---|---|---|---|---|---|---|
| blissful | blue | eager | cross | dismayed | amazed | agitated |
| cheerful | dejected | enthusiastic | disgruntled | distraught | astonished | anxious |
| chirpy *(informal)* | depressed | feverish | exasperated | distressed | astounded | apprehensive |
| contented | despairing | frenzied | indignant | disturbed | dumbfounded | concerned |
| delighted | despondent | high *(informal)* | irritated | grieved | dumbstruck | distracted |
| ecstatic | doleful | hyper *(informal)* | miffed *(informal)* | hurt | flabbergasted | distracted |
| elated | down | hysterical | needled | pained | *(informal)* | frantic |
| euphoric | forlorn | overwrought | *(informal)* | shaken | gobsmacked | fretful |
| glad | gloomy | restless | vexed | shattered | *(slang)* | nervous |
| gleeful | glum | thrilled | | | incredulous | on edge |
| jolly | grief-stricken | worked up | **angry** | **scared** | open-mouthed | perturbed |
| joyful | heartbroken | | enraged | afraid | shocked | tense |
| jubilant | low | **bored** | fuming | alarmed | speechless | troubled |
| light-hearted | melancholy | apathetic | furious | frightened | staggered | uneasy |
| optimistic | miserable | fed up | incensed | horrified | startled | |
| overjoyed | mournful | *(informal)* | infuriated | panicky | stunned | **confused** |
| perky | sorrowful | indifferent | irate | panic-stricken | stupefied | baffled |
| pleased | tearful | jaded | livid | petrified | taken aback | bewildered |
| rapturous | unhappy | listless | outraged | terrified | thunderstruck | dazed |
| thrilled | wistful | weary | seething | | | disorientated |
| | | | | | | fazed |
| | | | | | | flummoxed |
| | | | | | | flustered |
| | | | | | | muddled |
| | | | | | | mystified |
| | | | | | | nonplussed |
| | | | | | | perplexed |
| | | | | | | puzzled |

*listless* · *petrified*

*jubilant* · *despondent* · *livid* · *perplexed*

---

**ferocious** *see* **fierce** 1, 2.

**fertile**
*(adj) A fertile field.* fruitful, productive, rich, lush, well-manured, flourishing.
OPPOSITE: barren.

**festival**
*(n) Our town is planning a festival to mark the end of the war.* celebration, carnival, festivities *(plural)*, jamboree, fête, gala day, feast, holiday, jubilee, commemoration.

**fetch**
1 *(v) Would you fetch Dad's suit from the cleaner's?* go and get, get, collect, pick up, call for, go for, bring, carry, retrieve.
2 *(v) This painting will fetch a fortune.* sell for, go for, bring in, make, yield, earn.

**feud** *see* **quarrel** 3.

**feverish**
1 *(adj) You seem feverish; have you got a temperature?* hot, flushed, fevered, burning, shivery, trembling.
2 *(adj) The classroom was filled with feverish activity.* frenzied, frenetic, frantic, hectic, excited, agitated, restless.

**few**
*(adj) Few people have walked on the moon.* not many, hardly any, scarcely any, one or two, a handful of, a small number of, a couple of *(informal)*.
OPPOSITES: many, lots of.

**fiasco** *see* **failure** 2.

**fictional** *see* **imaginary** 1.

**fiddle with**
*(v) Don't fiddle with your pencil case!* fidget with, play with, toy with, finger, tinker with, tamper with, interfere with.

**fidget**
*(v) Sit still and don't fidget!* wriggle, squirm, jiggle, fiddle, jerk about, twitch, jitter *(informal)*, mess about.

**fidgety**
*(adj) Waiting makes me fidgety.* restless, nervous, nervy, on edge, edgy, jumpy, twitchy, jittery *(informal)*, uneasy, impatient, agitated, restive.

**field**
1 *(n) The cows are grazing in the field.* meadow, pasture, paddock, enclosure.
2 *(n) The players gathered on the sports field.* pitch, playing field, ground, arena.
3 *(n) Professor Peabody is an expert in the field of physics.* area, subject, sphere, discipline, department, domain.

**fierce**
1 *(adj) A fierce tiger.* ferocious, vicious, savage, wild, dangerous, fearsome, angry.
OPPOSITES: docile, tame.
2 *(adj) A fierce warrior.* ferocious, brutal, savage, violent, fearsome, cruel, ruthless, grim, bloodthirsty, menacing, threatening, barbaric, murderous, tigerish, wolfish.
OPPOSITES: gentle, kind.

3 *(adj) A fierce storm. See* **violent** 3.
4 *(adj) Fierce competition.* strong, intense, keen, cutthroat, relentless, furious.

**fiery**
1 *(adj) Fiery coals. See* **burning** 1.
2 *(adj) A fiery personality.* hot-headed, passionate, impetuous, excitable, irritable, irascible, peppery, choleric, violent.
OPPOSITES: even-tempered, docile.

**fight**
1 *(v) The two armies prepared to fight.* do battle, take up arms, go to war, wage war, attack, mount an attack, cross swords, engage in hostilities, clash, struggle.
2 *(v) The boys began to fight in the playground.* brawl, scuffle, tussle, scrap *(informal)*, grapple, spar, wrestle, box.
3 *(v) We fight all the time. See* **argue** 1.
4 *(v) We will fight the decision to close our school.* oppose, contest, resist, campaign against, protest against, take a stand against, dispute, defy, object to.
5 *(n) Many soldiers were wounded in the fight.* conflict, battle, skirmish, encounter, confrontation, struggle, clash, combat, action, raid, war, hostilities *(plural)*.
6 *(n) There was a fight in the playground.* brawl, scuffle, tussle, punch-up *(informal)*, scrap *(informal)*, bust-up *(informal)*, set-to *(informal)*, free-for-all *(informal)*, riot.
7 *(n) I've had a fight with my sister. See* **argument** 1.

# fight back

**fight back**
(v) *Should you fight back if someone punches you?* defend yourself, hit back, put up a fight, retaliate, give tit for tat.

**figure**
1 (n) *Our phone number starts with the figure 8.* number, digit, numeral, symbol.
2 (n) *Sasha has a slim figure.* build, frame, shape, physique, body.
3 (n) *I saw a dim figure in the mist.* shape, shadow, form, outline, silhouette.
4 (n) *Queen Victoria is a famous historical figure.* personality, character, person, personage, celebrity.

**figure out**
1 (v) (informal) *Can you figure out the cost?* work out, calculate, count up, add up, tot up, compute, reckon up.
2 (v) (informal) *I can't figure out these instructions.* See **understand** 2.

**fill**
1 (v) *Don't fill your bag with rubbish.* pack, stuff, cram, load, overload.
OPPOSITE: empty.
2 (v) *Can I fill your glass?* fill up, fill to the brim, replenish, refill, top up (informal).
OPPOSITES: empty, drain.
3 (v) *Fill the hole with earth.* close up, block up, bung up, plug, stop up, seal.
4 (v) *The scent of roses seemed to fill the air.* pervade, permeate, suffuse, saturate.

**fill in**
1 (v) *Please fill in this questionnaire.* complete, answer, fill out.
2 **fill in for** (v) *Can you fill in for James while he's ill?* See **stand in for**.
3 **fill you in on** (phrase) (informal) *Can I fill you in on what's happened?* update you on, bring you up to date with, give you the facts about, brief you about, inform you about, acquaint you with.

**filling**
(adj) *A filling meal.* satisfying, substantial, hearty, ample, heavy, stodgy, square.

**film**
1 (v) *A camera crew are going to film the wedding.* record on film, capture on film, photograph, take pictures of, make a film of, video, televise, shoot.
2 (n) *This book has been made into a film.* motion picture, movie (informal), picture.
TYPES OF FILM: action film, adventure film, animated film, black-and-white film, blockbuster, cartoon, comedy, detective film, disaster film, drama, epic, fantasy film, feature film, gangster film, horror film, martial arts film, musical, romantic film, sci-fi (science fiction) film, silent film, spoof (informal), 3-D film, thriller, war film, weepy (informal), Western. ❖ *Also see* **television & film**.
3 (n) *A film of dust.* See **layer** 1.

**filthy** see **dirty** 1, 2.

**final**
1 (adj) *The final episode.* See **last** 1.

2 (adj) *The referee's decision is final.* absolute, conclusive, decisive, indisputable, unalterable, irrevocable, definitive, definite.

**finally**
1 (adv) *Finally, the bus arrived.* eventually, at last, at long last, at length, at the last minute, in the end, ultimately.
2 (adv) *Finally, I'd like to thank you all for coming.* lastly, in conclusion, to conclude, to sum up, in summary.

**find**
1 (v) *Pirate Peg was lucky to find the treasure.* discover, come across, stumble upon, hit upon, spot, catch sight of, locate, uncover, unearth, turn up, chance upon.
2 (v) *Did you manage to find your pencil case?* locate, track down, trace, get back, recover, retrieve, regain.
OPPOSITES: lose, mislay.

**find out** see **discover** 1, 3.

**fine**
1 (adj) *That's a fine painting.* great, magnificent, splendid, superb, excellent, first-class, exceptional, outstanding, exquisite, beautiful, admirable, masterly, superior.
OPPOSITES: poor, second-rate.
2 (adj) *It's fine for you to come on Saturday.* all right, O.K. (informal), convenient, acceptable, satisfactory.
3 (adj) *The weather will be fine tomorrow.* dry, bright, sunny, fair, pleasant, clear, cloudless, clement.
OPPOSITES: bad, unpleasant.
4 (adj) *A fine crack appeared in the wall.* thin, narrow, hairline, threadlike.
OPPOSITES: wide, thick.
5 (adj) *The bride wore a veil of fine silk.* delicate, sheer, thin, lightweight, light, flimsy, floaty, translucent, transparent, gauzy, gossamer, chiffony, filmy, cobwebby, diaphanous.
OPPOSITES: heavy, thick.
6 (adj) *Granny collects fine china.* dainty, delicate, exquisite, elegant, fragile.
OPPOSITE: coarse.
7 (n) *Mum had to pay a fine for speeding.* penalty, charge.

**finish**
1 (v) *You must finish your project today.* complete, finalize, conclude, get done, round off, put the finishing touches to, bring to a close, end, wind up, wrap up (informal), sew up (informal).
OPPOSITES: start, begin.
2 (v) *When does school finish for the summer?* See **end** 6.
3 (v) *How quickly can you finish your dinner?* eat up, get through, polish off (informal), dispose of, consume, devour.
4 (n) *We waited to see the finish of the match.* See **end** 1.

**finished**
(adj) *I'm glad that job is finally finished.* completed, done, accomplished, wrapped up (informal), sewn up (informal), ended, over and done with, in the past.

**fire**
1 (n) *The fire could be seen for miles around.* blaze, flames (plural), inferno, conflagration.
2 (n) *The troops came under heavy fire.* gunfire, shelling, bombardment, sniping.
3 (v) *Watch the soldiers fire the rocket.* launch, let off, set off, trigger, discharge.
4 (v) (informal) *I hope the boss doesn't fire you.* See **dismiss** 1.
5 **on fire** (phrase) *Look! The forest is on fire!* blazing, burning, in flames, flaming, alight, ablaze, aflame.

## fire words

| fires... | flames... | you hear... |
|---|---|---|
| blaze | dance | crack |
| burn | dart | crackle |
| consume | flash | hiss |
| damage | flare | murmur |
| destroy | flicker | pop |
| devastate | gleam | roar |
| devour | glitter | rustle |
| dwindle | glow | snap |
| engulf | leap | whisper |
| glow | lick | |
| grow | play | **after the fire you see...** |
| ignite | shimmer | |
| kindle | | |
| rage | **smoke...** | ashes |
| rampage | belches | blackened walls |
| ravage | billows | blistered paint |
| raze to the ground | blinds | buckled iron |
| scorch | chokes | charred wood |
| singe | coils | debris |
| smoke | curls | embers |
| smoulder | envelops | gutted buildings |
| sweep | obscures | rubble |
| | spirals | scorched earth |
| | suffocates | smouldering ruins |
| | swirls | |
| | twists | |
| | wreathes | |
| **smoke smells...** | | |
| acrid | | |
| bitter | | |
| pungent | | |
| sooty | | |

## fireworks

**types of firework**

banger
cascade
Catherine wheel
firecracker
fountain
rocket
Roman candle
shooting star
sparkler

**fireworks...**

blaze
burst
cascade
dazzle
explode
fizzle out
flare
flash
flicker
glitter
rocket

shimmer
shoot
shower
sink
soar
sparkle
spin
spiral
spray
twirl
zoom

**fireworks can be...**

colourful
dazzling
deafening
ear-splitting
magical
multicoloured
spectacular
stunning (informal)

**you hear...**

bang
crack
crackle
fizz
hiss
pop
scream
screech
splutter
squeal
thud
wail
whine
whistle
whiz
whoosh

## firm

1 (adj) The ground felt firm underfoot. hard, solid, unyielding, resistant, rigid, compacted, compressed, frozen, stony.
OPPOSITE: soft.
2 (adj) Make sure the ladder is firm. steady, stable, secure, fixed, anchored, fastened, immovable, unshakable.
OPPOSITES: unsteady, wobbly.
3 (adj) Do you have any firm plans for the future? definite, fixed, settled, established, unalterable, unchangeable, inflexible.
OPPOSITES: vague, flexible.
4 (adj) Ed and I are firm friends. See **loyal**.
5 (adj) Jess is firm in her ideas about animal rights. adamant, resolute, inflexible, unbending, obstinate, unshakable, unfaltering, unwavering, unswerving.
OPPOSITES: wavering, irresolute.
6 (n) Mum works for a big electronics firm. company, business, organization, concern, corporation, conglomerate, multinational, outfit (informal).

## first

1 (adj) The first computers seem very basic now. earliest, original, initial, primitive.
OPPOSITE: latest.
2 (adj) Read the first chapter for homework. opening, introductory, initial.
OPPOSITES: last, closing.
3 (adj) United play in the first division. top, premier, highest, foremost, leading, main.
OPPOSITES: lowest, bottom.
4 (adj) Rudi has mastered the first steps in ballet. basic, elementary, rudimentary, primary, fundamental, key, cardinal.
5 (adv) First, think of a title for your story. firstly, first of all, to start with, to begin with, before anything else, in the first place, at the outset, beforehand.
OPPOSITES: last, lastly.

## fish

(n) TYPES OF FISH: angelfish, brill, carp, catfish, clown fish, cod, eel, flounder, flying fish, goldfish, guppy, haddock, hake, halibut, herring, lamprey, mackerel, minnow, mullet, perch, pike, pilchard, piranha, plaice, ray, roach, salmon, sardine, sea horse, shark, skate, sole, sprat, stickleback, sturgeon, swordfish, tiddler (informal), trout, tuna, whitebait, whiting.

## fishy (informal) see **suspicious** 2.

## fit

1 (v) Do you think these jeans will fit? be the right size, be big enough, be small enough, be the right shape.
2 (v) Fit the parts of the puzzle together. piece, put, join, connect, fix, place, lay, position, arrange.
3 (v) The punishment should fit the crime. suit, correspond to, match, be fitting for.
4 (adj) Swimming keeps me fit. healthy, in shape, in good shape, in good condition, in trim, toned up, strong, in good health.
OPPOSITES: unfit, out of shape.
5 (adj) This video isn't fit for children. See **suitable** 1.
6 (n) Fido had a fit and died. seizure, convulsion, attack, turn (informal).
7 (n) Den had a fit of coughing. attack, bout, spell, outbreak, outburst.

## fix

1 (v) I need to fix my bike. See **repair** 1.
2 (v) Did you fix a date for the party? agree on, decide on, set, settle, arrange, arrive at, establish, name, specify.
3 (v) Fix the pieces together. attach, join, link, fasten, connect, secure, stick, glue, paste, pin, nail, screw, bolt, tie, cement.
4 (v) I must fix my hair. tidy, neaten, arrange, see to, sort out, put in order.

5 (v) (informal) The goalie tried to fix the result of the match. rig, fiddle (informal), manipulate, influence, set up (informal).

## fixed

1 (adj) We have our meals at fixed times. See **set** 7.
2 (adj) Ed has very fixed views. See **set** 8.
3 (adj) Is my bike fixed yet? mended, repaired, sorted, in working order, going.

## fizzy

(adj) A fizzy drink. sparkling, bubbly, gassy, carbonated, effervescent, frothy, foaming.
OPPOSITES: still, flat.

## flabby

(adj) Flabby thighs. flaccid, slack, fleshy, sagging, soft, unfirm, out of shape.

## flag

(n) banner, standard, pennant, ensign.

## flake

1 (n) A flake of paint peeled off. chip, sliver, shaving, peeling, wafer, fragment.
2 (v) This paint is beginning to flake. peel, peel off, blister, chip, fall off.

## flame

(n) A flame of fire. tongue, flicker, blaze.

## flaming see **burning** 1.

## flap

1 (v) Watch the bird flap its wings. beat, flutter, flail, thrash, waggle, shake.
2 (v) The sail began to flap in the breeze. flutter, sway, wave, swish, swing, thrash about, flail about, whip around.
3 (n) (informal) The chef was in a flap. panic, state (informal), tizzy (informal), fluster, flutter, stew (informal), sweat (informal), dither.

## flash

1 (n) A flash of light lit up the sky. blaze, flare, burst, streak, shaft, ray, glare, glint, gleam, flicker, sparkle, shimmer, glimmer.
2 (n) Mehmet had a flash of inspiration. burst, rush, surge, touch, sudden show.
3 (v) I saw a light flash on the horizon. flicker, flare, wink, blink, blaze, beam, gleam, glint, sparkle, twinkle, shimmer.
4 (v) I saw a car flash past. See **shoot** 3.

## flashy see **vulgar** 2.

## flat

1 (adj) Find a flat surface to work on. level, horizontal, even, smooth.
OPPOSITES: uneven, sloping, vertical.
2 (adj) Oz lay flat on the ground. stretched out, full length, prostrate, outstretched, prone, spread-eagled, reclining.
3 (adj) You can't cycle with a flat tyre. deflated, burst, punctured, blown out.
4 (adj) After the show, the actors felt flat. deflated, let down, low, down, dejected, despondent, depressed, dispirited.
OPPOSITES: high (informal), elated.
5 (adj) Cyril has a flat voice. monotonous, boring, lifeless, unvarying, dull, lacklustre.
6 (n) We live in a flat on the fifth floor. apartment, bedsit, studio, penthouse, set of rooms, rooms (plural), pad (slang).

# **f**latten

**flatten**
1 *(v) Please flatten this cloth.* smooth out, make flat, level, iron out, even out, press.
2 *(v) Someone should flatten those tower blocks. See* **demolish**.
3 *(v) Don't flatten the roses.* trample, squash, crush, compress, press down.

**flatter**
1 *(v) I always flatter you when I want something.* compliment, butter you up, praise, cajole, soft-soap *(informal),* sweet-talk *(informal),* play up to, suck up to *(informal),* toady to, fawn on.
2 *(v) Those jeans really flatter your figure.* suit, set off, enhance, do something for, show to advantage.

**flavour**
1 *(v) You need to flavour this soup.* season, spice, ginger up, pep up.
2 *(n) This soup needs more flavour.* taste, zest, zing *(informal),* seasoning, flavouring, savour, relish, piquancy.

**flawless** *see* **perfect** 1, 2.

**fleck** *see* **speck** 1.

**flexible**
1 *(adj) This rod is quite flexible.* pliable, bendy, supple, springy, pliant.
OPPOSITE: rigid.
2 *(adj) Our plans must be flexible.* open, fluid, adaptable, adjustable, elastic.
OPPOSITES: fixed, settled.
3 *(adj) Karen won't mind; she's very flexible.* adaptable, accommodating, amenable, open-minded, compliant.
OPPOSITE: inflexible.

**flicker**
*(v) The flame began to flicker.* blink, gutter, tremble, quiver, waver, glimmer, shimmer, flutter, glitter, sparkle, flash.

**flimsy**
1 *(adj) A flimsy chair.* weak, insubstantial, fragile, rickety, shaky, tottery, jerry-built.
OPPOSITES: sturdy, strong.
2 *(adj) Flimsy fabric. See* **fine** 5.
3 *(adj) A flimsy excuse. See* **feeble** 3.

**flinch**
*(v) I always flinch at the sight of a needle.* cringe, wince, draw back, recoil, cower, quail, shrink, baulk, shy away, start, jump.

**fling** *see* **throw** 1.

**flippant**
*(adj) Don't make flippant remarks.* cheeky, impertinent, glib, pert, offhand, frivolous, flip *(informal),* disrespectful, irreverent.
OPPOSITES: serious, respectful.

**flirt with**
*(v) Did Lydia flirt with you at the party?* tease, chat you up *(informal),* make eyes at, lead you on, make advances to, ogle.

**float**
1 *(v) The bottle started to float down the stream.* sail, drift, glide, slip, bob, swim.
2 *(v) I watched the balloon float through the air.* waft, sail, glide, drift, hover.

**flood**
1 *(v) I hope the river doesn't flood.* overflow, burst its banks, brim over.
2 *(v) The river may flood the valley.* engulf, swamp, submerge, drown, deluge, immerse, cover, fill.
3 *(v) I'll try not to flood you with letters.* swamp, overwhelm, inundate, deluge, shower, bog you down, snow you under.
4 *(n) Our village was cut off by the flood.* torrent, deluge, tide, flood water.
5 *(n) We received a flood of complaints.* torrent, stream, deluge, rush, mass, spate.

**floor**
*(n) Our flat is on the second floor.* storey, level, landing.

**flop**
1 *(v) Don't let your hood flop over your face.* fall, droop, hang, sag, dangle, flap, drop, collapse, slump, tumble, topple.
2 *(n) (informal) The play was a flop. See* **failure** 2.

**floppy**
*(adj) Fido has floppy ears.* droopy, sagging, dangling, limp, pendulous, flapping, soft, loose, flaccid, flabby.

**flow**
1 *(v) Watch the water flow over the rocks.* glide, stream, gush, rush, surge, pour, run, swirl, spill, cascade, sweep, course, trickle, ripple, drift, spurt, seep, ooze, leak.
2 *(v) Complaints have started to flow in.* flood, pour, stream, trickle.
3 *(n) There was a steady flow of water from the roof.* stream, cascade, flood, torrent, spurt, gush, surge, trickle, leak.

**flower**
1 *(n) What's your favourite flower?* bloom, blossom, plant.
TYPES OF FLOWER: bluebell, buttercup, carnation, chrysanthemum, cowslip, crocus, cyclamen, daffodil, dahlia, daisy, dandelion, forget-me-not, foxglove, freesia, geranium, hollyhock, hyacinth, iris, lily, lupin, marigold, nasturtium, orchid, pansy, passionflower, poppy, primrose, rose, snowdrop, sunflower, sweet pea, tulip, violet, wallflower, water lily.
2 *(v) Our tree will flower soon.* blossom, bloom, be in flower, produce flowers, burst into bloom.

**flowing**
*(adj) A flowing robe.* loose, swirling, floating, sweeping, trailing, cascading.

**fluent**
*(adj) Max is a fluent public speaker.* articulate, eloquent, polished, confident, natural, self-assured, glib, smooth-talking.
OPPOSITES: tongue-tied, hesitant.

**fluffy**
*(adj) Fluffy baby animals.* furry, fuzzy, woolly, fleecy, downy, feathery, soft.

**fluid** *see* **liquid** 1, 2.

**fluke** *see* **chance** 1, 5.

**flushed**
*(adj) You look flushed.* red, crimson, hot, red in the face, hot and bothered, feverish, flustered, burning, glowing, rosy.

**flustered**
*(adj) All this attention makes me feel flustered.* agitated, hot and bothered, disconcerted, rattled *(informal),* ruffled, confused, fazed, unnerved, upset.

**flutter** *see* **flap** 1, 2, 3.

**fly**
1 *(v) Watch those birds fly!* soar, swoop, glide, flit, hover, circle, sail, coast, flutter, take to the air, take wing, take off.
2 *(v) See how the flags fly in the breeze.* flutter, wave, flap, swirl, stream, float.
3 *(v) The time seemed to fly by.* rush, race, whiz *(informal),* zoom, hurtle, slip, roll.
4 *(v) Elliot is learning to fly a plane.* pilot, operate, control, navigate.
5 *(v) I must fly or I'll be late! See* **hurry** 1.

**foam**
1 *(n) The bowl was full of foam.* bubbles *(plural),* froth, suds *(plural),* lather, scum.
2 *(n) Fill the cushion with foam.* sponge.
3 *(v) The potion began to foam.* bubble, froth, fizz, effervesce, seethe, lather.

**foggy**
*(adj) A foggy night.* misty, smoggy, murky, hazy, cloudy, shadowy, soupy.

**fold**
1 *(v) Fold the cloth.* double over, turn over, bend, crease, pleat, tuck, gather.
2 *(n) There's a fold in this material.* pleat, gather, tuck, crease, wrinkle, crinkle.

**follow**
1 *(v) The detectives decided to follow Burglar Beryl.* pursue, go after, tail, trail, shadow, stalk, chase, track, hunt, hound.
2 *(v) Who will follow Lisa as captain?* come after, go after, succeed, take over from, take the place of, replace, supplant, supersede, step into the shoes of.
3 *(v) Follow these instructions.* obey, observe, pay attention to, comply with, be guided by, attend to, keep to, heed.
4 *(v) The lecture was hard to follow.* understand, keep up with, take in, comprehend, grasp, catch on to *(informal).*

**follower** *see* **fan** 2.

**fond**
1 *(adj) A fond mother. See* **loving**.
2 **fond of** *(adj) Efra is fond of her boyfriend.* attached to, keen on, devoted to, in love with, stuck on *(slang),* crazy about *(informal),* mad about, besotted by.
3 **fond of** *(adj) Gus is fond of sweets.* keen on, partial to, crazy about *(informal),* mad about, hooked on, addicted to.

**food**
*(n) I need food.* nourishment, sustenance, refreshment, provisions *(plural),* rations *(plural),* grub *(informal),* nosh *(informal),* tuck *(informal),* victuals *(plural),* fodder.

## food and flavours

| nice food is... | food can be... | food can feel... | food can taste... |
|---|---|---|---|
| appetizing | burnt | chewy | acid |
| delicious | charred | creamy | bitter |
| luscious | dry | crisp | bland |
| moreish *(informal)* | fatty | crumbly | fiery |
| mouthwatering | filling | crunchy | fruity |
| scrumptious *(informal)* | fresh | glutinous *(gluey)* | hot |
| tasty | healthy | gooey *(informal)* | insipid *(tasteless)* |
| yummy *(slang)* | indigestible | greasy | peppery |
| | juicy | | salty |
| **nasty food is...** | lukewarm | leathery | savoury |
| disgusting | mouldy | lumpy | sharp |
| foul | nourishing | mushy | sickly |
| inedible | piping hot | oily | sour |
| nauseating | raw | rubbery | spicy |
| revolting | rich | runny | sugary |
| unappetizing | satisfying | slimy | sweet |
| vile | scalding | sloppy | syrupy |
| yucky *(slang)* | sizzling | smooth | tangy |
| | stale | soggy | tart |
| | steaming | spongy | vinegary |
| | stodgy | squashy | |
| | succulent | squidgy | |
| | tepid | sticky | |
| | undercooked | stringy | |
| | unhealthy | tender | |
| | unsatisfying | tough | |
| | well-cooked | wobbly | |
| | wholesome | | |

*juicy grapes*

*gooey gateau*

*sticky jam tart*

*squidgy pizza*

*crisp lettuce*

*crunchy carrots*

### fool
1 *(v)* You can't fool me. See **deceive** 1.
2 *(n)* Dwayne's such a fool! See **idiot**.

### fool around
*(v) (informal)* Don't fool around in class. clown around, act the fool, mess about *(informal)*, lark about *(informal)*, muck about *(slang)*, waste time.

### foolish see **silly** 1, 2.

### forbid
*(v)* I love skating; please don't forbid it! ban, prohibit, rule out, veto, block.
OPPOSITES: allow, permit.

### forbidden
*(adj)* Smoking is forbidden. not allowed, banned, prohibited, outlawed, taboo.
OPPOSITES: permitted, allowed.

### force
1 *(v)* If you don't want to go, I won't force you. make, compel, pressurize, push, coerce, oblige, bring pressure to bear on, put the squeeze on *(informal)*, dragoon.
2 *(v)* We had to force the lock. prise open, break open, wrench open, smash.
3 *(n)* You'll need lots of force to open this door. See **strength** 1.

### foreign
1 *(adj)* Indy often travels to foreign lands. remote, distant, exotic, faraway, far-flung, unfamiliar, unknown, strange, alien.
OPPOSITE: native.
2 *(adj)* We have some foreign visitors. overseas, international.

### foresee see **predict**.

### forever see **always** 1, 2.

### forgery see **fake** 1.

### forget
1 *(v)* How could you forget my birthday? fail to remember, overlook, be oblivious to, lose track of, neglect, ignore.
OPPOSITE: remember.
2 *(v)* Try to forget this unfortunate incident. put out of your mind, pay no attention to, dismiss, discount, disregard.
OPPOSITES: remember, recall.
3 *(v)* Don't forget your lunch. go without, leave behind, fail to take, abandon.
OPPOSITE: remember.

### forgetful
*(adj)* Professor Peabody is so forgetful! absent-minded, scatterbrained, vague, abstracted, dreamy, inattentive.

### forgive
*(v)* I will forgive you for what you did. pardon, excuse, let you off, accept your apologies, exonerate, absolve.

### forgiveness
*(n)* I need your forgiveness. pardon, mercy.

### forlorn see **sad** 1.

### form
1 *(n)* What form of music do you like? kind, type, sort, style, variety, form.
2 *(n)* The enchanter took on the form of a serpent. See **shape** 3.
3 *(n)* What form are you in at school? See **class**.
4 *(n)* Please fill in this form. document, paper, sheet, questionnaire, application.
5 *(n)* I hope Linford is in good form. condition, shape, health, spirits *(plural)*.
6 *(v)* It takes centuries for stalactites to form. develop, take shape, grow, come into existence, appear, materialize.
7 *(v)* Let's form a computer club. create, establish, set up, start, found, organize.

### formal
1 *(adj)* The banquet will be a formal affair. dignified, stately, ceremonial, solemn, correct, proper, posh *(informal)*, stiff.
OPPOSITES: informal, casual.
2 *(adj)* Please wear formal clothes. smart, dressed-up *(informal)*, posh *(informal)*, proper, correct, conventional.
OPPOSITE: casual.
3 *(adj)* You'll need formal permission to emigrate. official, lawful, proper, legal.

### fortunate see **lucky** 1, 2.

### fortune
1 *(n)* Lord Lucre's fortune is phenomenal. wealth, riches *(plural)*, possessions *(plural)*, assets *(plural)*, inheritance, estate.
2 *(n)* Giles has won a fortune. huge amount, pile *(informal)*, packet *(informal)*, bundle *(informal)*, millions *(plural)*.
3 *(n)* We found the house by good fortune. See **luck** 1.

### foul
1 *(adj)* A foul heap of rubbish. filthy, squalid, disgusting, revolting, nauseating, loathsome, repulsive, rotten, putrid, stinking, vile, sordid, grotty *(slang)*.
2 *(adj)* Foul language. indecent, obscene, profane, blasphemous, filthy, offensive, smutty, lewd, crude, coarse, vulgar.
OPPOSITES: polite, decent, clean.
3 *(adj)* A foul crime. vile, horrible, monstrous, shocking, revolting, odious, sordid, despicable, contemptible, detestable, atrocious, abominable, wicked, villainous, evil, heinous, infamous.
4 *(adj)* Foul weather. rough, dirty, stormy, squally, rainy, foggy, drizzly, murky.
OPPOSITES: fair, fine.
5 *(adj)* Callum was sent off for foul play. unfair, rough, dirty, unsporting, violent, sneaky, unscrupulous, prohibited, illegal.
OPPOSITE: fair.

# fragile

**fragile**
(adj) Fragile china. delicate, breakable, brittle, thin, weak, flimsy, insubstantial, frail, dainty.
OPPOSITES: strong, durable.

**fragment** see **piece** 2, 3.

**frail**
(adj) A frail old lady. delicate, weak, feeble, infirm, unsteady, vulnerable, puny.
OPPOSITES: strong, robust.

**frank**
(adj) A frank answer. plain, straight, direct, candid, forthright, honest, truthful, blunt, no-nonsense, upfront (informal), sincere, open, outspoken, unreserved.
OPPOSITES: evasive, insincere.

**frantic**
1 (adj) You'll be frantic when you hear the news. beside yourself, at your wits' end, desperate, panic-stricken, distraught, hysterical, overwrought, worked up.
OPPOSITE: calm.
2 (adj) The classroom was filled with frantic activity. See **feverish** 2.

**fraud**
1 (n) Dodgy Dave was sentenced for fraud. swindling, cheating, deception, sharp practice, double-dealing, embezzlement, trickery, chicanery.
2 (n) (informal) That man is a fraud. impostor, phoney (informal), fake, cheat, hoaxer, con man (informal), swindler, double-dealer, charlatan, quack (doctor).

**freak**
1 (adj) Freak weather. See **unusual** 1.
2 (n) (informal) Nathan is a computer freak. See **fan** 1.

**free**
1 (adj) I'd like to go out tonight. Are you free? available, uncommitted, footloose, fancy-free, off the leash (informal), off the hook (informal), at liberty.
OPPOSITES: busy, tied up.
2 (adj) The prisoners longed to be free. released, set free, set loose, unconfined, at liberty, unrestrained, on the loose.
OPPOSITES: imprisoned, confined.
3 (adj) Is this seat free? vacant, empty, unoccupied, unused, spare, available.
OPPOSITES: occupied, reserved, engaged.
4 (adj) These tickets are free. free of charge, complimentary, cost-free, gratis, on the house.
5 (v) Let's campaign to free the hostages. See **release** 1.
6 (v) The judge decided to free Burglar Beryl. See **release** 2.
7 (v) Can you free the boot from your fishing line? untangle, untie, extricate, undo, disentangle, disengage, clear.

**freedom**
(n) Pandora's parents allow her lots of freedom. independence, liberty, autonomy, leeway, licence, latitude, personal space, privileges (plural).

**freeze**
1 (v) I think the pond will freeze tonight. ice up, ice over, go solid, harden, solidify.
2 (v) Don't go outside; you'll freeze! die of cold (informal), be chilled to the bone, perish (informal), go numb.
3 (v) "Freeze, or I'll shoot!" said Arnie. keep still, stay where you are, stand still, don't move a muscle, stand stock-still.

**freezing** see **cold** 1, 2, 3.

**frenzied** see **feverish** 2.

**frenzy**
(n) The news sent us into a frenzy. turmoil, uproar, furore, confusion, passion, rage, fury, fit, paroxysm, hysteria.

**frequent**
1 (adj) A frequent problem. persistent, recurrent, regular, repeated, continual, constant, incessant, oft-repeated.
2 (adj) A frequent sight. See **familiar** 1.

**fresh**
1 (adj) This magazine needs some fresh ideas. new, original, novel, innovative, creative, inventive, untried, unfamiliar, up-to-date, up-to-the-minute, modern.
OPPOSITES: stale, outdated.
2 (adj) You should eat lots of fresh food. natural, unprocessed, untreated, uncontaminated, uncooked, raw (fruit, vegetables), freshly picked, freshly cooked.
OPPOSITES: processed, cooked, stale.
3 (adj) Is this water fresh? pure, drinkable, unpolluted, uncontaminated, running.
OPPOSITES: polluted, salty, stagnant.
4 (adj) Start on a fresh sheet of paper. clean, new, blank, empty, unused, spare.
OPPOSITES: used, full.
5 (adj) Can you feel that fresh sea breeze? cool, refreshing, brisk, bracing, invigorating, keen, chilly, nippy.

**friend**
(n) It's great to have a friend to talk to. mate (informal), pal (informal), chum (informal), buddy (informal), companion, comrade, soul mate, bosom friend, kindred spirit, confidant (male), confidante (female), crony, ally, well-wisher.
OPPOSITE: enemy.

**friendly**
(adj) Sasha is a friendly girl. warm, outgoing, sociable, chummy (informal), matey (informal), pally (informal), companionable, hospitable, neighbourly, welcoming, open, approachable, warm-hearted, affectionate, sympathetic, kind-hearted, considerate, understanding, supportive, generous, helpful, convivial.
OPPOSITES: unfriendly, cold.

**fright**
1 (n) I shrank back in fright. See **fear** 1.
2 (n) You gave me a fright. See **scare** 3.
3 (n) (informal) What a fright you look! See **sight** 4.

**frighten** see **scare** 1, 2.

**frightened** see **scared** 1, 2.

**frightening**
(adj) What a frightening experience! scary (informal), terrifying, petrifying, spine-chilling, hair-raising, bloodcurdling, horrifying, fearsome, ghastly, creepy (informal), eerie, spooky (informal), alarming, daunting, unnerving, sinister.
OPPOSITES: comforting, reassuring.

**frilly**
(adj) A frilly dress. flouncy, ruffled, ruched, flounced, lacy, frothy, fancy.

**frisky**
(adj) A frisky puppy. lively, playful, high-spirited, sprightly, bouncy, skittish, active.

**frivolous**
(adj) Frivolous remarks. empty-headed, foolish, fatuous, superficial, shallow, flippant, flip (informal), silly, trivial, puerile, childish, inane, dizzy, giddy, pointless, worthless, insignificant, idle, trifling.
OPPOSITES: serious, sensible.

**front**
1 (n) Put some people in the front of your painting. foreground, forefront.
OPPOSITES: background, back.
2 (n) Ivy grew up the front of the house. face, façade, frontage.
OPPOSITES: rear, back.
3 (n) Go to the front of the queue. top, head, beginning.
OPPOSITES: end, back.
4 (n) Dean's self-confidence is just a front. pretence, show, mask, façade, cover, disguise, cover-up, sham, blind, screen.

**frosty**
1 (adj) It's frosty this morning. icy, freezing, hoary, crisp, wintry, keen, chilly, nippy, cold. ❖ Also see **ice**, **frost & snow**.
2 (adj) Aunt Bertha gave a frosty reply. cold, icy, chilly, glacial, unfriendly, cool, standoffish, stiff, aloof, discouraging.
OPPOSITES: warm, friendly.

**frown**
(v) Mum will frown at you if you snigger. scowl, glare, glower, grimace, look daggers, give you a dirty look, look stern.

**frozen**
1 (adj) The roads are frozen. icy, frosty, icebound, ice-covered, frozen solid.
2 (adj) My nose is frozen. freezing, numb, icy, chilled, dead, frostbitten, frozen solid.

**fruit**
(n) TYPES OF FRUIT: apple, apricot, avocado, banana, bilberry, blackberry, blackcurrant, blueberry, cherry, clementine, crab apple, cranberry, damson, date, elderberry, fig, gooseberry, grape, grapefruit, greengage, guava, kiwi fruit, kumquat, lemon, lime, loganberry, lychee, mandarin, mango, melon, nectarine, olive, orange, papaya, passion fruit, peach, pear, pineapple, plum, pomegranate, prickly pear, quince, raspberry, redcurrant, rhubarb, satsuma, star fruit, strawberry, tangerine, tomato, ugli fruit.

**frustrated**
*(adj) I felt frustrated that I couldn't go to the party.* disgruntled, vexed, annoyed, peeved *(informal)*, miffed *(informal)*, resentful, thwarted, foiled, disappointed, embittered, sick as a parrot *(informal)*.

**full**
1 *(adj) The box is full.* full up, filled, full to the brim, overflowing, packed, crammed, stuffed, jam-packed, chock-a-block, full to bursting, bursting at the seams, brimming over, chock-full, jammed, crowded, laden, loaded, teeming, swarming, well-stocked. OPPOSITE: empty.
2 *(adj) I want a full explanation.* thorough, complete, detailed, comprehensive, exhaustive, unabridged, uncut, unedited. OPPOSITES: incomplete, partial.
3 *(adj) Charlotte felt full after her lunch.* satisfied, well-fed, sated, satiated, gorged, stuffed *(informal)*, replete. OPPOSITES: empty, hungry.

**fun**
1 *(n) Let's have some fun!* amusement, enjoyment, entertainment, fun and games *(plural)*, pleasure, recreation, diversion, distraction, high jinks *(plural)*, sport.
2 *(n) Oz is full of fun.* merriment, laughter, sparkle, high spirits *(plural)*, verve, zest, mirth, jollity, hilarity.
3 *(adj) The party was fun.* See **enjoyable**.

**funny**
1 *(adj) A funny comedian.* amusing, comical, witty, humorous, hilarious, entertaining, satirical, ironic, droll, sarcastic, facetious, hysterical *(informal)*, side-splitting, absurd, ludicrous, laughable, farcical, ridiculous, riotous.
2 *(adj) A funny habit. See* **strange** 1.
3 *(adj) A funny noise. See* **strange** 2.

**furious** *see* **angry**.

**furry**
*(adj) A furry creature.* fluffy, fuzzy, hairy, woolly, fleecy.

**fuss**
*(v) Don't fuss about petty details.* worry, fret, get worked up, flap *(informal)*, be agitated, be in a stew *(informal)*, niggle.

**fussy**
*(adj) Di is fussy about her food.* particular, choosy *(informal)*, fastidious, hard to please, difficult, picky *(informal)*, finicky, pernickety *(informal)*, faddy *(informal)*.

**future**
*(n) Your future looks bright.* prospects *(plural)*, expectations *(plural)*, outlook.

**fuzzy**
1 *(adj) It's hard to control my fuzzy hair.* frizzy, fluffy, woolly, wiry, bushy.
2 *(adj) Without my glasses, everything looks fuzzy. See* **blurred**.

**gabble**
*(v) Don't gabble! I can't understand you.* jabber, babble, rabbit on *(informal)*, rattle on, prattle, spout *(informal)*, blabber, gush.

**gadget**
*(n) This gadget slices apples.* device, tool, instrument, utensil, contraption, appliance, widget *(informal)*, gizmo *(slang)*, invention.

**gaffe** *see* **mistake** 2.

**gain** *see* **win** 2.

**gale** *see* **storm** 1.

**gamble**
1 *(v) If you gamble, you may lose.* bet, place a bet, have a flutter *(informal)*, speculate, take a risk, take a chance, try your luck, stick your neck out *(informal)*. OPPOSITE: play safe.
2 **gamble on** *(v) Flash Frank loves to gamble on the horses.* bet on, put money on, back, have a flutter on *(informal)*.

**game**
1 *(n) Don't take it so seriously; it's only a game.* amusement, diversion, distraction, entertainment, romp, lark *(informal)*, prank, jest, joke, bit of fun.
2 *(n) Football is a popular game.* sport, pastime, recreation, entertainment, amusement, leisure activity.
3 *(n) When does the rugby game start?* match, competition, tournament, contest.

**gang**
*(n) Can I join your gang?* group, crowd, club, set, bunch *(informal)*, circle, crew *(informal)*, clique, posse *(informal)*, mob, team, squad.

**gap**
1 *(n) We found a gap in the wall.* hole, crack, opening, space, chink, crevice, cranny.
2 *(n) There will be a gap between each act.* interval, pause, break, rest, breathing space, lull, interlude, intermission.
3 *(n) Measure the gap between the two houses.* space, distance, interval.

**gape** *see* **stare** 1.

**gaping**
*(adj) Beneath us stretched a gaping hole.* yawning, cavernous, vast, wide, wide-open, enormous.

**garden**
*(n)* patch, plot, lawn, grounds *(plural)*, back yard, yard.

**garish** *see* **gaudy**.

**gash** *see* **cut** 1, 9.

**funfair** *(n)* fair, fairground, amusement park, theme park.

**funfair rides**

| | |
|---|---|
| big dipper | ghost train |
| big wheel | helter-skelter |
| bumper cars | merry-go-round |
| carousel | roller coaster |
| Dodgems | simulator |
| Ferris wheel | swingboat |

**on a ride you...**

| | |
|---|---|
| bounce | revolve |
| bump | rock |
| climb | slide |
| crash | speed |
| dive | spin |
| drop | sway |
| hang | swerve |
| hurtle | swing |
| jerk | swoop |
| jolt | tilt |
| lurch | twist |
| plummet | whirl |
| plunge | zoom |

**rides can be...**
exciting
exhilarating
hair-raising
nail-biting
scary *(informal)*
spine-tingling
stomach-churning
terrifying
thrilling

**other amusements**
amusement arcade
bouncy castle
coconut shy
fortune-teller
hall of mirrors
laser show
shooting gallery
skittles
slot machine
stall

**people at a funfair...**
gape
gasp
gaze
jostle
mill about
push
queue
scream
screech
shove
shriek
squeal
yell

**funfair lights can be...**
blazing
colourful
dazzling
flashing
glittering
magical
whirling

**funfair music can be...**
blaring
booming
jangling
pounding
rhythmic
strident
tinny

# **g**asp

**gasp**
1 (v) This icy water will make you gasp. catch your breath, gulp, splutter, choke.
2 (v) Jogging makes me gasp. See **pant**.

**gate**
(n) entrance, exit, gateway, doorway, way in, way out, door, opening, turnstile, stile.

**gather**
1 (v) A crowd began to gather at the end of the pitch. See **collect** 3.
2 (v) I gather I'm next. See **understand** 3.

**gaudy**
(adj) A gaudy tie. garish, loud, lurid, bright, glaring, flashy, vulgar, showy, tasteless.

**gaunt**
(adj) After their ordeal, the prisoners looked gaunt. haggard, wasted, scrawny, emaciated, sunken-cheeked, hollow-eyed, drawn, pinched, skeletal, cadaverous.

**gaze** see **stare** 1.

**gear**
1 (n) Climbing gear. See **equipment**.
2 (n) (informal) Oz looks great in his party gear. clothes (plural), outfit, things (plural), togs (plural) (informal), strip (sport).

**general**
1 (adj) Untidiness is a general problem among teenagers. common, widespread, normal, typical, everyday, usual, universal.
OPPOSITES: individual, unusual.
2 (adj) Chloë gave a general outline of the story. broad, rough, vague, loose, approximate, imprecise, sweeping.
OPPOSITES: precise, detailed.

**generation**
1 (n) I get on best with people of my own generation. age, age group, peer group.
2 (n) Steam trains belong to a different generation. era, age, time, period, epoch.

**generous**
(adj) Lord Lucre is generous with his money. open-handed, liberal, ungrudging, unstinting, free, lavish, magnanimous, kind, charitable, bountiful.
OPPOSITES: mean, stingy.

**genius**
(n) Imran is a genius at maths. mastermind, marvel, ace (informal), whiz (informal), brainbox (slang), whiz kid (informal), hotshot (informal), prodigy (child).

**gentle**
1 (adj) Neesha has a gentle nature. mild, sweet-tempered, peaceful, placid, tender, meek, docile, unassertive, kind.
OPPOSITES: violent, aggressive.
2 (adj) The leaves stirred in the gentle breeze. light, soft, faint, slight, mild, balmy, caressing.
OPPOSITES: strong, violent.
3 (adj) Dad spoke to me in a gentle voice. soft, soothing, quiet, low, reassuring.
OPPOSITES: harsh, loud.
4 (adj) We cycled down a gentle slope. gradual, slight, imperceptible, easy, steady.
OPPOSITES: steep, sudden.

5 (adj) A gentle hint. See **subtle** 2.

**genuine**
1 (adj) Is that a genuine gold nugget? real, actual, authentic, bona fide, true, veritable, solid, pure, natural, original (art).
OPPOSITES: fake, imitation, artificial.
2 (adj) Sophie's enthusiasm seems to be genuine. See **sincere** 1.

**gesture**
1 (n) I don't know what Sam's gesture means. sign, signal, action, gesticulation.
2 (v) I tried to gesture to you that the branch wasn't safe. See **signal** 2.

**get**
1 (v) Where did you get those jeans? buy, get hold of, obtain, acquire, come by.
2 (v) Please get me a chair. See **fetch** 1.
3 (v) When will we get our exam results? receive, be given, hear, be told, be sent.
4 (v) Oz hopes to get first prize. win, gain, take, obtain, earn, achieve, attain, pick up.
5 (v) It should get warmer in the afternoon. become, grow, turn.
6 (v) When did you finally get home? arrive, come, reach, make it (informal).
7 (v) Shall I get supper? make, prepare, fix (informal), get ready, organize, cook.
8 (v) I wish I could get you to go out with me. persuade, convince, induce, coax, talk you into, wheedle you into, make, force.
9 (v) I mustn't get a cold. See **catch** 3.
10 (v) I don't get what you mean. See **understand** 1.
11 (v) (informal) I'm going to get you for stealing my hat! See **pay back** 2.

**get across**
1 (v) How will we get across the desert? See **cross** 4.
2 (v) It's important to get your message across. get over, put over, communicate, make clear, get through, bring home.

**get at**
1 (v) I can't get at that shelf. See **reach** 1.
2 (v) Can you see what I'm trying to get at? suggest, imply, lead up to, insinuate, convey, indicate, mean.
3 (v) Why does everyone always get at me? See **pick on**.

**getaway** see **escape** 4.

**get away**
1 (v) Burglar Beryl tried to get away from the police. See **escape** 1.
2 **get away with** (v) Don't try to cheat; you won't get away with it. get off scot-free, go unpunished, pull it off.

**get back**
1 (v) What time did you get back? See **return** 1.
2 (v) Did you manage to get your pencil case back? See **retrieve**.

**get better**
1 (v) You must take your medicine if you want to get better. See **recover** 1.
2 (v) The situation can only get better. See **improve** 2.

**get even** (informal) see **get your own back**.

**get off**
1 (v) Don't get off until the bus stops. get out, alight, disembark, dismount, exit.
2 (v) (informal) Did you get off with Jo at the party? make a date, get together, get lucky (informal), make out (informal).

**get on**
1 (v) I wonder how I'll get on at my new school. See **manage** 1.
2 (v) The driver told us to get on. get in, board, climb aboard, embark, enter.
3 (v) Did you and Sarah get on? get along, hit it off (informal), become friends, make friends, see eye to eye, agree.

**get out**
(v) If there's a fire, get out as fast as you can! leave, clear out (informal), escape, make your escape, exit, evacuate, free yourself, extricate yourself, break out.

**get out of** see **avoid** 2.

**get over**
1 (v) It didn't take long for Alice to get over her illness. recover from, get better from, shake off, convalesce, recuperate.
2 (v) It can be hard to get over losing a friend. recover from, survive, bounce back from, put behind you, forget.

**get rid of**
(v) Please get rid of that mouldy sandwich. throw away, dispose of, remove, bin, chuck (slang), dump (informal), ditch (slang), do away with, discard.

**get together** see **meet** 3.

**get up**
(v) It's time to get up! get out of bed, rise and shine (informal), wake up, surface (informal), get dressed, rise, stand up.

**get worse**
(v) Your marks will get worse if you don't work harder. deteriorate, worsen, go downhill (informal), take a turn for the worse, slip, slide, fall, slump, decline, lapse.
OPPOSITES: get better, improve.

**get your own back**
(phrase) (informal) Don't try to get your own back. take revenge, get your revenge, retaliate, get even (informal), settle the score, be avenged, give tit for tat.

**ghastly**
1 (adj) A ghastly crime. See **horrible** 1.
2 (adj) I saw a ghastly face in the moonlight. deathly pale, ashen, spectral, deathlike, cadaverous, gruesome.

**ghost**
(n) Max says he saw a ghost on the stairs. spirit, spook (informal), spectre, phantom, apparition, wraith, poltergeist, ghoul.

**ghostly**
1 (adj) A ghostly sound. See **spooky**.
2 (adj) A ghostly figure. ghostlike, spectral, phantom, wraithlike, shadowy, supernatural, unearthly, ghoulish.

## ghosts and hauntings

### ghosts and ghouls

apparition
banshee
bogeyman
ghost
ghoul
gremlin
phantom
poltergeist
  (mischievous spirit)
spectre
spirit
spook (informal)
vampire
werewolf
wraith
zombie

*haunted house*

*panelled room*

*grand staircase*

### in a haunted house

attic
bats
candelabra
cellar
chains
cobwebs
fluttering curtains
four-poster bed
grandfather clock
grand staircase
guttering candles
library
locked door
looking glass
manacles
  (handcuffs)
mice
oak chest
panelled room
portrait
secret door
secret passageway
shadows
sliding panel
spiral staircase
stone steps
study
suit of armour
sword
tapestry
trap door
turret
west wing
winding corridor

### ghosts and ghouls may...

appear
avenge (take revenge for)
beckon
creep
disappear
drift
flit
float
flutter
glide
glow
haunt
hover
loom
lurk
materialize
pace
pester
plague
possess
shimmer
skim
slide
slink
slither
stalk
sway
torment
trouble
vanish into thin air
waft
wander

### ghostly sounds

bang
bump
cackle
chime
clank
clatter
clink
crash
creak
cry
grate
grind
groan
hammer
hoot
howl
knock
moan
murmur
mutter
rattle
rustle
scream
screech
shriek
sigh
sob
thud
wail
whisper

### ghostly sounds can be...

bloodcurdling
chilling
creepy (informal)
disturbing
echoing
eerie
hair-raising
haunting
heart-stopping
high-pitched
lingering
long-drawn-out
melancholy
petrifying
piercing
reverberating
spine-chilling
uncanny
unearthly
unnerving
weird

### haunted houses can be...

bleak
creepy (informal)
crumbling
cursed
derelict
deserted
dilapidated
forbidding
gloomy
grim
isolated
lonely
menacing
moonlit
mysterious
neglected
rambling
ramshackle
remote
spooky (informal)
swathed in mist
tumbledown
uninhabited

*guttering candle*

### ghosts and ghouls may be...

anguished
ghastly
ghostly
ghoulish
grisly
grotesque
gruesome
horrifying
invisible
luminous
malevolent
mournful
restless
scary (informal)
shadowy
sinister
slimy
spectral
supernatural
tormented

*candelabra*

*manacle*

65

# giant

**giant**
1 (n) Jack dreamt about a fearsome giant. ogre, monster, hulk, titan.
2 (adj) Giant sale now on. See **huge**.

**gibberish** see **nonsense** 1.

**giddy** see **dizzy**.

**gift**
1 (n) Dad gave me this book as a gift. See **present** 1.
2 (n) Lord Lucre gave the school a generous gift. donation, contribution, grant, hand-out, offering, bequest, legacy.
3 (n) Mark has a gift for languages. talent, aptitude, flair, ability, facility, knack, bent, genius, skill, expertise.

**gifted** see **talented** 1, 2.

**gigantic** see **huge**.

**giggle**
(v) You'll giggle when you see Dad in his tank top. titter, snigger, chuckle, chortle, laugh, cackle, snicker.

**gimmick**
(n) This toy is just a gimmick to make you buy the cereal. novelty, ploy, trick, stunt, publicity device, dodge, wheeze (slang).

**girl**
(n) schoolgirl, lass, young woman, maiden (old-fashioned), damsel (old-fashioned).

**gist**
(n) Do you get the gist of what I'm saying? idea, general sense, drift, point, meaning, essence, substance, significance.

**give**
1 (v) Give your ticket to the driver. hand, pass, hand over, present, submit, deliver.
2 (v) Lord Lucre offered to give some money to our fund. donate, contribute, grant, present, allocate, make over, fork out (slang), provide, supply, entrust, bestow, bequeath (after death).
OPPOSITES: take away, receive.
3 (v) A graph is a good way to give information. communicate, convey, put across, display, show, set out, deliver, express, explain, demonstrate, impart.
4 (v) Let's give a party! throw, have, organize, arrange, put on, host, stage.
5 (v) Please let me come; I won't give any trouble. cause, make, create, produce.

**give away** see **betray** 1, 3.

**give in**
(v) Why don't you just give in and end the argument? give up, admit defeat, back down, climb down, throw in the towel, concede defeat, capitulate, surrender.

**give out**
(v) Mrs Badger asked me to give out the books. hand out, hand round, pass round, dish out (informal), distribute, dole out, share out, circulate.
OPPOSITES: collect, take in.

**give up**
1 (v) I'm determined to give up biting my nails. See **stop** 3.

2 (v) This assault course is tough, but I'm not going to give up. give in, admit defeat, quit, lose heart, despair, drop out, throw in the towel, throw in the sponge, pack it in (informal), call it a day (informal).
3 (v) Would you give up your pocket money for a good cause? sacrifice, forfeit, relinquish, forgo, surrender, offer.

**give way** see **collapse** 1.

**glad** see **pleased**.

**glamorous**
1 (adj) Helen looks glamorous in her ballgown. dazzling, alluring, stunning (informal), smart, elegant, sophisticated, snazzy (informal), charming, enchanting, bewitching, entrancing, irresistible, captivating, sexy (informal), seductive.
OPPOSITES: dull, dowdy.
2 (adj) The party was a glamorous affair. glittering, dazzling, glitzy (slang), ritzy (slang), colourful, fascinating, exciting.
OPPOSITES: humdrum, mundane.

**glamour**
(n) The glamour of Hollywood. glitter, dazzle, razzmatazz (slang), razzle-dazzle (slang), glitz (slang), magic, fascination, allure, appeal, attraction, charm, elegance.

**glance**
1 (n) Take a quick glance. See **look** 4.
2 (v) Would you glance at my homework? See **look at** 2.

**glare**
(v) Aunt Bertha will glare at you if you interrupt. give you a hard stare, glower, look daggers, give you a dirty look, frown, scowl, give you a black look.

**glaring**
1 (adj) Glaring headlights. See **bright** 1.
2 (adj) A glaring mistake. See **obvious**.

**glass**
(n) Fill the glass to the brim. tumbler, wineglass, goblet, flute (champagne).

**gleam**
1 (v) As Aladdin rubbed the lamp, it began to gleam. shine, glisten, glint, shimmer, glimmer, glow, sparkle, glitter, twinkle.
2 (n) A gleam of light. See **flash** 1.

**gleaming** see **shiny** 1, 2.

**glide**
1 (v) I'd like to glide through the air like a bird. float, drift, sail, soar, fly, coast, hover.
2 (v) Watch me glide across the ice! skate, slide, skim, sail, slip, skid.

**glimmer** see **gleam** 1.

**glimpse**
(n) I got a glimpse of something shiny in the grass. quick look, brief view, glance, peep, peek, sight, squint.

**glint** see **gleam** 1.

**glisten** see **gleam** 1.

**glitter**
1 (v) The light made the diamonds glitter. sparkle, shimmer, twinkle, glisten, shine, glint, gleam, glimmer, flash.

2 (n) The glitter of the treasure dazzled me. sparkle, brilliance, lustre, brightness.
3 (n) Jodie is fascinated by the glitter of Hollywood. See **glamour**.

**gloat**
(v) Don't gloat if you win. crow, brag, rub it in (informal), boast, show off (informal).

**globe**
1 (n) The sun is a globe of fire. See **ball** 1.
2 (n) Indiana has travelled round the globe. See **world** 1.

**gloom**
(n) When she heard the news, Emma was filled with gloom. melancholy, sorrow, sadness, unhappiness, despondency, dejection, misery, depression, despair, desolation, hopelessness, woe, pessimism.
OPPOSITES: happiness, delight.

**gloomy**
1 (adj) It was a gloomy winter's day. dismal, dreary, dull, dark, murky, cheerless, overcast, cloudy, sunless, dim, sombre.
OPPOSITES: bright, sunny.
2 (adj) Wet weather makes me feel gloomy. See **depressed**.

**glorious**
1 (adj) A glorious victory. magnificent, splendid, triumphant, heroic, honourable, famous, celebrated, renowned, illustrious.
OPPOSITES: shameful, humiliating.
2 (adj) Glorious weather. See **gorgeous** 3.

**glossy**
1 (adj) Glossy paintwork. shiny, shining, gleaming, bright, sparkling, shimmering, brilliant, smooth, polished, glazed.
OPPOSITES: dull, matt.
2 (adj) Glossy hair. shiny, shining, gleaming, sleek, silky, smooth, lustrous.
OPPOSITE: dull.

**glow**
1 (n) I saw a strange glow in the sky. light, gleam, glimmer, brightness, burning.
2 (n) The wind will bring a glow to your cheeks. bloom, blush, rosiness, pinkness, redness, flush.
3 (v) We watched the coals glow in the hearth. glimmer, burn, redden, smoulder.
4 (v) These stickers glow in the dark. shine, shimmer, gleam, glimmer, show up.

**glowing**
1 (adj) Glowing coals. See **burning** 1.
2 (adj) Glowing colours. See **bright** 2.
3 (adj) A glowing complexion. rosy, pink, healthy, radiant, reddish, ruddy, florid.
OPPOSITES: pale, wan.
4 (adj) A glowing report. complimentary, enthusiastic, ecstatic, rave (informal).
OPPOSITES: critical, scathing.

**glue** see **stick** 5.

**glum** see **depressed**.

**gnarled**
(adj) Gnarled hands. twisted, misshapen, knobbly, knotted, distorted, contorted, weather-beaten, leathery, wrinkled.

**gnash** see **grind** 2.

**gnaw**
(v) Carrots are nice to gnaw. chew, bite, nibble, munch, crunch.

**go**
1 (v) Do you want to go to London? travel, journey, make your way, drive, fly, take the train, cycle, walk, motor, ride, sail, cruise, voyage, move.
2 (v) It's time to go. See **leave** 1.
3 (v) The time seemed to go so quickly. See **pass** 2.
4 (v) Wind up the toy to make it go. See **work** 4.
5 (v) Where do these books go? belong, stay, live (informal), fit in, have a place.
6 (v) Will this belt go round my waist? reach, extend, stretch, fit.
7 (v) Let's wait and see how things go. work out, turn out, develop, unfold, progress, end up, pan out (informal).
8 (v) This cake will go mouldy if you don't eat it. become, grow, turn, get.
9 (v) If you use this cream, your rash will soon go. See **go away** 3.
10 (v) That chair will have to go. be thrown away, be got rid of, be disposed of, be discarded, be chucked out (informal), be dumped (informal).
OPPOSITE: stay.
11 (v) Granny's eyesight is beginning to go. See **fail** 5.
12 (v) Do these shorts and socks go? match, go together, coordinate, complement each other, blend, harmonize.
13 (n) (informal) Have a go! See **try** 1.
14 (n) (informal) Matty has lots of go. energy, drive, vitality, get-up-and-go (informal), oomph (informal), push (informal), vigour, life, spirit, verve.

**go about**
(v) I'm not sure how to go about this task. approach, tackle, begin, set about.

**go after** see **follow** 1, 2.

**go-ahead** (informal) see **permission**.

**go ahead**
(v) We decided to go ahead without you. start, begin, proceed, go on, continue.

**goal** see **aim** 1.

**go along with**
1 (v) David asked me to go along with him. See **go with** 1.
2 (v) Let's hope Nat will go along with our plan. See **agree** 6.

**go away**
1 (v) Go away and leave me alone! clear off (informal), shove off (informal), push off (informal), get lost (informal), scram (informal), beat it (slang), hop it (slang).
OPPOSITES: come here, stay.
2 (v) Do you have to go away so soon? See **leave** 1.
3 (v) I wish these spots would go away. go, clear up, disappear, vanish, fade away, die down, melt away.
OPPOSITES: stay, appear.

**go back** see **return** 1, 2.
**gobble**
(v) Don't gobble your food. bolt, guzzle, gulp, scoff (informal), wolf down, shovel down, devour, pig out on (slang).

**gobsmacked** (slang) see **astonished**.
**god**
(n) deity, divine being, divinity, Creator.

**go down**
1 (v) As we approached land, the plane began to go down. See **descend** 1.
2 (v) Prices are expected to go down. See **decrease** 2.
3 (v) I watched the sun go down over the sea. See **set** 5.

**go for**
1 (v) Did you see our goalie go for the ball? reach for, stretch for, lunge for, dive for, clutch at, grab at, fetch, go and get.
2 (v) I'm scared the dog might go for me. attack, set upon, rush at, spring at.
3 (v) Mel will really go for you in that shirt. See **fancy** 3.

**go in** see **enter** 1.
**golden**
1 (adj) Golden treasure. gilded, gilt, shining, gleaming, brilliant.
2 (adj) Golden hair. See **blonde** 2.

**gone**
(adj) All the food's gone. finished, eaten, consumed, used up, done, missing, disappeared, vanished, lost.

**good-looking** see **attractive**.
**gooey**
(adj) (informal) A gooey mixture. sticky, squidgy, gluey, glutinous, tacky, syrupy.

**go off**
1 (v) This bomb could go off at any moment. See **explode**.
2 (v) Don't go off without saying goodbye. See **leave** 1.
3 (v) (informal) This cheese will go off soon. go mouldy, go bad, rot, decay, decompose, putrefy, go stale, go sour.
4 (v) (informal) At present Tom likes the Howlers, but he'll soon go off them. get bored with, tire of, get sick of (informal), take a dislike to, turn against.

**go on** see **continue** 1, 2.
**go out**
1 (v) I just saw Samantha go out. leave, walk out, walk off, depart, exit.
OPPOSITES: come in, enter.
2 (v) It took ages for the fire to go out. die down, be extinguished, be quenched.
OPPOSITES: kindle, ignite.

**go out with**
(v) I don't want to go out with you any more. see, go with, go steady with (informal), date (informal).

**go over**
(v) Go over this topic carefully before the test. look over, revise, review, read through, work through, study, examine, check, scan, skim.

| good | | | | |
|---|---|---|---|---|
| **a good person** | **a good deed** | **a good footballer** | **good work** | **a good excuse** |
| blameless | altruistic | accomplished | admirable | adequate |
| decent | (unselfish) | capable | careful | genuine |
| honest | caring | competent | commendable | legitimate |
| honourable | charitable | expert | competent | proper |
| just | considerate | fine | excellent | reasonable |
| kind | generous | first-class | first-rate | satisfactory |
| law-abiding | helpful | gifted | pleasing | valid |
| moral | humane | proficient | satisfactory | |
| righteous | kind | skilful | sound | **good food** |
| saintly | thoughtful | skilled | splendid | appetizing |
| trustworthy | | talented | thorough | delicious |
| upright | **a good film** | | | mouthwatering |
| virtuous | brilliant | **good weather** | **a good mood** | scrumptious |
| | excellent | | buoyant | (informal) |
| **a good child** | fantastic | bright | carefree | tasty |
| angelic | (informal) | calm | cheerful | well-cooked |
| cooperative | great | clear | cheery | yummy |
| docile | impressive | cloudless | chirpy | (informal) |
| helpful | marvellous | fabulous | (informal) | |
| obedient | outstanding | (informal) | contented | **Fruit is good for you.** |
| obliging | sensational | fair | happy | beneficial |
| polite | (informal) | fine | jolly | healthy |
| well-behaved | superb | glorious | jovial | nourishing |
| well-mannered | terrific | mild | light-hearted | nutritious |
| willing | (informal) | sunny | optimistic | wholesome |
| | wonderful | | positive | |

# gorgeous

**gorgeous**
1 *(adj) The queen wore a gorgeous diamond necklace.* magnificent, beautiful, splendid, superb, dazzling, glittering, stunning *(informal)*, brilliant, breathtaking, resplendent, opulent, sumptuous, showy.
OPPOSITES: plain, ugly.
2 *(adj) You look gorgeous in that dress.* beautiful, lovely, stunning *(informal)*, dazzling, ravishing, attractive, sexy *(informal)*, drop-dead gorgeous *(slang)*.
OPPOSITES: plain, unattractive.
3 *(adj) The weather was gorgeous.* glorious, wonderful, lovely, beautiful, marvellous, terrific *(informal)*, fantastic *(informal)*, superb, excellent, fine.
OPPOSITE: awful.

**go round**
*(v) Take the new road, if you want to go round the town.* bypass, skirt, avoid, steer clear of, get round, make a detour round.

**gory**
*(adj) This film contains some gory scenes.* bloody, bloodthirsty, grisly, gruesome, brutal, violent, horrific, sickening, savage.

**gossip**
1 *(v) It's unkind to gossip about other people.* spread rumours, spread gossip, circulate rumours, spread stories, spread scandal, tittle-tattle, bad-mouth *(slang)*.
2 *(v) Don't gossip in class. See* **talk** 1.
3 *(n) Have you heard the gossip?* rumours *(plural)*, latest *(informal)*, scandal, tittle-tattle, hearsay, idle talk, dirt *(slang)*.
4 *(n) Mrs Bunn is a real gossip.* scandalmonger, gossipmonger, busybody, telltale, tattler, chatterbox *(informal)*.

**go through**
1 *(v) This arrow will never go through the dragon's skin. See* **pierce**.
2 *(v) I can't go through another day of this misery. See* **suffer** 3.
3 *(v) Try not to go through your pocket money so quickly.* spend, use up, exhaust, squander, fritter away, consume.

**go under**
1 *(v) Pirate Peg was scared her ship would go under.* sink, go down, be submerged.
2 *(v) Dad's firm may go under. See* **fail** 4.

**go up** *see* **rise** 1, 2.

**govern**
*(v) Who will govern the country after the next election?* rule, run, be in charge of, lead, control, administer, manage, conduct the affairs of, be in power over, direct, steer, command, preside over, reign over.

**go with**
1 *(v) Oz asked me to go with him to the party.* accompany, escort, go along with.
2 *(v) Does this top go with my skirt? See* **match** 2.

**go without**
*(v) Could you go without chocolate, if you had to?* do without, survive without, abstain from, deny yourself, go short of.

**go wrong**
1 *(v) Where did I go wrong in this maths question?* make a mistake, miscalculate, slip up *(informal)*, go astray, blunder.
2 *(v) Why do my brilliant ideas always go wrong?* turn out badly, end in disaster, come to grief, come to nothing, fail, misfire, fall flat, flop *(informal)*.

**grab**
1 *(v) I felt someone grab my arm.* clutch, seize, grip, clasp, grasp, catch hold of.
2 *(v) Burglar Beryl managed to grab the jewels. See* **snatch**.

**graceful**
1 *(adj) A graceful ballerina.* elegant, poised, supple, lithe, agile, nimble.
OPPOSITES: clumsy, awkward.
2 *(adj) Graceful dance steps.* smooth, elegant, flowing, fluid, balletic.
OPPOSITES: clumsy, awkward.

**grade**
1 *(n) I hope I get a good grade for my homework. See* **mark** 4.
2 *(n) Mum was promoted to a higher grade in the company. See* **level** 6.
3 *(v) Mrs Badger didn't have time to grade our tests.* assess, evaluate, classify, rate.

**gradual**
1 *(adj) There's been a gradual improvement in your work.* steady, continuous, progressive, systematic, step-by-step, slow, moderate, unspectacular.
OPPOSITE: sudden.
2 *(adj) There's a gradual slope down to the river. See* **gentle** 4.

**grand**
1 *(adj) Lord Lucre lives in a grand mansion.* magnificent, imposing, impressive, splendid, superb, palatial, stately, sumptuous, opulent, luxurious.
OPPOSITE: modest.
2 *(adj) The king made a grand entrance.* dignified, stately, majestic, regal.
3 *(adj) Our new neighbours seem very grand.* posh *(informal)*, upper class, upper crust *(informal)*, distinguished, aristocratic, haughty, high and mighty *(informal)*, lordly, imperious, pompous, pretentious.
OPPOSITES: ordinary, common.

**grapple**
1 *(v) Indiana had to grapple with the monster. See* **struggle** 2.
2 *(v) I'm too tired to grapple with this problem now. See* **tackle** 2.

**grasp**
1 *(v) Grasp my hand so you don't fall! See* **grip**.
2 *(v) I don't quite grasp what you're saying. See* **understand** 1.
3 *(n) Winter held the country in its icy grasp.* grip, embrace, clasp, clutches *(plural)*, hold.
4 *(n) Rick has a good grasp of the subject.* understanding, comprehension, awareness, knowledge, mastery, grip, appreciation, perception, insight.

**grass**
1 *(n) Don't walk on the grass!* lawn, turf, green, pitch, playing field.
2 *(n) The cows roamed through the grass.* meadow, pasture, field.
3 *(v) (slang) Burglar Beryl didn't want to grass on her friends. See* **inform** 2.

**grate**
1 *(v) Please grate this carrot.* shred, mince.
2 *(v) I heard the door grate across the tiles.* scrape, grind, rasp, scratch, rub, creak, squeak.

**grateful**
*(adj) I'm grateful for your help.* thankful, appreciative of, obliged to you, indebted to you.
OPPOSITE: ungrateful.

**grave**
1 *(n) We visited the grave of Queen Victoria.* burial place, tomb, sepulchre, burial chamber, mausoleum, crypt, vault.
2 *(adj) Mrs Badger looked grave as she gave us the news. See* **serious** 1.
3 *(adj) A grave problem. See* **serious** 3.
4 *(adj) A grave illness. See* **serious** 4.

**graveyard**
*(n)* cemetery, burial ground, churchyard.

**graze**
1 *(v) How did you graze your knee?* scrape, scratch, cut, skin, chafe.
2 *(v) Cows graze in fields.* feed, browse.

**greasy**
1 *(adj) I hate greasy chips.* fatty, oily.
2 *(adj) The mud made the path greasy. See* **slippery** 1.
3 *(adj) Flash Frank is such a greasy character. See* **slimy** 2.

**great**
1 *(adj) The explorers crossed a great stretch of desert.* immense, vast, large, huge, extensive, boundless, unlimited.
OPPOSITES: small, short.
2 *(adj) A great boulder blocked the cave entrance.* large, huge, enormous, massive, immense, gigantic, colossal, stupendous, tremendous, mammoth, gargantuan.
OPPOSITE: small.
3 *(adj) Clare's broken leg caused her great pain.* extreme, intense, considerable, acute, excessive, exceptional, inordinate.
OPPOSITES: slight, little.
4 *(adj) This is a great day for the school.* important, significant, momentous, historic, red-letter.
OPPOSITES: unimportant, insignificant.
5 *(adj) Anji is a great tennis player.* skilful, skilled, expert, first-class, ace *(informal)*, capable, proficient, able, talented, gifted, outstanding, impressive, crack *(slang)*.
OPPOSITES: poor, terrible.
6 *(adj) Charles Dickens was a great writer.* remarkable, outstanding, exceptional, talented, gifted, superb, excellent, distinguished, illustrious, eminent, famous, celebrated, renowned, notable.
OPPOSITES: second-rate, insignificant.

**7** (adj) Zoë is a great fan of Famous Fred. devoted, enthusiastic, keen, zealous.
**8** (adj) Paris is one of the world's great cities. See **major** 1.
**9** (adj) (informal) The party was really great. excellent, superb, fantastic (informal), terrific (informal), tremendous (informal), marvellous, decent (informal), cool (informal), mega (slang), crucial (slang), wicked (slang), neat (slang).

**greed**
**1** (n) Kevin's tummyache was the result of his greed. greediness, gluttony, overeating, self-indulgence, piggishness, insatiability.
OPPOSITE: self-restraint.
**2** (n) The sight of the gold filled Pirate Peg with greed. avarice, covetousness, desire, hunger, longing, craving, eagerness.
OPPOSITE: generosity.

**greedy**
**1** (n) Don't be so greedy! Leave some ice cream for me! gluttonous, self-indulgent, piggish, hoggish, insatiable, voracious.
OPPOSITES: self-restrained, abstemious.
**2** (adj) The greedy miser wouldn't share his money. selfish, avaricious, grasping, covetous, rapacious, miserly, tightfisted, niggardly, money-grubbing (informal).
OPPOSITES: generous, unselfish.

**green**
**1** (n) SHADES OF GREEN: acid green, apple green, bottle green, emerald, grass green, jade, khaki, lime green, Lincoln green, moss green, olive green, pea green, racing green, sage green, sea green.
**2** (adj) Daniel is interested in green issues. environmental, ecological, conservationist.
**3** (adj) Unleaded petrol is supposed to be green. environmentally friendly, non-polluting, eco-friendly, ecologically sound.
OPPOSITE: environmentally harmful.
**4** (adj) The cottage nestled in a green valley. grassy, verdant, leafy, flourishing.
**5** (adj) Sian looked green when she saw my new bike. See **envious**.

**greet**
(v) Mrs Badger was waiting to greet us as we arrived. welcome, say hello to, meet, receive, shake hands with, acknowledge, give a greeting to, salute, hail (old-fashioned), nod to, wave to.

**grey**
**1** (n) SHADES OF GREY: charcoal grey, dove grey, gunmetal, iron grey, pearl grey, pewter, silver, slate grey, smoke grey, steel grey.
**2** (adj) Winter days are often grey. dull, cloudy, overcast, foggy, misty, murky, dark, dim, sunless, dreary, dismal, gloomy, drab, depressing, cheerless.
OPPOSITES: bright, sunny.
**3** (adj) Granddad's hair is grey. silver, silvery, grizzled, greying, hoary, white.
**4** (adj) Cyril has such a grey personality. colourless, anonymous, nondescript, dull, characterless, uninteresting.

**5** (adj) Natasha's face turned grey. See **pale** 2.

**grief**
(n) Alice couldn't hide her grief when her dog died. sorrow, sadness, unhappiness, misery, dejection, distress, anguish, despair, heartache, pain, agony, suffering, regret, mourning, woe.
OPPOSITES: joy, delight.

**grieve**
(v) It's natural to grieve when someone dies. be sad, mourn, sorrow, weep, cry, sob, be heartbroken, pine, ache, mope, lament (old-fashioned), go into mourning.
OPPOSITE: rejoice.

**grim**
**1** (adj) Mrs Badger looked grim as she gave us our test results. serious, stern, sombre, severe, forbidding, formidable, fierce, cross, implacable, merciless.
OPPOSITES: cheerful, sympathetic.
**2** (adj) The witch's castle looked grim in the moonlight. forbidding, menacing, ominous, sinister, bleak, gloomy.
OPPOSITES: pleasant, welcoming.
**3** (adj) This film contains some grim battle scenes. grisly, gruesome, ghastly, shocking, harrowing, horrible, horrendous, hideous, frightful, appalling, unspeakable.
OPPOSITE: pleasant.

**grimy** see **dirty** 1.

**grin** see **smile** 1, 2.

**grind**
**1** (v) We need to grind some coffee. crush, mill, pulverize, pound, powder, crumble, granulate, mash, smash, grate.
**2** (v) I hate it when you grind your teeth. gnash, grate, rub together, scrape, grit.
**3** (n) (informal) I'm dreading the grind of revising. hard work, slog, drudgery, chore, toil, sweat (informal), exertion.

**grip**
(v) Grip my hand so you don't fall. grab, clutch, grasp, clasp, hold, hold on to, hang on to, seize, take hold of, clench.

**gripe** (informal) see **complaint**.

**gripping** see **fascinating**.

**grisly** see **gruesome**.

**groan**
**1** (v) I heard Bruno groan with pain. moan, cry, murmur, whimper, sigh, whine.
**2** (v) (informal) My parents groan about the mess in my room. See **complain**.

**groggy** (informal) see **dizzy**.

**groom**
**1** (n) I work as a groom at the local stables. stableboy, stablegirl, stable lad, ostler (old-fashioned).
**2** (v) Groom your pony regularly. rub down, curry, brush, clean.

**groove**
(n) Make a groove in the wood. channel, cut, score, slot, track, scratch, hollow, trench, rut, trough, furrow, indentation.

**grope**
(v) I had to grope around in the dark for my key. fumble, feel, scrabble, pick, fish, search, hunt.

**gross**
(adj) (slang) That pink shirt is really gross. disgusting, revolting, vile, repulsive, foul, tasteless, tacky (informal), naff (slang), yucky (slang).

**grotesque**
(adj) hideous, repulsive, ugly, misshapen, deformed, strange, bizarre, weird, outlandish, freakish, unnatural, monstrous.

a grotesque gargoyle

**grotty**
**1** (adj) (slang) Ziggy lives in a grotty flat. horrible, disgusting, dingy, shabby, tatty, scruffy, run-down, dilapidated, seedy, dirty, filthy, grubby, squalid, sordid, stinking, crummy (slang), scuzzy (slang).
OPPOSITES: smart, attractive.
**2** (adj) (slang) I feel really grotty this morning. See **rotten** 3.

**ground**
**1** (n) Lie flat on the ground! floor, deck (informal), earth.
**2** (n) Plant the seeds in the ground. See **earth** 2.
**3** (n) The council is building a new football ground. pitch, field, stadium, arena, park.
**4** (v) This storm could ground the ship. run ashore, beach, wreck, shipwreck, strand.
**5** (v) (informal) Dad will ground you if you misbehave. keep you in, forbid you to go out, confine you to the house, restrict.
**6** grounds (plural n) Lord Lucre's house is set in extensive grounds. gardens (plural), parkland, surroundings (plural), estate, land, property, acres (plural), fields (plural).
**7** grounds (plural n) Bella has good grounds for complaint. See **reason** 1.

**group**
**1** (v) Group round your team leaders. gather, collect, get together, congregate, assemble, come together, cluster, crowd, get into groups.
OPPOSITES: split up, disperse.
**2** (v) Group the photos according to size. See **sort** 3.
**3** (n) You're welcome to join our group. gang, band, clique, posse (informal), circle, set, bunch (informal), crowd, crew (informal), mob, club, community, party, company, meeting, gathering, assembly, society, association, organization.
**4** (n) A group of animals. herd, horde, brood (chicks), colony (ants, rabbits), flock (birds, sheep), gaggle (geese), litter (kittens, piglets, puppies), pack (hounds, wolves), pride (lions), school (dolphins, whales), shoal (fish), swarm (insects).
**5** (n) A group of things. bunch, bundle, cluster, clump, set, batch, assortment, collection, array, arrangement.

**grovel**
(v) There's no need to grovel to Lord Lucre. crawl, creep, toady, kowtow, bow and scrape, bootlick (informal), fawn, suck up (informal), curry favour with, ingratiate yourself with, humble yourself before.

**grow**
1 (v) I hope I'll grow this year. get bigger, get taller, fill out, shoot up.
OPPOSITES: shrink, get smaller.
2 (v) Before our eyes, the puddle began to grow. expand, get bigger, get larger, spread, swell, enlarge, increase, extend, stretch, fill out, widen, lengthen, deepen.
OPPOSITES: shrink, dwindle.
3 (v) Mum hopes that her business will grow. expand, develop, progress, advance, increase, prosper, flourish, boom, thrive.
OPPOSITES: contract, decline.
4 (v) These seeds will grow in the spring. germinate, sprout, bud, develop, spring up, shoot up, flourish, thrive.
5 (v) We grow orchids in our greenhouse. cultivate, produce, propagate, breed, raise, nurture, farm.
6 (v) Eventually, Luke will grow more sensible. become, get, come to be, turn.

**grown-up** see **adult** 1, 2.

**growth**
1 (n) The rapid growth in technology has changed the world. expansion, rise, increase, development, evolution, progress, advance, improvement.
OPPOSITE: decline.
2 (n) There has been a marked growth in crime. See **increase** 4.

**grow up**
(v) The prince waited for the princess to grow up. mature, develop, come of age, become an adult, reach adulthood.

**grub**
1 (n) It's cruel to keep that grub in a jam jar. caterpillar, maggot, larva.
2 (n) (informal) I'm desperate for some grub. See **food**.

**grubby** see **dirty** 1.

**grudge**
(n) This grudge of yours will eat you up inside. resentment, bitterness, grievance, hard feelings (plural), spite, malice, ill will, envy, hatred, malevolence, venom, hostility, animosity, antipathy, dislike.

**grudging**
(adj) Ellie gave me a grudging smile when I won. reluctant, half-hearted, unenthusiastic, lukewarm, unwilling, ungracious, resentful, envious.
OPPOSITES: enthusiastic, wholehearted.

**gruelling** see **exhausting**.

**gruesome**
(adj) A gruesome monster. grisly, ghastly, ghoulish, horrible, hideous, loathsome, repulsive, monstrous, horrifying, frightful, fearful, terrible, dreadful, spine-chilling, hair-raising, macabre, grim.

**gruff**
1 (adj) Uncle Arthur has a gruff voice. husky, low, hoarse, croaky, rough, gravelly, harsh, rasping, throaty, guttural.
2 (adj) Aunt Bertha has a gruff manner. blunt, brusque, curt, abrupt, ungracious, crusty, crabby, grumpy, grouchy (informal), crotchety (informal), surly, bad-tempered.
OPPOSITES: gracious, pleasant.

**grumble** see **complain**.

**grumpy**
(adj) Max gets grumpy when he's tired. irritable, bad-tempered, grouchy (informal), cross, ratty (informal), crabby, crotchety (informal), tetchy, peevish, surly, sullen, sulky, huffy, cantankerous.
OPPOSITES: good-humoured, cheerful.

**grungy** (slang) see **scruffy** 2.

**guarantee** see **promise** 1, 2.

**guard**
1 (v) We must guard the house. protect, keep watch over, safeguard, defend, patrol, police, mind, secure, shield.
2 (n) A guard is on patrol. watchman, lookout, sentinel, sentry (army), warder (prison), jailer (prison), bodyguard, escort.

**guess**
1 (v) Try to guess the weight of the doll. estimate, hazard a guess at, have a stab at (informal), work out, calculate, speculate about, predict, second-guess (informal).
2 (v) (informal) I guess I should go now. See **think** 2.
3 (n) Your guess was quite right. estimate, conjecture, speculation, guesswork, guesstimate (informal), prediction, shot in the dark, supposition, theory, hypothesis.

**guest**
(n) Try to be polite in front of our guest. visitor, caller, company.

**guidance**
(n) You need guidance when choosing a career. advice, counselling, direction, help, briefing, instruction, guidelines (plural), pointers (plural), tips (plural), hints (plural).

**guide**
1 (v) Guide me to the nearest shelter. lead, take, show, escort, accompany, direct, conduct, steer, shepherd.
2 (v) Try to guide the ship into harbour. steer, pilot, navigate, manoeuvre, direct.
3 (v) You need someone to guide you as you choose a career. advise, give you advice, counsel, give you direction, give you pointers, help, inform, instruct.
4 (n) We followed the guide through the mountains. leader, scout, escort, courier.
5 (n) Use this as a guide when you do your drawing. model, example, pattern, master, standard, benchmark, yardstick.

**guilt**
1 (n) Gregory was tormented by guilt. feelings of guilt (plural), remorse, regret, shame, self-reproach, self-condemnation, guilty conscience, bad conscience.

2 (n) The fingerprints proved Burglar Beryl's guilt. culpability, responsibility, wrongdoing, misconduct, criminality.
OPPOSITE: innocence.

**guilty**
1 (adj) Burglar Beryl was guilty. to blame, at fault, responsible, culpable, convicted.
OPPOSITES: innocent, guiltless.
2 (adj) Gregory felt guilty. ashamed, conscience-stricken, guilt-ridden, filled with regret, remorseful, repentant, rueful, sheepish, shamefaced, hangdog.
OPPOSITES: unrepentant, unashamed.

**gullible**
(adj) Letty is so gullible, she'd believe anything. naive, trusting, easily taken in, unsuspecting, credulous, innocent, green.
OPPOSITES: suspicious, cynical.

**gulp**
1 (v) Don't gulp your cola so quickly. swallow, swig (informal), knock back (informal), down (informal), swill, slurp (informal), guzzle, toss off.
2 (v) Don't gulp your food. See **gobble**.
3 (v) The icy water made me gulp. See **gasp** 1.
4 (n) A gulp of water might cure your hiccups. mouthful, swallow, swig (informal), slurp (informal), draught.

**gun**
(n) firearm, artillery (heavy military guns).
TYPES OF GUN: airgun, automatic pistol, blunderbuss, cannon, handgun, howitzer, machine gun, mortar, musket, pistol, revolver, rifle, sawn-off shotgun, shotgun, stun gun, sub-machine-gun.

**gunman**
(n) armed robber, sniper, assassin, hit man (slang), terrorist, gangster, killer, murderer.

**gurgle**
1 (v) Can you hear the baby gurgle? burble, crow, chuckle, laugh.
2 (v) Listen to the stream gurgle over the stones. babble, bubble, burble, splash, murmur, tinkle, ripple, lap, plash.

**gush**
(v) Water began to gush from the pipe. pour, cascade, stream, flow, flood, spurt, spout, squirt, splash, surge, overflow.

**gust**
(n) A gust of wind blew my hat off. puff, blast, flurry, rush, squall, gale, breeze.

**gusty** see **windy** 1.

**gut**
1 (n) I have a pain in my gut. stomach, belly, tummy (informal), guts (plural), insides (plural) (informal), intestines (plural), innards (plural) (informal).
2 (adj) (informal) I didn't think about it; it was a gut reaction. instinctive, intuitive, spontaneous, involuntary, unthinking, natural, emotional, deep-seated.
3 **guts** (plural n) (informal) It takes guts to face up to a bully. See **courage**.

**guzzle** see **gobble**.

## habit

**1** *(n) Cindy has a habit of biting her nails.* practice, way, tendency, quirk, mannerism.
**2** *(n) It's our habit to spend Christmas with Grandma.* custom, practice, tradition, routine, convention, procedure, rule.
**3** *(n) Mum wants to kick her habit of smoking.* addiction to, dependence on, craving for, weakness for, obsession with, fixation with.

## haggard

*(adj) The rescued sailors looked haggard.* drawn, drained, exhausted, worn out, tired out, thin, gaunt, hollow-cheeked, hollow-eyed, pinched, wasted, emaciated, all skin and bone *(informal)*, cadaverous.

## haggle *see* **bargain** 3.

## hair

**1** *(n) Sharmila's hair reaches her waist.* locks *(plural)*, tresses *(plural)*, curls *(plural)*, mop *(informal)*, mane, shock, head of hair.
**2** *(n) Craig is starting to get some hair on his chin.* whiskers *(plural)*, bristles *(plural)*, stubble, down, fuzz *(informal)*.
**3** *(n) The animal's hair was matted.* fur, coat, wool, fleece *(sheep)*, mane *(horse)*.

## hair-raising *see* **frightening**.

## hairy

**1** *(adj) A hairy animal.* furry, shaggy, long-haired, fleecy, woolly, fuzzy.
OPPOSITE: hairless.
**2** *(adj) A hairy face.* bearded, whiskery, bristly, stubbly, unshaven, fuzzy.
OPPOSITE: clean-shaven.

## half-hearted

**1** *(adj) I feel half-hearted about this plan.* lukewarm, unenthusiastic, apathetic, indifferent, unconcerned, unemotional, neutral, passive, uncommitted.
OPPOSITE: enthusiastic.
**2** *(adj) The goalie made a half-hearted attempt to reach the ball.* listless, lacklustre, perfunctory, cursory, superficial.
OPPOSITES: wholehearted, determined.

## hall

**1** *(n) The dining room is at the far end of the hall.* hallway, entrance hall, lobby, foyer *(hotel, theatre)*, passage, corridor.
**2** *(n) Over a hundred people gathered in the hall.* meeting hall, assembly hall, village hall, church hall, concert hall, auditorium, conference hall, exhibition hall.

## halt *see* **stop** 1, 4, 9.

## hammer

**1** *(n) Len dropped the hammer on his foot.* mallet, sledgehammer, gavel.
**2** *(v) Hammer this nail into the wood.* bang, drive, hit, knock, tap.

## hamper *see* **hinder** 1.

## hand

**1** *(n) Raise your hand if you disagree.* fist, palm, paw *(informal)*, mitt *(slang)*.
**2** *(n) I need a hand to move this table.* helping hand, help, assistance, aid.
**3** *(n) The audience gave me a big hand.* clap, round of applause, ovation.
**4** *(v) Hand your ticket to the bus driver.* give, hand over, pass, present, submit, offer, deliver, reach *(informal)*.

## handcuffs

*(plural n)* cuffs *(plural)* *(informal)*, bracelets *(plural)* *(slang)*, manacles *(plural)* *(old-fashioned)*, fetters *(plural)* *(old-fashioned)*, shackles *(plural)* *(old-fashioned)*.

## hand down

**1** *(v) I hand down my clothes to my younger sister.* pass on, pass down, give.
**2** *(v) Lord Lucre plans to hand down his fortune to his children.* leave, pass on, bequeath, will, transfer, give.

## handicap

**1** *(n) Deafness is a physical handicap.* disability, impairment.
**2** *(n) It's a handicap to live a long way from school.* disadvantage, drawback, inconvenience, nuisance, obstacle, hindrance, impediment, stumbling block.
OPPOSITE: advantage.

## hair and hairstyles

| hair colours | hairstyles | you can have your hair... | hair can be... | |
|---|---|---|---|---|
| auburn | Afro | backcombed | bouncy | unkempt |
| black | beehive | bleached | bushy | wavy |
| blonde | bob | braided | coarse | wild |
| brown | braids | crimped | curly | windswept |
| carroty | bun | cropped | dishevelled | wiry |
| chestnut | bunches | dyed | fine | wispy |
| coppery | chignon | flicked back | floppy | |
| dark | cornrows | gelled | flowing | |
| fair | crew cut | hennaed | frizzy | |
| flaxen | dreadlocks | highlighted | glossy | **other hair** |
| (golden) | flat-top | layered | greasy | **words** |
| ginger | French plait | permed | lank | bald patch |
| grey | hippy braids | plaited | limp | blue rinse |
| greying | mohican | scraped back | matted | fringe |
| mousy | pageboy | shaved | neat | hair band |
| platinum | perm | slicked back | receding | hair extension |
| blonde | pigtail | streaked | shaggy | hairline |
| raven (black) | plaits | tinted | shining | hairnet |
| red | ponytail | undercut | sleek | hairpiece |
| sandy | pudding-bowl | | smooth | hair ribbon |
| silver | quiff | | spiky | hair slide |
| snowy | ringlets | | straggly | parting |
| strawberry | short back | | straight | sideburns |
| blonde | and sides | | tangled | toupee (man's |
| white | skinhead | | thinning | hairpiece) |
| | wedge | | tousled | wig |

*braids*

*beehive*

*cornrows*

*chignon*

*quiff*

*bob*

*dreadlocks*

*mohican*

*hairpin*

*beads*

*hairgrip*

*gel*

**handicapped** see **disabled**.

**handle**
1 (v) Be careful how you handle your guinea pig. hold, pick up, touch, stroke, fondle, caress, feel, finger, paw (informal).
2 (v) This machine is easy to handle. control, operate, manage, work, use, run, manoeuvre, drive, steer, manipulate.
3 (v) Mrs Badger can handle our class. deal with, manage, control, cope with.

**hand out** see **give out**.

**handsome**
(adj) Ryan is so handsome! attractive, good-looking, gorgeous, hunky (informal).
OPPOSITES: ugly, unattractive.

**handwriting** see **writing**.

**handy**
1 (adj) This gadget is really handy. useful, practical, helpful, easy to use, user-friendly, convenient, well-designed, neat (slang).
OPPOSITES: awkward, impractical.
2 (adj) Do you have your ruler handy? within easy reach, close at hand, nearby, accessible, convenient, available, ready.
OPPOSITES: inaccessible, out-of-the-way.

**hang**
1 (v) I'd like the streamers to hang from the ceiling. hang down, be suspended, dangle, swing, trail, drape, sway.
2 (v) Look how the trees hang over the pond. lean, bend, bow, droop, sag, loll.
3 (v) Is this a good place to hang the picture? put up, fix, pin up, nail, stick, hook, suspend, fasten, attach.
4 (v) The eagle seemed to hang in the air. See **hover**.

**hang around**
1 (v) Is this where you like to hang around? hang about, hang out (informal), spend your time, loiter, linger, hang loose (informal), frequent, haunt.
2 (v) Don't hang around - we'll be late! See **delay** 1.

**hang on** see **hold on** 1, 2.

**hang-up**
(n) (informal) I have a hang-up about flying. phobia, fear of, problem with, thing (informal), mental block, inhibition.

**happen**
1 (v) Anything could happen if you make a wish. occur, take place, come about, come to pass (old-fashioned), follow, result, transpire, come up, crop up (informal).
2 (v) Did you happen to see Vanessa? chance, have the good fortune, have the luck, have the misfortune.
3 happen to (v) What will happen to me if I fail my exams? become of, befall.

**happiness**
(n) The thought of his holiday filled Mac with happiness. joy, delight, pleasure, contentment, bliss, glee, elation, ecstasy, jubilation, rejoicing, exuberance, euphoria, high spirits (plural), rapture, merriment.
OPPOSITES: sadness, sorrow.

**happy**
1 (adj) I feel happy. cheerful, contented, in good spirits, light-hearted, jolly, joyful, jubilant, elated, ecstatic, euphoric, on cloud nine (informal), over the moon (informal), in seventh heaven, walking on air (informal).
OPPOSITES: sad, miserable.
2 (adj) I'm so happy you could come. See **pleased**.
3 (adj) We had a happy holiday. blissful, heavenly, idyllic, jolly, merry, enjoyable.
OPPOSITE: miserable.

**harass** see **pester**.

**harbour** see **port**.

**hard**
1 (adj) We tried to dig a hole, but the ground was too hard. firm, solid, stony, rocky, unyielding, impenetrable, resistant, rigid, dense, compacted, frozen.
OPPOSITE: soft.
2 (adj) This sum is hard! See **difficult** 1.
3 (adj) Gardening is such hard work. exhausting, gruelling, strenuous, backbreaking, tough, killing (informal), demanding, laborious, uphill, heavy.
OPPOSITES: easy, light.
4 (adj) Barney has had a hard year. difficult, tough, rough (informal), unpleasant, painful, distressing, grim, unbearable, intolerable, disastrous, calamitous, dark, black.
OPPOSITES: easy, pleasant.
5 (adj) The boxer suffered a hard blow to the head. heavy, violent, powerful, driving, forceful, severe, strong, fierce, sharp.
OPPOSITES: gentle, light.
6 (adj) Miss Blackheart is a hard woman. hardhearted, heartless, unsympathetic, unfeeling, cold, callous, cruel, ruthless, pitiless, merciless, inflexible, unrelenting, stern, strict, brutal.
OPPOSITES: kind, softhearted.
7 (adv) Greg works hard. diligently, industriously, conscientiously, energetically, strenuously, vigorously, untiringly, persistently, doggedly, unceasingly, steadily, resolutely, furiously.

**harden**
(v) Wait for the mixture to harden. set, solidify, go hard, stiffen, freeze, jell, congeal, cake.
OPPOSITE: soften.

**hardly**
(adv) I hardly recognized you in that hat! scarcely, only just, barely, with difficulty.
OPPOSITE: easily.

**hard-wearing**
(adj) Hard-wearing fabric. tough, strong, sturdy, durable, long-lasting, rugged, resilient, stout.

**hard-working**
(adj) Libby is so hard-working! industrious, diligent, conscientious, energetic, tireless, productive, busy, indefatigable, keen.
OPPOSITES: lazy, workshy.

**harm**
1 (v) Casper wouldn't harm anyone. hurt, injure, ill-treat, abuse, wound, inflict pain on, inflict suffering on.
2 (v) Reading in poor light can harm your eyesight. See **damage** 3.
3 (n) The fire caused a lot of harm. See **damage** 1.
4 (n) The rumours caused a lot of harm. damage, distress, suffering, pain, ill feeling, mischief, upset, trauma.
OPPOSITE: benefit.

**harmful**
1 (adj) Smoking is harmful. damaging, bad for you, dangerous, detrimental, injurious.
OPPOSITES: beneficial, healthy.
2 (adj) Bleach contains harmful substances. See **dangerous** 4.

**harmless**
1 (adj) This mixture is harmless. safe, innocuous, nontoxic, nonpoisonous.
OPPOSITES: dangerous, deadly.
2 (adj) It was just a bit of harmless fun. gentle, innocent, inoffensive, innocuous, blameless, unobjectionable.
OPPOSITES: hurtful, offensive.

**harrowing** see **disturbing**.

**harsh**
1 (adj) The commander spoke in a harsh voice. grating, rasping, rough, strident, raucous, jarring, guttural, gruff, hoarse.
OPPOSITES: soft, gentle.
2 (adj) Life in the prison was harsh. hard, tough, austere, grim, Spartan, bleak, comfortless, brutal.
OPPOSITES: easy, comfortable.
3 (adj) Aunt Bertha's criticisms were harsh. severe, stern, unsparing, unkind, caustic, abrasive, stringent, ruthless, cruel.
OPPOSITES: gentle, compassionate.
4 (adj) The station lights were harsh. glaring, dazzling, garish, over-bright.
OPPOSITES: restful, subdued.

**hassle**
1 (n) (informal) I got my ticket without any hassle. bother, trouble, difficulty, fuss, inconvenience, problem, struggle.
2 (v) (informal) I wish you wouldn't hassle me! See **pester**.

**hassled**
(adj) (informal) After the shopping trip, Mum looked hassled. harassed, stressed, strained, uptight (informal), worried, careworn, troubled, distraught, harried.
OPPOSITES: carefree, relaxed.

**hasty**
1 (adj) You'll make mistakes if you're too hasty. rash, impetuous, impulsive, impatient, hot-headed, reckless, foolhardy.
OPPOSITES: cautious, careful.
2 (adj) The robbers made a hasty getaway. See **fast** 1.
3 (adj) I had a hasty glance at the paper. quick, brief, rapid, hurried, fleeting, passing, cursory, perfunctory.
OPPOSITES: leisurely, thorough.

## hat
(n) headdress, headgear, head covering.

*stetson*

*deerstalker*

*boater*

*pillbox*

*Panama hat*

*pith helmet*

*fez*

*trilby*

*cloche*

**TYPES OF HAT:**
balaclava, baseball cap, beanie, bearskin (*soldier*), beret, boater, bobble hat, bonnet, bowler, cap, cloche, coronet, crash helmet, crown, deerstalker, fez, hard hat, homburg, hunting cap, jockey cap, mitre (*bishop*), nightcap, Panama hat, peaked cap, pillbox, pith helmet, skullcap, sombrero, sou'wester, stetson, sunhat, tiara, top hat, trilby, turban, wimple (*nun*).

## hate
1 (v) *I hate bad language.* detest, loathe, despise, cannot stand, cannot bear, have an aversion to, dislike, abhor, abominate.
OPPOSITES: love, adore.
2 (n) *Miss Blackheart is full of hate.* hatred, hostility, loathing, dislike, ill will, malice, venom, animosity, antagonism, vindictiveness, antipathy, enmity, rancour.
OPPOSITE: love.

## haughty see proud 2.

## haul see pull.

## haunted
1 (adj) *Do you think that Greystone Grange is haunted?* visited by spirits, cursed, jinxed, ghostly, spooky (*informal*), eerie. ❖ *Also see* **ghosts & hauntings**.
2 (adj) *I was haunted by the memory of Samantha's smile.* obsessed, preoccupied, plagued, tormented, troubled, worried.

## have
1 (v) *I have six pets.* own, possess, keep.
2 (v) *How many chapters does your book have?* contain, consist of, include, comprise, incorporate.
3 (v) *You will have good and bad times in your life.* experience, go through, live through, undergo, encounter, meet with, endure, enjoy, suffer.
4 (v) *Everyone will have a prize.* get, receive, be given, win, gain, obtain, acquire, secure, take.
5 (v) *Let's have a party! See* **give** 4.
6 (v) *Let's have tea.* eat, take, consume.
7 (v) *Mum's going to have another baby.* give birth to, produce, bring into the world, bear, deliver, bring up, raise.

## have to
1 (v) *I have to do my homework.* must, should, ought to, have got to, need to.
2 (v) *There's no escaping. You'll have to pay.* be forced to, be compelled to, be made to, be obliged to, be required to.

## havoc
(n) (*informal*) *The pigs caused havoc in the pantry.* chaos, confusion, mayhem, turmoil, upheaval, disruption, disorder.

## haze
(n) *I can hardly see you through the haze.* mist, fog, murk, fumes (*plural*), clouds (*plural*), smog, smoke, dust.

## hazy
1 (adj) *It's so hazy I can hardly see.* misty, foggy, smoky, cloudy, dim, smoggy.
OPPOSITES: clear, bright.
2 (adj) *Without my glasses, everything looks hazy. See* **blurred**.
3 (adj) *I have a hazy memory of that weekend. See* **vague** 2.

## head
1 (n) *I bumped my head.* forehead, temple, skull, pate, cranium, crown, nut (*slang*), bonce (*slang*), block (*slang*).
2 (n) *Why don't you use your head!* brain, brains (*plural*) (*informal*), intelligence, intellect, common sense, wits (*plural*), reason, loaf (*slang*), noddle (*informal*).
3 (n) *Our school has a new head.* headteacher, principal, headmaster, headmistress.
4 (n) *Dad is the head of his company.* boss (*informal*), chief executive, director, president, chairman, MD (managing director), manager, chief, leader.
5 (n) *The problem came to a head at the end of term.* climax, crisis, critical point, turning point, crossroads, culmination.
6 (v) *Who will head the team? See* **lead** 2.

## headache
(n) *I've got a headache.* splitting headache, migraine, sick headache, sore head.

## head for
(v) *Let's head for home.* make for, aim for, go towards, make a beeline for, set off for.

## heal
1 (v) *Will this heal my rash? See* **cure**.
2 (v) *I hope your broken arm will heal soon.* get better, mend, recover, improve, be cured, knit (*bones*).

## health
(n) *Exercise is good for your health.* wellbeing, fitness, strength, constitution.

## healthy
1 (adj) *My parents have always been healthy.* fit, well, in good shape, hale and hearty, strong, active, vigorous, bursting with health, blooming.
OPPOSITES: sickly, unwell.
2 (adj) *Try to eat foods that are healthy.* nutritious, wholesome, nourishing, good for you, healthgiving, beneficial.
OPPOSITES: unhealthy, harmful.

## heap
1 (v) *Heap the leaves together. See* **pile** 2.
2 (n) *A heap of papers. See* **pile** 1.
3 **heaps** (*plural n*) (*informal*) *Lord Lucre has heaps of money. See* **plenty**.

## hear
1 (v) *Did you hear what I said?* catch, pick up, listen to, pay attention to, take in, overhear, eavesdrop on, listen in on.
2 (v) *I hear that you're leaving. See* **understand** 3.

## heart
1 (n) *I like living in the heart of the city. See* **centre** 1, 2.
2 (n) *Andrew has a kind heart.* nature, temperament, character, disposition.

## heartbreaking
(adj) *A heartbreaking story.* heart-rending, tragic, distressing, harrowing, poignant, pitiful, agonizing, tear-jerking (*informal*).

## heartless see cruel 1, 2.

## hearty
1 (adj) *We gave the explorers a hearty welcome.* enthusiastic, effusive, friendly, warm, cordial, sincere, genuine, heartfelt, genial, unreserved, back-slapping.
OPPOSITES: cool, lukewarm.
2 (adj) *After our walk, we'll need a hearty meal.* substantial, filling, satisfying, sizable, nourishing, solid, square.
OPPOSITES: meagre, modest.

## heat
1 (n) *This heat is making me ill.* warmth, high temperature, sultriness, hot weather, warm weather, heatwave, hot spell.
OPPOSITE: cold.
2 (v) *I'll heat some soup for lunch.* heat up, warm up, reheat, cook, make hot.
OPPOSITES: chill, cool.

## heated see passionate 1.

## heath see moor 1.

## heave
1 (v) *Heave the chest onto the deck.* haul, lug, pull, lift, raise, hoist, tug.
2 (v) *Heave the rubbish overboard. See* **throw** 1.
3 (v) *I'm going to heave! See* **vomit**.

## heaven
1 (n) *Do you believe that there is a heaven?* paradise, afterlife, hereafter, next world, life to come, life everlasting.
OPPOSITE: hell.
2 (n) *Our holiday was pure heaven!* bliss, delight, joy, ecstasy, paradise, happiness, seventh heaven.
OPPOSITES: hell (*informal*), misery.

## heavenly
1 (adj) *A heavenly messenger.* divine, angelic, celestial, holy, blessed.
OPPOSITE: earthly.
2 (adj) (*informal*) *A heavenly scent.* glorious, exquisite, delightful, sublime, out of this world, blissful, divine (*informal*), gorgeous, wonderful.
OPPOSITES: vile, disgusting.

# heavy

**heavy**
1 *(adj) I struggled with the heavy suitcase.* weighty, bulky, unwieldy, cumbersome, hefty, massive, top-heavy, immovable.
OPPOSITE: light.
2 *(adj) Ed is heavy for his age.* overweight, hefty, large, beefy *(informal)*, stout, portly.
OPPOSITES: light, slight.
3 *(adj) Mrs Badger has a heavy workload.* demanding, exhausting, gruelling, killing *(informal)*, taxing, onerous, tough, backbreaking, arduous, intolerable.
OPPOSITES: light, undemanding.
4 *(adj) Heavy rain forced us to stay indoors.* torrential, continuous, nonstop, steady, unremitting, severe, penetrating.
OPPOSITE: light.
5 *(adj) The bush was heavy with berries.* laden, weighed down, loaded, burdened.
6 *(adj) This film is too heavy for me.* serious, deep, difficult, profound, dry.
OPPOSITES: lightweight, light-hearted.
7 *(adj) The sky was heavy before the snowstorm.* leaden, louring, gloomy, dull, overcast, threatening, oppressive.

**hectic**
*(adj) The shops are hectic.* busy, bustling, chaotic, frenzied, frantic, frenetic.

**heir, heiress**
*(n) Who is the heir to the throne?* next in line, successor, inheritor of.

**hell**
1 *(n) Do you believe that there is a hell?* underworld, nether world, lower world, infernal regions *(plural)*, inferno.
OPPOSITE: heaven.
2 *(n) (informal) Mum went through hell worrying about Alice.* See **torture** 2.

**help**
1 *(v) I'd like to help you.* give you a hand, assist, lend you a hand, be of use to, be of assistance to, be helpful to, cooperate with, collaborate with, support, advise, give you moral support, back, stand by.
OPPOSITES: obstruct, hinder.
2 *(v) I'll help you if you get into trouble.* rescue, save, come to your rescue, come to your aid, save you from danger.
3 *(v) We raised money to help starving children.* support, aid, assist, benefit.
4 *(v) Will this help my toothache?* cure, relieve, ease, soothe, calm, make better, alleviate, do a world of good for.
5 *(n) I'm grateful for my parents' help.* support, assistance, backing, guidance, advice, cooperation, friendship, aid, encouragement, helping hand.

**helpful**
1 *(adj) Yusuf is always helpful.* obliging, cooperative, supportive, kind, friendly, considerate, caring, neighbourly.
OPPOSITES: unhelpful, uncooperative.
2 *(adj) Cam had some helpful suggestions.* useful, constructive, practical, handy, valuable, worthwhile, beneficial, positive.
OPPOSITES: useless, unhelpful.

**helping**
*(n) Mo wants another helping of pudding.* portion, serving, plate, bowl, plateful, bowlful, dollop *(informal)*, share, ration.

**helpless**
1 *(adj) Jon's injuries left him helpless.* weak, feeble, incapacitated, disabled, debilitated, paralysed, incapable, bedridden, laid up *(informal)*, dependent.
2 *(adj) Without weapons the soldiers were helpless.* powerless, impotent, useless, ineffective, defenceless, unprotected, vulnerable, exposed to danger.

**herb**
*(n)* TYPES OF HERB: basil, bay leaf, chives *(plural)*, coriander, dill, fennel, fenugreek, marjoram, mint, oregano, parsley, rosemary, sage, tarragon, thyme.

**hero**
1 *(n) Write about a sporting hero.* champion, celebrity, star, superstar, megastar, great man, great woman.
2 *(n) Famous Fred is my hero.* idol, role model, ideal, shining example, heart-throb.
3 *(n) I'm playing the hero in the school play.* lead, leading man, good guy *(informal)*, protagonist.
OPPOSITE: villain.

**heroic**
*(adj) Indiana has performed many heroic deeds.* brave, courageous, daring, adventurous, fearless, bold, intrepid, death-defying, swashbuckling, gallant, chivalrous, valiant *(old-fashioned)*.
OPPOSITES: cowardly, faint-hearted.

**heroine**
1 *(n) Miranda is my heroine.* idol, role model, ideal, shining example.
2 *(n) I'm playing the heroine in the school play.* lead, leading lady, protagonist.
OPPOSITE: villain.

**hesitant**
*(adj) Judd was hesitant at first, but in the end he joined in.* tentative, cautious, wary, unsure, uncertain, diffident, reluctant, indecisive, half-hearted, wavering, timid.
OPPOSITES: decisive, resolute.

**hesitate**
*(v) Don't hesitate; just do it!* falter, dither, delay, think twice, waver, hang back.

**hidden**
1 *(adj) Make sure that Mum's present is hidden.* concealed, out of sight, covered up, invisible, unseen, shrouded, veiled.
OPPOSITES: visible, exposed.
2 *(adj) Can you find the hidden message?* secret, obscure, cryptic, coded, mysterious.

**hide**
1 *(v) Quick! It's time to hide!* take cover, lie low, go into hiding, hole up *(informal)*, go to ground, keep out of sight, find a hiding place, conceal yourself, hide out.
2 *(v) Let's hide the present under these clothes.* conceal, put out of sight, cover up, bury, secrete, stow, stash *(informal)*.

3 *(v) It's hard to hide your feelings.* conceal, disguise, cover up, mask, keep secret, suppress, keep under your hat.
OPPOSITES: reveal, show.
4 *(v) The soldiers used bushes to hide the tank.* See **disguise** 3.

**hideous**
1 *(adj) A hideous monster.* See **ugly** 1.
2 *(adj) A hideous crime.* See **horrible** 1.

**high**
1 *(adj) A high tower.* See **tall** 2.
2 *(adj) Your work is of high quality.* excellent, outstanding, exceptional, top, first-class, superior.
OPPOSITES: low, poor.
3 *(adj) Jo has a high voice.* high-pitched, shrill, piercing, piping, soprano, treble.
OPPOSITES: low, deep.
4 *(adj) The price of the meal was rather high.* excessive, steep *(informal)*, exorbitant, extortionate, unreasonable.
OPPOSITES: low, reasonable.
5 *(adj) Lord Lucre moves in high society.* distinguished, exalted, aristocratic, upper class, eminent, leading, influential.
OPPOSITES: humble, lower class.
6 *(adj) (informal) We were all high after the concert.* See **excited**.
7 *(adj) (informal) Ziggy was high after taking drugs.* stoned *(slang)*, spaced out *(slang)*, on a trip *(informal)*, delirious.

**highlight**
1 *(n) Leonora's solo was the highlight of the show.* high spot, climax, high point.
OPPOSITE: low point.
2 *(v) Use make-up to highlight your best features.* emphasize, play up, draw attention to, accentuate, set off, spotlight.
OPPOSITES: conceal, disguise.
3 *(v) The report will highlight the importance of safety.* See **emphasize**.

**highly strung**
*(adj) Try not to upset Bo; she's very highly strung.* nervous, excitable, temperamental, easily upset, sensitive, twitchy, nervy *(informal)*, uptight *(informal)*, tense, hypersensitive, neurotic, wired *(slang)*.

**hijack**
*(v) Terrorists have threatened to hijack the plane.* seize, skyjack, take over, commandeer, hold up, divert, waylay.

**hike**
1 *(v) We had to hike all the way home.* walk, trek, tramp, backpack, trudge, slog, march, ramble, plod, hoof it *(slang)*.
2 *(n) It's a short hike home.* See **walk** 3.

**hilarious**
*(adj) The clowns were hilarious.* side-splitting, hysterical *(informal)*, uproarious, riotous, funny, entertaining.

**hill**
1 *(n) Let's run to the top of the hill.* hillside, mound, hillock, hummock, knoll, dune, bank, peak, ridge, tor, fell.
2 *(n) This hill is too steep for our old van.* slope, incline, rise, gradient.

## hinder
1 (v) That suitcase will hinder you terribly. hamper, get in your way, slow you down, hold you up, delay, handicap, encumber.
2 (v) If you want to go, I won't hinder you. deter, stand in your way, hold you back, prevent, thwart, oppose, obstruct, curb.

## hint
1 (n) There was no hint that Megan was planning to leave. clue, indication, suggestion, inkling, whisper, tip-off, intimation, insinuation, innuendo, allusion.
2 (n) I've picked up a handy hint from this book. tip, suggestion, piece of advice.
3 (n) Is there a hint of garlic in the sauce? trace, suggestion, touch, suspicion, whiff, tinge, dash, soupçon, taste.
4 (v) I did hint that I wanted a bike. imply, suggest, indicate, insinuate, let it be known, mention, signal, give you a tip-off.

## hit
1 (v) I hope Bozo won't hit you. punch, thump, strike, belt (slang), clobber (slang), biff (slang), whop (informal), deck (slang), clout (informal), bash (informal), wallop (informal), sock (slang), take a swipe at (informal), beat you up (informal), kick, knee, slap, smack, spank, beat, club, cosh, batter, pummel, hammer, jab, prod, poke.
2 (v) Don't hit your head! bump, bang, bash (informal), knock, strike, whack, thump, smash, hurt.
3 (v) Hit the ball hard. strike, slam, wham, whack, drive, smash, sock (slang), knock, swat, swipe at (informal), kick, head, punch, tap, volley, lob, putt (golf).
4 (v) I hope our car doesn't hit anything. bump into, crash into, run into, collide with, smash into, bash into (informal), knock, strike, bang into, meet head-on.
5 (v) The bad weather will hit tourism this summer. damage, affect, have an impact on, influence, make an impression on, leave its mark on, knock for six (informal).
6 (n) (informal) This film will be a hit. See success 1.

## hitch
(n) I'm sorry I'm late; there's been a hitch. problem, snag, complication, difficulty, hold-up, setback, hiccup (informal), delay.

## hoard
(v) Jamal loves to hoard his sweets. save, keep, hold on to, hang on to, save up, stockpile, store up, accumulate, amass, stack up, stash away (informal), stow away, set aside, set by, squirrel away.

## hoarse
(adj) My voice is hoarse from shouting. croaky, husky, rough, gruff, rasping, cracked, throaty, raucous, gravelly, harsh.

## hobble
(v) These new shoes make me hobble. limp, shuffle, stumble, totter, stagger.

## hobby
(n) Do you have a hobby? pastime, leisure activity, interest, pursuit, sideline.

## hoist see heave 1.

## hold
1 (v) I want to hold the baby. cuddle, embrace, hug, cradle, carry.
2 (v) Hold my hand. See hold on to.
3 (v) I can't hold your weight. carry, take, support, bear, sustain, shoulder.
4 (v) The police will hold the suspect. detain, confine, keep, remand in custody. OPPOSITES: release, let go.
5 (v) We decided to hold a meeting. call, organize, arrange, convene.
6 (v) The hall will hold six hundred people. seat, take, accommodate, contain, sit.
7 (v) I hope this weather will hold until the weekend. last, hold out, continue, hang on, carry on, stay, persist, keep up, endure.
8 (n) Leya couldn't get a hold on the rock. grip, foothold, footing, purchase.
9 (n) Polly's parents have no hold over her. control, authority, influence, power, clout.

## hold back
(v) Try to hold back your giggles. keep back, control, check, suppress, stifle, smother, restrain, bite back.

## hold on
1 (v) Try to hold on until help comes. hang on, hold out, keep going, persevere, stick it out (informal), hang in there (informal).
2 (v) (informal) Hold on! I'm coming. hang on (informal), wait a minute, stay there, don't go away, hold the line (telephone).

## hold on to
(v) Hold on to my hand. hold, take, hang on to, grip, grasp, clasp, clutch, seize, cling on to, clench.

## hold-up see delay 4.

## hold up
1 (v) I hope the traffic doesn't hold you up. See delay 2.
2 (v) These pillars hold up the roof. See support 1.
3 (v) The robbers planned to hold up the train. rob, hijack, stick up (slang), waylay.

## hole
1 (n) Don't fall into that hole! pit, crater, trench, hollow, dip, depression, burrow, tunnel, pothole, abyss, shaft, excavation.
2 (n) We found a hole in the wall. gap, opening, cavity (wall, tooth), crack, crevice, cranny, chink, fissure, slit, space.
3 (n) There's a hole in my tyre. puncture, slit, tear, split, cut, gash, rent, pinprick.
4 (n) The creature returned to its hole. lair, den, burrow (rabbit), warren (rabbit), earth (fox), sett (badger), cave, tunnel, nest.

## holiday
1 (n) You deserve a holiday. break, rest, vacation, time off, leave.
2 (n) Let's plan a holiday. vacation, trip, tour, cruise, package holiday, self-catering holiday, camping holiday, beach holiday, skiing trip, adventure holiday, safari.
❖ Also see **journey words**, **mountain words**, **sea & seashore**, **seaside words**.

## hollow
1 (n) We found a hollow in the ground. dip, depression, indentation, dent, recess, hole, crater, pit, cavity, trough, basin. OPPOSITES: rise, hill.
2 (adj) The tube was hollow. empty, unfilled, void, hollowed out, vacant. OPPOSITES: solid, filled.
3 (adj) The drum made a hollow sound. deep, low, echoing, reverberating, rumbling, muffled, muted, dull, dead.
4 (adj) The prisoner had hollow cheeks. sunken, caved-in, concave, deep-set (eyes).
5 (adj) I can't trust your hollow promises. empty, meaningless, false, insincere. OPPOSITES: genuine, sincere.

## holy
1 (adj) A holy person. saintly, pious, devout, God-fearing, religious, spiritual, virtuous, pure, godly.
2 (adj) A holy place. sacred, blessed, consecrated, sanctified, divine, hallowed (old-fashioned).

## home
(n) Is this your home? house, residence, pad (slang), dwelling, dwelling place, domicile, abode (old-fashioned), home town, birthplace, native land.
TYPES OF HOME: apartment, bedsit, bungalow, cabin, caravan, castle, chalet, chateau, cottage, council house, detached house, farmhouse, flat, high-rise flat, hostel, houseboat, hut, lodge, log cabin, maisonette, manor house, mansion, mill, mobile home, palace, prefabricated house, ranch, semi-detached house, shack, stately home, studio flat, tenement building, tent, terraced house, tower block, villa, windmill. ❖ Also see **houses & homes**.

## homeless
(adj) You can't imagine what it's like to be homeless. destitute, down-and-out, outcast, abandoned, without a roof over your head, on the streets.

## homely
(adj) Granny's cottage has a homely feel. cosy, comfortable, friendly, welcoming, snug, modest, unassuming, unpretentious, plain, simple.
OPPOSITES: grand, pretentious.

## honest
1 (adj) I want an honest answer to my question. truthful, sincere, straight, frank, candid, plain, direct, open, forthright, straightforward, upfront (informal).
OPPOSITES: false, insincere.
2 (adj) Mr Badger wouldn't cheat; he's an honest man. truthful, honourable, trustworthy, upright, moral, scrupulous, virtuous, law-abiding, principled.
OPPOSITE: dishonest.
3 (adj) I must find an honest way to earn money. above board, legitimate, on the level (informal), ethical, moral, legal, lawful, genuine, bona fide.
OPPOSITES: dishonest, fraudulent.

# honour

**honour**
1 (n) *Mr Badger wouldn't cheat; he's a man of honour.* integrity, principle, high principles *(plural)*, honesty, morality, scruples *(plural)*, decency, virtue.
2 (n) *I will fight to defend my honour. See* **reputation**.
3 (n) *It's an honour to be chosen for the team.* privilege, credit, achievement, source of pride, compliment.

**honourable** *see* **honest** 2.

**hooked** *see* **addicted** 1, 2.

**hooligan**
(n) vandal, delinquent, yob *(informal)*, yobbo *(informal)*, thug, ruffian, roughneck *(slang)*, tough, rowdy, lout, lager lout.

**hop** *see* **skip** 1.

**hope**
1 (v) *We hope that we will arrive on time.* expect, anticipate, believe, trust.
2 (v) *I hope to be a star.* long, want, wish, yearn, aspire, intend, plan, expect, dream.
3 (n) *This result should give you some hope.* confidence, faith, optimism, belief, trust, assurance, expectations *(plural)*.
4 (n) *Cassandra's hope is to be a star. See* **wish** 1.
5 (n) *Try this door; it's our only hope.* chance, opportunity, prospect, possibility.

**hopeful**
1 (adj) *We are hopeful that we will win.* optimistic, confident, expectant.
OPPOSITES: pessimistic, despairing.
2 (adj) *The future looks hopeful.* promising, encouraging, heartening, reassuring, bright, rosy, favourable.
OPPOSITES: hopeless, grim.

**hopeless**
1 (adj) *The situation is hopeless.* beyond hope, beyond repair, beyond remedy, impossible, irredeemable, irreparable.
OPPOSITES: promising, hopeful.
2 (adj) *All our efforts proved to be hopeless.* futile, useless, pointless, worthless, in vain, worth nothing.
OPPOSITES: worthwhile, useful.
3 (adj) *The bad news made us feel hopeless. See* **pessimistic**.
4 (adj) *(informal) I'm hopeless at French.* useless *(informal)*, no good, clueless *(slang)*, incompetent, pathetic *(informal)*, rotten *(informal)*, lousy *(slang)*.
OPPOSITES: expert, proficient.

**horrible**
1 (adj) *We were shocked by the horrible crime.* dreadful, appalling, horrifying, horrific, horrendous, terrible, shocking, ghastly, vile, gruesome, grisly, monstrous, sickening, harrowing, awful, frightful, atrocious, hideous, loathsome, despicable.
2 (adj) *What a horrible meal!* revolting, disgusting, foul, nasty, awful, terrible, dreadful, horrid, vile, yucky *(slang)*, nauseating, stomach-turning, inedible.
OPPOSITES: lovely, delicious.

3 (adj) *Don't be so horrible to me!* mean, nasty, beastly *(informal)*, horrid *(informal)*, unkind, disagreeable, unpleasant, hateful, cruel, spiteful, vicious, offensive, hostile.
OPPOSITES: kind, considerate.

**horrific** *see* **horrible** 1.

**horrified**
(adj) *Mum will be horrified when she hears the news.* shocked, appalled, aghast, outraged, scandalized, disgusted, revolted, sickened, nauseated, offended.

**horrify**
1 (v) *The sight of the monster will horrify you. See* **scare** 1.
2 (v) *Your jokes will horrify Aunt Bertha. See* **shock** 2.

**horror**
(n) *Ellie gazed at the scene in horror.* shock, alarm, dismay, dread, fear, terror, fright, fear and trembling, disgust, loathing, revulsion, consternation, panic.

**horse**
(n) pony, stallion (male), mare (female), foal (baby), colt (young male), filly (young female), gelding (castrated male), mount, steed, nag *(informal)*, charger.
TYPES OF HORSE: carthorse, cob, dressage horse, driving horse, event horse, hunter, polo pony, racehorse, show horse.
COLOURS OF HORSE: bay, chestnut, dapple-grey, dun, grey, palomino, piebald, roan, skewbald.

**hostile**
(adj) *Why are you so hostile?* antagonistic, aggressive, anti *(informal)*, belligerent, unsympathetic, unfriendly, unwelcoming.
OPPOSITES: friendly, peaceable.

**hot**
1 (adj) *I can't stand this hot weather.* sweltering, baking, boiling, scorching, roasting, blistering, burning, blazing, searing, sultry, humid, steamy, torrid.
OPPOSITES: cold, freezing, icy.
2 (adj) *Be careful! This food is hot.* boiling, boiling hot, scalding, piping hot, steaming, sizzling, red-hot, bubbling.
OPPOSITES: cold, chilled.
3 (adj) *I feel hot.* flushed, feverish, sweaty, perspiring, boiling, boiling hot, overheated.
OPPOSITES: cold, freezing.
4 (adj) *Bozo has a hot temper.* fiery, violent, fierce, savage, flaming, impetuous.
OPPOSITES: mild, sweet.
5 (adj) *This curry has a hot taste.* spicy, peppery, fiery, piquant, sharp, strong, pungent, biting.
OPPOSITE: mild.

**house**
1 (n) *Is this your house?* home, residence, pad *(slang)*, dwelling, dwelling place, domicile, abode *(old-fashioned)*.
2 (v) *You need someone to house you.* take you in, put you up, give you a roof over your head, shelter, accommodate.

## horse words

**horse moves**

amble, bolt, buck, canter, gallop, jump, kick, leap, pace, plod, prance, rear, roam

stride, stumble, trek, trot, walk

**horse sounds**

blow, neigh, puff, snort, whinny

**a horse can look...**

beautiful, dainty, elegant, graceful, muscular, powerful, solid, stocky, strong, sturdy

**a horse's coat can be...**

dull, glossy, mangy, matted, rough, shaggy, shiny, silky, sleek, smooth, tangled, thick, velvety

forelock, mane, neck, hindquarters, withers, muzzle, shoulder, breast, belly, foreleg, hindleg, fetlock, piebald

*glossy bay*

*palomino*

*stocky pony*

**a horse can be...**

alert, brave, calm, courageous, docile, excitable, fractious, friendly, frisky, gentle, good-natured, hardy, highly strung, intelligent, lively

nervous, nimble, obedient, playful, skittish, strong-willed, stubborn, surefooted, timid, tireless, uncontrollable, well-behaved, well-schooled, well-trained, wild

## houses and homes

### types of home

apartment
bedsit
bungalow
caravan
castle
cottage
council house
detached house
farmhouse
high-rise flat
hostel
houseboat
maisonette
mansion
mill
mobile home
semi-detached
   house
stately home
tenement
   building
terraced house
tower block
villa

### homes can be made of...

brick
concrete
glass
slate
steel
stone
timber

### homes can be...

half-timbered
ivy-covered
painted
pebble-dashed
plastered
thatched
timber-framed
whitewashed

*half-timbered cottage*   *high-rise flats*   *futuristic house*

### OUTSIDE THE HOME

#### homes may have...

balcony
bay window
casement window
   (hinged window)
chimney pots
dormer window
   (window in roof)
French windows
picture window
sash window
   (push-up
   window)
satellite dish
shutters
skylight
sliding doors
solar panel
TV aerial
window box

#### outside you may see...

crazy paving
creeper
drive
dustbin
fence
fire escape
flowerbed
flower tub
garage
garden
gate
graffiti
hedge
lawn
parking spaces
patio
railings
trellis
washing line

*mobile home*

### INSIDE THE HOME

#### at the windows

bamboo blinds
faded curtains
floor-length
   curtains
net curtains
roller blinds
ruched curtains
tattered curtains
Venetian blinds
vertical blinds

### homes can look...

dilapidated
drab
dreary
elegant
futuristic
gloomy
grand
imposing
modern
neat
neglected
palatial ●
pretty
quaint
rambling
ramshackle
shabby
tumbledown

### on the floors

bare boards
carpet
cork tiles
flagstones
lino
marble floor
parquet floor
quarry tiles
rugs
rush matting
wooden floor

### on the walls

bare plaster
ceramic tiles
damp patch
fancy border
flaking paint
gleaming
   paintwork
mould
peeling wallpaper
picture rail
wood panelling

### homes can feel...

airy
chilly
cluttered
cosy
cramped
damp
dank
draughty
homely
lived-in
luxurious
musty
roomy
snug
spacious
stuffy
sunny
warm
welcoming

*sash window*   *dormer window*   *casement window*

**hover**
(v) The eagle seemed to hover in the air. hang, be suspended, float, drift, be poised, flutter.

**howl**
1 (v) The baby began to howl. bawl, wail, cry, scream, yell, shriek, caterwaul, bellow.
2 (v) Can you hear the wolves howl? bay, yelp, yowl.

**huddle**
1 (v) Let's huddle together to stay warm. bunch, cluster, squeeze, snuggle, nestle, cuddle, press, pack, crowd, herd, throng. OPPOSITES: scatter, disperse.
2 (n) The players formed a huddle in the centre of the pitch. cluster, group, mass, crowd, pack, throng, jumble, heap.

**huff** see **mood** 2.

**hug**
(v) I long to hug you. take you in my arms, hold you close, cuddle, embrace, squeeze, hold, enfold, clasp, cling to.

**huge**
(adj) A huge building. enormous, immense, massive, vast, extensive, colossal, gigantic, monumental, mighty, lofty, towering, mammoth, giant, monstrous, monster, gargantuan, stupendous, ginormous (informal), humongous (informal). OPPOSITES: tiny, minute.

**hum**
(n) Can you hear the hum of the engine? buzz, drone, murmur, purr, whir, throb, thrum, pulsing, vibration.

**humble**
1 (adj) Carl was humble about his success. See **modest** 1.
2 (adj) The emperor expects his subjects to be humble. meek, submissive, docile, respectful, polite, courteous, deferential, servile, slavish, subservient, obsequious. OPPOSITES: proud, arrogant.
3 (adj) The woodcutter lived in a humble cottage. poor, simple, modest, ordinary, plain, unpretentious, lowly (old-fashioned), small, insignificant, unremarkable. OPPOSITES: grand, ostentatious.

**humid**
(adj) It was humid in the jungle. sultry, muggy, steamy, sticky, clammy, close, sweltering, sweaty, damp, dank, misty. OPPOSITES: dry, arid.

**humiliate**
(v) Your mum would never humiliate you in public. degrade, demean, put you down, make you feel small, take you down a peg (informal), make you eat humble pie, debase, deflate, disgrace, discredit, shame, make you ashamed, embarrass.

**humiliating**
(adj) A humiliating defeat. crushing, degrading, demeaning, ignominious, shameful, disgraceful, discreditable, embarrassing, mortifying, undignified.

**humorous** see **funny** 1.

# hunger

**hunger**
(n) *The refugees were dying of hunger.* starvation, malnutrition, lack of food.

**hungry**
1 (adj) *After the match, we were all hungry.* ravenous, famished, starving (informal), peckish (informal), in need of food, half-starved, empty (informal).
OPPOSITES: full, satisfied.
2 (adj) *Fred is hungry for success.* eager, longing, yearning, desperate, greedy.

**hunt**
1 (v) *Foxes hunt small animals.* prey on, stalk, track, trail, chase, pursue, hunt down, hound, capture, kill.
2 (v) *I must hunt for my tie.* See **search** 2.
3 (n) *The police organized a hunt for the escaped prisoner.* See **search** 3.

**hurl** see **throw** 1.

**hurricane** see **storm** 1.

**hurry**
1 (v) *We must hurry or we'll be late.* rush, be quick, get a move on (informal), hurry up, lose no time, dash, fly, run, step on it (informal), make haste (old-fashioned).
OPPOSITES: dawdle, delay.
2 (v) *You can't hurry this process.* rush, hasten, speed up, accelerate, quicken.
OPPOSITES: slow down, delay.
3 (n) *Jessica left in a hurry.* rush, flurry, flap (informal), commotion, bustle.

**hurt**
1 (v) *How did you hurt your arm?* injure, wound, bruise, cut, scratch, graze, scrape, burn, scald, sprain, break, damage.
2 (v) *My comment wasn't meant to hurt you.* hurt your feelings, upset, wound, distress, cause you pain, offend, grieve, sadden, sting, cut you to the quick.
3 (v) *This won't hurt.* be painful, be sore, sting, smart, burn, ache, throb, be tender.
4 (adj) *I felt hurt when Ben ignored me.* upset, wounded, saddened, distressed, cut to the quick, aggrieved, offended, put out.

**hurtful**
(adj) *A hurtful remark.* upsetting, distressing, offensive, unkind, cruel, nasty, spiteful, malicious, vicious, cutting, biting, scathing, wounding, sarcastic, withering.

**hurtle** see **speed** 4.

**husky** see **hoarse**.

**hut**
(n) *The refugees lived in a tiny hut.* shack, shelter, shed, cabin, hovel, shanty, den.

**hype**
1 (n) *After all the hype, the film was disappointing.* See **build-up**.
2 (v) *Famous Fred is trying to hype his new release.* See **promote** 2.

**hypocritical**
(adj) *It's hypocritical of Burglar Beryl to condemn stealing.* two-faced, insincere, deceitful, dishonest, duplicitous, phoney (informal), inconsistent, self-righteous, sanctimonious, holier-than-thou.

**hysterical**
1 (adj) *You'll be hysterical when you hear the news.* frantic, frenzied, in a frenzy, berserk, beside yourself, distraught, overwrought, in a panic, out of control, wild, out of your mind, crazed.
2 (adj) (informal) *The comedy act was hysterical.* See **hilarious**.

# Ii

**icy**
1 (adj) *The weather was icy.* See **cold** 1, 2.
2 (adj) *The pavement was icy.* slippery, like glass, frosty, frozen over, treacherous, glassy, slippy (informal).
3 (adj) *Aunt Bertha gave me an icy stare.* cold, chilly, frosty, glacial, frigid, stony, steely, hard, disapproving, withering, forbidding, hostile, unfriendly.
OPPOSITES: warm, friendly.

**idea**
1 (n) *The idea came to me in the bath.* thought, notion, inspiration, brainwave, plan, scheme, design, concept, theory, hypothesis, solution.

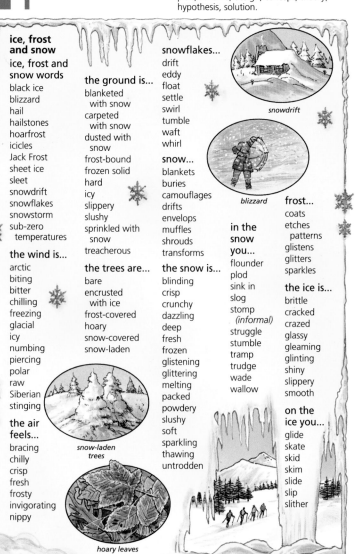

**ice, frost and snow**

**ice, frost and snow words**
black ice
blizzard
hail
hailstones
hoarfrost
icicles
Jack Frost
sheet ice
sleet
snowdrift
snowflakes
snowstorm
sub-zero temperatures

**the wind is...**
arctic
biting
bitter
chilling
freezing
glacial
icy
numbing
piercing
polar
raw
Siberian
stinging

**the air feels...**
bracing
chilly
crisp
fresh
frosty
invigorating
nippy

**the ground is...**
blanketed with snow
carpeted with snow
dusted with snow
frost-bound
frozen solid
hard
icy
slippery
slushy
sprinkled with snow
treacherous

**the trees are...**
bare
encrusted with ice
frost-covered
hoary
snow-covered
snow-laden

*snow-laden trees*

*hoary leaves*

**snowflakes...**
drift
eddy
float
settle
swirl
tumble
waft
whirl

**snow...**
blankets
buries
camouflages
drifts
envelops
muffles
shrouds
transforms

**the snow is...**
blinding
crisp
crunchy
dazzling
deep
fresh
frozen
glistening
glittering
melting
packed
powdery
slushy
soft
sparkling
thawing
untrodden

*snowdrift*

*blizzard*

**in the snow you...**
flounder
plod
sink in
slog
stomp (informal)
struggle
stumble
tramp
trudge
wade
wallow

**frost...**
coats
etches patterns
glistens
glitters
sparkles

**the ice is...**
brittle
cracked
crazed
glassy
gleaming
glinting
shiny
slippery
smooth

**on the ice you...**
glide
skate
skid
skim
slide
slip
slither

**2** *(n) I had an idea that Aunt Bertha was angry.* feeling, notion, suspicion, hunch, inkling, sense, impression.
**3** *(n) Give me an idea about what you'd like for your birthday.* clue, hint, indication, suggestion, inkling, intimation.
**4** *(n) What was the idea of running off like that?* point, purpose, aim, object, intention, meaning, sense, use.
**5** *(n) We all had the same idea about the film.* opinion, thoughts *(plural)*, view, viewpoint, feeling, attitude, impression, judgment, interpretation, conclusion.

**ideal**
**1** *(adj) Edward is an ideal pupil.* model, perfect, faultless, exemplary, dream.
**2** *(adj) This is the ideal time to buy a house.* best, perfect, right, most suitable, correct, most advantageous, optimum.
**3** *(adj) In my ideal world it would always be summer.* imaginary, dream, fantasy, hypothetical, perfect, Utopian.

**idealistic**
*(adj) Jamie has an idealistic view of life.* unrealistic, romantic, over-optimistic, impractical, starry-eyed, perfectionist.
OPPOSITES: realistic, down-to-earth.

**identical**
*(adj) These socks are identical.* the same, matching, indistinguishable, similar, alike.
OPPOSITE: different.

**identify**
**1** *(v) Can you identify these flowers?* recognize, name, put a name to, classify, catalogue, label.
**2** *(v) Try to identify the differences between the two pictures. See* **spot** 1.
**3** **identify with** *(v) Can you identify with the hero in the film?* relate to, sympathize with, feel for, empathize with, put yourself in the shoes of, see through the eyes of.

**idiot**
*(n) Don't be such an idiot!* fool, imbecile *(informal)*, nincompoop, twit *(informal)*, nitwit *(informal)*, numskull, dimwit *(informal)*, twerp *(informal)*, wally *(slang)*, prat *(slang)*, plonker *(slang)*, nerd *(slang)*, jerk *(slang)*, dork *(slang)*, airhead *(slang)*.

**idiotic** *see* **stupid** 1, 2.

**idle** *see* **lazy** 1.

**idol**
**1** *(n) Who is your idol at the moment?* hero, heroine, heart-throb, pin-up *(slang)*, favourite, darling, ideal, star.
**2** *(n) Indiana found a golden idol in the tomb.* image, statue, effigy, god.

**idolize**
*(v) I idolize Famous Fred.* adore, worship, hero-worship, look up to, admire, revere.

**ignorant**
**1** *(adj) I'm totally ignorant about politics.* uninformed, unaware, unknowledgeable, clueless *(slang)*, unenlightened, naive, green, uneducated, unlearned, illiterate.
OPPOSITES: well-informed, educated.

**2** *(adj) That was a very ignorant remark.* stupid, thoughtless, insensitive, shallow, superficial, crass, rude, crude, coarse.
OPPOSITES: intelligent, astute.
**3** **ignorant of** *(adj) Ziggy is ignorant of the dangers of taking drugs.* unaware of, oblivious to, blind to, unfamiliar with, unacquainted with, in the dark about, unconscious of, ill-informed about.
OPPOSITES: aware of, conscious of.

**ignore**
**1** *(v) Try to ignore Theo's nasty remarks.* take no notice of, pay no attention to, disregard, overlook, pass over, turn a deaf ear to, turn a blind eye to, be oblivious to.
OPPOSITES: pay attention to, heed.
**2** *(v) If you try to spoil our game, we'll ignore you.* take no notice of, pay no attention to, send you to Coventry, shut you out, ostracize, shun, reject, snub, give you the cold shoulder *(informal)*, freeze you out *(informal)*, cut you dead *(informal)*.
OPPOSITE: pay attention to.

**ill**
**1** *(adj) Are you ill?* sick, unwell, poorly *(informal)*, off colour, ailing, indisposed, under the weather *(informal)*, out of sorts.
OPPOSITES: well, healthy.
**2** *(adj) I came off the boat feeling ill.* sick, queasy, groggy *(informal)*, nauseous, green around the gills *(informal)*, peculiar, funny *(informal)*, queer, rough *(informal)*, grotty *(slang)*, weak, faint, delicate, fragile, frail.
OPPOSITES: well, strong.

**illegal**
**1** *(adj) Have you ever done anything illegal?* unlawful, criminal, against the law, illicit, forbidden, outlawed, banned, prohibited, proscribed.
OPPOSITES: legal, above board.
**2** *(adj) Dodgy Dave sells illegal whisky.* unlicensed, black market, bootleg, under-the-counter *(informal)*, contraband.
OPPOSITE: legal.

**illegible**
*(adj) Mrs Badger says my handwriting is illegible.* impossible to read, hard to make out, indecipherable, unreadable, unclear, unintelligible, scribbled, scrawled, squiggly.
OPPOSITES: legible, clear.

**illness**
**1** *(n) Araminta is absent with a mysterious illness.* ailment, complaint, disorder, sickness, disease, infection, virus, bug *(informal)*, lurgy *(slang)*, malady, indisposition, affliction, attack.
**2** *(n) Our family has been plagued by illness.* ill health, poor health, sickness, disease, disability, infirmity.
OPPOSITES: good health, fitness.

**illusion**
**1** *(n) That white lady you saw was just an illusion.* hallucination, apparition, figment of your imagination, phantom, spectre, fantasy, dream, mirage (illusion of water).
OPPOSITE: reality.

**2** *(n) One line looks longer than the other, but that's an illusion.* trick, optical illusion, false impression, deception, misperception.

**illustrate**
*(v) Write out your poem and illustrate it.* add pictures to, add drawings to, provide artwork for, depict, decorate, adorn, embellish, ornament.

**illustration**
**1** *(n) Look at the illustration on page 14.* picture, drawing, sketch, artwork, graphics *(plural)*, figure, plate, diagram, graph.
**2** *(n) Give me an illustration of what you mean. See* **example** 1.

**image**
**1** *(n) Can you see an image on your computer screen?* picture, symbol, figure, icon, photograph, reflection.
**2** *(n) You're the image of your dad.* double, living image, spitting image *(informal)*, twin, clone, dead ringer for *(slang)*, chip off the old block *(informal)*.
**3** *(n) People have the wrong image of me.* idea, impression, picture, perception.
**4** *(n) Flash Frank is worried about his image.* public persona, reputation, public perception, outward appearance, aura.

**imaginary**
**1** *(adj) Dragons aren't real; they're imaginary.* make-believe, fictional, nonexistent, unreal, fantastic, legendary, mythical, mythological, fairy-tale.
OPPOSITE: real.
**2** *(adj) Justin has an imaginary illness.* made-up, pretend, invented, imagined, notional, nonexistent.
OPPOSITES: real, actual.

**imagination**
**1** *(n) Designers need imagination.* creativity, inventiveness, originality, inspiration, vision, flair, ingenuity, insight.
**2** *(n) The monster only exists in your imagination.* mind, fantasies *(plural)*, dreams *(plural)*, head.

**imaginative**
*(adj) Jabir is full of imaginative ideas.* creative, original, inspired, inventive, innovative, ingenious, resourceful.
OPPOSITES: unimaginative, unoriginal.

**imagine**
**1** *(v) Can you imagine a world without flowers?* picture, envisage, visualize, see in your mind's eye, conceive of, think of, conjure up, dream up.
**2** *(v) I imagine you'd like some lunch. See* **assume**.

**imitate**
**1** *(v) Felix can imitate Elvis Presley.* do an impression of, impersonate, mimic, do *(informal)*, take off *(informal)*, send up *(informal)*, parody, ape, caricature.
**2** *(v) Try to imitate the style of this poem.* copy, match, duplicate, emulate, follow, take as a model, follow the example of.
**3** *(v) Do soaps on TV imitate real life?* reflect, mirror, echo, parallel, simulate.

## imitation
1 *(n) Is this painting real or is it an imitation? See* **copy** 2.
2 *(n) Bobby does a good imitation of Elvis Presley. See* **impression** 4.
3 *(adj) My bag is made of imitation leather.* synthetic, artificial, mock, fake, man-made, simulated, sham.
OPPOSITES: real, genuine.

## immature
*(adj) Act your age and don't be so immature!* childish, babyish, juvenile, infantile, puerile, adolescent, callow, unsophisticated, inexperienced, green.
OPPOSITES: mature, grown-up.

## immediate
*(adj) I received an immediate reply.* instant, instantaneous, prompt, quick, speedy, swift, direct, punctual.

## immediately
*(adv) Come here immediately!* at once, straightaway, right away, instantly, without delay, promptly, directly, now, right now, this minute, this instant, in the twinkling of an eye.

## immense *see* **huge**.

## immerse *see* **dip** 3.

## immoral
1 *(adj) How could anyone be so immoral?* unprincipled, dishonest, unscrupulous, amoral, unethical, depraved, perverted, corrupt, debauched, degenerate, dissolute, promiscuous, evil, wicked, sinful, bad.
OPPOSITES: moral, upright, virtuous.
2 *(adj) It's immoral to show violent films to young children. See* **wrong** 2.

## immortal
*(adj) An immortal being.* eternal, undying, everlasting, indestructible, timeless, ageless, deathless, divine.
OPPOSITE: mortal.

## impact
1 *(n) The car headlights were shattered by the impact.* blow, collision, crash, bump, bang, jolt, smash, knock, clash.
2 *(n) What sort of impact did the book have?* effect, influence, significance, consequences *(plural)*, repercussions *(plural)*, impression, splash *(informal)*.

## impartial *see* **neutral**.

## impatient
1 *(adj) Waiting makes me feel impatient.* restless, fidgety, edgy, on edge, irritable, agitated, fretful, anxious, nervous, tense, wound up *(informal)*, jittery *(informal)*, excited, like a caged lion.
OPPOSITES: patient, calm.
2 *(adj) Aunt Bertha was very impatient with me.* abrupt, brusque, curt, snappy, short, intolerant, short-tempered, peevish.
OPPOSITES: patient, tolerant.
3 *(adj) I was impatient to open my presents. See* **eager** 2.

## impersonate *see* **imitate** 1.

## impertinent *see* **cheeky**.

## imply *see* **hint** 4.

## importance
*(n) Mrs Badger stressed the importance of the situation.* significance, seriousness, gravity, momentousness, urgency.

## important
1 *(adj) This is an important decision.* significant, major, serious, momentous, vital, critical, crucial, key, grave, weighty, far-reaching, historic, once-in-a-lifetime, earthshaking *(informal)*.
OPPOSITES: insignificant, trivial.
2 *(adj) It's important that you come on time.* essential, vital, necessary, crucial.
OPPOSITES: unimportant, unnecessary.
3 *(adj) Underline the important points in your notes. See* **main**.
4 *(adj) I'd like to be an important person.* influential, powerful, prominent, high-ranking, leading, eminent, distinguished, outstanding, notable, famous.
OPPOSITES: unimportant, insignificant.

## impose on
*(v) I don't want to impose on you.* be a nuisance to, take advantage of, inconvenience, put you out, make you go out of your way, abuse your hospitality, exploit, burden, saddle *(informal)*.

## imposing *see* **impressive** 1.

## impossible
1 *(adj) Pigs can't fly - it's impossible!* out of the question, beyond the bounds of possibility, unthinkable, inconceivable, unimaginable, not to be thought of.
OPPOSITE: possible.
2 *(adj) Don't set yourself impossible goals.* unrealistic, unreasonable, unachievable, unattainable, impractical, unworkable, ridiculous, ludicrous, preposterous, crazy.
OPPOSITES: reasonable, realistic.
3 *(adj) I'm in an impossible situation.* hopeless, intolerable, unbearable, unacceptable, catch-22, no-win *(slang)*.
4 *(adj) (informal) Evie is being impossible again! See* **awkward** 4.

## impractical
1 *(adj) An impractical plan.* unworkable, impossible, unrealistic, useless, wild, crazy.
OPPOSITES: practical, viable.
2 *(adj) Daisy is so impractical.* unrealistic, unbusinesslike, up in the clouds, idealistic, romantic, starry-eyed.
OPPOSITES: sensible, down-to-earth.

## impress
1 *(v) Did the film impress you?* make an impression on, affect, inspire, move, touch, excite, stir, leave its mark on, stick in your mind *(informal)*, grab *(informal)*, influence.
2 *(v) Justin wore a smart suit in order to impress.* make an impact, stand out, cause a stir, be conspicuous, arouse comment, attract attention, make a hit *(informal)*.

## impression
1 *(n) This book made a big impression on me.* impact, effect, influence, mark.

2 *(n) What was your impression of the film?* opinion, view, memory, recollection.
3 *(n) I got the impression something was wrong. See* **feeling** 2.
4 *(n) Do your impression of Elvis Presley.* impersonation, imitation, takeoff *(informal)*, send-up *(informal)*, parody.

## impressive
1 *(adj) An impressive view of the mountains.* striking, imposing, magnificent, splendid, majestic, awe-inspiring, breathtaking, remarkable, grand.
2 *(adj) An impressive film.* powerful, inspiring, remarkable, memorable, magnificent, great, stunning *(informal)*, stirring, moving, touching, thrilling.

## imprison *see* **jail** 2.

## improbable *see* **unlikely**.

## improve
1 *(v) Jamal has begun to improve this term.* make progress, get better, develop, make strides, make headway, progress, come on, advance, shape up *(informal)*.
OPPOSITES: get worse, fall behind.
2 *(v) Mum hopes that business will improve soon.* get better, pick up, perk up, look up, recover, rally, take a turn for the better *(informal)*.
OPPOSITES: worsen, fall off.
3 *(v) I'm doing my best to improve the situation.* make better, put right, rectify, correct, help, mend, ameliorate.
OPPOSITES: make worse, aggravate.
4 *(v) The patient is starting to improve.* get better, recover, be on the mend, be on the road to recovery, recuperate, rally, convalesce, heal, turn the corner.
OPPOSITES: get worse, deteriorate.

## improvement
1 *(n) I've seen some improvement in your work.* progress, development, advance.
OPPOSITE: deterioration.
2 *(n) Our flat needs some improvement.* renovation, refurbishment, redecoration, modernization, alterations *(plural)*.

## improvise
*(v) If you haven't prepared a speech, you'll have to improvise.* ad-lib, make it up as you go along, wing it *(informal)*, speak off the cuff *(informal)*, extemporize.

## impudent *see* **cheeky**.

## impulsive
1 *(adj) Letty is such an impulsive person.* impetuous, unpredictable, spontaneous, hot-headed, rash, reckless, capricious.
OPPOSITES: cautious, prudent.
2 *(adj) Jen took an impulsive decision to become a vegetarian. See* **sudden** 2.

## inaccessible *see* **remote**.

## inaccurate
*(adj) This account is inaccurate.* incorrect, inexact, imprecise, untrue, false, wrong, flawed, unreliable, unsound, misleading, vague, full of errors, wide of the mark.
OPPOSITES: accurate, exact.

**inadequate**
1 *(adj) Our supplies are inadequate.* insufficient, not enough, meagre, scanty, sparse, in short supply, low.
OPPOSITES: adequate, sufficient.
2 *(adj) Mrs Badger said my essay was inadequate.* unsatisfactory, unacceptable, not good enough, not up to scratch *(informal),* incomplete, deficient, sketchy.
OPPOSITES: adequate, satisfactory.
3 *(adj) My older sister makes me feel inadequate.* See **inferior** 2.

**incessant** *see* **constant** 1.

**in charge** *see* **responsible** 3.

**incident**
1 *(n) That was a memorable incident! See* **event** 1.
2 *(n) I hope there won't be an incident at the match.* disturbance, clash, skirmish, confrontation, scene, commotion, row, fracas, fight, contretemps.

**include**
1 *(v) This kit should include everything you need.* contain, incorporate, hold, consist of, comprise, involve, take in, encompass, embrace.
OPPOSITES: exclude, leave out.
2 *(v) Try to include this point in your essay.* incorporate, bring in, build in, cover, take into account, deal with, introduce, put in, insert, slip in, add, enter.
OPPOSITES: leave out, omit.

**incompetent**
*(adj) Mum thinks her boss is totally incompetent.* incapable, inept, inadequate, ineffectual, inexpert, useless *(informal),* hopeless *(informal),* inefficient, unqualified.
OPPOSITES: competent, capable.

**inconsiderate** *see* **thoughtless**.

**inconvenient**
1 *(adj) You've picked an inconvenient moment to arrive.* awkward, inopportune, ill-timed, untimely, unfortunate, unsuitable, embarrassing, bad.
OPPOSITES: convenient, suitable.
2 *(adj) It's inconvenient when the water is cut off.* awkward, tiresome, annoying, irritating, troublesome, a nuisance, a bore.
OPPOSITES: convenient, handy.
3 *(adj) This parcel is an inconvenient shape. See* **awkward** 3.

**increase**
1 *(v) Pupil numbers should increase.* rise, grow, multiply, escalate, climb, soar, shoot up, rocket, snowball, spiral, mushroom.
OPPOSITES: decrease, decline.
2 *(v) The noise began to increase when Mrs Badger left the room.* grow, rise, build up, intensify, mount, escalate, heighten.
OPPOSITES: decrease, diminish.
3 *(v) Jet wants to increase her CD collection.* expand, extend, enlarge, build up, widen, broaden, develop, add to, boost, swell, enhance, augment.
OPPOSITES: reduce, decrease.

4 *(n) There has been an increase in crime.* rise, growth, explosion, escalation, upsurge, upturn, leap.
OPPOSITES: decrease, fall.

**incredible**
1 *(adj) Jojo told an incredible tale about meeting an alien.* unbelievable, far-fetched, unlikely, implausible, improbable, impossible, unconvincing, amazing, extraordinary, absurd, preposterous.
2 *(adj) (informal) I had an incredible time at the party. See* **fantastic** 3.

**indecent**
1 *(adj) An indecent joke. See* **rude** 2.
2 *(adj) Indecent clothes.* immodest, improper, unseemly, revealing, titillating, outrageous, shocking, tasteless, vulgar.
OPPOSITES: decent, respectable.

**indecisive**
*(adj) Bart is so indecisive, he just can't make up his mind.* irresolute, dithery, tentative, hesitant, undecided, uncertain, vacillating, in two minds.
OPPOSITES: decisive, certain.

**independent**
1 *(adj) Europe is made up of many independent countries.* separate, distinct, unconnected, individual, self-governing, autonomous, sovereign, non-aligned.
2 *(adj) Fenella is too independent to work well in a team.* self-reliant, self-sufficient, self-contained, individualistic, unconventional, free-thinking, liberated.

**indicate** *see* **show** 2, 5.

**indifferent**
*(adj) How can you be so indifferent when people are suffering?* unconcerned, unfeeling, apathetic, unsympathetic, uncaring, unmoved, impassive, heedless, blasé, detached, unemotional, cold.
OPPOSITES: caring, concerned.

**indignant** *see* **annoyed**.

**indirect**
*(adj) I took an indirect route home.* roundabout, circuitous, winding, meandering, rambling, tortuous, long.
OPPOSITES: direct, straight.

**individual**
1 *(adj) You can buy individual portions of butter.* single, separate, personal.
2 *(adj) Maisie has an individual style.* unique, distinctive, personal, idiosyncratic, particular, characteristic, special, singular.

**indulge**
1 *(v) Gran loves to indulge us. See* **spoil** 3.
2 **indulge in** *(v) Why don't you indulge in a relaxing bath?* treat yourself to, wallow in, luxuriate in, revel in, bask in.

**indulgent**
*(adj) I wish my parents were as indulgent as yours.* lenient, permissive, tolerant, liberal, easy-going, understanding, sympathetic, forbearing, generous, doting, fond, overindulgent, soft.
OPPOSITE: strict.

**inevitable**
*(adj) This disaster was inevitable.* unavoidable, unpreventable, inescapable, bound to happen, certain, fated, destined, ordained, decreed, out of your hands.

**inexperienced**
*(adj) An inexperienced team member.* new, untried, untrained, untutored, unpractised, unseasoned, unqualified, green, raw.
OPPOSITE: experienced.

**infatuated** *see* **in love with**.

**infect**
*(v) This virus could infect our water supply.* contaminate, poison, pollute, blight, taint.

**infectious** *see* **catching**.

**inferior**
1 *(adj) This is inferior work. See* **poor** 2.
2 *(adj) My older sister makes me feel inferior.* inadequate, useless *(informal),* worthless, ineffectual, small, no good.

**infinite**
1 *(adj) Infinite time.* unlimited, endless, never-ending, eternal, everlasting.
2 *(adj) Infinite space.* boundless, limitless, bottomless, immeasurable, fathomless.
3 *(adj) There are an infinite number of stars in the sky.* countless, incalculable, untold, numberless, unimaginable.

**inflate** *see* **blow up** 3.

**influence**
1 *(n) Jak has a lot of influence in my life.* control, clout, pull, sway, impact, effect, authority, dominance, mastery.
2 *(v) I don't want to influence your decision.* affect, sway, control, bring pressure to bear on, prejudice, guide, determine, direct, manipulate, alter.

**inform**
1 *(v) We need to inform everyone of the new arrangements. See* **tell** 1.
2 **inform on** *(v) Burglar Beryl doesn't want to inform on her friends.* betray, denounce, incriminate, accuse, tell on *(informal),* blow the whistle on *(informal),* grass on *(slang),* shop *(slang),* squeal on *(slang),* snitch on *(slang),* rat on *(informal).*

**informal**
1 *(adj) The party will be quite informal.* casual, relaxed, simple, unpretentious, cosy, unceremonious, unofficial, easy.
OPPOSITES: formal, official.
2 *(adj) Sanjay has an informal manner. See* **casual** 1.
3 *(adj) Don't use informal language in your essay.* colloquial, slangy, chatty.
OPPOSITE: formal.

**information**
1 *(n) Computers store information.* data, facts *(plural),* statistics *(plural),* details *(plural),* material, knowledge.
2 *(n) I'd like some information about camping.* details *(plural),* advice, info *(informal),* bumf *(informal),* gen *(informal),* inside knowledge, lowdown *(informal).*

**infuriating** *see* **annoying**.

## initiative

*(n) You need lots of initiative to set up a theatre company.* resourcefulness, enterprise, get-up-and-go *(informal)*, dynamism, drive, ambition, push *(informal)*, leadership, inventiveness, originality, creativity.

## injection

*(n) My arm was sore after the injection.* jab *(informal)*, inoculation, vaccination, shot *(informal)*, booster.

## injure

*(v) Did the terrorists injure many people?* hurt, harm, wound, maim, stab, shoot, beat up *(informal)*, bruise, cripple, disable, mutilate, mangle, damage.

## injustice

*(n) Todd wants to fight against injustice.* unfairness, discrimination, prejudice, inequality, oppression, partisanship, bias.
OPPOSITES: justice, fairness.

## in love with

*(phrase) Maisie is in love with Famous Fred.* attracted to, infatuated with, head over heels in love with, besotted with, passionate about, crazy about *(informal)*, smitten with, devoted to, enamoured of.

## innocent

1 *(adj) Burglar Beryl insists that she is innocent.* not guilty, in the clear *(informal)*, free from blame, blameless, guiltless, above suspicion, clean *(slang)*.
OPPOSITE: guilty.
2 *(adj) It was just an innocent remark. See* **harmless** 2.
3 *(adj) When Jet left home she was still very innocent.* naive, inexperienced, childlike, gullible, credulous, trusting, unworldly, wet behind the ears *(informal)*.
OPPOSITES: sophisticated, worldly.

## inquire *see* **ask** 1.

## inquisitive

1 *(adj) Don't you hate inquisitive neighbours? See* **nosy**.
2 *(adj) Lara has an inquisitive approach to life.* inquiring, questioning, interested, curious, lively, alert, probing, sceptical.

## insane *see* **mad** 1, 2, 3.

## inscription

*(n) Can you read the inscription on this stone?* writing, lettering, words *(plural)*, engraving, carving, etching.

## insect

*(n)* creepy-crawly *(informal)*, bug.

## insensitive *see* **thoughtless**.

## inside

1 *(n) We cleaned the inside of the car.* interior, contents *(plural)*.
OPPOSITES: outside, exterior.
2 *(adv) Stay inside!* indoors, under cover.
OPPOSITE: outside.
3 *(adj) The inside walls are flimsy.* interior, internal, indoor, inner, innermost.
OPPOSITE: outside.

## insignificant *see* **unimportant**.

## insincere

1 *(adj) I despise insincere politicians.* hypocritical, two-faced, deceitful, devious, evasive, untruthful, dishonest, shifty.
OPPOSITES: sincere, honest.
2 *(adj) Jessie gave me an insincere smile.* false, artificial, feigned, affected, put-on, phoney *(informal)*, flattering.
OPPOSITES: sincere, genuine.

## insist

1 *(v) I insist that you tidy your room.* demand, require, command, urge, order.
2 *(v) If anyone objects, you must insist.* stand firm, stand your ground, make a stand, put your foot down, be resolute, be determined, not take no for an answer.
OPPOSITES: back down, give way.
3 *(v) Beryl continues to insist that she is innocent.* claim, assert, maintain, affirm, emphasize, stress, swear, vow.

## inspect

*(v) Experts came to inspect our school.* examine, check, monitor, look over, check out, scrutinize, investigate, study, survey, view, observe, appraise.

## inspiration

1 *(n) What was the inspiration for your poem?* stimulus, idea, spur, motivation, starting point, influence, encouragement.
2 *(n) I've had an inspiration! See* **idea** 1.

## inspire

*(v) This book should inspire you.* stimulate, fire your imagination, motivate, spark you off, spur you on, encourage, enthuse, energize, galvanize, stir, hearten.

## instant

1 *(n) I'll go in an instant. See* **moment** 1.
2 *(adj) An instant reply. See* **immediate** 1.

## instinct

1 *(n) Oscar has an instinct for saying the right thing.* knack, gift, talent, genius, intuition, aptitude, capacity, predisposition.
2 *(n) I had an instinct that someone was following me.* feeling, hunch, sense, gut feeling *(informal)*, presentiment, intuition, sixth sense, gut reaction *(informal)*.

## instructions

*(plural n) Follow the instructions carefully.* directions *(plural)*, rules *(plural)*, guidelines *(plural)*, recommendations *(plural)*, advice.

## instrument *see* **musical instrument**.

## insult

1 *(v) I hope the boys won't insult you.* be rude to, call you names, slag you off *(slang)*, put you down, sneer at, abuse, offend, snub, slight, hurt your feelings, mortify, humiliate, wound, revile, slander.
2 *(n) Your insult really hurt me.* abuse, taunt, gibe, put-down, snub, slur, slight.

## insulting

*(adj) Insulting comments.* rude, abusive, hurtful, wounding, offensive, snide, disparaging, patronizing, scornful, humiliating, slanderous, scurrilous.

## intelligent

1 *(adj) An intelligent pupil. See* **clever** 1.
2 *(adj) An intelligent comment.* astute, perceptive, discerning, sensible, shrewd, apt, well-informed, profound, wise, clever.
OPPOSITES: stupid, ignorant.

## intend *see* **mean** 3.

## intense

1 *(adj) I felt an intense pain in my leg.* sharp, agonizing, excruciating, severe, acute, violent, extreme, great, fierce.
OPPOSITES: slight, mild.
2 *(adj) Jan was seized by an intense desire to win. See* **strong** 6.

## intentional *see* **deliberate**.

## interest

1 *(n) The poster has attracted lots of interest.* attention, curiosity, notice, concern, suspicion, scrutiny, awareness, response, reaction, sympathy.
2 *(n) The lecture was of no interest to me.* relevance, concern, importance, significance, consequence, value, note.
3 *(n) Taking up a new interest is a good way to meet people. See* **hobby**.
4 *(v) I think this game should interest you.* appeal to, arouse your curiosity, capture your imagination, hold your attention, amuse, attract, intrigue, turn you on *(slang)*, grab *(informal)*, fascinate, captivate, enthral, absorb, engross, rivet.
OPPOSITE: bore.

## interested

1 *(adj) I'm interested to know how the story ends.* curious, fascinated, intrigued, keen, eager, excited, concerned.
2 *(adj) Benji is an interested pupil.* enthusiastic, keen, attentive, responsive.
OPPOSITES: apathetic, bored.
3 **interested in** *(adj) Yoko is interested in science fiction.* into *(informal)*, keen on, fascinated by, enthusiastic about, fond of.

## interesting

1 *(adj) This TV programme is really interesting.* fascinating, intriguing, compelling, enthralling, absorbing, gripping, riveting, engrossing, thought-provoking, stimulating, entertaining, spell-binding, captivating, compulsive.
OPPOSITES: boring, dull.
2 *(adj) Barney has an interesting job.* fascinating, varied, stimulating, exciting, challenging, unpredictable, unusual.
OPPOSITES: boring, tedious.

## interfere

1 *(v) It's best not to interfere.* get involved, poke your nose in *(informal)*, stick your oar in *(informal)*, intervene, be a busybody, meddle, tamper, intrude, pry, butt in.
2 **interfere with** *(v) Bad weather will interfere with our plans. See* **upset** 2.

## international

*(adj) Pollution is an international problem.* global, worldwide, universal.
OPPOSITES: national, regional, local.

**interrogate** *see* **question** 5.

**interrupt**
1 *(v) Don't interrupt when I'm talking.* butt in, barge in *(informal)*, cut in, chip in *(informal)*, chime in *(informal)*, heckle, muscle in *(informal)*, disturb, intrude.
2 *(v) We must interrupt this programme to bring you a newsflash.* break off, break into, suspend, cut short, discontinue.

**interview**
1 *(v) We will interview six candidates for the job.* talk to, sound out, question, quiz.
2 *(v) The detective was keen to interview Burglar Beryl. See* **question** 5.
3 *(n) I had an interview with the careers teacher. See* **talk** 6.

**intimate**
1 *(adj) Jade is an intimate friend of mine.* close, dear, bosom, treasured, special.
2 *(adj) My diary contains my most intimate secrets. See* **private** 2.
3 *(adj) This cottage has an intimate feel.* cosy, friendly, warm, welcoming, inviting.

**intimidate** *see* **scare** 2.

**intolerable** *see* **unbearable**.

**intolerant**
*(adj) Why is Aunt Bertha so intolerant?* critical, disapproving, narrow-minded, small-minded, bigoted, prejudiced, illiberal, racist, sexist, ageist, homophobic, chauvinist, xenophobic.
OPPOSITES: tolerant, broad-minded.

**intriguing** *see* **fascinating**.

**introduce**
1 *(v) May I introduce you to Jon?* present, make you known, acquaint you with.
2 *(v) Simon will introduce the magic act. See* **announce** 2.
3 *(v) Mrs Badger wants to introduce a new system of rewards.* bring in, set up, start, establish, initiate, launch, inaugurate, institute, set in motion, pioneer.

**introduction**
*(n) Listen to this introduction.* opening, intro *(informal)*, lead-in, preamble, opening remarks *(plural)*, foreword *(book)*, preface *(book)*, overture *(music)*, opening bars *(plural)* *(music)*, prologue *(play)*.
OPPOSITE: conclusion.

**invade**
*(v) The soldiers will invade the city.* attack, storm, march into, enter, descend on, take over, overrun, occupy, raid, plunder.

**invasion** *see* **attack** 4.

**invent**
*(v) Gita loves to invent new recipes.* make up, think up, devise, create, concoct, dream up, come up with, improvise, formulate, design.

**invention**
*(n) Professor Peabody has come up with a new invention.* creation, discovery, innovation, design, brainchild *(informal)*, gadget, contraption, contrivance, device.

**investigate**
*(v) We need to investigate the causes of the accident.* inquire into, look into, go into, make inquiries about, gather evidence about, study, examine, consider, explore, research, probe, scrutinize, analyse, inspect, check out.

**investigation**
1 *(n) Please work on this investigation for homework.* study, exploration, research, analysis, survey, review, examination.
2 *(n) The police are conducting an investigation.* inquiry, postmortem (examination of a dead body), hearing, inquest, fact-finding exercise, review.

**invisible**
*(adj) The camouflaged soldiers were invisible in the bushes.* hidden, concealed, disguised, undetectable, indiscernible, inconspicuous, out of sight.
OPPOSITES: visible, conspicuous.

**invite**
*(v) The king and queen invite you to the ball.* ask, request the pleasure of your company at, summon, bid *(old-fashioned)*.

**inviting** *see* **tempting**.

**involve**
1 *(v) The pantomime will involve everyone.* affect, concern, draw in, include, touch.
OPPOSITE: exclude.
2 *(v) I won't involve you in this crazy plan.* include, mix you up, implicate, embroil.
3 *(v) What will the job involve?* entail, require, demand, necessitate, mean, imply.

**involved**
1 *(adj) I don't like story lines that are too involved. See* **complicated**.
2 *(adj) Do you know who was involved in the robbery?* mixed up, implicated, caught up, in on *(informal)*, included, associated, concerned, taking part, participating.

**irrelevant**
*(adj) Your comments are irrelevant to the subject.* unrelated, unconnected, beside the point, neither here nor there, inappropriate, unnecessary, inessential, immaterial, pointless, extraneous.
OPPOSITES: relevant, pertinent.

**irresistible**
*(adj) I felt an irresistible urge to laugh.* powerful, overpowering, overwhelming, compelling, uncontrollable, urgent.

**irresponsible**
*(adj) You're too irresponsible to be trusted.* unreliable, untrustworthy, reckless, careless, immature, harebrained, wild, scatterbrained, erratic, flighty, feckless.
OPPOSITES: responsible, reliable.

**irritable** *see* **bad-tempered**.

**irritate**
1 *(v) Seb's jokes irritate me. See* **annoy** 1.
2 *(v) Will this cardigan irritate the baby's skin?* chafe, rub, scratch, itch *(informal)*, hurt, tickle, inflame, redden, make itchy.

**irritated** *see* **annoyed**.

**irritating** *see* **annoying**.

**isolated**
1 *(adj) The cottage was very isolated.* remote, out-of-the-way, inaccessible, lonely, in the middle of nowhere, secluded, off the beaten track, cut off.
2 *(adj) Imogen felt isolated in her new school. See* **alone** 2.

**issue**
1 *(n) Gus feels strongly about the issue of whaling. See* **subject**.
2 *(n) Have you read the November issue of "Rap Weekly"?* edition, copy, instalment, publication, number.
3 *(v) The police will issue a description of Burglar Beryl. See* **release** 3.
4 *(v) The prison will issue you with a uniform.* supply, provide, furnish, equip.

**itch**
1 *(n) I've got an itch on my back.* tickle, prickle, tingling, itchiness, irritation.
2 *(v) Chickenpox makes your skin itch.* tickle, prickle, tingle, crawl, burn.

**itchy**
*(adj) The nettles gave me an itchy rash.* prickly, tickly, irritating, maddening, uncomfortable, painful, burning.

**item**
1 *(n) Jen added another item to her list.* object, article, thing, point, detail, entry.
2 *(n) I saw an interesting item in the newspaper. See* **article** 1.

**jab**
1 *(v) Jo began to jab at the paper with her brush.* stab, poke, lunge, thrust, punch.
2 *(n) Andy gave me a jab in the ribs.* dig, poke, prod, nudge, stab, punch.
3 *(n) (informal) Did the doctor give you a jab? See* **injection**.

**jacket** *see* **clothes**.

**jagged**
1 *(adj) The knife had a jagged edge.* uneven, serrated, ragged, notched, barbed, toothed, irregular, zigzag, spiky.
2 *(adj) I walked carefully over the jagged rocks.* craggy, sharp, uneven, spiky, pointed, ridged, rough, angular.

**jail**
1 *(n) Burglar Beryl spent a month in the local jail.* gaol, prison, detention centre, cells *(plural)*, nick *(slang)*, can *(slang)*, slammer *(slang)*, clink *(slang)*.
2 *(v) The judge decided to jail Burglar Beryl.* send to prison, lock up, send down *(informal)*, imprison, put away, put behind bars, detain, incarcerate, confine.
OPPOSITES: free, release.

# jam

**jam**
1 *(n) The accident caused a jam on the bypass.* traffic jam, hold-up, snarl-up *(informal)*, tailback, bottleneck, blockage, obstruction, gridlock, congestion.
2 *(v) I tried to jam all my clothes into the case. See* **cram** 1.
3 *(v) All these cars will jam the town centre.* clog, congest, block, obstruct, overcrowd, bung up.

**jangle**
*(v) I heard the keys jangle in the lock.* clink, clank, clang, rattle, clatter, chime *(bell)*.

**jealous**
1 *(adj) I was jealous when I saw Liam's new bike. See* **envious**.
2 *(adj) Clarissa's boyfriend is so jealous.* possessive, suspicious, distrustful, doubting, insecure, clingy, overprotective.

**jealousy**
1 *(n) I was filled with jealousy when I saw Carl's new bike. See* **envy** 1.
2 *(n) Jon's jealousy drove his girlfriend away.* suspicion, suspiciousness, distrust, possessiveness, insecurity.

**jeer**
1 *(v) Let's jeer at the villain! See* **boo**.
2 **jeer at** *(v) I'm scared Bozo will jeer at me. See* **make fun of**.

**jerk**
1 *(v) Jerk the rope when you're ready.* tug, yank, pull, twitch, tweak, jiggle, wrench.
2 *(v) I felt the train jerk. See* **jolt** 1.

**jerky**
*(adj) The robot moved with jerky steps.* jumpy, twitchy, shaky, jolting, lurching, fitful, spasmodic, convulsive.
OPPOSITES: smooth, gliding.

**jet**
*(n) A jet of water gushed from the pipe.* spurt, fountain, stream, spout, spray, gush.

**jewel**
*(n)* gem, precious stone, gemstone, stone, rock *(slang)*, sparkler *(informal)*.
TYPES OF JEWEL: amethyst, aquamarine, diamond, emerald, garnet, jade, jasper, jet, lapis lazuli, moonstone, onyx, opal, pearl, ruby, sapphire, topaz, turquoise, zircon.
❖ *Also see* **treasure words**.

**jewellery**
*(n) Shall I wear my jewellery?* jewels *(plural)*, trinkets *(plural)*, finery, gems *(plural)*, regalia, costume jewellery.
TYPES OF JEWELLERY: anklet, bangle, beads *(plural)*, bracelet, brooch, chain, charm bracelet, choker, crucifix, cuff links *(plural)*, earring, engagement ring, eternity ring, locket, medallion, necklace, nose ring, pendant, pin, signet ring, tiara, tiepin, watch, wedding ring.

**jingle**
1 *(v) Can you hear the sleigh bells jingle?* ring, tinkle, jangle, chime, clink, clank.
2 *(n) I can't get that jingle out of my head.* song, tune, melody, ditty, chorus.

**jittery** *(informal) see* **nervous**.

**job**
1 *(n) It's my job to keep the classroom tidy.* responsibility, duty, task, chore, role, function, contribution.
2 *(n) What type of job are you interested in?* work, career, employment, occupation, profession, trade, business, line of work.
3 *(n) Mum is looking for a new job.* post, position, situation, appointment.

**jog**
1 *(v) I jog every day.* run, go running, go jogging, exercise.
2 *(v) Don't jog me when I'm writing.* nudge, prod, poke, push, knock, tap, elbow, jiggle, jolt, jerk, jar, jostle.
3 *(v) This picture should jog your memory.* refresh, jolt, prompt, stir, stimulate, prod.

**join**
1 *(v) Join the pieces together.* attach, fasten, fix, fit, link, connect, stick, glue, tie, bind, pin, nail, fuse, weld, solder, cement.
OPPOSITES: detach, separate.
2 *(v) Do you want to join our club?* become a member of, enrol in, sign up for, register with, enlist in, affiliate with.
3 *(v) Where do the two roads join?* meet, come together, converge, cross, intersect.
OPPOSITES: fork, divide.

**join in**
*(v) I want you all to join in.* take part, participate, contribute, pitch in, pull your weight, do your bit, lend a hand.

**joint**
*(adj) The garden is our joint responsibility.* shared, mutual, common, collective, combined, united, communal, cooperative.
OPPOSITE: individual.

**joke**
1 *(n) Have you heard the joke about the purple cat?* gag *(informal)*, wisecrack *(informal)*, one-liner *(informal)*, quip, pun.
2 *(n) Let's play a joke on Joel. See* **trick** 2.
3 *(v) It's a serious matter; don't joke.* make jokes, crack jokes, jest, fool around *(informal)*, tease, mock, be facetious.

**jolly** *see* **merry**.

**jolt**
1 *(v) I felt the train jolt as it moved off.* lurch, jerk, jar, start, bump, shake, jounce.
2 *(v) Don't jolt me! See* **jog** 2.

**jostle**
*(v) Don't let the others jostle you out of the way.* push, shove, elbow, crowd, hustle, press, squeeze, force, knock, bump.

**journalist** *see* **reporter**.

**journey**
1 *(n) The explorers set out on their journey.* voyage, travels *(plural)*, expedition, trek, safari, adventure, odyssey.
2 *(n) Write about your journey to France.* trip, excursion, outing, jaunt, tour, flight, crossing, cruise, drive, voyage.
3 *(v) I must journey home. See* **travel** 1.

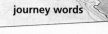

## journey words

**for your journey you may need...**
boarding pass
foreign currency
hand luggage
luggage
map
passport
phrasebook
travel games
traveller's cheques
travel tickets
visa

**journeys can be...**
boring
bumpy
dramatic
eventful
exhilarating
fascinating
nerve-racking
relaxing
rough
smooth
tedious
thrilling
tiring
turbulent *(air)*

*luggage sticker*

**on a journey you may feel...**
airsick
bored
excited
exhausted
expectant
fed up *(informal)*
fidgety
hot
jet-lagged
jittery *(informal)*

nervous
queasy
restless
seasick
sticky
sweaty
tired
travel-sick
worn out

**AIR**

**at the airport**
air-traffic control tower
arrivals hall
bureau de change
check-in desk
customs
departure lounge
duty-free shop
flight indicator board
information desk
luggage carousel
luggage trolley
observation terrace
passenger bus
passenger terminal
passport control
restaurant
runway
X-ray machine

**you can travel by...**
aeroplane
airliner
executive jet
helicopter
jumbo jet *(informal)*
light aircraft

**planes...**
ascend
bank
circle
climb
cruise
descend
drop
glide
land
mount
nose-dive
rise
soar
take off
taxi

*hovering helicopter*

## RAIL

### at the station
arrivals and
  departures board
concourse
  (large central area)
left-luggage office
luggage locker
luggage trolley
platform
railway track
snack bar
station
  announcement
taxi rank
ticket machine
ticket office
waiting room

### you can
### travel by...
commuter train
express train
high-speed train
locomotive
monorail
overnight train
steam train
tube
underground
  train

*luggage
label*

### trains...
glide
grind to a halt
hurtle
jerk
jolt
judder
  (informal)
lurch
pull away
pull in
rock
shake
shudder
sway
trundle

### train sounds
clank
clatter
click
creak
grind
hum
rattle
squeal
swish
whistle
whoosh

*rail
tickets*

### trains can be...
airless
comfortable
cramped
crowded
draughty
jam-packed
shabby
stuffy

### rail problems
cancellation
derailment
obstruction on
  the line
points failure
rail strike
signal failure

*network
map*

*high-speed
train*

## SEA

### you can
### travel by...
catamaran
cruise ship
ferry
hovercraft
hydrofoil
liner

### ships...
berth
cruise
dock
glide
list
pitch
plough through
  the waves
put to sea
roll
sail
set sail
skim
steam
tilt
toss
wallow

### on the ship
bridge
cabin
cafeteria
car deck
cinema
control room
deck
duty-free shop
engine room
funnel
lifeboat
lookout tower
passenger lounge
porthole
restaurant
snack bar
sun deck

### problems at sea
cancelled crossing
choppy seas
delayed crossing
engine failure
running aground
stormy seas

*cruising
catamaran*

*airliner leaving
the runway*

### plane
### sounds
drone
hum
roar
shriek
throb
vibrate
whine

### on the plane
air steward
aisle
captain
emergency exit
flight deck
foldaway table
galley (kitchen)
in-flight
  entertainment
life jacket
overhead
  compartment
safety
  demonstration
seat belt
window seat

*foreign
coins*

### air travel
### problems
air pockets
bad weather
cancelled flight
delayed flight
lost luggage
turbulence

*hire car
key*

## ROAD

### you can
### travel by...
bicycle
bus
camper van
car
coach
hire car
minibus
moped
motorcycle
scooter
taxi

### vehicles...
accelerate
brake
crawl
cruise
nose forward
overtake
park
pass
reverse
skid
speed
stall
swerve

### traffic
### sounds
beep
chug
cough
growl
honk
hum
purr
rev
roar
screech
splutter
toot
vroom

### roads can be...
bumpy
busy
chock-a-block
congested
empty
endless
hazardous
narrow
scenic
single-track
smooth
steep
straight
treacherous
tree-lined
twisting
wide
winding

### problems on
### the road
accident
bad weather
breakdown
hold-up
pile-up (informal)
roadworks
tailback
traffic diversion
traffic jam

*camper
van*

*Also see **aircraft**, **boat**.*

# joy

**joy** *see* **happiness**.

**joyful** *see* **happy** 1.

**judge**

1 *(v) Who will judge Burglar Beryl's case?* try, hear, examine, give a verdict on, pass sentence on.

2 *(v) Mrs Badger will judge the competition entries.* assess, evaluate, appraise, size up, examine, weigh up, review, criticize.

3 *(v) It was hard to judge if Seb was lying.* gauge, decide, work out, guess, determine, discern, ascertain.

4 *(n) I like this painting, but I'm not much of a judge.* expert, authority, critic, connoisseur.

**judgment**

1 *(n) What was the court's judgment?* verdict, ruling, decision, conclusion, finding, decree, sentence.

2 *(n) Sam showed a complete lack of judgment.* common sense, good sense, intelligence, discernment, understanding, wisdom, shrewdness, discretion, taste.

**jug**

*(n) A jug of water.* pitcher, ewer, carafe, decanter, flagon, crock, urn.

**juicy**

1 *(adj) Juicy plums.* succulent, luscious, moist, squelchy, soft.
OPPOSITES: dry, shrivelled.

2 *(adj) Juicy gossip.* sensational, spicy *(informal)*, tasty *(informal)*, racy, hot *(informal)*, scandalous, risqué, fascinating, exciting, colourful.

**jumble**

1 *(v) Don't jumble my papers!* muddle, muddle up, mix up, mess up, make a mess of, shuffle, tangle, disturb, disorganize.

2 *(n) Tidy up this jumble!* mess, chaos, confusion, muddle, clutter, litter, shambles, hotchpotch, hodgepodge, mishmash.

**jump**

1 *(v) Look at the frog jump!* leap, bound, spring, bounce, hop, skip.

2 *(v) Watch me jump that fence!* clear, vault, hurdle, leap over, sail over.

3 *(v) The noise of the fireworks made me jump.* flinch, start, jerk, recoil, wince, twitch, quiver.

4 *(v) I could jump for joy! See* **dance** 4.

5 *(n) The horse cleared the final jump.* hurdle, fence, gate, rail, hedge, obstacle, barrier, ditch, gap.

6 *(n) I woke with a jump.* jolt, start, jerk, twitch, shudder, shake, quiver.

7 *(n) We predict a jump in prices. See* **rise** 5.

**jumper**

*(n) Put on your jumper.* sweater, jersey, pullover, woolly. ❖ *Also see* **clothes**.

**jumpy** *see* **nervous**.

## jungle

*(n)* rainforest, tropical forest, equatorial forest.

**jungle words**

clearing (open space)
foliage
forest floor
leaf canopy
quagmire
river
stream
swamp
undergrowth

**jungles can be...**

airless
claustrophobic
damp
dank
dark
dim
gloomy
humid
misty
muddy
muggy
murky
rainy
shady
slimy
squelchy
steamy
sticky
stifling
swampy
treacherous
unexplored

*orchid*

**jungle trees and plants**

avocado tree
banana tree
cacao tree
ebony tree
fern
liana (creeper)
mahogany tree
mangrove (shrub growing in a swamp)
moss
orchid
palm tree
pineapple tree
rubber tree
teak tree

**jungle foliage can be...**

bushy
dense
impenetrable
knotted
lush
luxuriant
rotting
tangled

*tree frog*

*chameleon*

**jungle creatures**

alligator
ant
anteater
armadillo
beetle
bird of paradise
butterfly
chameleon
crocodile
gorilla
hummingbird
jaguar
leech (bloodsucker)
leopard
macaw
monkey
mosquito
parrot
piranha (flesh-eating fish)
porcupine
snake
spider
termite
tiger
toucan
tree frog
tree snake

*tree snake*

**jungle creatures may...**

attack
bite
crawl
creep
dart
flit
flutter
hover
hunt
lie in wait
pad
pounce
prey on other creatures
prowl
scamper
scuttle
slither
spring
stalk
sting
suck blood
swarm
swoop

*macaw*

**jungle sounds**

burble
buzz
croak
growl
grunt
gurgle
hiss
rustle
screech
shriek
splash
squawk
squeak
squeal
squelch

*toucan*

**in the jungle you might...**

become disorientated
be eaten alive
break into a run
develop a fever
climb
creep
crouch
faint
forage (search for food)
get stuck in a swamp
hack through the undergrowth
hide
itch
lose your way
panic
pant
scrabble
scramble
scratch
slither
slog
splash through streams
squirm
stagger
stumble
sweat
swim
swing from creepers
trek
trip
trudge
wade through mud

*hummingbird*

*liana*

*armadillo*

*forest floor*

*jaguar*

**junk**
*(n) Please throw out this junk.* rubbish, trash, garbage, litter, scrap, clutter, odds and ends *(plural)*, bric-a-brac.

**just**
1 *(adj) Mrs Badger is strict but she's always just. See* **fair** 2.
2 *(adj) Burglar Beryl received a just sentence.* fitting, appropriate, suitable, proper, apt, rightful, well-deserved.
OPPOSITES: unjust, inappropriate.

**justify** *see* **excuse** 2.

**keen**
1 *(adj) Tejal is a keen student.* committed, motivated, enthusiastic, eager, interested, willing, conscientious, diligent, ambitious.
OPPOSITES: unenthusiastic, apathetic.
2 *(adj) Kate is keen to open her birthday presents. See* **eager** 2.
3 **keen on** *(adj) Jenny is keen on football. See* **interested** 3.

**keep**
1 *(v) Keep the champagne for a special occasion.* hold on to, keep hold of, hang on to, save, put aside, reserve, put away, store, stash away *(informal)*.
OPPOSITES: get rid of, use.
2 *(v) Oil the wood to help it keep its shine.* retain, maintain, hold, preserve, conserve, keep intact, prolong.
OPPOSITE: lose.
3 *(v) Just keep walking. See* **continue** 1.
4 *(v) Keep off the grass!* stay, remain.
5 *(v) It costs a lot to keep a family.* provide for, feed, support, maintain, nourish.
6 *(v) Does your dad keep pigeons?* have, own, care for, look after, tend, mind.

**keep on** *see* **continue** 1.

**keep up with**
*(v) I'm doing my best to keep up with the others.* keep pace with, keep abreast of, compete with, rival, match, vie with.

**key**
1 *(n) This key will open the door.* latchkey, master key, pass key, skeleton key.
2 *(n) Detectives are looking for a key to the mystery. See* **clue**.
3 *(adj) Select the key facts. See* **main**.

**kick**
1 *(v) Kick the ball.* boot, dribble, pass.
2 *(v) (informal) Mum is trying to kick smoking. See* **stop** 3.

**kid**
1 *(n) (informal) Stop acting like a kid! See* **child**.
2 *(v) (informal) Who are you trying to kid? See* **deceive** 1.

**kidnap**
*(v) In fairy tales, elves sometimes kidnap babies.* snatch, seize, abduct, carry off, steal, hold to ransom, hold hostage.

**kill**
1 *(v) A hit man was paid to kill the President.* murder, assassinate, take the life of, do away with, bump off *(slang)*, do in *(slang)*, take out *(slang)*, top *(slang)*.
2 *(v) The soldiers were ordered to kill the enemy troops.* put to death, slaughter, massacre, butcher, slay, wipe out, destroy, annihilate, obliterate, eradicate, exterminate, liquidate, decimate, waste *(informal)*, execute, hang, behead.
3 *(v) (informal) Don't run the marathon - it'll kill you!* tire you out, exhaust, wear you out, overtire, overtax, strain.

**killer** *see* **murderer**.

**killing**
1 *(n) Police are investigating the killing.* murder, assassination, homicide, manslaughter, massacre, slaying.
2 *(n) The killing must stop.* bloodshed, slaughter, carnage, butchery, genocide.
3 *(adj) (informal) The runners set off at a killing pace. See* **exhausting**.

**kind**
1 *(adj) Mr Badger is a kind person.* kind-hearted, kindly, caring, thoughtful, considerate, sympathetic, understanding, unselfish, compassionate, warm-hearted, softhearted, generous, charitable, hospitable, helpful, obliging, neighbourly, friendly, gentle, patient, well-meaning.
OPPOSITES: unkind, cruel.
2 *(n) What kind of food do you like?* sort, type, style, variety, make, brand.
3 *(n) What kind of bird is that?* sort, type, breed, species, family, class, category.

**kindness**
*(n) I appreciate your kindness.* helpfulness, thoughtfulness, consideration, generosity, hospitality, sympathy, compassion, understanding, patience, tolerance.

**king**
*(n)* monarch, sovereign, ruler.

**kingdom** *see* **country** 1.

**kiss**
1 *(v) I don't mind if people kiss in public.* embrace, exchange kisses, blow a kiss, smooch *(informal)*, neck *(informal)*, snog *(slang)*, canoodle *(slang)*.
2 *(n) Ned gave me a kiss on the cheek.* peck *(informal)*, smacker *(slang)*.

**kit**
1 *(n) The explorers packed their kit into rucksacks.* gear, equipment, tackle, stuff, paraphernalia, apparatus, instruments *(plural)*, tools *(plural)*, supplies *(plural)*, provisions *(plural)*, baggage, luggage.
2 *(n) I like your new sports kit.* gear, strip, rigout *(informal)*, outfit, colours *(plural)*, clothes *(plural)*, uniform.

**knack**
*(n) I'd love to be able to juggle, but I don't have the knack.* skill, ability, talent, aptitude, expertise, capability, gift, flair.

**kneel**
*(v) Kneel before the king!* get down on your knees, fall to your knees, bow down.

**knock**
1 *(v) Knock the nails into the wood.* tap, hammer, bang, drive, rap, pound, hit.
2 *(v) Don't knock your head on that shelf. See* **hit** 2.
3 *(n) I heard a loud knock on the door.* tap, rap, bang, thud, ratatat-tat.

**knock down**
1 *(v) The builders were told to knock down this house. See* **demolish**.
2 *(v) If you insult me again, I'll knock you down!* knock you to the floor, throw you to the ground, floor, deck *(slang)*.
3 *(v) Be careful that bus doesn't knock you down! See* **run over**.

**knock out**
*(v) A blow on the head could knock you out.* make you unconscious, knock you out cold, floor, knock you for six *(informal)*, put you out for the count, KO *(slang)*.

**knot**
1 *(n) I can't undo this knot in my shoelace.* loop, twist, bow, tangle.
2 *(v) Knot the two ropes together.* tie, loop, bind, twist, weave, braid, secure.

**know**
1 *(v) You need to know these facts for the test.* be familiar with, be acquainted with, be conversant with, have a knowledge of, be aware of, have memorized, have learnt by heart, understand.
OPPOSITE: be ignorant of.
2 *(v) How can you know that ghosts exist?* know for certain, be sure, be certain, be positive, be confident.
3 *(v) You can't possibly know what I'm going through.* realize, understand, comprehend, tell, be aware of, be conscious of, sense, have experience of.
4 *(v) I used to know Famous Fred.* be acquainted with, have dealings with, socialize with, associate with, be friends with, be on good terms with, be close to.

**knowledge**
1 *(n) Books are a great source of knowledge.* information, facts *(plural)*, data, learning, wisdom, enlightenment.
2 *(n) Penny's knowledge of the subject is good.* understanding, grasp, awareness, comprehension, expertise in.
OPPOSITE: ignorance.

**knowledgeable**
1 *(adj) The professor is a knowledgeable person.* well-informed, educated, well-read, learned, scholarly, erudite, intelligent.
2 **knowledgeable about** *(adj) Are you knowledgeable about the rules of football? See* **familiar** 2.

# label

**label**
1 *(n) The price is on the label.* tag, tab, sticker, ticket, docket, marker.
2 *(v) Label your luggage.* attach a label to, put a sticker on, name, mark, tag, stamp.
3 *(v) It's unfair to label a child as "difficult".* identify, describe, define, brand, class, categorize, classify, call, term, dub.

**lack**
1 *(n) There's a distinct lack of books in our school. See* **shortage**.
2 *(v) The refugees seem to lack basic medicines.* be without, be lacking, be short of, be missing, need, require, want.
OPPOSITES: have, possess.

**lacy**
*(adj) Lacy material.* gauzy, cobwebby, wispy, gossamer, delicate, frilly, meshy.

**lag behind** *see* **drop behind**.

**laid-back** *(informal) see* **relaxed** 1, 2.

**lair**
*(n) The creature returned to its lair.* den, hole, haunt, cave, tunnel, burrow *(rabbit)*, warren *(rabbit)*, earth *(fox)*, sett *(badger)*.

**lake**
*(n) We paddled in the lake.* loch *(Scottish)*, lough *(Irish)*, lagoon, tarn (mountain lake), reservoir, boating lake, pool, pond.

**land**
1 *(n) The sailors were glad to be back on land.* dry land, solid ground, terra firma.
2 *(n) This land is very fertile.* ground, soil, earth, clay, loam, farmland, countryside.
3 *(n) Lord Lucre's wealth comes from his land.* property, real estate, estate, grounds *(plural)*, acres *(plural)*, farmland.
4 *(n) Indiana is visiting a distant land. See* **country** 1.
5 *(v) When will the plane land?* touch down, come in to land, arrive.
OPPOSITE: take off.

**landscape**
*(n) We admired the landscape.* countryside, scenery, view, panorama, scene, vista, outlook.

**lane**
*(n) Our garden opens on to a narrow lane.* path, pathway, footpath, track, passageway, passage, alley, alleyway.

**lank**
*(adj) Lank hair.* limp, straggly, straight, long, dull, lifeless, lustreless, drooping.
OPPOSITES: bouncy, shiny.

**lanky**
*(adj) A lanky youth.* tall, long-legged, rangy, gangling, thin, skinny, scrawny, bony, spindly, weedy *(informal)*.
OPPOSITES: dumpy, squat.

**lap**
1 *(n) Pickles settled on my lap.* knee.
2 *(n) I ran a lap of the track.* circuit, circle.
3 *(v) Look at Pickles lap his milk.* drink, lick up, sip, slurp *(informal)*, sup.
4 *(v) Listen to the water lap against the boat.* wash, slap, splash, slosh, plash, swish, ripple, gurgle.

**large**
1 *(adj) Mum gave me a large helping of chips.* big, huge, enormous, substantial, generous, liberal, sizable, ample, massive, immense, colossal, gigantic, giant, mammoth, mountainous, prodigious, outsize, king-size, whopping *(informal)*.
OPPOSITES: small, modest.
2 *(adj) Aunt Bertha is a large woman.* big, well-built, big-boned, stout, hefty, thickset, heavy, burly, strapping, fat, corpulent.
OPPOSITES: small, slight.
3 *(adj) Lord Lucre lives in a large mansion.* great, huge, enormous, spacious, roomy, vast, immense, massive, extensive, sizable, palatial, towering, monumental.
OPPOSITES: small, poky.

**last**
1 *(adj) Read the last chapter of the book.* final, concluding, closing, ultimate.
OPPOSITES: first, opening.
2 *(adj) Why am I always last?* at the end, at the back, at the rear, last in line.
OPPOSITE: first.
3 *(adj) What was the last film you saw?* most recent, latest.
4 *(v) That plant won't last much longer.* live, survive, hold out, hold on, live on, linger, endure, continue.
5 *(v) The rain could last for hours. See* **continue** 2.

**lasting** *see* **permanent** 2.

**lastly** *see* **finally** 2.

**late**
1 *(adj) Why was the train late?* behind schedule, not on time, delayed.
OPPOSITES: early, on time.
2 *(adj) Minty is always late.* unpunctual, behind time, behind, tardy, slow.
OPPOSITES: early, punctual.
3 *(adj) I'm sorry about your late birthday present.* belated, overdue.
OPPOSITE: early.
4 *(adj) The funeral of the late Mr Ray was held yesterday.* deceased, departed, dead.

**later**
*(adv) I'll come over later.* later on, in a while, afterwards, in a bit, by and by, at a later date, at some point in the future.

**lather** *see* **foam** 1, 3.

**laugh**
1 *(v) This joke will make you laugh.* chuckle, giggle, chortle, titter, snigger, roar with laughter, guffaw, split your sides, crack up *(informal)*, fall about *(informal)*, crease up *(informal)*, have hysterics *(informal)*, be in stitches *(informal)*.
2 *(n) Bruce is such a laugh!* clown, joker, comedian, comic, scream *(informal)*, hoot *(informal)*, card *(informal)*, wit.
3 **laugh at** *(v) Don't laugh at me. See* **make fun of**.

**laughable** *see* **ridiculous**.

**laughter**
1 *(n) The sound of laughter filled the air.* laughing, giggling, chuckling, chortling, tittering, sniggering, guffawing.
2 *(n) Dom's jokes are a great source of laughter.* amusement, hilarity, mirth, merriment, entertainment.

**lavatory** *see* **toilet**.

**lavish**
1 *(adj) Lord Lucre is lavish with his money. See* **generous**.
2 *(adj) Posy spooned on a lavish amount of cream.* copious, abundant, plentiful, profuse, generous, liberal, extravagant, excessive, immoderate, wasteful.
OPPOSITES: meagre, frugal.

**law**
*(n) This new law prohibits smoking in public places.* rule, regulation, order, directive, command, decree, edict, pronouncement, bill, statute, act.

**lawful** *see* **legal**.

**lay**
1 *(v) Lay the photos on the table.* put, place, spread, leave, arrange, set out, set, set down, position, deposit.
2 *(v) Hens don't normally lay golden eggs.* produce, bring forth, bear, deposit.
3 *(v) Please lay the table. See* **set** 3.

**layer**
1 *(n) A layer of snow settled on the ground.* covering, coating, sheet, film, blanket, mantle, sprinkling, dusting, coat.
2 *(n) Each layer of rock was a different colour.* stratum, seam, vein, bed, thickness, level, row, tier.

**lay into** *(informal) see* **attack** 2, 3.

**layout** *see* **design** 3.

**lay out** *see* **set out** 2.

**laze**
*(v) I'm going to laze on the beach all day.* sit about, lie about, lounge, loll about, loaf about, do nothing, relax, unwind, rest, veg out *(slang)*.

**lazy**
1 *(adj) Mrs Badger says I'm lazy.* idle, slothful, workshy, indolent, slack, lax.
OPPOSITES: industrious, hard-working.
2 *(adj) I feel really lazy today.* sluggish, listless, lethargic, languid, inactive, drowsy.
OPPOSITE: energetic.

**lead**
1 *(v) I can lead you to the treasure.* take, show you the way, lead the way, guide, conduct, escort, steer, usher, pilot.
2 *(v) Will you lead the team?* be in charge of, head, direct, command, manage, supervise, oversee, head up *(informal)*.

3 (v) Sally managed to lead until the last lap. be in the lead, head the field, be in front, be out in front, be ahead, come first, blaze a trail.
4 (v) Rob seems to lead a lonely life. live, have, spend, pass, experience, undergo.
5 (v) Your behaviour might lead me to change my mind. cause, persuade, influence, prompt, induce, incline, move, dispose, sway, make.
6 (n) Follow Amanda's lead. example, direction, guidance, leadership, model.
7 (n) After the first lap, Harry was in the lead. first place, leading position, front.
8 (n) Sally has quite a lead over the others. advantage, edge, margin, start, head start.
9 (n) I was desperate to play the lead in the school play. leading role, starring role, title role, principal character, main part, male lead, female lead, hero, heroine.
10 (n) The police need a lead. See clue.
11 (n) Connect this lead to the television. wire, flex, cable.
12 (n) Fasten the lead to your dog's collar. leash, strap, chain, rope, cord, tether, rein.

**leader**
1 (n) The country needs a strong leader. ruler, premier, prime minister, president, governor, chancellor, dictator, figurehead.
2 (n) Take me to your leader! chief, boss (informal), skipper, captain, commander, superior, director, manager, supervisor, number one (informal), ringleader.
OPPOSITE: follower.

**lead to** see **cause** 1.

**leaflet**
(n) Someone pushed a leaflet through the door. hand-out, circular, flyer, pamphlet, booklet, brochure, handbill, mailshot.

**leak**
1 (n) There's a leak in this pipe. hole, crack, chink, break, fissure, puncture, cut, gash, slit, crevice, opening.
2 (v) Water began to leak from the pipe. escape, drip, dribble, seep, trickle, ooze, spill, gush, percolate.
3 (v) Someone is bound to leak this story to the press. tell, reveal, disclose, divulge, pass on, make known, make public, let slip, let the cat out of the bag, spill the beans (informal), blow wide open (slang).

**leaky**
(adj) We must fix this leaky pipe. leaking, dripping, cracked, split, broken, punctured, perforated, holey.

**lean**
1 (v) The tower began to lean. tilt, tip, heel over, slant, slope, incline, list (ship).
2 (v) Lean against the wall if you feel tired. support yourself, prop yourself up, rest, recline, steady yourself.
3 (adj) The gymnast had a lean, muscular body. See thin 1.
4 (adj) I prefer lean meat. low-fat, unfatty.
OPPOSITE: fatty.

**lean on** see **depend on** 1.

leaping frog

**leap**
1 (v) Watch that frog leap! jump, hop, bound, bounce, skip, spring.
2 (v) Sita began to leap about when she heard the news. See dance 4.
3 (n) With one giant leap, I cleared the fence. jump, bound, spring, vault, hop.
4 (n) We'll see a leap in prices. See rise 5.

**learn**
1 (v) Chinese is a hard language to learn. study, grasp, master, become competent in, take in, absorb, pick up, acquire.
2 (v) Try to learn the words of the song. memorize, learn by heart, remember, commit to memory, get off pat, get word-perfect, swot up on (informal).
3 (v) I was sorry to learn that Tom was leaving. hear, discover, find out, be told, get word, gather, become aware.

**learner**
(n) beginner, novice, pupil, student, trainee, apprentice, greenhorn, L-driver.

**leave**
1 (v) Do you have to leave so soon? go, set off, set out, depart, make tracks, get going, start, be on your way, be off, disappear, say goodbye, go away, go off.
OPPOSITES: arrive, come.
2 (v) The demoralized soldiers decided to leave. run away, abscond, desert, make off, clear off (informal), take off (informal), slope off, pull out, disappear, split (informal), flit (informal), scarper (slang), do a bunk (slang), hook it (slang).
OPPOSITE: stay.
3 (v) If you don't like your job you should leave. See resign 1.
4 (v) Don't leave me! See desert 1.
5 (v) Leave your bag in the hall. See put 1.
6 (v) Did you leave your umbrella on the train? leave behind, forget, lose, mislay.
7 (v) The sauce will leave a stain on your skirt. leave behind, produce, cause, make.
8 (v) You can leave this job to Mr Badger. entrust, assign, hand over, consign, refer.
9 (v) Did your grandma leave you any money? bequeath, hand down, will.
10 (n) How much leave do you have? holiday, vacation, time off, leave of absence, furlough, sabbatical.

**leave out**
1 (v) Leave out chapter three. See omit.
2 (v) Don't leave me out! See exclude.

**lecture**
1 (n) I went to an interesting lecture on astronomy. talk, speech, address.
2 (n) I got a real lecture when I stayed out late. scolding, reprimand, telling-off (informal), talking-to (informal), going-over (informal), dressing-down (informal).
3 (v) Please don't lecture me. See tell off.

**ledge**
(n) The climbers sheltered under a rocky ledge. overhang, shelf, sill, ridge.

**leftover**
(adj) What will we do with the leftover food? remaining, extra, surplus, excess, spare, uneaten, unused, unwanted.

**leftovers** see **scraps**.

**legal**
(adj) Are Dodgy Dave's activities legal? lawful, legitimate, above board, permissible, allowed, permitted, acceptable, authorized, valid, legit (slang).
OPPOSITES: illegal, unlawful.

**legalize**
(v) Should the government legalize the use of cannabis? make legal, permit, allow, decriminalize, ratify, authorize, sanction.
OPPOSITES: ban, outlaw.

**legend**
(n) Do you know the legend of the glass mountain? story, tale, myth, folk tale, saga, fairy tale, fable, epic.

**leisure**
(n) Everyone needs some leisure. free time, spare time, time off, relaxation, recreation, rest, breathing space, holiday, vacation.
OPPOSITE: work.

**leisurely**
(adj) A leisurely walk. relaxed, unhurried, gentle, easy, laid-back (informal), restful, comfortable, slow, lazy, lingering.
OPPOSITES: brisk, hasty, rushed.

**lend**
(v) I'd be happy to lend you my bike. loan, let you use, give you the loan of, let you have the use of, advance (money).
OPPOSITE: borrow.

**length**
1 (n) Work out the length of the bridge from end to end. extent, span, distance, reach, measurement.
2 (n) Burglar Beryl spent a length of time in jail. period, stretch, spell, term, space, span, duration.

**lengthen**
1 (v) I asked Mum to lengthen my skirt. let down, make longer.
OPPOSITES: shorten, take up.
2 (v) This detour will lengthen our journey. make longer, increase, extend, add to, prolong, stretch out, draw out, protract.
OPPOSITES: shorten, cut down.

**lengthy** see **long** 1, 2.

**lenient**
(adj) Pandora's parents are really lenient. easy-going, tolerant, indulgent, soft, gentle, kind, forgiving, forbearing, compassionate, merciful.
OPPOSITE: strict.

**lesson**
1 (n) When does the next lesson start? period, class, lecture, tutorial, seminar.
2 (n) This story contains a lesson for us all. message, moral, warning, rebuke, deterrent, example, model.

# let

**let**
*(v) Will your parents let you go to the disco?* allow, give you permission, permit, give you the go-ahead *(informal)*, give you the green light, give you the thumbs up, authorize, agree to, consent to.
OPPOSITE: forbid.

**letdown**
*(n) After all the hype, the concert was a letdown.* anticlimax, disappointment, comedown *(informal)*, fiasco, washout *(informal)*.

**let down**
1 *(v) If you trust me, I won't let you down.* disappoint, fail, leave you in the lurch, leave you stranded, desert, forsake.
2 *(adj) I felt let down when I learnt the truth about Mark. See* **disappointed**.

**let go** *see* **release** 1, 2.

**lethal** *see* **deadly** 1, 2.

**lethargic**
*(adj) This heat makes me feel lethargic.* listless, sluggish, languid, lazy, weary, slow, drowsy, sleepy, heavy, torpid, slothful, apathetic, passive, unenthusiastic.
OPPOSITES: lively, energetic.

**let in**
*(v) We can't let you in without a ticket.* allow you to enter, admit, give you access, take you in, receive, welcome.

**let off**
1 *(v) It's your turn to wash up, but I'll let you off.* excuse, spare, exempt.
2 *(v) The judge may let Burglar Beryl off. See* **release** 2.
3 *(v) Don't let off the fireworks yet.* set off, detonate, light, ignite, explode.

**let on**
*(v) (informal) Don't let on that you know Justin's secret.* let slip, give away, let out, reveal, divulge, disclose, tell, admit, let the cat out of the bag.

**letter**
1 *(n) What's the last letter in the alphabet?* character, symbol.
2 *(n) Thank you for your letter.* note, message, reply, answer, epistle, communication.

*medieval decorated letter*

**level**
1 *(adj) The football pitch should be level.* flat, even, smooth, horizontal.
OPPOSITES: uneven, sloping.
2 *(adj) Is this picture level?* straight, horizontal, flush, square, in line, aligned.
OPPOSITES: crooked, tilted.
3 *(adj) The two teams are level.* equal, evenly balanced, well-matched, all square, on a level, neck and neck, at level pegging *(informal)*, on a par, the same.
OPPOSITE: unequal.
4 *(v) Level the icing on the cake.* level out, even out, smooth out, smooth, flatten.

5 *(n) The river rose to an alarming level.* height, depth, altitude.
6 *(n) Mr Badger has reached a senior level at work.* position, grade, rank, status.

**lick**
1 *(v) Can I lick your ice cream?* taste, suck.
2 *(v) The flames began to lick around the curtains.* flicker, dart, flick, ripple, play.

**lid**
*(n) Put the lid on the toothpaste.* cap, top, stopper, cover, plug, cork *(bottle)*.

**lie**
1 *(v) I love to lie in front of the fire.* stretch out, recline, sprawl, loll, lounge, relax, rest, be prostrate, be horizontal.
2 *(v) Where is the treasure supposed to lie?* be, be situated, be located, be found.
3 *(v) Don't lie, if you want to be trusted.* tell lies, tell untruths, fib, falsify the facts, make up stories, bluff, perjure yourself, be economical with the truth.
OPPOSITE: tell the truth.
4 *(n) Bo told a lie.* fib, untruth, falsehood, barefaced lie, white lie, whopper *(informal)*, porky *(slang)*, cock-and-bull story *(informal)*, tall tale *(informal)*.
5 **lies** *(plural n) That rumour is pure lies.* fabrication, fiction, invention, deceit.
OPPOSITE: truth.

**life**
1 *(n) There's no life in a stone statue.* animation, vitality, breath, growth.
2 *(n) You will have many adventures in your life.* lifetime, career, the course of your life, lifespan, time on earth, existence.
3 *(n) Could there be life on Mars?* living things *(plural)*, living creatures *(plural)*, living beings *(plural)*, flora, fauna, wildlife.
4 *(n) What do you know about the life of the Vikings?* way of life, lifestyle, daily life, everyday life, activities *(plural)*, behaviour, habits *(plural)*, customs *(plural)*.
5 *(n) Aisha is so full of life.* energy, vitality, enthusiasm, get-up-and-go *(informal)*, vigour, verve, dynamism, exuberance, high spirits *(plural)*, sparkle, pizzazz *(informal)*, oomph *(informal)*, zip *(informal)*.

**lifelike** *see* **realistic** 2.

**lift**
1 *(v) Can you lift this case?* pick up, carry, lift up, raise, hoist.
2 *(v) The balloon began to lift off the ground. See* **rise** 1.
3 *(v) Wait for the fog to lift. See* **clear** 10.
4 *(n) Can I have a lift in your car?* ride, run, drive, trip, spin *(informal)*.

**light**
1 *(v) We waited for Mum to light the bonfire.* set light to, set fire to, set alight, put a match to, kindle, ignite.
OPPOSITES: put out, extinguish.
2 *(n) I saw a strange light in the sky.* flash, flare, glare, blaze, glow, gleam, shimmer, glint, sparkle, twinkle, glitter, ray of light, beam of light, shaft of light, brightness, illumination, radiance.

3 *(n) You need a light to see at night.* lamp, bulb, torch, flashlight, lantern, candle, taper, flare, beacon.
4 *(n) I woke as soon as it was light.* day, daylight, daytime, daybreak, morning, sunrise, dawn, first light.
OPPOSITES: dark, dusk.
5 *(adj) Big windows make a room really light.* bright, full of light, sunny, well-lit.
OPPOSITES: dark, gloomy.
6 *(adj) My shirt is light blue. See* **pale** 3.
7 *(adj) This box is really light.* lightweight, insubstantial, flimsy, easy to carry, portable, underweight *(person)*.
OPPOSITES: heavy, weighty.
8 *(adj) I just had a light lunch.* small, modest, frugal, scanty, snack, digestible.
OPPOSITES: heavy, rich.
9 *(adj) The dancer moved with light steps.* agile, graceful, nimble, lithe, deft, sprightly, light-footed, airy, sylphlike.
OPPOSITES: heavy, clumsy.
10 *(adj) A light breeze. See* **gentle** 2.
11 *(adj) A light workload. See* **easy** 2.

**light up**
*(v) Those lamps light up the street beautifully.* illuminate, lighten, brighten, shed light on, flood with light, floodlight.

**likable** *see* **pleasant** 3.

**like**
1 *(v) I used to like mushy peas.* love, be partial to, have a taste for, enjoy, be keen on, be fond of, adore *(informal)*, relish.
OPPOSITES: hate, loathe.
2 *(v) I'm sure Robbie will like badminton.* enjoy, be keen on, be interested in, go in for, be into *(informal)*, love, take pleasure in, get a kick out of *(informal)*.
OPPOSITES: dislike, hate.
3 *(v) I used to like Melissa.* be fond of, have a soft spot for, admire, think a lot of, think highly of, respect, have a high regard for, love, be attracted to, fancy *(informal)*.
OPPOSITES: dislike, detest.
4 *(v) Choose whichever cake you like.* want, wish, fancy, please, prefer, desire.
5 *(adj) Our house is like yours.* similar to, much the same as, not unlike, identical to, comparable to, equivalent to, resembling.
OPPOSITES: unlike, different from.

**likely**
1 *(adj) It's likely that we'll win.* probable, to be expected, anticipated, on the cards, odds-on, possible, plausible, feasible.
OPPOSITE: unlikely.
2 *(adj) Jon is likely to lose his temper if we are late.* liable, apt, inclined, prone.
OPPOSITE: unlikely.

**limit**
1 *(n) This fence marks the limit of our property.* boundary, border, edge, end, furthest extent, cut-off point, frontier, perimeter, periphery, confines *(plural)*.
2 *(n) There's a limit on how fast you can drive.* limitation, restriction, constraint, check, curb, ceiling, maximum.

**3** (v) Mum is going to limit my TV viewing. restrict, ration, curb, keep within bounds, hold in check, control, regulate, reduce.

**limited**
(adj) Our time at the pool is limited. restricted, rationed, fixed, controlled, finite, insufficient, inadequate, minimal.
OPPOSITES: unlimited, unrestricted.

**limp**
**1** (v) I hurt my leg and had to limp. hobble, shuffle, shamble, hop.
**2** (adj) Let your arms go limp. floppy, relaxed, slack, loose, droopy, soft, flexible, flabby, flaccid.
OPPOSITES: stiff, firm, tense.

**line**
**1** (n) Draw a line on the page. rule, stroke, underline, slash, dash, hyphen.
**2** (n) My shirt has a red line on the collar. stripe, band, strip, bar, streak, mark.
**3** (n) The pupils formed a line. queue, column, row, crocodile (informal), file, procession, cordon, chain, string.
**4** (n) Copy this line of figures. row, column, list, series, sequence.
**5** (n) Don't step over the line. boundary, borderline, demarcation line, mark, limit, edge, border, frontier.
**6** (n) Mum spotted a new line on her face. wrinkle, crease, furrow, crow's foot, groove, scar.
**7** (n) Throw me a line. See **rope**.

**linger**
**1** (v) The smell of garlic tends to linger. hang around, stay around, stick around (informal), persist, endure, last, remain.
OPPOSITES: go, disappear.
**2** (v) Don't linger on your way to school. See **dawdle**.

**link**
**1** (n) Our town has a close link with yours. connection, association, relationship, tie, attachment, affiliation, liaison, bond.
**2** (v) The police will link Burglar Beryl with the robbery. See **associate** 2.
**3** (v) Link the two ends of the chain. See **join** 1.

**liquid**
**1** (n) Drink this liquid. fluid, juice, solution.
OPPOSITE: solid.
**2** (adj) Liquid gold. liquified, fluid, runny, flowing, molten, wet, watery, sloppy.
OPPOSITES: solid, solidified.

**list**
**1** (n) Is there a list of items for sale? listing, record, inventory, catalogue, register, directory, file, index, schedule.
**2** (v) List everything that you will need. write down, note down, jot down, itemize, record, log, enter, set down, catalogue.

**listen**
**1** (v) The music is about to start, so please listen. pay attention, prick up your ears, keep your ears open, pin back your ears (informal), be all ears, lend an ear, concentrate, attend, be attentive.

**2** (v) Listen when I tell you what to do! pay attention, take notice, take heed, obey, do as you are told.
**3** listen to (v) Did you listen to what I said? See **hear** 1.

**listless** see **lethargic**.

**litter**
**1** (n) Don't drop litter. See **rubbish** 1.
**2** (v) Don't litter the room with your magazines. See **mess up** 3.

**little**
**1** (adj) A little speck of dust. small, tiny, minute, minuscule, microscopic, infinitesimal, wee, titchy (slang), teeny.
OPPOSITE: large.
**2** (adj) A little dancer. petite, diminutive, dainty, small-boned, slight, slender, elfin, short, pint-sized (informal), Lilliputian.
OPPOSITE: large.
**3** (adj) Little kittens. young, baby, infant, immature, undeveloped.
OPPOSITES: adult, mature.
**4** (adj) A little helping of ice cream. small, modest, meagre, measly (informal), inadequate, insufficient, mean, stingy, mingy (informal), scant, skimpy.
OPPOSITES: large, generous.
**5** (adj) A little problem. trivial, minor, unimportant, insignificant, trifling, paltry.
OPPOSITES: major, important.
**6** (n) There's only a little left. small amount, bit, spot, scrap, trace, dash, smidgen (informal), pinch, taste, touch, dab, tad (informal), speck, grain.
OPPOSITES: lot, plenty.

**live**
**1** (v) I will love you for as long as I live. have life, draw breath, breathe, exist, have being, walk the earth.
OPPOSITE: die.
**2** (v) Where will you live when you grow up? have your home, reside, dwell (old-fashioned), settle, stay, hang out (informal), lodge, hang your hat (informal).
**3** (v) Can you live on your salary? survive, support yourself, make a living, make ends meet, get by (informal), pay the bills.
**4** (v) The memory of this will live for ever. last, endure, survive, persist, stay alive, be remembered, abide (old-fashioned).
OPPOSITES: die, fade.
**5** (adj) I saw a live snake. living, alive.
OPPOSITE: dead.

**lively**
**1** (adj) Mo is so lively. full of life, vivacious, high-spirited, energetic, bubbly, bouncy, feisty (informal), animated, enthusiastic, exuberant, cheerful, chirpy (informal).
OPPOSITES: lifeless, listless.
**2** (adj) Our puppies are really lively. frisky, active, energetic, boisterous, playful, alert.
OPPOSITES: inactive, sluggish.
**3** (adj) The film provoked a lively discussion. animated, heated, enthusiastic, excited, spirited, interesting, stimulating.
OPPOSITES: dull, apathetic.

**4** (adj) This café looks lively. buzzing, bustling, jumping (slang), busy, crowded, swarming, thronging, hectic, astir.
OPPOSITES: dull, quiet.

**livid** see **angry**.

**living** see **alive** 1, 2.

**load**
**1** (n) Customs officers inspected the load. cargo, consignment, shipment, vanload, lorryload, containerload, freight.
**2** (n) You've taken a load off my mind. weight, burden, worry, millstone, strain.
**3** (v) Load the car with shopping. fill, fill up, pack, cram, stuff, pile, heap, stack.
OPPOSITE: unload.

**loathe** see **hate** 1.

**loathing** see **disgust** 1.

**local**
(adj) Let's meet in the local hall. nearby, neighbourhood, community, municipal, district, regional, village, parish, town, city.

**lock**
**1** (v) Make sure you lock the gate. bolt, bar, padlock, secure, chain up, fasten.
OPPOSITE: unlock.
**2** (n) I'd love to have a lock of Famous Fred's hair. strand, tuft, curl, ringlet.

**logical**
(adj) Try to think in a logical way. rational, systematic, methodical, clear, coherent, consistent, well-organized, reasonable, sensible, intelligent.
OPPOSITES: illogical, unsystematic.

**loiter** see **hang around** 1.

**lonely**
**1** (adj) A lonely person. friendless, solitary, lonesome, alone, neglected, abandoned, outcast, rejected, forsaken, forlorn.
**2** (adj) A lonely cottage. See **isolated** 1.

**loner**
(n) Don't expect Nicholas to join in; he's a loner. outsider, individualist, lone wolf, recluse, hermit.

**long**
**1** (adj) Nasim crawled down a long tunnel. lengthy, extensive, endless, never-ending.
OPPOSITE: short.
**2** (adj) Aunt Bertha is recovering from a long illness. lengthy, prolonged, long-drawn-out, lingering, protracted, seemingly endless, interminable.
OPPOSITES: short, brief.
**3** long for (v) It's pointless to long for something you can't have. yearn for, wish for, hanker after, eat your heart out over, pine for, dream of, crave, hunger for, thirst for, ache for, hope for, want, desire.

**longing** see **desire** 2.

**long-winded**
(adj) A long-winded speech. long, lengthy, overlong, rambling, wordy, verbose, long-drawn-out, repetitious, boring, tedious.
OPPOSITES: brief, concise.

**loo** (informal) see **toilet**.

# look

## look
1 (v) *Please don't look!* watch, stare, peep, peek, gape, gawp (slang), ogle.
2 (v) *Do I look tired?* seem, appear, strike you as, give the impression of being.
3 (v) *Let's look for clues. See* **search** 2.
4 (n) *Take a look over here!* glance, peek, peep, glimpse, squint (informal), look-see (slang), butcher's (slang), shufti (slang).
5 (n) *Famous Fred has the look of a film star.* appearance, air, manner, bearing, demeanour, face, expression.
6 (n) *What a sad look! See* **expression** 1.

## look after
(v) *Please look after my rat while I'm away.* take care of, care for, mind, keep an eye on, watch, guard, protect, attend to.

## lookalike
(n) *Sidney is a lookalike of Elvis Presley.* double, living image, clone, twin, spitting image (informal), dead ringer for (slang).

## look at
1 (v) *Look at those acrobats!* take a look at, watch, see, check out (informal), get a load of (informal), clock (slang).
2 (v) *Could you look at my homework?* take a look at, glance at, cast your eye over, run your eyes over, skim through, scan, check, read, scrutinize, examine.
3 (v) *I love to look at the waves crashing on the shore.* watch, gaze at, stare at, contemplate, study, survey, observe, view.

## look down on *see* **scorn** 1.

## look forward to
(v) *I look forward to your next letter.* long for, count the days until, await, anticipate, wait for, hope for.

## look like
(v) *Don't the girls look like their mum?* resemble, take after, remind you of, bear a resemblance to, look similar to, put you in mind of, have a look of, favour (informal).

## look out
(v) *Look out or you'll get hurt!* watch out, pay attention, keep your eyes open, be careful, beware, be alert, keep an eye out.

## look up to *see* **admire** 1.

## loop
1 (n) *Make a loop in the rope.* coil, circle, hoop, ring, spiral, twist, kink, curl, curve.
2 (v) *Loop the rope round this post.* coil, wind, twist, knot, entwine, circle, spiral, curl, bend.

## loose
1 (adj) *Wear loose clothing on the plane.* loose-fitting, baggy, sloppy, loosened, unbuttoned, slack, flowing.
OPPOSITES: tight, close-fitting.
2 (adj) *Don't let the leads become loose.* free, unattached, unfastened, untied, detached, disconnected, insecure, wobbly.
OPPOSITES: secure, firm.
3 (adj) *Tighten the rope so it isn't loose.* slack, floppy, dangling, hanging, free.
OPPOSITES: taut, tight.

4 (adj) *My hamster is loose in the kitchen!* on the loose, free, at large, at liberty, roaming, unconfined, unrestricted.

## loosen
(v) *Uncle Walter had to loosen his belt.* let out, slacken, undo, release, unfasten, unbutton, unhook, untie.
OPPOSITE: tighten.

## loot
1 (n) *Burglar Beryl ran home with the loot.* booty, spoils (plural), swag (slang), haul, plunder, stolen goods (plural), takings (plural), ill-gotten gains (plural).
2 (v) *The rioters began to loot the shops.* raid, steal from, ransack, rob, plunder, burgle, pillage.

## lopsided
(adj) *That clay pot looks lopsided.* off-balance, crooked, uneven, cockeyed (informal), skewwhiff (informal), askew, asymmetrical, warped, out of true.
OPPOSITES: symmetrical, straight.

## lorry
(n) *Tim's dad drives a lorry.* truck, HGV (heavy goods vehicle), articulated lorry, artic (informal), van, juggernaut, tanker.

## lose
1 (v) *I'm scared I might lose my bus fare.* mislay, misplace, drop, be unable to find.
OPPOSITE: find.
2 (v) *I knew I would lose.* be beaten, be defeated, be the loser, be thrashed, lose out (informal), suffer defeat, take a licking (informal), come a cropper (informal).
OPPOSITE: win.
3 (v) *Don't lose your chance to go on the outing. See* **miss** 3.

## lose your temper
(phrase) *There's no need to lose your temper!* fly into a rage, blow up (informal), blow your top (informal), throw a fit (informal), fly off the handle (informal), go off the deep end (informal), go berserk, blow a fuse (informal), go mad (informal), go crazy (informal), see red (informal), lose your cool (slang), lose it (slang).

## loss
1 (n) *You may notice a loss of sound.* lack, absence, disappearance, failure.
2 (n) *Granny never recovered from the loss of her home.* ruin, destruction, wrecking, demolition, eradication.
3 (n) *I sent my friend a card consoling her on her loss.* bereavement, misfortune.
4 (n) *The company made a loss last year.* deficit, shortfall.
OPPOSITES: profit, gain.

## lost
1 (adj) *I'm sad because my kitten's lost.* missing, disappeared, vanished, gone, strayed, untraceable.
OPPOSITE: found.
2 (adj) *We keep lost items in this cupboard.* mislaid, misplaced, missing, forgotten, unclaimed, abandoned.
OPPOSITE: found.

3 (adj) *The explorers realized they were lost.* off-course, off-track, adrift, astray, disoriented, going round in circles, at sea.
4 (adj) *You may feel lost when you start at your new school.* confused, bewildered, baffled, at a loss, out of your depth, at sea, helpless, mystified, perplexed.
5 (adj) *Joel was lost in his own thoughts.* absorbed, engrossed, deep, rapt, preoccupied, distracted, spellbound.
6 (adj) *Think of those lost opportunities.* wasted, missed, squandered, frittered away, misspent, misused.

## lots (informal) *see* **many**.

## loud
1 (adj) *Loud music came from the disco.* noisy, deafening, ear-splitting, booming, blaring, piercing, ear-piercing, thunderous, resounding, clamorous, strident.
OPPOSITES: quiet, soft.
2 (adj) *I hate loud shirts. See* **gaudy**.
3 (adj) *Barry can't help being loud.* brash, vulgar, loudmouthed (informal), rowdy, boisterous, raucous, offensive, brazen, coarse, crude, crass, pushy (informal).
OPPOSITES: quiet, retiring.

## lovable *see* **adorable**.

## love
1 (v) *I will always love you.* adore, be devoted to, be in love with, think the world of, dote on, worship, idolize, be infatuated with, care for, have a soft spot for, be fond of, be attached to, treasure, cherish, desire, fancy (informal).
OPPOSITES: hate, loathe.
2 (v) *I used to love fudge. See* **like** 1.
3 (n) *My love for you will never die.* affection, passion, fondness, tenderness, desire, devotion to, infatuation with, adoration, yearning, adulation, regard.
OPPOSITES: hatred, loathing.
4 (n) *Pirate Peg's love for adventure is well known.* fondness, liking, taste, relish, soft spot, weakness, enjoyment of.
5 fall in love with *see* **fall in love with**.
6 in love with *see* **in love with**.

## lovely
1 (adj) *Laura looks lovely.* beautiful, gorgeous, stunning (informal), enchanting, ravishing, bewitching, captivating, appealing, adorable, alluring, charming, pretty, elegant, attractive, glamorous.
OPPOSITES: unattractive, hideous.
2 (adj) *We had a lovely day at the seaside.* delightful, blissful, enjoyable, wonderful, fabulous (informal), fantastic (informal), marvellous, brilliant, glorious, pleasant.
OPPOSITES: awful, terrible.
3 (adj) *Mrs Honey is a lovely person.* delightful, engaging, warm, charming, sweet, agreeable, pleasant, amiable.
OPPOSITES: obnoxious, disagreeable.

## loving
(adj) *Loving parents.* affectionate, caring, devoted, fond, adoring, doting, kind, warm-hearted, tender, demonstrative.

# low

1 *(adj) A low hedge.* small, little, short, stumpy, stubby, squat, stunted, knee-high. OPPOSITES: high, tall.

2 *(adj) A low salary.* small, meagre, paltry, inadequate, pathetic *(informal)*, poor. OPPOSITE: high.

3 *(adj) A low rank.* junior, inferior, humble, menial, lowly *(old-fashioned)*. OPPOSITES: high, senior.

4 *(adj) This work is of a low standard.* inferior, poor, mediocre, second-rate, unacceptable, substandard. OPPOSITE: high.

5 *(adj) Supplies are low.* meagre, scanty, inadequate, sparse, few, depleted, reduced, diminished, wanting, deficient. OPPOSITE: ample.

6 *(adj) A low whisper. See* **quiet** 1.

7 *(adj) Low prices.* reasonable, cheap, modest, inexpensive, economical. OPPOSITES: high, exorbitant.

8 *(adj) Low notes. See* **deep** 3.

9 *(adj) I'm feeling low. See* **miserable** 1.

# lower

1 *(adj) We offer lower prices.* reduced, decreased, slashed, pruned, cut, diminished, pared down. OPPOSITES: higher, increased.

2 *(adj) These soldiers are in the lower ranks.* junior, subordinate, inferior, minor. OPPOSITES: higher, senior.

3 *(v) Lower your speed. See* **reduce** 3.

4 *(v) Lower your voice.* tone down, soften, quieten, moderate, hush, muffle. OPPOSITE: raise.

5 *(v) Lower the sail.* take down, let down, pull down, haul down, drop, let fall. OPPOSITE: raise.

## lower yourself

*(v) Don't lower yourself by answering back.* demean yourself, degrade yourself, humiliate yourself, debase yourself, belittle yourself, humble yourself, discredit yourself, stoop, sink, condescend.

## loyal

*(adj) A loyal friend.* faithful, devoted, firm, true, steadfast, staunch, trustworthy, constant, dependable, unwavering. OPPOSITES: disloyal, fickle.

**lucid** *see* **clear** 7.

## luck

1 *(n) We found the right path by luck.* chance, accident, coincidence, fluke, good fortune, a stroke of luck, serendipity.

2 *(n) I wish you luck.* good luck, good fortune, success, happiness, prosperity.

## lucky

1 *(adj) Who are the lucky winners?* fortunate, favoured, jammy *(slang)*, successful, happy.

2 *(adj) This book was a lucky find.* fortunate, happy, fluky *(informal)*, chance, accidental, fortuitous, providential, opportune, timely.

**ludicrous** *see* **ridiculous**.

# luggage

*(n) Don't forget your luggage!* baggage, bags *(plural)*, cases *(plural)*, belongings *(plural)*, things *(plural)*, gear.

## lukewarm

1 *(adj) This water is lukewarm.* tepid, warm, at room temperature.

2 *(adj) I feel lukewarm about this plan. See* **half-hearted** 1.

## lump

1 *(n) A lump of cheese.* piece, wedge, slab, chunk, hunk, block, bit, nugget, wodge *(informal)*, mass.

2 *(n) Robyn has a lump on her knee.* bump, bruise, bulge, swelling, growth, cyst, tumour, hump.

## lumpy

1 *(adj) This custard is lumpy.* full of lumps, granular, clotted, curdled. OPPOSITE: smooth.

2 *(adj) My mattress is lumpy.* bumpy, uneven, knobbly, bulging. OPPOSITES: flat, even.

## lunge

*(n) Bozo made a lunge at me.* charge, rush, dive, swipe *(informal)*, swing, jab, stab.

## lurch

1 *(v) The drunk began to lurch towards us.* stagger, totter, teeter, stumble, sway, reel, weave, lunge, jerk.

2 *(v) The storm made the ship lurch.* wallow, roll, pitch, tilt, list, lean, heel.

## lure

*(v) The wizard tried to lure the princess into his castle.* entice, tempt, ensnare, inveigle, draw, seduce, cajole, attract.

**lurid** *see* **sensational** 1.

## lurk

*(v) Wolves lurk in this forest.* skulk, lie in wait, lie low, hide, crouch, wait, prowl, slink, steal, take cover.

**luscious** *see* **delicious**.

## lush

*(adj) We pushed our way through the lush vegetation.* luxuriant, flourishing, overgrown, dense, thick, verdant, green, profuse, abundant, teeming, riotous. OPPOSITE: sparse.

## luxurious

*(adj) A luxurious hotel.* comfortable, sumptuous, plush *(informal)*, lavish, opulent, ritzy *(slang)*, de luxe, grand, magnificent, posh *(informal)*, swish *(informal)*, swanky *(informal)*, up-market. OPPOSITES: basic, Spartan.

## luxury

1 *(n) Let's have a day of luxury.* comfort, pleasure, indulgence, ease, enjoyment, bliss, self-indulgence, opulence, affluence, high living, splendour, hedonism. OPPOSITES: discomfort, self-denial.

2 *(n) Caviar is a luxury.* treat, extravagance, indulgence, extra, frill, nonessential. OPPOSITE: essential.

# Mm

## machine

*(n) Is there a machine to do this job?* appliance, contraption, device, gadget, instrument, tool, mechanism, apparatus.

## machinery

*(n) Do you have the machinery for this job?* machines *(plural)*, apparatus, equipment, gear, tackle, mechanism, tools *(plural)*.

## macho

*(adj) Bozo thinks it's good to be macho.* virile, manly, butch *(slang)*, hard, tough, masculine, muscular, Ramboesque, strong, strapping, chauvinist, sexist.

## mad

1 *(adj) The doctor thought her patient might be mad.* insane, deranged, psychotic, manic, of unsound mind, unbalanced, mentally ill. OPPOSITES: sane, rational.

2 *(adj) You must be mad to dress up as a gorilla.* crazy, insane, demented, out of your mind, raving mad *(informal)*, unhinged, barmy *(slang)*, bonkers *(slang)*, batty *(slang)*, screwy *(slang)*, loopy *(informal)*, nuts *(slang)*, bananas *(slang)*, off your head *(slang)*, off your trolley *(slang)*, round the twist *(slang)*, nutty as a fruitcake *(slang)*, out to lunch *(slang)*.

3 *(adj) Bathing in baked beans is a mad thing to do.* crazy, absurd, ridiculous, insane, daft *(informal)*, ludicrous, nonsensical, preposterous, wild.

4 *(adj) (informal) Mum was mad that I'd broken her best vase. See* **angry**.

5 *(adj) Kevin is mad about football.* crazy *(informal)*, fanatical, passionate, wild, nuts *(slang)*, bonkers *(slang)*, hooked on, devoted to, keen on, into *(informal)*.

## made-up

1 *(adj) Is that a made-up story?* invented, fictional, make-believe, imaginary, fantasy, mythical, fairy-tale. OPPOSITES: true, real-life.

2 *(adj) I don't want to hear any of your made-up excuses.* fabricated, invented, trumped up, concocted, manufactured, false, untrue, spurious. OPPOSITES: true, genuine.

## magazine

*(n)* journal, weekly, monthly, quarterly, glossy, fanzine, mag *(informal)*, paper, comic, colour supplement, periodical.

## magic

1 *(n) The witch was an expert in magic.* sorcery, enchantment, witchcraft, wizardry, black magic, the black arts *(plural)*, voodoo, spell-making.

2 *(n) Miraculous Marvello produced a rabbit by magic.* conjuring, hocus-pocus, illusion, sleight of hand, trickery, wizardry.

# magician

## magician
1 (n) *The magician cast a spell.* sorcerer, wizard, enchanter, sorceress, enchantress.
2 (n) *The magician did an amazing trick.* conjurer, illusionist.

## magnificent
1 (adj) *What a magnificent palace!* splendid, impressive, imposing, majestic, superb, grand, noble, stately, regal, resplendent, sumptuous, opulent, ornate, lavish, elegant, awe-inspiring, stunning (informal), striking.
2 (adj) *Maggie gave a magnificent performance.* splendid, superb, stunning (informal), masterly, excellent, accomplished, skilful, brilliant, terrific (informal), wonderful, virtuoso.

## magnify
(v) *The scientist used a microscope to magnify the cells.* enlarge, make larger, expand, increase, blow up (informal).

## mail see post 2, 4.

## main
(adj) *What are the main arguments in your essay?* major, central, principal, chief, leading, important, key, basic, essential, fundamental, critical, pivotal, vital, prime, primary, foremost.

## mainly see mostly 1, 2.

## maintain
1 (v) *I can't maintain this effort for long.* keep up, sustain, continue, uphold, prolong, keep alive, perpetuate.
2 (v) *Oil the wood to help it maintain its shine. See* keep 2.
3 (v) *Do you know how to maintain your bike?* look after, take care of, service, keep in good repair, keep in good condition.
4 (v) *Burglar Beryl continues to maintain that she is innocent. See* insist 3.

## major
1 (adj) *New York is one of the world's major cities.* largest, biggest, great, most important, main, principal, leading, chief.
OPPOSITE: minor.
2 (adj) *We're making some major changes.* great, significant, wide-ranging, extensive, drastic, radical, serious, important, crucial, large-scale, wholesale.
OPPOSITES: minor, insignificant.
3 (adj) *The play was a major success.* great, outstanding, huge, enormous, phenomenal, notable, mega (informal).

## make
1 (v) *Kim loves to make things.* construct, put together, assemble, build, produce, create, fashion, shape, model, mould, devise, form, manufacture, mass-produce.
2 (v) *I don't want to go, so don't make me! See* force 1.
3 (v) *Can you make this sheet into a ghost costume? See* turn 3.
4 (v) *Let's make some money. See* earn 1.
5 (v) *Five and five make ten.* add up to, come to, amount to, total.

6 (v) *We want to make you captain.* appoint, elect, nominate, name, create.
7 (v) *We must make some new rules.* draw up, decide on, agree on, formulate, put together, frame, introduce, bring in.
8 (v) *Joe may make trouble. See* cause 1.
9 (v) *Anne will make a good doctor.* be, become, grow into, develop into.
10 (v) *You might make the train if you run.* catch, get, arrive in time for.
OPPOSITE: miss.
11 (v) *I make the total to be 65.* calculate, estimate, reckon, work out, judge, gauge.
12 (n) *Which make of chocolate do you prefer?* brand, type, sort, kind, variety.

## make a mess of
(phrase) *I hope I don't make a mess of this.* muff, botch, mess up, bungle, fudge, make a hash of (informal), screw up (informal), muck up (slang), cock up (slang), make a pig's ear of (slang).

## make-believe
1 (n) *Josephine lives in a world of make-believe.* fantasy, imagination, invention, romance, pretence, play-acting, illusion, unreality, dreams (plural).
OPPOSITE: reality.
2 (adj) *A dragon is a make-believe animal. See* imaginary 1.

## make believe see pretend 1.

## make better
1 (v) *How can we make the situation better? See* improve 3.
2 (v) *This ointment will make your rash better. See* cure.

## make fun of
(phrase) *Don't make fun of me because I'm small.* laugh at, poke fun at, tease, take the mickey out of (informal), taunt, scoff at, jeer at, sneer at, mock, ridicule.

## make love
(phrase) have sex, sleep together, go to bed together, have sexual intercourse, copulate.

## make out
1 (v) *I could just make out a figure coming through the fog.* distinguish, recognize, see, perceive, discern, detect, pick out.
2 (v) *Can you make out what this means? See* understand 2.
3 (v) *Edwin tried to make out that he was 18.* pretend, bluff, claim, suggest, give the impression, let on (informal), imply.
4 (v) *I wonder how Marco will make out as an actor.* fare, get on, shape up (informal), manage, cope, succeed.

## make-up
(n) *Put on your make-up and let's go out!* cosmetics (plural), war paint (informal), greasepaint (theatre), face paint.

## make up
1 (v) *Oz will make up a silly excuse.* invent, fabricate, manufacture, cook up (informal), trump up, concoct, dream up, hatch, come up with, conjure up.

2 (v) *Ruby loves to make up new songs.* compose, invent, write, originate, devise, create, think up, dream up.
3 (v) *How many players make up a team?* form, constitute, comprise, compose.
4 (v) *I'm sick of fighting; let's make up.* be friends, shake hands, call it quits, bury the hatchet, forgive and forget, make peace.

## make up for
(v) *How can I make up for forgetting your birthday?* compensate for, make amends for, atone for, recompense you for.

## make up your mind
(phrase) *You'll have to make up your mind soon.* decide, make a decision, come to a decision, reach a decision, choose.

## make worse
(v) *Arguing will only make the situation worse.* worsen, exacerbate, aggravate.

## malicious see spiteful.

## man
1 (n) *Who's that man over there?* guy (informal), bloke (informal), chap (informal), gentleman, fellow.
2 (n) *Sonia joined a dating agency to find herself a man.* boyfriend, partner, husband, lover, spouse, bloke (informal).
3 (n) *Man is descended from the apes.* human beings (plural), people (plural), mankind, the human race, humankind.

## manage
1 (v) *I wonder how I'll manage at my new school?* cope, get on, get along, survive, make out, fare.
2 (v) *Mum has always wanted to manage her own business.* run, be in charge of, be in control of, be the manager of, preside over, direct, administer, organize, oversee, supervise, head up (informal).
3 (v) *See what you can manage in an hour. See* achieve.
4 (v) *A large family can be hard to manage.* look after, cope with, deal with, handle, organize, control.

## man-made see artificial 1.

## manners
1 (plural n) *Haven't you learnt any manners?* etiquette, good manners (plural), social graces (plural), politeness, courtesy, civility, refinement, decorum.
2 (plural n) *Pip's manners are terrible.* behaviour, conduct.

## manufacture see make 1.

## many
(adj) *Nadya received many presents.* lots of (informal), a lot of, masses of (informal), a great many, loads of (informal), scores of, tons of (informal), heaps of (informal), stacks of (informal), piles of (informal), oodles of (informal), countless, innumerable, numerous.

## map
(n) *We need a map to find the way.* plan, guide, street map, town plan, road atlas, route map, atlas, chart (sea, air).

## march

1 *(v)* We watched the soldiers march past. file, troop, parade, strut.
2 *(v)* Dan loves to march across the moors. stride, pace, stomp *(informal)*, walk, hike, trek, tramp, slog, stalk.
3 *(n)* Please join our march against war. demonstration, demo *(informal)*, protest march, protest, parade, procession.

*banner*

*protest march*

## mark

1 *(n)* What's that mark on the wall? spot, blot, blotch, smear, smudge, streak, splotch, speck, dot, stain, scribble, line, scratch, dent, nick, chip, notch, pit, pock, score, gash, cut, blemish, flaw, impression.
2 *(n)* Ed has a mark on his face. blemish, birthmark, scar, scratch, bruise, tattoo.
3 *(n)* Did the thief leave any mark? trace, sign, trail, tracks *(plural)*, footprints *(plural)*, fingerprints *(plural)*, vestige.
4 *(n)* Zanzi got a good mark for her test. grade, percentage, rating, valuation.
5 *(n)* Did the experience leave a mark on you? lasting impression, scar, impression, effect, impact, influence, imprint.
6 *(v)* Don't mark the paintwork! damage, make a mark on, dirty, stain, smear, smudge, scratch, dent, chip, nick, score, cut, scribble on, spoil, blemish, deface.
7 *(v)* Mrs Badger will mark our tests fairly. correct, assess, grade, evaluate, appraise.
8 *(v)* Mark the spot clearly. identify, label, show, tag, signpost, flag, highlight, name, initial, stamp.

## market

*(n)* You'll find great bargains in the market. open-air market, covered market, flea market, bazaar, fair, marketplace.

## marooned *see* **stranded**.

## marriage

1 *(n)* My parents are celebrating 15 years of marriage. matrimony, wedlock, union.
2 *(n)* We've been invited to Simon's marriage. wedding, wedding ceremony, marriage ceremony, nuptials *(plural)*.

## marry

*(v)* Luke and Lucy are planning to marry. get married, become man and wife, wed, tie the knot *(informal)*, walk down the aisle *(informal)*, get hitched *(slang)*, get spliced *(informal)*, take the plunge *(informal)*.
OPPOSITES: stay single, divorce.

## marsh

*(n)* We squelched through the marsh. bog, swamp, marshland, fen, wetland, morass, quagmire, mire, mud flats *(plural)*.

## marshy

*(adj)* Marshy ground. swampy, boggy, soggy, waterlogged, squelchy, spongy, muddy, wet.

## marvel

1 *(n)* The pyramids were a marvel of the Ancient World. *See* **wonder** 2.
2 *(n)* Oz is a marvel at art. *See* **genius**.
3 marvel at *(v)* You'll marvel at the skill of the acrobats. be amazed by, be astonished by, be filled with amazement at, wonder at, gape at, goggle at, admire, applaud, not believe your eyes.

## marvellous *see* **wonderful** 1, 2.

## mash

*(v)* Did you mash the vegetables? purée, pulp, crush, pound, pulverize, squash, smash, beat, reduce to a pulp.

## mask

1 *(n)* Ben wore a gruesome mask to the Hallowe'en party. false face, disguise.
2 *(n)* Wear this mask to protect your face. protective mask, visor, shield, safety goggles *(plural)*.
3 *(n)* Dean's charming manner is just a mask. *See* **front** 4.
4 *(v)* The soldiers used bushes to mask the tank. *See* **disguise** 3.

## mass

1 *(n)* A mass of papers covered the desk. load, lot, quantity, heap, mound, pile, stack, bundle, bunch, collection.
2 *(n)* A mass of people packed the stadium. *See* **crowd** 1.
3 *(n)* The statue was carved from a mass of rock. block, lump, piece, chunk, hunk.
4 *(v)* A crowd began to mass in the square. *See* **collect** 3.
5 *(adj)* There was mass rioting after the match. widespread, general, large-scale, wholesale, extensive, indiscriminate.
6 masses *(plural n)* *(informal)* Gita has masses of CDs. *See* **many**.

## massive *see* **huge**.

## master

1 *(v)* Greek is hard to master. *See* **learn** 1.
2 *(v)* Indy will master the situation. take command of, gain control of, take charge of, get the better of, manage, control, handle, get the upper hand.
3 *(n)* Jan is a master at golf. *See* **expert** 2.

## match

1 *(n)* When does the match start? game, contest, competition, tournament, event, trial, head-to-head, tie, bout *(boxing, wrestling)*, test match *(cricket)*.
2 *(v)* This top should match my leggings. go with, coordinate with, tone in with, be the same colour as, complement, blend with, team with, harmonize with.
3 *(v)* The coach will match you with a suitable partner. link you up, pair, put you together, team you up, join you up.
4 *(v)* Nothing can match a steaming hot bath. *See* **equal** 5.

## matching

*(adj)* The twins wore matching clothes. identical, similar, the same, coordinating, corresponding, toning, harmonizing.

## material

*(n)* What sort of material is your shirt made of? fabric, cloth, stuff, textile.
TYPES OF MATERIAL: acrylic, calico, canvas, cashmere, chambray, cheesecloth, chiffon, chintz, corduroy, cotton, crêpe de chine, damask, denim, felt, flannel, gauze, gingham, hessian, jersey, lace, lamé, linen, lycra, muslin, net, nylon, oilcloth, polyester, rayon, satin, seersucker, silk, taffeta, tulle, tweed, velours, velvet, viscose, wool.

## matter

1 *(v)* Will the way I dress matter? make a difference, be important, carry weight, count, be relevant, signify, be of any consequence, make any odds.
2 *(n)* What's the matter, Kirsty? trouble, problem, difficulty, worry, wrong.
3 *(n)* Mrs Badger dealt with the matter quickly. situation, incident, episode, affair, occurrence, subject, issue, question.

## matter-of-fact

*(adj)* Guy gave a matter-of-fact account of the accident. factual, straightforward, down-to-earth, sober, unemotional, prosaic, mundane, unimaginative, plain, unvarnished, unsentimental, humdrum.
OPPOSITES: emotional, imaginative.

## mature

*(adj)* Carl is mature for his age. grown-up, advanced, well-developed, adult, sensible, responsible, sophisticated, wise, shrewd.
OPPOSITES: immature, childish.

## meadow *see* **field** 1.

## meal

*(n)* What a delicious meal! spread *(informal)*, feast, banquet, snack, picnic, barbecue, blowout *(slang)*, nosh-up *(slang)*, tuck-in *(informal)*, beanfeast *(informal)*, repast *(old-fashioned)*. ❖ Also see **food & flavours**.

## mean

1 *(v)* What do those initials mean? stand for, indicate, represent, signify, symbolize, denote, convey, communicate, spell, say.
2 *(v)* What does Hamlet mean in this speech? suggest, imply, hint at, drive at, insinuate, indicate, allude to, say, convey.
3 *(v)* Did you mean to break the record? intend, plan, set out, want, resolve, determine, have plans, aim, wish, hope, aspire, have in mind, have the intention.
4 *(v)* Being in the team will mean a lot of work. involve, entail, necessitate, require, lead to, result in, give rise to.
5 *(adj)* Scrooge was too mean to share his money. miserly, stingy, tightfisted, niggardly, tight, mingy *(informal)*, selfish, grasping, penny-pinching *(informal)*.
OPPOSITE: generous.
6 *(adj)* That was a mean thing to do. nasty, horrible, spiteful, malicious, cruel, unkind, shabby, cheap, sneaky, shameful, despicable, contemptible, lousy *(slang)*, rotten *(informal)*, beastly *(informal)*, low-down *(informal)*.

# meaning

**meaning**
1 *(n) Use a dictionary to find the meaning of this word.* definition, sense, explanation.
2 *(n) Did you grasp the meaning of my poem?* sense, gist, drift, message, thrust, implication, significance, import.
3 *(n) What's the meaning of your awful behaviour?* reason for, explanation for, point, purpose, aim, objective, intention.

**meaningless**
1 *(adj) I can't understand Ziggy's meaningless babble.* unintelligible, incomprehensible, incoherent, senseless.
2 *(adj) I wasted the day in meaningless pursuits. See* **empty 4**.

**meant**
1 *(adj) You're not meant to walk here.* supposed, allowed, permitted, authorized.
2 *(adj) I don't know what we're meant to do.* supposed, expected, required.
3 *(adj) We seem to be meant for each other.* made, destined, intended, fated, suited to, cut out, designed.

**measure**
*(v) Can you measure the amount of sugar in this cup?* determine, find out, quantify, calculate, work out, compute, gauge, estimate, assess, judge, evaluate, weigh, calibrate, mark off, pace off, time.

**measurement**
1 *(n) Your measurement must be accurate.* calculation, estimation, assessment, reckoning, computation, calibration, timing, survey.
2 **measurements** *(plural n) Work out the measurements of this box.* dimensions *(plural)*, size, length, width, height, depth, area, volume, capacity, mass, weight.

**meat**
*(n)* flesh, red meat, white meat.
**TYPES OF MEAT:** bacon, beef, beefburger, chicken, chop, corned beef, cutlet, duck, escalope, game, gammon, goose, ham, hamburger, joint, kebab, kidney, lamb, liver, meatloaf, mince, mutton, offal, pâté, pheasant, pork, poultry, rissole, roast, salami, sausage, smoked ham, sparerib, steak, tripe, turkey, veal, venison.

**mechanical**
1 *(adj) Ken's dad drives a mechanical digger.* automatic, automated, motor-driven, power-driven, machine-driven. **OPPOSITE:** manual.
2 *(adj) Blinking is a mechanical response. See* **automatic 2**.

**meddle** *see* **interfere 1**.

**medicine**
*(n) Take your medicine!* medication, medicament, drug, remedy, cure.
**TYPES OF MEDICINE:** antibiotic, antiseptic, capsule, cream, decongestant, drops *(plural)*, herbal remedy, linctus, lotion, lozenge, ointment, over-the-counter drug, painkiller, pill, powder, prescription drug, spray, syrup, tablet, tonic, tranquillizer.

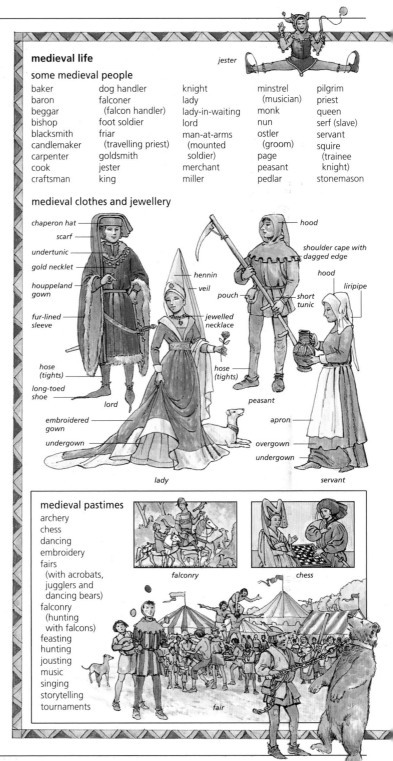

## medieval life

*jester*

### some medieval people

| | | | | |
|---|---|---|---|---|
| baker | dog handler | knight | minstrel | pilgrim |
| baron | falconer | lady | (musician) | priest |
| beggar | (falcon handler) | lady-in-waiting | monk | queen |
| bishop | foot soldier | lord | nun | serf (slave) |
| blacksmith | friar | man-at-arms | ostler | servant |
| candlemaker | (travelling priest) | (mounted | (groom) | squire |
| carpenter | goldsmith | soldier) | page | (trainee |
| cook | jester | merchant | peasant | knight) |
| craftsman | king | miller | pedlar | stonemason |

### medieval clothes and jewellery

chaperon hat
scarf
undertunic
gold necklet
houppeland gown
fur-lined sleeve
hose (tights)
long-toed shoe
*lord*

hood
shoulder cape with dagged edge
hood
liripipe
short tunic

hennin
veil
pouch
jewelled necklace
hose (tights)
*peasant*

embroidered gown
undergown
*lady*

apron
overgown
undergown
*servant*

### medieval pastimes

archery
chess
dancing
embroidery
fairs
  (with acrobats, jugglers and dancing bears)
falconry
  (hunting with falcons)
feasting
hunting
jousting
music
singing
storytelling
tournaments

*falconry*

*chess*

*fair*

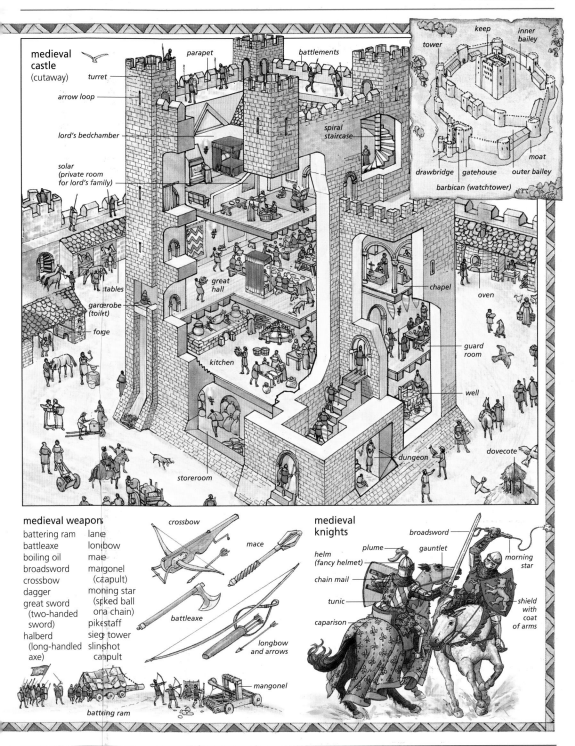

medieval
castle
(cutaway)

turret

parapet

battlements

arrow loop

lord's bedchamber

spiral
staircase

solar
(private room
for lord's family)

stables

garderobe
(toilet)

forge

great
hall

kitchen

chapel

oven

guard
room

well

dungeon

dovecote

storeroom

tower

keep

inner
bailey

moat

drawbridge    gatehouse    outer bailey

barbican (watchtower)

**medieval weapons**

| | |
|---|---|
| battering ram | lance |
| battleaxe | longbow |
| boiling oil | mace |
| broadsword | mangonel |
| crossbow | (catapult) |
| dagger | morning star |
| great sword | (spiked ball |
| (two-handed | on a chain) |
| sword) | pikestaff |
| halberd | siege tower |
| (long-handled | slingshot |
| axe) | catapult |

crossbow

mace

battleaxe

longbow
and arrows

mangonel

battering ram

**medieval
knights**

broadsword

plume

gauntlet

morning
star

helm
(fancy helmet)

chain mail

tunic

caparison

shield
with
coat
of arms

# mediocre

**mediocre** see **average** 2.

**medium**
(adj) Susie is of medium height. average, moderate, middling, normal, middle.

**meek**
(adj) A meek tone of voice. timid, humble, mild, submissive, docile, quiet, soft, gentle, unassuming, deferential, resigned.
OPPOSITES: arrogant, assertive.

**meet**
1 (v) I didn't expect to meet you here! bump into (informal), run into, come across, run across, find, see, come upon, encounter, come face to face with.
2 (v) Is anyone coming to meet you? fetch, pick you up, greet, welcome.
3 (v) On Fridays all the pupils meet in the hall. gather, assemble, congregate, come together, get together, collect, convene.
OPPOSITES: disperse, scatter.
4 (v) The two paths meet here. See **join** 3.

**meeting**
1 (n) Al's parents arranged a meeting with his teacher. appointment, get-together (informal), interview, chat, rendezvous.
2 (n) We all attended the meeting about animal rights. discussion group, gathering, seminar, rally, conference, convention, forum, assembly, council, congress.
3 (n) Tim had an unexpected meeting with a bull. encounter, confrontation, brush.

**melancholy**
1 (adj) Melancholy music makes me feel low. mournful, sombre, sad, depressing, gloomy, dismal, doleful, lugubrious.
OPPOSITES: cheerful, lively.
2 (adj) I feel melancholy. See **depressed**.

**melt**
1 (v) The ice will melt soon. thaw, defrost.
OPPOSITE: freeze.
2 (v) If you heat the butter it will melt. soften, dissolve, liquefy, run.
OPPOSITES: harden, solidify.

**memorize** see **learn** 2.

**menace**
(n) That driver is a menace to other motorists. threat, danger, hazard, risk.

**menacing**
(adj) Bozo gave me a menacing look. threatening, intimidating, ominous, forbidding, grim, sinister, frightening, dark.

**mend**
1 (v) I must mend my bike. See **repair** 1.
2 (v) Can you mend my trousers? sew up, stitch, darn, patch, repair.
3 (v) Broken bones mend slowly. See **heal** 2.

**mention**
1 (v) Mrs Badger happened to mention that she was leaving. say, remark, observe, let slip, let on (informal), reveal, divulge, disclose, make known, declare, state.
2 (v) Don't mention this subject again! bring up, raise, broach, refer to, speak about, allude to, touch upon, hint at.

**merciful**
(adj) Burglar Beryl hoped the judge would be merciful. compassionate, lenient, forgiving, pitying, forbearing, sympathetic, humane, tenderhearted, generous, kind.
OPPOSITES: merciless, hardhearted.

**merciless** see **ruthless**.

**mercy**
(n) The judge showed no mercy. pity, compassion, leniency, forgiveness, sympathy, understanding, feeling, kindness, charity, clemency.
OPPOSITES: severity, harshness.

**merge**
1 (v) The two schools are going to merge. amalgamate, join together, unite, link up, combine, integrate, join forces, team up.
OPPOSITES: separate, split up.
2 (v) The trees seemed to merge into the background. blend, melt, mingle, fuse, mix, become lost in, be swallowed up by.

**merry**
(adj) A merry smile. happy, cheerful, cheery, chirpy (informal), carefree, bright, jolly, jovial, joyful, gleeful.
OPPOSITES: sad, serious.

**mess**
1 (n) Clear up this mess! clutter, rubbish, jumble, litter, dirt, muck, gunge (informal), gunk (informal), grot (slang).
2 (n) My room is in a total mess. muddle, shambles, jumble, state (informal), chaos, confusion, disarray, disorder, turmoil.
3 (n) You got me into this mess! predicament, difficulty, quandary, dilemma, muddle, mix-up, fix (informal), jam (informal), pickle (informal), stew (informal), tight spot, hot water (informal).
4 make a mess of see **make a mess of**.

**mess about**
1 (v) I like to mess about on the beach. potter about, play about, footle about (informal), muck about (slang), loaf about, lounge about, fiddle about (informal).
2 (v) Don't mess about with my computer! interfere, tamper, meddle, tinker, fiddle (informal), play about, muck about (slang).
3 (v) (informal) Don't mess about in class. See **fool around**.

**message**
1 (n) I sent you a message. note, memo, communication, letter, fax, e-mail, text message, bulletin, dispatch, communiqué, report, statement, announcement, news.
2 (n) The message of this story is clear. meaning, moral, point, theme, thrust, idea.

**messenger**
(n) A messenger delivered the parcel. courier, carrier, dispatch rider, runner, delivery boy (old-fashioned), go-between.

**mess up**
1 (v) I hope I don't mess up this exam. See **make a mess of**.
2 (v) Don't mess up my papers. See **jumble** 1.

3 (v) Don't mess up the room with your comics. clutter, litter, strew, make untidy, throw into disorder, dirty.
OPPOSITES: tidy up, clean up.

**messy**
1 (adj) Josie's room always looks messy. untidy, cluttered, chaotic, in a muddle, shambolic (informal), in disarray, littered, dirty, grubby, filthy, mucky.
OPPOSITES: neat, tidy.
2 (adj) Why do you always look so messy? untidy, scruffy, unkempt, dishevelled, rumpled, crumpled, slovenly, shambolic (informal), tousled (hair), windswept.
OPPOSITES: neat, tidy.
3 (adj) Mrs Badger criticized my messy work. untidy, careless, slapdash, sloppy (informal), slipshod, disorganized.
OPPOSITES: neat, meticulous.

**metal**
(n) TYPES OF METAL: aluminium, brass, bronze, chrome, copper, gold, iron, lead, mercury, nickel, pewter, platinum, silver, steel, tin, zinc.

**method**
(n) What method did you use in your experiment? procedure, process, approach, technique, system, practice, scheme, plan.

**methodical**
(adj) Jo has a methodical approach to her work. orderly, well-organized, systematic, structured, logical, disciplined, businesslike, efficient, careful, painstaking, meticulous.
OPPOSITES: haphazard, chaotic.

**middle**
1 (n) We ate our picnic in the middle of the wood. centre, heart, thick, depths (plural), midst (old-fashioned), core.
2 (n) Tie this scarf around your middle. waist, midriff, tummy (informal), waistline.
3 (adj) The middle window is smaller than the others. central, inner, inside.
4 (adj) Find the middle point of the line. mid, halfway, midway, central, median.

**miffed** (informal) see **annoyed**.

**mighty** see **strong** 1.

**mild**
1 (adj) Mr Badger has a mild manner. gentle, placid, meek, docile, calm, easy-going, peaceable, serene, amiable, affable.
OPPOSITES: aggressive, violent.
2 (adj) It was a mild evening. warm, balmy, pleasant, temperate (climate).
OPPOSITES: cool, cold.
3 (adj) This soup has a mild flavour. delicate, subtle, faint, bland, insipid.
OPPOSITE: strong.

**mime**
(v) Can you mime the title of the film? act out, use gestures to indicate, gesture.

**mimic**
1 (v) Dominic can mimic Elvis Presley. See **imitate** 1.
2 (n) Tony is an excellent mimic. impressionist, impersonator, imitator.

## mind
1 *(n) Use your mind to work out the answer.* brain, head, intelligence, intellect, brains *(plural) (informal)*, brainpower, powers of reasoning *(plural)*, wits *(plural)*, judgment, grey matter *(informal)*.
2 *(n) Don't let your mind wander.* attention, thoughts *(plural)*, concentration.
3 *(n) I must be losing my mind!* sanity, wits *(plural)*, senses *(plural)*, judgment, reason, marbles *(plural) (informal)*.
4 *(v) I won't mind if you go without me.* object, take offence, be upset, care, worry, be bothered, be resentful, disapprove.
5 *(v) Mind the cars!* watch out for, look out for, be careful of, beware of, be wary of, remember, pay attention to.
6 *(v) Please mind my rat while I'm away.* See **look after**.
7 change your mind see **change your mind**.
8 make up your mind see **make up your mind**.

## mingle
1 *(v) Trina likes to mingle with people of her own age.* See **mix** 3.
2 *(v) Let the paints mingle together on the page.* See **merge** 2.

## minor
*(adj) Don't worry about such a minor mistake.* small, slight, trivial, insignificant, unimportant, negligible, trifling, petty.
OPPOSITE: major.

## minute
1 *(n) I'll be with you in a minute.* See **moment** 1.
2 *(adj) A minute speck of dust.* See **tiny** 2.

## miracle
*(n) It's a miracle how I passed my exams!* wonder, mystery, marvel, phenomenon.

## miraculous see **wonderful** 2.

## mischievous
1 *(adj) A mischievous child.* See **naughty** 1.
2 *(adj) A mischievous smile.* impish, playful, teasing, roguish, wicked, arch.

## miserable
1 *(adj) Carl is feeling miserable.* depressed, unhappy, low, down, blue, glum, gloomy, down in the dumps *(informal)*, down in the mouth *(informal)*, dejected, despondent, melancholy, tearful, mournful, downcast, forlorn, doleful, wretched, heartbroken, grief-stricken, brokenhearted.
OPPOSITES: cheerful, happy.
2 *(adj) It was a miserable day.* dismal, dreary, depressing, gloomy, grey, dull.
OPPOSITES: fine, bright.
3 *(adj) Conditions in the prison were miserable.* grim, hard, harsh, cheerless, filthy, squalid, sordid, desperate, wretched, inhuman, unbearable, distressing, pitiful, disgraceful, shameful, deplorable.
OPPOSITES: comfortable, pleasant.

## miserly see **mean** 5.

## misery
1 *(n) Gemma couldn't hide her misery when her dog died.* sadness, sorrow, unhappiness, grief, anguish, pain, agony, despair, heartache, distress, suffering, torment, torture, desolation, depression.
OPPOSITES: joy, happiness.
2 *(n) The film showed the misery of the refugees' lives.* hardship, wretchedness, poverty, squalor, deprivation, discomfort, trials *(plural)*, tribulations *(plural)*.
OPPOSITES: ease, comfort.
3 *(n) (informal) Don't be such a misery!* wet blanket *(informal)*, misery guts *(informal)*, moaner, spoilsport *(informal)*, killjoy, grouch, pessimist.

## misfortune
*(n) I had the misfortune to be ill on my birthday.* bad luck, hard luck.
OPPOSITES: good fortune, good luck.

## misjudge
1 *(v) It's easy to misjudge how fast traffic is moving.* miscalculate, underestimate, overestimate, make a mistake about, be wrong about, guess wrongly.
2 *(v) People misjudge Ziggy because of how he looks.* get the wrong idea about, jump to the wrong conclusion about, underrate, undervalue, overrate.

## mislead see **deceive** 1.

## misleading
1 *(adj) A misleading signpost.* confusing, ambiguous, muddling, puzzling, deceptive.
OPPOSITE: clear.
2 *(adj) A misleading answer.* deceitful, deceptive, ambiguous, evasive, tricky, dishonest, false, wrong.
OPPOSITES: straightforward, honest.

## miss
1 *(v) That shot will miss the dartboard by a mile.* be wide of, fall short of, fail to hit.
OPPOSITE: hit.
2 *(v) Hurry up or you'll miss the train.* be too late for, fail to catch.
OPPOSITE: catch.
3 *(v) You mustn't miss the chance to go skiing.* miss out on, pass up *(informal)*, forgo, let slip, lose, let go, fail to grasp.
OPPOSITES: take, seize.
4 *(v) I hope you won't miss school tomorrow.* be away from, be absent from, play truant from, skip *(informal)*, skive off *(informal)*, bunk off *(slang)*, dodge, avoid.
OPPOSITE: attend.
5 *(v) I know I'll miss my mum when I'm away.* be homesick for, want, need, long to see, long for, pine for, yearn for.

## missing see **lost** 1, 2.

## miss out
1 *(v) Don't miss out any questions in the exam.* leave out, omit, skip, overlook, pass over, fail to notice, forget, ignore.
2 miss out on *(v) If you go now, you'll miss out on all the fun.* miss, be deprived of, lose out on *(informal)*, be left out of, forgo, pass up *(informal)*.

## mist
*(n) I couldn't see through the mist.* fog, haze, spray, steam, vapour, condensation.

## mistake
1 *(n) Rani spotted a mistake in her maths homework.* error, inaccuracy, slip, fault, miscalculation, slip-up *(informal)*, boob *(informal)*, blunder, howler *(informal)*, bloomer *(informal)*, oversight, flaw, lapse.
2 *(n) It was a mistake to invite Stan to the party.* error of judgment, faux pas, gaffe, misjudgment, blunder, clanger *(informal)*.
3 mistake for *(v) I often mistake you for your sister.* See **confuse** 2.

## misty
1 *(adj) A misty day.* hazy, foggy, murky.
OPPOSITE: clear.
2 *(adj) Misty glass.* steamy, cloudy, opaque, frosted.
OPPOSITE: clear.

## mix
1 *(v) Mix the sugar and butter in a bowl.* combine, blend, stir together, mingle.
OPPOSITE: separate.
2 *(v) Mix the two packs of cards.* shuffle, jumble, combine, join, merge, mingle.
OPPOSITE: separate.
3 *(v) Zoë prefers to mix with people of her own age.* socialize, associate, go around, hang out *(informal)*, mingle, hobnob, rub shoulders *(informal)*, circulate, meet.

## mixed
1 *(adj) I'd like a bag of mixed sweets.* assorted, different, various, miscellaneous.
2 *(adj) I have mixed feelings about moving house.* confused, ambivalent, uncertain.
3 *(adj) Do you go to to a mixed school?* coeducational, co-ed.
OPPOSITE: single-sex.

## mixed-up
*(adj) After her parents' divorce, Lucy was really mixed-up.* confused, disturbed, screwed up *(informal)*, bewildered, upset, untogether *(slang)*, maladjusted.

## mixture
1 *(n) This box contains a mixture of chocolates.* assortment, selection, variety, range, choice, collection.
2 *(n) The house was a mixture of styles.* blend, combination, fusion, amalgamation, mix, jumble, hotchpotch, mishmash, mixed bag, potpourri, hybrid, conglomeration.
3 *(n) We created a horrible mixture.* concoction, brew, potion, compound.
4 *(n) Drink up your cough mixture.* medicine, syrup, linctus.

## mix-up
*(n) We need to sort out this mix-up.* mistake, misunderstanding, confusion, muddle, mess, snarl-up *(informal)*.

## moan
1 *(v) Tom began to moan with pain.* groan, whimper, whine, sob, wail, sigh.
2 *(v) Samantha will moan if we're late.* See **complain**.

## mob
1 (n) The police tried to control the angry mob. crowd, rabble, throng, horde, swarm, pack, mass, gang.
2 (v) The fans will mob Famous Fred when he appears. crowd around, swarm around, surround, besiege, jostle, converge on.

## mock see **make fun of**.

## mocking
(adj) Jacinta gave me a mocking smile. sneering, scornful, disdainful, contemptuous, disparaging, sardonic, ironic, sarcastic, taunting, teasing.

## model
1 (n) This dinosaur is only a model. copy, imitation, replica, dummy, mock-up.
2 (n) Our car is the latest model. version, type, design, style, shape, mark.
3 (adj) Helen collects model aeroplanes. miniature, toy, scaled down, imitation.
OPPOSITES: real, full-size.
4 (adj) Jason is a model pupil. perfect, ideal, exemplary, dream.
5 (v) Can you model a hippo out of clay? mould, shape, form, make, create, fashion (old-fashioned), sculpt, carve, chisel, cast.
6 (v) Claudia will model the latest style in beachwear. wear, display, show off, sport (informal).

## moderate
1 (adj) I have a moderate amount of homework. fair, average, middling, reasonable, normal, ordinary, unexceptional, modest, limited, adequate.
OPPOSITE: excessive.
2 (adj) My parents have moderate views. middle-of-the-road, reasonable, restrained, rational, fair, sensible, temperate, mild.
OPPOSITE: extreme.

## modern
(adj) Do you like modern music? contemporary, current, present-day, recent, new, up-to-date, up-to-the-minute, the latest, fashionable, trendy (informal).
OPPOSITES: ancient, old-fashioned.

## modernize
(v) The editor wants to modernize the magazine. bring up to date, update, revamp, remodel, give a face-lift to, make over, refresh, renovate (building).

## modest
1 (adj) Akin was modest about his success. humble, self-effacing, self-deprecating, unassuming, unpretentious, reticent, quiet.
OPPOSITES: conceited, boastful.
2 (adj) Di is too modest to get undressed with the others. self-conscious, shy, embarrassed, bashful, diffident, demure, coy, reserved, prudish, prim and proper.
3 (adj) I've saved a modest sum of money. See **moderate** 1.

## moist
1 (adj) The cave walls felt moist. damp, dank, dripping, wettish, wet.
OPPOSITE: dry.
2 (adj) The air feels moist. humid, clammy, muggy, steamy, sticky, damp, dank, misty.
OPPOSITES: dry, arid.

## moisten see **wet** 5.

## moisture
1 (n) I could feel the moisture in the air. humidity, dampness, dankness, wetness, condensation, steam, vapour.
2 (n) Drops of moisture ran down Garth's face. perspiration, sweat, water, liquid.

## moment
1 (n) I'll be with you in a moment. minute, second, bit, tick (informal), instant, jiffy (informal), two shakes of a lamb's tail (informal), flash, trice, the twinkling of an eye, no time.
2 (n) At that moment, the clock struck midnight. minute, second, instant, point, point in time, juncture, stage.

## money
1 (n) Lord Lucre may leave his money to the dogs' home. cash, wealth, riches (plural), funds (plural), capital, hard cash, gold, silver, dosh (slang), lolly (slang), dough (slang), readies (plural) (informal).
2 (n) Take some foreign money with you. currency, coins (plural), notes (plural).

## monotonous
1 (adj) Harvey has such a monotonous voice. boring, dull, flat, droning, toneless, colourless, unvarying, samey (informal).
OPPOSITES: animated, lively.
2 (adj) A monotonous job. See **boring**.

## monster
1 (n) I dreamt about a big green monster. creature, beast, dragon, sea monster, giant, ogre, troll, goblin, ghoul, werewolf, zombie, vampire, gremlin, mutant.
2 (n) Heidi's brother is a little monster. terror, horror, devil, demon, fiend, brute.
3 (adj) I had a monster portion of ice cream. See **enormous**.

## monstrous
1 (adj) I dreamt of a monstrous creature with two heads. hideous, gruesome, grotesque, repulsive, horrible, frightful, fiendish, hellish, freakish, mutant.
2 (adj) A monstrous crime. See **horrible** 1.
3 (adj) A monstrous amount of chocolate. See **enormous**.

## monument
(n) This monument is dedicated to those who died in battle. memorial, statue, column, pillar, shrine, cenotaph, obelisk, cairn, mausoleum, sepulchre, tombstone.

## mood
1 (n) What sort of mood are you in? frame of mind, state of mind, humour, temper.
2 (n) I wish you'd snap out of this mood. bad mood, bad temper, sulk, huff, grumps (plural) (informal), depression, blues (plural), doldrums (plural), melancholy.
3 (n) How would you describe the mood of the film? atmosphere, feel, tone, flavour, character, ambience.

## moody
1 (adj) Tricia gets moody if she doesn't have her own way. cross, grumpy, bad-tempered, irritable, ratty (informal), sulky, in a huff, peevish, touchy, snappy, crotchety (informal), crabby, sullen, miserable, depressed, down in the dumps (informal), down in the mouth (informal), in the doldrums, glum, gloomy.
OPPOSITES: cheerful, contented.
2 (adj) Jason is so moody, you can't tell how he'll react. unpredictable, erratic, temperamental, volatile, mercurial, impulsive, capricious, unstable.
OPPOSITES: steady, predictable.

## moor
1 (n) We hiked across the moor. heath, moorland, fell.
2 (v) Moor the dinghy or it will drift away. tie up, secure, make fast, anchor, berth.

## mope
1 (v) Don't mope; it will all come right in the end. be miserable, be despondent, be dejected, fret, pine, be down in the mouth (informal), eat your heart out, brood, sulk.
2 **mope about** (v) Barney tends to mope about on his own. drift about, mooch about (slang), hang around, knock around, wander about, languish, idle.

## moral
(n) What is the moral of this story? lesson, teaching, message, meaning, point.

## morbid
1 (adj) Don't be so morbid! pessimistic, gloomy, glum, melancholy, morose, obsessed with death, preoccupied with death, fixated with death.
OPPOSITE: cheerful.
2 (adj) Carla has a morbid fascination with graveyards. unhealthy, unwholesome, grim, ghoulish, macabre, grisly, gruesome, horrible, sick (informal), brooding.
OPPOSITE: healthy.

## more
(adj) This extension will give us more space. extra, additional, added, further, supplementary, spare, fresh, new.
OPPOSITE: less.

## morning
(n) dawn, daybreak, break of day, sunrise, morn (old-fashioned), forenoon (old-fashioned).

## mostly
1 (adv) Mostly I shop at the supermarket. usually, normally, generally, as a rule, mainly, in general, on the whole, typically, most often, for the most part, in the main.
2 (adv) Miranda's bedroom is mostly blue. mainly, almost entirely, predominantly, largely, primarily, for the most part, chiefly.

## mother
1 (n) Jemima lives with her mother. mum (informal), mummy (informal), ma (informal), mamma (informal), old woman (informal), old lady (informal).

**2** (v) Alexander likes to mother his little sister. look after, care for, protect, comfort, nurse, fuss over, baby, pamper, indulge, spoil.

**motionless** see **still** 1, 2.

**motivate**
**1** (v) Maybe this news will motivate you to take some action. See **prompt** 1.
**2** (v) A good teacher should be able to motivate you. inspire, get you going, spur you on, give you some incentive, stimulate.

**motive**
(n) There seemed to be no motive for the murder. reason, cause, motivation, rationale, grounds (plural), purpose, stimulus, spur, incentive.

**mould**
**1** (n) The damp walls were covered in mould. fungus, mildew.
**2** (n) Pour the jelly into a mould. cast, form, shape.
**3** (v) Can you mould a hippo out of clay? See **model** 5.

**mouldy**
**1** (adj) This plum is mouldy. bad, rotten, mildewed, spoiled, decaying, putrefying.
OPPOSITE: fresh.
**2** (adj) I hate the smell of mouldy clothes. mildewed, musty, fusty.

**mound**
**1** (n) A mound of dirty clothes. See **pile** 1.
**2** (n) A grassy mound. bank, hill, hillock, hummock, knoll, embankment, dune.

**mountain**
**1** (n) The mountain was hidden by clouds. peak, hill, fell, pinnacle, alp.
**2** (n) Please move this mountain of rubbish. See **pile** 1.

**mountainous**
(adj) The picture shows a mountainous landscape. alpine, highland, hilly, rugged, craggy, rocky.
OPPOSITE: flat.

**mourn** see **grieve**.

**move**
**1** (v) Stay there and don't move! budge, stir, shift, fidget, change position.
**2** (v) Please move your things into the spare room. shift, take, carry, bring, transfer, switch, transport.
**3** (v) Try to move steadily through the forest. advance, proceed, walk, make your way, go, march, journey, pass.
**4** (v) I may have to move to Spain. move house, relocate, move away, emigrate.
**5** (v) It's time to move! go, set off, get moving, make tracks, get started, get going, make a move, take action, act.
**6** (v) This film will really move you. touch, affect, upset, make you cry, reduce you to tears, tug at your heartstrings, get to (informal), disturb, have an effect on, make an impression on, stir, inspire.
**7** (v) I hope this news will move you to take some action. See **prompt** 1.
**8** (n) One move and I'll shoot! movement, motion, gesture, change of position.
**9** (n) Taking the train was a good move. step, thing to do, manoeuvre, tack, plan, stratagem, tactic, ploy, trick.
**10** (n) It's your move now. go, turn.

**movement**
(n) I saw some movement in the bushes. activity, motion, action, moving, stirring.

**moving**
**1** (adj) This model car has moving parts. movable, mobile, working.
OPPOSITES: fixed, immovable.
**2** (adj) The film was so moving it made me cry. touching, emotional, poignant, heart-rending, inspiring, stirring, heart-warming, tear-jerking (informal), sentimental.

**muck**
(n) Clean that muck off your shoes! dirt, filth, mud, grime, slime, sludge, gunge (informal), gunk (informal), manure, dung.

**mucky** see **dirty** 1.

**mud**
(n) My boots are covered in mud. clay, dirt, soil, silt, muck, sludge, slime, slurry, ooze.

**muddle**
**1** (v) Please don't muddle my papers. See **jumble** 1.
**2** (v) Complex instructions muddle me. See **confuse** 1.
**3** (n) Tabitha's room is in a total muddle. See **mess** 2.

**muddled**
**1** (adj) All these instructions make me feel muddled. See **confused**.
**2** (adj) Your essay is very muddled. disorganized, confused, jumbled, chaotic, incoherent, woolly, unclear, mixed-up, scrambled, higgledy-piggledy (informal).
OPPOSITES: clear, well-organized.

**muddy**
**1** (adj) How did your boots get so muddy? dirty, mucky, filthy, grubby, grimy, caked with mud, mud-spattered.
OPPOSITE: clean.
**2** (adj) We squelched across a muddy field. marshy, mucky, soggy, waterlogged, swampy, boggy, miry, sodden, slimy.
OPPOSITES: dry, firm.
**3** (adj) The water in our pond is muddy. cloudy, murky, dirty, opaque.
OPPOSITES: clear, clean.

**muffled**
(adj) I heard a muffled cry from the cellar. faint, indistinct, dull, smothered, stifled, muted, suppressed, strangled.

**mug**
**1** (n) Wash up your mug. cup, beaker, tankard, jug, flagon (old-fashioned).
**2** (v) (informal) Someone tried to mug Dodgy Dave. attack, rob, set upon, beat up (informal), assault, lay into (informal), rough up (informal), duff up (slang), do over (slang), work over (slang).

---

## mountain words

### mountains can be...
awe-inspiring  massive
bare  rocky
barren  rugged
breathtaking  shrouded in
craggy  mist
forbidding  snowcapped
jagged  soaring
lofty  spectacular
looming  towering
majestic  treacherous

*glacier*

### in the mountains
alpine flowers  ice field
alpine meadow  ledge
avalanche  log cabin
boulder  mountain
cable car  pass
cave  mountain
chair lift  range
chalet  peak
conifers  precipice
crevasse  ridge
  (crack in  scree (loose
  glacier)  stones)
crevice (crack  slope
  in rock face)  stream
glacier  summit
  (river of ice)  tunnel
gorge  waterfall

### in the mountains you may feel...
alone
awestruck
breathless
chilled to
  the bone
daunted
dazzled
dizzy
dwarfed
exhilarated
insignificant
overawed

### mountain activities
abseiling  snowblading
bobsleighing  snowboarding
climbing  tobogganing
hang-gliding  walking
hiking  white-water
mountain  rafting
  biking
mountaineering
paragliding
skiing

*snowboarding*

**muggy**
*(adj) This muggy weather makes me sweat.*
sticky, sultry, humid, steamy, clammy,
oppressive, close, stuffy, airless.

**mumble**
*(v) Speak up and don't mumble!* mutter,
murmur, stutter, stammer, hem and haw.

**munch** *see* **chew**.

**murder**
1 *(n) The police are investigating the
murder. See* **killing** 1.
2 *(v) A hit man was paid to murder the
President. See* **kill** 1.

**murderer**
*(n)* killer, assassin, hit man *(slang)*,
cutthroat, butcher, slayer, slaughterer.

**murky**
1 *(adj) It was a murky Autumn day.* dark,
dull, foggy, misty, grey, cloudy, overcast,
gloomy, dismal, dreary, cheerless.
OPPOSITES: bright, clear.
2 *(adj) I won't swim in such murky water.*
cloudy, muddy, dirty, opaque.
OPPOSITE: clear.

**murmur**
1 *(v) Did you murmur something?* mutter,
mumble, whisper, say under your breath.
2 *(n) The hall was filled with the murmur
of voices.* hum, buzzing, whispering,
muttering, drone, mumble, babble, burble.

**muscular** *see* **strong** 1.

**mushy**
1 *(adj) Mushy peas.* pulpy, squashy,
squelchy, slushy, squidgy, soft.
2 *(adj) (informal) A mushy love story.
See* **sentimental** 2.

**music**
*(n)* melody, harmony, rhythm.

**musical**
*(adj) The bells made a musical sound.*
tuneful, melodious, melodic, harmonious,
lilting, sweet-sounding, dulcet.
OPPOSITES: discordant, cacophonous.

**musical instrument**
*(n)* TYPES OF MUSICAL INSTRUMENT:
BRASS: bugle, cornet, euphonium, French
horn, sousaphone, trombone, trumpet,
tuba. KEYBOARD: accordion,
harpsichord, organ, piano, synthesizer.
PERCUSSION: bass drum, bongos, cabasa,
castanets, chime bars, claves, cymbals,
finger cymbals, glockenspiel, guiro *(West
Indies)*, maracas, rattle, side drum, sleigh
bells, steel drum *(West Indies)*, tabla
*(India)*, tambourine, tam-tam (gong),
timpani (kettle drums), triangle, tubular
bells, vibraphone, wood block, xylophone.
STRINGS: balalaika *(Russia)*, banjo, cello,
double bass, guitar, harp, lute, lyre,
mandolin, sitar *(India)*, ukulele, viola, violin,
zither. WIND: bagpipes, bassoon, clarinet,
cor anglais, didgeridoo *(Australia)*, fife,
flute, harmonica (mouth organ), oboe,
panpipes *(South America)*, penny whistle,
piccolo, recorder, saxophone.

**musician**
*(n)* performer, player, instrumentalist,
minstrel *(old-fashioned)*, singer.
TYPES OF MUSICIAN: accompanist,
bandsman, bassoonist, bugler, busker,
cellist, clarinettist, composer, conductor,
cornetist, drummer, fiddler, flautist,
guitarist, harpist, oboist, organist,
percussionist, pianist, piper, soloist,
timpanist, trombonist, trumpeter, violinist.
*Also see* **singer**.

**must**
1 *(v) I must go now. See* **have to** 1.
2 *(n) Sensible shoes are a must if you
want to go hiking.* necessity, essential,
requirement, prerequisite.
OPPOSITE: option.

**musty**
*(adj) The cellar smells musty.* mouldy,
mildewy, fusty, damp, dank, stale, stuffy,
airless, frowsty.
OPPOSITES: fresh, airy.

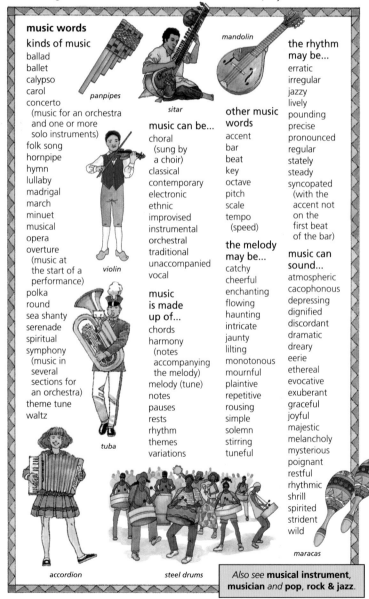

**music words**

**kinds of music**
ballad
ballet
calypso
carol
concerto
  (music for an orchestra
  and one or more
  solo instruments)
folk song
hornpipe
hymn
lullaby
madrigal
march
minuet
musical
opera
overture
  (music at
  the start of a
  performance)
polka
round
sea shanty
serenade
spiritual
symphony
  (music in
  several
  sections for
  an orchestra)
theme tune
waltz

*panpipes*

*sitar*

*mandolin*

*violin*

**music can be...**
choral
  (sung by
  a choir)
classical
contemporary
electronic
ethnic
improvised
instrumental
orchestral
traditional
unaccompanied
vocal

**music
is made
up of...**
chords
harmony
  (notes
  accompanying
  the melody)
melody (tune)
notes
pauses
rests
rhythm
themes
variations

*tuba*

**other music
words**
accent
bar
beat
key
octave
pitch
scale
tempo
  (speed)

**the melody
may be...**
catchy
cheerful
enchanting
flowing
haunting
intricate
jaunty
lilting
monotonous
mournful
plaintive
repetitive
rousing
simple
solemn
stirring
tuneful

**the rhythm
may be...**
erratic
irregular
jazzy
lively
pounding
precise
pronounced
regular
stately
steady
syncopated
  (with the
  accent not
  on the
  first beat
  of the bar)

**music can
sound...**
atmospheric
cacophonous
depressing
dignified
discordant
dramatic
dreary
eerie
ethereal
evocative
exuberant
graceful
joyful
majestic
melancholy
mysterious
poignant
restful
rhythmic
shrill
spirited
strident
wild

*maracas*

*accordion*

*steel drums*

*Also see* **musical instrument**,
**musician** *and* **pop, rock & jazz**.

**mutter**
*(v) Did I hear you mutter that you weren't satisfied?* mumble, murmur, say under your breath, grumble, complain, grouse.

**mysterious**
*(adj) A mysterious crime.* baffling, puzzling, perplexing, mystifying, unexplained, inexplicable, insoluble, cryptic, enigmatic, strange, curious, bizarre, weird, uncanny.

**mystery**
1 *(n) Can you solve the mystery of the green cat?* enigma, puzzle, riddle, conundrum, problem, secret.
2 *(n) Nadia reads one mystery after another.* detective story, crime story, whodunit *(informal)*, thriller.

**nag**
*(v) Don't nag me!* scold, keep on at, go on at *(informal)*, harp on at, find fault with, badger, pester, hassle *(informal)*, henpeck.

**naive**
*(adj) Emily is so naive, she trusts everybody.* gullible, unsuspecting, trusting, credulous, innocent, green, inexperienced, unworldly, unsophisticated, childlike.
OPPOSITES: experienced, cynical.

**naked**
*(adj) It's normal to be naked in the bath.* nude, bare, in the nude, undressed, stark naked, starkers *(informal)*, in your birthday suit *(informal)*, in the altogether *(informal)*, without a stitch on.
OPPOSITES: dressed, fully clothed.

**name**
1 *(v) What shall we name our gang?* call, entitle, label, term, style, tag, dub.
2 *(v) Can you name all the European capitals?* identify, list, cite, reel off, recite.
3 *(n) What is your name?* first name, given name, Christian name, surname, family name, middle name, maiden name, married name, nickname, alias, pseudonym (pen name), handle *(informal)*.

**nap** *see* **sleep** 3.

**narrow**
1 *(adj) What a narrow space!* tight, confined, cramped, restricted, limited.
OPPOSITES: wide, ample.
2 *(adj) This chair has narrow legs.* thin, slim, slender, tapering, fine.
OPPOSITES: wide, broad.

**nasty**
1 *(adj) What a nasty smell!* disgusting, revolting, horrible, unpleasant, foul, repulsive, nauseating, sickening, vile, loathsome, odious, obnoxious, offensive, repugnant, repellent, yucky *(slang)*.
OPPOSITES: pleasant, nice.

2 *(adj) Don't be nasty! See* **horrible** 3.
3 *(adj) Ria has a nasty illness.* unpleasant, serious, bad, severe, major, critical, painful.
4 *(adj) Should nasty videos be banned?* pornographic, obscene, blue, dirty, smutty, indecent, off colour, violent, offensive.

**national**
*(adj) Tomorrow will be a national holiday.* public, state, nationwide, countrywide, general, widespread, coast-to-coast.

**natter** *see* **talk** 1, 5.

**natural**
1 *(adj) It's natural to grieve when someone dies.* normal, healthy, understandable, usual, common, typical.
OPPOSITES: abnormal, unnatural.
2 *(adj) Dom has a natural musical ability.* innate, inborn, instinctive, intuitive, intrinsic, inherent, inherited.
3 *(adj) I prefer to eat natural foods.* unprocessed, pure, organic, additive-free, chemical-free, unrefined, uncoloured, unbleached, whole, plain, wholesome.
OPPOSITES: processed, synthetic.
4 *(adj) Jenny has a natural manner.* unaffected, artless, genuine, open, frank, spontaneous, easy, unselfconscious, unsophisticated, unpretentious, unstudied.
OPPOSITES: affected, artificial.

**nature**
*(n) I enjoy learning about nature.* the environment, the countryside, natural history, wildlife, the living world, the natural world, the earth.

**naughty**
1 *(adj) A naughty child.* disobedient, badly behaved, mischievous, unruly, defiant, unmanageable, wild, wilful, wayward, undisciplined, cheeky, exasperating.
OPPOSITES: well-behaved, obedient.
2 *(adj) A naughty joke. See* **rude** 2.

**near**
1 *(prep) I live near the shops.* close to, not far from, next to, adjacent to, handy for, within sniffing distance of *(informal)*.
OPPOSITE: far from.
2 *(adj) Winter is near.* coming, approaching, looming, just around the corner, close at hand, imminent.
OPPOSITES: far off, distant.

**nearly**
*(adv) I've nearly finished.* almost, just about, practically, virtually, as good as, to all intents and purposes, not quite.

**neat**
1 *(adj) Ned's room looks neat. See* **tidy** 2.
2 *(adj) The carpenter did a neat job.* careful, precise, meticulous, skilful, deft, expert, competent, accurate, efficient.
OPPOSITES: clumsy, messy.

**necessary**
*(adj) A hard hat is necessary for riding.* essential, vital, compulsory, obligatory, needed, indispensable, mandatory.
OPPOSITES: unnecessary, optional.

**need**
1 *(v) This project will need a lot of work.* require, demand, call for, necessitate, entail, want.
2 *(v) Come back - I need you!* want, miss, rely on, depend on, yearn for, pine for.
3 *(n) There's a need for qualified teachers.* demand, call, lack of, shortage of, want of.
4 **needs** *(plural n) Will this money satisfy your needs?* requirements *(plural)*, demands *(plural)*, wants *(plural)*, wishes *(plural)*, desires *(plural)*.
5 **need to** *(v) I need to revise for the test. See* **have to** 1.

**neglect**
1 *(v) Don't neglect your dog.* fail to look after, fail to care for, abandon, leave alone, forsake.
OPPOSITES: look after, care for.
2 *(v) If you neglect your studies, you'll fail the exam.* let slide, pay no attention to, skimp on, leave undone, shirk, avoid.
OPPOSITES: pay attention to, attend to.

**neglected**
1 *(adj) A neglected animal.* abandoned, uncared-for, unfed, mistreated, unloved.
2 *(adj) A neglected flowerbed.* untended, overgrown, unweeded, uncared-for, derelict *(building)*, run-down *(building)*.

**neighbourhood** *see* **area** 1.

**nervous**
*(adj) I'm always nervous before a concert.* anxious, apprehensive, worried, scared, frightened, on edge, uneasy, edgy, tense, jittery *(informal)*, uptight *(informal)*, twitchy, jumpy, fidgety, nervy *(informal)*, hyper *(informal)*, agitated, overwrought, flustered, highly strung, excitable.
OPPOSITES: calm, confident.

**neutral**
*(adj) A referee must remain neutral.* impartial, objective, detached, unbiased, nonpartisan, unprejudiced, dispassionate, uninvolved, sitting on the fence.
OPPOSITE: biased.

**never**
*(adv) Do you tell lies? No, never!* certainly not, no way, not at all, under no circumstances, on no account, not ever, at no time, not on your life *(informal)*.
OPPOSITES: sometimes, always.

**new**
1 *(adj) We have some new information.* fresh, recent, up-to-date, current, up-to-the-minute, extra, additional, more.
OPPOSITES: old, outdated.
2 *(adj) Have you tried this new product?* brand-new, state-of-the-art, revolutionary, innovative, ground-breaking, advanced, modern, ultramodern, novel, original.
OPPOSITES: obsolete, out of date.
3 *(adj) Start a new page. See* **fresh** 4.
4 *(adj) Let's explore a new path.* different, unfamiliar, unknown, untried, unexplored, uncharted, untouched, untrodden, fresh.
OPPOSITE: familiar.

## news

1 (n) *The news from the war zone shocked the nation.* report, bulletin, news item, newsflash, story, press release, announcement, communiqué, dispatch, message, account, statement, information, facts (plural), intelligence, info (informal), update, leak, disclosure, revelation.
2 (n) *Have you heard the news about Jason?* latest (informal), rumours (plural), gossip, lowdown (informal), word, talk, stories (plural), tittle-tattle, gen (informal), scandal, dirt (slang).
3 the news (n) *I like to keep up with the news.* current affairs (plural), world events (plural).

## newspaper

(n) paper, daily, weekly, Sunday paper, national paper, local paper, tabloid, broadsheet, rag (informal).

## next

1 (adj) *We planned our work for the next four weeks.* following, succeeding, ensuing, subsequent, coming.
OPPOSITES: previous, past.
2 (adj) *Can you hear voices in the next room?* adjacent, adjoining, neighbouring, nearest, closest.
3 (adv) *Next add the sugar.* then, after that, afterwards, later, subsequently.

## nibble

1 (v) *The mouse began to nibble the cheese.* bite, gnaw, peck at, chew on, munch, pick at, eat, taste.
2 (n) *I've only had a nibble of my sandwich.* See **bite** 3.

## night

(n) dark, darkness, night-time, small hours (plural), hours of darkness (plural).

| night... | the night is... | the moon is... | in the sky you see... | night-time creatures |
|---|---|---|---|---|
| closes in | moonless | bright | clouds | badger |
| descends | moonlit | ghostly | constellations | bat |
| falls | pitch-black | gleaming | crescent | firefly |
| settles | shadowy | hazy | moon | frog |
| **darkness...** | silent | hidden | full moon | glow-worm |
| blots out | starless | luminous | Milky Way | hedgehog |
| cloaks | starlit | pale | planets | mosquito |
| conceals | still | remote | shooting stars | moth |
| engulfs | | shining | **night-time sights** | nightingale |
| envelops | **the sky is...** | silvery | | owl |
| hides | clear | veiled | Catseyes | **night-time sounds** |
| masks | cloudy | | (reflectors on roads) | bats squeaking |
| obscures | illuminated | **the stars...** | city lights | cats yowling |
| swallows up | inky | flicker | floodlit buildings | clocks chiming |
| veils | jet-black | glimmer | headlights | frogs croaking |
| | lit up | glitter | illuminations | mosquitoes whining |
| | starry | shimmer | neon signs | owls hooting |
| | star-studded | sparkle | streetlights | sirens wailing |
| | vast | twinkle | | |
| | velvety | wink | | |

## nice

| a nice person | a nice meal | a nice view | I had a nice time. | You look nice. |
|---|---|---|---|---|
| agreeable | appetizing | beautiful | agreeable | attractive |
| amiable | delectable | breathtaking | amusing | beautiful |
| caring | delicious | glorious | brilliant | divine (informal) |
| charming | lovely | gorgeous | enjoyable | gorgeous |
| considerate | luscious | impressive | entertaining | handsome |
| delightful | mouthwatering | lovely | excellent | lovely |
| friendly | scrumptious (informal) | magnificent | fabulous (informal) | pretty |
| generous | tasty | picturesque | fantastic (informal) | ravishing |
| gentle | yummy (slang) | spectacular | fun | stunning (informal) |
| good-natured | **nice weather** | splendid | good | wonderful |
| helpful | beautiful | superb | great (informal) | **Nice people don't swear.** |
| kind | bright | wonderful | interesting | courteous |
| likable | dry | **a nice piece of work** | lovely | genteel |
| lovely | fair | accurate | marvellous | gentlemanly |
| obliging | fine | careful | pleasant | ladylike |
| pleasant | glorious | methodical | super (informal) | polite |
| sweet | gorgeous | meticulous | terrific (informal) | refined |
| sympathetic | lovely | neat | wonderful | respectable |
| thoughtful | mild | painstaking | | well-bred |
| understanding | pleasant | pleasing | | |
| unselfish | sunny | well-presented | | |
| warm-hearted | warm | well-written | | |

## nightmare

(n) *You've had a nightmare.* bad dream.
2 (n) *The test was a nightmare.* ordeal, torment, torture, agony, horror, trial.

## nimble

(adj) *You must be nimble to be a good footballer.* light on your feet, agile, lithe, nippy (informal), speedy, quick, swift, supple, acrobatic, deft, skilful, proficient.

## noble

(adj) *Many noble lords attended the banquet.* aristocratic, titled, highborn, blue-blooded, distinguished.

## nod

(v) *Nod your head if you agree.* incline, bow, bob, dip, duck, shake up and down.

## noise

1 (n) *I heard a faint noise.* sound.
2 (n) *The noise in the classroom was unbelievable.* din, racket, row, clamour, uproar, hullabaloo, tumult, rumpus, hubbub, commotion, pandemonium.

## noisy

1 (adj) *A noisy aeroplane.* See **loud** 1.
2 (adj) *A noisy gang of kids.* boisterous, riotous, rowdy, uproarious, raucous, clamorous, rackety, talkative, vociferous.
OPPOSITES: quiet, subdued.

**nonsense**
1 (n) *Don't talk nonsense.* rubbish, drivel, garbage, rot, guff (informal), baloney (informal), twaddle, balderdash, piffle, claptrap (informal), codswallop (slang), poppycock (informal), gibberish, double Dutch (informal), gobbledegook (informal). OPPOSITE: sense.
2 (n) *Mum won't stand for any nonsense.* silliness, foolishness, stupidity, tomfoolery, monkey business (informal), misbehaviour, mischief, antics (plural), high jinks (plural).

**normal**
1 (adj) *It's normal for babies to cry.* common, usual, commonplace, natural, typical, standard, accepted, expected. OPPOSITES: unusual, unnatural.
2 (adj) *Our normal routine was disrupted.* See **usual**.
3 (adj) *A normal person wouldn't behave like that.* sane, well-adjusted, rational, well-balanced, reasonable. OPPOSITES: abnormal, insane.

**nosy**
(adj) (informal) *Nosy neighbours.* inquisitive, prying, snooping (informal), eavesdropping, curious, overcurious, interfering, meddlesome, intrusive.

**note**
1 (n) *I must send Henry a note.* message, letter, reminder, memo, memorandum, line (informal), communication.
2 (v) *Note down this date.* See **write** 1.

**nothing**
1 (pronoun) *There's nothing in the box.* not a thing, nothing at all, zilch (slang), not a sausage (informal).
2 (pronoun) *We scored nothing.* nought, zero, nil, love (tennis), a duck (cricket).

**notice**
1 (v) *Did you notice Burglar Beryl's new brooch?* see, spot, observe, catch sight of, note, take in, take note of, spy, detect, discern, perceive, get a load of (informal).
2 (n) *Have you seen the notice about the sale?* announcement, poster, sign, advertisement, circular, leaflet, pamphlet, brochure, bulletin, communication.

**noticeable**
(adj) *There has been a noticeable change in Toni's behaviour.* distinct, perceptible, discernible, unmistakable, obvious, clear, marked, visible, pronounced, striking, conspicuous, definite, significant, evident. OPPOSITE: imperceptible.

**now**
1 (adv) *I must go now.* See **immediately**.
2 (adv) *Most families now have a TV.* nowadays, these days, today, in this day and age, at the moment, at present.

**nude** see **naked**.

**nudge**
(v) *Don't nudge me when I'm writing.* poke, prod, jog, jolt, bump, knock, jab, push, shove, touch, elbow.

**nuisance**
1 (n) *It's a nuisance when you miss the bus.* inconvenience, problem, pain (informal), pain in the neck (informal), hassle (informal), drag (informal), headache (informal), bore, disadvantage.
2 (n) *Jemima is such a nuisance.* pest, pain (informal), pain in the neck (informal), problem, bother, plague, bore.

**numb**
(adj) *My fingers feel numb.* dead, paralysed, frozen, chilled, anaesthetized, without feeling, asleep, desensitized.

**number**
1 (n) *Think of a number between one and ten.* figure, digit, numeral, integer, unit.
2 (n) *Count the number of sweets in the bag.* amount, quantity, total, sum, tally.
3 (n) *A large number of people gathered in the hall.* group, crowd, throng, horde, mass, collection, company, multitude.

**obedient**
(adj) *An obedient child.* well-behaved, dutiful, respectful, biddable, submissive, compliant, manageable, amenable, docile, meek, well-trained (animal). OPPOSITES: disobedient, rebellious.

**obey**
1 (v) *You must obey the school rules.* observe, follow, keep to, stick to, abide by, comply with, adhere to, respect, submit to, conform to, be ruled by, heed. OPPOSITES: disobey, defy.
2 (v) *You'll get into trouble if you don't obey.* do as you are told, follow orders, toe the line, knuckle under (informal). OPPOSITES: rebel, revolt.

**object**
1 (n) *What's that red object?* See **thing** 1.
2 (v) *My parents object when I play loud music.* See **disapprove** 1.

**obscene**
(adj) *An obscene film.* indecent, pornographic, blue, immoral, corrupting, offensive, shocking, sickening, vile, lewd, vulgar, smutty, suggestive, raunchy (slang), dirty, filthy, kinky (slang), sick (informal). OPPOSITE: decent.

**observant**
(adj) *Spies need to be observant.* watchful, alert, eagle-eyed, sharp-eyed, perceptive, attentive, vigilant, wide-awake, aware. OPPOSITES: unobservant, oblivious.

**observe**
1 (v) *The police will observe Beryl's actions.* watch, keep an eye on, monitor, keep under observation, keep tabs on (informal), keep under surveillance, spy on.

2 (v) *Did you observe that the clock was five minutes fast?* See **notice** 1.

**obsessed**
(adj) *Leo is obsessed by the fear of failing.* consumed, gripped, possessed, haunted, tormented, plagued, preoccupied with.

**obstacle**
(n) *Mum's disapproval could be a major obstacle.* difficulty, problem, stumbling block, hurdle, impediment, drawback, disadvantage, snag, deterrent, barrier.

**obstinate** see **stubborn**.

**obstruct** see **block** 2, 3.

**obtain** see **get** 1, 4.

**obvious**
(adj) *Ziggy's boredom is obvious.* plain, clear, evident, self-evident, easy to see, crystal clear, visible, apparent, noticeable, conspicuous, striking, unmistakable, undisguised, unconcealed, undeniable, transparent, blatant, glaring, flagrant. OPPOSITES: imperceptible, hidden.

**occasion** see **event** 1, 2.

**occasional**
(adj) *I heard an occasional rumble of thunder.* intermittent, periodic, infrequent, sporadic, irregular, odd, rare. OPPOSITES: frequent, continuous.

**occupation** see **job** 2.

**occupy**
1 (v) *This puzzle will occupy you for hours.* See **amuse** 2.
2 (v) *Does sport occupy a lot of your time?* take up, fill, use up, eat up, consume.
3 (v) *The Smiths occupy a small house.* live in, inhabit, dwell in, reside in, rent, own.

**occur**
1 (v) *When did this occur?* See **happen** 1.
2 occur to (v) *When did the idea occur to you?* come to, dawn on, enter your head, cross your mind, spring to mind, strike.

**ocean** see **sea** 1.

**odd**
1 (adj) *Odd behaviour.* See **strange** 1.
2 (adj) *An odd noise.* See **strange** 2.
3 (adj) *Why is there always one odd sock in the wash?* spare, unmatched, leftover, remaining, single, solitary, lone.

**off**
1 (adj) *Mrs Badger says the trip is off.* cancelled, called off, postponed, shelved.
2 (adj) *Tom is off today.* See **away** 1.
3 (adj) *This yoghurt is off.* bad, mouldy, sour, rancid, turned, curdled, rotten.
4 (adj) (informal) *That comment was really off.* out of order, uncalled-for, unjustified, unwarranted, unacceptable, in bad taste, objectionable, non-pc (informal).

**offend**
(v) *I didn't mean to offend you.* upset, hurt your feelings, put your back up, give offence, insult, slight, snub, tread on your toes (informal), put your nose out of joint (informal), annoy, anger, provoke, rile.

**offended**
*(adj) Dad looked offended when I criticized his cooking.* hurt, upset, wounded, put out, piqued, affronted, miffed *(informal)*, insulted, resentful, disgruntled, in a huff, annoyed, incensed, outraged.

**offensive**
1 *(adj) An offensive smell. See* **nasty** 1.
2 *(adj) Offensive remarks. See* **rude** 1, 2.

**offer**
1 *(v) Most schools offer a good education.* provide, supply, give, give the opportunity of, place at your disposal, make available.
2 *(v) Did Jo offer to help? See* **volunteer**.
3 *(v) Did you offer Grandma some cake?* give, hand, proffer, pass, present with.

**official**
1 *(adj) Is that an official certificate?* authorized, approved, recognized, valid, bona fide, authentic, legitimate, legal.
2 *(adj) The mayor attends many official functions.* formal, ceremonial, solemn.

**often**
*(adv) Fifi is often late.* frequently, regularly, usually, generally, repeatedly, constantly, habitually, again and again, time after time, over and over again, time and again.
OPPOSITES: rarely, seldom.

**O.K.** *(informal) see* **all right** 1, 2, 3.

**old**
1 *(adj) I'll look after you when you're old.* older, elderly, getting on, advanced in years, grey-haired, aged, past your prime, over the hill *(informal)*, past it *(informal)*, doddery *(informal)*, decrepit.
OPPOSITE: young.
2 *(adj) Our school buildings are old.* ancient, historic, antiquated, dilapidated, crumbling, decaying, run-down.
OPPOSITES: new, modern.
3 *(adj) Do you have to wear those old clothes?* ancient, worn-out, shabby, scruffy, moth-eaten, ragged, tattered, cast-off, second-hand.
OPPOSITE: new.
4 *(adj) Flash Frank collects old cars.* vintage, veteran, antique.
OPPOSITES: new, modern.
5 *(adj) Life was harder in the old days.* bygone, former, olden *(old-fashioned)*, early, past, forgotten, of old, of yore.
OPPOSITES: recent, modern.
6 *(adj) Kissing under the mistletoe is an old custom.* ancient, age-old, long-established, long-standing, time-honoured, traditional, enduring, antiquated.
OPPOSITES: modern, recent.

**old-fashioned**
*(adj) Aunt Bertha's ideas are really old-fashioned.* out of date, behind the times, dated, outdated, outmoded, out of fashion, unfashionable, backward-looking, reactionary, old-fogyish, square *(informal)*, ancient, archaic, antiquated, quaint, medieval, out of the ark *(informal)*.
OPPOSITES: up-to-date, modern.

**ominous**
*(adj) An ominous silence.* forbidding, menacing, threatening, grim, sinister, dark, unpromising, inauspicious, baleful, fateful.
OPPOSITES: encouraging, promising.

**omit**
*(v) We'll sing the song, but omit verse three.* leave out, miss out, skip, pass over, exclude, drop, forget about, cut.

**on purpose**
*(phrase) You did that on purpose!* deliberately, intentionally, purposely, wilfully, knowingly, consciously, wittingly.
OPPOSITES: accidentally, by accident.

**ooze**
*(v) Fat began to ooze from the sausage.* seep, dribble, trickle, drip, escape, leak.

**open**
1 *(v) Could you open this for me?* undo, unfasten, untie, unwrap, unlock, unbolt, unbar, unseal, uncork, unroll, unfold.
OPPOSITES: close, shut.
2 *(v) Will you open the discussion? See* **start** 4.
3 *(adj) The door was left open.* ajar, wide-open, unlocked, unfastened, unbolted, unbarred, unlatched, gaping, yawning.
OPPOSITES: closed, locked.
4 *(adj) When are the tennis courts open?* available, free, accessible, usable, public.
OPPOSITES: unavailable.
5 *(adj) We reached some open country.* wide-open, empty, clear, undeveloped, unbuilt-up, uncrowded, spacious, unenclosed, unfenced, exposed, wild.
OPPOSITES: enclosed, built-up.
6 *(adj) Please be open with me. See* **honest** 1.

**opinion** *see* **view** 2.

**opportunity**
1 *(n) Take every opportunity that you're offered.* chance, opening, break *(informal)*.
2 *(n) Is this a good opportunity to talk?* moment, time, occasion.

**oppose**
*(v) No one dares to oppose Aunt Bertha.* defy, challenge, resist, stand up to, take a stand against, cross, contradict, disagree with, take issue with, confront, quarrel with, argue with, gainsay, thwart.

**opposite**
1 *(adj) I sat opposite Sandy.* facing, face-to-face with, across from.
2 *(adj) We have opposite views.* opposing, conflicting, contradictory, incompatible, differing, different, diametrically opposed.
OPPOSITES: identical, similar.

**optimistic**
*(adj) Ryan is optimistic about the future.* positive, confident, hopeful, cheerful, sanguine, buoyant, upbeat *(informal)*.
OPPOSITES: pessimistic, cynical.

**orange**
*(n)* SHADES OF ORANGE: amber, apricot, ginger, ochre, peach, tangerine.

**ordeal**
*(n) I never want to go through this ordeal again.* torture, torment, agony, nightmare, distress, anguish, suffering, hardship, trial, tribulation, struggle, difficulty, trouble.

**order**
1 *(v) Didn't I order you to go home?* tell, command, instruct, direct, bid, charge.
2 *(v) Did you order tickets for the concert?* apply for, send away for, book, reserve, request, ring for, place an order for.
3 *(n) The general gave the order to advance.* command, instruction, direction.
4 *(n) Can you see any order in this group of numbers?* pattern, structure, sequence, progression, system, plan, organization, regularity, grouping, arrangement.
OPPOSITES: chaos, muddle.
5 *(n) Mrs Badger quickly restored order.* discipline, control, peace and quiet, calm, tranquillity, harmony, neatness, tidiness, obedience, law and order.
OPPOSITES: disorder, pandemonium.
6 *(n) Try to keep your bicycle in good order.* condition, shape, nick *(informal)*.

**ordinary**
1 *(adj) Guitar practice is part of my ordinary routine. See* **usual**.
2 *(adj) I live in an ordinary terraced house.* typical, standard, conventional, run-of-the-mill, common or garden *(informal)*, commonplace, simple, modest, humble.
OPPOSITES: unusual, extraordinary.
3 *(adj) This is a rather ordinary piece of work.* average, mediocre, indifferent, nondescript, unexceptional, unremarkable, unimpressive, unimaginative, uninspired, dull, run-of-the-mill, banal, pedestrian.
OPPOSITES: exceptional, outstanding.

**organize**
1 *(v) Let's organize a trip. See* **arrange** 3.
2 *(v) Mrs Badger asked me to organize the cake stall.* take charge of, be responsible for, set up, run, manage, coordinate, look after, see to, take care of.
3 *(v) Try to organize your essay more clearly.* structure, plan, construct, put together, shape.
4 *(v) I must organize my CDs. See* **sort** 3.

**original**
1 *(adj) Who were the original inhabitants of Australia?* first, earliest, initial, native, indigenous, aboriginal, primitive, primeval.
2 *(adj) Your essay contains lots of original ideas.* new, fresh, unique, individual, innovative, novel, ground-breaking, imaginative, ingenious, inspired, inventive, creative, unusual, unconventional.
OPPOSITES: old, familiar.
3 *(adj) Is this an original painting?* genuine, authentic, real, unique.
OPPOSITES: copied, fake.

**ornament**
*(n) Hang the ornament on the tree.* trinket, knick-knack, bauble, decoration, trimming.

**outgoing** *see* **extrovert**.

**outing** see **trip** 1.

**outline**
1 *(n) Show me an outline of your design.* rough draft, sketch, drawing, tracing, plan, diagram, layout.
2 *(n) Give me an outline of the story.* rough idea, quick rundown, summary, shortened version, résumé, synopsis, main points *(plural)*, bare bones *(plural)*.
3 *(n) I saw the outline of a man through the mist.* shape, silhouette, figure, profile.

**outrageous**
1 *(adj) Conditions in the prison were outrageous.* shocking, scandalous, atrocious, barbaric, monstrous, disgraceful, intolerable, unbearable, abominable, vile.
2 *(adj) Dodgy Dave sells his cars at outrageous prices.* exorbitant, excessive, preposterous, scandalous, unreasonable, over the top, extravagant, OTT *(slang)*.
OPPOSITES: reasonable, fair.

**outside**
1 *(n) We need to paint the outside of our house.* exterior, façade, front, surface.
OPPOSITE: inside.
2 *(adv) Let's play outside.* outdoors, out-of-doors, in the open air, in the fresh air.
OPPOSITE: inside.
3 *(adj) The outside walls look damp.* external, exterior, outer, outermost.
OPPOSITE: inside.

**outspoken** see **blunt** 2.

**outstanding**
*(adj) An outstanding writer.* exceptional, great, first-class, superlative, excellent, remarkable, impressive, distinguished, notable, important, celebrated, eminent.
OPPOSITES: unremarkable, insignificant.

**over**
1 *(adj) I'm glad that unpleasant affair is over.* over and done with, at an end, finished, ended, past, closed, concluded, settled, ancient history *(informal)*.
2 *(prep) We've invited over 20 people.* more than, in excess of, above.

**overcome** see **conquer** 1, 2.

**overhear**
*(v) Did you overhear our conversation?* listen in on, eavesdrop on, pick up, catch.

**overpowering**
1 *(adj) I felt an overpowering urge to laugh. See* **irresistible**.
2 *(adj) The smell of Wayne's aftershave is overpowering.* suffocating, sickening, nauseating, stifling, unbearable.

**overtake**
*(v) Let's try to overtake that car.* pass, get past, get by, go past, outdistance, outstrip, outdo, go faster than, leave behind.

**overweight**
*(adj) Dad is getting overweight.* heavy, chubby, tubby, plump, podgy, stout, portly, paunchy, fleshy, hefty, corpulent, fat, obese, huge, massive, outsize, gross.
OPPOSITE: underweight.

**own**
1 *(v) I hope to own a pony one day.* have, be the owner of, possess, keep, be in possession of, be responsible for.
2 *(adj) Everyone needs their own space.* personal, individual, private, particular.

**own up** see **confess** 1, 2.

**pace**
1 *(n) Take one pace forwards. See* **step** 2.
2 *(v) Don't pace about; it makes me nervous.* march, walk, stride, tramp, pad.

**pack**
*(v) Can you pack all your books in this box?* put, place, load, stow, fit, stuff, cram, bundle, squeeze, jam, wedge, ram.

**paddle**
*(v) Let's paddle in the sea.* wade, splash about, slosh about, dabble.

**page**
*(n) Take a new page for each question.* side, sheet, piece of paper, leaf, folio.

**pain**
1 *(n) You may feel a little pain.* soreness, discomfort, tenderness, irritation, twinge, pang, spasm, throbbing, ache, cramp.
2 *(n) This behaviour will cause your parents great pain. See* **distress** 1.

**painful**
1 *(adj) Is your arm painful? See* **sore**.
2 *(adj) Splitting up with your boyfriend can be painful.* upsetting, distressing, unpleasant, hard, tough, heartbreaking, traumatic, agonizing, harrowing.

**paint**
1 *(n) This paint will hide the dirt.* colour, pigment, dye, tint, stain, emulsion, gloss, whitewash, undercoat, primer.
2 *(v) Can you paint the sunset?* depict, portray, represent.
3 *(v) Dad plans to paint the house himself.* decorate, redecorate, do up *(informal)*.

**painting**
*(n) TYPES OF PAINTING:* abstract painting, altarpiece, fresco, landscape, miniature, mural, oil painting, portrait, seascape, self-portrait, still life, watercolour.

**pair**
*(n) Sam and Seb are a good pair.* couple, match, combination, partnership, double act, twosome, duo, team.

**palace**
*(n)* chateau, stately home, mansion, castle, official residence. ❖ *Also see* **building**.

**pale**
1 *(adj) Megan has a pale complexion.* fair, light, creamy, ivory, pallid, waxen, pasty.
OPPOSITES: rosy, ruddy.

2 *(adj) You look pale.* peaky *(informal)*, washed out *(informal)*, drained, white, ashen, anaemic, sickly, grey, green, like death warmed up *(informal)*.
OPPOSITES: flushed, blooming.
3 *(adj) Claire's room is decorated in pale shades of blue.* light, soft, subtle, pastel, muted, subdued, faint, faded, bleached.
OPPOSITES: dark, bright, strong.

**pamper** see **spoil** 3.

**panic**
1 *(n) The sight of the fire filled us with panic.* alarm, horror, fear, terror, dread, consternation, hysteria, confusion, dismay.
2 *(v) Don't panic!* be alarmed, be scared, become hysterical, overreact, go to pieces, lose your head, lose your nerve, freak out, get into a tizzy *(informal)*, lose your cool *(slang)*, throw a wobbly *(slang)*.

**pant**
*(v) Exercise makes me pant.* gasp, wheeze, breathe heavily, puff, huff and puff.

**paper**
1 *(n) I need some more paper.* writing paper, notepaper, stationery, file paper, rough paper, scrap paper, cartridge paper, graph paper, tracing paper.
2 *(n) Which paper do your parents read? See* **newspaper**.
3 **papers** *(plural n) These papers prove that Dodgy Dave is guilty.* documents *(plural)*, records *(plural)*, files *(plural)*, certificates *(plural)*, forms *(plural)*, deeds *(plural)*, diaries *(plural)*, archives *(plural)*.

**parade**
*(n) Crowds lined the street to watch the parade.* procession, cavalcade, march past *(troops)*, motorcade, cortege *(funeral procession)*, display, spectacle, pageant.

**paradise** see **heaven** 1, 2.

**parcel**
*(n) Is this parcel for me?* package, packet, box, carton, pack, bundle.

**pardon** see **forgive**.

**park**
*(n) Let's walk around the park.* public park, recreation ground, gardens *(plural)*, botanical gardens *(plural)*, green, common, woodland, parkland, grounds *(plural)*.

**part**
1 *(n) Have a part of my orange. See* **bit** 2.
2 *(n) Which part of the course do you prefer?* bit, section, element, unit, module, component, constituent.
3 *(n) Which part of the company interests you?* bit, area, branch, division, section, department, sector, segment.
4 *(n) Which part of the country are you from?* bit, area, region, district, neck of the woods *(informal)*, neighbourhood.
5 *(n) I'd love to play a part in the pantomime.* role, character, starring role, lead, supporting role, speaking part, bit part, walk-on part, extra, cameo role.
6 **take part** see **take part**.

# participate

**participate** *see* **take part.**

**particular**
1 *(adj) This sauce has a particular flavour.* distinct, unique, special, unmistakable, specific, definite, individual, certain.
OPPOSITES: vague, general.
2 *(adj) Aunt Bertha is particular about her food. See* **fussy**.

**partner**
1 *(n) Bring your partner to the dance.* boyfriend, girlfriend, wife, husband, spouse, other half *(informal)*, mate.
2 *(n) Dad had a business lunch with his partner.* associate, colleague, collaborator, ally, sidekick *(informal)*, accomplice.

**party**
1 *(n) Let's have a party!* celebration, gathering, get-together *(informal)*, bash *(informal)*, thrash *(informal)*, do *(informal)*, rave-up *(slang)*, shindig *(informal)*, knees-up *(informal)*, function, reception.
2 *(n) Which party do you belong to?* group, faction, alliance, association, camp, side, team, gang, crew *(informal)*, band.

**pass**
1 *(v) The guard let us pass.* go by, go past, pass by, move past, move on, proceed, go on, go ahead, go through, enter.
2 *(v) The time seemed to pass so quickly.* go, go by, go past, pass by, elapse, slip by, tick away, fly by, glide by, flow by, roll by.
3 *(v) Can we pass that car? See* **overtake**.
4 *(v) Your anger will pass.* blow over, run its course, come to an end, die away, fade away, disappear, evaporate, peter out.
5 *(v) How do you pass the time?* occupy, fill, spend, while away, fritter away, kill.
6 *(v) Pass me your plate. See* **hand** 4.
7 *(v) This exam is so hard; I hope I'll pass.* succeed, get through, come up to scratch *(informal)*, pass muster, qualify, graduate.
OPPOSITE: fail.

**passage**
1 *(n) The thieves escaped down a narrow passage.* passageway, alley, alleyway, lane, path, track, corridor, tunnel.
2 *(n) Listen to this passage from "Oliver Twist".* excerpt, extract, quotation, piece, section, episode, scene, paragraph, verse.

**passion**
1 *(n) The actor played his part with passion.* feeling, emotion, intensity, fervour, zeal, warmth, fire, zest, gusto, enthusiasm, energy, animation.
2 *(n) Jason is consumed with passion for Jodie.* love, adoration, desire, lust, longing, yearning, hunger, the hots *(plural) (slang)*.

**passionate**
1 *(adj) A passionate argument.* heated, emotional, impassioned, intense, fierce, vehement, furious, violent, fiery, stormy.
OPPOSITES: cool, dispassionate.
2 *(adj) A passionate embrace.* loving, ardent, amorous, steamy *(informal)*, sensual, lustful, urgent, burning, frenzied.
OPPOSITE: cool.

**past**
1 *(adj) Those times are past. See* **over** 1.
2 *(adj) You can learn a lot from past events.* former, bygone, earlier, previous, prior, recent, historical, ancient.
OPPOSITE: future.
3 **the past** *(n) I like learning about the past.* history, past times, former times, days gone by, the olden days, the good old days, yesteryear *(old-fashioned)*, recent history, ancient history, prehistory.
OPPOSITE: the future.

**pastel** *see* **pale** 3.

**pastime** *see* **hobby**.

**pat**
1 *(v) Come and pat Fido.* stroke, pet.
2 *(v) Pat Joe on the back; he's coughing!* slap, thump, hit, smack, bang, clap, tap.

**patch**
1 *(v) I must patch my jeans.* mend, sew up, stitch up, reinforce, darn, repair, fix.
2 *(n) We grow turnips on this patch.* plot, piece of land, spot, bed, lot, allotment, ground, area, stretch, tract, clearing.

**path**
*(n)* footpath, pathway, pavement, towpath, bridle path, track, trail, lane.

**pathetic**
1 *(adj) Fido gave a pathetic whimper.* pitiful, plaintive, forlorn, doleful, mournful, woeful, touching, moving, poignant, heart-rending, heartbreaking, distressing.
2 *(adj) Dad made a pathetic attempt to be trendy.* feeble, unsuccessful, unconvincing, pitiful, dismal, woeful, sorry, sad *(slang)*.
3 *(adj) (informal) I'm pathetic at maths. See* **hopeless** 4.

**patient**
1 *(adj) Mrs Badger is always patient with us.* tolerant, long-suffering, forbearing, understanding, sympathetic, calm, even-tempered, accommodating, indulgent.
OPPOSITES: impatient, short-tempered.
2 *(adj) Try to be patient; you'll get there in the end.* persistent, persevering, steady, unhurried, resolute, determined, dogged, resigned, philosophical, stoical.
OPPOSITES: impatient, restless.

**patronizing** *see* **condescending**.

**pattern**
1 *(n) Use this as a pattern for your sketch.* guide, model, example, master, blueprint, template, stencil, standard.
2 *(n) A floral pattern. See* **design** 2.

**pause**
1 *(v) Don't pause at the end of every sentence.* stop, break off, hesitate, wait, delay, rest, take a break, have a rest, halt.
2 *(n) There will be a pause between each act. See* **gap** 2.

**pay**
1 *(v) Who will pay for the party?* foot the bill, pay up, settle the bill, meet the cost, shell out *(informal)*, cough up *(informal)*, stump up *(informal)*, fork out *(slang)*.
2 *(v) I didn't pay much. See* **spend** 1.
3 *(v) Mum said she'd pay me if I washed the car.* reward, reimburse, compensate.
4 *(v) You'll pay for this!* suffer, be punished, answer, pay the price, make amends, get your comeuppance *(informal)*.
5 *(n) At your interview, ask about the pay.* salary, wages *(plural)*, earnings *(plural)*, fee, payment, remuneration.

**pay attention**
*(v) Pay attention or you won't know what to do.* listen, watch, concentrate, take notice, listen up *(slang)*.

**pay back**
1 *(v) You must pay back the money.* repay, return, refund, reimburse.
2 *(v) I'll pay you back for taking my pen!* repay, get revenge on, get even with *(informal)*, get *(informal)*, settle the score with, retaliate against, hit back at.

**peace**
1 *(n) I wish there could be peace all over the world.* harmony, goodwill, agreement, accord, friendship, reconciliation.
2 *(n) The two armies agreed to a permanent peace.* truce, ceasefire, armistice, cessation of hostilities, reconciliation, alliance, treaty, pact.
3 *(n) I love the peace of the countryside.* peace and quiet, tranquillity, peacefulness, calm, stillness, quietness, silence, hush.

**peaceful**
1 *(adj) It's so peaceful here.* tranquil, restful, quiet, still, calm, relaxing, soothing.
OPPOSITES: noisy, bustling.
2 *(adj) Alice looks so peaceful.* tranquil, serene, at peace, relaxed, untroubled, unruffled, unworried, calm, placid.

**peak**
1 *(n) A snowy mountain peak. See* **top** 1.
2 *(n) Famous Fred is at the peak of his career.* height, high point, climax, zenith.

**peculiar**
1 *(adj) Peculiar behaviour. See* **strange** 1.
2 *(adj) A peculiar noise. See* **strange** 2.
3 *(adj) I feel peculiar. See* **ill** 2.

**peep**
*(v) Did you peep at your presents?* peek, steal a look, sneak a look, take a sly look.

**peer**
*(v) I saw you peer through the window.* spy, peek, peep, squint, snoop, try to see, look closely, screw up your eyes.

**people**
1 *(plural n) What makes people different from animals?* humans *(plural)*, human beings *(plural)*, the human race, mankind.
2 *(plural n) How many people were hurt?* men and women *(plural)*, children *(plural)*, individuals *(plural)*, persons *(plural)*.
3 *(plural n) The king addressed the people.* nation, citizens *(plural)*, populace, general public, community, population, crowd, masses *(plural)*, multitude, mob, rabble, rank and file, hoi polloi.

**perceptive**
(adj) Perceptive comments. shrewd, discerning, astute, penetrating, incisive, observant, sensitive, understanding.

**perfect**
1 (adj) If you buy something new, you expect it to be perfect. flawless, in mint condition, undamaged, unblemished, unscratched, unbroken, clean, spotless, immaculate, intact, complete, whole.
OPPOSITES: imperfect, faulty.
2 (adj) Ali gave a perfect performance. flawless, faultless, exemplary, unerring, impeccable, consummate, unrivalled, matchless, unequalled, ideal, definitive.
OPPOSITES: flawed, poor.
3 (adj) A perfect copy. See **exact** 3.
4 (adj) A perfect choice. See **ideal** 2.

**perform**
1 (v) Will you perform in the concert? take part, appear, play, act, dance, sing, star.
2 (v) Let's perform a play. See **stage** 3.

**performance**
(n) I'm sure you'll enjoy the performance. show, production, play, concert, recital, gig (informal), act, presentation, display, spectacle, entertainment, matinée, debut, premiere, preview, dress rehearsal.

**perfume** see **scent** 1, 2.

**period**
1 (n) I spent a period in Spain. See **time** 1.
2 (n) We're studying the medieval period. See **age** 1.

**permanent**
1 (adj) Billy has a permanent cough. constant, continual, perpetual, persistent.
2 (adj) Is this a permanent arrangement? fixed, firm, definite, unalterable, unchangeable, irreversible, immutable, binding, lasting, enduring, stable.
OPPOSITES: short-lived, temporary.

**permission**
(n) We need police permission to hold a street party. authorization, approval, authority, consent, leave, go-ahead (informal), rubber stamp, green light.

**permit** see **allow** 1, 2.

**perplexing** see **puzzling**.

**persecute**
(v) The refugees feared the officials would persecute them. hound, plague, pursue, harass, harry, bully, terrorize, victimize, oppress, ill-treat, torment, molest, torture.

**persevere**
(v) Try to persevere when life gets hard. keep going, carry on, soldier on, stick at it, keep at it, hang in there (informal), be resolute, persist, plug away (informal).

**person**
(n) Each person is different. human being, individual, character, living being, soul.

**personal**
1 (adj) Cynthia has her own personal style. See **individual** 2.
2 (adj) Don't open that letter; it's personal! See **private** 2.
3 (adj) Don't make personal comments. insulting, offensive, rude, nasty, critical, negative, hurtful, disparaging, derogatory.

**personality** see **character** 1.

**perspire** see **sweat** 2.

**persuade**
(v) Can I persuade you to try some squid? coax, tempt, entice, induce, cajole, urge, prompt, prevail on, convince, talk you into, wheedle you into, sweet-talk you into (informal), win you over, bring you round.
OPPOSITES: dissuade, deter.

**persuasive**
(adj) The salesman was very persuasive. convincing, compelling, forceful, plausible, credible, believable, eloquent, silver-tongued, seductive, coaxing, winning.
OPPOSITES: unconvincing, implausible.

**pessimistic**
(adj) I feel pessimistic about the future. gloomy, hopeless, negative, despondent, despairing, depressed, glum, melancholy, fatalistic, defeatist, resigned, cynical.
OPPOSITES: optimistic, positive.

**pester**
(v) Answer my question and I won't pester you anymore. badger, bother, plague, torment, hound, harass, harry, hassle (informal), disturb, annoy, nag, be on your back (slang), get in your hair (informal).

**petrified** see **scared** 1.

**phase** see **stage** 2.

**phone**
1 (v) Did Sid phone you? call, telephone, ring you up, ring, give you a call, give you a bell (slang), give you a tinkle (informal), give you a buzz (informal), get on the blower to you (informal).
2 (n) We've bought a new phone. telephone, mobile phone, cordless phone, car phone, cellphone, answerphone, videophone, handset, blower (informal).

**photograph**
1 (n) Look at this photograph of Granddad. photo (informal), picture, print, snap (informal), snapshot, shot, slide, transparency, enlargement, likeness.
2 (v) I want to photograph you in your clown suit. take a photograph of, take a picture of, capture you on film, get a shot of, shoot, film, snap (informal), record.

**phrase** see **expression** 2.

**pick**
1 (v) Pick a number. See **choose** 1.
2 (v) Shall I pick some flowers? gather, cut, collect, pluck, harvest (fruit).

**pick on**
(v) Pick on someone else for a change! criticize, find fault with, blame, nag, get at, tease, torment, badger, bully.

**pick up**
1 (v) Pick up that box. See **lift** 1.

2 (v) I'll pick you up at two o'clock. call for, come for, collect, give you a lift, fetch.
3 (v) Did you pick up any French on holiday? acquire, learn, get the hang of (informal), grasp, master.

**picture**
1 (n) That's a good picture of your dad. likeness, portrayal, depiction, representation, study, portrait, photograph, drawing, sketch, painting, caricature, cartoon, silhouette, etching, engraving, print, poster.
2 (v) I can't picture Aunt Bertha as a teenager. See **imagine** 1.

**picturesque** see **pretty** 2.

**piece**
1 (n) I'd like a piece of cheese. See **bit** 1.
2 (n) I dropped a piece of food on the floor. bit, scrap, morsel, mouthful, fragment, crumb, speck, particle.
3 (n) I cut my foot on a piece of glass. bit, fragment, sliver, splinter, shard, chip.
4 (n) Do you need that piece of material? bit, scrap, snippet, shred, remnant, length.
5 (n) Have a piece of my apple. See **bit** 2.
6 (n) This kit has a piece missing. bit, part, section, element, component.
7 (n) I'm learning a new piece for the concert. work, composition, item.
8 (v) Piece the parts together. See **fit** 2.

**pierce**
(v) Did the spear pierce the dragon's skin? puncture, penetrate, make a hole in, enter, go through, pass through, perforate, prick, wound, stab, spike, skewer.

**pile**
1 (n) Matt has a huge pile of magazines in his room. stack, heap, mound, mountain, mass, bundle, load, hoard, store, stockpile.
2 (v) Pile the papers here. stack, heap, gather, collect, amass, assemble, store.

**pill**
(n) tablet, capsule, lozenge.

**pillar**
(n) That pillar holds up the roof. column, post, pole, support, upright, prop, shaft.

**pinch**
1 (v) Don't pinch my leg. nip, squeeze.
2 (v) These shoes pinch my feet. hurt, cramp, squeeze, crush, confine, chafe.
3 (n) Add a pinch of salt. bit, taste, touch, dash, smidgen (informal), soupçon, small amount, trace, tad (informal), speck.

**pink**
(adj) Pink cheeks. rosy, flushed.
SHADES OF PINK: cerise, coral, flesh-colour, rose, salmon, shell pink, shocking pink.

**pipe**
(n) Water flowed through the pipe. tube, hose, duct, water main, pipeline, drainpipe, channel, conduit.

**pirate**
(n) buccaneer, raider, marauder, freebooter, cutthroat. ❖ Also see **pirates & shipwrecks**.

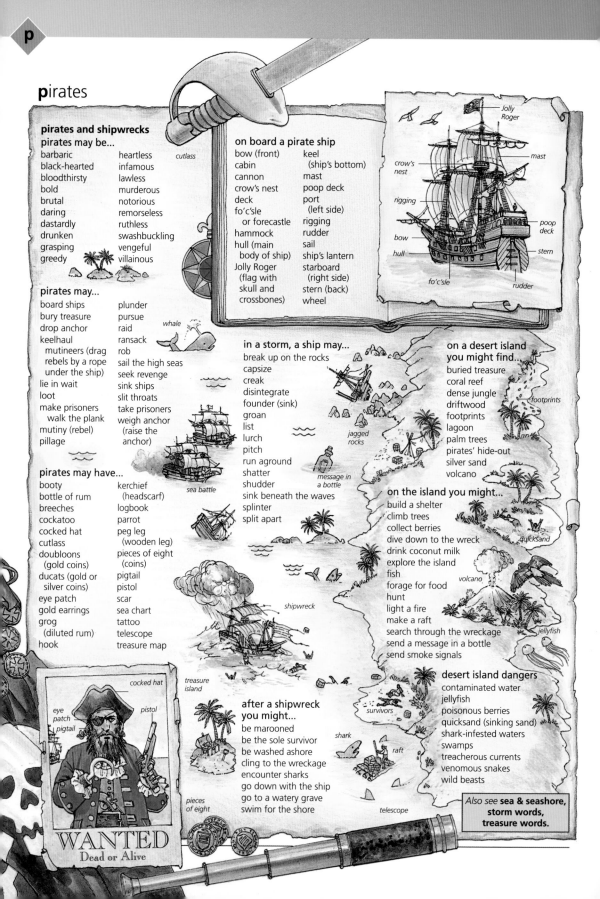

# pirates

## pirates and shipwrecks

### pirates may be...

barbaric
black-hearted
bloodthirsty
bold
brutal
daring
dastardly
drunken
grasping
greedy
heartless
infamous
lawless
murderous
notorious
remorseless
ruthless
swashbuckling
vengeful
villainous

*cutlass*

### pirates may...

board ships
bury treasure
drop anchor
keelhaul
  mutineers (drag
  rebels by a rope
  under the ship)
lie in wait
loot
make prisoners
  walk the plank
mutiny (rebel)
pillage
plunder
pursue
raid
ransack
rob
sail the high seas
seek revenge
sink ships
slit throats
take prisoners
weigh anchor
  (raise the
  anchor)

*whale*

### pirates may have...

booty
bottle of rum
breeches
cockatoo
cocked hat
cutlass
doubloons
  (gold coins)
ducats (gold or
  silver coins)
eye patch
gold earrings
grog
  (diluted rum)
hook
kerchief
  (headscarf)
logbook
parrot
peg leg
  (wooden leg)
pieces of eight
  (coins)
pigtail
pistol
scar
sea chart
tattoo
telescope
treasure map

*sea battle*

## on board a pirate ship

bow (front)
cabin
cannon
crow's nest
deck
fo'c'sle
  or forecastle
hammock
hull (main
  body of ship)
Jolly Roger
  (flag with
  skull and
  crossbones)
keel
  (ship's bottom)
mast
poop deck
port
  (left side)
rigging
rudder
sail
ship's lantern
starboard
  (right side)
stern (back)
wheel

*Jolly Roger* — *mast*
*crow's nest*
*rigging*
*bow* — *poop deck*
*hull* — *stern*
*fo'c'sle* — *rudder*

## in a storm, a ship may...

break up on the rocks
capsize
creak
disintegrate
founder (sink)
groan
list
lurch
pitch
run aground
shatter
shudder
sink beneath the waves
splinter
split apart

*jagged rocks*
*message in a bottle*

## on a desert island you might find...

buried treasure
coral reef
dense jungle
driftwood
footprints
lagoon
palm trees
pirates' hide-out
silver sand
volcano

*footprints*
*quicksand*

## on the island you might...

build a shelter
climb trees
collect berries
dive down to the wreck
drink coconut milk
explore the island
fish
forage for food
hunt
light a fire
make a raft
search through the wreckage
send a message in a bottle
send smoke signals

*volcano*
*jellyfish*
*shipwreck*

## desert island dangers

contaminated water
jellyfish
poisonous berries
quicksand (sinking sand)
shark-infested waters
swamps
treacherous currents
venomous snakes
wild beasts

*cocked hat*
*treasure island*
*eye patch*
*pistol*
*pigtail*

## after a shipwreck you might...

be marooned
be the sole survivor
be washed ashore
cling to the wreckage
encounter sharks
go down with the ship
go to a watery grave
swim for the shore

*survivors*
*shark*
*raft*
*pieces of eight*
*telescope*

Also see **sea & seashore, storm words, treasure words.**

## WANTED
### Dead or Alive

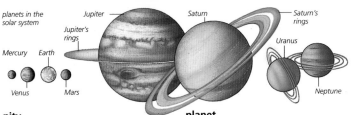

planets in the solar system — Jupiter — Jupiter's rings — Saturn — Saturn's rings — Uranus — Mercury — Earth — Venus — Mars — Neptune

## pity
1 *(n) The judge showed no pity.* sympathy, compassion, understanding, fellow feeling, mercy, charity, kindness, emotion, feeling.
2 *(n) It's a pity you can't come.* shame, crying shame, stroke of bad luck, bummer *(slang)*, misfortune, tragedy, sin.
3 *(v) I pity anyone out in this blizzard.* feel sorry for, sympathize with, feel for, commiserate with, feel pity for, have compassion for, weep for, grieve for.

## place
1 *(n) What a good place for a picnic!* spot, position, site, location, situation, setting.
2 *(n) Riverdale is an interesting place to visit.* village, town, city, neighbourhood, district, area, region, spot, locality.
3 *(n) Save me a place!* seat, chair, space.
4 *(v) Place the fruit in the bowl. See* **put** 1.

## placid
*(adj) Anna is a placid child.* calm, even-tempered, docile, easy-going, peaceable, serene, self-possessed, composed, level-headed, unexcitable, steady.
OPPOSITES: excitable, temperamental.

## plain
1 *(adj) The room was decorated in a plain style.* simple, basic, restrained, subdued, unpretentious, austere, stark, severe, Spartan, unadorned, unembellished, undecorated, unpatterned.
OPPOSITES: fancy, ornate.
2 *(adj) Aunt Bertha likes plain food.* simple, basic, ordinary, homely, everyday, unsophisticated, unexciting, frugal.
OPPOSITES: fancy, elaborate.
3 *(adj) Martha is a plain child.* ordinary-looking, unattractive, unprepossessing.
OPPOSITES: attractive, good-looking.
4 *(adj) Mrs Badger's feelings were plain. See* **obvious**.

## plan
1 *(n) That sounds like a sensible plan.* idea, scheme, plan of action, suggestion, proposal, proposition, strategy, procedure, system, method, tactic.
2 *(n) Look at this plan of our new house.* drawing, scale drawing, blueprint, layout, diagram, sketch, outline, representation, illustration, map, chart, bird's-eye view.
3 *(v) I didn't plan to cheat. See* **mean** 3.
4 *(v) Plan your project before you start.* think out, sketch out, map out, outline, organize, prepare, draft, design, formulate, devise, shape, frame.

## plane *see* **aircraft**.

## planet
*(n) The planet floated in space.* sphere, orb, globe, satellite, heavenly body.
**PLANETS IN THE SOLAR SYSTEM:**
Earth, Jupiter, Mars, Mercury, Neptune, Saturn, Uranus, Venus. ❖ *Also see* **space adventure**.

## plant
*(n) What's that unusual plant?* flower, bloom, seedling, weed, shrub, bush, climber, creeper, herb, vegetable, grass, fern, cactus, moss, lichen.

## plaster *see* **smear** 1.

## play
1 *(v) You have all day to play.* amuse yourself, entertain yourself, enjoy yourself, have fun, play games, mess about.
2 *(v) The others won't let me play.* join in, take part, participate, be in the game.
3 *(v) Rangers will play United.* play against, take on, challenge, compete against, rival, vie with, contend with.
4 *(v) Gill will play Cinderella.* act, be, take the part of, take the role of, portray.
5 *(n) Did you enjoy the play?* show, production, performance, drama.
**TYPES OF PLAY:** comedy, farce, historical play, melodrama, mime, musical, nativity play, pageant, pantomime, puppet show, radio play, satire, tragedy, TV play.

## play about *see* **mess about** 1, 2.

## playful
1 *(adj) Playful puppies. See* **lively** 2.
2 *(adj) A playful grin. See* **mischievous** 2.

## plead with *see* **beg** 2.

## pleasant
1 *(adj) A pleasant day out. See* **enjoyable**.
2 *(adj) What pleasant weather!* lovely, beautiful, glorious, delightful, fine, mild, warm, sunny, balmy.
OPPOSITES: unpleasant, nasty.
3 *(adj) Mrs Honey is a pleasant person.* likable, lovely, good-natured, amiable, delightful, charming, agreeable, friendly.
OPPOSITES: unpleasant, obnoxious.
4 *(adj) This makes a pleasant change.* agreeable, welcome, refreshing, pleasing, satisfying, appreciated.
OPPOSITES: unwelcome, unpleasant.

## please
1 *(v) I'm doing my best to please you.* make you happy, give you pleasure, satisfy, cheer you up, delight, charm, entertain, amuse, indulge, gratify, humour, suit.
2 *(v) Do as you please. See* **like** 4.

## pleased
*(adj) Kim was pleased when she passed her exams.* happy, delighted, glad, contented, satisfied, thrilled, overjoyed, jubilant, elated, euphoric, over the moon *(informal)*, thrilled to bits *(informal)*, chuffed *(slang)*.

## pleasure
*(n) Lord Lucre leads a life of pleasure.* enjoyment, contentment, satisfaction, comfort, ease, gratification, entertainment, amusement, bliss, delight.
OPPOSITES: misery, suffering.

## plenty
*(n) Lord Lucre has plenty of money.* a great deal, a lot, lots *(plural) (informal)*, a large amount, more than enough, enough, sufficient, a fund, heaps *(plural) (informal)*, loads *(plural) (informal)*, masses *(plural) (informal)*, oodles *(plural) (informal)*, piles *(plural) (informal)*, stacks *(plural) (informal)*.

## plot
1 *(n) The pirates hatched a plot.* scheme, conspiracy, plan, stratagem, intrigue.
2 *(n) Can you follow the plot of this play?* storyline, story, narrative, thread, structure.
3 *(v) Let's plot to get our revenge.* plan, scheme, conspire, intrigue, manoeuvre.

## plough
1 *(v) Farmer Phyllis plans to plough this field.* cultivate, till, turn over, dig up.
2 *(v) We tried to plough through the mud.* plunge, push, wallow, wade, cut, drive.

## plump
*(adj) Mrs Honey is rather plump.* chubby, tubby, podgy, dumpy, pudgy, roly-poly, well-rounded, stout, portly, corpulent, fat, well-padded, fleshy, buxom, matronly.
OPPOSITES: slim, slender.

## plunge *see* **dive** 1, 2.

## plush *(informal) see* **luxurious**.

## poem
*(n)* rhyme, verse, ditty, ballad, ode, sonnet, limerick, haiku, elegy, epic, jingle.

## poetic
*(adj) This story is written in a poetic style.* lyrical, imaginative, creative, artistic, flowing, lilting, graceful, songlike, flowery.

## poignant *see* **sad** 2.

## point
1 *(n) This is the point where we started.* spot, place, position, site, location.
2 *(n) At that point, Zak left.* moment, very moment, instant, second, stage, juncture.
3 *(n) This spear has a sharp point.* tip, end, spike, prong, sharp end.
4 *(n) What is the point of this game?* purpose, aim, objective, object, use.
5 *(n) I don't understand the point of this story.* meaning, significance, relevance, thrust, drift, theme, main idea, substance.
6 *(n) I covered that point in my talk.* detail, aspect, item, feature, particular, facet.
7 *(v) Point me to the station. See* **direct** 6.
8 *(v) Point your arrow at the bull's-eye. See* **aim** 3.

# **p**ointless

**pointless** see **useless** 1.

**point out**
(v) Why didn't you point out this problem earlier? draw attention to, mention, bring up, allude to, refer to, indicate, identify.

**poisonous**
(adj) Bleach is a poisonous substance. toxic, noxious, lethal, deadly, harmful, venomous (snakes, spiders).
OPPOSITES: harmless, nontoxic.

**poke**
1 (v) Don't poke your finger in the trifle! See **stick** 6.
2 (v) Poke me if I start to snore. prod, jab, nudge, elbow, butt, hit.

**poky**
(adj) This room is so poky. cramped, small, tiny, narrow, confined, cell-like.
OPPOSITES: spacious, large.

**pole**
(n) rod, bar, post, stake, stick, staff, spar.

**polish**
1 (n) Look at the polish on that table! See **shine** 4.
2 (v) Polish your shoes. shine, buff up, rub, wax, brush, clean, burnish (metal).

**polite**
1 (adj) Cyril is always polite. courteous, well-behaved, well-mannered, civil, tactful, diplomatic, respectful, deferential, obliging, considerate, thoughtful.
OPPOSITES: rude, discourteous.
2 (adj) It's not polite to gobble your food. acceptable, done, proper, seemly, nice, genteel, civilized, ladylike, gentlemanly.
OPPOSITES: rude, ignorant.

**pollute**
(v) Cars pollute the air. contaminate, poison, dirty, foul up, taint, blight, infect.

**pool**
(n) puddle, pond, fish pond, duck pond, millpond, oasis, water hole, lake, tarn, swimming pool, paddling pool.

**poor**
1 (adj) I hate being poor. short of money, badly off, hard up (informal), penniless, poverty-stricken, destitute, down-and-out, on the rocks, impoverished, broke (informal), flat broke (informal), stony-broke (slang), skint (slang).
OPPOSITES: rich, wealthy.
2 (adj) This is a poor piece of work. inadequate, unsatisfactory, second-rate, mediocre, inferior, substandard, below average, disappointing, feeble, worthless, dismal, rubbishy, shoddy, rotten (informal).
OPPOSITES: good, excellent.
3 (adj) The poor kitten was soaked! unfortunate, unlucky, wretched, luckless, hapless, miserable, pathetic, pitiable.
4 (adj) Eva earns a poor salary. See **low** 2.

**pop**
(v) Can you hear the firecrackers pop? bang, crack, snap, go bang, explode, go off, go off with a bang, detonate, burst.

## **pop, rock and jazz**

### musical styles
| | | | |
|---|---|---|---|
| acid jazz | dub | hip-hop | rave |
| beat | easy listening | house | reggae |
| bebop | folk | indie | rhythm |
| big band | funk | jazz | and blues |
| blues | garage | jungle | rock 'n' roll |
| country and | glam rock | pop | salsa |
| western | gospel | psychedelia | ska |
| dance | hardcore | punk | soul |
| disco | hard rock | ragga | swing |
| doo-wop | heavy metal | rap | techno |

jazz musician

drummer

volume control, tempo control (changes speed), display screen, sound editing buttons, pitch blend (changes pitch), vibrato, synthesizer, keyboard

### you might listen to...
| | |
|---|---|
| acoustic version | live recording |
| album | new release |
| chart music | remix |
| compilation album | single |
| concept album | soundtrack |
| cover version | track |
| hit single | unplugged |
| live performance | version |

### a band may use...
| | |
|---|---|
| acoustic guitar | PA system |
| amplifier | record deck |
| bass guitar | sampler |
| drum kit | (equipment to |
| drum machine | mix in sounds) |
| electric guitar | sequencer |
| headphones | (equipment to |
| keyboard | memorize a |
| microphone | sequence of |
| mixing desk | notes) |
| multitrack tape | speakers |
| machine | synthesizer |

crash cymbal, ride cymbal, tom-toms, hi-hat cymbal, snare drum, floor tom, pedal, bass drum, pedal
drum kit

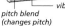
vocalist

punk

### on a track you might hear...
| | |
|---|---|
| backing vocals | key change |
| bass line | lyrics |
| beat | melody |
| bridge (link) | refrain (chorus) |
| chords | rhythm |
| drum break | riff (repeated |
| (drum solo) | chord |
| echo effects | sequence) |
| fade | sample |
| harmony | (mixed-in |
| hook | extract from |
| (catchy phrase) | another record) |
| improvisation | scratching |
| instrumental | sound effects |
| section | theme |
| intro (informal) | vocals (singing) |

### a track may sound...
| | |
|---|---|
| bland | original |
| catchy | polished |
| dreamy | raucous |
| fresh | repetitive |
| funky | rhythmic |
| (informal) | sexy (informal) |
| futuristic | slick |
| haunting | smooth |
| laid-back | soulful |
| (informal) | tinny |
| manic | tribal |
| melancholy | tuneless |
| mellow | unoriginal |
| melodic | upbeat |
| (tuneful) | (informal) |
| monotonous | weird |

**the beat may be...**

| | |
|---|---|
| booming | pumping |
| bouncy | rhythmic |
| energetic | shuffling |
| frenetic | steady |
| frenzied | throbbing |
| hypnotic | thumping |
| insistent | unhurried |
| jazzy | |
| mesmerizing | |
| pounding | |
| pulsating | |

*electric guitar*

*tuning peg*

*head*

*fret*

*neck*

*string*

*body*

*fingerplate*

*tremolo*

*bridge*

*output socket (leads to loudspeaker)*

**the lyrics may be...**

| | |
|---|---|
| aggressive | romantic |
| bleak | sentimental |
| brooding | simple |
| clever | soppy *(informal)* |
| clichéd | suggestive |
| dark | superficial |
| despairing | trite |
| funny | witty |
| heartfelt | |
| imaginative | |
| inane (silly) | |
| incomprehensible | |
| jokey | |
| moving | |
| offensive | |
| pessimistic | |
| provocative | |
| quirky | |
| raunchy *(slang)* | |

*rapper*

*reggae singer*

*heavy metal guitarist*

*Also see **musical instrument**, **musician**, **music words**, **singer**.*

**popular**
1 *(adj) Josie has always been popular.* well-liked, admired, in demand, in favour, sought-after, accepted, loved, idolized. OPPOSITE: unpopular.
2 *(adj) Short hair is popular at the moment.* fashionable, in fashion, in, in favour, trendy *(informal)*, hip *(slang)*. OPPOSITES: unfashionable, out.
3 *(adj) There's a popular theory that chocolate gives you spots.* common, widespread, general, well-known, current, prevailing, prevalent.

**port**
*(n) The ship approached the port.* harbour, dock, seaport, marina, anchorage, wharf, quay, landing stage, dockyard, dry dock.

**portion** see **helping**.

**portrait**
*(n) Do you like this portrait of Fergus?* picture, self-portrait, painting, drawing, sketch, photograph, study, likeness, portrayal, image, depiction, impression.

**posh**
1 *(adj) (informal) We stayed in a posh hotel.* grand, luxurious, plush *(informal)*, up-market, classy *(slang)*, swish *(informal)*, swanky *(informal)*, ritzy *(slang)*, high-class. OPPOSITES: modest, humble.
2 *(adj) (informal) Araminta is much too posh to talk to us.* grand, superior, swanky *(informal)*, upper class, refined, genteel, snooty *(informal)*, toffee-nosed *(slang)*, stuck-up *(informal)*, la-di-da *(informal)*.

**position**
1 *(n) What a perfect position for a house!* See **place** 1.
2 *(n) Ben's request put me in a difficult position.* situation, predicament, spot, plight, dilemma, state.
3 *(n) What's your mum's position in the company?* See **rank**.
4 *(n) Mrs Badger applied for the position of deputy head.* See **job** 3.
5 *(n) I can't hold this position for much longer.* pose, stance, posture, attitude.

**positive**
1 *(adj) Are you positive that you saw a ghost?* See **certain** 1.
2 *(adj) Do you have any positive proof?* real, actual, definite, clear-cut, firm, concrete, categorical, absolute, conclusive, indisputable, undeniable, irrefutable.
3 *(adj) Mrs Badger made some positive suggestions.* helpful, constructive, encouraging, useful, practical, beneficial. OPPOSITES: negative, unhelpful.

**possible**
1 *(adj) Anything is possible if you try.* achievable, attainable, feasible, within reach, practicable, workable, doable. OPPOSITES: impossible, unattainable.
2 *(adj) This story has only one possible ending.* conceivable, imaginable, plausible, credible, likely, probable, potential. OPPOSITES: inconceivable, unthinkable.

**post**
1 *(n) Stick the post in the ground.* stake, pole, upright, support, pillar, gatepost.
2 *(n) Don't open my post.* mail, letters *(plural)*, correspondence.
3 *(n) May I apply for this post?* See **job** 3.
4 *(v) I must post this parcel.* mail, send, send off, dispatch.

**postpone**
*(v) We'll have to postpone the match.* put off, put back, defer, hold over, delay, shelve, suspend, adjourn, put on the back burner *(informal)*, take a rain check on *(informal)*, put on ice *(informal)*.

**potion**
*(n) A magic potion.* brew, concoction, mixture, drink, draught, elixir, drug.

**potter about** see **mess about** 1.

**pounce**
1 *(v) The eagle will pounce when it sees its prey.* strike, attack, swoop down, drop down, descend.
2 **pounce on** *(v) Ed is waiting to pounce on you.* jump on, leap out at, spring on, swoop on, lunge at, make a grab for, ambush, attack, take you by surprise.

**pour**
1 *(v) Water began to pour from the pipe.* See **flow** 1.
2 *(v) Please pour the tea.* pour out, serve.
3 *(v) It's going to pour.* See **rain** 1.

**powdery**
*(adj) Powdery earth.* crumbly, fine, dry, loose, dusty, sandy, chalky, grainy.

**power**
1 *(n) You'll need all your power to lift that sack.* See **strength** 1.
2 *(n) I wish I had the power to fly.* ability, capacity, capability, potential.
3 *(n) The king has power over his people.* control, authority, command, mastery, supremacy, dominance, sovereignty, influence, sway, clout.
4 *(n) Nuclear power.* energy, fuel.

**powerful**
1 *(adj) A powerful leader.* strong, forceful, influential, dominant, commanding, high-powered, authoritative, mighty, supreme, invincible, all-powerful, omnipotent. OPPOSITES: weak, powerless.
2 *(adj) A powerful wrestler.* See **strong** 1.
3 *(adj) A powerful film.* compelling, effective, impressive, convincing, forceful, inspiring, stirring, moving, disturbing.

**powerless** see **helpless** 2.

**practical**
1 *(adj) Mandy is a practical person.* sensible, down-to-earth, matter-of-fact, no-nonsense, hard-headed, businesslike, efficient, realistic, pragmatic. OPPOSITES: impractical, idealistic.
2 *(adj) Your idea isn't really practical.* practicable, workable, feasible, viable, doable, possible, realistic, sensible, sound. OPPOSITES: impractical, unworkable.

# practice

**practice**
1 (n) *To be a good pianist you must do lots of practice.* training, exercises (plural), drill, repetition, preparation.
2 (n) *This is the last practice before the concert.* See **rehearsal**.

**practise**
1 (v) *Let's practise our performance.* rehearse, work at, go over, run through, go through, prepare, polish, fine-tune.
2 (v) *Dancers practise daily.* See **train** 3.

**praise**
1 (n) *Neesha would flourish if you gave her more praise.* compliments (plural), approval, appreciation, congratulations (plural), acclaim, applause, admiration.
OPPOSITES: criticism, censure.
2 (v) *I'm sure the critics will praise your performance.* compliment you on, congratulate you on, commend, acclaim, rave about (informal), sing the praises of, eulogize about, admire, applaud, cheer.
OPPOSITES: criticize, revile.

**prance**
(v) *Look how the ponies prance about!* leap, jump, skip, caper, cavort, romp, frisk, dance, gambol.

**prank** see **trick** 2.

**prattle**
(v) *Sophie can prattle for hours.* chatter, natter, gossip, gabble, jabber, twitter, babble, rattle on, rabbit on (informal), waffle, witter on (informal), go on (informal), yak (slang), jaw (slang).

**precarious**
(adj) *Indy is in a precarious position.* dangerous, risky, hazardous, perilous, tricky, dicey (informal), dodgy (informal), hairy (slang), vulnerable, insecure, unstable, uncertain, touch and go.
OPPOSITES: safe, secure.

**precious**
1 (adj) *Precious jewels.* See **valuable** 1.
2 (adj) *Don't hurt my precious child.* beloved, adored, cherished, treasured, darling, dearest, idolized, valued, prized.

**precise**
1 (adj) *Please take precise measurements.* See **accurate** 1.
2 (adj) *At that precise moment, Eve burst in.* very, exact, specific, particular, actual.
3 (adj) *Jo is so precise; she even keeps her CDs in alphabetical order.* particular, methodical, meticulous, careful, exact, finicky, fastidious, fussy, prim.
OPPOSITES: sloppy (informal), careless.

**predicament** see **mess** 3.

**predict**
(v) *It's hard to predict what problems may arise.* foresee, foretell, anticipate, forecast, prophesy, guess, second-guess (informal).

**prefer**
(v) *Which team do you prefer?* like better, favour, fancy, incline towards, support, back, go for, opt for, recommend.

**pregnant**
(adj) *Auntie Penny is pregnant.* expecting (informal), having a baby, in the family way (informal), in the club (slang), in the pudding club (slang), preggers (informal).

**prejudiced**
(adj) *Don't be so prejudiced; try to keep an open mind.* bigoted, biased, intolerant, narrow-minded, opinionated, partisan, one-sided, unfair, racist, sexist, chauvinist, ageist, homophobic, xenophobic.
OPPOSITES: open-minded, tolerant.

**prepare**
1 (v) *We must prepare for the play.* get ready, plan, make arrangements, gear up, practise, rehearse, train, get into shape.
2 (v) *Let's prepare this room for our visitors.* get ready, make ready, arrange, sort out, organize, fix up, set up.
3 **prepare yourself** (v) *Prepare yourself for a shock.* get ready, be prepared, brace yourself, steel yourself, gear yourself up, psych yourself up (informal).

**present**
1 (n) *Thank you for the present.* gift, pressie (informal), offering, contribution, donation, hand-out, freebie (informal).
2 (n) *Try to live for the present.* here and now, present day, today, this day and age.
OPPOSITES: past, future.
3 (adj) *Let's consider the present situation.* current, existing, immediate.
OPPOSITES: past, future.
4 (adj) *Is everyone present?* here, there, on the spot, at hand, ready, in attendance, available, accounted for.
OPPOSITES: absent, away.
5 (v) *Lord Lucre will present the prizes.* give, hand out, distribute, give out, hand over, award, bestow, donate, grant.

**press**
1 (v) *Press the mixture into the tin.* push down, squeeze, compress, force down, cram, jam, crush, flatten, smooth out.
2 (v) *Look how the fans press round their team.* push, crowd, surge, swarm, cluster, throng, flock, mill, huddle, squeeze.
3 **the press** (n) *What does the press say?* papers (plural), newspapers (plural), media, journalists (plural), reporters (plural).

**pressure**
1 (n) *The ice will break under the pressure.* weight, force, load, burden, stress, strain.
2 (n) *I can't stand all this pressure!* stress, strain, tension, anxiety, worry, hassle (informal), demands (plural).
3 (n) *I only came here under pressure.* duress, obligation, constraint, compulsion, coercion, force.

**pressurize**
(v) *I don't want to go, so don't pressurize me.* push, pressure, put pressure on, press, browbeat, bully, force, drive, compel, coerce, bulldoze (informal), dragoon, try to persuade, lean on (informal).

**presume** see **assume**.

**pretence** see **front** 4.

**pretend**
1 (v) *Let's pretend we're space aliens.* imagine, make believe, suppose, fantasize.
2 (v) *I don't know how to speak Chinese, but I could pretend.* bluff, fake it, put on an act, play-act, put it on, sham, feign.

**pretentious**
(adj) *Araminta is so pretentious; she's always putting on airs.* affected, phoney (informal), false, unnatural, pseudo (informal), showy, ostentatious, stagy.
OPPOSITES: unpretentious, unassuming.

**pretty**
1 (adj) *Yasmin is really pretty.* attractive, good-looking, cute, beautiful, lovely, fetching (informal), striking, appealing.
OPPOSITES: plain, ugly.
2 (adj) *What a pretty village!* picturesque, quaint, charming, beautiful, old-world, scenic, chocolate-box (informal).
OPPOSITES: ugly, unattractive.
3 (adv) (informal) *I did pretty well.* See **quite** 1.

**prevent**
1 (v) *Try to prevent any accidents.* avoid, avert, ward off, head off, stave off, pre-empt, forestall, nip in the bud (informal).
OPPOSITE: cause.
2 (v) *We must prevent Joel from leaving.* stop, deter, hinder, hamper, impede, obstruct, thwart, deflect, foil, hold back.

**price**
1 (n) *I can't afford such a high price.* cost, charge, amount, figure, sum, rate, payment, fee, outlay, expenditure.
2 (n) *Fred has discovered the price of being famous.* cost, consequence, result, outcome, penalty, sacrifice, punishment.

**priceless**
(adj) *Don't break that vase; it's priceless.* beyond price, irreplaceable, precious, valuable, expensive, costly, worth a king's ransom, worth its weight in gold, rare, treasured, cherished, prized.
OPPOSITE: worthless.

**prick**
(v) *Prick the balloon with a pin.* jab, stab, puncture, pierce, put a hole in, perforate, spike, nick, jag (informal).

**prickly**
1 (adj) *Ned scratched himself on a prickly branch.* thorny, spiky, spiny, brambly, barbed, bristly, briery.
2 (adj) *This rash gives me a prickly feeling.* itchy, scratchy, tingly, stinging, crawling.

**pride**
1 (n) *It hurts my pride when people laugh at me.* self-esteem, self-respect, self-worth, dignity, self-image, ego, feelings (plural).
2 (n) *Pride is one of the seven deadly sins.* conceit, vanity, arrogance, haughtiness, self-importance, bigheadedness (informal), self-love, egotism.
OPPOSITE: humility.

**3** (n) You can take pride in a job well done. pleasure, satisfaction, delight, joy.
OPPOSITES: shame, dissatisfaction.

**prim**
(adj) Aunt Bertha is too prim to join in the fun. strait-laced, starchy, stuffy, proper, prissy, priggish, prudish, stiff, formal.

**prison** see **jail** 1.

**prisoner**
**1** (n) Burglar Beryl shared a cell with another prisoner. convict, jailbird, con (slang), lifer (informal).
**2** (n) Granddad was a prisoner during the war. captive, hostage, POW (prisoner of war), detainee.

**private**
**1** (adj) Flash Frank has his own private jet. personal, individual, special, exclusive, particular, privately owned.
OPPOSITE: public.
**2** (adj) This letter contains private information. confidential, personal, intimate, secret, restricted, classified, unofficial, off the record, hush-hush (informal), inside.
OPPOSITE: public.
**3** (adj) This beach seems very private. secluded, solitary, remote, isolated, secret, quiet, sequestered, unknown, hidden.

**prize**
**1** (n) Kirsty won a prize on Sports Day. award, trophy, cup, medal, shield, badge, rosette, certificate, reward, accolade.
**2** (n) How did you spend your prize from the lottery? winnings (plural), jackpot, windfall, haul.

**probable** see **likely** 1.

**problem**
**1** (n) I can't cope with this problem alone. difficulty, dilemma, predicament, mess, setback, snag, complication, worry, burden, trouble, quandary.
**2** (n) Mrs Badger gave us a problem to solve. question, puzzle, riddle, brain-teaser (informal), conundrum, poser, mystery.

**procession** see **parade**.

**prod** see **poke** 2.

**produce**
**1** (v) How many cars can the factory produce in a week? turn out, manufacture, make, put together, build, assemble, construct, supply, churn out (informal).
**2** (v) We produce all our own vegetables. grow, cultivate, supply.
**3** (v) The police can't produce any evidence. supply, provide, furnish, offer, put forward, reveal, show, present, display.
**4** (v) This decision will produce a lot of ill feeling. cause, give rise to, result in, lead to, provoke, generate, bring about, make for, engender, spark off, trigger.

**programme**
**1** (n) What's the programme for today? plan, schedule, timetable, order of events, agenda, line-up, order of the day.

**2** (n) Would you like to buy a programme? brochure, leaflet, guide, list of events, list of performers, list of players.
**3** (n) What's your favourite TV programme? show, broadcast, production.
❖ Also see **television & film**.

**progress**
**1** (n) Have you made any progress on your project? headway, advance, improvement, steps forward (plural), progression, development, breakthrough.
**2** (v) You've really begun to progress this term. See **improve** 1.

**prohibit** see **forbid**.

**project**
**1** (n) Have you finished your science project? assignment, topic, task, activity, investigation, research, piece of work.
**2** (n) I'm involved in a project to clean up the pond. scheme, campaign, venture, operation, programme, plan, undertaking.

**promise**
**1** (v) Promise you'll love me always! vow, swear, give your word, pledge, guarantee, take an oath, undertake, cross your heart.
**2** (n) I give you my promise. word, word of honour, assurance, guarantee, pledge, vow, oath, commitment, undertaking.
**3** (n) Your work shows promise. potential, ability, aptitude, talent, flair.

**promising**
**1** (adj) The future looks promising. See **hopeful** 2.
**2** (adj) Benji is a promising young actor. talented, gifted, up-and-coming, budding.

**promote**
**1** (v) If you work hard the company may promote you. give you promotion, upgrade, advance, move you up, move you up the ladder, give you a rise.
OPPOSITES: demote, downgrade.
**2** (v) Famous Fred is keen to promote his new album. publicize, advertise, push, plug (informal), hype, market, sell.

**prompt**
**1** (v) This news may prompt Judd to take some action. motivate, induce, lead, cause, move, persuade, influence, encourage, inspire, rouse, stir, stimulate, provoke.
**2** (v) I'll prompt you if you forget your lines. See **remind** 1.
**3** (adj) I need a prompt reply. See **quick** 2.

**proof**
(n) Is there any proof that Burglar Beryl is guilty? evidence, confirmation, verification, corroboration, testimony.

**proper**
**1** (adj) I need the proper equipment for diving. right, correct, appropriate, suitable.
OPPOSITES: inappropriate, unsuitable.
**2** (adj) This is the proper way to use chopsticks. right, correct, usual, normal, conventional, accepted, established, acceptable, orthodox.
OPPOSITES: wrong, unconventional.

**3** (adj) Aunt Bertha expects proper behaviour. decent, seemly, respectable, polite, fitting, genteel, refined, ladylike, gentlemanly, sedate, decorous, dignified.
OPPOSITES: improper, unseemly.

**property**
(n) Keep your hands off my property! possessions (plural), belongings (plural), things (plural), personal effects (plural), land, ground, estate, house, money, wealth, riches (plural), assets (plural).

**protect**
**1** (v) Don't worry; I'll protect you. look after, watch over, keep you safe, take care of, shield, shelter, guard, defend, save, stick up for (informal), cover up for.
OPPOSITES: expose to danger, betray.
**2** (v) The soldiers did their best to protect the city. See **defend** 1.
**3** (v) These goggles will protect your eyes. shield, cover, safeguard, save, preserve, screen, mask, conceal.
OPPOSITES: expose, endanger.

**protest**
**1** (n) If there's any protest we'll go home. objection, opposition, complaint, dissent, disagreement, disapproval, outcry, fuss.
**2** (n) Mel took part in a protest against fox-hunting. See **demonstration** 2.
**3** **protest against** (v) We will protest against the education cuts. oppose, fight, take a stand against, object to, say no to, speak out against, raise objections to, put up a fight against, kick up a fuss about (informal), complain about, grumble about, demonstrate against.
OPPOSITES: accept, go along with.

**proud**
**1** (adj) I felt proud to be chosen. pleased, gratified, full of pride, honoured, chuffed (slang), satisfied, contented, happy.
OPPOSITE: ashamed.
**2** (adj) Araminta is so proud; she looks down on everyone. arrogant, haughty, high and mighty (informal), supercilious, disdainful, conceited, vain, self-satisfied, self-important, overbearing, snobbish, stuck-up (informal), snooty (informal), toffee-nosed (slang), uppity (informal).
OPPOSITES: humble, unassuming.

**prove**
(v) This letter will prove that I am right. demonstrate, show, establish, confirm, provide evidence, give proof, bear out.
OPPOSITES: disprove, refute.

**provide**
**1** (v) Can you provide enough food for everyone? supply, lay on, offer, produce, contribute, deliver, donate, grant.
**2** **provide for** (v) Uncle Pete works hard to provide for his family. See **support** 2.

**provoke**
**1** (v) Don't provoke me! See **annoy** 1.
**2** (v) This news may provoke a riot. cause, start, spark off, trigger, incite, give rise to, lead to, produce, prompt, precipitate.

# public

**public**
1 *(adj) I think education should be a public service.* state, national, social, civic, nationwide, countrywide, universal.
OPPOSITE: private.
2 *(adj) Is this road public?* open to the public, free to all, accessible to all, unrestricted, communal.
OPPOSITES: private, restricted.
3 *(adj) Charles's secret soon became public.* widely known, well-known, publicized, famous, notorious, obvious, apparent, evident, plain, exposed, visible.
OPPOSITES: secret, unknown.
4 *(n) What will the public say about this?* people *(plural)*, country, nation, society, community, citizens *(plural)*, populace, voters *(plural)*, electorate, masses *(plural)*, hoi polloi, rank and file, Joe Public *(slang)*.

**pudding** see **dessert**.

**puff**
1 *(n) Did you feel that puff of wind?* gust, breath, blast, whiff, flurry, draught.
2 *(v) Running makes me puff.* See **pant**.

**puffy** see **swollen**.

**puke** *(slang)* see **vomit**.

**pull**
*(v) Pull the sledge up the hill.* drag, haul, tug, heave, lug, tow, trail, draw, yank, jerk.
OPPOSITE: push.

**pull through** see **recover** 1.

**pull yourself together**
*(phrase)* get a grip on yourself, control yourself, snap out of it *(informal)*.

**pump**
1 *(v) Pump the water through the pipe.* siphon, force, push, drive, send, drain.
2 **pump up** *(v) You need to pump up your tyres.* inflate, blow up.

**punch**
*(v) Let me past or I'll punch you!* hit, thump, sock *(slang)*, bash *(informal)*, belt *(slang)*, biff *(slang)*, whack, thwack, slug, clout *(informal)*, strike, clobber *(slang)*, wallop *(informal)*, hammer, pummel.

**punctual**
*(adj) Carly is always punctual.* on time, prompt, early, in good time, on the dot.
OPPOSITES: unpunctual, late.

**punish**
*(v) The head will punish you if you cheat in exams.* penalize, discipline, teach you a lesson, correct, scold, chastise, slap your wrists, rap your knuckles, sentence.

**pure**
1 *(adj) Is this water pure?* clean, fresh, uncontaminated, unpolluted, clear, untainted, natural, germ-free, uninfected, sterilized, pasteurized *(milk)*, undiluted.
OPPOSITES: contaminated, polluted.
2 *(adj) Despite temptations, Eve remained pure.* chaste, virtuous, uncorrupted, undefiled, unstained, blameless, innocent, true, upright, squeaky-clean *(informal)*.
OPPOSITES: impure, corrupt.

3 *(adj) That goal was pure magic!* See **absolute**.

**purple**
*(n)* SHADES OF PURPLE: aubergine, burgundy, grape, lavender, lilac, maroon, mauve, mulberry, plum, puce, violet.

**purpose**
1 *(n) What was your purpose in cycling to Rome?* aim, object, goal, objective, target, motive, intention, plan, reason, rationale.
2 *(n) What is the purpose of this machine?* use, function, point, value, advantage.
3 **on purpose** see **on purpose**.

**pursue** see **follow** 1.

**push**
1 *(n) Give the door a push.* shove, nudge, prod, jolt, thrust.
OPPOSITE: pull.
2 *(v) Push this button.* press, press down, push down, depress, put pressure on.
3 *(v) Bozo tried to push me into the pool.* shove, propel, force, drive, thrust, ram.
4 *(v) Can you push through the crowd?* force your way, squeeze, press, shove, barge *(informal)*, elbow, shoulder, jostle.
5 *(v) Mum has to push me to do my piano practice.* See **pressurize**.
6 *(v) Famous Fred is keen to push his new album.* See **promote** 2.

**pushy**
*(adj) (informal) Jemima is so pushy; she's invited herself to the party!* assertive, forceful, forward, aggressive, bumptious, brash, loud, bold, cocksure, ambitious.
OPPOSITES: timid, retiring.

**put**
1 *(v) Put the files on the desk.* place, lay, leave, set, stand, rest, plonk, dump, park *(informal)*, set down, deposit.
2 *(v) Don't put your finger in the trifle!* See **stick** 6.
3 *(v) I bet Mrs Badger will put you in the top stream.* place, assign you to, consign you to, allocate you to, rank, grade.

**put away**
*(v) Put away your clothes.* tidy away, clear away, tidy up, put back, replace.

**put down**
1 *(v) The vet had to put down the sick animal.* put to sleep, put out of its misery, destroy, do away with, put away.
2 *(v) My friends never put me down.* belittle, humiliate, disparage, denigrate, sneer at, deflate, crush.

**put off**
1 *(v) We'll have to put off the match until next week.* See **postpone**.
2 *(v) Don't let the spectators put you off.* See **distract**.
3 *(v) Don't let this one setback put you off.* discourage, dissuade, deter, dishearten, dismay, daunt, perturb, faze, throw *(informal)*, rattle *(informal)*.
4 *(v) Doesn't lumpy custard really put you off?* See **disgust** 2.

**put on**
1 *(v) Why don't you put on your jeans?* slip into, change into, don, get dressed in.
OPPOSITE: take off.
2 *(v) It doesn't matter if you put on a bit of weight.* gain, add.
OPPOSITES: take off, lose.
3 *(v) Araminta likes to put on a posh accent.* affect, fake, feign, assume.
4 *(v) We're hoping to put on a pantomime.* See **stage** 3.

**put out**
1 *(v) Put out the flames!* extinguish, quench, douse, smother, stifle, stamp out, blow out, snuff out *(candle)*.
2 *(adj) Kim felt put out that she hadn't been invited.* See **offended**.

**put up**
1 *(v) Dad plans to put up a new garage.* See **build** 1.
2 *(v) We can easily put you up for the night.* take you in, give you a bed, give you a room, accommodate, give you lodging.

**put up with** *(informal)* see **stand** 4.

**puzzle**
1 *(n) I can't get my head round this puzzle.* problem, question, brain-teaser *(informal)*, poser, riddle, conundrum, mystery, enigma, paradox, crossword.
2 *(v) The crime seemed to puzzle the police.* baffle, mystify, perplex, flummox, floor *(informal)*, stump, bewilder, confuse, confound, defeat, nonplus.

**puzzling**
*(adj) A puzzling code.* baffling, perplexing, mystifying, cryptic, bewildering, confusing, mindboggling *(informal)*, insoluble, incomprehensible, mysterious, strange.
OPPOSITES: simple, straightforward.

**quaint**
*(adj) Tourists think our village is quaint.* old-fashioned, picturesque, charming, old-world, antiquated, twee *(informal)*.

**quality**
1 *(n) This work is of a poor quality.* standard, level, grade, class.
2 *(n) Aren't you impressed by the quality of the acting?* high standard, calibre, excellence, superiority, distinction, merit.
3 *(n) Honesty is a quality I value in a friend.* See **characteristic**.

**quantity** see **amount** 1, 2.

**quarrel**
1 *(v) My sisters quarrel all the time.* See **argue** 1.
2 *(n) We had a quarrel about who should pay.* See **argument** 1.

3 *(n) The quarrel between the two families lasted for years.* feud, dispute, disagreement, misunderstanding, argument, hostility, enmity, conflict, vendetta, bad blood, rivalry.

**quarrelsome**
*(adj) Andy is so quarrelsome; he's always fighting with someone.* argumentative, belligerent, aggressive, pugnacious, cantankerous, irritable, irascible.
OPPOSITES: easy-going, even-tempered.

**quay**
*(n) We tied up our boat at the quay.* jetty, wharf, landing stage, dock, harbour.

**queasy** see **sick** 2.

**queen**
*(n)* monarch, sovereign, ruler.

**quest**
*(n) The white knight set out on a perilous quest.* mission, search, hunt, expedition, adventure, voyage, journey, crusade.

**question**
1 *(n) Do you have a question?* query, inquiry.
OPPOSITES: answer, reply.
2 *(n) Mrs Badger set us a difficult question. See* **problem** 2.
3 *(n) There's some question about who won the race.* doubt, uncertainty, dispute, debate, argument, controversy, confusion.
4 *(n) That's an interesting question for a debate. See* **subject**.
5 *(v) Detectives want to question Burglar Beryl.* interview, interrogate, cross-examine, cross-question, quiz, grill *(informal)*, pump, give the third degree to.
6 *(v) Why do you question everything I say?* query, call into question, challenge, dispute, raise objections to, oppose, throw doubt on, suspect.
OPPOSITES: accept, believe.

**queue**
1 *(n) There was a long queue of traffic at the lights.* line, string, column, row, tailback, chain, file.
2 *(v) You must queue for tickets.* line up, wait in line, stand in line, form a queue.

**quick**
1 *(adj) The sprinter ran at a quick pace.* fast, swift, rapid, brisk, speedy, spanking *(informal)*, breakneck, headlong.
OPPOSITES: slow, sluggish.
2 *(adj) I need a quick response.* instant, immediate, instantaneous, prompt, early, swift, rapid, speedy.
OPPOSITES: slow, delayed.
3 *(adj) We paid a quick visit to Aunt Bertha. See* **short** 3.
4 *(adj) Let's go home the quick way. See* **short** 4.
5 *(adj) Ed will see the problem right away; he's very quick.* bright, sharp, astute, quick on the uptake *(informal)*, quick-witted, shrewd, clever, perceptive, discerning, intelligent, able, all there *(informal)*.
OPPOSITES: slow, stupid.

6 *(adj) Sharmeen is always quick to help. See* **willing**.

**quiet**
1 *(adj) Ellen spoke in a quiet voice.* soft, low, hushed, scarcely audible, muted.
OPPOSITE: loud.
2 *(adj) Toni crept past with quiet steps.* silent, soundless, noiseless, inaudible.
OPPOSITES: noisy, loud.
3 *(adj) Frances is a quiet member of the class.* reserved, uncommunicative, unforthcoming, taciturn, silent, shy, retiring, diffident, unassertive, introverted, unobtrusive, subdued, restrained.
OPPOSITES: noisy, talkative.
4 *(adj) Everything was quiet before the storm.* still, calm, peaceful, tranquil.
OPPOSITES: restless, agitated.
5 *(adj) The cottage stood in a quiet valley.* peaceful, sleepy, secluded, isolated, lonely, remote, out-of-the-way, private.
OPPOSITES: bustling, crowded.
6 **be quiet** *(phrase) Be quiet and listen!* stop talking, shut up *(informal)*, shush, quieten down, don't say a word, don't make a sound, hush, hold your tongue, put a sock in it *(slang)*, belt up *(slang)*, shut your trap *(slang)*, pipe down *(slang)*.

**quite**
1 *(adv) It's quite windy today.* rather, fairly, pretty *(informal)*, moderately, reasonably, relatively, a bit, somewhat.
OPPOSITE: very.
2 *(adv) Your answer is quite correct.* absolutely, completely, totally, perfectly, entirely, wholly, utterly.
OPPOSITES: partly, more or less.

**quiver** see **shiver**.

**quote**
1 *(v) Try to quote plenty of examples in your essay.* give, mention, cite, refer to, allude to, name.
2 *(v) Can you quote any lines from Shakespeare?* recite, repeat, recall, recollect, reel off.

**race**
1 *(n) Lateefah took part in the race.* competition, contest, heat, final, relay race, sprint, marathon, cross-country, steeplechase, hurdles.
2 *(n) The Ancient Greeks were a civilized race.* people, nation, tribe, ethnic group.
3 *(v) I must race for my bus. See* **run** 1.
4 *(v) I'll race you to the corner.* have a race with, try to beat, compete with, take you on, run faster than.

**racket** see **noise** 2.

**rage** see **anger** 1.

**ragged**
1 *(adj) The little boy's trousers were ragged.* tattered, torn, frayed, worn-out, in tatters, in holes, in shreds, in ribbons, threadbare, patched, shabby, tatty.
2 *(adj) The torn page had a ragged edge.* uneven, rough, jagged, irregular, serrated.
OPPOSITES: smooth, even.

**raid**
1 *(n) There's been a raid at the bank.* robbery, hold-up, heist *(slang)*, smash-and-grab *(informal)*, stick-up *(slang)*, break-in, ram raid *(informal)*.
2 *(n) We hid underground during the raid. See* **attack** 4.
3 *(v) Pirate Peg planned to raid the enemy's hide-out.* attack, invade, break into, storm, charge, rush, swoop on, rob, loot, plunder, pillage, ransack, rifle.

**rain**
1 *(v) Suddenly it began to rain.* pour, pelt down, bucket down, lash down, teem, rain cats and dogs *(informal)*, come down in torrents, spit, drizzle, sleet, hail.
2 *(n) I wish this rain would stop.* shower, drizzle, downpour, deluge, thunderstorm, cloudburst, torrential rain, driving rain, rainfall, raindrops *(plural)*, sleet, hail.

**rainforest** see **jungle**.

**rainy**
*(adj) I like to stay inside on rainy days.* wet, drizzly, showery, damp.
OPPOSITES: dry, fine, sunny.

**raise**
1 *(v) We'll need a crane to raise those girders.* lift, hoist, pick up, heave up, jack up, put up, elevate, set upright.
OPPOSITE: lower.
2 *(v) Supermarkets may raise their prices.* put up, increase, hike *(informal)*, inflate.
OPPOSITES: lower, reduce, cut.
3 *(v) We need to raise a lot of money for our new computer.* make, collect, get together, gather together, scrape together, pull in, drum up, obtain.
4 *(v) This campaign will raise awareness about drugs.* heighten, increase, promote, boost, strengthen, improve, enhance.
5 *(v) How can we raise some enthusiasm for the campaign?* arouse, awaken, stimulate, stir up, whip up, drum up, summon up, excite, kindle, foster.
6 *(v) It's hard to raise a family on your own. See* **bring up** 1.
7 *(v) Please don't raise that subject again. See* **mention** 2.

**ram**
1 *(v) Saul tried to ram my Dodgem car.* crash into, slam into, smash into, bump into, drive into, run into, collide with, hit.
2 *(v) Ram your stuff in here. See* **cram** 1.

**ramshackle**
*(adj) A ramshackle cottage.* tumbledown, dilapidated, run-down, derelict, neglected, decrepit, crumbling, rickety, unsafe, falling to pieces, gone to rack and ruin.

# random

**random**
*(adj) I jotted down my ideas in a random way.* haphazard, arbitrary, indiscriminate, casual, unplanned, unsystematic, unmethodical, aimless, desultory.
OPPOSITES: deliberate, orderly.

**range**
1 *(n) This shop stocks a wide range of CDs.* variety, assortment, selection, choice, collection, array.
2 *(n) The ship is outside the range of our radar.* reach, scope, field, span, sweep, radius, limits *(plural)*, bounds *(plural)*.
3 *(v) Your marks range from good to excellent.* vary, fluctuate, stretch, extend.

**rank**
*(n) Mum has a high rank in the company.* grade, status, position, level, standing.

**rapid** *see* **fast 1**.

**rare**
*(adj) Vases like this one are rare.* unusual, out of the ordinary, scarce, few and far between, uncommon, exceptional, remarkable, thin on the ground, sparse, irreplaceable, unique, valuable, precious.
OPPOSITES: common, plentiful.

**rarely**
*(adv) We rarely see Lucy.* hardly ever, seldom, scarcely ever, almost never, once in a while, once in a blue moon *(informal)*, on rare occasions, infrequently.
OPPOSITES: often, frequently.

**rash**
1 *(n) Your rash should soon clear up.* spots *(plural)*, allergy, itch, hives *(plural)*.
2 *(adj) Don't make any rash decisions.* reckless, impetuous, impulsive, hasty, sudden, hurried, foolhardy, harebrained, madcap, imprudent, ill-considered, ill-advised, risky, careless, thoughtless.
OPPOSITES: careful, considered.

**rate**
1 *(n) Gus raced off at a tremendous rate.* speed, pace, velocity.
2 *(n) What's the rate for a single room?* charge, cost, price, fee, tariff, payment, damage *(informal)*, figure.
3 *(v) Would you rate my performance as good?* regard, consider, judge, count, evaluate, assess, appraise, classify, rank.
4 *(v) (slang) I don't rate our new teacher at all. See* **admire 1**.

**rather** *see* **quite 1**.

**rattle**
*(v) The wind made the shutters rattle.* clatter, bang, clank, clink, clunk, clack, shake, vibrate, jiggle.

**rave**
1 *(adj) (informal) Our play got rave reviews.* rapturous, enthusiastic, ecstatic, excellent, favourable.
OPPOSITES: lukewarm, critical.
2 *(n) (slang) I hear there was a rave last night.* party, warehouse party, disco, rave-up *(slang)*, bash *(informal)*.

**ravenous** *see* **hungry 1**.

**raw**
1 *(adj) Raw meat.* uncooked, unprepared, bloody, underdone, rare, fresh *(vegetables, fruit)*.
OPPOSITES: cooked, well-done.
2 *(adj) Raw materials.* unprocessed, unrefined, untreated, natural, basic, crude, unfinished, coarse, rough.
OPPOSITES: refined, processed.
3 *(adj) Raw skin.* chafed, grazed, scraped, scratched, red, inflamed, sensitive, sore.
4 *(adj) A raw winter's day. See* **cold 1**.

**ray**
*(n) A ray of sunlight.* beam, shaft, stream, gleam, streak, flash, glimmer, glint, flicker.

**reach**
1 *(v) Can you reach that book on the top shelf?* get at, get hold of, touch, grab, grasp, catch at, clutch at, seize.
2 *(v) Did the explorers reach the North Pole?* get to, make, make it to *(informal)*, get as far as, arrive at, set foot on, land at.
3 *(v) The mountains seemed to reach the sky.* touch, stretch to, extend to.
4 *(v) (informal) Please reach me that book.* pass, hand, give, hand over.
5 *(v) I tried to reach you yesterday, but you were out. See* **contact**.

**reach out**
*(v) Reach out and grab the railing.* stretch out, hold out your hand, stick out your hand, lean out, lean over.

**react**
*(v) How did Zak react when he heard the news?* respond, behave, act, cope, reply.

**reaction**
*(n) Did you get any reaction to your suggestion?* response, reply, answer, feedback, comeback *(informal)*, backlash.

**read**
1 *(v) Did you read the paper yesterday?* look at, study, browse through, scan, skim through, glance at, run your eye over, dip into, pore over, wade through, peruse.
2 *(v) I have to read a poem in assembly.* read out, read aloud, recite, say, deliver.
3 *(v) Your writing is hard to read.* make out, decipher, understand, interpret, comprehend, decode.

**ready**
1 *(adj) Is everything ready?* prepared, arranged, organized, set up, finished, completed, finalized, ready and waiting, in readiness, primed, all set, fitted out.
OPPOSITES: unprepared, unfinished.
2 *(adj) Grandma is always ready to babysit. See* **willing**.
3 *(adj) Have you got your bus fare ready? See* **handy 2**.
4 *(adj) Louise looked ready to cry.* about, likely, liable, close, in danger of, on the brink of, on the point of, on the verge of.

**real**
1 *(adj) Is that real gold? See* **genuine 1**.

2 *(adj) These are the real facts.* true, actual, veritable, unquestionable, correct, certain, positive, tangible, truthful, factual.
OPPOSITES: false, imaginary.
3 *(adj) I can't hide my real feelings.* true, genuine, sincere, honest, heartfelt.
OPPOSITES: feigned, insincere.

**realistic**
1 *(adj) You must be realistic about your job prospects.* practical, sensible, level-headed, clear-sighted, rational, objective, pragmatic, down-to-earth, businesslike, hard-headed, unromantic, unsentimental.
OPPOSITES: unrealistic, idealistic.
2 *(adj) What a realistic model!* lifelike, convincing, true-to-life, naturalistic, authentic, faithful, accurate, precise.
OPPOSITES: unrealistic, unconvincing.

**realize**
*(v) I didn't realize what had happened.* understand, appreciate, grasp, comprehend, take in, absorb, twig *(informal)*, catch on to *(informal)*, cotton on to *(informal)*, notice, recognize.

**really**
1 *(adv) This film is really gruesome.* totally, utterly, absolutely, truly, extremely, thoroughly, completely, positively, very.
2 *(adv) Archie says that he's nine, but he's really only seven.* actually, in fact, in reality, in truth, as a matter of fact.

**reason**
1 *(n) Do you have any reason for being late?* grounds *(plural)*, cause, explanation, excuse, justification, pretext, rationale.
2 *(n) What is the reason behind your visit? See* **purpose 1**.
3 **reason with** *(v) It's a waste of time trying to reason with you.* argue with, persuade, dissuade, talk you round, win you over, bring you round, plead with, show you the error of your ways.

**reasonable**
1 *(adj) That sounds like a reasonable explanation.* sensible, logical, rational, credible, plausible, believable, intelligent, well-thought-out, reasoned, sound.
OPPOSITES: irrational, incredible.
2 *(adj) Mr Badger is a reasonable man.* moderate, fair, just, sensible, rational, wise, open to reason.
OPPOSITE: unreasonable.
3 *(adj) Your exam results are reasonable. See* **all right 3**.
4 *(adj) Reasonable prices. See* **low 7**.

**reassure**
*(v) Did Mrs Badger's comments reassure you?* put your mind at rest, comfort, calm, soothe your fears, encourage, give you confidence, cheer up, hearten, bolster.
OPPOSITES: discourage, worry.

**reassuring**
*(adj) Dad gave me a reassuring smile.* encouraging, supportive, comforting, heartening, sympathetic, soothing.
OPPOSITES: discouraging, disturbing.

## rebel
1 (v) *The citizens threatened to rebel.* revolt, riot, rise up, mutiny, take to the streets, take up arms, man the barricades, take a stand, resist.
2 **rebel against** (v) *Teenagers sometimes rebel against their parents. See* **disobey** 1.

## rebellion *see* **revolution** 1.

## rebellious
1 (adj) *A rebellious teenager.* defiant, disobedient, unruly, difficult, stroppy (informal), obstinate, uncontrollable, wild.
OPPOSITES: obedient, compliant.
2 (adj) *Rebellious soldiers.* mutinous, insubordinate, rioting, disloyal, disaffected, rebel, revolutionary, insurgent.
OPPOSITES: loyal, obedient.

## receive
1 (v) *I was thrilled to receive a prize.* be given, be awarded, get, accept, collect, pick up, obtain, gain, come by.
OPPOSITE: give.
2 (v) *I hope to receive some good news.* hear, be given, be told, be informed of.

## recent
(adj) *A recent invention.* new, modern, present-day, contemporary, fresh, novel, up-to-the-minute, current, up-to-date.
OPPOSITES: old, early.

## recite
(v) *Can you recite the alphabet backwards?* say, repeat, reel off, read aloud, run through, go through, perform, deliver.

## reckless *see* **rash** 2.

## reckon *see* **think** 1, 2.

## recognize
1 (v) *I didn't recognize you with short hair.* know, spot, identify, notice, pick you out, remember, recall, place.
2 (v) *Do you recognize what you've done wrong?* realize, see, understand, know, accept, acknowledge, appreciate, admit to.

## recommend
1 (v) *What did the doctor recommend?* advise, suggest, propose, advocate, urge.
2 (v) *All my friends recommend this film.* speak highly of, praise, rave about (informal), approve of, commend, vouch for, put in a good word for, applaud.

## record
1 (n) *Is there a record of this trip?* account, report, chronicle, diary, log, journal, note, memo, file, dossier, document, archives (plural).
2 (n) *Have you heard Famous Fred's new record? See* **release** 4.
3 (n) *Leo has a good record of punctuality.* track record (informal), history, background, past performance, reputation.
4 (v) *Record your progress every day.* document, log, note, write down, set down, enter, chronicle, put on record, put in writing, jot down, tape, video.
5 (v) *The band hope to record a single.* cut, make a recording of, lay down (slang).

## recover
1 (v) *I'm sure you'll soon recover.* get better, get well, improve, get back on your feet, bounce back, rally, pull through, recuperate, convalesce, heal, mend.
OPPOSITES: deteriorate, get worse.
2 (v) *I tried to recover my lost suitcase. See* **retrieve**.

## red
1 (n) SHADES OF RED: beetroot red, blood red, brick red, burgundy, cardinal red, cherry red, crimson, flame red, magenta, maroon, pillar-box red, poppy red, puce, ruby, scarlet, tomato, vermilion.
2 (adj) *Red hair.* ginger, auburn, carroty, chestnut, coppery, sandy, reddish, flame-coloured, rust-coloured, russet, Titian.
3 (adj) *A red face.* flushed, flaming, burning, rosy, glowing, ruddy, florid, sunburnt, rosy-cheeked, apple-cheeked.
4 (adj) *Red eyes.* bloodshot, red-rimmed.

## reduce
1 (v) *We will reduce our prices.* lower, bring down, cut, slash, discount, trim, halve, mark down, knock down (informal).
OPPOSITES: raise, increase.
2 (v) *Earplugs will reduce the sound.* cut down, decrease, lessen, lower, diminish, minimize, tone down, muffle, dull.
OPPOSITES: increase, amplify.
3 (v) *Please reduce your speed.* lower, decrease, cut down, cut, lessen, ease off.
OPPOSITE: increase.

## refer to
1 (v) *Who could this rude note refer to?* apply to, relate to, concern, be aimed at, be directed at, be relevant to, pertain to.
2 (v) *Did the letter refer to our visit?* mention, make reference to, speak about, touch on, allude to, comment on, hint at.
3 (v) *Refer to your textbooks.* consult, look at, turn to, look up.

## reflect
1 (v) *The lakes reflect the trees.* mirror.
2 (v) *Do soaps on TV reflect real life? See* **imitate** 3.
3 (v) *Your marks reflect your ability.* do justice to, demonstrate, display, reveal, indicate, bear out, speak volumes about.

## refreshing
1 (adj) *This drink is very refreshing.* thirst-quenching, cooling, reviving, revitalizing, rejuvenating, fortifying, restorative.
2 (adj) *I've just had a refreshing swim.* bracing, invigorating, cooling, freshening, exhilarating, revitalizing.

## refuse
1 (v) *Here's an offer you can't refuse.* turn down, say no to, decline, reject, pass up (informal), resist, spurn, rebuff, dismiss.
OPPOSITE: accept.
2 (v) *Damian's parents refuse him nothing. See* **deny** 2.

## region
(n) *A mountainous region.* area, place, district, land, country, province, territory.

## regret
1 (v) *Don't you regret that you lied to me?* feel sorry, feel ashamed, feel remorse, reproach yourself, have qualms, repent.
2 (v) *When you're older you'll regret this lost opportunity.* feel sorry about, pine over, fret over, bemoan, weep over.
3 (n) *Amir was filled with regret.* remorse, shame, guilt, self-reproach, contrition, repentance, sadness, sorrow, grief.
OPPOSITES: satisfaction, pleasure.

## regular
1 (adj) *Guitar practice is part of my regular routine. See* **usual**.
2 (adj) *You'll receive a regular progress report.* periodic, frequent, yearly, quarterly, termly, monthly, weekly, daily, hourly.
OPPOSITES: occasional, infrequent.
3 (adj) *The trees were planted at regular intervals.* constant, fixed, set, equal, even, uniform, unvarying, consistent, measured.
OPPOSITES: irregular, erratic.

## rehearsal
(n) *We need another rehearsal before the performance.* practice, practice session, run-through, trial run, dress rehearsal, dummy run, dry run (informal).

## reign
(v) *Who will reign when the king dies?* be king, be queen, sit on the throne, wear the crown, rule, govern, hold power.

## reinforce *see* **strengthen** 2, 3.

## reject
1 (v) *I bet the head will reject our plans.* say no to, veto, disallow, give the thumbs down to, throw out, scrap, discard, bin.
OPPOSITES: accept, approve.
2 (v) *How could you reject your best friend?* disown, turn your back on, spurn, abandon, cast aside, forsake, drop (informal), dump (informal), ditch (slang).
3 (v) *Don't reject my offer. See* **refuse** 1.

## rejoice
(v) *The whole school will rejoice if we win.* be happy, be pleased, be glad, be delighted, be jubilant, be overjoyed, jump for joy, celebrate, triumph, exult.
OPPOSITES: mourn, grieve.

## related
(adj) *The two crimes seem to be related.* connected, linked, interconnected, associated, similar, comparable, parallel.

## relation
(n) *Aunt Bertha is a close relation.* relative, member of the family, family member, blood relative, relative by marriage.

## relax
1 (v) *Relax your grip.* loosen, slacken, ease, weaken, unclench, lessen, reduce, release.
OPPOSITE: tighten.
2 (v) *You can relax after the exams.* unwind, take it easy, rest, ease up, put your feet up, laze about, chill out (slang), hang loose (informal), let your hair down, lighten up (slang).

**relaxed**

1 *(adj) Bianca has a relaxed attitude to her work.* easy-going, laid-back *(informal)*, casual, free and easy, leisurely, nonchalant, blasé, unconcerned, slack.
OPPOSITES: uptight *(informal)*, serious.
2 *(adj) We had a relaxed lunch.* leisurely, unhurried, restful, informal, laid-back *(informal)*, cosy, comfortable.
OPPOSITES: formal, tense.

**relaxing**

*(adj) We spent a relaxing day on the beach.* restful, peaceful, quiet, leisurely, unhurried, lazy, languid, soothing.
OPPOSITE: stressful.

**release**

1 *(v) Let's campaign to release the hostages.* free, set free, liberate, deliver, emancipate, let go, let out, turn loose.
OPPOSITE: imprison.
2 *(v) The judge decided to release Burglar Beryl.* free, let go, let off, spare, excuse, acquit, discharge, pardon, absolve.
OPPOSITE: detain.
3 *(v) The police will release a description of the criminal.* issue, put out, publish, broadcast, circulate, distribute, make public, make known, reveal, disclose.
OPPOSITES: withhold, suppress.
4 *(n) Listen to this new release.* recording, record, disc, tape, CD, single, album, EP (extended play), 12-inch, remix, rerelease.

**relevant**

*(adj) Is that remark relevant to the discussion?* related, pertinent, connected, linked, applicable, essential, significant.
OPPOSITES: irrelevant, beside the point.

**reliable**

1 *(adj) Lateefah is a reliable friend.* dependable, trustworthy, trusty, staunch, faithful, loyal, devoted, unfailing, constant, steady, true, responsible, honest.
OPPOSITES: unreliable, fickle.
2 *(adj) Is your information reliable?* dependable, well-founded, sound, tried and tested, trustworthy, credible, true.
OPPOSITES: unreliable, dodgy *(informal)*.

**relieve**

1 *(v) This ointment will relieve the pain.* ease, alleviate, soothe, lessen, reduce, deaden, dull, numb, blunt.
OPPOSITES: increase, intensify.
2 *(v) A substitute will relieve you at half-time.* take over from, replace, stand in for, take your place, give you a break.

**religion**

*(n) What is your religion?* faith, belief, creed, denomination, sect.

**religious**

1 *(adj) Religious books.* theological, devotional, spiritual, sacred, holy, divine.
OPPOSITE: secular.
2 *(adj) A religious woman.* pious, devout, God-fearing, godly, churchgoing.

**reluctant** *see* **unwilling**.

**rely on** *see* **depend on** 1, 2.

**remain** *see* **stay** 1, 4.

**remains**

1 *(plural n) What shall we do with the remains of this meal?* leftovers *(plural)*, scraps *(plural)*, remnants *(plural)*, crumbs *(plural)*, dregs *(plural) (drink)*, rest, residue.
2 *(plural n) Experts sifted through the remains.* rubble, debris, wreckage, ruins *(plural)*, ashes *(plural)*, bones *(plural)*.

**remark** *see* **comment** 1, 2.

**remarkable**

*(adj) What a remarkable painting!* amazing, astonishing, incredible, extraordinary, astounding, surprising, startling, striking, distinctive, unusual, strange, outstanding, exceptional.
OPPOSITES: ordinary, unremarkable.

**remember**

1 *(v) Can you remember my name?* think of, recall, recollect, call to mind, place.
OPPOSITE: forget.
2 *(v) It took me ages to remember my lines. See* **learn** 2.
3 *(v) Granny likes to remember her youth.* reminisce about, think about, think back on, look back on, hark back to, recall, recollect, talk about, be nostalgic about.
OPPOSITE: forget about.

**remind**

1 *(v) I'll remind you when it's time to go.* prompt, jog your memory, refresh your memory, give you a reminder, prod.
2 **remind you of** *(v) This song will remind you of our holiday.* make you think of, bring back memories of, take you back to, awaken memories of, put you in mind of.

**remote**

*(adj) Pirate Peg landed on a remote island.* faraway, far-off, distant, far-flung, outlying, out-of-the-way, isolated, lonely, inaccessible, secluded, godforsaken.
OPPOSITES: accessible, nearby.

**remove**

1 *(v) Please do not remove these books.* take, take away, take out, carry away, move, shift, dislodge, withdraw, borrow, throw out, steal.
2 *(v) This liquid will remove stains.* get rid of, eradicate, eliminate, dislodge, shift, move, budge, erase, wipe out, root out.
3 *(v) Remove your hat. See* **take off** 1.

**repair**

1 *(v) Can you repair my radio?* fix, mend, put right, restore to working order, patch up, sort out, overhaul, rebuild, recondition.
2 *(v) I must repair my jeans. See* **mend** 2.

**repay** *see* **pay back** 1, 2.

**repeat**

1 *(v) Don't repeat this story to anyone!* tell, pass on, quote, relate, recount, reiterate, retell, restate, recite.
2 *(v) Listen to the violins repeat the tune.* echo, reiterate, re-echo, restate, replay, play back, copy, duplicate, reproduce.

**replace**

1 *(v) Please replace the knives and forks.* put back, put away, return.
2 *(v) You must replace those worn tyres.* change, renew, exchange, swap, switch.
3 *(v) Who will replace Jodie on the team?* take the place of, stand in for, substitute for, deputize for, cover for, take over from, succeed, follow, supplant, supersede.

**reply** *see* **answer** 1, 2, 3.

**report**

1 *(n) Have you read this report?* account, description, statement, write-up, article, news story, piece, message, communiqué, communication, note, summary, narrative.
2 *(v) The committee will report their findings.* present, state, announce, declare, publish, make public, communicate, outline, document, detail, give an account of, put in writing, broadcast, circulate.
3 *(v) I'm going to report you to the head.* complain about, denounce, tell on *(informal)*, inform on, blow the whistle on *(informal)*, shop *(slang)*, snitch on *(slang)*.

**reporter**

*(n)* journalist, correspondent, hack, newshound *(informal)*, writer, investigator, commentator, broadcaster, feature writer, columnist, member of the press.

**represent**

1 *(v) What do the letters "PC" represent? See* **stand for**.
2 *(v) Rose will represent our class on the school council.* speak for, act on behalf of, be the voice of, be the spokesperson for.

**repulsive** *see* **disgusting** 1.

**reputation**

*(n) This rumour could damage Famous Fred's reputation.* name, good name, character, honour, respectability, standing, status, position, prestige, fame, renown.

**request**

1 *(n) The police issued a request for information.* appeal, call, plea, demand.
2 *(v) The genie will do anything you request. See* **ask** 4.

**require**

1 *(v) This project will require a lot of work. See* **need** 1.
2 *(v) I expect Dad will require an apology. See* **demand** 1.

**rescue**

1 *(v) Don't panic; I'll rescue you!* save, save your life, help, come to your rescue, free, release, set you free, get you out, deliver you from danger, liberate.
2 *(v) Pirate Peg managed to rescue her map from the wreck.* recover, retrieve, salvage, save, extricate, fish out.
3 *(n) We watched the rescue on television.* rescue operation, rescue attempt, air-sea rescue, recovery, salvage operation, relief operation.
4 *(n) Please come to my rescue.* aid, help, assistance.

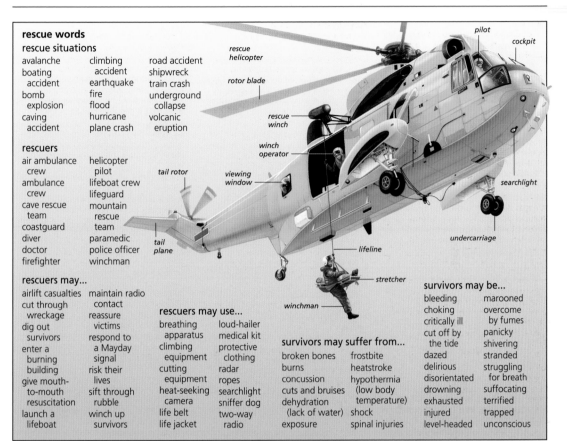

**rescue words**

**rescue situations**

| | | |
|---|---|---|
| avalanche | climbing | road accident |
| boating | accident | shipwreck |
| accident | earthquake | train crash |
| bomb | fire | underground |
| explosion | flood | collapse |
| caving | hurricane | volcanic |
| accident | plane crash | eruption |

*rescue helicopter*

*rotor blade*

*pilot*

*cockpit*

**rescuers**

| | |
|---|---|
| air ambulance | helicopter |
| crew | pilot |
| ambulance | lifeboat crew |
| crew | lifeguard |
| cave rescue | mountain |
| team | rescue |
| coastguard | team |
| diver | paramedic |
| doctor | police officer |
| firefighter | winchman |

*rescue winch*

*winch operator*

*tail rotor*

*viewing window*

*searchlight*

*tail plane*

*undercarriage*

*lifeline*

**rescuers may...**

| | |
|---|---|
| airlift casualties | maintain radio |
| cut through | contact |
| wreckage | reassure |
| dig out | victims |
| survivors | respond to |
| enter a | a Mayday |
| burning | signal |
| building | risk their |
| give mouth- | lives |
| to-mouth | sift through |
| resuscitation | rubble |
| launch a | winch up |
| lifeboat | survivors |

**rescuers may use...**

| | |
|---|---|
| breathing | loud-hailer |
| apparatus | medical kit |
| climbing | protective |
| equipment | clothing |
| cutting | radar |
| equipment | ropes |
| heat-seeking | searchlight |
| camera | sniffer dog |
| life belt | two-way |
| life jacket | radio |

*stretcher*

*winchman*

**survivors may suffer from...**

| | |
|---|---|
| broken bones | frostbite |
| burns | heatstroke |
| concussion | hypothermia |
| cuts and bruises | (low body |
| dehydration | temperature) |
| (lack of water) | shock |
| exposure | spinal injuries |

**survivors may be...**

| | |
|---|---|
| bleeding | marooned |
| choking | overcome |
| critically ill | by fumes |
| cut off by | panicky |
| the tide | shivering |
| dazed | stranded |
| delirious | struggling |
| disorientated | for breath |
| drowning | suffocating |
| exhausted | terrified |
| injured | trapped |
| level-headed | unconscious |

**research**
1 *(n) I need to do some research for my project.* reading, background reading, groundwork, fact-finding, investigation, study, experiments *(plural)*, tests *(plural)*.
2 *(v) I've decided to research my family history. See* **investigate**.

**resent**
1 *(v) Aunt Bertha will resent not being invited.* feel bitter about, feel aggrieved at, be offended at, take offence at, take umbrage at, put up with, bear a grudge about, have hard feelings about, take exception to.
2 *(v) Try not to resent your sister's success.* begrudge, feel bitter about, envy, be jealous of, feel aggrieved at.

**resentful** *see* **bitter** 2.

**reserve**
1 *(v) Please reserve a room. See* **book** 3.
2 *(n) Who will be the reserve?* substitute, replacement, stand-in *(informal)*, deputy.

**resign**
1 *(v) If you don't like your job, why don't you resign?* leave, hand in your notice, give notice, quit, stand down, step down *(informal)*, give up, pack it in *(informal)*.

2 **resign yourself to** *(phrase) Revising is dull, but you'll have to resign yourself to it.* reconcile yourself to, accept, come to terms with, put up with *(informal)*, grin and bear *(informal)*, make the best of.

**resigned**
*(adj) How can Dad be so resigned about losing his job?* accepting, philosophical, stoical, patient, long-suffering, calm, reasonable, unresisting, passive, defeatist.

**resist**
1 *(v) How can you resist eating that cake?* prevent yourself from, keep from, avoid, refrain from, abstain from, stop.
2 *(v) I can't resist your offer. See* **refuse** 1.
3 *(v) We will resist any attempt to close our school. See* **fight** 4.

**respect**
1 *(n) You should have more respect for people's feelings.* consideration, concern, regard, deference, appreciation, reverence.
OPPOSITES: contempt, disdain.
2 *(v) People respect Mr Badger.* think highly of, think well of, have a high opinion of, admire, look up to, revere.
OPPOSITES: look down on, scorn.

**respectable**
1 *(adj) Mr Badger is a respectable citizen.* respected, upstanding, decent, law-abiding, upright, honest, well-regarded.
OPPOSITE: disreputable.
2 *(adj) Put on your dressing gown; you're not respectable! See* **decent** 1.

**respond**
1 *(v) Didn't Ed respond when you tickled him?* react, retaliate, hit back, reciprocate.
2 *(v) I heard Kate respond. See* **answer** 2.
3 **respond to** *(v) I must respond to this letter. See* **answer** 1.

**response** *see* **answer** 3.

**responsible**
1 *(adj) We need a responsible babysitter.* reliable, dependable, trustworthy, sensible, level-headed, conscientious, mature.
OPPOSITES: irresponsible, unreliable.
2 *(adj) What a mess! Who is responsible?* guilty, to blame, at fault, culpable.
3 **be responsible for** *(phrase) Who will be responsible for the team's actions?* take responsibility for, be in charge of, take control of, be accountable for, be answerable for, take the blame for.

## rest

1 (n) *Granny is having a rest. See* **sleep** 3.
2 (n) *You deserve a rest after your hard work.* break, breather (informal), holiday, vacation, time off, leave, breathing space.
3 (n) *What shall I do with the rest?* remainder, surplus, excess, balance, residue, remains (plural), remnants (plural), leftovers (plural) (food), others (plural).
4 (v) *You should rest for a while.* take a break, have a breather (informal), relax, take it easy, sit down, lie down, put your feet up, take a nap, have forty winks (informal).
5 (v) *Rest your bike against the wall.* lean, prop, support, stand, balance, steady.

## restaurant

(n) TYPES OF RESTAURANT: bistro, brasserie, burger bar, café, cafeteria, canteen, carvery, diner, grill, pizzeria, snack bar, steakhouse, takeaway.

## restful *see* **relaxing**.

## restless

1 (adj) *Before the show, all the cast were restless.* unsettled, agitated, fidgety, jittery (informal), excitable, impatient, edgy, nervous, on edge, jumpy, anxious, fretful.
OPPOSITES: calm, composed.
2 (adj) *I had a restless night.* sleepless, wakeful, disturbed, unsettled, troubled.
OPPOSITES: peaceful, undisturbed.

## restrict *see* **limit** 3.

## result

1 (n) *The meeting had an unexpected result.* outcome, consequence, effect, upshot, aftermath, sequel, legacy, end product, repercussion, side effect, spin-off.
2 (v) *If the two countries can't agree, war may result.* follow, ensue, develop, come about, take place, happen, occur, arise.
3 **result in** (v) *These talks could result in a solution.* lead to, bring about, give rise to, produce, create, culminate in, end in, finish in, conclude in, terminate in.

## retreat

(v) *The soldiers were forced to retreat.* withdraw, draw back, back off, back away, pull back, pull out, give ground, flee, take flight, turn tail, bolt, retire, depart.
OPPOSITE: advance.

## retrieve

(v) *I tried to retrieve my lost suitcase.* get back, reclaim, recover, track down, find, salvage, rescue, regain, recapture.

## return

1 (v) *Dad said he would return after tea.* come back, be back, get back, go back, reappear, come home.
2 (v) *If you return the same way you may find your keys.* go back, walk back, retrace your steps, double back, backtrack, retreat.
3 (v) *I asked Shelley to return my pen.* give back, put back, replace, send back.
4 (n) *I couldn't wait for Dad's return.* homecoming, reappearance, arrival.

## reveal

1 (v) *Does this skirt reveal too much leg?* expose, show, display, bare, uncover.
OPPOSITES: cover up, conceal.
2 (v) *Will Melissa reveal her true feelings?* give away, betray, let out, let slip, disclose, divulge, declare, make known, make public, broadcast, display, lay bare, unveil.
OPPOSITES: hide, conceal.

## revenge

1 (n) *We think the attack was an act of revenge.* vengeance, retaliation, reprisal, retribution, vindictiveness, tit for tat.
2 **take revenge for** (phrase) *You must take revenge for this injustice.* avenge, wreak your revenge for, get your own back for (informal), even the score for, repay, retaliate against, hit back at.

## reverse

1 (v) *You'll have to reverse up the drive.* back, go backwards, drive backwards, go into reverse, back away, retreat, backtrack.
2 (v) *The head won't reverse her decision.* overturn, go back on, revoke, change, alter, undo, overrule, retract, repeal.
3 (n) *The instructions are on the reverse.* other side, back, rear, opposite side, flip side, underside, underneath.

## review

1 (n) *Write a review of this book.* criticism, critique, appreciation, evaluation, assessment, appraisal, report, write-up.
2 (v) *Will you review the school play for our magazine?* give your opinion of, comment on, discuss, write a critique of, evaluate, assess, appraise, criticize.

## revise

(v) *I must revise these facts before the test.* go over, run through, memorize, learn, swot up on (informal), mug up on (slang), reread, study.

## revive

1 (v) *Doctors tried to revive the patient.* resuscitate, bring back to life, breathe life into, save, bring round, rouse, awaken.
2 (v) *The patient began to revive.* come round, regain consciousness, rally, recover.

## revolt

1 (n) *An armed revolt. See* **revolution** 1.
2 (v) *The citizens will revolt. See* **rebel** 1.

## revolting *see* **disgusting** 1.

## revolution

1 (n) *Troops were brought in to crush the revolution.* uprising, rebellion, revolt, coup, coup d'état, mutiny, riot, insurrection, insurgency, armed struggle, civil war.
2 (n) *Computers have caused a revolution in the way we work.* complete change, radical change, transformation, sea change, turnaround, shift, upheaval.

## revolve

1 (v) *Watch the cogs revolve. See* **turn** 1.
2 **revolve around** (v) *Satellites revolve around the earth.* circle, orbit, travel round, spin round, rotate around.

## reward

1 (n) *Do we get a reward for effort?* prize, payment, remuneration, recompense, bonus, tip, compensation, award.
OPPOSITES: penalty, punishment.
2 (v) *The leader will reward you if you succeed.* repay, pay, compensate, make it worth your while, recompense, honour.
OPPOSITES: penalize, punish.

## rhythm

(n) *Listen to the rhythm of the music.* beat, pulse, throbbing, pounding, tempo, phrasing, pattern, lilt, swing, syncopation.

## rich

1 (adj) *Lord Lucre is rich.* wealthy, well-off, affluent, prosperous, well-to-do, well-heeled (informal), made of money (informal), stinking rich (informal), loaded (slang), rolling in it (slang).
OPPOSITE: poor.
2 (adj) *The walls were hung with rich tapestries.* costly, expensive, valuable, priceless, sumptuous, luxurious, opulent, lavish, ornate, elaborate, fine, exquisite, magnificent, splendid, gorgeous.
OPPOSITES: worthless, shabby.
3 (adj) *Red is a rich colour.* strong, deep, warm, vivid, vibrant, bright, intense.
OPPOSITES: pale, insipid.
4 (adj) *This sauce is too rich for me.* heavy, fatty, creamy, spicy, highly flavoured, indigestible, full-bodied (wine).
OPPOSITES: light, bland.

## rickety

(adj) *A rickety bridge.* broken-down, wobbly, tumbledown, ramshackle, flimsy, unstable, unsafe, weak, decrepit.
OPPOSITES: strong, stable.

## riddle *see* **puzzle** 1.

## ride

1 (v) *Rod's moped is hard to ride.* control, handle, manage, steer, pedal, drive.
2 (v) *I love to ride on the bus.* travel, go, take a trip on, journey, sit, stand.
3 (n) *Come for a ride in our new car! See* **drive** 4.

## ridiculous

(adj) *The idea of a flying pig is ridiculous.* absurd, ludicrous, crazy, mad, incredible, preposterous, outrageous, unbelievable, laughable, farcical, comical, hilarious, daft (informal), foolish, silly, nonsensical, zany.
OPPOSITE: sensible.

## right

1 (adj) *Is this the right answer?* correct, proper, true, exact, precise, perfect, most accurate, valid, spot-on (informal).
OPPOSITES: wrong, incorrect.
2 (adj) *I try to do what's right.* just, fair, honourable, good, honest, decent, ethical, moral, proper, legal, above board.
OPPOSITES: wrong, immoral.
3 (adj) *Is this outfit right for a funeral?* suitable, appropriate, fitting, fit, proper, seemly, sensible.
OPPOSITES: inappropriate, unsuitable.

**4** (n) Do you have the right to do that? authority, power, entitlement, prerogative, privilege, permission, authorization, justification, licence, freedom, liberty.

**rigid**
1 (adj) Rigid plastic. See **stiff** 1.
2 (adj) Rigid rules. See **strict** 2.

**ring**
1 (n) Make a paper ring. circle, disc, hoop, loop, band, cordon.
2 (n) The police are investigating a drugs ring. circle, gang, group, organization, band, syndicate, cartel, cell, mob.
3 (v) Listen to the bells ring. chime, peal, toll, tinkle, jingle, jangle, clang, ding, ping, sound, resound, reverberate, fill the air.
4 (v) Please ring me tonight. See **phone** 1.

**riot**
1 (n) This news may cause a riot. uprising, revolt, breach of the peace, insurrection, rebellion, upheaval, disturbance, street fight, brawl, scuffle, free-for-all (informal), violence, unrest, fighting, uproar, anarchy.
2 (v) The people will riot when they hear the news. run riot, rise up, take to the streets, revolt, rebel, take the law into their own hands, run amok, go on the rampage.

**rip** see **tear** 1, 2, 4.

**ripe**
(adj) Wait until the fruit is ripe. matured, mellow, ready to eat, fully developed, seasoned, perfect, fully grown.

**rise**
1 (v) Watch the plane rise into the air. lift, climb, ascend, soar, go up, fly up, shoot up, rocket, mount, spiral, take off.
OPPOSITES: fall, descend.
2 (v) House prices may rise. increase, go up, climb, escalate, spiral, soar, shoot up, rocket, surge, jump, leap, grow.
OPPOSITES: fall, drop.
3 (v) Can you see the mountain rise above us? tower, loom, soar, rear up, stand out.
4 (v) The path began to rise. get steeper, climb, incline, go uphill, slope upwards.
OPPOSITE: fall.
5 (n) I predict a rise in prices. jump, increase, leap, surge, escalation, upturn.
OPPOSITES: drop, fall.

**risk**
1 (n) There's a risk of snow. See **chance** 2.
2 (n) Dodgy Dave took a risk. gamble, chance, leap in the dark, speculation.
3 (n) There's some risk involved in motor racing. danger, hazard, peril, uncertainty.
4 (v) Don't risk all your money on a bet. gamble, hazard, chance, speculate with.
5 (v) Would you risk your life to save me? endanger, put at risk, put in jeopardy, imperil, jeopardize, gamble with.

**risky**
(adj) Skating on thin ice is risky. dangerous, hazardous, fraught with danger, perilous, unsafe, precarious, dicey (informal), chancy (informal), dodgy (informal), iffy (informal).
OPPOSITE: safe.

---

**river**
(n) stream, brook, creek, rivulet, tributary, waterway, torrent.

**along a river you might see...**
estuary (river mouth)
ford (crossing)
gorge (deep river valley)
island
lock
meander (loop)
pool
rapids (fast-moving water)
reeds
river bank
river bed
rushes
stepping stones
towpath
waterfall
weeds
weir

**rivers may be...**
choked up
clean
contaminated
crystal clear
dark
deep
fast-flowing
foaming
frothing
glassy
glittering
icy
muddy
polluted
shallow
shimmering
silted up
silvery
slow-moving
sluggish
sparkling
turbulent
wide

**rivers may...**
babble
bubble
burble
cascade
eddy
flood
flow
glide
gurgle
gush
meander
murmur
plunge
race
ripple
roar
rush
snake
splash
stream
surge
sweep
swirl
thunder
trickle
tumble
twist
wind

**river activities**
angling
canoeing
cruising
fishing
paddling
punting
rowing
sailing
swimming
wading
white-water rafting

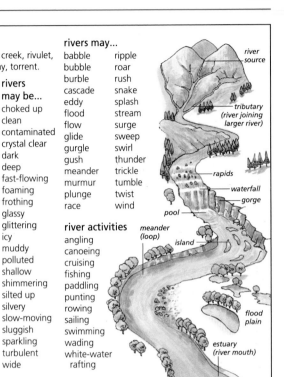

river source
tributary (river joining larger river)
rapids
waterfall
gorge
pool
meander (loop)
island
flood plain
estuary (river mouth)

---

**road**
(n) Which road do we take? route, way, direction, course.
TYPES OF ROAD: alley, avenue, backstreet, boulevard, bypass, close, crescent, cul-de-sac, drive, dual carriageway, high street, highway, lane, main road, minor road, motorway, one-way street, ring road, side street, single-track road, street, track.

**roar**
1 (v) The giant began to roar. bellow, thunder, shout, yell, bawl, howl, shriek.
2 (v) Listen to the thunder roar. boom, rumble, roll, growl, crash, thunder.

**rob**
1 (v) Someone tried to rob the post office. burgle, break into, hold up, raid, loot, steal from, ransack, ram raid (informal).
2 (v) Don't let anyone rob you. steal from, pick your pocket, mug (informal), swindle, con (informal), defraud, cheat, diddle (informal), rip you off (slang).

**robber**
(n) thief, burglar, pickpocket, shoplifter, housebreaker, looter, mugger (informal), bandit, brigand, highwayman, pirate.

**robbery**
1 (n) Beryl was found guilty of robbery. burglary, theft, stealing, housebreaking, ram raiding (informal), shoplifting, pilfering, swindling, fraud, embezzlement.

2 (n) There's been a robbery in town. burglary, break-in, smash-and-grab (informal), hold-up, raid, heist (slang), stick-up (slang), ram raid (informal).

**robot**
(n) android, automaton, machine.

**rock**
1 (n) Crispin sat on a rock. boulder, stone, crag, rocky outcrop.
2 (v) The waves made the boat rock. sway, roll, toss, pitch, lurch, wobble, swing.

**rocky**
(adj) We scrambled over the rocky ground. stony, boulder-strewn, pebbly, rough, hard, rugged, craggy, jagged, barren.

**rod**
(n) A wooden rod. stick, pole, switch, cane, birch, wand, baton, staff, crook, bar.

**roll**
1 (v) Look at the coin roll across the floor. trundle, travel, spin, wheel, twirl, whirl.
2 (v) Let's roll in the snow! tumble, somersault, go head over heels.
3 (v) The wheels roll smoothly. See **turn** 1.
4 (v) Roll your hair around your fingers. curl, coil, wind, wrap, twist, entwine, bind.
5 (v) Use a rolling pin to roll the dough. roll out, flatten, smooth, even out, level, spread out, press down.
6 (n) I need another roll of paper. spool, reel, cylinder, drum, scroll, tube, bobbin.

# Roman life

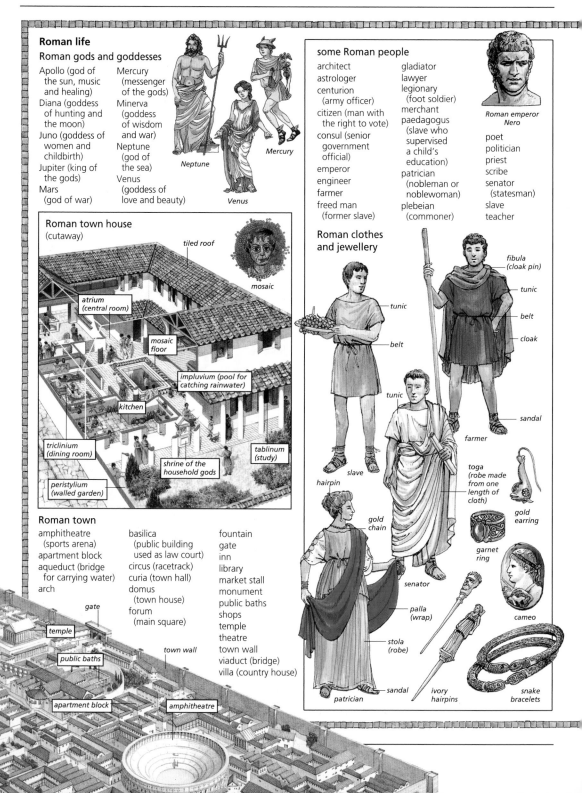

## Roman life

### Roman gods and goddesses

Apollo (god of the sun, music and healing)
Diana (goddess of hunting and the moon)
Juno (goddess of women and childbirth)
Jupiter (king of the gods)
Mars (god of war)
Mercury (messenger of the gods)
Minerva (goddess of wisdom and war)
Neptune (god of the sea)
Venus (goddess of love and beauty)

Mercury

Neptune

Venus

### some Roman people

architect
astrologer
centurion (army officer)
citizen (man with the right to vote)
consul (senior government official)
emperor
engineer
farmer
freed man (former slave)
gladiator
lawyer
legionary (foot soldier)
merchant
paedagogus (slave who supervised a child's education)
poet
politician
priest
scribe
senator (statesman)
slave
teacher
patrician (nobleman or noblewoman)
plebeian (commoner)

Roman emperor Nero

### Roman town house

(cutaway)

tiled roof

mosaic

atrium (central room)

mosaic floor

impluvium (pool for catching rainwater)

kitchen

triclinium (dining room)

tablinum (study)

shrine of the household gods

peristylium (walled garden)

### Roman town

amphitheatre (sports arena)
apartment block
aqueduct (bridge for carrying water)
arch
basilica (public building used as law court)
circus (racetrack)
curia (town hall)
domus (town house)
forum (main square)
fountain
gate
inn
library
market stall
monument
public baths
shops
temple
theatre
town wall
viaduct (bridge)
villa (country house)

gate

temple

public baths

town wall

apartment block

amphitheatre

### Roman clothes and jewellery

fibula (cloak pin)
tunic
belt
cloak
tunic
belt
tunic
sandal
farmer
slave
hairpin
toga (robe made from one length of cloth)
gold chain
gold earring
garnet ring
senator
palla (wrap)
cameo
stola (robe)
sandal
ivory hairpins
snake bracelets
patrician

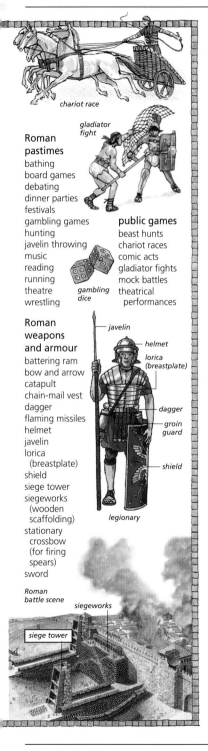

chariot race

gladiator fight

## Roman pastimes

bathing
board games
debating
dinner parties
festivals
gambling games
hunting
javelin throwing
music
reading
running
theatre
wrestling

### public games

beast hunts
chariot races
comic acts
gladiator fights
mock battles
theatrical performances

gambling dice

## Roman weapons and armour

battering ram
bow and arrow
catapult
chain-mail vest
dagger
flaming missiles
helmet
javelin
lorica
  (breastplate)
shield
siege tower
siegeworks
  (wooden
  scaffolding)
stationary
  crossbow
  (for firing
  spears)
sword

javelin

helmet

lorica (breastplate)

dagger

groin guard

shield

legionary

Roman battle scene

siegeworks

siege tower

## romantic

1 *(adj) Romantic films make me cry.* sentimental, lovey-dovey, emotional, heart-warming, soppy *(informal),* slushy *(informal),* schmaltzy, mushy *(informal).*
2 *(adj) Ed held Eve in a romantic embrace.* loving, tender, fond, amorous, passionate.
3 *(adj) Daisy is hopelessly romantic.* dreamy, starry-eyed, unrealistic, idealistic, optimistic, impractical.
OPPOSITES: down-to-earth, realistic.
4 *(adj) Paris is a romantic city.* colourful, fascinating, glamorous, exciting, exotic, charming, picturesque, idyllic, inspiring.
OPPOSITES: unromantic, banal.

## room

1 *(n) I need more room. See* **space** 2.
2 *(n) A secret room.* chamber.
TYPES OF ROOM: attic, ballroom, basement, bathroom, bedroom, boudoir *(old-fashioned),* breakfast room, cellar, cloakroom, conservatory, den, dining room, drawing room, dressing room, gallery, games room, guest room, hall, kitchen, landing, larder, lavatory, library, living room, loft, loo *(informal),* lounge, music room, nursery, office, pantry, parlour, playroom, scullery *(old-fashioned),* sitting room, spare room, store room, studio, study, toilet, utility room, WC (water closet). ❖ *Also see* **building**.

## rope

*(n) Pull the rope tight.* cord, cable, line, string, twine, guy rope, lasso.

## rot

1 *(v) These tomatoes will rot if we don't eat them soon.* go bad, go mouldy, spoil, deteriorate, go off *(informal),* decay, perish, decompose, fester, putrefy.
2 *(v) The wallpaper had started to rot.* fall apart, disintegrate, crumble, perish, decay.
3 *(v) Sweets can rot your teeth.* eat away, eat into, decay, erode, corrode *(metal).*

## rotten

1 *(adj) These tomatoes are rotten.* bad, mouldy, spoiled, off, sour *(milk),* putrid, festering, foul, fetid, decomposing.
OPPOSITE: fresh.
2 *(adj) Be careful! The floorboards are rotten.* decayed, decaying, crumbling, disintegrating, unsound, corroded *(metal).*
OPPOSITE: sound.
3 *(adj) (informal) I feel rotten.* ill, unwell, sick, off colour, ghastly, rough *(informal),* under the weather *(informal),* poorly *(informal),* grotty *(slang),* lousy *(slang).*
OPPOSITE: well.
4 *(adj) (informal) That was a rotten trick! See* **mean** 6.
5 *(adj) (informal) This is a rotten piece of homework. See* **poor** 2.

## rough

1 *(adj) The cave walls felt rough.* uneven, bumpy, irregular, jagged, craggy, pitted, ridged, lumpy, rugged, rocky, stony.
OPPOSITE: smooth.

2 *(adj) The sea is rough today.* choppy, stormy, turbulent, tempestuous, wild.
OPPOSITES: calm, smooth.
3 *(adj) Granddad's skin feels rough.* scratchy, bristly, unshaven, leathery, callused, chapped, wrinkled.
OPPOSITES: smooth, soft.
4 *(adj) My dog has a rough coat.* coarse, bristly, wiry, fuzzy, shaggy, tangled.
OPPOSITES: smooth, silky.
5 *(adj) Peg has a rough voice. See* **gruff** 1.
6 *(adj) Cynthia hates rough games.* rowdy, boisterous, violent, tough, unruly, wild.
OPPOSITES: gentle, quiet.
7 *(adj) Nat made a rough drawing.* basic, quick, sketchy, crude, clumsy, rough-and-ready, hasty, incomplete, unfinished.
OPPOSITES: detailed, precise.
8 *(adj) I only have a rough idea of what to do. See* **vague** 2.

## round

1 *(adj) I saw a round object in the sky.* circular, spherical, ball-shaped, balloon-like, curved, globular, bulbous, cylindrical.
2 *(adj) Augustus has a round face.* rounded, full, chubby, plump, podgy, fat, fleshy, moon-shaped, babyish.
3 *(n) I got to the last round of the contest.* stage, phase, level, heat, game, lap.

## routine

1 *(n) My normal routine was disrupted.* procedure, schedule, pattern, programme, system, practice, custom, habit.
2 *(adj) This is just a routine checkup.* normal, ordinary, standard, typical, regular, everyday, usual, customary, conventional.
OPPOSITES: unusual, special.

## row

1 *(v) I hate it when we row. See* **argue** 1.
2 *(n) Anita and Alice are having a row. See* **argument** 1.
3 *(n) What's that awful row? See* **noise** 2.
4 *(n) Look at that long row of cars.* line, queue, string, column, file, chain.
5 *(v) Let's row down the river.* paddle, scull, canoe, punt, boat.

## rowdy

*(adj) A rowdy class.* unruly, noisy, boisterous, loud, riotous, obstreperous, disorderly, rough, loutish, wild.
OPPOSITES: quiet, subdued.

## rub

1 *(v) Rub the lamp until it gleams.* polish, buff up, scrub, clean, shine, burnish, scour.
2 *(v) I knew the label would rub my neck.* chafe, irritate, scratch, scrape, graze.
3 *(v) Shall I rub suntan lotion on to your back?* smear, smooth, massage, spread, stroke, apply, work in.

## rubbish

1 *(n) Put the rubbish in the bin.* litter, waste, refuse, garbage, trash, junk *(informal),* scraps *(plural),* leftovers *(plural),* dregs *(plural),* debris.
2 *(n) Don't talk rubbish! See* **nonsense** 1.

**rub out** *see* **erase**.

# rude

**rude**
1 *(adj) That was a rude remark.* insolent, impertinent, cheeky, impudent, impolite, insulting, offensive, abusive, discourteous, disrespectful, inconsiderate, tactless.
OPPOSITES: polite, civil.
2 *(adj) Bozo told a rude joke.* dirty, smutty, crude, coarse, vulgar, filthy, indecent, obscene, blue, lewd, suggestive, risqué, naughty, saucy, tasteless, offensive.
OPPOSITES: clean, decent.

**rugged**
*(adj) A rugged coastline.* rocky, craggy, jagged, rough, stony, irregular, uneven.

**ruin**
1 *(v) This haircut could ruin my image.* wreck, destroy, shatter, spoil, damage, play havoc with, harm, mar, undermine, screw up *(informal)*, blow *(slang)*.
2 *(v) Earthquakes can ruin whole cities.* See **destroy** 1.
3 *(v) If your business fails, it could ruin you.* bankrupt, break, destroy, crush, make you a pauper, impoverish, bring you down.
4 *(n) This mistake could lead to ruin.* disaster, defeat, failure, collapse, breakdown, destruction, devastation, bankruptcy, insolvency, destitution.

**ruined**
*(adj) The ruined castle looked ghostly in the moonlight.* crumbling, derelict, dilapidated, ramshackle, tumbledown.

**ruins**
*(plural n) Rescuers searched the ruins.* rubble, wreckage, debris, remains *(plural)*.

**rule**
1 *(n) You must obey this rule.* regulation, ruling, guideline, directive, order, commandment, law, decree, statute.
2 *(v) Who will rule the country?* See **govern**.

**rumble**
1 *(v) I felt the ground rumble under my feet.* thunder, reverberate, boom, roar, murmur, groan, shake.
2 *(v) My tummy began to rumble.* gurgle, grumble, growl, murmur.

**rumour**
*(n) Have you heard the rumour about Famous Fred?* gossip, talk, word, news, story, buzz, hearsay, scandal, dirt *(slang)*.

**run**
1 *(v) You'll have to run to catch the bus.* race, sprint, jog, dash, hurry, rush, hotfoot it, leg it *(informal)*, get a move on *(informal)*, tear along, speed along, charge along, hare along *(informal)*, career along, scoot, scurry, scamper, gallop.
2 *(v) Does this car run on unleaded petrol?* go, work, function, operate, perform.
3 *(v) Water began to run down the walls.* trickle, dribble, drip, pour, flow, stream, cascade, course, spill, gush, spout.
4 *(v) These skis run smoothly over the snow.* glide, skim, slide, move, go.

5 *(v) I hope to run a music shop one day.* See **manage** 2.
6 *(v) I hope the colours don't run.* bleed, mix, spread, wash out.
7 *(n) Let's go for a run around the park.* jog, sprint, race, trot, gallop, marathon.

**run after** see **chase**.

**run away**
*(v) Run away or you'll get caught!* run off, take off *(informal)*, make a run for it, take to your heels, bolt, escape, flee, scram *(informal)*, scarper *(slang)*, beat it *(slang)*, do a runner *(slang)*, do a bunk *(slang)*.

**runny**
1 *(adj) This paint is too runny.* thin, watery, liquid, fluid, diluted, flowing.
OPPOSITES: thick, solid.
2 *(adj) I've got a runny nose.* streaming.

**run out**
1 *(v) When does your season ticket run out?* expire, lapse, finish, end, terminate.
2 *(v) Our supplies will soon run out.* be finished, be used up, dry up, be exhausted, give out, peter out.

**run over**
*(v) Watch out or that bus will run you over.* knock you down, run you down, knock you over, hit, bump into.

**rush**
1 *(v) We must rush or we'll be late.* See **hurry** 1.
2 *(v) You can't rush such an important decision.* See **hurry** 2.
3 *(n) It was a rush to get there on time.* race, scramble, struggle, mad dash.
4 *(n) Take your time; there's no rush.* hurry, urgency, pressure.

**rustle**
*(v) The wind made the leaves rustle.* swish, whisper, crackle, crinkle.

**ruthless**
*(adj) The king was ruthless in his revenge.* merciless, pitiless, heartless, remorseless, relentless, without pity, cruel, hardhearted, callous, unfeeling, unrelenting, implacable, inhuman, ferocious.
OPPOSITES: merciful, compassionate.

**sack** *(informal)* see **dismiss** 1.

**sad**
1 *(adj) Leah felt sad.* unhappy, miserable, depressed, down, blue, low, glum, gloomy, down in the dumps *(informal)*, dejected, melancholy, mournful, sorrowful, forlorn, wistful, despondent, upset, tearful, heartbroken, brokenhearted, grief-stricken, sick at heart, wretched, despairing.
OPPOSITES: happy, cheerful.

2 *(adj) This film has a sad ending.* unhappy, poignant, tear-jerking *(informal)*, heartbreaking, heart-rending, touching, moving, tragic, depressing, sombre, dark.
OPPOSITE: happy.
3 *(adj) I have some sad news for you.* bad, serious, grave, unfortunate, upsetting, painful, regrettable, distressing, tragic, heartbreaking, grim, harrowing.
OPPOSITES: happy, good.
4 *(adj) (slang) Dad made a sad attempt to be trendy.* See **pathetic** 2.

**sadden**
*(v) It will sadden you to hear this tragic news.* upset, grieve, distress, break your heart, pain, dismay, make you cry, bring tears to your eyes, make your heart bleed.
OPPOSITES: cheer, comfort.

**sadness** see **sorrow**.

**safe**
1 *(adj) All the explorers are safe.* unharmed, unhurt, uninjured, unscathed, safe and sound, alive and well, in one piece *(informal)*, out of danger, all right.
OPPOSITES: hurt, injured.
2 *(adj) The villagers were safe inside the castle.* secure, protected, out of harm's way, sheltered, defended, shielded, guarded, invulnerable, unassailable, out of danger, free from harm.
OPPOSITES: in danger, at risk.
3 *(adj) Mum is a safe driver.* careful, prudent, sensible, responsible, reliable, dependable, cautious, unadventurous.
OPPOSITES: dangerous, reckless.
4 *(adj) This snake is quite safe.* harmless, docile, tame, nonpoisonous, innocuous.
OPPOSITE: dangerous.
5 *(adj) Is the tap water safe?* pure, uncontaminated, unpolluted, drinkable, nontoxic, wholesome, edible *(food)*.
OPPOSITES: unsafe, harmful.
6 *(n) Put your valuables in the safe.* safe-deposit box, cash box, deposit box, strongbox, coffer, strongroom, vault.

**sag**
*(v) My bed is starting to sag in the middle.* sink, slump, droop, dip, cave in, give way, subside, hang down, drop, fall.

**sail**
1 *(v) Pirate Peg is ready to sail.* set sail, put to sea, leave port, weigh anchor, hoist sail, get under way, embark.
2 *(v) Did you sail to France?* go by boat, cruise, go by sea, steam, ride the waves, voyage.
3 *(v) Watch the balloon sail through the air.* See **glide** 1.

**same**
1 *(adj) That's the same tune I heard before.* selfsame, very same, very, identical.
OPPOSITE: different.
2 **the same** *(adj) Our hats are the same.* identical, alike, matching, like peas in a pod *(informal)*, indistinguishable.
OPPOSITES: different, dissimilar.

**3 the same** *(adj) These two experiments should give the same results.* identical, matching, corresponding, equivalent, parallel, comparable, similar.
OPPOSITES: different, dissimilar.
**4 the same** *(adj) At the North Pole, the weather is always the same.* unchanging, unvarying, consistent, constant, uniform.
OPPOSITES: variable, changeable.

**sarcastic**
*(adj) Sarcastic comments.* cutting, scathing, caustic, biting, withering, acerbic, sharp-tongued, disparaging, contemptuous, scornful, mocking, sneering, taunting, jeering, sarky *(informal)*, ironic, sardonic.

**satisfactory** *see* **all right** 3.

**satisfied**
1 *(adj) After his enormous tea, Augustus felt satisfied. See* **full** 3.
2 *(adj) Once she's won the prize, Lucy will feel satisfied.* content, contented, pleased, gratified, happy, glad, at ease, self-satisfied, complacent, smug, like the cat that swallowed the cream *(informal)*.
OPPOSITES: dissatisfied, discontented.

**savage**
1 *(adj) Savage animals.* wild, ferocious, fierce, vicious, untamed, undomesticated.
OPPOSITES: tame, gentle.
2 *(adj) A savage attack.* brutal, vicious, ferocious, violent, bloody, bloodthirsty, barbaric, murderous, sadistic, cruel, callous, cold-blooded, merciless, pitiless, ruthless, inhuman, diabolical, bestial.

**save**
1 *(v) Don't panic; I'm coming to save you! See* **rescue** 1.
2 *(v) Try to save your money.* hold on to, hang on to, be sparing with, be thrifty with, be frugal with, economize, set aside, put aside, put away, stash away *(informal)*, keep for a rainy day, hoard, accumulate, amass, bank, deposit, invest.
OPPOSITES: squander, waste.
3 *(v) Let's campaign to save the whales.* protect, preserve, conserve, safeguard, defend, guard, keep safe, look after.
OPPOSITES: endanger, imperil.

**say**
1 *(v) Sam couldn't say what was bothering her.* put into words, articulate, express, communicate, give voice to, convey, put across, mention, tell, relate, reveal, disclose, divulge, come out with.
2 *(v) Say your lines out loud.* recite, repeat, speak, deliver, perform, rehearse, declaim, read.
3 *(v) What does the recipe say?* specify, state, suggest, indicate.
4 *(v) I would say it's about four o'clock. See* **think** 2.
5 *(v) People say Dodgy Dave is a crook.* claim, allege, suggest, put about, report.
6 *(n) Do I have any say in this decision?* input, voice, share, part, vote, influence, clout, sway, weight.

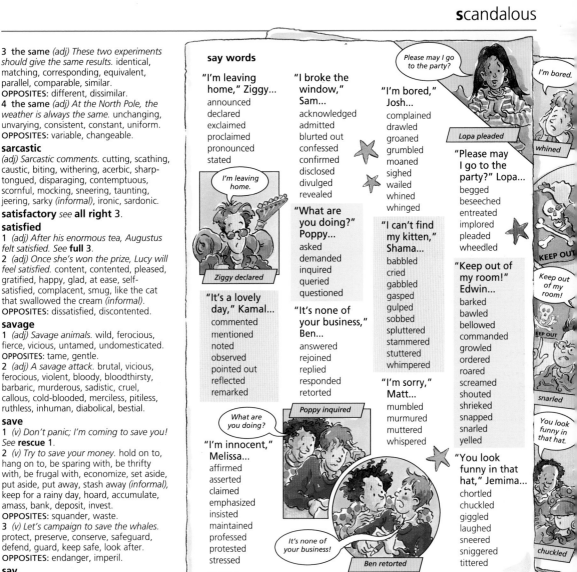

**say words**

**"I'm leaving home,"** Ziggy...
announced
declared
exclaimed
proclaimed
pronounced
stated

*I'm leaving home.*

*Ziggy declared*

**"It's a lovely day,"** Kamal...
commented
mentioned
noted
observed
pointed out
reflected
remarked

*What are you doing?*

**"I'm innocent,"** Melissa...
affirmed
asserted
claimed
emphasized
insisted
maintained
professed
protested
stressed

*It's none of your business!*

**"I broke the window,"** Sam...
acknowledged
admitted
blurted out
confessed
confirmed
disclosed
divulged
revealed

**"What are you doing?"** Poppy...
asked
demanded
inquired
queried
questioned

**"It's none of your business,"** Ben...
answered
rejoined
replied
responded
retorted

*Poppy inquired*

*Ben retorted*

**"I'm bored,"** Josh...
complained
drawled
groaned
grumbled
moaned
sighed
wailed
whined
whinged

**"I can't find my kitten,"** Shama...
babbled
cried
gabbled
gasped
gulped
sobbed
spluttered
stammered
stuttered
whimpered

**"I'm sorry,"** Matt...
mumbled
murmured
muttered
whispered

*Please may I go to the party?*

*Lopa pleaded*

**"Please may I go to the party?"** Lopa...
begged
beseeched
entreated
implored
pleaded
wheedled

**"Keep out of my room!"** Edwin...
barked
bawled
bellowed
commanded
growled
ordered
roared
screamed
shouted
shrieked
snapped
snarled
yelled

**"You look funny in that hat,"** Jemima...
chortled
chuckled
giggled
laughed
sneered
sniggered
tittered

*I'm bored.*

*whined*

*KEEP OUT*

*Keep out of my room!*

*EEP OUT*

*snarled*

*You look funny in that hat.*

*chuckled*

---

**scalding** *see* **hot** 2.

**scamper**
1 *(v) Watch the mouse scamper across the floor.* scurry, scuttle, scoot, scramble, dart, dash, run, sprint, race, beetle *(informal)*.
2 **scamper about** *(v) My rabbit loves to scamper about in the grass.* run about, romp, frisk, frolic, gambol, cavort.

**scan**
1 *(v) Scan the front page. See* **look at** 2.
2 *(v) Beryl stopped to scan the street for police.* survey, search, scrutinize, scour, inspect, take stock of, check out *(informal)*, recce *(informal)*, look up and down.

**scandal**
1 *(n) Don't believe the scandal you read in the papers.* gossip, rumours *(plural)*, dirt *(slang)*, tittle-tattle, libel *(written)*, slander *(spoken)*, muckraking, smear campaign.
2 *(n) It's a scandal that so many people are homeless.* disgrace, outrage, crime, sin, shame, crying shame.

**scandalous**
1 *(adj) Dodgy Dave's behaviour is scandalous. See* **disgraceful** 1.
2 *(adj) Who started that scandalous rumour?* slanderous *(spoken)*, libellous *(written)*, scurrilous, malicious, untrue.

## scarce

(adj) Bananas were scarce during the war. in short supply, few and far between, seldom seen, hard to find, thin on the ground, rare, uncommon.
OPPOSITES: plentiful, common.

## scarcely see hardly.

## scare

1 (v) This film will scare you. frighten, scare you out of your wits, scare you stiff, terrify, horrify, petrify, make your hair stand on end, send shivers down your spine, make your blood run cold, make your flesh creep, unnerve, alarm, startle.
2 (v) Don't let Bozo scare you. intimidate, frighten, terrorize, bully, threaten, menace, put the wind up (informal), cow, daunt.
3 (n) The news gave me a real scare. fright, shock, panic, start, jolt.
4 (n) The shops are closed because of a bomb scare. alert, alarm, hoax.

## scared

1 (adj) Weren't you scared when the lights went out? afraid, frightened, terrified, petrified, scared stiff, scared out of your wits, panic-stricken, terror-stricken, panicky, apprehensive, alarmed, anxious, fearful, startled, horrified, horrorstruck.
2 be scared of (phrase) There's no need to be scared of spiders. be afraid of, be frightened of, fear, have a phobia about, have a horror of, dread, shudder at, tremble at, live in fear of, shake in your shoes, be in a blue funk (informal).

## scarred

(adj) A scarred face. disfigured, blemished, marked, pockmarked, pitted.

## scary (informal) see frightening.

## scatter

1 (v) Don't scatter your magazines over the floor. strew, spread, throw, fling, toss, drop, shower, sprinkle, distribute.
2 (v) The crowd began to scatter. break up, disperse, disband, separate, dissolve.

## scatterbrained

(adj) Don't rely on Kylie; she's much too scatterbrained! absent-minded, forgetful, muddleheaded, disorganized, vague, scatty (informal), featherbrained, bird-brained (informal), empty-headed, giddy, dizzy, flighty, unreliable, not with it (informal).

## scene

1 (n) We admired the scene. See view 1.
2 (n) Let's investigate the scene of the crime. site, location, setting, place, area, spot, position, whereabouts, locality, locale, neighbourhood, region.
3 (n) In this scene the hero dies. act, episode, sequence, shot, clip, take.
4 (n) The curtain rose on a stunning scene. set, stage, setting, tableau, backdrop.

## scenery

1 (n) Isn't the scenery beautiful! landscape, countryside, surroundings (plural), terrain, view, vista, panorama.

2 (n) Natalie designed the scenery for our school play. set, stage set, staging, setting, backdrop, backcloth, décor.

## scent

1 (n) Don't these roses have a wonderful scent! perfume, fragrance, smell, bouquet, aroma (food, drink).
2 (n) Do you like my new scent? perfume, fragrance, eau de Cologne, cologne, body spray, toilet water, aftershave.

## schedule

(n) Try to keep to the schedule. plan, programme, timetable, agenda, itinerary.

## scheme

1 (n) The government announced a scheme to cut crime. See plan 1.
2 (n) Dodgy Dave has a new scheme to make money. plan, idea, stratagem, ploy, plot, ruse, intrigue, dodge, manoeuvre, subterfuge, conspiracy, racket (informal).
3 (v) Let's scheme to get our revenge. See plot 3.

## school

(n) college, academy.
TYPES OF SCHOOL: boarding school, co-ed (coeducational school), comprehensive school, day school, grammar school, grant-maintained school, high school, independent school, infant school, junior school, kindergarten, middle school, mixed school, nursery school, prep school (preparatory school), primary school, private school, public school, secondary school, selective school, single-sex school, sixth-form college, state school, technology college.

## scold see tell off.

## scorch

(v) Don't scorch the paintwork! burn, singe, char, blacken, blister, sear, roast.

## scorching see hot 1.

## score

1 (n) What was the score at half-time? tally, result, number of points, total, mark.
2 (v) We need to score ten points. win, earn, gain, achieve, make, total, chalk up (informal), notch up (informal), amass.
3 (v) Don't score your name in the desk! See cut 5.

## scorn

1 (v) Don't scorn my efforts at sewing. sneer at, scoff at, jeer at, look down on, despise, be contemptuous of, turn up your nose at (informal), mock, deride.
OPPOSITES: admire, respect.
2 (n) Hilda viewed my painting with scorn. contempt, derision, disdain, disgust, mockery, ridicule, sarcasm.
OPPOSITES: admiration, respect.

## scornful

(adj) Maddy gave her brother a scornful look. disdainful, contemptuous, scathing, withering, condescending, supercilious, sneering, derisive, sarcastic, mocking.
OPPOSITES: admiring, respectful.

## scowl

(v) Mum will scowl at you if you snigger. frown, grimace, glower, glare, look daggers, give you a dirty look.

## scramble

1 (v) Can you scramble up this cliff? clamber, scrabble, climb, crawl, struggle, swarm, scale, scurry.
2 (v) Watch the fans scramble for a seat. jostle, scrabble, fight, scuffle, struggle, jockey, battle, vie, rush, dash, scurry.

## scrap

1 (n) Pick up that last scrap. piece, bit, fragment, crumb, morsel, speck, grain, snippet, sliver, remnant, mouthful, drop.
2 (n) (informal) The boys had a scrap in the playground. See fight 6.
3 (v) Don't scrap that paper! See throw away 1.
4 (v) Let's scrap the match. See cancel.

## scrape

1 (v) How did you scrape your knee? graze, scratch, skin, scuff.
2 (v) Scrape the food off the floor. scoop, shovel, scrub, scour, clean.
3 (v) Can you hear my fingernails scrape against the blackboard? grate, scratch, rasp, squeak, grind, screech.

## scraps

(plural n) Leave the scraps for the birds. leftovers (plural), remains (plural), leavings (plural), pickings (plural), scrapings (plural), crumbs (plural), remnants (plural).

## scratch

1 (v) Don't scratch the table. score, mark, scrape, cut, gouge, claw at, damage.
2 (n) I have a scratch on my leg. cut, graze, scrape, gash, nick, abrasion, mark.

## scrawl see scribble 1, 2.

## scrawny see thin 1.

## scream

(v) I'll scream if you put that spider down my neck. shriek, screech, squeal, squawk, cry out, yell, howl, yelp, yowl, wail, holler (informal), bawl, bellow, shout.

## scribble

1 (v) I just had time to scribble a message. scrawl, dash off, jot down, write, pen.
2 (v) Don't scribble on the walls! doodle, scrawl, write, draw, write graffiti.

## scrounge

(v) (informal) Let's scrounge some money off Dad. cadge, sponge, beg for, wheedle.

## scrub

(v) We'll have to scrub the floor to get the dirt off. scour, wash, clean, rub, swab.

## scruffy

1 (adj) Barney always looks scruffy. dishevelled, unkempt, untidy, messy, down-at-heel, bedraggled, shabby.
OPPOSITES: smart, neat.
2 (adj) I like wearing scruffy jeans. tatty, shabby, worn, tattered, ragged, holey, sloppy, grungy (slang).
OPPOSITE: smart.

3 *(adj) Ziggy lives in a scruffy part of town.*
shabby, tatty, run-down, dilapidated,
seedy, disreputable, squalid, dirty, dingy,
grotty *(slang)*, rough.
OPPOSITE: smart.

**scrumptious** *(informal) see* **delicious**.

**scuffle** *see* **fight** 2, 6.

**sea**

1 *(n) Pirate Peg sailed across the sea.*
ocean, waves *(plural)*, high seas *(plural)*,
briny *(informal)*, deep, drink *(informal)*.
2 *(adj) An octopus is a sea creature.*
saltwater, aquatic, marine.

**seal**

1 *(v) Seal the bottle.* stop up, plug, cork,
make airtight, make waterproof, bung.
2 *(v) The police decided to seal the room.*
close up, shut up, lock, secure, seal off,
close off, board up, wall up, cordon off.

**search**

1 *(v) Rescuers had to search the wreckage.*
hunt through, look through, comb, scour,
sift through, rummage through, rifle
through, examine, scrutinize, investigate,
go over with a fine-tooth comb, turn
upside down, turn inside out, ransack.

2 *(v) The police began to search for clues.*
look, hunt, poke about, nose about, ferret
around, scout around, cast around, look
high and low, seek, probe, pry, leave no
stone unturned.
3 *(n) Hundreds of people joined in the
search.* hunt, pursuit, quest, investigation,
inquiry, exploration, chase.

**seaside**

*(n) We spent our holiday at the seaside.*
beach, coast, shore, seashore, sands
*(plural)*, seaside resort, coastal resort.
❖ *Also see* **seaside words**.

---

## sea and seashore

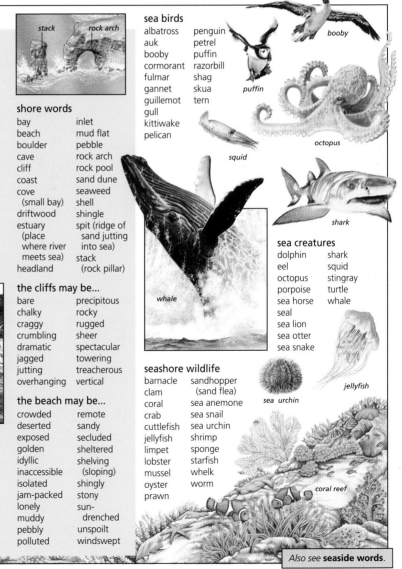

stack    rock arch

### sea words

| | |
|---|---|
| breaker | spume (foam) |
| crest (top | surf |
| of wave) | swell |
| current | tidal wave |
| high tide | white horses |
| low tide | (waves with |
| spray | white crests) |

### the sea may be...

| | |
|---|---|
| aquamarine | rough |
| billowing | sapphire blue |
| calm | shimmering |
| choppy | silvery |
| crystal clear | sparkling |
| emerald | stormy |
| green | tempestuous |
| glassy | tranquil |
| grey | turbulent |
| heaving | turquoise |
| raging | wild |

*raging sea*

### the waves may...

| | | |
|---|---|---|
| billow | plash | spill |
| break | plunge | splash |
| churn | pound | surge |
| crash | race | swirl |
| curl | ripple | swish |
| foam | roar | thunder |
| froth | roll | tumble |
| lap | rush | wash |

### shore words

| | |
|---|---|
| bay | inlet |
| beach | mud flat |
| boulder | pebble |
| cave | rock arch |
| cliff | rock pool |
| coast | sand dune |
| cove | seaweed |
| (small bay) | shell |
| driftwood | shingle |
| estuary | spit (ridge of |
| (place | sand jutting |
| where river | into sea) |
| meets sea) | stack |
| headland | (rock pillar) |

### the cliffs may be...

| | |
|---|---|
| bare | precipitous |
| chalky | rocky |
| craggy | rugged |
| crumbling | sheer |
| dramatic | spectacular |
| jagged | towering |
| jutting | treacherous |
| overhanging | vertical |

### the beach may be...

| | |
|---|---|
| crowded | remote |
| deserted | sandy |
| exposed | secluded |
| golden | sheltered |
| idyllic | shelving |
| inaccessible | (sloping) |
| isolated | shingly |
| jam-packed | stony |
| lonely | sun- |
| muddy | drenched |
| pebbly | unspoilt |
| polluted | windswept |

## sea birds

| | |
|---|---|
| albatross | penguin |
| auk | petrel |
| booby | puffin |
| cormorant | razorbill |
| fulmar | shag |
| gannet | skua |
| guillemot | tern |
| gull | |
| kittiwake | |
| pelican | |

booby

puffin

squid

octopus

whale

shark

### sea creatures

| | |
|---|---|
| dolphin | shark |
| eel | squid |
| octopus | stingray |
| porpoise | turtle |
| sea horse | whale |
| seal | |
| sea lion | |
| sea otter | |
| sea snake | |

## seashore wildlife

| | |
|---|---|
| barnacle | sandhopper |
| clam | (sand flea) |
| coral | sea anemone |
| crab | sea snail |
| cuttlefish | sea urchin |
| jellyfish | shrimp |
| limpet | sponge |
| lobster | starfish |
| mussel | whelk |
| oyster | worm |
| prawn | |

sea urchin

jellyfish

coral reef

*Also see* **seaside words**.

# seaside

*Pick up*

## seaside words

### at a seaside resort
amusement arcade
aquarium
boating lake
campsite
caravan park
disco
fairy lights
funfair
guesthouse
harbour
hotel
ice-cream kiosk
jetty
marina
nightclub
pier
promenade
souvenir shop

### on the beach
beach ball
beach café
beach hut
breakwater
bucket and spade
deckchair
parasol
Punch and Judy show
sandcastle
sun-lounger
volleyball net
windbreak

### seaside food
candyfloss
fish and chips
ice cream
ice lolly *(informal)*
seafood
seaside rock
shellfish

*mask*
*snorkel*

### a resort may be...
bustling
busy
buzzing
crowded
elegant
fashionable
jumping *(slang)*
lively
noisy
packed
peaceful
picturesque
quiet
shabby
sleepy
smart
tacky *(informal)*
tatty
touristy *(informal)*
up-market

### seaside activities
beachcombing
boat trips
collecting shells
donkey rides
exploring caves
fishing trips
jet skiing
paddling
parasailing
sailing
sandsailing
scuba diving
shrimping
snorkelling
sunbathing
surfing
swimming
volleyball
water-skiing
windsurfing

*candy floss*

Also see **sea & seashore**.

---

**seat**
(n) *Find yourself a seat.* chair, stool, bench, place. *Also see* **chair**, **sofa**.

**second**
1 (adj) *I asked for a second helping of pudding.* extra, additional, further, other.
2 (n) *The butterfly was gone in a second.* See **moment** 1.

**secret**
1 (adj) *This information must remain secret.* hidden, concealed, under wraps, unpublished, undisclosed, private, confidential, restricted, classified, off the record, hush-hush *(informal)*.
OPPOSITES: public, well-known.
2 (adj) *Agent Arthur was sent on a secret mission.* undercover, covert, cloak-and-dagger, underground, clandestine, hush-hush *(informal)*, furtive, surreptitious.
OPPOSITES: open, well-known.
3 (adj) *The treasure chamber had a secret entrance.* concealed, hidden, camouflaged, disguised, invisible.
OPPOSITES: obvious, visible.
4 (adj) *Can you read this secret message?* cryptic, encoded, mysterious, hidden.
OPPOSITE: straightforward.
5 (n) *Don't tell Mum - it's a secret!* private matter, confidential matter, confidence.
6 (n) *What is the secret of eternal youth?* formula, recipe, key, solution, answer.

**section**
1 (n) *Have a section of my pear.* See **bit** 2.
2 (n) *What section of the company do you work in?* See **part** 3.
3 (n) *Read the next section for homework.* bit, part, passage, paragraph, chapter, unit, module, page, instalment.

**secure**
1 (adj) *I feel secure at my new school.* safe, confident, at ease, unworried, relaxed, comfortable, reassured.
OPPOSITES: insecure, uneasy.
2 (adj) *Is that ladder secure?* firm, steady, stable, fixed, immovable, safe, strong.
OPPOSITES: unsafe, precarious.
3 (adj) *Make sure the windows are secure.* fastened, locked, shut, closed, barred.
4 (adj) *The villagers were secure inside the castle.* See **safe** 2.
5 (v) *Secure your bike to the railings.* See **fasten** 1.

**see**
1 (v) *Did you see the comet?* catch sight of, catch a glimpse of, spot, notice, glimpse, make out, identify, observe, sight, note, spy, witness, clap eyes on *(informal)*.
2 (v) *It was hard to see what Alice meant.* understand, grasp, follow, take in, make out, know, make sense of, comprehend, get the drift of, get the hang of *(informal)*, catch on to *(informal)*, get, twig *(informal)*.

3 (v) *Mrs Badger wants to see my parents.* talk to, speak to, meet, consult, confer with, interview, visit.
4 (v) *Can you see when the film starts?* find out, have a look, ask, discover, ascertain, determine, investigate.
5 (v) *See that Tommy doesn't hurt himself.* make sure, mind, see to it, take care, make certain, ensure.
6 (v) *"Can I go to the disco?" "I'll see."* think about it, give it some thought, think it over, consider it, mull it over.
7 (v) *I'll see you to your car.* show, walk, accompany, escort, lead, usher.
8 (v) *I can't quite see you as a film star.* picture, imagine, visualize, envisage.
9 (v) *I see problems ahead.* foresee, envisage, anticipate, predict, foretell.

**seem**
(v) *Do I seem sad?* appear, look, strike you as, give the impression of being, sound.

**see-through** see **transparent**.

**see to**
(v) *Can you see to the baby?* attend to, check up on, look after, take care of, be responsible for, manage, take charge of.

**seize**
1 (v) *I felt someone seize me by the arm.* See **grab** 1.
2 (v) *Customs officials were quick to seize the drugs.* See **confiscate**.

**seldom** see **rarely**.

**select** see **choose** 1.

**selection**
1 (n) *This shop stocks a wide selection of CDs.* See **choice** 2.
2 (n) *This book contains a selection of poems.* collection, anthology, miscellany, choice, variety, range, medley, potpourri.

**self-centred** see **selfish**.

**self-confident** see **confident** 1.

**self-conscious**
(adj) *Zoë feels self-conscious when she has to sing in public.* awkward, embarrassed, uncomfortable, ill at ease, shy, diffident, nervous, insecure, bashful, mortified.

**self-control**
(n) *It took great self-control not to shout at my brother.* self-discipline, self-restraint, restraint, willpower, strength of mind, patience, composure, coolness, calmness.

**selfish**
(adj) *Nev is so selfish; he never thinks of others.* self-centred, egocentric, egotistical, self-absorbed, demanding, greedy, mean.
OPPOSITES: unselfish, generous.

**self-satisfied** see **smug**.

**sell**
1 (v) *We're planning to sell our house.* put up for sale, put on the market, auction off.
OPPOSITE: buy.
2 (v) *Dodgy Dave is trying to sell stolen goods.* sell off, dispose of, peddle, hawk, tout, exchange, deal in, traffic in, handle.

3 *(v) Does this shop sell balloons?* stock, keep *(informal)*, supply, carry, trade in, deal in, offer for sale, retail.
4 *(v) Famous Fred is keen to sell his new single. See* **promote** 2.

**send**
1 *(v) Don't forget to send your card to Granny. See* **post** 4.
2 *(v) Can you send this message for me?* convey, relay, forward, transmit, dispatch, radio, fax, e-mail, broadcast.
3 *(v) Will your parents send you to boarding school?* pack you off, ship you off, farm you out, dispatch, consign.

**send for** *see* **summon**.

**sensational**
1 *(adj) A sensational newspaper article.* dramatic, melodramatic, lurid, shocking, scandalous, electrifying, startling, staggering, spectacular, astounding, horrifying, alarmist, shock-horror.
2 *(adj) (informal) A sensational party. See* **fantastic** 3.

**sense**
1 *(n) I had a sense that something was wrong.* feeling, impression, hunch, sensation, awareness, instinct, intuition, premonition, presentiment.
2 *(n) I can't work out the sense of this poem. See* **meaning** 2.
3 *(n) Adrian has no sense.* common sense, brains *(plural) (informal)*, wit, judgment, understanding, intelligence, nous *(slang)*.
4 *(v) Didn't you sense that Mrs Badger was annoyed?* feel, get the impression, get the feeling, have a hunch, suspect, notice, pick up, perceive, observe, realize.

**sensible**
1 *(adj) A sensible girl.* level-headed, down-to-earth, practical, matter-of-fact, serious-minded, thoughtful, mature, steady.
OPPOSITES: silly, foolish.
2 *(adj) A sensible choice.* wise, prudent, intelligent, logical, rational, reasonable, sound, realistic, shrewd, well-thought-out.
OPPOSITES: foolish, stupid.
3 *(adj) Sensible shoes.* practical, comfortable, functional, suitable, hard-wearing, serviceable.
OPPOSITES: impractical, unsuitable.

**sensitive**
1 *(adj) Don't tease Mary; she's very sensitive.* thin-skinned, touchy, easily upset, oversensitive, hypersensitive.
OPPOSITES: thick-skinned, tough.
2 *(adj) My skin is sensitive.* easily irritated, delicate, soft, tender, painful, sore, raw.
OPPOSITE: tough.
3 *(adj) Karen will notice if you're unhappy; she's very sensitive.* perceptive, discerning, receptive, responsive, impressionable.
OPPOSITES: obtuse, insensitive.
4 *(adj) Try to deal with this situation in a sensitive way.* discreet, diplomatic, tactful, sympathetic, thoughtful, understanding.
OPPOSITES: insensitive, heavy-handed.

5 *(adj) This is a sensitive issue.* delicate, difficult, awkward, controversial, contentious, problematic, thorny, ticklish.

**sentimental**
1 *(adj) Old love songs make Granny feel sentimental.* emotional, nostalgic, tearful, weepy *(informal)*, dewy-eyed, maudlin, softhearted, tenderhearted, warm.
2 *(adj) I hate sentimental poetry.* romantic, lovey-dovey, mawkish, soppy *(informal)*, slushy *(informal)*, corny *(slang)*, mushy *(informal)*, schmaltzy, sugary, syrupy, weepy *(informal)*, tear-jerking *(informal)*.

**separate**
1 *(v) The police tried to separate the fighting fans.* split up, break up, part, disentangle, divide, come between, keep apart, segregate, isolate, scatter, disperse.
2 *(v) Be careful! The pieces could separate in your hands.* come apart, fall apart, break apart, come away, detach, split, divide, disconnect, disintegrate, scatter.
3 *(v) I'm sorry that you and Jason have decided to separate.* split up, break up, part, part company, go your separate ways, live apart, divorce.
4 *(v) At the big tree, the two paths separate. See* **divide** 1.
5 *(adj) The two schools are quite separate.* unconnected, unrelated, distinct, different, independent, autonomous, detached.

**series**
*(n) A series of disasters.* sequence, string, chain, run, row, succession, train, procession, progression, set, cycle.

**serious**
1 *(adj) Edwin is a serious boy.* solemn, earnest, sober, grave, pensive, thoughtful, sedate, staid, humourless, sombre.
OPPOSITES: frivolous, cheerful.
2 *(adj) We had a serious discussion.* earnest, grave, weighty, heavy, deep, profound, sincere, important, significant.
OPPOSITES: frivolous, trivial.
3 *(adj) Pollution is a serious problem.* grave, major, urgent, pressing, acute, critical, far-reaching, worrying, alarming.
OPPOSITES: minor, insignificant.
4 *(adj) Aunt Bertha has a serious illness.* major, severe, grave, critical, dangerous, acute, incapacitating, crippling, incurable, inoperable, fatal, terminal, malignant.
OPPOSITES: mild, minor.
5 *(adj) A serious accident occurred.* major, catastrophic, calamitous, tragic, fatal.
OPPOSITE: minor.
6 *(adj) You must be serious if you want to learn ballet.* committed, determined, in earnest, sincere, resolved, resolute, dedicated, single-minded, unwavering, conscientious, hard-working, diligent.
OPPOSITES: half-hearted, casual.

**servant**
*(n)* attendant, helper, assistant, help, hired help, retainer, hireling, domestic, dogsbody *(informal)*, skivvy, drudge, slave.

**serve**
1 *(v) The genie will serve the owner of the lamp.* work for, obey, assist, help, be of use to, wait on, attend to, minister to.
2 *(v) Shall I serve tea?* put out, set out, dish up, give out, hand round, pass round.
3 *(v) Do you serve refreshments?* supply, provide, offer, sell, lay on.

**service**
*(n) We all joined in the service.* ceremony, act of worship, worship, prayers *(plural)*, celebration, assembly, meeting.

**serving** *see* **helping**.

**set**
1 *(v) Set the dish on the table. See* **put** 1.
2 *(v) Let's set a date. See* **fix** 2.
3 *(v) Please set the table for tea.* lay, spread, prepare, arrange, make ready.
OPPOSITE: clear.
4 *(v) Wait for the jelly to set.* jell, harden, solidify, thicken, stiffen, take shape, congeal, crystallize, cake, coagulate.
5 *(v) The sun began to set.* go down, sink, drop below the horizon, disappear, vanish.
OPPOSITE: rise.
6 *(v) Can you set the video timer?* adjust, regulate, fix, programme, synchronize.
7 *(adj) We have our meals at set times.* fixed, established, agreed, definite, appointed, arranged, scheduled, regular.
OPPOSITES: flexible, varying.
8 *(adj) Aunt Bertha has set views.* fixed, definite, hard and fast, inflexible, unbending, firm, strict, entrenched, deep-seated, hidebound, narrow-minded.
OPPOSITES: flexible, open-minded.
9 *(adj) The story is set in India.* located, supposed to take place, situated, placed.
10 *(n) I'm collecting the whole set.* series, range, collection, group, batch, class, kit.
11 *(n) Tanya designed the set for our play. See* **scenery** 2.
12 *(n) Which set are you in for English? See* **class**.

**setback**
*(n) Don't let this setback discourage you.* hitch, difficulty, problem, snag, hiccup *(informal)*, complication, obstacle, disappointment, misfortune, blow, relapse.

**set fire to** *see* **light** 1.

**set free** *see* **release** 1.

**set off**
1 *(v) It's time to set off. See* **leave** 1.
2 *(v) Don't set off the fireworks.* let off, detonate, light, ignite, trigger off, explode.

**set out**
1 *(v) It's time to set out. See* **leave** 1.
2 *(v) Set out your work neatly.* lay out, present, arrange, organize, display, exhibit.
3 *(v) I didn't set out to cheat. See* **mean** 3.

**setting**
*(n) Paris is the ideal setting for a romantic weekend.* place, location, situation, venue, backdrop, scene, background, environment, surroundings *(plural)*.

# settle

**settle**
1 *(v) Do you plan to settle in Australia?* stay, set up home, make your home, put down roots, take up residence, become established, move to, emigrate to, live.
2 *(v) The moth may settle on your hand.* come to rest, stop, rest, stay, land, alight.
3 *(v) We need to settle this dispute.* sort out, resolve, clear up, put an end to, end, patch up, decide, deal with.
4 *(v) Wait for the dust to settle.* die down, subside, sink, clear.
5 **settle on** *(v) Let's settle on a date. See* **agree** 2.

**settle down**
1 *(v) Settle down and get on with your work.* calm down, quieten down, be quiet.
2 *(v) Settle down and enjoy the film.* sit down, relax, make yourself comfortable, snuggle down, curl up.

**set up** *see* **start** 5.

**severe**
1 *(adj) Aunt Bertha always looks so severe. See* **stern** 1.
2 *(adj) Jamie is recovering from a severe illness. See* **serious** 4.
3 *(adj) We should expect severe weather conditions.* bad, extreme, harsh, rough, violent, fierce, drastic, dangerous, freezing.
OPPOSITES: mild, moderate.

**sew**
1 *(v) Can you teach me how to sew?* stitch, tack, embroider, do needlework, make clothes, do dressmaking.
2 **sew up** *(v) I need to sew up this hole in my shirt. See* **mend** 2.

**sex**
1 *(n) What sex is your kitten?* gender.
2 *(n) Should children be taught about sex at school?* the facts of life *(plural)*, sexual intercourse, sexuality, reproduction.
3 **have sex** *see* **make love**.

**sexy**
1 *(adj) (informal) Sam is really sexy.* desirable, sexually attractive, seductive, sultry, sensuous, voluptuous *(female)*, shapely, kissable, fit *(slang)*.
2 *(adj) (informal) Mum thinks my dress is too sexy.* slinky, seductive, titillating, provocative, revealing.
3 *(adj) (informal) This song has very sexy lyrics.* suggestive, raunchy *(slang)*, erotic, risqué, pornographic, obscene.

**shabby**
1 *(adj) Your jeans are looking shabby.* worn, faded, threadbare, tatty, scruffy, worn-out, frayed, ragged, tattered.
OPPOSITES: smart, new.
2 *(adj) Ziggy lives in a shabby part of town. See* **scruffy** 3.

**shade**
1 *(n) Those trees will provide some shade.* shadow, shelter, protection, coolness.
2 *(n) That shade of green suits you.* colour, tone, hue, tint, tinge.

**shadow**
1 *(n) Emma sat in the shadow of a tree. See* **shade** 1.
2 *(n) I saw a shadow on the wall.* shape, silhouette, outline, figure, image.
3 **shadows** *(plural n) I saw a figure lurking in the shadows.* dark, darkness, gloom, dimness, blackness, dusk, semi-darkness.
4 *(v) The detectives decided to shadow Burglar Beryl. See* **follow** 1.

**shadowy** *see* **dim** 2.

**shady**
1 *(adj) We walked through a shady wood.* shadowy, shaded, dim, dark, cool, leafy, sunless, gloomy, sun-dappled.
OPPOSITES: sunny, sunlit.
2 *(adj) (informal) Dodgy Dave is a shady character. See* **suspicious** 2.

**shaggy**
*(adj) Shaggy hair.* bushy, thick, tousled, tangled, unkempt, untidy, rough, woolly.

**shake**
1 *(v) The earthquake made the buildings shake.* vibrate, quake, shudder, judder *(informal)*, tremble, totter, sway, wobble, quiver, shiver, jiggle, joggle, convulse.
2 *(v) Shake the mixture.* shake up, stir up, churn up, agitate, swirl, jiggle, joggle.
3 *(v) Don't shake that stick at me.* brandish, flourish, wave, waggle, jiggle.

**shaky**
1 *(adj) Don't stand on that shaky chair.* wobbly, rickety, unsteady, rocky, flimsy, unsafe, unstable, tottery, teetering, weak.
OPPOSITES: steady, firm.
2 *(adj) I answered the questions in a shaky voice.* faltering, tremulous, trembling, quavering, quivery, quivering, unsteady, wavering, wobbly, weak, nervous.
OPPOSITES: steady, firm.
3 *(adj) I felt shaky when I got up this morning. See* **dizzy**.

**shallow**
*(adj) Mrs Badger said my essay was too shallow.* superficial, trivial, empty, flimsy, slight, lightweight, insubstantial, glib, frivolous, facile, unconvincing, skin-deep.
OPPOSITES: thoughtful, thorough.

**shame**
1 *(n) Casper was filled with shame for what he had done.* remorse, self-reproach, guilt, guilty conscience, disgust, self-loathing, mortification, chagrin.
OPPOSITE: pride.
2 *(n) I can't bear the shame of losing.* humiliation, disgrace, ignominy, degradation, indignity, embarrassment, dishonour, scandal, stigma, stain, infamy.
OPPOSITES: honour, glory.
3 *(n) It's a shame that Dad is so strict.* pity, crying shame, hard luck, disgrace, outrage, scandal, tragedy, sin.
4 *(v) Your mum would never shame you in public. See* **humiliate**.

**shameful** *see* **humiliating**.

**shape**
1 *(n) TYPES OF SHAPE:* circle, cone, cube, cylinder, diamond, hexagon, oblong, octagon, oval, parallelogram, pentagon, prism, pyramid, rectangle, rhombus, sphere, square, trapezium, triangle.
2 *(n) Can you recognize the shape of France on a map?* outline, form, contours *(plural)*, profile, silhouette, lines *(plural)*.
3 *(n) The enchanter took on the shape of a serpent.* form, guise, likeness, look, semblance, aspect.
4 *(n) I try to keep in good shape. See* **condition** 1.
5 *(v) Can you shape a hippo out of clay? See* **model** 5.

**shapeless**
1 *(adj) A shapeless cloud.* nebulous, formless, vague, undefined, unformed, ill-defined, amorphous, indeterminate.
2 *(adj) A shapeless dress.* loose, baggy, sack-like, sloppy, unfitted, ill-fitting.

**share**
1 *(n) We all had a share of the profits.* portion, part, fraction, proportion, percentage, quota, ration, cut *(informal)*, helping, whack *(informal)*, piece, slice.
2 *(v) Share the sweets between you.* share out, divide, split, distribute, deal out, dole out, allocate, apportion, measure out, go halves, go fifty-fifty *(informal)*.

**sharp**
1 *(adj) Don't cut yourself on that sharp knife.* razor-sharp, pointed, keen-edged, serrated, sharpened, jagged, barbed.
OPPOSITE: blunt.
2 *(adj) The rocks are sharp. See* **jagged** 2.
3 *(adj) I felt a sharp pain.* piercing, stabbing, shooting, violent, excruciating, agonizing, intense, severe, acute.
OPPOSITE: dull.
4 *(adj) Aunt Bertha gave a sharp reply.* cutting, stinging, caustic, scathing, sarcastic, barbed, curt, tart, acid, acerbic.
OPPOSITE: gentle.
5 *(adj) Lemons taste sharp. See* **sour** 1.
6 *(adj) We came to a sharp bend.* tight, sudden, abrupt, unexpected, hairpin.
OPPOSITES: gentle, gradual.
7 *(adj) In front of us was a sharp drop. See* **steep** 1.
8 *(adj) Try to get a sharp picture on the TV. See* **clear** 5.

**shatter** *see* **smash** 2.

**shattered**
1 *(adj) Kim was shattered by the news.* devastated, stunned, dazed, crushed, heartbroken, destroyed, upset, shocked.
2 *(adj) (informal) I was shattered after the race. See* **exhausted**.

**shed**
*(n)* garden shed, tool shed, potting shed, woodshed, hut, shack, shelter, outhouse.

**sheer**
1 *(adj) That goal was sheer magic! See* **absolute**.

**2** *(adj) In front of us was a sheer drop.* See **steep** 1.
**3** *(adj) The bride wore a veil of sheer silk.* See **fine** 5.

### sheet
**1** *(n) Start each question on a new sheet.* piece of paper, page, side, leaf, folio.
**2** *(n) A metal sheet covered the window.* panel, plate, piece, slab, pane *(glass).*
**3** *(n) A sheet of snow covered the ground.* See **layer** 1.

### shelf
*(n) Put the clock on that shelf.* ledge, mantelpiece, windowsill, bracket.

### shell
*(n) Some seeds are protected by a hard shell.* casing, covering, case, pod, husk, exterior, outside, outer layer.

### shelter
**1** *(v) The trees will shelter us from the rain.* protect, shield, screen, provide cover for, provide protection for, provide refuge for, safeguard.
**2** *(v) Where can we shelter from the storm?* take cover, take shelter, take refuge, seek refuge, seek protection.
**3** *(n) The refugees looked for shelter.* cover, protection, refuge, safety, asylum, sanctuary, safe haven.

### sheltered
**1** *(adj) Our garden is sheltered because of the trees.* protected, shielded, shaded, screened, secluded, snug, windless.
OPPOSITES: exposed, open.
**2** *(adj) Mary had a sheltered childhood.* quiet, protected, cloistered, unadventurous, unexciting, secluded, isolated, reclusive.

### shield *see* **protect** 1, 3.

### shift
**1** *(v) Shift your things into the spare room.* See **move** 2.
**2** *(v) You'll need hot water to shift that stain.* See **remove** 2.

### shimmer *see* **shine** 2.

### shine
**1** *(v) Light bulbs are supposed to shine.* give out light, shed light, emit light, be bright, be luminous.
**2** *(v) I saw something shine in the sky.* gleam, glow, shimmer, glimmer, twinkle, sparkle, glint, glitter, glisten, blaze, flash, flicker, beam, glare.
**3** *(v) Jo manages to shine at everything she does.* excel, do well, stand out, be brilliant, be expert, show talent, star.
**4** *(n) Look at the shine on that table!* polish, sheen, gloss, gleam, sparkle, lustre, finish, patina.

### shining
*(adj) I saw a shining light in the sky.* bright, brilliant, dazzling, blazing, radiant, luminous, glowing, beaming, gleaming, shimmering, sparkling, glittering, glistening, glaring, fluorescent.

### shiny
**1** *(adj) A shiny golden goblet.* gleaming, shining, sparkling, glistening, glittering, dazzling, bright, polished, burnished.
OPPOSITES: dull, matt.
**2** *(adj) Shiny hair.* glossy, shining, gleaming, sleek, lustrous, silky, satiny.
OPPOSITE: dull.

### ship *see* **boat**.

### shiver
*(v) Ghost stories make me shiver.* shudder, shake, tremble, quiver, quake.

### shock
**1** *(v) This news may shock you.* stun, stagger, startle, take your breath away, amaze, astonish, astound, surprise, alarm, dismay, shake, shake you up *(informal),* shatter, devastate, disturb, distress, traumatize, perturb, daze, numb, stupefy.
**2** *(v) Rude jokes shock Aunt Bertha.* horrify, disgust, offend, scandalize, appal, outrage, revolt, sicken, nauseate.
**3** *(n) You gave me a shock! See* **scare** 3.
**4** *(n) The news came as a shock.* surprise, blow, bombshell, bolt from the blue, revelation, eye-opener *(informal).*

### shocking
**1** *(adj) Have you heard the shocking news about Mrs Badger?* astonishing, surprising, startling, staggering, stunning, stupefying, unexpected, disturbing, perturbing, upsetting, disquieting, unsettling.
**2** *(adj) Bozo's behaviour is shocking.* outrageous, disgusting, scandalous, appalling, disgraceful, offensive, revolting, repugnant, sickening, nauseating, atrocious, monstrous, indecent.
**3** *(adj) There has been a shocking accident.* horrific, horrendous, horrifying, appalling, ghastly, harrowing, grisly, gruesome, terrible, dreadful, frightening.

### shoddy
*(adj) Mrs Badger criticized my shoddy work.* second-rate, poor-quality, inferior, careless, messy, slapdash, sloppy *(informal),* slovenly, slipshod, untidy, tatty.
OPPOSITES: careful, meticulous.

### shoe
*(n) footwear.*
TYPES OF SHOE: ballet shoe, boot, bootee, brogue, clog, court shoe, deck shoe, dolly shoe, espadrille, flip-flop, gym shoe, high-heeled shoe, lace-up, loafer, moccasin, mule, patent shoe, peep-toe, platform shoe, plimsoll, pump, running shoe, sandal, slingback, slip-on, slipper, sneaker, stiletto, suede shoe, tennis shoe, trainer, winklepicker.

### shoot
**1** *(v) "Don't move or I'll shoot you!" Arnie said.* fire at, open fire on, gun you down, snipe at, blow your brains out, take a pot shot at, pump you full of lead *(slang),* riddle you with bullets, zap *(slang),* shell.
**2** *(v) Shoot the arrows at the target.* fire, aim, launch, propel, let fly.
**3** *(v) Watch the comet shoot through the sky.* fly, hurtle, streak, flash, speed, whiz *(informal),* zoom, zip, tear, race, dash.
**4** *(n) A shoot will grow.* bud, offshoot, tendril, sprout, new growth, stem, twig.

### shop
*(n) corner shop, supermarket, store, department store, superstore, megastore, hypermarket, boutique, market, cash-and-carry, emporium (old-fashioned).*

### shore
*(n) We walked along the shore.* seashore, beach, coast, sand, sands *(plural),* water's edge, waterside, waterfront, lakeside, seafront, foreshore, shingle, strand. ❖ *Also see* **sea & seashore**, **seaside words**.

### short
**1** *(adj) Dil is rather short.* small, squat, little, tiny, petite, diminutive, dumpy, stubby, stumpy, pint-sized *(informal).*
OPPOSITE: tall.
**2** *(adj) Write a short account of your trip.* brief, concise, succinct, pithy, compressed, to the point, abridged, abbreviated.
OPPOSITES: long, long-winded.
**3** *(adj) We paid a short visit to Aunt Bertha.* brief, quick, fleeting, hurried, hasty, short-lived, cursory.
OPPOSITES: long, leisurely.
**4** *(adj) Shall we go home the short way?* quick, direct, straight, obvious.
OPPOSITES: long, indirect.

### shortage
*(n) There's a noticeable shortage of books in our school.* lack, scarcity, shortfall, absence, dearth, deficiency.
OPPOSITES: abundance, surplus.

### shorts *see* **clothes**.

### shot
**1** *(n) Did you hear that shot?* gunshot, crack, bang, pop, report, explosion, blast.
**2** *(n) That was a great shot!* hit, stroke, volley, lob, smash, throw, pass, kick, header, drive, putt, pot, pot shot.
**3** *(n) (informal) Have a shot! See* **try** 1.

### shout
*(v) Please don't shout.* yell, raise your voice, bawl, bellow, holler *(informal),* scream, shriek, screech, roar, call out, cry out.

brogue  deck shoe  loafer  slingback  winklepicker  espadrille  mule  stiletto

# shove

**shove** see **push** 1, 3, 4.

**show**
1 *(v) Will this mark show?* show up, be visible, be seen, stand out, be noticeable, catch the eye, attract attention.
2 *(v) Todd tried not to show his true feelings.* display, make obvious, make plain, make known, indicate, express, betray, reveal, expose, disclose, divulge.
3 *(v) I want to show an alien in my painting.* depict, portray, illustrate, represent, feature.
4 *(v) Delia will show you how to make an omelette. See* **demonstrate** 1.
5 *(v) This letter will show that I am telling the truth.* indicate, demonstrate, make clear, prove, establish, confirm, clarify.
6 *(n) Enjoy the show! See* **performance**.
7 *(n) You'll see all kinds of cars at the show.* exhibition, fair, expo *(informal)*, display, demonstration, presentation.
8 *(n) Nina put on a show of affection for Aunt Bertha.* display, appearance, pretence, pose, affectation, illusion.

**shower**
1 *(n) The sudden shower surprised us.* downpour, cloudburst, deluge, rainfall.
2 *(v) Be careful the elephants don't shower you with water! See* **spray** 1.

**show-off**
*(n) (informal) Jeremy is such a show-off.* bighead *(informal)*, boaster, poser *(informal)*, exhibitionist, braggart.

**show off**
1 *(v) Al is keen to show off his computer.* flaunt, parade, display, demonstrate.
2 *(v) (informal) Don't show off about all your prizes. See* **boast**.

**show up**
1 *(v) This orange shirt will certainly show up.* be visible, stand out, be conspicuous, catch the eye, leap out at you.
2 *(v) Bright light will show up my spots.* accentuate, draw attention to, highlight, expose, reveal.
3 *(v) (informal) Don't you hate it when your parents show you up!* let you down, embarrass, humiliate, disgrace, shame, mortify, show you in a bad light.

**shred**
1 *(n) The detectives found a shred of cloth.* scrap, snippet, strip, bit, piece, fragment, ribbon, rag, tatter, wisp.
2 *(n) There isn't a shred of evidence against Burglar Beryl.* scrap, bit, jot, iota, trace, grain, speck, crumb, atom, particle.

**shriek** see **scream**.

**shrill**
*(adj) A shrill sound.* high-pitched, piercing, ear-piercing, ear-splitting, penetrating, strident, screeching, piping, sharp.

**shrink**
1 *(v) This balloon is starting to shrink.* grow smaller, deflate, contract, shrivel up.
OPPOSITES: expand, swell.

2 *(v) Famous Fred's record sales may shrink.* decrease, decline, dwindle, drop off, fall off, diminish, contract, reduce.
OPPOSITES: expand, increase.
3 *(v) Don't shrink away from me. See* **cower**.

**shrivel**
*(v) The flowers will shrivel in the sun.* wither, dry up, wilt, droop, dry out, dehydrate, shrink, wrinkle up, pucker up.

**shudder** see **shiver**.

**shuffle**
1 *(v) Shuffle the cards.* mix, mix up, jumble up, rearrange, reorganize.
2 *(v) I hate the way you shuffle around in those shoes.* shamble, drag your feet, paddle, pad, hobble, stumble, limp.

**shut**
1 *(v) Shut the door.* close, slam, lock, bolt, bar, secure, fasten, latch, pull to, push to.
OPPOSITE: open.
2 *(v) Shut the curtains.* close, draw, pull.
OPPOSITE: open.
3 *(v) Why did the king shut the princes in the tower?* lock, imprison, incarcerate, shut up, keep, confine, detain, enclose, coop up, wall up, cage, box.
4 *(adj) Is the shop shut?* closed, locked up, shut up, bolted and barred, closed down.
OPPOSITE: open.

**shut down**
*(v) The car factory may have to shut down.* close down, cease operating, cease production, cease trading *(shop, business)*.

**shut out** see **exclude**.

**shut up**
*(v) (informal) Shut up and listen!* be quiet, stop talking, keep quiet, shush, hush, hold your tongue, put a sock in it *(slang)*, belt up *(slang)*, shut your trap *(slang)*.

**shy**
*(adj) Amy is too shy to come to the party.* timid, diffident, reserved, retiring, mousy, bashful, self-conscious, inhibited, reticent, introverted, wary, coy.
OPPOSITES: self-assured, assertive.

**sick**
1 *(adj) Kamilah can't come to school because she's sick. See* **ill** 1.
2 *(adj) I feel sick.* nauseous, queasy, bilious, green around the gills *(informal)*.
3 *(adj) Bozo's behaviour makes me sick.* disgusted, sickened, appalled, revolted, nauseated, upset, distressed, outraged, repelled, offended, horrified.
4 *(adj) (informal) Harriet has a sick sense of humour.* twisted, black, perverted, morbid, macabre, ghoulish, sadistic.
5 **sick of** *(adj) (informal) I'm sick of staying at home. See* **fed up with**.
6 **be sick** *(v) I'm going to be sick! See* **vomit**.

**sickening**
1 *(adj) The smell from the drains was sickening. See* **disgusting** 1.

2 *(adj) The way Araminta sucks up to Mrs Badger is sickening.* loathsome, disgusting, nauseating, distasteful, cringe-making *(informal)*, repellent, repulsive, obnoxious, odious, objectionable, stomach-turning.

**sickly**
1 *(adj) A sickly baby. See* **delicate** 2.
2 *(adj) A sickly dessert.* sugary, syrupy, treacly, cloying, nauseating, saccharine.

**side**
1 *(n) Paint one side of the box.* face, surface, facet, flank, elevation *(building)*.
2 *(n) Stand at the side of the pool.* edge, rim, brink, perimeter, periphery, boundary, verge *(road)*, kerb *(pavement)*.
3 *(n) The side of the page was covered with notes.* edge, margin, border.
4 *(n) Start each question on a new side. See* **page**.
5 *(n) Which side won?* team, group, faction, camp, party, army, sect, cause.
6 *(n) Try to look at the problem from every side.* angle, aspect, perspective, point of view, viewpoint, standpoint, position.
7 **side with** *(v) Did you side with Dalal in the argument?* agree with, support, back, take the part of, go along with, team up with, ally with, champion, second.

**sieve**
1 *(v) Sieve the mixture.* strain, sift, filter, separate, pan *(gold)*.
2 *(n) Pass me the sieve.* strainer, colander.

**sigh**
1 *(v) Did I hear you sigh?* exhale, let out your breath, moan, groan.
2 *(v) The wind began to sigh through the branches.* whisper, rustle, moan.

**sight**
1 *(n) I'm worried about Matty's sight.* eyesight, vision, eyes *(plural)*, short-sightedness, long-sightedness.
2 *(n) We watched the balloon until it was out of sight.* view, range, eyeshot, range of vision, field of vision.
3 *(n) What a beautiful sight!* scene, vision, spectacle, picture, image, view, vista, panorama, display, prospect, outlook.
4 *(n) (informal) You look a sight!* fright *(informal)*, mess *(informal)*, wreck, eyesore.

**sign**
1 *(n) Is there any sign that Burglar Beryl has been here?* indication, hint, suggestion, clue, evidence, proof, pointer, trace, vestige, giveaway, telltale sign.
2 *(n) Did you read the sign?* notice, poster, placard, board, signpost.
3 *(n) Let's design a secret sign for our gang.* symbol, badge, emblem, identification mark, logo, insignia.
4 *(n) Give me a sign when it's time to begin.* signal, indication, tip-off, cue, message, hint, reminder, warning, wave, nod, wink, gesture, go-ahead *(informal)*.
5 *(n) Arthur knew the pile of bones was a sign.* warning, omen, portent, forewarning, message, token, pointer.

**6** (v) *Please sign this postcard.* write your name on, autograph, initial, inscribe, put your name to, put your mark on.

**signal**
**1** (n) *Give me a signal when it's time to begin. See* **sign** 4.
**2** (v) *I'll signal to you when it's safe.* indicate, make a sign, gesture, sign, motion, wave, nod, beckon, gesticulate.

**significant** *see* **important** 1.

**silence**
**1** (n) *I love the silence of evening.* quietness, stillness, calm, tranquillity, peacefulness, peace, quiet, hush.
OPPOSITE: noise.
**2** (n) *Sarah's silence puzzled us.* lack of speech, dumbness, muteness, reticence, uncommunicativeness.
**3** (v) *How can we silence the sound of Paula's trumpet?* quieten, muffle, stifle, smother, deaden, suppress, subdue.

**silent**
**1** (adj) *Ravi approached with silent steps.* soundless, noiseless, inaudible, muffled.
OPPOSITES: noisy, loud.
**2** (adj) *The shock made me silent for a while.* speechless, tongue-tied, dumbstruck, unable to get a word out, mute, dumb, mum.
**3** (adj) *Edward is a rather silent member of the class. See* **quiet** 3.
**4** (adj) *Everything was silent before the storm. See* **still** 3.
**5** (adj) *We watched with silent approval.* unspoken, unvoiced, unexpressed, wordless, tacit, implied, implicit.

**silhouette** *see* **outline** 3.

**silky**
(adj) *I stroked the horse's silky coat.* sleek, smooth, velvety, satiny, shiny, glossy, soft.
OPPOSITES: rough, matted.

**silly**
**1** (adj) *What a silly idea!* stupid, foolish, daft (informal), idiotic, crazy, absurd, ridiculous, preposterous, ludicrous, senseless, nonsensical, brainless, irrational, illogical, misguided, half-baked (informal), inane, harebrained, foolhardy, reckless.
OPPOSITES: sensible, clever.
**2** (adj) *Daisy can be so silly.* idiotic, brainless, daft (informal), foolish, stupid, senseless, dotty (slang), dippy (slang), dopey (slang), goofy (informal), immature, childish, infantile, puerile, irresponsible, featherbrained, giddy, flighty, frivolous.
OPPOSITES: sensible, mature.

**silver**
(adj) *A silver moon.* silvery, pearly, ivory.

**similar**
(adj) *Our answers are similar.* alike, comparable, much the same, close, in agreement, corresponding, matching.
OPPOSITES: different, dissimilar.

**simple**
**1** (adj) *The test was simple! See* **easy** 1.

**2** (adj) *The instructions are written in simple language.* clear, straightforward, uncomplicated, plain, intelligible, understandable, comprehensible, easy to follow, foolproof, uninvolved.
OPPOSITES: complicated, complex.
**3** (adj) *The peasants lived in a simple cottage.* modest, ordinary, humble, plain, basic, unpretentious, undecorated, austere, stark, Spartan, poor, lowly, rustic.
OPPOSITES: grand, fancy.
**4** (adj) *I like simple meals. See* **plain** 2.
**5** (adj) *Give me the simple truth.* plain, honest, naked, stark, bald, basic, unvarnished, unembellished, unadorned.

**sincere**
**1** (adj) *Peter's sympathy seems to be sincere.* genuine, real, wholehearted, heartfelt, in earnest, unfeigned, bona fide.
OPPOSITES: insincere, feigned.
**2** (adj) *Mr Badger is a sincere person.* truthful, honest, frank, candid, open, straightforward, genuine, artless, guileless, upfront (informal), plain-dealing.
OPPOSITES: insincere, deceitful.

**sing**
**1** (v) *Dad likes to sing in the shower.* warble, croon, carol, yodel, chant, serenade, hum, whistle.
**2** (v) *The nightingale began to sing.* trill, warble, twitter, chirrup, cheep, chirp, whistle, pipe, peep, squawk.

**singer**
(n) vocalist, songster, songstress.
TYPES OF SINGER: alto, backing singer, baritone, bass, choirboy, choirgirl, chorister, contralto, countertenor, crooner, folk singer, jazz singer, lead singer, mezzo-soprano, opera singer, pop singer, prima donna (leading female opera singer), rapper, rock singer, soloist, soprano, tenor, treble, troubadour (old-fashioned).

**single**
**1** (adj) *Do you have single rooms?* individual, separate, personal, unshared.
OPPOSITES: shared, double.
**2** (adj) *A single tree stood on the hill.* lone, solitary, isolated, unique, individual, unaccompanied, on its own, solo.
**3** (adj) *Do you think you'll stay single?* unattached, unmarried, celibate, on your own, unwed, partnerless, not tied down, free, fancy-free, footloose.
OPPOSITES: attached, married.

**sinister**
(adj) *The shadows looked sinister.* threatening, menacing, ominous, forbidding, frightening, disturbing, spooky (informal), malevolent, evil, malign.

**sink**
**1** (v) *The ship is going to sink!* go down, go under, founder, submerge, go to the bottom, go to Davy Jones's locker, drown.
OPPOSITE: float.
**2** (v) *The plane began to sink. See* **drop** 2.
**3** (v) *We watched the sun sink. See* **set** 5.

**4** (v) *Oliver tried to sink his toy boat.* submerge, scupper, scuttle, capsize, drown, swamp, flood, immerse, engulf, dunk, duck, torpedo.
**5** (v) *How could you sink to that level of meanness?* lower yourself, stoop, be reduced, debase yourself, succumb, yield.
OPPOSITES: aspire, rise.
**6** (n) *Fill the sink.* washbasin, basin.

**sit**
(v) *You can sit here.* sit down, be seated, seat yourself, take a seat, settle down, perch, squat, rest, take the weight off your feet, loll, sprawl, flop, collapse.

**situation** *see* **position** 2.

**sketch**
**1** (v) *Why don't you sketch your cat? See* **draw** 1.
**2** (n) *We admired Meg's sketch.* drawing, picture, study, design, outline, diagram, plan, representation, rough drawing.

**skid**
(v) *The car began to skid.* slide, slip, spin, go into a skid, go into a spin, go out of control, sideslip, veer, glide, aquaplane.

**skilful**
(adj) *Ryan is a skilful footballer.* skilled, accomplished, talented, expert, capable, proficient, deft, versatile, ace (informal).
OPPOSITES: inept, incompetent.

**skill**
(n) *We admired the potter's skill.* expertise, technique, prowess, talent, ability, artistry, craftsmanship, workmanship, art, craft, deftness, dexterity, versatility, finesse.

**skim**
**1** (v) *Watch me skim over the ice!* glide, slide, skate, sail, fly, float, coast.
**2** (v) *See how the dragonflies skim the surface of the pond.* brush, graze, touch.
**3** **skim through** (v) *Skim through this booklet.* glance through, look through, run your eye over, leaf through, scan, flip through, skip through, thumb through.

**skin**
**1** (n) *With your fair skin you should avoid the sun.* complexion, colouring, skin tone.
**2** (n) *This fruit has a tough skin.* rind, peel, outer layer, exterior, surface, casing, covering, shell, husk, pod.
**3** (n) *Is this jacket made from an animal's skin?* hide, pelt, coat, fleece, fur.
**4** (n) *I hate custard with a skin on top.* film, coating, layer, crust, scum.

**skinny** *see* **thin** 1.

**skip**
**1** (v) *I love to see the children skip around the garden!* prance, dance, bounce, frolic, gambol, cavort, bound, jump, leap, hop.
**2** (v) *Let's skip this page. See* **miss out** 1.
**3** (v) (informal) *You mustn't skip school.* miss, play truant from, dodge, skive off (informal), bunk off (slang), cut (informal), play hooky from (informal).

**skirt** *see* **clothes**.

# skulk

**skulk** *see* **lurk**.

**sky**
*(n) My balloon floated up into the sky.* air, atmosphere, skies *(plural)*, space, heavens *(plural)*, stratosphere, blue, firmament.

**slab** *see* **block** 1.

**slag off** *(slang) see* **criticize** 1.

**slant**
1 *(v) That chimney seems to slant to one side. See* **lean** 1.
2 *(n) Look at the slant of that table top! See* **slope** 1.
3 *(n) Veena gave the story a new slant.* angle, emphasis, twist, perspective, bias.

**slap**
1 *(v) Don't slap Caroline! See* **smack**.
2 *(v) Sam started to slap paint on the walls.* slop, splash, slosh *(informal)*, daub, dollop *(informal)*, plaster, spread.

**slapdash** *see* **careless** 1.

**slash**
1 *(v) The vandals began to slash the furniture.* cut, slit, gash, rip, tear, lacerate, score, knife, hack at.
2 *(v) Supermarkets may slash their prices. See* **reduce** 1.

**slaughter**
1 *(n) The slaughter must be stopped. See* **killing** 2.
2 *(v) The farmers had to slaughter their sick cattle. See* **kill** 2.
3 *(v) (informal) We'll slaughter the other team. See* **beat** 2.

**sleazy**
*(adj) The street was full of sleazy bars.* sordid, seedy, disreputable, squalid, run-down, tacky *(informal)*, crummy *(slang)*.
OPPOSITES: respectable, up-market.

**sleek** *see* **silky**.

**sleep**
1 *(v) You can sleep at my house.* spend the night, stay, sleep over, kip *(slang)*, doss down *(slang)*, crash out *(slang)*.
2 *(v) Aunt Bertha likes to sleep after lunch.* doze, take a nap, snooze *(informal)*, catnap, drowse, have forty winks *(informal)*, get some shuteye *(informal)*, drop off *(informal)*, nod off *(informal)*, rest.
3 *(n) Granny is having a sleep.* nap, rest, siesta, snooze *(informal)*, doze, catnap, lie-down, forty winks *(plural) (informal)*, kip *(slang)*, shuteye *(informal)*, zizz *(informal)*.

**sleeping** *see* **asleep**.

**sleepy**
1 *(adj) Do you feel sleepy?* tired, drowsy, half-asleep, weary, exhausted, unable to keep your eyes open, lethargic, sluggish, dozy, dopey *(informal)*, ready for bed.
OPPOSITES: wide-awake, alert.
2 *(adj) Nothing ever happens in this sleepy town.* quiet, peaceful, dozy, unexciting, boring, dull, dreary, dead.
OPPOSITES: lively, bustling.

**slender** *see* **slim** 1, 2.

**slice**
1 *(n) Have a slice of cake.* piece, segment, slab, wedge, sliver, doorstep *(informal)*, chunk, portion, helping, wodge *(informal)*.
2 *(v) Will you slice the pineapple?* cut up, divide, carve, segment, dissect.

**slide**
*(v) Felix began to slide across the ice.* slip, slither, skid, glide, skate, skim, sideslip, veer, toboggan, ski.

**slight**
*(adj) There's been a slight improvement in your work.* small, minor, modest, negligible, imperceptible, insignificant, trivial, tiny, trifling, measly *(informal)*.
OPPOSITES: great, considerable.

**slim**
1 *(adj) Natasha has a slim figure.* slender, trim, slight, lean, thin, willowy, sylphlike, svelte, graceful.
OPPOSITES: chubby, fat.
2 *(adj) There's a slim chance that we might survive.* slight, small, slender, faint, remote, outside.

**slimy**
1 *(adj) We squelched through a slimy swamp.* slippery, sludgy, oozy, gooey *(informal)*, sticky, muddy, mucky.
2 *(adj) Flash Frank is a slimy character.* smooth, smarmy *(informal)*, oily, greasy, obsequious, ingratiating, grovelling, fawning, toadying, sycophantic, unctuous.

**sling** *see* **throw** 1.

**slink**
*(v) The thieves tried to slink through the bushes.* creep, sneak, steal, slip, sidle, prowl, skulk, tiptoe, pussyfoot *(informal)*.

**slinky**
*(adj) Naomi wore a slinky black dress.* clinging, figure-hugging, skintight, close-fitting, sleek, sexy *(informal)*.

**slip**
1 *(v) It's easy to slip if the pavement is icy.* skid, lose your balance, lose your footing, fall, trip, slide, slither, glide, skate.
2 *(v) Try to slip out of the house unnoticed. See* **creep** 2.
3 *(n) I made a slip in my calculations. See* **mistake** 1.
4 *(n) Write your phone number on this slip of paper.* scrap, piece, bit, strip, snippet.
5 *(n) Your slip is showing.* petticoat, underskirt.

**slippery**
1 *(adj) The path is slippery.* icy, greasy, oily, slimy, slithery, slippy *(informal)*, skiddy *(informal)*, glassy, treacherous.
2 *(adj) Dodgy Dave is a slippery character. See* **deceitful**.

**slip up** *(informal) see* **go wrong** 1.

**slit**
1 *(n) Jamie has a slit in his trousers.* cut, split, slash, tear, rip, gash.
2 *(n) I peeped through a slit in the rock. See* **crack** 2.

**slither**
*(v) Watch the snake slither over the sand!* slide, glide, slip, wriggle, squirm, skitter, slink, writhe, twist, snake, worm, creep.

**slobber**
*(v) Look at Fido slobber over his bone.* drool, slaver, dribble, salivate.

**slope**
1 *(n) Look at the slope of that roof!* slant, angle, tilt, rake, pitch, skew, incline, gradient, camber *(road)*.
2 *(n) Our house is built on a slope.* hill, hillside, bank, rise, incline, ramp.
3 *(v) The path began to slope steeply.* rise, fall, drop, descend, ascend, incline, shelve.
4 *(v) That chimney seems to slope to one side. See* **lean** 1.

**sloppy**
1 *(adj) A sloppy trifle.* runny, slushy, watery, soggy, squidgy, oozy, liquid.
OPPOSITES: firm, solid.
2 *(adj) (informal) Sloppy work. See* **careless** 1.
3 *(adj) A sloppy jumper. See* **loose** 1.

**slot**
*(n) Insert a knife in the slot.* slit, crack, opening, hole, groove, notch, channel.

**slouch**
*(v) Sit up and don't slouch!* slump, stoop, droop, hunch, loll, lounge, sprawl, sag.

**slow**
1 *(adj) Tortoises move at a slow pace.* unhurried, steady, plodding, sluggish, ponderous, snail-like, dawdling, crawling, leisurely, easy, lazy, measured, deliberate.
OPPOSITES: fast, quick.
2 *(adj) Aunt Bertha's recovery was slow.* gradual, long-drawn-out, protracted, prolonged, lingering, interminable.
OPPOSITES: fast, rapid.
3 *(adj) Rory was slow in handing in his project.* late, delayed, unpunctual, tardy, behind, dilatory.
OPPOSITE: prompt.
4 *(adj) This film is so slow!* slow-moving, uneventful, tedious, monotonous, dull, boring, tiresome, wearisome.
OPPOSITES: fast-moving, action-packed.

**slow down**
1 *(v) Slow down; you're going too fast!* reduce your speed, slacken your speed, decelerate, put the brakes on, brake.
OPPOSITES: speed up, accelerate.
2 *(v) Don't slow me down. See* **delay** 2.

**sly**
*(adj) That was a sly trick you played.* crafty, sneaky, cunning, wily, artful, devious, deceitful, underhand, stealthy, furtive, insidious, scheming, clever, smart, shrewd.
OPPOSITES: straightforward, honest.

**smack**
*(v) Should parents smack their children?* slap, hit, strike, whack, spank, wallop *(informal)*, belt *(slang)*, thump, cuff, clout *(informal)*, biff *(slang)*, beat.

## small

| a small person | a small child | a small helping of pudding | a small space | a small mistake |
|---|---|---|---|---|
| dainty | little | inadequate | confined | insignificant |
| diminutive | teeny | insubstantial | cramped | minor |
| elfin | tiny | meagre | limited | negligible |
| Lilliputian | wee | mean | narrow | slight |
| little | young | measly | poky | trifling |
| petite | | *(informal)* | restricted | trivial |
| pint-sized | **a small radio** | mingy | | unimportant |
| *(informal)* | compact | *(informal)* | **a small speck** | |
| puny | dinky | moderate | infinitesimal | **Don't make me feel small!** |
| short | *(informal)* | modest | microscopic | foolish |
| slender | mini | scanty | minuscule | humiliated |
| slight | miniature | skimpy | minute | ridiculous |
| squat | pocket-sized | stingy | teeny | sheepish |
| tiny | tiny | tiny | teeny-weeny | silly |
| titchy *(slang)* | toy | titchy *(slang)* | tiny | stupid |
| undersized | | | | |

**smart**
1 *(adj)* Ellie always looks smart. elegant, stylish, chic, well-dressed, well-groomed, presentable, spruce, neat, tidy, dashing, dapper, natty *(informal)*, snazzy *(informal)*.
OPPOSITES: scruffy, dowdy.
2 *(adj)* That was a smart move. clever, intelligent, shrewd, crafty, astute, quick-witted, bright, ingenious, wise, sensible.
OPPOSITES: stupid, idiotic.
3 *(adj)* Oliver loves to make smart remarks. clever, witty, facetious, impertinent, cheeky, saucy, smart-alecky *(informal)*, clever-clever *(informal)*, clever-Dick *(informal)*, droll, waggish.
4 *(v)* If you get soap in your eyes it will smart. See **sting**.

**smash**
1 *(n)* Was anyone injured in the smash? See **crash** 2.
2 *(v)* If you drop that bowl it will smash. shatter, splinter, smash to smithereens, break, break into pieces, crack, split, fracture, disintegrate.
3 smash into *(v)* Try not to smash into that tree. See **hit** 4.

**smear**
1 *(v)* Don't smear paint on the walls! spread, daub, plaster, smudge, wipe, rub.
2 *(n)* You've got a smear of paint on your nose. streak, smudge, splodge, blotch, splotch, daub, spot, mark.

**smell**
1 *(n)* What a wonderful smell! fragrance, scent, perfume, aroma, bouquet, odour.
2 *(n)* What a horrible smell! stink, stench, pong *(informal)*, odour, whiff, reek.
3 *(v)* Your feet smell! See **stink** 1.
4 *(v)* A fox can smell chickens from miles away. scent, sniff out, nose out, sense, detect, track down, get wind of *(informal)*.
5 *(v)* Smell that lovely aroma! inhale, breathe in, take in, sniff, get a whiff of.

**smelly**
*(adj)* Throw away that smelly cheese. stinking, reeking, pongy *(informal)*, whiffy *(slang)*, stinky *(informal)*, pungent, strong-smelling, foul-smelling, evil-smelling, malodorous, high, putrid, fetid.
OPPOSITES: sweet-smelling, fragrant.

**smile**
1 *(v)* Smile for the camera! grin, beam, look happy, smirk, simper, say cheese.
2 *(n)* The witch gave a horrible smile. grin, smirk, leer, grimace, sneer.

**smoke**
1 *(v)* Please don't smoke. light up, chain-smoke, puff away, have a drag *(informal)*, have a fag *(slang)*, inhale.
2 *(v)* The fire started to smoke. smoulder, give off smoke, emit smoke, billow.
3 *(n)* The air was filled with smoke. clouds of smoke *(plural)*, exhaust fumes *(plural)*, pollution, smog, haze.

**smooth**
1 *(adj)* You need a smooth lawn for bowls. level, flat, even, horizontal, flush.
OPPOSITES: bumpy, uneven.
2 *(adj)* Clare has smooth skin. soft, velvety, silky, downy, flawless, unlined, unwrinkled.
OPPOSITES: rough, coarse.
3 *(adj)* This table has a smooth surface. polished, shiny, glossy, satiny, sleek, even.
OPPOSITES: rough, bumpy.
4 *(adj)* Nothing disturbed the smooth surface of the lake. calm, still, unruffled, glassy, mirror-like, tranquil, placid, flat.
OPPOSITES: choppy, rough.
5 *(adj)* You'll love the smooth taste of this sauce. mild, mellow, creamy, velvety, pleasant, agreeable, bland.
6 *(adj)* I hope you have a smooth journey. easy, comfortable, straightforward, effortless, peaceful, uneventful, uninterrupted, trouble-free, stress-free.
OPPOSITES: difficult, stressful.

7 *(adj)* Ballet dancers should have smooth movements. easy, effortless, flowing, fluid, graceful, steady, rhythmic, regular.
OPPOSITES: jerky, erratic.
8 *(adj)* Flash Frank has a smooth manner. suave, polished, glib, charming, persuasive, flattering, ingratiating, sophisticated, urbane, slick, smarmy *(informal)*, slimy.
OPPOSITES: rough, abrasive.
9 *(v)* Smooth the sheets before you fold them. smooth out, flatten, iron, press.
OPPOSITES: crumple, crease.
10 *(v)* I must smooth the edges of this box. file, sand, plane, even, level off.

**smother**
1 *(v)* Don't smother me with that pillow! suffocate, stifle, asphyxiate, choke.
2 *(v)* Try to smother your giggles. stifle, suppress, hold back, keep in, muffle, hide.
3 *(v)* Let's smother the cake with cream. cover, plaster, heap, pile, envelop, drown, swamp, engulf, surround, blanket.

**smudge**
1 *(n)* There's a smudge on the front of this book. smear, streak, dirty mark, blotch, splotch, blot, spot, stain, smut.
2 *(v)* Try not to smudge the glass. smear, streak, blur, dirty, mark, blotch, stain.

**smug**
*(adj)* Don't look so smug when you get the answer right. self-satisfied, pleased with yourself, complacent, superior, conceited, self-righteous, holier-than-thou, priggish.

**snake**
1 *(n)* I saw a snake in the grass. serpent.
TYPES OF SNAKE: adder, boa constrictor, cobra, grass snake, python, rattlesnake, sea snake, sidewinder, tree snake, viper.
2 *(v)* The path began to snake up the mountain. See **wind** 2.

**snap**
1 *(v)* I hope this rope doesn't snap! break, break in two, give way, split, come apart.
2 *(v)* Can you hear the twigs snap under your feet? crack, crackle, pop, crunch.
3 snap at *(v)* Did the dog snap at you? bite, nip, go for, have a go at *(informal)*, snarl at, yap at, bark at, growl at.

**snarl**
1 *(v)* Don't snarl, Fido! growl, show your teeth, bare your teeth.
2 *(n)* "Clear off!" the man said with a snarl. growl, scowl, sneer, grimace.

**snatch**
*(v)* A thief tried to snatch my bag. grab, seize, take, wrench away, make off with, run off with, steal, nick *(slang)*, nab *(informal)*, swipe *(slang)*.

**sneak**
1 *(v)* Try to sneak past the guard. See **creep** 2.
2 *(v)* I tried to sneak the kitten into my bedroom. smuggle, slip, spirit.
3 sneak on *(v)* *(informal)* Will your sister sneak on us? See **tell on**.

# **s**neaky

**sneaky** see **sly**.

**sneer**
1 (n) "It's your own fault," said Edwin with a sneer. smirk, snigger, curl of the lip.
2 sneer at (v) Don't sneer at my efforts. See **scorn** 1.

**sniff**
(v) Don't sniff! sniffle, snuffle, snort, snivel.

**snigger** see **giggle**.

**snobbish**
(adj) Araminta is so snobbish; she looks down on everyone. condescending, snooty (informal), stuck-up (informal), superior, haughty, arrogant, disdainful, patronizing, hoity-toity (informal), toffee-nosed (slang).

**snooze** (informal) see **sleep** 2, 3.

**snub**
(v) Did Araminta snub you at the party? ignore, cut, cut you dead (informal), give you the cold shoulder, give you the brush-off (slang), put you down, humiliate, slight.

**snug** see **cosy**.

**snuggle**
(v) Watch the piglets snuggle against their mother. cuddle, nestle, nuzzle, curl up.

**soak**
1 (v) Soak the fruit in the liquid. immerse, steep, saturate, marinate, submerge, wet.
2 (v) This rain will soak my shoes. saturate, drench, seep through, penetrate.
3 soak up (v) This cloth will soak up the water. absorb, mop up, take in, take up.

**soaking**
(adj) My shoes are soaking. wet through, sopping wet, dripping wet, wringing wet, sodden, saturated, drenched, dripping, soggy, waterlogged (ground).
OPPOSITES: dry, bone-dry (informal).

**soar** see **rise** 1, 2, 3.

**sob** see **cry** 1.

**sofa**
(n) settee, couch, sofa bed, divan, chaise longue, futon, ottoman.

**soft**
1 (adj) Clare's skin is so soft. smooth, delicate, tender, silky, velvety, downy.
OPPOSITES: rough, tough.
2 (adj) The baby animals felt soft. fluffy, furry, fleecy, silky, downy, feathery, velvety, satiny, sleek, smooth.
OPPOSITES: rough, coarse.
3 (adj) This sofa is really soft. comfortable, well-padded, well-cushioned, squashy, bouncy, springy, yielding.
OPPOSITES: hard, uncomfortable.
4 (adj) Uri rubbed the spoon until it was soft. bendy, pliable, flexible, supple, malleable, bendable, limp, floppy.
OPPOSITES: hard, rigid.
5 (adj) This biscuit is soft. See **soggy** 2.
6 (adj) Be careful! The ground is soft. spongy, boggy, swampy, marshy, waterlogged, muddy, crumbly, yielding.
OPPOSITES: hard, firm.

7 (adj) Mum spoke in a soft voice. quiet, low, gentle, soothing, hushed, faint, scarcely audible, whispered, murmured.
OPPOSITES: loud, harsh.
8 (adj) The room was bathed in a soft light. gentle, dim, subdued, faint, low, pale, subtle, muted, restful, diffuse.
OPPOSITES: harsh, glaring.

**soggy**
1 (adj) The rain has made my shoes soggy. See **soaking**.
2 (adj) These biscuits are soggy. soft, mushy, spongy, squashy, pulpy, doughy.
OPPOSITES: crisp, crunchy.

**soil** see **earth** 2.

**soldier**
(n) fighter, trooper, serviceman, warrior (old-fashioned), marine, paratrooper, commando, guardsman, sentry, gunner, rifleman, cavalryman, infantryman, mercenary, conscript.

**solemn**
1 (adj) Sara looks solemn. See **serious** 1.
2 (adj) The coronation was a solemn occasion. stately, ceremonial, formal, grand, dignified, majestic, imposing, awe-inspiring, momentous, impressive.
OPPOSITES: frivolous, informal.

**solid**
1 (adj) Cement becomes solid when it sets. hard, firm, rigid, set, unyielding, thick, dense, compact.
OPPOSITES: liquid, powdery.
2 (adj) The castle walls are solid. thick, strong, sturdy, firm, substantial, stout, sound, unshakable, well-built, well-made.
OPPOSITES: flimsy, shaky.
3 (adj) My ring is solid silver. pure, real, genuine, unalloyed, unadulterated.
4 (adj) The traffic formed a solid line. continuous, unbroken, uninterrupted.

**solve**
(v) Can you solve this mystery? work out, figure out (informal), unravel, clear up, decipher, get to the bottom of, find the answer to, resolve, crack, find the key to, find the solution to, suss out (slang).

**song**
(n) Listen to this song. tune, ditty, air, melody, number, chorus.
TYPES OF SONG: anthem, aria, ballad, calypso, canon, carol, chant, folk song, hymn, jingle, love song, lullaby, madrigal, nursery rhyme, pop song, psalm, round, sea shanty, serenade, spiritual. ❖ Also see **music words** and **pop, rock & jazz**.

**soothing**
(adj) Let's listen to some soothing music. restful, relaxing, peaceful, calming, gentle.

**sophisticated**
(adj) Eva has become quite sophisticated since she went to Paris. stylish, poised, cultured, cultivated, urbane, refined, cosmopolitan, worldly, worldly-wise, blasé.
OPPOSITES: unsophisticated, naive.

**soppy** (informal) see **sentimental** 2.

**sore**
(adj) My knee is sore where I scraped it. painful, tender, raw, hurting, smarting, stinging, throbbing, aching, bruised, burning, inflamed, chafed, irritated.

**sorrow**
(n) Demi's sorrow was unbearable. sadness, grief, misery, anguish, despair, distress, unhappiness, heartache, heartbreak, wretchedness, woe, melancholy, gloom, despondency.
OPPOSITES: happiness, joy.

**sorry**
1 (adj) I hope you're sorry about breaking that window! repentant, remorseful, regretful, conscience-stricken, penitent, contrite, apologetic, ashamed, guilt-ridden.
OPPOSITES: unrepentant, unapologetic.
2 (adj) I was sorry when I heard that your cat had died. sad, upset, distressed, unhappy, miserable, sorrowful, grieved, concerned, disconsolate, crestfallen.
OPPOSITES: unconcerned, unmoved.
3 feel sorry for (phrase) You should feel sorry for the losing team. feel for, feel pity for, feel compassion for, sympathize with, commiserate with, condole with.

**sort**
1 (n) What sort of bread shall I buy? See **kind** 2.
2 (n) What sort of dog is that? See **kind** 3.
3 (v) Sort your books according to subject. organize, group, put in order, order, arrange, file, separate, divide, subdivide, classify, categorize, grade, rank, catalogue.

**sound**
1 (n) Can you hear a sound? noise.
2 (adj) Are these old floorboards sound? solid, sturdy, strong, substantial, intact, whole, undamaged, in good condition.
OPPOSITES: flimsy, weak.
3 (adj) Nadia gave me some sound advice. See **sensible** 2.

**sour**
1 (adj) Lemons taste sour. sharp, tangy, acid, tart, bitter, vinegary, piquant, unripe.
OPPOSITE: sweet.
2 (adj) This milk is sour. curdled, rancid, off, turned, bad, spoiled, fermented.
OPPOSITE: fresh.

**space**
1 (n) How can we fill this space? gap, hole, opening, blank, blank space, interval, area, expanse, stretch, vacuum.
2 (n) We need more space for our activities. room, scope, capacity, freedom, elbow room, room to manoeuvre, leeway.
3 (n) Vijay stared into space. infinity, emptiness, nothingness, the distance, thin air, the void, the blue.
4 (n) I'm reading a book about space. the universe, outer space, interplanetary space, interstellar space, intergalactic space, the galaxy, the solar system, the stars (plural), the planets (plural), astronomy.

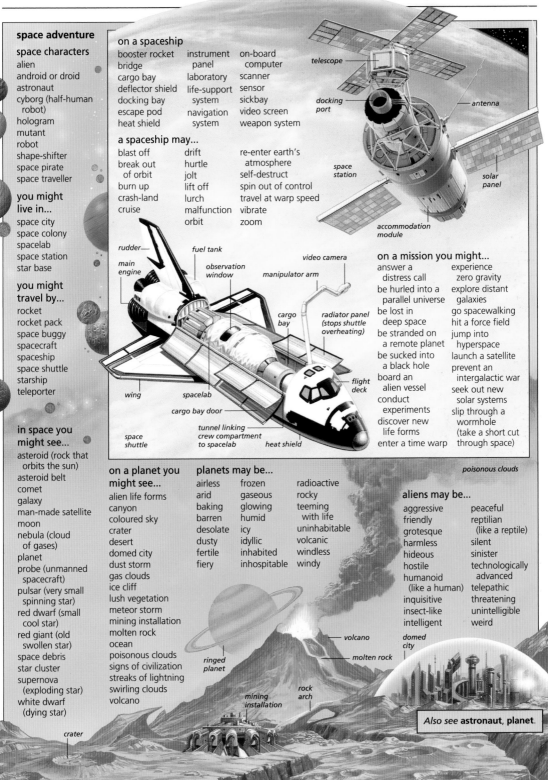

## space adventure

### space characters
alien
android or droid
astronaut
cyborg (half-human robot)
hologram
mutant
robot
shape-shifter
space pirate
space traveller

### you might live in...
space city
space colony
spacelab
space station
star base

### you might travel by...
rocket
rocket pack
space buggy
spacecraft
spaceship
space shuttle
starship
teleporter

### in space you might see...
asteroid (rock that orbits the sun)
asteroid belt
comet
galaxy
man-made satellite
moon
nebula (cloud of gases)
planet
probe (unmanned spacecraft)
pulsar (very small spinning star)
red dwarf (small cool star)
red giant (old swollen star)
space debris
star cluster
supernova (exploding star)
white dwarf (dying star)

### on a spaceship
booster rocket
bridge
cargo bay
deflector shield
docking bay
escape pod
heat shield
instrument panel
laboratory
life-support system
navigation system
on-board computer
scanner
sensor
sickbay
video screen
weapon system

### a spaceship may...
blast off
break out of orbit
burn up
crash-land
cruise
drift
hurtle
jolt
lift off
lurch
malfunction
orbit
re-enter earth's atmosphere
self-destruct
spin out of control
travel at warp speed
vibrate
zoom

### on a planet you might see...
alien life forms
canyon
coloured sky
crater
desert
domed city
dust storm
fiery
gas clouds
ice cliff
lush vegetation
meteor storm
mining installation
molten rock
ocean
poisonous clouds
signs of civilization
streaks of lightning
swirling clouds
volcano

### planets may be...
airless
arid
baking
barren
desolate
dusty
fertile
fiery
frozen
gaseous
glowing
humid
icy
idyllic
inhabited
inhospitable
radioactive
rocky
teeming with life
uninhabitable
volcanic
windless
windy

### on a mission you might...
answer a distress call
be hurled into a parallel universe
be lost in deep space
be stranded on a remote planet
be sucked into a black hole
board an alien vessel
conduct experiments
discover new life forms
enter a time warp
experience zero gravity
explore distant galaxies
go spacewalking
hit a force field
jump into hyperspace
launch a satellite
prevent an intergalactic war
seek out new solar systems
slip through a wormhole (take a short cut through space)

### aliens may be...
aggressive
friendly
grotesque
harmless
hideous
hostile
humanoid (like a human)
inquisitive
insect-like
intelligent
peaceful
reptilian (like a reptile)
silent
sinister
technologically advanced
telepathic
threatening
unintelligible
weird

**Labels on spaceship diagram:**
telescope
docking port
antenna
space station
solar panel
accommodation module
rudder
fuel tank
main engine
observation window
video camera
manipulator arm
cargo bay
radiator panel (stops shuttle overheating)
flight deck
wing
spacelab
cargo bay door
tunnel linking crew compartment to spacelab
space shuttle
heat shield

**Labels on planet scene:**
poisonous clouds
volcano
molten rock
domed city
ringed planet
mining installation
rock arch
crater

*Also see astronaut, planet.*

# spank

**spank** see **smack**.

**spare**
1 *(adj)* Take some spare socks. extra, additional, supplementary, reserve.
2 *(adj)* Is that sandwich spare? left over, going begging, unwanted, unneeded, superfluous, surplus to requirements.
3 *(adj)* In my spare time I play tennis. free, leisure, unoccupied, remaining, available.
4 *(v)* I can spare a few pounds for a good cause. afford, part with, donate, give up, sacrifice, let you have, give, provide.
5 *(v)* I can spare this piece of cake. let you have, do without, manage without, get along without, dispense with.
6 *(v)* The judge decided to spare Burglar Beryl. have mercy on, be lenient towards, go easy on *(informal)*, pardon, let off, reprieve, release, free, let go.
OPPOSITES: punish, condemn.

**spark**
*(n)* The firework sent out a spark of light. flash, flicker, flare, glint, gleam, glimmer.

**sparkle**
*(v)* Look how the stars sparkle in the sky. twinkle, flicker, shimmer, flash, glitter, glisten, glint, glimmer, gleam, shine, glow.

**speak**
1 *(v)* Why didn't you speak earlier? say something, speak out, speak up, make yourself heard, open your mouth, have your say, express yourself, pipe up.
2 *(v)* Can you speak Chinese? talk, communicate in, express yourself in, hold a conversation in, get by in *(informal)*.
3 *(v)* Please speak your words more clearly. pronounce, enunciate, articulate.
4 *(v)* Dad can speak for hours on any subject. talk, hold forth, lecture, spout *(informal)*, sermonize, spiel, speechify, give a talk, give a speech, deliver an address.

**speak to**
*(v)* Mrs Badger would like to speak to you. talk to, have a word with, chat to, have words with, have a discussion with, converse with, bend your ear *(informal)*.

**special**
1 *(adj)* Eliza has a special talent for drawing. extraordinary, exceptional, remarkable, unusual, rare, outstanding, notable, unique, singular.
OPPOSITES: unexceptional, commonplace.
2 *(adj)* This is a special day for our school. important, momentous, significant, noteworthy, memorable, red-letter, gala.
OPPOSITES: normal, ordinary.
3 *(adj)* Soy sauce has a special flavour. distinctive, unique, unmistakable, characteristic, distinct, definite, specific, particular, individual, peculiar.
OPPOSITES: unremarkable, undistinctive.

**speck**
1 *(n)* I've got a speck of paint on my shirt. spot, fleck, speckle, dot, smudge, mark.
2 *(n)* There isn't a speck of food left. bit, crumb, grain, shred, trace, jot, iota, atom.

**speckled**
*(adj)* A speckled egg. flecked, freckled, spotted, spotty, stippled, mottled, dappled.

**spectacular**
*(adj)* The acrobats gave a spectacular display. breathtaking, dazzling, eye-catching, dramatic, daring, extraordinary, remarkable, staggering, striking, stunning *(informal)*, sensational, magnificent, impressive, astonishing, amazing.

**spectator**
*(n)* onlooker, viewer, observer, looker-on, bystander, passer-by, witness, eyewitness.

**speech**
1 *(n)* The speech lasted for hours. talk, address, lecture, sermon, oration, spiel.
2 *(n)* Mum says my speech isn't clear. pronunciation, diction, enunciation, articulation, accent, voice, dialect.

**speechless**
*(adj)* Your news left me speechless. dumbstruck, dumbfounded, thunderstruck, stunned, at a loss for words, tongue-tied, silent, mute.

**speed**
1 *(n)* The speed of the car amazed us. pace, swiftness, rapidity, quickness, velocity, acceleration, momentum.
OPPOSITES: sluggishness, slowness.
2 *(n)* Jo walks at a great speed. rate, pace.
3 *(v)* You may be fined if you speed. break the speed limit, exceed the speed limit, go over the speed limit, drive too fast.
4 *(v)* I saw you speed past on your bike. race, zoom, flash, fly, whiz *(informal)*, whoosh *(informal)*, zip, hurtle, tear, bomb, belt *(slang)*, streak, career, dash, go like the wind, go like a bat out of hell *(slang)*.
OPPOSITES: dawdle, crawl.

**speed up**
1 *(v)* The train began to speed up. accelerate, pick up speed, gather speed, go faster, quicken, gain momentum, put on a spurt, get a move on *(informal)*.
OPPOSITES: slow down, decelerate.
2 *(v)* We need to speed up the wedding preparations. See **hurry** 2.

**speedy** see **fast** 1, 2.

**spell**
*(n)* The witch used a spell to turn the prince into a frog. charm, incantation, magic formula, magic words *(plural)*, curse.

**spend**
1 *(v)* How much money did you spend? pay, pay out, get through, part with, lay out *(informal)*, shell out *(informal)*, fork out *(slang)*, cough up *(informal)*, lash out *(informal)*, splurge, blow *(slang)*, squander, waste, fritter away.
OPPOSITE: save.
2 *(v)* How shall we spend the day? occupy, fill, pass, while away, use up.
3 *(v)* You should spend more time on your homework. put in, concentrate, invest, lavish, devote.

**spice**
*(n)* This curry needs more spice. flavouring, seasoning, taste, flavour, bite, piquancy.
TYPES OF SPICE: allspice, caraway seed, cardamom, cayenne, chilli, cinnamon, clove, coriander, cumin, curry powder, ginger, mace, nutmeg, paprika, pepper, pimento, saffron, star anise, turmeric.

**spicy**
1 *(adj)* A spicy curry. hot, peppery, fiery, piquant, aromatic, highly seasoned.
OPPOSITES: bland, mild.
2 *(adj)* *(informal)* Spicy gossip. See **juicy** 2.

**spike**
*(n)* Be careful of that spike! point, prong, barb, stake, nail, thorn, prickle, needle.

**spiky** see **prickly** 1.

**spill**
1 *(v)* Try not to spill your drink. knock over, overturn, tip over, upset.
2 *(v)* Lift the bucket slowly so the water doesn't spill. spill out, slop over, run over, brim over, overflow, pour out, flow out.

**spin**
*(v)* Open the music box and watch the ballerina spin. go round, turn, twirl, whirl, pirouette, revolve, rotate, gyrate, wheel.

**spine** see **back** 1.

**spine-chilling** see **frightening**.

**spirit**
1 *(n)* Do you think your spirit will live on after you die? soul, inner self, psyche.
2 *(n)* The castle was haunted by a spirit. See **ghost**.
3 *(n)* The explorers showed great spirit in the face of danger. See **courage**.
4 *(n)* It's hard to suppress Lydia; she's got so much spirit. energy, life, enthusiasm, sparkle, fire, vigour, zest, verve, zip *(informal)*, willpower, determination.

**spit**
1 *(v)* Don't spit on the floor! gob *(informal)*, spew, expectorate, hawk.
2 *(v)* Graham tends to spit when he talks. splutter, sputter, spray, hiss.

**spiteful**
*(adj)* Tania's spiteful comments upset me. malicious, snide, hurtful, cruel, nasty, unkind, catty *(informal)*, bitchy *(informal)*, vicious, vindictive, poisonous, venomous.

**splash**
1 *(v)* Marcus began to splash paint on the walls. slap, slop, slosh *(informal)*, spatter, splatter, sprinkle, squirt, spray, shower, spill, daub, splodge.
2 *(v)* Can you hear the waves splash against the rocks? break, dash, wash, surge, smack, swish, swash, plash, plop.
3 *(v)* I love to splash in the river. paddle, wallow, wade, dabble, bathe, plunge.

**splendid**
1 *(adj)* Splendid tapestries. magnificent, gorgeous, impressive, rich, costly, sumptuous, opulent, ornate, dazzling, glittering, resplendent, lavish, luxurious.

**2** *(adj) A splendid essay.* See **excellent**.

**splinter**
**1** *(n) A small splinter broke off the table.* See **chip** 2.
**2** *(v) The explosion made the glass splinter.* See **smash** 2.

**split**
**1** *(v) I hope this bag doesn't split.* burst, tear, rip, come apart, break, give way.
**2** *(v) The ground seemed to split beneath my feet.* open, crack, gape, yawn, part.
**3** *(v) Where does the path split in two?* See **divide** 1.
**4** *(v) Let's split the money between us.* See **divide** 3.
**5** *(n) I have a split in my jeans.* See **tear** 4.

**split up** see **separate** 1, 3.

**spoil**
**1** *(v) One mistake could spoil your chances of winning.* See **ruin** 1.
**2** *(v) I didn't mean to spoil your painting.* damage, ruin, wreck, deface, mess up, smudge, blemish, mark, stain, botch.
**3** *(v) I wish Granny wouldn't spoil you.* indulge, overindulge, pamper, mollycoddle, wait on you hand and foot, cosset, spoon-feed, baby, pander to.

**spoilsport**
*(n) Don't be such a spoilsport!* killjoy, wet blanket *(informal)*, party pooper *(informal)*, misery *(informal)*, dog in the manger.

**spoof**
*(n) (informal) This film is a spoof of a disaster movie.* takeoff *(informal)*, send-up *(informal)*, parody, pastiche, satire.

**spooky**
*(adj) (informal) The castle looks spooky in the moonlight.* eerie, creepy *(informal)*, mysterious, ghostly, uncanny, unearthly, weird, frightening, spine-chilling, haunted.
❖ *Also see* **ghosts & hauntings**.

**sport**
*(n) Sport is good for you.* exercise, games *(plural)*, physical activity, PE (physical education), physical recreation.
TYPES OF SPORT: aikido, American football, angling, archery, athletics, badminton, baseball, basketball, beach volleyball, billiards, bobsleighing, bowls, boxing, canoeing, cricket, croquet, curling, cycling, darts, diving, dressage, eventing, fencing, Gaelic football, golf, greyhound racing, gymnastics, handball, hockey, horse racing, hurling, ice hockey, judo, jujitsu, karate, lacrosse, luge, motorcycle racing, motor racing, mountaineering, netball, orienteering, polo, pool, rallycross, rock climbing, rounders, rowing, rugby league, rugby union, sailing, shooting, show jumping, skating, skiing, snooker, soccer, softball, squash, surfing, swimming, synchronized swimming, table tennis, tae kwon do, tennis, trampolining, volleyball, water polo, water-skiing, weightlifting, windsurfing, wrestling, yachting. *Also see* **athletics**.

## sport words

### types of sporting event

| | |
|---|---|
| challenge | play-off |
| championship | preliminary |
| competition | round |
| contest | qualifying |
| final | round |
| fixture | quarterfinal |
| friendly match | race |
| game | regatta |
| head-to-head | replay |
| heat | semifinal |
| match | test match |
| Olympic Games | time trial |
| Paralympics | tournament |

*gymnasts tumble*

*fencers lunge*

*foil*

*mask*

*goalkeepers leap*

### sport moves

| | | | |
|---|---|---|---|
| attack | evade | pass | speed |
| block | field | pitch | spin |
| bowl | glide | punch | sprint |
| catch | hurtle | race | stretch |
| chase | intercept | reach | strike |
| corner | jump | retrieve | swerve |
| dart | kick | save | swing |
| defend | leap | score | tackle |
| deflect | lob | shoot | throw |
| dive | lunge | skim | tumble |
| dodge | mark | slam | twist |
| dribble | overtake | slide | vault |
| duck | parry | smash | volley |

*motorcyclists corner*

*basketball players dribble*

### competitors may...

| | | |
|---|---|---|
| be disqualified | go flat out | storm ahead |
| be stretchered off | miss a shot | take a penalty |
| break a record | play safe | take evasive |
| cheat | put on a spurt | action |
| clinch the match | reach a new | take the lead |
| commit a foul | personal best | use tactics |
| draw level | run out of steam | work as a |
| equalize | score a hat-trick | team |
| fend off a tackle | set the pace | |
| follow a game plan | | |

*tennis court*

*sports complex*

### sporting events can be...

| | |
|---|---|
| dangerous | hotly |
| demanding | contested |
| draining | nail-biting |
| dramatic | nerve-racking |
| dull | punishing |
| electrifying | strenuous |
| emotional | tedious |
| exhausting | tense |
| exhilarating | testing |
| frustrating | thrilling |
| gruelling | uneventful |

*skaters spin*

*ski pole*

*skiers swerve*

*mast*

*sail*

*baseball players swing at the ball*

*batten*

*boom*

*window*

*board*

*judo players throw their opponents*

*windsurfers skim the waves*

### sporting events can end in...

| | |
|---|---|
| celebration | humiliation |
| controversy | injury time |
| dead heat | photo finish |
| defeat | riot |
| disaster | success |
| draw | tie |
| extra time | triumph |
| failure | victory |

*stadium*

*tiered seating*

*track*

*sports hall*

*field*

*swimming pool*

**sporty**
*(adj) Tabby is very sporty.* athletic, active, energetic, fit, hearty, outdoorsy *(informal).*

**spot**
1 *(v) Did you spot the difference between the pictures?* notice, detect, identify, pinpoint, discover, pick out, single out, observe, put your finger on *(informal).*
2 *(v) Did you spot my note? See* **notice** 1.
3 *(n) Try to rub that spot off the wall.* mark, stain, speck, fleck, smudge, blotch, blob, blot, splotch, patch, blemish.
4 *(n) Jilly has a spot on her chin.* pimple, zit *(slang),* blackhead, boil, pustule, mole.
5 *(n) We found a perfect spot to camp. See* **place** 1.
6 **spots** *(plural) Our curtains are blue with yellow spots.* dots *(plural),* polka dots *(plural),* circles *(plural),* blobs *(plural).*

**spotless** *see* **clean** 2.

**spotty**
*(adj) Spike has a spotty face.* pimply, acne-covered, blotchy, blemished, freckled.

**sprawl**
*(v) I love to sprawl in front of the telly.* stretch out, lie around, lounge, loll, flop, slouch, slump, spread-eagle.

**spray**
1 *(v) Don't spray water over me!* sprinkle, shower, spatter, splash, scatter, squirt.
2 *(n) The fountain sent out a spray of water.* jet, shower, sprinkling, mist, drizzle, squirt, droplets *(plural),* vapour.

**spread**
1 *(v) Spread the rug on the ground.* spread out, stretch out, open out, lay out, unroll, unfold, arrange, display.
2 *(v) Spread the glue thickly.* apply, smear on, plaster on, lay on, daub, coat.
3 *(v) See the puddle spread! See* **grow** 2.
4 *(v) The violence may spread.* increase, escalate, mushroom, grow, proliferate.
5 *(v) Spread the news!* pass on, circulate, broadcast, publicize, make known, make public, proclaim, disseminate, transmit.

**spring** *see* **jump** 1.

**springy** *see* **bouncy** 1.

**sprinkle**
1 *(v) Sprinkle sugar over the cake.* scatter, strew, shower, spread, dust, pepper.
2 *(v) Don't sprinkle water everywhere! See* **spray** 1.

**sprint** *see* **run** 1.

**spurt**
1 *(v) Water began to spurt from the pipe. See* **squirt.**
2 *(n) I felt a spurt of speed as the car accelerated.* burst, surge, rush, explosion.

**spy**
1 *(n) Could Stanley be a spy?* secret agent, undercover agent, enemy agent, mole *(informal),* double agent, infiltrator.
2 **spy on** *(v) Let's spy on Leo!* keep watch on, keep an eye on, follow, shadow, tail, trail, snoop on, eavesdrop on.

**squabble** *see* **argue** 1.

**squash**
1 *(v) Don't squash the strawberries!* crush, squeeze, squish, flatten, pulp, pulverize, smash, mash, mangle, compress, pound, stamp on, tread on, trample on, crumple.
2 *(v) I can't squash any more food into the fridge. See* **squeeze** 1.

**squashy**
*(adj) I hate squashy bananas.* soft, squishy, squidgy, mushy, pulpy, spongy, soggy.

**squat**
1 *(v) Squat behind this bush! See* **crouch.**
2 *(adj) Angus has a squat figure.* dumpy, stocky, chunky, stubby, thickset, short.
OPPOSITE: lanky.

**squawk**
*(v) The parrot began to squawk.* screech, shriek, squeal, cackle, crow, cheep, hoot.

**squeak**
*(v) Can you hear my brakes squeak?* squeal, screech, creak, scrape, grate, peep.

**squeal** *see* **scream.**

**squeeze**
1 *(v) I can't squeeze any more food into the fridge.* squash, cram, stuff, pack, crowd, jam, ram, force, wedge.
2 *(v) Try to squeeze the water out of the cloth.* wring, force, twist, screw, extract.
3 *(v) Don't squeeze my hand like that!* grip, clasp, clutch, pinch, nip, press, crush, squash, compress.
4 *(v) Try to squeeze your way through the crowd.* edge, shoulder, worm, wriggle, squirm, wiggle, elbow, jostle, push, shove.
5 *(n) I gave Anna a friendly squeeze.* hug, embrace, cuddle, clasp, grasp, bear hug.

**squirm**
1 *(v) Don't squirm about! See* **wriggle** 1.
2 *(v) Dad's jokes make me squirm.* cringe, wince, die of shame *(informal),* curl up and die *(informal),* flinch, blench, writhe.

**squirt**
*(v) Watch the water squirt out of the hose.* spurt, shoot, gush, spout, jet, spray, splash, spatter, pour, spit, spew, shower.

**stab**
*(v) Stab the dragon through the heart!* pierce, spear, knife, spike, lance, skewer, impale, run through, gore, transfix.

**stack** *see* **pile** 1, 2.

**stage**
1 *(n) Stand on the stage to recite your poem.* platform, dais, rostrum, podium.
2 *(n) We completed the final stage of our journey.* phase, leg, section, step, lap.
3 *(v) Let's stage a play next term.* perform, put on, produce, present, mount.

**stagger**
1 *(v) The weight of the parcel made me stagger.* totter, teeter, reel, lurch, stumble, wobble, sway, falter.
2 *(v) The height of the skyscrapers will stagger you. See* **astonish.**

**stagnant**
*(adj) A pool of stagnant water.* motionless, still, stale, foul, dirty, filthy, polluted.
OPPOSITES: flowing, fresh.

**stain**
1 *(n) I must get this stain off my shirt.* mark, spot, blotch, smudge, smear, blot.
2 *(n) The rumour left a stain on my reputation.* smear, slur, blot, blemish, taint.
3 *(v) Those sweets will stain your tongue blue.* dye, colour, tinge, tint, discolour.

**stairs**
*(plural n)* steps *(plural),* flight of stairs, staircase, stairway.

**stale**
1 *(adj) This bread is stale.* old, dry, dried up, dried out, hard, mouldy.
OPPOSITE: fresh.
2 *(adj) The air in the cellar smelt stale.* musty, fusty, frowsty, stuffy, foul, damp.
OPPOSITE: fresh.

**stammer**
*(v) I always stammer when I'm nervous.* stutter, splutter, falter, hesitate, stumble.

**stamp**
1 *(n) Look for the maker's stamp on the vase.* mark, imprint, hallmark, seal, label, logo, signature, impression, brand.
2 *(v) Please don't stamp around the house.* stomp *(informal),* clump, clomp, tramp, pound, thump, thud.
3 **stamp on** *(v) Don't stamp on the flowers! See* **trample on.**

**stand**
1 *(v) Stand when the judge comes in.* stand up, rise, get to your feet, get up.
OPPOSITES: sit, sit down.
2 *(v) Don't stand on my toes! See* **step** 5.
3 *(v) Stand the photograph on the shelf.* put, place, set, position, set upright, prop.
4 *(v) I can't stand the sight of blood!* bear, stick *(slang),* endure, abide, tolerate, stomach, take, handle, cope with, put up with *(informal).*

**standard**
1 *(n) Are you pleased with the standard of my work? See* **quality** 1, 2.
2 *(n) Steve's tennis is below standard.* average, the norm, par.
3 *(adj) It's standard practice to brush your teeth in the morning. See* **normal** 1.

**stand by**
1 *(v) I'll stand by you whatever happens.* support, be loyal to, stay with, stick with *(informal),* back, take your side, defend.
2 *(v) Stand by for takeoff!* be prepared, be ready, wait, wait in the wings.

**stand for**
*(v) What does "PC" stand for?* represent, mean, indicate, denote, signify, symbolize.

**stand in for**
*(v) I'll stand in for you if you're ill.* take your place, fill in for, cover for, deputize for, take over from, substitute for, replace, represent, understudy *(theatre).*

**stand out**
(v) You'll certainly stand out in that orange shirt! stick out, be noticed, attract attention, be conspicuous, be eye-catching, stand out from the crowd.

**stand up for**
(v) I'll stand up for you. stick up for (informal), defend, come to your defence, back, support, take your side, stand by.

**star**
1 (n) Astronomers have sighted a new star. ❖ See **space adventure**.
2 (n) Jodie longs to be a star. celebrity, superstar, megastar, big name, top draw, idol, screen goddess, starlet, celeb (informal), VIP (very important person).
3 (v) Who will star in this film? take the lead, play the starring role, head the cast, top the bill, co-star, feature.

**stare**
1 (v) When I met Famous Fred, all I could do was stare. gape, gaze, look, gawp (slang), gawk, goggle, be open-mouthed, ogle, rubberneck (slang).
2 (n) A hard stare. glare, look, dirty look.

**start**
1 (v) You've got lots to do, so you'd better start soon. get started, make a start, make a beginning, begin, get going, get moving, get weaving (informal), take the plunge (informal), get the show on the road (informal), pull your finger out (informal). OPPOSITE: stop.
2 (v) When did life on earth first start? See **begin** 4.
3 (v) Are you packed and ready to start? See **leave** 1.
4 (v) Who will start the discussion? begin, commence, open, initiate, kick off (informal), set in motion, kick-start, get going, get under way, start the ball rolling. OPPOSITES: end, finish.
5 (v) Mum wants to start her own business. set up, establish, launch, create, found, form, pioneer, get off the ground (informal), get going, set in motion. OPPOSITES: wind up, close down.
6 (n) Danni missed the start of the show. beginning, opening, commencement, kickoff (informal), introduction. OPPOSITE: end.
7 (n) Greg got a start on the others at the beginning of the race. head start, lead, advantage, edge, margin.
8 (n) Bo woke with a start. See **jump** 6.

**startle**
(v) Did the firecracker startle you? alarm, scare, frighten, make you jump, give you a start, catch you unawares, shock, surprise, unnerve, unsettle, disturb, disconcert.

**starving**
1 (adj) The refugees were starving. hungry, starved, famished, underfed, malnourished, dying of starvation.
2 (adj) (informal) I'm starving! ravenous, famished, hungry.

**state**
1 (v) Did Beryl state that she was innocent? declare, say, assert, affirm, announce, proclaim, profess, reveal.
2 (v) You'll have a chance to state your opinion. put, express, voice, present, put across, explain, communicate, submit.
3 (n) The castle is owned by the state. nation, country, government, people (plural), citizens (plural), republic, kingdom, realm (old-fashioned), commonwealth.
4 (n) What sort of state are the survivors in? condition, shape, frame of mind, mood, spirits (plural), form, health.

**stay**
1 (v) Don't stay in town too long. remain, hang around, linger, loiter, delay, stop, wait around, dally.
2 (v) We're hoping to stay in a luxury hotel. spend the night, stop over, take a room, put up, lodge, board.
3 (v) If we like Australia we might stay there. See **settle** 1.
4 (v) Please stay standing. remain, keep, continue, carry on, go on.
5 (n) Enjoy your stay in London! holiday, break, stopover, visit, vacation.

**steady**
1 (adj) This chair isn't very steady. firm, stable, safe, secure, solid. OPPOSITES: unsteady, wobbly.
2 (adj) The steady rain kept us indoors. continuous, constant, incessant, nonstop, endless, persistent, ceaseless, unremitting. OPPOSITES: intermittent, sporadic.
3 (adj) The drummer kept up a steady beat. regular, rhythmic, even, constant, repeated, unvarying, uniform, unhurried. OPPOSITES: irregular, uneven.

**steal**
1 (v) It's wrong to steal. thieve, pilfer, shoplift, pick pockets, commit a theft.
2 (v) Someone tried to steal my purse. take, make off with, walk off with, pocket, filch, misappropriate, pinch (informal), nick (slang), lift (informal), swipe (slang).

**steep**
1 (adj) There's a steep drop down to the beach. sheer, precipitous, sharp, sudden, abrupt, vertical, perpendicular. OPPOSITES: gentle, gradual.
2 (v) Steep your shirt in water. See **soak** 1.

**steer**
(v) The car was hard to steer. control, handle, drive, direct, navigate, pilot.

**step**
1 (n) My foot slipped off the step. stair, rung (ladder), doorstep, tread (staircase).
2 (n) Take one step forwards. pace, stride.
3 (n) We must plan our next step carefully. move, manoeuvre, course of action, act.
4 (n) Learning to read is an important step for a child. step forward, advance, development, progression, stage, phase.
5 (v) Don't step on my toes! tread, stand, tramp, trample, walk, stamp.

**stern**
1 (adj) A stern look. severe, grim, forbidding, serious, disapproving, tight-lipped, steely-eyed, frowning, unsmiling, unsympathetic, sombre, sober, austere.
2 (adj) A stern teacher. See **strict** 1.

**stick**
1 (n) Throw another stick on the bonfire. branch, twig, switch, piece of wood.
2 (n) Grandpa uses a stick when he walks. walking stick, cane, crutch, staff, crook.
3 (n) Don't hit me with that stick! rod, cane, switch, birch, truncheon, baton, club, cudgel, cosh.
4 (n) Tie the ivy to a stick so it won't droop. cane, pole, stake, post.
5 (v) Stick the pieces together. glue, tape, paste, gum, fix, fasten, attach, join, bond.
6 (v) Don't stick your finger in the trifle! put, poke, jab, stab, dig, thrust, insert.
7 (v) Let's hope the car doesn't stick in the mud. get stuck, get bogged down, get embedded, get lodged, get clogged up.
8 (v) I felt a bone stick in my throat. catch, lodge, wedge, jam, get trapped, snag.
9 (v) (informal) Stick your trainers in the wardrobe. See **bung**.
10 (v) (slang) I can't stick this noise any longer! See **stand** 4.

**stick at** see **persevere**.

**stick out**
1 (v) How far does the ledge stick out? jut out, extend, project, protrude, overhang.
2 (v) You'll certainly stick out in that orange shirt! See **stand out**.

**sticky**
1 (adj) A sticky label. gummed, adhesive.
2 (adj) A sticky mixture. gluey, gooey (informal), tacky, glutinous, viscous.
3 (adj) A sticky bun. gooey (informal), syrupy, treacly, sugary, creamy, jammy.
4 (adj) Sticky weather. See **muggy**.

**stiff**
1 (adj) I can't bend this plastic; it's too stiff. rigid, hard, firm, inflexible, unbending, unyielding, inelastic, brittle. OPPOSITES: flexible, pliable.
2 (adj) After the climb my muscles felt stiff. tight, tense, taut, unsupple, painful, aching, sore, creaky (informal), arthritic. OPPOSITE: supple.
3 (adj) The robot's movements looked stiff. See **awkward** 2.

**stifle** see **smother** 1, 2.

**still**
1 (adj) Andy stood still and stared. motionless, stock-still, rooted to the spot, without moving, immobile, stationary, paralysed, transfixed, spellbound, frozen.
2 (adj) The clouds were reflected in the still water. calm, motionless, smooth, unruffled, undisturbed, stagnant. OPPOSITE: turbulent.
3 (adj) What a still evening! quiet, silent, calm, tranquil, peaceful, windless, airless. OPPOSITES: stormy, noisy.

# sting

**sting**
(v) *If you get soap in your eyes it will sting.* smart, burn, prick, hurt, tingle, irritate.

**stingy** *see* **mean 5.**

**stink**
1 (v) *Those rotten eggs really stink.* smell, reek, pong *(informal)*, stink to high heaven *(informal)*, hum *(slang)*, whiff *(slang)*.
2 (n) *What's making that stink?* stench, bad smell, foul odour, pong *(informal)*.

**stir**
1 (v) *Stir the ingredients together.* mix, blend, whisk, beat, whip.
2 (v) *The leaves began to stir in the breeze.* move, quiver, tremble, flutter, rustle, shake, twitch.
3 **stir up** (v) *Oscar loves to stir up trouble.* make, cause, start, provoke, spark off, trigger off, incite, instigate, inflame.

**stomach**
1 (n) *Tabitha has a pain in her stomach.* tummy *(informal)*, belly, abdomen, insides *(plural)* *(informal)*, guts *(plural)*.
2 (n) *Trevor has a huge stomach.* tummy *(informal)*, paunch, gut *(slang)*, beer belly *(slang)*, spare tyre *(informal)*, potbelly.

**stone**
1 (n) *I found a smooth stone on the beach.* pebble, rock, boulder.
2 (n) *Flash Frank wears a ring with a huge stone in it. See* **jewel.**
3 (n) *Don't eat the stone in the middle of the fruit.* pip, seed, kernel, nut.
4 (n) *The grave was marked by a stone.* gravestone, headstone, tombstone, monument, memorial stone, tablet.
5 **stones** *(plural n) Don't slip on the stones!* gravel, scree, shingle, pebbles *(plural)*, cobbles *(plural)*.

**stony**
(adj) *We struggled over the stony ground.* rocky, rough, pebbly, gravelly, shingly *(beach)*, boulder-strewn, hard, flinty.

**stoop**
1 (v) *You'll have to stoop to get into the cave.* duck, crouch, bend down, lean down, bow down, bend your head, lower your head, hunch your shoulders, squat.
2 (v) *How could you stoop to playing such a mean trick? See* **lower yourself.**

**stop**
1 (v) *Wait for the bus to stop before you get off.* come to a stop, come to a halt, come to a standstill, pull up, draw up, halt, come to rest, grind to a halt.
OPPOSITES: go, start.
2 (v) *Let's stop now; I'm tired.* pause, have a break, rest, finish, call it a day *(informal)*, knock off *(informal)*, down tools.
OPPOSITES: keep going, carry on.
3 (v) *Dad has decided to stop smoking.* finish, cease, quit, give up, desist from, refrain from, leave off, cut out *(informal)*, pack in *(informal)*, kick *(informal)*.
OPPOSITES: start, take up.

4 (v) *The college may stop our pottery classes.* put an end to, call a halt to, end, finish, wind up, shut down, discontinue, cut short, break off, axe *(informal)*, drop.
OPPOSITES: start, set up.
5 (v) *You can't stop me from going to the disco. See* **prevent 2.**
6 (v) *Stop that man!* catch, seize, restrain, hold, capture, intercept, arrest, detain.
7 (v) *We must stop the bleeding.* stem, staunch, check, shut back, control.
8 (v) *Will you stop anywhere on your way to Paris?* break your journey, spend time, stay, spend a night, stay over, put up, visit.
9 (n) *Is this your stop?* bus stop, station, halt, terminus, destination, depot.

**store**
1 (v) *Farmers have to store hay for the winter.* stock up on, set aside, put by, lay in, save, reserve, stash away *(informal)*, salt away, accumulate, amass, hoard, stockpile.
2 (n) *Pirate Peg has a huge store of gold.* hoard, stock, stockpile, quantity, supply, fund, reserve, cache, accumulation.

**storm**
1 (n) *The storm wrecked our garden.* gale, squall, tempest, thunderstorm, blizzard, hurricane, typhoon, cyclone, tornado, whirlwind, twister *(informal)*, monsoon.
2 (v) *Why did Josie storm out of the room like that?* flounce, stamp, stomp *(informal)*, rush, charge, fly, stalk, march, stride.

**stormy**
1 (adj) *Stormy weather.* rough, windy, squally, blustery, gusty, thundery, rainy, foul, dirty, wild, violent.
OPPOSITES: calm, fine.
2 (adj) *Stormy seas. See* **rough 2.**

**story**
1 (n) *Tell me the story of the giant octopus!* tale, yarn *(informal)*, anecdote, account, history, narrative.
TYPES OF STORY: adventure story, allegory, crime story, detective story, fable, fairy tale, fantasy story, folk tale, ghost story, historical romance, horror story, legend, love story, mystery, myth, novel, parable, romance, saga, science fiction story, spy story, thriller, whodunit *(informal)*.
2 (n) *Clark wrote a good story for "Rap Weekly". See* **article 1.**

**stout** *see* **plump.**

**straight**
1 (adj) *This wall isn't straight.* level, even, horizontal, perpendicular, vertical, upright, true, flush, plumb, square, aligned, in line.
OPPOSITES: crooked, bent.
2 (adj) *We took the straight route to the coast.* direct, short, undeviating, quick.
OPPOSITES: indirect, circuitous.
3 (adj) *Our team has had five straight wins.* consecutive, successive, unbroken, uninterrupted, continuous, in a row.
4 (adj) *A straight answer. See* **honest 1.**

## storm words

| in a storm | thunder may... | the rain may... | storms can... | storms can be... |
|---|---|---|---|---|
| billowing clouds | boom | beat down | block roads | awe-inspiring |
| cloudburst | crack | bucket down | bring down power lines | cataclysmic |
| deluge | crash | lash down | cut off villages | catastrophic |
| downpour | echo | pelt down | damage crops | deafening |
| driving rain | growl | pour down | destroy buildings | destructive |
| forked lightning | resound | teem down | flatten fences | devastating |
| gale | reverberate | **the wind may...** | flood homes | dramatic |
| gust of wind | roar | batter | mangle cars | ear-splitting |
| hailstones | roll | blast | maroon motorists | fierce |
| inky sky | rumble | blow | rip off roof tiles | frightening |
| lashing rain | **lightning may...** | buffet | smash windows | furious |
| leaden sky | flare | gust | start fires | powerful |
| peal of thunder | flash | howl | swell rivers | raging |
| sheet of lightning | flicker | moan | topple chimneys | savage |
| streak of lightning | light up the sky | rage | uproot trees | short-lived |
| thunderbolt | streak across the sky | roar | wreck ships | spectacular |
| thunderclap | strike | shriek | | squally |
| torrential rain | zigzag | swirl | | tempestuous |
| | | wail | | turbulent |
| | | whirl | | unrelenting |
| | | | | violent |
| | | | | wild |

**5** *(adv) Go straight to school.* directly, immediately, at once, instantly, without delay, by the shortest route.

**straightaway** *see* **immediately**.

**strain**

**1** *(n) I can't take the strain any longer! See* **pressure** 2.

**2** *(v) Did you strain a muscle?* pull, sprain, injure, damage, hurt, twist, tear, wrench.

**3** *(v) Reading in the dark can strain your eyes.* tire, weaken, tax, fatigue, damage.

**4** *(v) Strain the mixture.* sieve, sift, filter, separate, percolate *(coffee)*.

**stranded**

*(adj) Pirate Peg was stranded on a desert island.* marooned, shipwrecked, cast away, left high and dry, stuck, abandoned.

**strange**

**1** *(adj) Ziggy wears some really strange clothes.* unusual, extraordinary, remarkable, funny, odd, peculiar, curious, queer, weird, bizarre, outlandish, eccentric, way-out *(informal)*, wacky *(slang)*, off-the-wall *(slang)*, uncommon, abnormal. OPPOSITES: normal, standard.

**2** *(adj) I heard a strange noise outside the window.* odd, peculiar, funny, weird, mysterious, eerie, spooky *(informal)*, uncanny, unnatural, unearthly, puzzling, perplexing, mystifying, inexplicable. OPPOSITES: ordinary, unremarkable.

**3** *(adj) The new school seemed strange to me.* unfamiliar, alien, foreign, different, new, novel, unknown. OPPOSITES: familiar, well-known.

**4** *(adj) Indiana was alone in a strange land.* unfamiliar, foreign, alien, exotic, remote, little-known, unexplored. OPPOSITES: familiar, well-known.

**5** *(adj) I felt strange being the only girl in the class.* odd, awkward, ill at ease, uncomfortable, out of place, lost. OPPOSITES: at ease, comfortable.

**strangle**

*(v) Don't strangle yourself with that scarf!* choke, throttle, strangulate, garrotte.

**strap**

*(v) Strap the parcel to your bicycle rack.* buckle, lash, fasten, attach, secure, tie.

**stray**

**1** *(adj) We're looking after a stray dog.* abandoned, lost, homeless, unclaimed.

**2** *(v) Don't stray too far from the path.* wander, roam, ramble, drift, straggle, rove, range, deviate, go off course, go astray.

**streak**

**1** *(n) Our car has a black streak down the side.* stripe, strip, line, band, slash, zigzag, smear, smudge, mark.

**2** *(n) Look at that streak of lightning!* flash, bolt, fork, stroke, sheet.

**stream**

**1** *(n) Gregory paddled in the stream.* brook, river, spring, beck, burn, creek, rivulet, tributary. ❖ *Also see* **river**.

**2** *(n) A stream of water poured from the washing machine.* flood, torrent, cascade, jet, gush, rush, surge, flow, outpouring.

**3** *(v) Tears began to stream down Anji's face. See* **run** 3.

**street** *see* **road**.

**strength**

**1** *(n) Wilf hasn't the strength to lift a paper bag!* power, might, muscle, brawn, force, energy, stamina, vigour. OPPOSITES: weakness, frailty.

**2** *(n) Jade showed great strength under pressure.* courage, bravery, fortitude, strength of character, spirit, grit, determination, firmness, backbone. OPPOSITE: weakness.

**3** *(n) Don't underestimate the strength of my feelings.* intensity, depth, force, vehemence, ardour.

**strengthen**

**1** *(v) Fluoride can strengthen your teeth.* harden, toughen, make stronger, build up. OPPOSITE: weaken.

**2** *(v) The soldiers tried to strengthen the castle walls.* reinforce, fortify, make stronger, support, brace up, buttress. OPPOSITE: weaken.

**3** *(v) This success should strengthen your desire to do well.* reinforce, increase, heighten, deepen, intensify, confirm. OPPOSITES: weaken, undermine.

**strenuous** *see* **exhausting**.

**stress**

**1** *(n) Too much stress can make you ill.* pressure, strain, tension, anxiety, worry, hassle *(informal)*, nervous tension.

**2** *(n) Put the stress on the first word.* emphasis, accent, weight, beat.

**3** *(v) I must stress the importance of safety. See* **emphasize**.

**stressed**

*(adj) I always feel stressed at exam time.* under pressure, pressurized, hassled *(informal)*, tense, anxious, overworked, overstretched, pushed to the limit. OPPOSITE: relaxed.

**stressful**

**1** *(adj) The exam period can be a stressful time.* tense, worrying, anxious, nerve-racking, nail-biting, agonizing, traumatic.

**2** *(adj) Teaching is a stressful job.* pressurized, high-pressure, demanding, tough, taxing, challenging, difficult, trying.

**stretch**

**1** *(v) Stretch the elastic.* pull, extend, draw out, tighten, tauten, lengthen, elongate.

**2** *(v) Balloons stretch when you blow them up.* expand, inflate, swell, distend.

**3** *(v) I hope this jumper doesn't stretch.* pull out of shape, get larger, get bigger, widen, lengthen. OPPOSITE: shrink.

**4** *(v) How far does the desert stretch?* extend, spread, reach, continue, range.

**5** *(v) This test will stretch you.* challenge, push you to the limit, tax, extend.

**stretchy**

*(adj) Rubber bands are stretchy.* elastic, stretchable, rubbery, springy.

**strict**

**1** *(adj) Jason's dad is really strict.* stern, firm, severe, harsh, hard, tough, inflexible, uncompromising, authoritarian, autocratic, iron-handed, iron-fisted, tyrannical. OPPOSITES: lenient, lax.

**2** *(adj) Our school has strict rules about uniform.* stringent, rigid, hard and fast, rigorous, exacting, inflexible, tight, set. OPPOSITES: flexible, lax.

**stride**

**1** *(v) We watched the sentry stride up and down.* pace, march, pound, parade, strut.

**2** *(n) With one stride the giant crossed the river.* step, pace, bound, leap.

**strike**

**1** *(v) Should parents ever strike their children? See* **hit** 1.

**2** *(v) Strike the ball hard. See* **hit** 3.

**3** *(v) I saw the car strike a tree. See* **hit** 4.

**4** *(v) When did it strike you that you'd forgotten your key? See* **occur** 2.

**5** *(v) The workers decided to strike.* go on strike, walk out, take industrial action, stop work, down tools, come out.

**6** *(n) Do you support the teachers' strike?* industrial action, walkout, stoppage, sit-in.

**striking**

**1** *(adj) The similarity between the sisters is striking.* obvious, unmistakable, evident, noticeable, conspicuous, visible, remarkable, extraordinary, incredible.

**2** *(adj) That's a striking painting.* eye-catching, distinctive, unusual, arresting, dazzling, stunning *(informal)*, memorable.

**string**

**1** *(n) Tie the parcel up with string.* cord, twine, yarn, rope.

**2** *(n) Sasha is wearing a string of pearls.* row, strand, rope, necklace.

**3** *(n) I had a string of disasters. See* **series**.

**strip**

**1** *(v) You have to strip before you shower.* take your clothes off, get undressed, undress, strip off *(slang)*, peel off *(slang)*, remove your clothes, strip naked. OPPOSITES: get dressed, dress.

**2** *(v) Strip the paper off the walls.* peel, scrape, tear, rip, flake, remove, clear.

**3** *(n) My sweatshirt has a red strip round the bottom.* stripe, band, line, bar.

**4** *(n) Cut off a strip of material.* band, piece, bit, ribbon, swathe, slip, shred.

**stripe** *see* **strip** 3.

**stroke**

**1** *(v) Fido loves it when you stroke his ears.* rub, pat, fondle, caress, pet.

**2** *(n) What a brilliant stroke! See* **shot** 2.

**stroll**

*(v) Why don't you stroll into town?* amble, wander, saunter, walk, make your way, mooch *(slang)*, mosey *(informal)*, ramble.

# strong

**strong**
1 *(adj) A strong giant has uprooted the trees!* powerful, mighty, muscular, brawny, hefty, strapping, athletic, sinewy, wiry, sturdy, burly, Ramboesque.
OPPOSITES: weak, puny.
2 *(adj) Clint is a strong character who always gets his way.* forceful, strong-willed, assertive, aggressive, tough, determined, tenacious, unyielding.
OPPOSITES: weak, spineless.
3 *(adj) Ellie has been very strong since her mum fell ill.* brave, courageous, plucky, resilient, gutsy *(informal)*, resourceful.
OPPOSITES: feeble, pathetic.
4 *(adj) The walls are strong. See* **solid** 2.
5 *(adj) Farmer Phyllis wears strong boots.* stout, sturdy, hard-wearing, heavy, heavy-duty, durable, indestructible, robust.
OPPOSITES: lightweight, flimsy.
6 *(adj) Karen has a strong desire to win.* deep, deep-seated, passionate, fervent, intense, keen, fierce, heartfelt, ardent.
OPPOSITES: superficial, half-hearted.
7 *(adj) There are strong arguments against smoking.* compelling, convincing, persuasive, forceful, cogent, potent.
OPPOSITES: unconvincing, weak.
8 *(adj) Ziggy's room is painted in strong colours.* bright, bold, vivid, loud, glaring, dazzling, brilliant, stark, clear, intense.
OPPOSITES: pale, muted.
9 *(adj) This soup has a strong flavour.* intense, concentrated, overpowering, spicy, tangy, piquant, pungent, sharp, biting, fiery, highly flavoured.
OPPOSITES: bland, delicate.
10 *(adj) This drink is too strong for me.* concentrated, overpowering, alcoholic, intoxicating, potent, heady.
OPPOSITES: weak, nonalcoholic.
11 *(adj) A strong wind blew in off the sea.* stiff, high, brisk, fresh, gusting, gale-force.
OPPOSITES: light, gentle.

**stroppy** *(informal) see* **awkward** 4.

**struggle**
1 *(v) You will have to struggle to stay in the race.* work hard, strain every muscle, exert yourself, do your utmost, make a huge effort, go all out *(informal)*, bust a gut *(informal)*, break your neck *(informal)*.
2 *(v) Indiana had to struggle with the monster.* grapple, wrestle, tussle, fight, scuffle, skirmish, brawl, scrap *(informal)*, clash, do battle, slog it out, spar, vie.
3 *(v) The puppy will struggle when you put him on the lead.* strain, wriggle, squirm, writhe, flail about.
4 *(n) It was a struggle to complete the assault course.* effort, grind *(informal)*, battle, challenge, slog, long haul.

**strut** *see* **swagger**.

**stubborn**
*(adj) Don't be so stubborn!* obstinate, pig-headed, headstrong, wilful, self-willed, inflexible, defiant, determined.

**stuck**
1 *(adj) Should the pieces be stuck together?* fixed, fastened, joined, attached, glued, taped, pasted, gummed, cemented.
2 *(adj) I'm stuck in a hole!* stuck fast, stuck tight, wedged, jammed, stranded.
3 *(adj) (informal) Ask Mrs Badger to help you if you're stuck.* stumped, baffled, at a loss, at a standstill, bogged down, beaten, up against a brick wall, at your wits' end.

**stuck-up** *(informal) see* **snobbish**.

**study**
1 *(v) Study this chapter for the test.* work on, look at, revise, read up on, swot up on *(informal)*, mug up on *(slang)*, cram *(informal)*, burn the midnight oil.
2 *(v) Dustin wants to study Spanish at college.* learn, take, read, master.
3 *(v) The detectives will study the evidence. See* **examine**.
4 *(n) We're doing a study of local traffic problems. See* **survey**.

**stuff**
1 *(n) Pick up all your stuff! See* **things**.
2 *(n) The alien's clothes were made of some odd green stuff.* substance, material, fabric, cloth, textile, fibres *(plural)*.
3 *(v) I can't stuff anything more into this case. See* **squeeze** 1.

**stuffy**
*(adj) It was stuffy in the attic.* airless, fusty, musty, stale-smelling, frowsty, fuggy, stifling, suffocating, oppressive, poorly ventilated, close, muggy.
OPPOSITES: airy, well-ventilated.

**stumble** *see* **trip** 2.

**stunned**
1 *(adj) The blow from the cricket ball left Ian stunned.* dazed, semiconscious, reeling, seeing stars, dizzy, groggy *(informal)*, senseless, in a stupor, unconscious, knocked out, out for the count *(informal)*.
2 *(adj) The news left us stunned.* amazed, astonished, staggered, dazed, shocked, numb, dumbstruck, flabbergasted *(informal)*, dumbfounded, thunderstruck, stupefied, gobsmacked *(slang)*, devastated.

**stupid**
1 *(adj) Andy isn't usually so stupid!* dim, dense, idiotic, brainless, thick, slow, clueless *(slang)*, gormless *(informal)*, dopey *(slang)*, dumb *(informal)*, dull, obtuse.
OPPOSITES: clever, intelligent.
2 *(adj) What a stupid idea!* idiotic, foolish, daft *(informal)*, crackbrained, ludicrous, silly, senseless, pointless, irresponsible, foolhardy, rash, half-baked *(informal)*.
OPPOSITES: sensible, clever.

**sturdy** *see* **strong** 1, 5.

**stutter** *see* **stammer**.

**style**
1 *(n) I love the style of this skirt.* cut, design, shape, lines *(plural)*.
2 *(n) These jeans are the latest style. See* **fashion** 1.

**subject**
*(n) Choose a subject to debate.* topic, issue, question, theme, point, motion.

**subtle**
1 *(adj) A subtle shade of green.* delicate, understated, gentle, pale, muted, unobtrusive, low-key, tasteful.
2 *(adj) A subtle hint.* gentle, indirect, veiled, implied, tactful, insinuated, crafty.

**succeed**
1 *(v) I'm sure you'll succeed.* do well, be successful, prosper, thrive, flourish, get on, get to the top, make it *(informal)*, make good, arrive *(informal)*, triumph.
OPPOSITES: fail, be unsuccessful.
2 *(v) My scheme didn't succeed.* work, work out, turn out well, produce results, come off *(informal)*, bear fruit.
OPPOSITES: fail, fall flat.

**success**
1 *(n) I hope our play will be a success.* hit *(informal)*, smash hit *(informal)*, sensation, triumph, winner, crowd puller *(informal)*, sellout *(informal)*, blockbuster *(informal)*.
OPPOSITES: failure, flop *(informal)*.
2 *(n) Success hasn't spoiled Famous Fred.* stardom, fame, good fortune, glory, honour, acclaim, recognition, prosperity.
OPPOSITE: failure.

**successful**
1 *(adj) Mum runs a successful business.* profitable, thriving, flourishing, booming, lucrative, fruitful, productive, profit-making, moneymaking, rewarding.
OPPOSITES: failing, unsuccessful.
2 *(adj) Mr Mustafa is a successful businessman.* wealthy, prosperous, well-off, high-earning, high-flying, high-powered, top, best-selling *(writer)*.
OPPOSITES: unsuccessful, failed.
3 *(adj) Our team has been successful all year.* victorious, unbeaten, on a winning streak, out in front *(informal)*, triumphant.
OPPOSITES: unsuccessful, defeated.

**suck**
*(v) Suck your drink through a straw.* drink, suck up, slurp *(informal)*, draw up, take in.

**suck up** *(informal) see* **crawl** 3.

**sudden**
1 *(adj) A sudden noise.* unexpected, startling, surprising, unforeseen.
OPPOSITES: expected, anticipated.
2 *(adj) A sudden decision.* instant, quick, speedy, hasty, snap, spur-of-the-moment, immediate, hurried, impetuous, impulsive, spontaneous, rash, unconsidered.
OPPOSITES: considered, careful.
3 *(adj) Sudden movements.* abrupt, jerky, rapid, quick, unpredictable, unexpected.
OPPOSITES: slow, gradual.

**suddenly**
*(adv) Suddenly the car swerved.* all of a sudden, all at once, without warning, unexpectedly, out of the blue *(informal)*, on the spur of the moment, abruptly.

**suffer**
1 *(v) The vet made sure that Fido wouldn't suffer.* be in pain, feel any pain, be hurt, be in agony, be racked with pain, be sore.
2 *(v) If parents fight, their children will suffer.* be distressed, be upset, be hurt, feel miserable, feel wretched, have a bad time, go through hell *(informal)*, grieve.
3 *(v) I can't suffer another day of this misery.* go through, endure, tolerate, put up with *(informal)*, bear, stand, take, stick *(slang)*, cope with, handle.

**suffocate** *see* **smother** 1.

**suggest**
1 *(v) What did Dr Honey suggest?* propose, advise, recommend, advocate, put forward, counsel, urge, prescribe.
2 *(v) The pictures suggest that the hotel has a pool.* give the impression, give the idea, lead you to believe, make you think, indicate, show, imply, hint, insinuate.

**suit**
1 *(n) That's a very smart suit.* outfit, ensemble. ❖ *Also see* **clothes**.
2 *(v) Those jeans suit you.* look good on, look right on, do something for, flatter, suit your image, become *(old-fashioned)*.
3 *(v) Would three o'clock tomorrow suit you?* be convenient for, be good for, be acceptable to, do for, meet your requirements, please, satisfy.

**suitable**
1 *(adj) This video isn't suitable for children.* appropriate, fit, acceptable, meant, cut out, right, fitting, relevant to.
OPPOSITES: unsuitable, inappropriate.
2 *(adj) Is this a suitable moment to talk?* convenient, appropriate, opportune, good.
OPPOSITES: inappropriate, awkward.

**sulky**
*(adj) There's no need to be sulky just because you lost.* in a sulk, in a huff, resentful, disgruntled, put out, piqued, grumpy, cross, petulant, peevish, grouchy *(informal)*, sullen, moody, bad-tempered, in a strop *(slang)*, morose, surly, sour.

**summary**
*(n) Write a summary of what happened in the first chapter.* outline, résumé, précis, synopsis, overview, rundown, survey, analysis, review, summing-up.

**summon**
*(v) Summon the king's musicians!* send for, call for, call, fetch, call together, assemble, gather, muster, demand the presence of.

**sum up**
*(v) Can you sum up what happened in the last chapter?* summarize, give a summary of, outline, give a rundown of, give the main points of, put in a nutshell, encapsulate, précis, review.

**sunburnt**
*(adj) Dad looks sunburnt.* red, scarlet, like a lobster, burnt, blistered, peeling, tanned, suntanned, brown as a berry, bronzed.

**sunny**
*(adj) Sunny weather.* sunshiny, fine, summery, bright, clear, cloudless, brilliant.
OPPOSITES: cloudy, dull.

**sunrise** *see* **dawn** 1.

**sunset** *see* **dusk**.

**sunshine**
*(n) Open the curtains and let in the sunshine.* sun, sunlight, sunbeams *(plural)*, sun's rays *(plural)*, daylight, light.

**supple**
*(adj) A supple gymnast.* lithe, agile, loose-limbed, nimble, flexible, lissom, limber.
OPPOSITES: stiff, awkward.

**supply**
1 *(v) Can you supply some backing for our project?* provide, contribute, produce, give, offer, donate, come up with, fork out *(slang)*, grant, pass on.
2 *(v) The school will supply you with books.* provide, equip, furnish, kit you out.
3 *(n) Anjali keeps a supply of chocolate in her bedroom.* hoard, store, stock, stockpile, quantity, fund, reserve, cache.
4 **supplies** *(plural n) Do we have enough supplies for the trip?* food, rations *(plural)*, provisions *(plural)*, stores *(plural)*, equipment, materials *(plural)*.

**support**
1 *(v) These pillars support the ceiling.* hold up, keep up, prop up, carry, bear, underpin, shore up, strengthen, reinforce.
2 *(v) Uncle Pete works hard to support his family.* provide for, keep, take care of, look after, finance, maintain, sustain, nourish.
3 *(v) Do you support animal rights?* agree with, go along with, back, defend, uphold, stand up for, stick up for *(informal)*, speak out for, argue for, promote, champion.
OPPOSITE: oppose.
4 *(n) I'm grateful for the support of my parents.* encouragement, moral support, backing, backup, help, assistance, approval, reassurance, loyalty, friendship.

**suppose**
1 *(v) I suppose Tom is ill. See* **assume**.
2 *(v) Let's suppose that pigs could fly!* imagine, pretend, make believe, fantasize.

**sure** *see* **certain** 1, 3.

**surface**
1 *(n) This fruit has a knobbly surface.* exterior, covering, outside, skin, outer face, wall, crust, coat.
2 *(n) The table has a shiny surface.* top, coating, finish, veneer, sheen, polish, patina, appearance, texture.
3 *(n) Paint each surface of the box a different colour. See* **side** 1.

**surge**
1 *(v) We watched the waves surge around the rocks.* gush, rush, swirl, eddy, billow, seethe, stream, well up, heave, roll.
2 *(v) Did you see the fans surge on to the pitch?* rush, charge, stampede, swarm, stream, throng, flood, sweep, push.

**surprise**
1 *(v) This news will surprise you.* amaze, astonish, astound, stun, stagger, shock, take your breath away, bowl you over *(informal)*, leave you open-mouthed, throw *(informal)*, wow *(slang)*.
2 *(v) Did Mum surprise you as you were raiding the fridge?* burst in on, catch you out, catch you unawares, take you by surprise, catch you in the act, catch you red-handed, startle, ambush.
3 *(n) Kate's eyes opened wide with surprise.* amazement, astonishment, incredulity, wonder, shock, bewilderment.
4 *(n) What a surprise! See* **shock** 4.

**surprised**
*(adj) I bet you're surprised to see me!* amazed, astonished, astounded, startled, taken aback, taken by surprise, shocked, stunned, staggered, thunderstruck, flabbergasted *(informal)*, gobsmacked *(slang)*, bowled over *(informal)*.

**surprising**
*(adj) A surprising result.* amazing, astonishing, astounding, incredible, staggering, startling, extraordinary, unexpected, unforeseen, unpredicted, unusual, remarkable, shocking.
OPPOSITES: predictable, unsurprising.

**surrender**
*(v) Will you surrender?* give in, admit defeat, give yourself up, submit, yield, cave in *(informal)*, lay down your arms, show the white flag, throw in the towel, quit.

**surround**
*(v) The soldiers planned to surround the castle.* circle, ring, close in on, encircle, hem in, fence in, hedge in, encompass, enclose, envelop, besiege, lay siege to.

**surroundings**
*(plural n) The hotel is situated in pleasant surroundings.* environment, location, neighbourhood, setting, vicinity, locality.

**survey**
*(n) Show the results of your survey in a graph.* study, investigation, inquiry, examination, analysis, research, review, poll, questionnaire, ballot, count, census.

**survive**
1 *(v) The explorers managed to survive.* stay alive, hold out, get by *(informal)*, cling to life, keep body and soul together *(informal)*, pull through, live, exist.
2 *(v) Did the daffodils survive the storm?* come through, withstand, weather, live through, outlast, outlive.

**suspect**
1 *(v) Why should Oz suspect you?* distrust, doubt, have suspicions about, have doubts about, have misgivings about, have qualms about, be sceptical about, disbelieve, mistrust, think you are guilty, smell a rat.
2 *(v) I suspect we'll lose.* have a feeling, have a hunch, have a sneaking suspicion, think, guess *(informal)*, imagine, suppose.

# suspense

**suspense**
*(n) The suspense is killing me!* tension, uncertainty, anticipation, expectation, excitement, anxiety.

**suspicious**
1 *(adj) Don't be so suspicious; you can trust me.* distrustful, wary, doubtful, uneasy, apprehensive, sceptical, jealous.
OPPOSITES: trusting, unsuspecting.
2 *(adj) That man in the dark glasses looks suspicious.* questionable, suspect, dubious, shifty, dodgy *(informal),* shady *(informal),* fishy *(informal),* disreputable, slippery.
OPPOSITES: above board, respectable.

**swagger**
*(v) Look at Bozo swagger about in his leather jacket!* strut, parade, prance, swank *(informal),* show off *(informal).*

**swallow**
1 *(v) Swallow your bun. See* **eat** 2.
2 *(v) Swallow your juice. See* **drink** 1.

**swamp**
*(n)* bog, marsh, marshland, morass, mire, quagmire, fen, quicksand.

**swap** *see* **exchange**.

**swarm** *see* **crowd** 1, 2.

**sway**
*(v) The wind made the trees sway.* bend, lean, wave, move to and fro, rock, swing.

**swear**
1 *(v) Don't swear!* use bad language, curse, be foul-mouthed, blaspheme, turn the air blue *(informal),* cuss *(informal).*
2 *(v) Swear you'll always love me! See* **promise** 1.

**sweat**
1 *(n) I'm covered in sweat.* perspiration.
2 *(v) The runners began to sweat.* perspire, break out in a sweat, drip with perspiration, swelter, glow, steam.

**sweaty**
*(adj) I was sweaty after the match.* sweating, perspiring, dripping with perspiration, drenched in sweat, sticky, clammy, glowing.

**sweep**
1 *(v) Sweep the crumbs off the table.* brush, clear, clean, dust, remove, push.
2 *(v) Fire began to sweep through the building.* spread, race, tear, rip, whip, whoosh *(informal),* fly, streak, course.

**sweet**
1 *(adj) This pudding tastes really sweet.* sugary, syrupy, sickly, cloying, treacly, sweetened, saccharine.
OPPOSITES: bitter, sour, savoury.
2 *(adj) The sweet smell of roses filled the air.* fragrant, sweet-smelling, aromatic, balmy, fresh, cloying, sickly.
OPPOSITES: foul, acrid.
3 *(adj) What a sweet child!* cute, appealing, lovable, charming, endearing, winsome, engaging, delightful, sweet-tempered, pretty, lovely, attractive.
OPPOSITES: nasty, obnoxious.

4 *(adj) I love the sweet sound of the lark's song.* tuneful, melodious, musical, dulcet, harmonious, mellow, soft, soothing.
OPPOSITES: harsh, discordant.
5 *(n) What's for sweet? See* **dessert**.
6 **sweets** *(plural n) Inga spends all her money on sweets.* confectionery, sweeties *(plural) (informal),* candy, bonbons *(plural).*

**swell**
1 *(v) My ankle started to swell.* puff up, balloon, bulge, blow up, become bloated.
2 *(v) The sails began to swell.* fill out, billow, inflate, expand, balloon, bulge.

**swerve**
*(v) The car had to swerve.* veer, turn aside, change direction, take evasive action, go off course, dodge, weave, swing, wheel.

**swift** *see* **fast** 1.

**swim**
1 *(v) I can't swim.* float, doggy-paddle, do breaststroke, do the crawl, do backstroke, do butterfly, tread water.
OPPOSITE: sink.
2 *(v) Let's swim in the lake.* go for a swim, go swimming, take a dip, bathe, splash about, go skinny-dipping, dive, plunge.

**swing**
1 *(v) Monkeys like to swing by their tails.* hang, dangle, move back and forth, rock, sway, be suspended.
2 *(v) Nola's mood can swing from one extreme to the other.* shift, fluctuate, veer, waver, seesaw, change, vary, alter.

**swirl** *see* **whirl**.

**switch** *see* **change** 4, 5, 6.

**swivel**
*(v) Press the button to make the robot's head swivel.* pivot, rotate, revolve, spin, turn, swing round, gyrate, twirl, wheel.

**swollen**
*(adj) After the fight, Rocky had a swollen nose.* puffy, inflamed, bulbous, enlarged, bulging, distended, bloated, puffed up.

**swoop**
*(v) Watch the eagles swoop.* dive, plunge, sweep down, drop, plummet, descend, fly down, nose-dive, pounce, lunge.

**sword**
*(n)* blade, steel.
TYPES OF SWORD: broadsword, cutlass, dagger, dirk, foil, machete, rapier, sabre, samurai sword, scimitar.

**symbol**
1 *(n) A horseshoe is a symbol of good luck.* sign, token, emblem, mark, image.
2 *(n) The school symbol is a swan.* badge, emblem, insignia, logo, sign, motif.

**sympathetic**
*(adj) Mum was sympathetic when I had to change schools.* understanding, supportive, caring, concerned, kind, comforting, considerate, consoling, sorry, compassionate, encouraging, approving.
OPPOSITES: unsympathetic, callous.

**tackle**
1 *(v) Try to tackle Simon before he scores.* challenge, intercept, block, take on, bring down, grab, seize, stop.
2 *(v) I'm ready to tackle the next question.* get to work on, embark on, set about, get stuck into *(informal),* wade into, attempt, try, have a go at *(informal),* have a stab at *(informal),* deal with, get to grips with, grapple with.
3 *(v) Who will tackle Dad about bedtimes?* confront, challenge, talk to, speak to, take on, have a go at *(informal),* face up to.

**tactful**
*(adj) It's not tactful of you to laugh at my hair.* diplomatic, discreet, polite, subtle, sensitive, considerate, thoughtful.
OPPOSITES: tactless, insensitive.

**tactless**
*(adj) Dom made a tactless remark about Dad's bald patch.* indiscreet, undiplomatic, unsubtle, indelicate, blundering, clumsy, heavy-handed, insensitive, thoughtless, inconsiderate, impolite, rude, hurtful.
OPPOSITES: tactful, diplomatic.

**take**
1 *(v) Take your suitcase upstairs.* carry, bring, move, cart, lift, haul.
2 *(v) Take my hand!* take hold of, hold on to, grab, grasp, grip, clutch, hang on to.
3 *(v) Dad will take you to school.* bring, drive, run, give you a lift, accompany, walk, escort, ferry, transport, convey.
4 *(v) Please take a piece of cake.* have, help yourself to, pick out, choose, select.
5 *(v) Did the burglars take anything valuable? See* **steal** 2.
6 *(v) Did the terrorists take any hostages?* capture, seize, abduct, kidnap, snatch, carry off, detain, arrest.
7 *(v) Take your medicine.* swallow, gulp down, get down, drink, consume, inhale.
8 *(v) Do you take the bus?* catch, travel by, go by, come by, use.
9 *(v) Card tricks take a lot of practice.* need, require, call for, demand.
10 *(v) I can't take this noise. See* **stand** 4.

**take advantage of**
*(phrase) Don't take advantage of your friends.* exploit, use, walk all over *(informal),* impose on, manipulate, milk, squeeze dry, rip off *(slang).*

**take away**
*(v) Take away three from eight.* subtract, take, deduct, minus, remove.
OPPOSITE: add.

**take in**
*(v) I can't take in all this information at once.* absorb, digest, assimilate, make sense of, grasp, understand, comprehend.

## take off
1 *(v) Take off your clothes.* remove, strip off, peel off, throw off, drop, discard.
OPPOSITE: put on.
2 *(v) We watched the plane take off.* leave the ground, take to the air, rise into the air, become airborne, lift off, climb.
OPPOSITE: land.

## take part
*(phrase) Do you want to take part?* join in, participate, be involved, contribute, play a part, be included, enter *(competition)*.

## talented
1 *(adj) I really envy Jemima; she's so talented.* gifted, accomplished, versatile, clever, able, brilliant, artistic, musical.
2 *(adj) Gary is a talented footballer.* accomplished, skilful, brilliant, gifted, skilled, expert, proficient, capable, deft.

## talk
1 *(v) Mum can talk for hours.* speak, chat, chatter, converse, hold forth, spout *(informal)*, natter, gossip, rattle on, prattle on, rabbit on *(informal)*, witter on *(informal)*, jabber on, go on *(informal)*, yak *(slang)*, jaw *(slang)*, spiel, gabble, babble.
2 *(v) Can you talk Italian? See* **speak** 2.
3 *(v) If you're upset it helps to talk.* express your feelings, discuss things, share your thoughts, get things off your chest *(informal)*, put things into words.
4 *(v) The police quizzed Burglar Beryl but she wouldn't talk.* blab, let the cat out of the bag, give the game away, speak out, confess, tell, tell tales, spill the beans *(informal)*, squeal *(slang)*, grass *(slang)*.
5 *(n) Sophie and I had a talk on the phone.* chat, conversation, word, gossip, natter, chinwag *(informal)*, confab *(informal)*, heart-to-heart, tête-à-tête.
6 *(n) I had a long talk with the careers teacher.* chat, conversation, discussion, meeting, interview, consultation.
7 *(n) Dad gave a talk. See* **speech** 1.

## talkative
*(adj) Zoë is so talkative, it's hard to shut her up.* chatty, gossipy, garrulous, loquacious, voluble, gushing, effusive.

## tall
1 *(adj) Fran is quite tall.* big, lanky, rangy, long-legged, leggy, gangling, statuesque.
OPPOSITES: short, small.
2 *(adj) Tall towers loomed over us.* high, lofty, giant, towering, soaring, sky-high.
OPPOSITES: small, low.

## tame
*(adj) Is your pet tame?* domesticated, used to humans, safe, docile, gentle, manageable, obedient, trained, house-trained, broken in *(horse)*.
OPPOSITES: wild, untamed.

## tamper
*(v) Don't tamper with my computer!* interfere, meddle, tinker, fiddle *(informal)*, mess about, muck about *(slang)*, monkey around, fool around *(informal)*, damage.

## tangle
1 *(n) Can you sort out this tangle of threads?* jumble, muddle, mass, mess, knot, snarl, coil, mesh, web, confusion.
2 *(v) Don't tangle yourself in that wire.* entangle, ensnare, enmesh, get tangled up, get snarled up, get muddled up, trap.
OPPOSITES: untangle, extricate, free.

## tangled
*(adj) I can't straighten out these tangled threads.* snarled, twisted, knotted, jumbled, scrambled, messy, matted, tousled *(hair)*, dishevelled *(hair)*.

## tanned
*(adj) Kit looks tanned.* suntanned, brown, bronzed, sunburnt, weather-beaten.

## tantrum *see* **temper** 1.

## tap
1 *(n) Water gushed out of the tap.* spout, valve, stopcock, mixer tap.
2 *(n) I heard a tap. See* **knock** 3.
3 *(v) Did you hear something tap against the window?* knock, rap, thud, bang, beat, drum, hammer, strike, hit.
4 *(v) Tap Ed on the back.* touch, pat, slap.

## tape
1 *(n) Wrap some tape round the parcel.* sticky tape, adhesive tape, ribbon, string.
2 *(n) What's on this tape?* cassette, video, video tape, video cassette, audiocassette.
3 *(v) Tape the pieces together.* stick, fasten, fix, attach, tie, bind, secure.
4 *(v) Did you tape the concert?* record, video, tape-record.

## target
1 *(n) Aim at the target.* bull's-eye, mark.
2 *(n) My target is to run a mile. See* **aim** 1.

## task
*(n) I have a task to complete.* job, chore, duty, assignment, activity, undertaking, piece of work, exercise, challenge, mission.

## taste
1 *(n) This dish doesn't have much taste.* flavour, tang, flavouring, savour, relish, character, zest, aftertaste. ❖ *Also see* **food & flavours**.
2 *(n) Give me a taste of your supper.* mouthful, spoonful, bite, nibble, sip, drop, morsel, titbit, nip, swallow.
3 *(n) Kylie has no taste!* style, flair, class, fashion sense, judgment, discernment, colour sense, design sense.
4 *(n) Flash Frank has a taste for fast cars.* liking, penchant, fondness, preference, appetite, desire, fancy, relish, weakness.
5 *(v) Taste this snack.* try, sample, try out, test, nibble, sip, relish, savour.
6 *(v) The sauce should taste of orange.* have a flavour, smack, savour, have a tang.
7 *(v) Can you taste the garlic in this dish?* make out, distinguish, identify, recognize.

## tasteless
1 *(adj) Tasteless soup.* flavourless, bland, insipid, unexciting, uninteresting, boring, weak, watery, mild, dull, watered down.

2 *(adj) A tasteless comment.* crude, vulgar, crass, uncouth, coarse, cheap, offensive, distasteful, insensitive, tactless.
3 *(adj) Tasteless clothes. See* **vulgar** 2.

## tasty *see* **delicious**.

## taunt *see* **make fun of**.

## taut *see* **tight** 1.

## teach
1 *(v) Dan wants to teach photography.* be a teacher of, give lessons in, give classes in, give instruction in, lecture in, demonstrate.
2 *(v) Mrs Badger aims to teach her students thoroughly.* educate, instruct, tutor, coach, train, drill, inform, enlighten.
3 *(v) Can you teach Daisy how to tie her shoelaces?* show, explain to, demonstrate to, train, instruct.

## teacher
*(n)* TYPES OF TEACHER: coach, don, governess, guide, guru, headteacher, instructor, lecturer, mentor, professor, schoolteacher, trainer, tutor.

## team
*(n) Please join our team.* side, crew, squad, troupe, line-up, club, gang, band, group, company, unit, staff, alliance, party.

## tear
1 *(v) The brambles will tear your dress.* rip, cut, rip to shreds, slit, slash, split, pull to pieces, snag, pierce, mangle, claw at.
2 *(v) Louis started to tear the paper off his present.* rip, pull, yank, wrench, peel.
3 *(v) I saw Jim tear past. See* **speed** 4.
4 *(n) There's a tear in my shorts.* rip, split, slit, slash, cut, hole, gash, snag, run.

## tease
*(v) Does your brother tease you?* pull your leg *(informal)*, wind you up *(informal)*, have you on *(informal)*, kid *(informal)*, make fun of, laugh at, taunt, mock, goad, torment, pester, annoy, provoke.

## teenager
*(n)* adolescent, young person, youngster, youth, juvenile.

## telephone *see* **phone** 1, 2.

## television
*(n) What's on the television tonight?* TV, telly *(informal)*, box *(informal)*, gogglebox *(slang)*, small screen *(informal)*.
TYPES OF TELEVISION PROGRAMME: arts programme, cartoon, chat show, children's programme, classic drama, comedy, costume drama, courtroom drama, current affairs programme, debate, detective series, discussion programme, docudrama, documentary, drama, film, game show, hospital drama, live show, magazine programme, miniseries, murder mystery, natural history programme, news broadcast, newsflash, play, police drama, quiz, real-life drama, serial, series, sitcom (situation comedy), soap (soap opera), sports programme, talk show, variety show, whodunit *(informal)*. ❖ *Also see* **television & film**.

# television and film

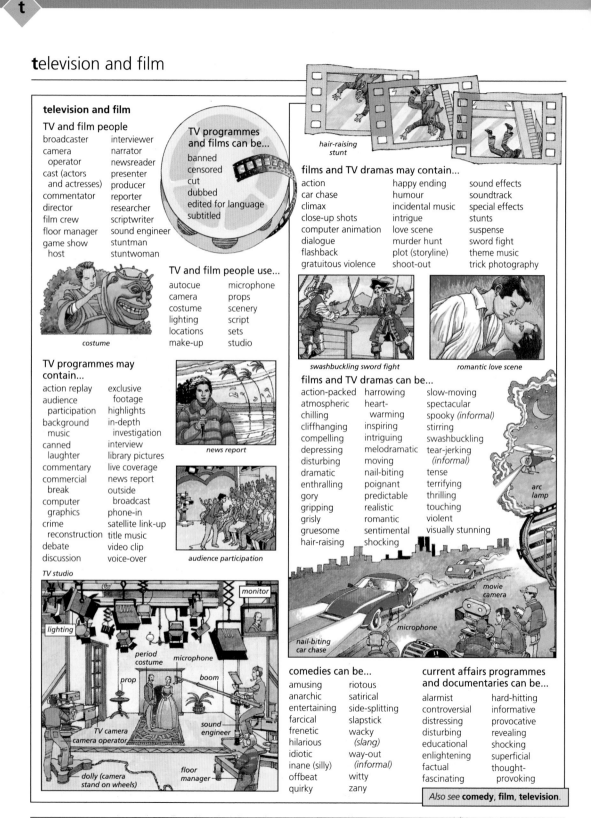

## television and film

### TV and film people

| | |
|---|---|
| broadcaster | interviewer |
| camera | narrator |
| operator | newsreader |
| cast (actors | presenter |
| and actresses) | producer |
| commentator | reporter |
| director | researcher |
| film crew | scriptwriter |
| floor manager | sound engineer |
| game show | stuntman |
| host | stuntwoman |

*costume*

### TV and film people use...

| | |
|---|---|
| autocue | microphone |
| camera | props |
| costume | scenery |
| lighting | script |
| locations | sets |
| make-up | studio |

### TV programmes and films can be...

banned
censored
cut
dubbed
edited for language
subtitled

*hair-raising stunt*

### films and TV dramas may contain...

| | | |
|---|---|---|
| action | happy ending | sound effects |
| car chase | humour | soundtrack |
| climax | incidental music | special effects |
| close-up shots | intrigue | stunts |
| computer animation | love scene | suspense |
| dialogue | murder hunt | sword fight |
| flashback | plot (storyline) | theme music |
| gratuitous violence | shoot-out | trick photography |

*swashbuckling sword fight*    *romantic love scene*

### TV programmes may contain...

| | |
|---|---|
| action replay | exclusive |
| audience | footage |
| participation | highlights |
| background | in-depth |
| music | investigation |
| canned | interview |
| laughter | library pictures |
| commentary | live coverage |
| commercial | news report |
| break | outside |
| computer | broadcast |
| graphics | phone-in |
| crime | satellite link-up |
| reconstruction | title music |
| debate | video clip |
| discussion | voice-over |

*news report*

*audience participation*

### films and TV dramas can be...

| | | |
|---|---|---|
| action-packed | harrowing | slow-moving |
| atmospheric | heart- | spectacular |
| chilling | warming | spooky (informal) |
| cliffhanging | inspiring | stirring |
| compelling | intriguing | swashbuckling |
| depressing | melodramatic | tear-jerking |
| disturbing | moving | (informal) |
| dramatic | nail-biting | tense |
| enthralling | poignant | terrifying |
| gory | predictable | thrilling |
| gripping | realistic | touching |
| grisly | romantic | violent |
| gruesome | sentimental | visually stunning |
| hair-raising | shocking | |

*arc lamp*

*TV studio*

*lighting*

*monitor*

*movie camera*

*microphone*

*nail-biting car chase*

*period costume*

*microphone*

*prop*

*boom*

*sound engineer*

*TV camera*
*camera operator*

*floor manager*

*dolly (camera stand on wheels)*

### comedies can be...

| | |
|---|---|
| amusing | riotous |
| anarchic | satirical |
| entertaining | side-splitting |
| farcical | slapstick |
| frenetic | wacky |
| hilarious | (slang) |
| idiotic | way-out |
| inane (silly) | (informal) |
| offbeat | witty |
| quirky | zany |

### current affairs programmes and documentaries can be...

| | |
|---|---|
| alarmist | hard-hitting |
| controversial | informative |
| distressing | provocative |
| disturbing | revealing |
| educational | shocking |
| enlightening | superficial |
| factual | thought- |
| fascinating | provoking |

*Also see* **comedy, film, television**.

# things

**tell**
1 (v) *I'll tell you where the treasure is buried.* let you know, inform, notify, reveal to, disclose to, divulge to, describe to, recount to, relate to, mention to, report to, confess to, own up to, tip you off about.
2 (v) *The signs tell you that it isn't safe to swim.* show, inform, advise, indicate to, warn, notify, tip you off, proclaim to.
3 (v) *Didn't I tell you to be home by ten o'clock? See* **order** 1.
4 (v) *I'll tell the story while you act it out.* relate, narrate, recount, recite, describe.
5 (v) *I couldn't tell which twin it was.* make out, work out, identify, recognize, distinguish, discern, discover, differentiate.

**tell off**
(v) *(informal) Dad will tell you off if you're late.* scold, reprimand, lecture, tick you off *(informal),* bawl you out *(informal),* tear you off a strip *(informal),* read you the riot act, give you a rocket *(informal),* give you a dressing-down *(informal),* haul you over the coals *(informal),* rebuke, castigate.

**tell on**
(v) *(informal) Your secret is safe; I won't tell on you!* betray, give you away, tell tales about, sneak on *(informal),* snitch on *(slang),* rat on *(informal),* grass on *(slang),* report, shop *(slang),* breathe a word.

**temper**
1 (n) *Dad's in a temper.* rage, fury, bad temper, foul temper, tantrum, bad mood.
2 (n) *People avoid Danielle because of her temper.* quick temper, hot temper, irritability, peevishness, irascibility, hot-headedness, unpredictability, volatility.
3 *lose your temper see* **lose your temper**.

**temporary**
1 (adj) *Jo's bad moods are only temporary.* short-lived, brief, passing, fleeting, momentary, a flash in the pan, transient, impermanent, ephemeral.
OPPOSITES: permanent, long-lasting.
2 (adj) *This is a temporary arrangement.* provisional, interim, stopgap, short-term.
OPPOSITES: permanent, long-term.

**tempt**
(v) *The witch tried to tempt the princess off the path.* lure, entice, draw, lead, coax, persuade, woo, inveigle, seduce, bribe.

**tempting**
(adj) *The thought of a tropical holiday is so tempting!* inviting, irresistible, enticing, attractive, alluring, tantalizing, seductive, appetizing *(food),* mouthwatering *(food).*

**tender**
1 (adj) *Cook the meat until it's tender.* soft, succulent, juicy, coming off the bone.
OPPOSITES: tough, chewy.
2 (adj) *Is your finger still tender? See* **sore**.
3 (adj) *Max gave me a tender look.* affectionate, loving, gentle, sympathetic, caring, tenderhearted, warm, kind, doting.
OPPOSITES: cold, unsympathetic.

**tense**
1 (adj) *I feel tense.* wound up *(informal),* worked up, keyed up, uptight *(informal),* stressed, under pressure, nervous, edgy, on edge, jumpy, jittery *(informal),* anxious.
OPPOSITE: relaxed.
2 (adj) *We had some tense moments waiting for the result. See* **stressful** 1.
3 (adj) *My muscles were tense as I waited for the race to start.* taut, tight, strained, stretched, rigid, flexed, braced, stiff.
OPPOSITE: relaxed.

**tension**
(n) *I can't bear the tension of waiting.* suspense, stress, strain, anxiety, worry, uncertainty, anticipation, excitement.

**terrible**
1 (adj) *A terrible crime. See* **dreadful** 1.
2 (adj) *A terrible essay. See* **dreadful** 2.
3 (adj) *A terrible smell. See* **horrible** 2.
4 (adj) *A terrible predicament. See* **desperate** 3.

**terrific**
1 (adj) *A terrific storm.* tremendous, enormous, gigantic, huge, great, mighty, fierce, violent, intense, severe, dreadful, awful, terrible, horrific, awesome.
2 (adj) *(informal) A terrific party. See* **great** 9.

**terrified** *see* **scared** 1.

**terrifying** *see* **frightening**.

**terror** *see* **fear** 1, 2.

**test**
1 (n) *Did you pass the test?* exam, examination, assessment, oral test, written test, practical, audition, medical *(informal).*
2 (v) *This quiz will test your general knowledge.* put to the test, assess, evaluate, check, examine, probe, appraise.
3 (v) *Scientists test medicines to make sure they are safe.* run tests on, investigate, analyse, experiment on, check, check out, research, inspect, scrutinize.

**thank**
(v) *Remember to thank Granny for the present.* say thank you to, show your appreciation to, express gratitude to.

**thankful** *see* **grateful**.

**thaw**
(v) *Don't let the ice cream thaw.* defrost, melt, soften, liquefy, warm up, unfreeze.
OPPOSITE: freeze.

**then** *see* **next** 3.

**theory**
(n) *The detective's theory was proved right.* idea, hypothesis, supposition, conjecture, speculation, notion, belief, assumption.

**thick**
1 (adj) *Thick walls.* broad, wide, deep, solid, substantial, sturdy, stout, chunky.
OPPOSITES: thin, flimsy.
2 (adj) *A thick book.* fat, chunky, bulky, heavy, weighty, big, large.
OPPOSITES: thin, slim.

3 (adj) *Thick hair.* abundant, luxuriant, bushy, shaggy, coarse, wiry, frizzy, woolly.
OPPOSITES: thin, sparse.
4 (adj) *Thick jungle.* dense, impenetrable, impassable, heavy, lush, closely packed.
OPPOSITES: thin, sparse.
5 (adj) *Thick fog.* dense, heavy, soupy, impenetrable, murky, smoggy, opaque.
OPPOSITES: thin, light.
6 (adj) *Thick custard.* condensed, concentrated, solid, viscous, gelatinous, congealed, coagulated, firm, stiff.
OPPOSITES: thin, runny.

**thicken**
(v) *Wait for the mixture to thicken.* set, jell, solidify, coagulate, congeal, cake, condense, reduce, clot *(blood).*

**thief**
(n) pickpocket, shoplifter, pilferer, poacher, burglar, housebreaker, robber, mugger *(informal),* swindler, embezzler, fraudster.

**thin**
1 (adj) *A thin girl.* slim, slender, slight, lean, lanky, skinny, underweight, spindly, scrawny, bony, gaunt, scraggy, flat-chested, waiflike, skeletal, emaciated, undernourished, anorexic.
OPPOSITES: plump, fat, obese.
2 (adj) *A thin crack. See* **fine** 4.
3 (adj) *Thin curtains.* light, lightweight, flimsy, fine, delicate, floaty, gauzy, filmy, gossamer, diaphanous, sheer, translucent, transparent, see-through, threadbare.
OPPOSITES: thick, heavy.
4 (adj) *Thin hair.* sparse, wispy, fine, straggly, thinning, scanty, scarce.
OPPOSITES: thick, luxuriant.
5 (adj) *Thin gravy.* runny, watery, diluted, wishy-washy *(informal),* weak.
OPPOSITES: thick, concentrated.

**thing**
1 (n) *What's that thing on the table?* object, article, item.
2 (n) *There's a thing crawling out of the swamp!* creature, being, entity.
3 (n) *We have a thing for crushing cans.* gadget, device, machine, contraption, appliance, tool, instrument, implement.
4 (n) *A funny thing happened.* incident, occurrence, happening, phenomenon.
5 (n) *There's one more thing I have to do.* job, task, chore.
6 (n) *What made you do such a crazy thing?* act, deed, exploit, feat.
7 (n) *A worrying thing occurred to me.* thought, idea, notion, theory.
8 (n) *What's the thing you like best about this book?* aspect, feature, quality, characteristic, attribute, detail, point.

**things**
(plural n) *Put your things away.* belongings *(plural),* stuff, paraphernalia, bits and pieces *(plural),* odds and ends *(plural),* possessions *(plural),* clothes *(plural),* gear, kit, equipment, tools *(plural),* tackle, junk *(informal),* clobber *(slang),* baggage.

# think

**think**
1 (v) *I used to think that girls were silly.* believe, consider, reckon, be convinced, be of the opinion, maintain, feel.
2 (v) *I think it's about four o'clock.* reckon, imagine, suppose, guess (informal), would say, estimate, assume, presume, believe.
3 (v) *I didn't think that you'd come.* expect, foresee, anticipate, envisage, suppose, imagine, dream.
4 (v) *Lauren likes to sit in her room and think.* meditate, contemplate, cogitate, deliberate, reflect, ponder, muse, brood.
5 **think about** (v) *You should think about your future.* consider, give thought to, put your mind to, concentrate on, reflect on, mull over, chew over, weigh up, work out.

**think up**
(v) *We must think up a cunning plan.* dream up, come up with, make up, concoct, devise, invent, create, contrive.

**thirsty**
(adj) *The explorers were thirsty.* parched, dry (informal), dehydrated, gasping, panting, dying of thirst (informal).

**thorough**
(adj) *A thorough investigation.* detailed, in-depth, extensive, comprehensive, exhaustive, full, complete, wide-ranging, meticulous, painstaking, methodical.

**thought**
1 (n) *This plan will need a lot of thought.* consideration, reflection, deliberation, thinking, brainwork, concentration, reasoning, contemplation, meditation.
2 (n) *An interesting thought. See* **idea** 1.

**thoughtful**
1 (adj) *It was thoughtful of you to visit Granny.* considerate, kind, caring, unselfish, friendly, helpful, compassionate.
OPPOSITES: thoughtless, selfish.
2 (adj) *Tessa wrote a thoughtful essay.* well-thought-out, perceptive, insightful, profound, penetrating, discerning.
OPPOSITES: superficial, shallow.
3 (adj) *Hanif is in a thoughtful mood.* pensive, reflective, contemplative, philosphical, meditative, introspective, brooding, wistful, dreamy.

**thoughtless**
(adj) *A thoughtless remark.* insensitive, tactless, inconsiderate, unkind, uncaring, unsympathetic, cruel, rude, indiscreet.
OPPOSITES: thoughtful, tactful.

**thrash** see **beat** 1, 2.

**thread**
(n) *Pull the thread tight.* strand, cotton, string, yarn, twine, wool, silk.

**threaten**
1 (v) *Did Bozo threaten you?* intimidate, bully, terrorize, make threats to, menace, browbeat, pressurize, lean on (informal).
2 (v) *Reckless drivers threaten lives.* put at risk, endanger, imperil, put in jeopardy.

**threatening** see **menacing**.

**thrill**
(n) *Luke gets a thrill out of surfing.* sense of excitement, feeling of exhilaration, kick (informal), buzz (slang), charge (slang).

**thrilling** see **exciting**.

**throb**
(v) *Loud music began to throb through the house.* pulsate, pound, thump, thud, beat, vibrate, reverberate, pulse.

**throw**
1 (v) *Throw the ball.* hurl, fling, chuck (informal), lob (informal), sling, toss, pitch, shy, heave, send, launch, propel, let fly.
2 (v) (informal) *Did Aunt Bertha's arrival throw you?* faze, disconcert, put you off, throw you off your stride, worry, unsettle, unnerve, upset, rattle (informal).

**throw away**
1 (v) *Throw away your rubbish.* get rid of, throw out, dispose of, chuck out (informal), bin, dump (informal), scrap, ditch (slang), discard, jettison.
2 (v) *Don't throw away this opportunity.* See **waste**.

**throw out**
(v) *Why did the football club throw you out?* expel, eject, kick you out (informal), turf you out (informal), oust, banish, evict.

**throw up** (informal) see **vomit**.

**thump**
1 (v) *Don't thump your brother! See* **hit** 1.
2 (v) *My heart began to thump loudly. See* **beat** 3.
3 (n) *Jack fell out of the tree with a thump.* thud, crash, bang, clunk, clonk, clump, clomp, thwack, smack, wham.

**tidy**
1 (adj) *Jo always looks tidy.* neat, smart, well-turned-out, well-groomed, trim, spruce, spick-and-span, presentable.
OPPOSITES: untidy, messy.
2 (adj) *Adam keeps his room tidy.* neat, uncluttered, clean, well-organized, in good order, shipshape, spick-and-span, immaculate, in apple-pie order (informal).
OPPOSITES: untidy, messy.
3 (v) *Please tidy your room.* sort out, tidy up, clear up, neaten up, put straight.

**tie**
1 (v) *Tie the boat to the post.* tie up, secure, fasten, attach, make fast, tether, lash, knot, moor, hitch, bind, rope, chain.
2 (v) *Please tie your shoelaces.* tie up, do up, knot, make a bow in, make a knot in.
3 (n) *The result was a tie. See* **draw** 6.
4 (n) *Dad wore a spotty tie.* necktie, bow tie, dicky bow, cravat, neckerchief.

**tight**
1 (adj) *Pull the rope until it's tight.* taut, rigid, stretched, strained, tense.
OPPOSITES: slack, loose.
2 (adj) *Mo wore a tight skirt.* tight-fitting, close-fitting, skintight, figure-hugging, snug, clinging, straining at the seams.
OPPOSITES: baggy, roomy.

3 (adj) *Screw the lid on until it's tight.* sealed, secure, airtight, watertight.
OPPOSITE: loose.
4 (adv) *Hold on tight!* tightly, firmly, fast.

**tilt** see **lean** 1.

**time**
1 (n) *Burglar Beryl spent a short time in prison.* period, while, spell, interval, stretch, term, season, session, duration.
2 (n) *What did people wear in the time of Queen Victoria? See* **age** 1.
3 (n) *The bomb could blow up at any time.* moment, minute, second, instant, point, point in time, stage, juncture.
4 (n) *What time would suit you?* day, date, time of day, hour, week, month, season, year, decade, century, millennium.
5 (v) *Time how long the journey takes.* measure, count, clock, record, calculate.

**timid** see **shy**.

**tingle**
(v) *Can you feel your skin tingle?* prickle, prick, tickle, itch, sting, come up in goose pimples, have pins and needles (informal).

**tinkle** see **jingle** 1.

**tiny**
1 (adj) *A tiny girl.* small, slight, petite, titchy (slang), undersized, pint-sized (informal), diminutive, Lilliputian.
OPPOSITES: big, tall, enormous.
2 (adj) *A tiny speck.* minute, minuscule, microscopic, infinitesimal, teeny, weeny, teeny-weeny, itsy-bitsy (informal).
OPPOSITES: huge, enormous.

**tip**
1 (n) *The tip of an iceberg.* top, peak, pinnacle, summit, point, cap, crown, apex.
2 (n) *A pencil tip.* end, point, sharp end.
3 (n) *A useful tip.* piece of advice, hint, suggestion, pointer, tip-off, clue.
4 (v) *Tip the scraps into the bin.* pour, empty, dump, unload, slide.
5 **tip over** (v) *Don't let the desk tip over!* fall over, topple over, keel over, overturn, upend, capsize (boat).

**tired**
1 (adj) *You must be tired after your hard work.* worn out, exhausted, weary, sleepy, drowsy, ready to drop, dead tired, drained, shattered (informal), done in (informal), dead on your feet (informal), whacked (informal), bushed (slang), zonked (slang).
OPPOSITES: wide-awake, rested.
2 **tired of** (adj) *I'm tired of your moaning.* See **fed up with**.

**tiring**
(adj) *Teaching is a tiring job.* exhausting, draining, wearing, wearying, taxing, demanding, tough, arduous, strenuous.

**toilet**
(n) lavatory, loo (informal), WC (water closet), public convenience, urinal, bog (slang), john (slang), khazi (slang), ladies (informal), gents (informal), cloakroom, bathroom, powder room, washroom.

## tolerant
1 *(adj) I try to be tolerant about other people's views.* open-minded, broad-minded, unprejudiced, unbigoted, fair, liberal, understanding, sympathetic.
OPPOSITES: intolerant, narrow-minded.
2 *(adj) Amy's dad is so tolerant; he lets her do anything.* easy-going, permissive, free and easy, indulgent, lenient, soft, patient, long-suffering, unshockable, forgiving.
OPPOSITES: strict, authoritarian.

## tolerate *see* **endure** 1.

## tomb
*(n)* grave, burial place, sarcophagus, burial chamber, vault, crypt, sepulchre, mausoleum, catacomb, final resting place.

## tool
*(n)* implement, instrument, device, utensil, gadget, appliance, machine, contraption.

## tooth
*(n) An animal's tooth.* fang, tusk.

## top
1 *(n) I climbed to the top of the mountain.* peak, summit, pinnacle, crest, tip, crown *(hill)*, brow *(hill)*, highest point, apex.
2 *(n) Put the top back on.* lid, cap, cover, stopper, cork, covering.
3 *(n) Paula has a new top.* ❖ *See* **clothes**.
4 *(adj) The jug is on the top shelf.* highest, topmost, upper, uppermost.
OPPOSITES: bottom, lowest.
5 *(adj) Who got the top marks in the test?* highest, best, most, maximum, winning.
OPPOSITES: lowest, bottom.
6 *(adj) Professor Peabody is a top scientist.* leading, eminent, outstanding, great, important, famous, celebrated, renowned, noted, high-ranking, crack *(slang)*.
OPPOSITES: second-rate, obscure.

## topic *see* **subject**.

## torment *see* **torture** 1, 2.

## torture
1 *(v) Will the kidnappers torture their prisoners?* inflict pain on, hurt, abuse, maltreat, ill-treat, be cruel to, torment, use force on, intimidate, persecute, bully.
2 *(n) You can't imagine the torture I went through.* agony, torment, anguish, pain, suffering, misery, distress, hell *(informal)*.

## toss
1 *(v) Toss the ball to me. See* **throw** 1.
2 *(v) Bad dreams made me toss around all night.* thrash, toss and turn, roll, twist and turn, writhe, wriggle, wallow, tumble.
3 *(v) Look at the boats toss on the waves.* bob, wallow, lurch, pitch, tumble, heave.

## total
1 *(n) Add up the figures and tell me the total.* tally, full amount, sum total, grand total, answer, sum, aggregate, gross.
2 *(adj) What's the total population of the two towns?* overall, complete, sum, full, gross, entire, whole, combined.
3 *(adj) A total disaster. See* **complete** 2.

## totter *see* **stagger** 1.

## touch
1 *(v) Don't let the wires touch!* come into contact, connect, meet, come together.
2 *(v) I felt the cobweb touch my face.* brush, graze, tickle, rub against.
3 *(v) Don't touch the animals!* lay a finger on, feel, stroke, pat, rub, fondle, caress, nuzzle, tickle, pick up.
4 *(v) Don't touch my radio!* lay a finger on, move, pick up, interfere with, fiddle with *(informal)*, tamper with, finger.
5 *(v) I only managed to touch the ball once in the match.* hit, strike, kick, head, tap, knock, come into contact with.
6 *(v) Never touch drugs!* get involved with, have anything to do with, concern yourself with, handle, consume, use.

## touchy
*(adj) Treat Amy carefully; she's very touchy.* sensitive, easily offended, thin-skinned, oversensitive, irritable, ratty *(informal)*, tetchy, grouchy *(informal)*, bad-tempered.
OPPOSITES: easy-going, thick-skinned.

## tough
1 *(adj) Bulletproof glass needs to be tough.* strong, hard, thick, solid, durable, resilient, hard-wearing, unbreakable, indestructible, sturdy, inflexible, firm, rigid.
OPPOSITES: flimsy, fragile.
2 *(adj) You must be tough to go on this expedition.* fit, strong, sturdy, hardy, robust, resilient, brawny, muscular.
OPPOSITES: feeble, delicate.
3 *(adj) Gangsters are pretty tough characters.* rough, hard, hardened, hard-bitten, ruffianly, wild, vicious, violent, lawless, rowdy, hard as nails.
OPPOSITES: gentle, civilized.
4 *(adj) This steak is tough.* chewy, leathery, rubbery, stringy, gristly, sinewy.
OPPOSITES: tender, succulent.
5 *(adj) A tough puzzle. See* **difficult** 1.
6 *(adj) A tough job. See* **difficult** 2.

## tower
*(n) Let's climb up this tower.* turret, keep, clock tower, bell tower, steeple, spire, belfry, minaret, column, pillar, obelisk.

## trace
1 *(n) There's just a trace of sherry in this trifle.* dash, touch, spot, bit, drop, splash, smattering, hint, whiff, tinge, soupçon.
2 *(n) Indy found no trace of the temple.* sign, evidence, indication, record, remains *(plural)*, remnants *(plural)*, vestiges *(plural)*.
3 *(v) Police are trying to trace Dodgy Dave.* find, locate, track down, hunt down, seek out, uncover, unearth, get in touch with.

## track
1 *(n) The fox left a track.* trail, scent, spoor, footprints *(plural)*, prints *(plural)*, marks *(plural)*, traces *(plural)*.
2 *(n) We cycled along a narrow track.* path, pathway, bridle path, footpath, trail.
3 *(n) The competitors sped round the track.* racetrack, circuit, running track, racecourse, speedway.

## tradition *see* **custom**.

## tragic
1 *(adj) A tragic ending. See* **sad** 2.
2 *(adj) A tragic accident.* catastrophic, disastrous, calamitous, terrible, appalling, dreadful, awful, shocking, fatal, deadly.

## trail
1 *(n) Angus left a trail of rubbish.* line, train, stream, track, path, wake, wash.
2 *(n) Follow the fox's trail. See* **track** 1.
3 *(v) Let the streamers trail from the ceiling. See* **hang** 1.
4 *(v) Watch the queen's robes trail behind her.* drag, sweep, fall, stream out, flow.
5 *(v) Don't trail behind. See* **drop behind**.

## train
1 *(n) The train pulled into the station.* locomotive, engine.
TYPES OF TRAIN: boat train, bullet train *(Japan)*, diesel train, electric train, express train, freight train, goods train, high-speed train, intercity train, maglev, monorail, steam train, tube train, underground train.
❖ *Also see* **journey words**.
2 *(v) Matt wants to train to be a nurse.* study, learn, qualify, prepare.
3 *(v) Athletes train regularly.* practise, exercise, work out, prepare, get fit.
4 *(v) Who will train the team?* coach, prepare, drill, instruct, guide, teach.

## tramp *see* **trudge**.

## trample on
*(v) Don't trample on the tulips!* tread on, tramp all over, step on, stamp on, walk on, squash, crush, flatten, grind under foot.

## transform *see* **change** 2.

## transparent
*(adj) Transparent material.* see-through, clear, glassy, crystal clear, translucent, sheer, filmy, gauzy, diaphanous.
OPPOSITE: opaque.

## trap
1 *(n) The creature was caught in a trap.* snare, noose, net, pit, mousetrap, mantrap, booby trap, web.
2 *(v) The police managed to trap Burglar Beryl.* catch, capture, snare, ensnare, corner, cut off, ambush, smoke out.

## travel
1 *(v) Which way will you travel?* go, journey, voyage, head, proceed, drive, walk, cycle, ride, fly, sail, cruise, motor, ramble, roam, wander, trek, commute.
❖ *Also see* **journey words**.
2 *(v) Uncle Walter loves to travel.* see the world, go abroad, go on trips, go on journeys, tour, go globetrotting, sightsee.

## treasure
1 *(n) Pirate Peg buried her treasure.* riches *(plural)*, valuables *(plural)*, fortune, hoard, jewels *(plural)*, coins *(plural)*, gold, silver, money. ❖ *Also see* **treasure words**.
2 *(v) Clare will treasure this gift.* cherish, value, prize, appreciate, love, adore, dote on, be careful with, keep safe, look after.

# treasure words

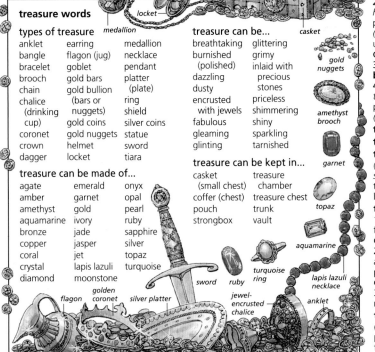

## treasure words

### types of treasure

| | | |
|---|---|---|
| anklet | earring | medallion |
| bangle | flagon (jug) | necklace |
| bracelet | goblet | pendant |
| brooch | gold bars | platter |
| chain | gold bullion | (plate) |
| chalice | (bars or | ring |
| (drinking | nuggets) | shield |
| cup) | gold coins | silver coins |
| coronet | gold nuggets | statue |
| crown | helmet | sword |
| dagger | locket | tiara |

### treasure can be made of...

| | | |
|---|---|---|
| agate | emerald | onyx |
| amber | garnet | opal |
| amethyst | gold | pearl |
| aquamarine | ivory | ruby |
| bronze | jade | sapphire |
| copper | jasper | silver |
| coral | jet | topaz |
| crystal | lapis lazuli | turquoise |
| diamond | moonstone | |

*locket*
*medallion*
*casket*
*gold nuggets*
*amethyst brooch*
*garnet*
*topaz*
*aquamarine*
*turquoise ring*
*lapis lazuli necklace*
*sword* *ruby* *jewel-encrusted chalice* *anklet*
*flagon* *golden coronet* *silver platter*

### treasure can be...

| | |
|---|---|
| breathtaking | glittering |
| burnished | grimy |
| (polished) | inlaid with |
| dazzling | precious |
| dusty | stones |
| encrusted | priceless |
| with jewels | shimmering |
| fabulous | shiny |
| gleaming | sparkling |
| glinting | tarnished |

### treasure can be kept in...

| | |
|---|---|
| casket | treasure |
| (small chest) | chamber |
| coffer (chest) | treasure chest |
| pouch | trunk |
| strongbox | vault |

## treat

1 (n) *I enjoyed my birthday treat.* present, gift, entertainment, party, outing, surprise, celebration, fun.
2 (v) *How did your penfriend's family treat you?* behave towards, act towards, relate to, look upon, talk to, deal with, handle.
3 (v) *Does the doctor treat outpatients?* look after, take care of, give treatment to, care for, see to, attend to, patch up.

## tree

(n) *Look at that tree!* conifer, evergreen, deciduous tree, fruit tree, sapling, bonsai.
TYPES OF TREE: alder, apple, apricot, ash, aspen, beech, birch, cedar, cherry, cypress, ebony, elder, elm, eucalyptus, fig, fir, hawthorn, hazel, holly, horse chestnut, juniper, laburnum, larch, lemon, lime, magnolia, mahogany, mango, maple, mimosa, monkey puzzle, oak, olive, orange, palm, peach, pear, pine, plane, plum, poplar, redwood, rowan, rubber, sequoia, spruce, sweet chestnut, sycamore, walnut, weeping willow, willow, yew.

## tremble see **shiver**.

## tremendous

1 (adj) *A tremendous bang.* terrific, enormous, colossal, mighty, stupendous, almighty (informal), dreadful, awful, terrible, frightful, deafening, ear-splitting.
2 (adj) (informal) *A tremendous experience. See* **fantastic** 3.

## trick

1 (n) *We were amazed by the magician's trick.* conjuring trick, illusion, magic trick, stunt, sleight of hand.
2 (n) *Mum wasn't amused by our trick.* joke, practical joke, prank, leg-pull (informal), wind-up (slang), hoax, gag (informal), stunt, jape, April fool.
3 (v) *Don't let Ed trick you. See* **deceive** 1.

## trickle see **dribble** 2.

## tricky see **awkward** 5, 6.

## trip

1 (n) *We're going on a trip to France.* outing, visit, excursion, jaunt, expedition, coach trip, day trip, field trip, tour, journey.
2 (v) *Be careful not to trip!* trip up, fall, fall over, lose your footing, lose your balance, go head over heels, stumble, take a tumble, slip, stagger, catch your foot.

## trivial

(adj) *Don't waste my time with trivial details.* unimportant, insignificant, inconsequential, petty, minor, negligible, trifling, piffling, worthless, frivolous.
OPPOSITES: important, significant.

## trouble

1 (n) *Our new car has caused us a lot of trouble.* bother, problems (plural), hassle (informal), inconvenience, difficulty, irritation, annoyance, worry, anxiety.
OPPOSITES: pleasure, convenience.

2 (n) *Granny has had a lot of trouble in her life.* difficulty, hardship, adversity, problems (plural), trials (plural), tribulations (plural), misfortune, bad luck, sadness, unhappiness, heartache, pain, suffering.
OPPOSITES: happiness, good fortune.
3 (v) *I didn't mean to trouble you. See* **bother** 1, 2.
4 in trouble (phrase) *Call me if you're in trouble.* in difficulty, having problems, in a predicament, in a mess, in hot water (informal), in dire straits, in danger.

## trousers see **clothes**.

## truck see **lorry**.

## trudge

(v) *I watched you trudge through the snow.* plod, tramp, slog, stomp (informal), traipse (informal), trek, hike, clomp, yomp, lumber, drag your feet, shuffle.

## true

1 (adj) *This is a true story.* real, real-life, factual, actual, based on real life.
OPPOSITES: fictional, made-up.
2 (adj) *Is your account true?* correct, accurate, right, truthful, faithful, exact, precise, reliable, genuine, confirmed.
OPPOSITES: false, fabricated.
3 (adj) *Tell me your true feelings. See* **real** 3.

## trust

(v) *You can trust me; I won't let you down.* put your trust in, have confidence in, have faith in, be sure of, rely on, depend on, count on, pin your hopes on, confide in.

## truthful see **honest** 1, 2.

## try

1 (n) *Have a try!* attempt, go (informal), bash (informal), stab (informal), shot (informal), crack (informal), effort.
2 (v) *You should try to break the record.* attempt, make an attempt, endeavour, aim, seek, strive, make an effort, do your best, exert yourself, go all out (informal), bend over backwards (informal).
3 (v) *Let's try that new restaurant.* try out, check out (informal), sample, investigate, experience, test, give it a whirl (informal).

## tug see **pull**.

## tumble see **fall** 1, 3, 6.

## tummy (informal) see **stomach** 1, 2.

## tune

(n) *A catchy tune.* melody, song, theme, air, refrain. ❖ *Also see* **music words**.

## tunnel

(n) passageway, passage, shaft, mine, burrow, hole, subway, underpass.

## turn

1 (v) *Watch the wheels turn.* go round, spin, revolve, rotate, gyrate, roll, circle, wheel, pivot, swivel, twirl, whirl.
2 (v) *It's unlikely that this frog will turn into a prince. See* **change** 3.
3 (v) *Let's turn the garage into a games room.* convert, adapt, transform, change, make, remodel, alter, make over.

**4** (n) We came to a turn in the road. bend, curve, twist, hairpin bend, U-turn, corner, turning, turn-off, angle, loop, zigzag.
**5** (n) Everyone will have a turn on the computer. go (informal), try, chance, shot (informal), opportunity, attempt, bash (informal), stab (informal), spell, stint.

**turn out**
(v) How did things turn out? work out, end up, develop, pan out (informal), evolve, come about, happen, transpire (informal).

**TV** see **television**.

**twinkle** see **sparkle**.

**twist**
**1** (v) Twist the threads together. weave, wind, entwine, intertwine, tangle, plait, braid, knot, loop, wreathe, coil, wrap.
**2** (v) The noise made Posy twist round in her seat. turn, spin, swivel, swing, pivot.
**3** (v) The path began to twist. See **wind** 2.
**4** (v) Try not to twist your ankle. sprain, turn, wrench, strain, rick (neck).
**5** (v) Reporters can twist what you say. distort, slant, warp, garble, misquote, misrepresent, falsify, change, alter.

**twisted**
**1** (adj) A twisted tree trunk. distorted, contorted, crooked, bent, deformed, misshapen, gnarled, knotted.
**2** (adj) Twisted threads. See **tangled**.

**twitch**
(v) Do you twitch in your sleep? jerk, fidget, wriggle, squirm, writhe, quiver, shiver, tremble, start, jump.

**type** see **kind** 2, 3.

**typical**
**1** (adj) It was a typical weekend at home. normal, average, standard, ordinary, usual, commonplace, everyday, run-of-the-mill.
OPPOSITES: extraordinary, remarkable.
**2** (adj) Woodchester is a typical English village. archetypal, quintessential, classic, characteristic, representative, stereotypical.
OPPOSITES: atypical, unique.
**3** (adj) It's typical of Dan to be late. characteristic, in character, true to type, true to form, in keeping, unsurprising.
OPPOSITE: unusual.

**ugly**
**1** (adj) You look ugly in that mask. hideous, grotesque, horrible, repulsive, disgusting, revolting, ghastly, monstrous, deformed, disfigured, misshapen.
OPPOSITES: beautiful, lovely.
**2** (adj) What an ugly building! unsightly, unattractive, hideous, horrible, ghastly, vile, grim, inelegant, tasteless, monstrous.
OPPOSITES: beautiful, lovely.

**unavoidable** see **inevitable**.
**unaware** see **ignorant** 1, 3.
**unbearable**
(adj) The noise is unbearable. intolerable, unendurable, insupportable, insufferable, unacceptable, too much (informal).

**unbelievable** see **incredible** 1.

**uncertain**
**1** (adj) I'm uncertain about what to do. unsure, doubtful, dubious, undecided, hesitant, in two minds, unclear, vague.
**2** (adj) It's uncertain who won the race. unclear, undecided, unresolved, unconfirmed, inconclusive, arguable, open to question, ambiguous, up in the air.

**unclear**
(adj) This message is unclear. hard to read, illegible, hard to understand, unintelligible, indecipherable, cryptic, ambiguous, vague, confused, garbled, mystifying, puzzling.

**uncomfortable**
**1** (adj) My new shoes are uncomfortable. tight, cramped, hard, stiff, painful.
OPPOSITE: comfortable.
**2** (adj) I feel uncomfortable in this situation. awkward, ill at ease, self-conscious, embarrassed, out of place, uneasy, tense, on edge, nervous, edgy.
OPPOSITES: comfortable, at ease.

**unconscious**
(adj) The patient lay unconscious. senseless, comatose, out cold, knocked out, concussed, stunned, sleeping.

**underground**
(adj) An underground chamber. subterranean, sunken, buried, covered.

**understand**
**1** (v) I didn't understand what you meant. realize, see, grasp, know, recognize, take in, comprehend, follow, get, catch on to (informal), cotton on to (informal), twig (informal), get the drift of.
**2** (v) I can't understand this code. make sense of, make head or tail of (informal), make out, work out, figure out (informal), suss out (slang), decipher, decode.
**3** (v) I understand that you're leaving. believe, hear, gather, learn.

**understanding**
**1** (n) Samirah has a good understanding of history. See **grasp** 4.
**2** (adj) My dad is very understanding. sympathetic, compassionate, tolerant, forgiving, forbearing, patient, kind, considerate, thoughtful, sensitive.

**undo**
(v) Can you undo this? unfasten, open, loosen, untie, unwrap, unbutton, unzip, unlace, unhook, unclip, unclasp, unscrew, unpin, unlock, unchain, disentangle, untangle, unravel, release.

**undress**
(v) Undress before you shower. get undressed, take your clothes off, strip, strip off (slang), peel off (slang), disrobe.

**unemployed**
(adj) Justin's dad is unemployed. out of work, out of a job, on the dole (informal), jobless, laid off, redundant.

**uneven** see **bumpy** 1.

**unexpected** see **surprising**.

**unfair**
(adj) An unfair decision. unjust, biased, prejudiced, one-sided, partisan, arbitrary, unreasonable, unjustified, uncalled-for.
OPPOSITES: fair, just.

**unfamiliar** see **strange** 3, 4.

**unfortunate**
(adj) An unfortunate accident. unlucky, regrettable, dreadful, disastrous, calamitous, tragic, lamentable.

**unfriendly**
(adj) Unfriendly neighbours. unsociable, aloof, distant, standoffish, cold, cool, chilly, disagreeable, unpleasant, uncivil, hostile, aggressive, antisocial.

**unhappy** see **sad** 1, 2.

**unhealthy**
**1** (adj) The stray dog looked unhealthy. ill, sick, in poor health, unwell, sickly, poorly (informal), ailing, infirm, weak, feeble, frail, undernourished, unfit, out of condition.
OPPOSITES: healthy, well.
**2** (adj) The refugees lived in unhealthy conditions. insanitary, unhygienic, squalid, dirty, disease-ridden, polluted, harmful.
OPPOSITES: clean, healthy.
**3** (adj) A diet of chips and fizzy drinks is unhealthy. bad for you, unwholesome, unnourishing, harmful, damaging.

**unimportant**
(adj) Leave out anything that is unimportant. of no importance, trivial, insignificant, inessential, inconsequential, of no consequence, irrelevant, immaterial.
OPPOSITES: important, significant.

**uninhabited**
**1** (adj) An uninhabited flat. See **empty** 3.
**2** (adj) An uninhabited planet. unpopulated, unpeopled, uncolonized, unsettled, deserted, desolate, barren.

**unique**
(adj) Ziggy's hairstyle is unique. distinctive, in a class of its own, one-off (informal), without equal, unparalleled, unrivalled.

**united**
**1** (adj) Let's make a united effort to win. combined, joint, concerted, cooperative, collaborative, collective, common, unified.
**2** (adj) We are united in our opposition to the plan. agreed, in agreement, undivided, at one, of one mind, unanimous.
OPPOSITES: divided, at odds.

**unkind**
(adj) It was unkind of you to laugh at me. cruel, nasty, mean, heartless, uncaring, callous, unfriendly, inconsiderate, insensitive, thoughtless, hurtful, spiteful.
OPPOSITES: kind, considerate.

# unknown

**unknown**
1 *(adj) The causes of the disease are unknown.* unidentified, undiscovered, undecided, unrecognized, mysterious, undisclosed, hidden, concealed, secret.
2 *(adj) This song is by an unknown band called Purple Pig.* little-known, obscure, unheard-of, unfamiliar, insignificant.
3 *(adj) Pirate Peg sailed into unknown waters.* unfamiliar, unexplored, uncharted, unmapped, undiscovered, new, strange.

**unlikely**
*(adj) It's unlikely that there's life on Venus.* improbable, not likely, doubtful, questionable, inconceivable, unimaginable.

**unlucky**
1 *(adj) You really are unlucky, aren't you?* unfortunate, accident-prone, jinxed, cursed, ill-fated, ill-starred, star-crossed, out of luck, down on your luck, luckless.
OPPOSITES: lucky, fortunate.
2 *(adj) Seeing a magpie is supposed to be unlucky.* bad luck, a bad sign, a bad omen, inauspicious, ominous, ill-omened.
OPPOSITES: lucky, auspicious.

**unnecessary**
*(adj) Smart clothes are unnecessary on a cycling holiday.* inessential, nonessential, uncalled-for, superfluous, surplus to requirements, redundant, dispensable.
OPPOSITES: necessary, essential.

**unpleasant**
1 *(adj) An unpleasant child.* disagreeable, objectionable, bad-tempered, unfriendly, unkind, nasty, spiteful, hateful, unlovable.
2 *(adj) An unpleasant smell. See **nasty** 1.*

**unpopular**
*(adj) You'll be unpopular if you start telling tales.* disliked, friendless, unwanted, unwelcome, out of favour, detested, hated, despised, avoided, ignored, rejected, shunned.
OPPOSITES: popular, well-liked.

**unrealistic** see **impractical** 1, 2.

**unreasonable**
*(adj) Don't be so unreasonable!* irrational, illogical, inconsistent, opinionated, obstinate, headstrong, biased, prejudiced.

**unreliable**
*(adj) Don't trust Oz; he's too unreliable.* undependable, irresponsible, erratic, inconsistent, unpredictable, untrustworthy.
OPPOSITES: reliable, dependable.

**unselfish**
*(adj) It was unselfish of you to give me your last chocolate.* self-sacrificing, selfless, noble, generous, magnanimous, kind, big-hearted, big, altruistic, charitable.

**unsuccessful**
*(adj) My attempts to talk Dad round were unsuccessful.* fruitless, futile, in vain, to no avail, useless, abortive, unproductive, ineffective, foiled, thwarted, frustrated.
OPPOSITES: successful, fruitful.

**unsure** see **uncertain** 1.

**untidy**
1 *(adj) My desk is untidy.* messy, chaotic, cluttered, disorganized, muddled, jumbled, littered, topsy-turvy, shambolic *(informal)*.
OPPOSITES: tidy, neat.
2 *(adj) You look untidy. See **messy** 2.*
3 *(adj) What untidy work! See **messy** 3.*

**unusual**
1 *(adj) Pat has an unusual ability to learn languages.* extraordinary, exceptional, rare, remarkable, phenomenal, singular, uncommon, abnormal, freak, atypical.
2 *(adj) Ziggy dresses in an unusual way.* strange, peculiar, odd, weird, bizarre, eccentric, unconventional, outlandish, curious, offbeat, original, different, exotic.

**unwilling**
*(adj) Andy was unwilling to volunteer.* reluctant, loath, slow, disinclined, not in the mood, ill-disposed, unenthusiastic.
OPPOSITES: willing, eager.

**upset**
1 *(v) I didn't mean to upset you.* hurt, distress, offend, rub you up the wrong way, annoy, irritate, worry, alarm, disturb, ruffle, fluster, faze, dismay, unsettle.
2 *(v) Don't upset our plans.* disrupt, interfere with, spoil, ruin, wreck, mess up, throw into confusion, turn upside down.
3 *(v) I can see that you're upset.* hurt, distressed, worried, troubled, disturbed, bothered, agitated, in a state *(informal)*, put out, offended, angry.

**urge**
*(n) I felt a sudden urge to scream.* impulse, desire, compulsion, need, drive, longing, yearning, inclination, wish, whim.

**urgent**
*(adj) I must see the doctor; it's urgent.* imperative, vital, essential, critical, crucial, important, high-priority, serious, pressing.

**use**
1 *(v) Can you use these empty boxes?* find a use for, make use of, put to good use, utilize, do something with.
2 *(v) This whisk is easy to use.* operate, control, work, manage, handle.
3 *(v) Fenella will use you to get what she wants. See **take advantage of**.*
4 *(n) What's the use of complaining?* point, purpose, good, advantage, benefit, value, usefulness, worth.

**used to**
*(adj) I'm used to coming last.* accustomed to, resigned to, hardened to, familiar with, at home with, in the habit of, given to.

**useful**
1 *(adj) A useful gadget.* practical, handy, convenient, effective, helpful, valuable, functional, multipurpose, all-purpose.
OPPOSITES: useless, ineffective.
2 *(adj) Useful suggestions.* helpful, practical, worthwhile, valuable, invaluable, constructive, positive, beneficial.
OPPOSITES: useless, unhelpful.

**useless**
1 *(adj) The search was useless.* futile, pointless, a waste of time, in vain, fruitless, unsuccessful, hopeless, unproductive.
OPPOSITES: worthwhile, fruitful.
2 *(adj) This knife is useless.* no use, unusable, ineffective, impractical, hopeless *(informal)*, faulty, defective, broken.
OPPOSITES: useful, effective.

**usual**
*(adj) Jogging is part of my usual routine.* normal, regular, customary, accustomed, everyday, daily, ordinary, typical, standard, general, familiar, set, fixed, established.

# Vv

**vacant**
1 *(adj) A vacant flat. See **empty** 3.*
2 *(adj) A vacant seat.* empty, available, free, unoccupied, not in use, not taken.
OPPOSITES: occupied, in use.
3 *(adj) A vacant stare.* blank, glazed, expressionless, faraway, dreamy, absent-minded, abstracted, vague, inattentive.

**vague**
1 *(adj) I could see a vague shape through the fog.* indistinct, hazy, shadowy, ill-defined, blurred, fuzzy, dim, faint.
OPPOSITES: clear, distinct.
2 *(adj) Justin has a vague idea of history.* hazy, woolly, foggy, inexact, imprecise, rough, broad, generalized.
OPPOSITES: clear, well-defined.
3 *(adj) Professor Peabody is terribly vague. See **absent-minded**.*

**vain**
*(adj) Too much praise can make you vain.* conceited, bigheaded *(informal)*, swollen-headed *(informal)*, self-satisfied, proud, arrogant, narcissistic, cocky, puffed up.
OPPOSITES: modest, humble.

**valuable**
1 *(adj) A valuable painting.* expensive, precious, costly, priceless, invaluable, dear, treasured, highly prized.
OPPOSITES: worthless, inexpensive.
2 *(adj) A valuable clue. See **useful** 2.*

**vanish**
*(v) The figure seemed to vanish.* disappear, become invisible, vanish into thin air, dematerialize, vanish off the face of the earth, fade away, melt away.
OPPOSITES: appear, materialize.

**vast**
1 *(adj) The universe is vast.* immense, huge, boundless, infinite, immeasurable, never-ending, limitless, unending, unbounded, sweeping, extensive.
OPPOSITES: tiny, limited.
2 *(adj) A vast appetite. See **enormous**.*

## vegetable
(n) greens (plural), garden produce.
TYPES OF VEGETABLE: artichoke, asparagus, aubergine, beetroot, broad bean, broccoli, Brussels sprout, cabbage, carrot, cauliflower, celery, chicory, courgette, cucumber, fennel, garlic, haricot bean, kale, leek, lettuce, mangetout, marrow, mushroom, okra, onion, parsnip, pea, potato, pumpkin, radish, rocket, runner bean, shallot, spinach, spring greens (plural), spring onion, squash, string bean, swede, sweet corn, sweet pepper, sweet potato, turnip, watercress.

## very
1 (adv) I was very sad to hear your news. extremely, really, terribly, dreadfully, deeply, truly, profoundly, intensely, acutely, awfully (informal).
2 (adv) Mrs Badger was very impressed with Oscar's work. extremely, really, tremendously, highly, greatly, most, exceedingly, enormously, hugely, mightily.

## vibrate see shake 1.

## vicious see fierce 1.

## victory
(n) The team were excited by their victory. win, success, triumph, conquest.
OPPOSITE: defeat.

## view
1 (n) What a beautiful view! vista, scene, sight, outlook, prospect, panorama, landscape, seascape, spectacle, picture.
2 (n) Kali shared my view that the film was awful. opinion, point of view, judgment, belief, conviction, assessment, way of thinking, idea, feeling, impression.

## viewpoint
(n) Try to see the problem from a different viewpoint. angle, perspective, point of view, standpoint, position, side, slant.

## vile see horrible 1, 2.

## violent
1 (adj) A violent attack. savage, vicious, brutal, bloody, bloodthirsty, ferocious, fierce, barbaric, murderous, frenzied.
2 (adj) Violent emotions. powerful, uncontrollable, passionate, burning, intense, vehement, tempestuous, overwhelming, ungovernable, extreme.
3 (adj) A violent storm. raging, tempestuous, tumultuous, turbulent, wild, blustery, fierce, severe, devastating.
4 (adj) A violent stab of pain. See sharp 3.

## visible see noticeable.

## visit
1 (v) May I visit you next summer? come to see, go to see, call in on, drop in on (informal), look you up, pay you a visit, stay with, be your guest, descend on.
2 (n) Enjoy your visit to Paris! See trip 1.

## vital
(adj) The doctor made a vital decision. critical, crucial, life-or-death, urgent, serious, significant, important, key, major.

## vivid
1 (adj) I love vivid colours. brilliant, vibrant, glowing, bright, bold, strong, rich, deep, clear, luminous, fluorescent, dazzling.
OPPOSITES: dull, pale.
2 (adj) Gita gave a vivid account of her travels. graphic, dramatic, colourful, lively, exciting, striking, powerful, expressive, imaginative, true-to-life, realistic, lifelike.
OPPOSITES: dull, lifeless.

### volcano
volcanoes...

| belch | growl | smoulder |
|---|---|---|
| blow up | grumble | spew |
| erupt | roar | spurt |
| explode | rumble | steam |
| flare up | smoke | thunder |

volcanoes send out...

| burning rock | smoke |
|---|---|
| cinders | steam |
| lava (molten rock) | suffocating |
| lava flow | clouds |
| poisonous gas | volcanic ash |

lava may...

| burn | flow | solidify |
|---|---|---|
| bury | gush | spread |
| destroy | harden | stream |
| devastate | pour | surge |
| engulf | slide | sweep |

lava can be..

| bubbling | glimmering | runny |
|---|---|---|
| fiery | glowing | sticky |
| flaming | lumpy | viscous |
| fluid | red-hot | (thick) |

volcanoes can be...

active
dormant
extinct
underwater

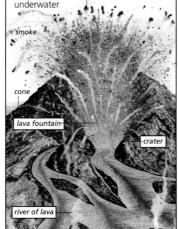

volcanic bomb (lump of solidified lava)

smoke

cone

lava fountain

crater

river of lava

## volunteer
(v) Did you volunteer to help? offer, put yourself forward, come forward, step forward, offer your services.

## vomit
(v) I think I'm going to vomit! be sick, throw up (informal), puke (slang), spew up, retch, heave, gag, bring up, do a technicolour yawn (slang).

## vote
1 (n) What was the result of the vote? poll, ballot, show of hands, election.
2 vote for (v) I didn't know who to vote for. cast a vote for, choose, elect, return, nominate, opt for, select, pick, support.

## voyage see journey 1, 2.

## vulgar
1 (adj) Vulgar jokes. See crude.
2 (adj) Vulgar jewellery. tasteless, flashy, showy, gaudy, garish, ostentatious, tawdry, tacky (informal), cheap and nasty.
OPPOSITE: tasteful.

## waffle
(v) Don't waffle! Stick to the point! ramble, witter (informal), rabbit on (informal), blather, beat about the bush.

## wail
(v) Babies wail when they're hungry. cry, howl, yowl, sob, weep, bawl, shriek, caterwaul, moan, whine, complain.

## wait
1 (v) Wait until it's your turn. be patient, hold on (informal), hang on (informal), sit tight, stand by, hold back, hold your horses, cool your heels, hang fire.
2 (v) Wait here until I get back. stay, stop, remain, stay put, hang around.

## wake up
(v) I didn't wake up until midday. wake, stir, surface (informal), get up, rise, come to life, awaken (old-fashioned).

## walk
1 (v) I usually walk to school. go on foot, travel on foot, foot it, hoof it (slang).
WAYS TO WALK: amble, crawl, creep, dodder, hike, hobble, limp, lope, march, mince, mooch (slang), pace, pad, parade, plod, prowl, ramble, saunter, scuttle, shamble, shuffle, slink, stagger, stalk, stomp (informal), stride, stroll, strut, stumble, swagger, teeter, tiptoe, toddle, totter, traipse (informal), tramp, trek, trot, trudge, waddle, wander.
2 (v) Don't walk on the tulips! tread, trample, tramp, step, stamp, walk all over.
3 (n) Let's go for a walk. stroll, saunter, wander, ramble, hike, tramp, trek, march.

## wander

1 *(v) I'll just wander round town.* drift, saunter, stroll, amble, mooch *(slang),* traipse *(informal),* roam, ramble, cruise.
2 *(v) Don't wander off! See* **stray** 2.

## want

*(v) The genie will give you whatever you want.* desire, wish for, fancy, like, dream of, crave, long for, yearn for, hanker after, set your heart on, covet, pine for, need.

## war

*(n) Many soldiers were killed in the war.* conflict, fighting, hostilities *(plural),* armed conflict, struggle, confrontation, combat.

## warm

1 *(adj) A warm evening.* mild, balmy, hot, sultry, sunny, summery, fine, pleasant.
OPPOSITES: cool, cold.
2 *(adj) Warm water.* lukewarm, tepid.
OPPOSITES: cool, cold.
3 *(adj) A warm coat.* thick, heavy, woolly, fleecy, cosy, snug, thermal, padded.
OPPOSITES: thin, lightweight.
4 *(adj) A warm welcome.* hearty, cordial, friendly, heartfelt, fervent, enthusiastic, emotional, effusive, ecstatic, rapturous.
OPPOSITES: cool, hostile.

## warn

1 *(v) I'll warn you if anyone comes.* alert, tip you off, let you know, inform, notify, give you fair warning, raise the alarm.
2 *(v) Didn't I warn you not to hitchhike?* caution, tell, advise, counsel, urge, remind.

## warning

*(n) Did you have any warning of what would happen?* advance notice, forewarning, tip-off, notification, word, sign, hint, indication, premonition, omen.

## wash

1 *(v) Did you wash before you went to bed?* have a wash, wash yourself, have a bath, have a shower, bath, shower.
2 *(v) We must wash our car.* clean, shampoo, sponge down, scrub, soap, swab down, wipe, mop, launder *(clothes).*

## waste

*(v) Don't waste all your money at the fair.* squander, fritter away, throw away, blow *(slang),* use up, run through, exhaust.

## watch

1 *(v) I like to watch the people.* look at, observe, see, gaze at, stare at, survey, view, contemplate, check out *(informal),* scrutinize, inspect, peer at, peep at, gape at, gawp at *(slang),* ogle, clock *(slang).*
2 *(v) Watch what I do first.* observe, look at, notice, pay attention to, mark, note.
3 *(v) I'll watch your bike for you.* keep watch over, keep an eye on, guard, mind, take care of, look after, protect.

## watch out

*(v) Watch out for signs of trouble.* look out, be on the lookout, keep a lookout, keep your eyes open, be on the alert, be on your guard, be vigilant, be watchful.

## wave

1 *(v) Wave when the coast is clear.* signal, indicate, gesture, motion, sign, beckon.
2 *(v) Don't wave that stick at me!* shake, waggle, brandish, flourish, swing, twirl.
3 *(v) Watch the grass wave in the breeze.* sway, stir, ripple, quiver, shake, flutter.
4 *(n) The surfer was carried along on the wave.* breaker, roller, billow, surf, swell, white horses *(plural),* tidal wave.

## way

1 *(n) Is this the right way home?* route, direction, road, path, street, lane, track.
2 *(n) Think of a way to solve the puzzle.* method, technique, procedure, system, means *(plural),* plan, approach, scheme.

## weak

1 *(adj) Mia felt weak after her illness.* frail, feeble, delicate, fragile, faint, shaky, unsteady, debilitated, infirm, incapacitated, sickly, tired, exhausted, wasted, puny.
OPPOSITES: strong, energetic.
2 *(adj) The bridge is too weak to support us.* flimsy, insubstantial, rickety, unsafe, shaky, unsteady, thin, fragile, delicate.
OPPOSITES: strong, sturdy.
3 *(adj) Don't be weak!* feeble, spineless, timid, cowardly, pathetic, wet *(informal),* soft, wimpish *(informal),* weedy *(informal).*
OPPOSITES: assertive, brave.
4 *(adj) This drink is too weak.* watery, diluted, watered down, wishy-washy *(informal),* tasteless, insipid, thin.
OPPOSITES: strong, concentrated.
5 *(adj) A weak excuse. See* **feeble** 3.
6 *(adj) A weak cry. See* **faint** 4.

## weakness

1 *(n) Nat's weakness is laziness.* failing, shortcoming, fault, flaw, defect, problem.
OPPOSITES: strength, asset.
2 *(n) Jo has a weakness for sweets.* liking, fondness, taste, passion, love, soft spot.

## wealthy *see* **rich** 1.

## weapons

*(plural n)* arms *(plural),* munitions *(plural),* armaments *(plural),* weaponry, offensive weapons *(plural).*
TYPES OF WEAPON: battering ram, battleaxe, bayonet, bazooka, biological weapons *(plural),* blowpipe, bomb, boomerang, bow and arrow, cannon, catapult, cosh, crossbow, cudgel, dagger, flame-thrower, grenade, guided missile, gun, harpoon, lance, longbow, missile, mortar, mustard gas, nerve gas, pike, rocket, shell, spear, sword, tear gas, tomahawk, torpedo, truncheon, warhead.
Also see **bomb, gun, sword.**

## wear

*(v) What will you wear?* put on, dress in, be dressed in, have on, sport *(informal).*

## wear away

*(v) The sea will slowly wear away the rocks.* erode, eat away, wear down, grind down, wash away, crumble, dissolve, corrode *(metal),* eat into, rot, decay.

## wear out

*(v) My shirt is starting to wear out.* become worn, show signs of wear, wear thin, fray, go into holes, become threadbare.

## weather

*(n)* climate, weather conditions *(plural).*

*a stormy day*

**it is hot**
baking
blistering
boiling
roasting
scorching
searing
sizzling
sweltering
torrid

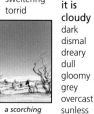

*a scorching day*

**it is humid**
clammy
close
muggy
oppressive
steamy
sticky
stifling
stuffy
suffocating
sultry

**it is fine**
balmy
bright
calm
clear
cloudless
dry
fair
mild
pleasant
still
summery
sunny
sunshiny
warm

*a frosty morning*

**it is cloudy**
dark
dismal
dreary
dull
gloomy
grey
overcast
sunless

**it is wet**
bucketing *(informal)*
coming down in torrents
damp
drizzly
lashing down
pelting down
pouring
rainy
showery
spitting
teeming
tipping down *(informal)*

**it is foggy**
hazy
misty
murky
smoggy

**it is windy**
blowy
blustery
breezy
gusty
squally
stormy

**it is cold**
bitter
bracing
chilly
cool
crisp
freezing
fresh
frosty
icy
nippy
numbing
parky *(informal)*
perishing *(informal)*
raw
snowy
wintry

*a murky evening*

*Also see* **ice, frost & snow, storm words.**

**wedding** *see* **marriage** 2.

**weird** *see* **strange** 1, 2.

**welcome**
*(adj) Emily's parents made me feel welcome.* at home, one of the family, accepted, appreciated, wanted, included.
OPPOSITES: unwelcome, excluded.

**well**
1 *(adj) You look well.* healthy, fit, in good health, blooming, strong, robust, thriving.
OPPOSITES: unwell, ill.
2 *(n) The well provided water for the village.* water hole, borehole, spring, water source, oasis, artesian well, wishing well.

**well-behaved**
*(adj) A well-behaved child.* good, obedient, cooperative, amenable, compliant, docile, polite, well-mannered, dutiful.
OPPOSITES: badly behaved, naughty.

**well-known** *see* **famous**.

**wet**
1 *(adj) My clothes are wet.* damp, soaking, dripping, sopping wet, sodden, drenched, wringing wet, saturated, wet through.
OPPOSITES: dry, bone-dry *(informal)*.
2 *(adj) After the rain, the ground was wet.* damp, moist, sodden, waterlogged, saturated, soggy, spongy, muddy, dewy.
OPPOSITES: dry, parched.
3 *(adj) If it's wet we won't go out.* rainy, raining, pouring, drizzly, showery, damp, misty, dank, clammy, humid.
OPPOSITES: dry, fine.
4 *(adj) (informal) Stand up for yourself and don't be so wet! See* **weak** 3.
5 *(v) Wet the cloth.* dampen, moisten, soak, drench, saturate, steep, douse, splash, sprinkle, spray, irrigate *(ground)*.

**whine**
1 *(v) The toddler began to whine.* whimper, wail, cry, grizzle *(informal)*.
2 *(v) Cecil always finds something to whine about. See* **complain**.

**whip** *see* **beat** 1, 4.

**whirl**
*(v) Watch the dancers whirl round the room.* spin, twirl, swirl, circle, wheel, reel, pirouette, gyrate, revolve, rotate, swivel.

**whisper**
1 *(v) I can't hear you when you whisper.* speak under your breath, speak in hushed tones, talk quietly, speak softly, keep your voice down, murmur, mutter.
2 *(n) Sandy spoke in a whisper.* low voice, quiet voice, soft voice, murmur, stage whisper, undertone, hushed tones *(plural)*.

**white**
1 *(adj) The statue looked white in the moonlight.* milky, chalky, pearly, silvery, snow-white, alabaster, ivory, ghostly.
2 *(adj) Granny has white hair.* snowy, snow-white, silver, silvery, hoary.
3 *(adj) Edmund's face was white with fear.* ashen, pale, pallid, bloodless, wan, pasty, waxen, chalky, drained.

**whole**
*(adj) Will the whole film be shown on television?* entire, complete, full, total, uncut, unedited, unabridged *(book)*.

**wicked**
1 *(adj) A wicked criminal.* evil, bad, sinful, immoral, corrupt, depraved, villainous, vicious, vile, fiendish, diabolical, devilish, black-hearted, lawless.
OPPOSITES: good, virtuous.
2 *(adj) A wicked grin. See* **mischievous** 2.

**wide** *see* **broad** 1, 2.

**wild**
1 *(adj) That dog is quite wild.* untamed, undomesticated, savage, fierce, ferocious.
OPPOSITES: tame, domesticated.
2 *(adj) We crossed some wild country.* uncultivated, unspoilt, untamed, natural, deserted, empty, waste, barren, desolate, bleak, rough, rugged, overgrown.
OPPOSITES: cultivated, inhabited.
3 *(adj) What wild weather! See* **stormy** 1.
4 *(adj) The boys are very wild.* rowdy, boisterous, unruly, uncontrollable, undisciplined, wayward, out of control, rough, noisy, violent, rude, riotous.
5 *(adj) Ziggy had a wild idea. See* **mad** 3.
6 *(adj) Al is wild about soccer. See* **mad** 5.

**willing**
*(adj) Helen is always willing to help.* glad, happy, pleased, ready, quick, prepared, eager, keen, game *(informal)*.
OPPOSITES: unwilling, reluctant.

**wilt** *see* **wither**.

**win**
1 *(v) I hope that I will win.* come first, be the winner, get first place, take first prize, finish first, be victorious, triumph, succeed.
OPPOSITES: lose, come last.
2 *(v) Mo wants to win a medal.* gain, earn, secure, obtain, receive, collect, pick up.

**wince** *see* **flinch**.

**wind**
1 *(n) A strong wind can cause a lot of damage.* breeze, gust, blast, squall, headwind, crosswind, tailwind, gale, tornado, cyclone, whirlwind, twister *(informal)*. ❖ *Also see* **storm words**.
2 *(v) The path began to wind up the mountain.* meander, snake, twist and turn, twist, zigzag, weave, spiral, corkscrew.
3 *(v) Wind the tinsel round the tree.* loop, twist, coil, entwine, wrap, curl, thread.

**window**
*(n) TYPES OF WINDOW:* bay window, bow window, casement window, dormer window, fanlight, French window, leaded window, louvred window, oriel window, picture window, plate-glass window, porthole, rose window, sash window, skylight, stained-glass window.

**windy**
1 *(adj) A windy day.* breezy, blustery, blowy, gusty, squally, stormy, wild.
OPPOSITES: calm, still.

2 *(adj) A windy spot.* exposed, open, unprotected, windswept, bleak, desolate.
OPPOSITE: sheltered.

**winner**
*(n) Who is the winner?* victor, champion, prizewinner, medallist, champ *(informal)*.
OPPOSITE: loser.

**wipe**
*(v) Wipe the surface.* clean, sponge, mop, swab, wash, dust, polish, rub, brush.

**wise**
1 *(adj) A wise ruler.* learned, clever, knowledgeable, intelligent, astute, shrewd, perceptive, discerning, understanding, enlightened, experienced, deep-thinking.
OPPOSITE: foolish.
2 *(adj) A wise choice. See* **sensible** 2.

**wish**
1 *(n) Josie has a secret wish to be famous.* desire, longing, hankering, yearning, craving, hunger, ambition, aspiration, hope, dream, fancy, whim.
2 *(n) The genie will carry out your every wish.* request, desire, demand, command, order, instruction, bidding.
3 *wish for (v) The genie will give you whatever you wish for. See* **want**.

**wistful**
*(adj) You look wistful; what are you thinking about?* sad, forlorn, melancholy, disconsolate, thoughtful, pensive, dreamy.

**witch**
*(n)* sorceress, enchantress, crone.

**wither**
*(v) The daffodils will wither if you don't water them.* wilt, dry up, shrivel up, fade, droop, go limp, flop, sag, flag, die.
OPPOSITES: flourish, bloom.

**witty**
*(adj) Tim's witty remarks made me laugh.* funny, humorous, amusing, clever, quick-witted, sparkling, lively, droll, facetious.

**wizard** *see* **magician** 1.

**wobble**
1 *(v) Can you make the bottle wobble without knocking it over?* teeter, totter, rock, sway, waver, seesaw, oscillate.
2 *(v) Look at the jelly wobble!* quiver, tremble, shake, vibrate, quake.

**woman**
*(n) Who's that woman?* lady, girl, female, dame *(slang)*, lass, maiden *(old-fashioned)*.

**wonder**
1 *(n) We gazed at the magician in wonder.* amazement, astonishment, awe, wonderment, admiration, curiosity, bewilderment, surprise, disbelief.
2 *(n) The pyramids were a wonder of the Ancient World.* marvel, phenomenon, miracle, spectacle, curiosity, attraction.
3 *(v) It's pointless to wonder what might have happened.* think about, ponder, speculate about, ask yourself, puzzle over, reflect on, meditate on, query, question, be curious about, be inquisitive about.

## wonderful

1 *(adj) What a wonderful party!* fantastic *(informal)*, marvellous, great *(informal)*, terrific *(informal)*, superb, excellent, fabulous *(informal)*, tremendous *(informal)*, amazing *(informal)*, sensational *(informal)*, magnificent, wicked *(slang)*, decent *(informal)*, cool *(informal)*.
OPPOSITES: terrible, dreadful.
2 *(adj) Modern medicine can do wonderful things.* amazing, astonishing, incredible, astounding, extraordinary, remarkable, staggering, marvellous, miraculous, phenomenal, awe-inspiring.
OPPOSITES: commonplace, unremarkable.

## wood

1 *(n) Don't get lost in the wood.* woods *(plural)*, woodland, copse, spinney, thicket, coppice, forest, trees *(plural)*.
2 *(n) The shed was made of wood.* timber, logs *(plural)*, planks *(plural)*, boards *(plural)*.

## word

1 *(n) What's the proper word for this thing?* name, term, expression.
2 *(n) Give me your word you'll be there.* See **promise** 2.

## work

1 *(v) You'll have to work if you want to pass your exams.* slog away, slave, graft *(informal)*, sweat *(informal)*, labour, toil, exert yourself, beaver away *(informal)*, peg away, keep your nose to the grindstone.
2 *(v) Lord Lucre doesn't need to work.* have a job, go to work, earn a living.
3 *(v) This whisk is easy to work.* See **use** 2.
4 *(v) Our CD player doesn't work properly.* function, go, perform, run, operate, play.
5 *(v) My plan might work.* See **succeed** 2.
6 *(n) I need a rest after all that work.* hard work, effort, toil, labour, exertion, drudgery, graft *(informal)*, hard grind *(informal)*, donkey-work, slavery.
7 *(n) What work do you do?* See **job** 2.

## work out

1 *(v) Can you work out the answer to this question?* figure out *(informal)*, calculate, deduce, puzzle out, suss out *(slang)*, find out, discover, solve, find the solution to.
2 *(v) We must work out a plan.* think up, come up with, concoct, devise, construct, put together, decide on, formulate.
3 *(v) Pamela likes to work out on the beach.* exercise, do exercises, train, keep fit, tone up, lift weights, pump iron *(slang)*.

## world

1 *(n) Captain Stardust travelled round the world.* earth, globe, planet.
2 *(n) How did the world begin?* earth, universe, cosmos, life, existence, human life, nature, creation, everything.

## worn out see **exhausted**.
## worried see **anxious** 1.
## worry

1 *(v) Don't worry about the exams.* fret, be anxious, be apprehensive, get in a state *(informal)*, get worked up, get in a stew *(informal)*, agonize, torment yourself.
2 *(v) Don't let this small problem worry you.* trouble, concern, bother, distress, upset, disturb, unsettle, make you anxious.
3 *(n) Ziggy has caused his parents a lot of worry.* anxiety, concern, unease, distress, bother, hassle *(informal)*, problems *(plural)*.

## worthwhile

*(adj) I want to do a job that's really worthwhile.* useful, valuable, helpful, worth the effort, constructive, beneficial, important, rewarding, profitable.
OPPOSITES: worthless, pointless.

## wound

1 *(n) The doctor examined the wound.* cut, gash, laceration, knife wound, stab wound, bullet wound, incision, injury.
2 *(v) Did the terrorists wound anyone?* See **injure**.

## wrap

1 *(v) Wrap the ornament in cotton wool.* pack, cover, bundle up, surround, swathe, drape, enfold, enclose, envelop, cocoon.
2 *(v) Wrap the tape round the pole.* wind, loop, twist, roll, coil, twine, bind.

## wreck

1 *(v) Don't wreck the furniture!* destroy, demolish, break, smash, trash *(slang)*, total *(slang)*, write off *(car) (informal)*.
2 *(v) One mistake could wreck our chances of winning.* See **ruin** 1.
3 *(n) Divers explored the wreck.* shipwreck, sunken ship, wreckage, hulk.

## wreckage

*(n) Rescuers sifted through the wreckage.* debris, remains *(plural)*, rubble, ruins *(plural)*, fragments *(plural)*.

## wriggle

1 *(v) Sit still and don't wriggle!* fidget, squirm, jiggle about, twist around, writhe around, shift around, jerk about.
2 *(v) Watch the snake wriggle across the grass.* wiggle, zigzag, twist and turn, writhe, snake, worm, slither, crawl, slink.

## wrinkled

1 *(adj) A wrinkled face.* lined, wrinkly, furrowed, wizened, crinkly, creased.
2 *(adj) A wrinkled shirt.* creased, crumpled, rumpled, crinkled, unironed.

## write

1 *(v) I'll write your number on this pad.* write down, note down, jot down, take down, make a note of, record, scribble, scrawl, print, put in writing, copy, inscribe.
2 *(v) I have to write a story for homework.* make up, invent, create, compose, draft, pen, dash off, put together, concoct.

## writer

*(n)* author, novelist, scriptwriter, dramatist, playwright, poet, biographer, journalist.

## writing

*(n) I can't read this writing.* handwriting, scrawl, scribble, script, print, letters *(plural)*, characters *(plural)*, calligraphy.

## wrong

1 *(adj) My theory turned out to be wrong.* incorrect, inaccurate, mistaken, off target, wide of the mark, erroneous, false, untrue, off beam *(informal)*, way out *(informal)*.
OPPOSITES: right, correct.
2 *(adj) It's wrong to sell stolen goods.* illegal, unlawful, criminal, immoral, unethical, dishonest, corrupt, deceitful, crooked *(informal)*, wicked, sinful, evil.
OPPOSITES: right, legal.
3 *(adj) It would be wrong to wear a bikini to school.* inappropriate, unsuitable, unfitting, unseemly, improper, unacceptable, not done, unconventional, funny, incongruous, incorrect.
OPPOSITES: right, proper.
4 go wrong see **go wrong** 1, 2.

## xylophone

*(n)* glockenspiel, chime bars *(plural)*.

## yearn see **long** 3.
## yell see **shout**.
## yellow

*(n)* SHADES OF YELLOW: amber, buttercup yellow, canary yellow, gold, lemon, mustard, ochre, primrose, saffron.

## young

1 *(adj) Young children can't look after themselves.* small, little, infant, newborn.
OPPOSITES: old, grown-up.
2 *(adj) Zak is so young for his age.* childish, babyish, immature, juvenile, infantile, puerile, adolescent.
OPPOSITES: mature, grown-up.
3 *(adj) My parents still seem young.* youthful, boyish, girlish, fresh-faced, sprightly, spry, well-preserved, active.
OPPOSITES: old, elderly.
4 *(plural n) Animals try to protect their young.* babies *(plural)*, offspring *(plural)*, little ones *(plural)*, litter, brood, family.

## zero see **nothing** 2.
## zoom see **speed** 4.

The publishers are grateful to the following: AppleCentre, Oxford; Cellmark Diagnostics (35); Central Broadcasting Ltd (150); Penny Dwyer (102); GKN Westland Helicopters Ltd (121); Korg (UK) Ltd (112); Martin Lunn (139); Anne Millard (10,11,13, 96-97,124-125); Basil Mustafa (22); Thames Valley Police Fingerprint Department (35). Cover photo credits: *rattlesnake* ©Robert Pickett/CORBIS; *French horn, high-speed train* ©Digital Vision; *puffin* ©Galen Rowell/CORBIS; *icy leaf* ©Stockmarket; *snowflakes* ©Jim Zuckerman/CORBIS.